Contents

Acknowledgements

It is always difficult when writing a book of this size to acknowledge all the support that has been given to make the process work, but listed below are those people who have offered the most important contributions. We have both been fortunate to receive grants from a wide range of funding bodies over the years and these have provided much of the data that has been used in this book. We would therefore like to mention grants from the Economic and Social Research Council, the Department of Trade and Industry, the Department of Health, the European Regional Development Fund and the Chartered Institute of Personnel and Development.

We are both immensely lucky to work with such good colleagues at what was the Manchester School of Management, UMIST (now Manchester Business School at the University of Manchester), and Loughborough University Business School who provide the space and the support that is needed when putting together a textbook. Special thanks go to co-researchers on the ESRC Future of Work Project, especially Jill Rubery, Damian Grimshaw and Fang Lee Cooke, with whom Mick has worked so closely over the last few years. Great support has also been received from people at CIPD in taking this book to publication in such a short time period, as well as colleagues in the PKI Group.

Lindsay Endell and Rebecca White have once again been heavily involved in the production of the manuscript and Lindsay has also pulled together the references. As usual, our families have been immensely supportive, so thanks again to Lorrie, Jack and Lucy, and Jackie, Erin and Aidan. Jackie has provided material for some chapters as well as legal expertise. However, the largest acknowledgement for this edition is to Lorrie Marchington. She has tracked down publications and websites and her contribution to the chapters on learning and development has been especially important. It is impossible to acknowledge just how much she has done.

Mick Marchington
Adrian Wilkinson
Manchester and Loughborough, October 2004

The Authors and Publishers would like to thank the following people for attending a focus group to discuss the new edition of this text:

- Paul Smith, University of Hertfordshire
- Adrian Murton, London Metropolitan University
- Andrew Leleux, Buckinghamshire and Chilterns University College
- Julia Pointon, De Montfort University
- Jan Rae, Bournemouth University
- Andrew Summers, London South Bank University.

Acronyms and weblinks

Acas	The Advisory, Conciliation and Arbitration Service: www.acas.org.uk
ALI	Adult Learning Inspectorate: www.ali.gov.uk
AMA	Advanced Modern Apprenticeship
APEL	Accreditation of Prior Experience and Learning
APL	Accreditation of Prior Learning
BACP	British Association for Counselling and Psychotherapy: www.counselling.co.uk
BCG	Boston Consulting Group
BPS	British Psychological Society: www.bps.org.uk
CAC	Central Arbitration Committee: www.cac.gov.uk
CAT	Credit Accumulation and Transfer
CBI	Confederation of British Industry: www.cbi.org.uk
CCT	compulsory competitive tendering
CEML	Council for Excellence in Management and Leadership: www.managementandleadershipcouncil.org
CEO	Chief Executive Officer
CIPD	Chartered Institute of Personnel and Development: www.cipd.co.uk
CPD	Continuing Professional Development
CPI	Californian Psychological Inventory
CR	corporate responsibility
CRE	Commission for Racial Equality: www.cre.gov.uk
CSR	corporate social responsibility
DB	defined benefit
DC	defined contribution
DDA	Disability Discrimination Act
DOCAS	deduction of contributions at source
DfES	Department for Education and Skills: www.dfes.gov.uk
DRC	Disability Rights Commission: www.drc-gb.org
DTI	Department of Trade and Industry: www.dti.gov.uk
E2E	Entry to Employment
EAP and EAPA	Employee Assistance Programmes and Employee Assistance Professionals Association: www.eapa.org.uk
EAT	Employment Appeals Tribunal: www.employmentappeals.gov.uk
EC	European Commission: www.europa.eu.int
ECJ	European Court of Justice: http://europa.eu.int/cj/en/
EDAP	Employee Development and Assessment Programmes
EEC	European Economic Community
EEF	Engineering Employers Federation: www.eef.org.uk
EI	employee involvement
EOC	Equal Opportunities Commission: www.eoc.org.uk
EPCA	Employment Protection (Consolidation) Act
ERA	Employment Rights Act
ESOP	employee share ownership plans
ETP	employer training pilots
ETUC	European Trade Union Confederation: www.etuc.org/
EU	European Union: www.europa.eu.int
EWC	European Works Council
FD	Foundation Degree

FE	further education
FMA	Foundation Modern Apprenticeship
GCHQ	Government Communications Headquarters
GCSE	General Certificate of Secondary Education
HASAWA	Health and Safety at Work Act
HCM	high commitment management
HE	higher education
HND	Higher National Diploma
HPW	high performance working
HQ	headquarters
HR	human resource
HRD	human resource development
HRM	human resource management
HSC	Health and Safety Commission: www.hse.gov.uk/aboutus/hse
HSE	Health and Safety Executive: www.hse.gov.uk
ICT	information and communication technology
IDS	Incomes Data Services: www.incomesdata.com
IiP	Investors in People: www.investorsinpeople.co.uk
ILO	International Labour Organization: www.ilo.org
IMF	International Monetary Fund: www.imf.org
IPA	Involvement and Participation Association: www.ipa-involve.com
IPR	individual performance review
IPRP	individual performance-related pay
IRS	Industrial Relations Services
IT	information technology
ITD	Institute of Training and Development
ITN	identification of training and learning needs
JCC	Joint Consultative Committee
KM	knowledge management
KRA	key result area
LEA	Local Education Authority
LFS	Labour Force Surveys
LO	learning organisation
LSC	Learning and Skills Council: www.lsc.gov.uk
MBA	Masters in Business Administration
MCI	Management Charter Initiative: www.mci.com
MD	management development
MNC	multinational corporation
NESS	National Employer Skills Survey
NHS	National Health Service
NIACE	National Institute for Adult and Continuing Education: www.niace.org.uk
NVQs/SVQs	National/Scottish Vocational Qualifications
OECD	Organisation for Economic Co-operation and Development: www.oecd.org
OFR	operating and financial review
OFSTED	Office for Standards in Education: www.ofsted.gov.uk
OHS	Occupational Health Services
OPI	Occupational Personality Inventory
PAQ	Position Analysis Questionnaire
PBR	payment by results
PDS	Professional Development Scheme

PFI	private finance initiative
PM	performance management
PM&D	people management and development
PMS	performance management system
PPP	public–private partnerships
PRP	performance-related pay
PVA	production value added
QCA	Qualifications and Curriculum Authority: www.qca.org.uk
QMV	qualified majority voting
R&D	research and development
RBV	resource-based view
RDAs	Regional Development Agencies (Department for Regional Development): www.drdni.gov.uk
SAYE	Save As You Earn
SME	small and medium-sized enterprises
SRI	socially responsible investment
SSA	Sector Skills Agreement/Single Status Agreement
SSCs	Sector Skills Councils: www.ssda.org.uk
SSDA	Sector Skills Development Agency: www.ssda.org.uk
STB	single table bargaining
TECs/LECs	Training and Enterprise Councils
TNA	training needs analysis
TQM	total quality management
TUC	Trades Union Congress: www.tuc.org.uk
TUPE	Transfer of Undertakings (Protection of Employment) Regulations
UCAS	Universities and Colleges Admissions Service: www.ucas.ac.uk
UKIP	UK Independence Party
ULF	Union Learning Fund
ULR	union learning representative
UNICE	Union of Industrial and Employers' Confederations of Europe: www.unice.org
VET	vocational education and training
VIP	Values in Practice
WAIS	Wechsler's Adult Intelligence Scale
WERS	Workplace Employee Relations Survey
WPS	Work Profiling System

Introduction to this edition

Readers of previous editions of this book will notice a number of changes this time around, not least in the title! For the third edition, we have reversed the order of the title and elevated *HRM at Work* from the subtitle in order to reflect the much wider usage of this term in academic and practitioner circles. These changes, as well as the substantive changes we talk about below, are all designed to increase the appeal of the book to wider, non-CIPD, audiences especially at final-year undergraduate and postgraduate levels. At the same time, however, the book remains ideal for those students on CIPD programmes such as the core module in *People Management and Development*, and the text follows the CIPD standards closely while many of the exercises are designed to cater for students studying on part-time as well as full-time routes into membership.

The organisation of the chapters has also changed somewhat with this edition. The first chapter – on HRM, strategy and the global context – is new; it provides an introduction to the background thinking about HRM, as well as considering how it relates to organisational strategies and global forces. The second chapter is a condensed version of what was three chapters in previous editions, and this provides a concise summary of the range of forces external to the organisation – such as legal regulation and third party agencies – that shape how HRM works in practice. It also reviews major issues concerned with job satisfaction, organisational commitment and loyalty, and work intensification that impinge on HRM. Chapters 3–5 develop the main strategic aspects of HRM, in much the same way as in previous editions, but with a much sharper focus on the factors that influence management choices about HRM and how these impact on performance. In these chapters we review major questions about HRM such as:

1   What does the high commitment model comprise and is it universally applicable?
2   How does HRM vary between different types of organisation and why?
3   Which HR practices and processes are most likely to lead to sustained competitive advantage?
4   How can line managers and HR specialists work in partnership with one another?
5   Does the HR function need to remain in-house or can it operate effectively through alternative forms of service delivery?

The main practice areas of HRM are dealt with in Chapters 6–13. As in previous editions, we focus on HR planning, recruitment and selection; performance management; learning and development; employment relations; reward management. These chapters are packed with essential guidance about how HRM works in practice, both in terms of academic underpinnings and contemporary organisational examples. We aim to provide readers with a substantial understanding of these areas that can be used as a base for more in-depth treatments of each part of the subject. These chapters combine a mixture of survey results and empirical research, and at all times readers are expected to draw conclusions about how HRM operates under very different employment regimes – say, between the public and private sectors, manufacturing and service, and small and large firms.

The final chapter contains a review of research methods, and we see this as a key element in the book. It offers a concise guide to the conduct of research which will be of immense value to final-year undergraduates undertaking a dissertation or project as part of their degree, as well as to postgraduates – whether or not they are studying for CIPD. Indeed, this chapter provides a summary of the key issues in research methods that would also be highly appropriate for people who are seeking CIPD membership through the professional assessment route.

The pedagogical features of the book have been greatly enhanced in this edition. As with previous editions, we have interspersed the text with mini-questions that give readers the opportunity to review their understanding of the material, undertake an exercise that requires some consolidation and extension of their reading, or engage in a debate in class about an issue of major importance to HRM. At the end of each chapter there are suggestions for further reading, typically comprising a mix of book chapters, refereed journal articles, professional magazines and surveys. A variety of organisations undertake annual surveys and it is essential that readers keep up-to-date with these as information is provided about the extensiveness of particular techniques, as well as guidance about how these work in practice. The bibliography offers a comprehensive list of materials that are available to consolidate learning, but of course this needs to be updated by readers each year through a review of literature.

The web pages accompanying the book are also an essential source of further information and advice to readers. Lecturers can download sets of Powerpoint slides that can help them plan sessions and further enhance student learning by integrating the book and the web support. In addition, there are short introductions to how each chapter might be used and suggestions for how the mini-questions might be addressed. At the same time, we do not assume that our 'answers' cover every possible explanation, and it is an essential element of study at this level that students engage with and explore alternative 'solutions'. After all, CIPD students who are taking the Professional Development Scheme are expected to act as 'thinking performers' and it goes without saying that final-year undergraduates and postgraduates should critically analyse everything they do. Our whole philosophy, which has been exemplified in each successive edition of the book, is that readers should continually review and question what is written about and what happens at work so that they improve organisational practice. It is only by integrating the best of academic work with how HRM works in practice that gains will be made; please read the book with this in mind.

How to use this book

For Masters and final-year undergraduate students studying HRM as a core module, the book can quite easily be used sequentially.

Chapter 1 provides a clear discussion of the multiple meanings of HRM, the relationship between strategy and HRM, and the value of seeing strategy in terms of multiple stake-holders. The final section then extends the argument by looking at HRM in multinational organisations and in different countries.

Chapter 2 provides a summary of the forces shaping HRM, and this may usefully supplement ideas they have picked up from other modules during their degree. It also explains clearly our approach, namely that institutional forces shape, but do not determine, HRM at work. There is interesting material in here about job satisfaction and the psychological contract, about flexibility and employment issues across organisational boundaries, and about the impact of the law.

These two chapters form an essential building block for modules at this level. Students might learn just as easily through seminar work and through reading prior to controlled learning sessions with the lecturer.

From Chapter 3 onwards we move more explicitly on to HRM, and the focus in Chapters 3–5 is on HRM, strategy and performance by analysing different theoretical frameworks – the universalist high commitment paradigm, the contingency best-fit approach and the resource-based view of the firm; all of these are presented as alternative ways in which to understand the link between strategy and HRM at work. They also raise issues that are developed and expanded at an operational level throughout the remainder of the book – issues to do with staffing, resourcing and performance management, issues relating to learning and development, to employee relations and to reward management.

Chapter 5 considers who has responsibility for HRM, and examines the links between line managers and HR specialists, as well as reviewing alternative forms of HR service delivery through external consultants and shared service operations.

These three chapters form the core of the book and they need to be understood before students embark on a more detailed analysis of specific aspects of HRM so that they are able to see the context in which HRM operates as well as gain understanding about the purpose of HRM. While this is explicitly and overtly about how HRM can contribute to business performance, the book also challenges simplistic assumptions about the contribution of HRM to employer goals in the short term. We consider the role of HRM in creating links with wider societal objectives such as fairness, equity, social exclusion and the contribution of people as citizens.

Depending on the length of the module and its principal focus, students may find that some of the following chapters (6–13) are more useful than others and lecturers may decide to spend more time on specific aspects of HRM – such as recruitment or training – than others. Alternatively, lecturers may decide the best way to use the book is as a basis for covering all components of HRM. Chapter 14, on research methods and change management, will be particularly useful for all students who are required to do projects or dissertations.

Students on CIPD programmes should also follow the book sequentially, again paying particular attention to the early chapters before moving on to look at other chapters as appropriate. For example, students doing People Management and Development (PM&D) will find the book contains everything they need to provide a sound base for their studies, and this can be supplemented – as with other groups – by readings from journals, the CIPD website and research findings. Chapter 14 is vitally important for these students and reading this relatively early on should help them to understand the basis of a management report, as well as its key elements. Looking through this chapter may also help them appreciate what other writers are trying to do through their research, especially in terms of how they approach a major project. Students who are taking generalist modules will find some chapters of more help than others; for example, those taking People Resourcing modules are likely to gain most from Chapters 6 and 7, learning and development modules are catered for in Chapters 8 and 9, employee relations in Chapters 10 and 11, and reward management is specifically dealt with in Chapters 12 and 13. Each of these groups of students will also find the early chapters of the book, especially Chapters 3 and 4, very useful for grounding their studies and for showing how each of the different components of HRM link together and can be used to support business goals. In each case, however, these chapters can do no more than provide a basic-level treatment, which is expanded by other CIPD books in the specific area.

Broadly, *HRM at Work* offers a comprehensive, analytical and systematic text to cater for the needs of students in the final year of their undergraduate studies as well as those on postgraduate courses, irrespective of whether or not they are taking CIPD examinations nationally or one that has exemption and the right to assess locally. It deals with all the main issues and its focus throughout encourages a critical awareness of HRM. Throughout the text there are mini-questions to check understanding. Tables provide further information, as do boxes, many of which contain case studies to show how HRM works in practice in a wide variety of different settings. The cases are drawn both from the UK and from other countries, in particular North America and Europe. Each chapter concludes with a set of useful readings and the extensive bibliography provides students with pointers to further reading as well as those that are central to the particular topic in hand. At this level, students must not rely on a textbook alone, however. It is essential they read journals to see how research is developing, visit websites and official sources of information for updating their knowledge, and engage in discussion with other class members. To achieve M-level understanding, they must eschew simple models and ideas, and consistently question both their own ideas and those of others, paying particular attention to the methods used to collect data as well as the results of research. Only by doing this are they likely to achieve an effective grounding in HRM.

Plan of the book

PART 1 HRM, STRATEGY AND PERFORMANCE

HRM, strategy and the global context

Forces shaping HRM at work

High commitment HRM and performance

Designing HRM to fit organisational goals

Changing responsibilities for HRM

PART 2 RESOURCING

Staffing and resourcing the organisation

Performance management

PART 3 DEVELOPMENT

Vocational education, training and skills

Learning and development at work

PART 4 RELATIONS

Managing worker voice

Procedures and workplace employee relations

PART 5 REWARD

Motivation and pay systems

Equity and fairness in reward management

PART 6 RESEARCH AND CHANGE MANAGEMENT SKILLS

Research and change management skills

Guided Tour

Chapter objectives outline the key learning outcomes of the chapter. This feature is designed to help students focus their learning and evaluate their progress.

Quotations explaining key terms or issues are highlighted to emphasise their meaning in students' minds.

Boxes provide additional information or research.

PART 4 RELATIONS

The purpose of this chapter is to examine management's role in employee relations focusing in particular on union recognition and the nature of union and non-union workplaces, as well as collective bargaining. Given its increasing prominence, the final part of the chapter analyses EI, consultation and social partnership.

By the end of the chapter, readers should be able to:

- provide advice to management on employee relations objectives appropriate for their own organisation
- design an employee relations policy explaining how trade unions and collective bargaining will be dealt with, or how a non-union strategy will be effected
- provide advice on the appropriateness of adopting different forms of employee involvement within their organisation.

In addition, they should understand and be able to explain:

- the way in which effective employee relations can contribute to increased employee potential and commitment
- the processes of union recognition and derecognition
- the nature and meaning of collective bargaining and employee involvement and their place within the employee relations framework.

MANAGEMENT'S ROLE IN EMPLOYEE RELATIONS

The centrepiece of employee relations is the relationship between employers and employees, with its common and divergent interests (Edwards 2003a). It is in neither party's interest for the organisation to perform poorly with consequent negative effects on profits (for the employer) or wages (for the employee). However, while there are clearly common goals there are also divergent interests. In simple terms, the employer is likely to wish to buy labour at the lowest possible price or cost so as to maximise profits, whereas employees wish to sell their labour at the highest possible price. This produces a conflict of interest, which not necessarily results in open conflict, but means that the arrangements reached may be unstable depending on relative bargaining power. Because employees are usually relatively weaker than employers, employees are likely to gain from organising themselves into trade unions so as to boost bargaining power.

Thus employee relations is characterised by both conflict and co-operation. Some people regard it as inextricably linked with conflict, since this is the only time employee relations obtains much media coverage. It is now accepted that the so-called 'British disease' of industrial conflict in the 1970s was largely a myth, as Britain had a record no worse than many other developed countries. Conflict may manifest itself through a strike or it may be contained or institutionalised through procedures (see Chapter 11).

Write two lists, one specifying the common interests of employers and the other the divergent interests. Apply this to an organisation you are see if it helps you to evaluate the quality of employee relations there.

266

---

6 Vocational Education, Training and Skills

apprenticeship training. In these sectors workers are usually trained to level 2 and managed by those qualified to level 4 and beyond.

While the aims of providing more training for those traditionally denied it is laudable, it is clear that the hybrid aims of the 'modern' apprenticeships are failing to meet the conflicting demands made upon it. The government would do well to look at the European model which is highly successful in that it provides an equitable funding system based on social agreements between employers, unions, the government and educators with quality underpinned by legislation guaranteeing minimum criteria. Further, without addressing the demand side from employers, it is likely that the reputation of modern apprenticeships will continue to suffer.

In order to fill the intermediate skills gap (at level 3) in the UK, vocational routes must become as attractive as academic routes to able young people. Do you agree with this statement? Do you think that modern apprenticeships will achieve this aim? If not why not?

Investors in People

The initiative that has probably had the greatest impact on cajoling employers to invest in training has been Investors in People (IiP; www.iipuk.co.uk). As the literature from IiP UK (2001) states:

The Standard provides a national framework for improving business performance and competitiveness, through a planned approach to setting and communicating business objectives and developing people to meet these objectives. The result is that what people can do and are motivated to do, matches what the organisation needs them to do. The process is cyclical and should engender the culture of continuous improvement.

IiP is based on four key principles that incorporate a total of 12 assessment indicators against which organisations are measured:

- fully committed to developing people in order to achieve aims and objectives
- clear about aims and objectives and what people need to do to achieve them
- develops people effectively in order to improve performance
- understands the impact of investment in people on performance.

Once the award has been made, there are regular reviews no more than three years apart. IiP Quality Centres are responsible for assessment and quality assurance with the LSCs responsible for advice and support. IiP UK commissions independent research periodically and respond to feedback. By 2004, 32,000 organisations had been accredited covering 27 per cent of the workforce with 87 per cent of organisations staying with the standard. Independent research for IiP among 2000 accredited organisations found t had increased customer satisfaction and 70 per cent had improved their c and productivity.

PART 2 RESOURCING

their potential role, and without them people would apply for jobs without any form of realistic job preview. Having to outline critical results areas or accountability profiles can help managers decide whether or not it is necessary to fill a post, and if so in what form and at what level. On the other hand, vague and 'flexible' accounts of what is needed in a job may only store up trouble if there are subsequent concerns about performance and whether or not people are doing what is expected of them. There is a danger that commentators are seduced by the language of liberation and empowerment that articulates these ideas, without being mindful that some employers exploit this newfound freedom to redesign people's jobs without consultation or negotiation.

Do job descriptions still exist in your organisation or one with which you are familiar? If they have been abandoned, has this led to greater autonomy or greater stress? If detailed job descriptions still exist, how well do these work?

BOX 20 A TRADITIONAL VIEW OF PERSON SPECIFICATIONS

Rodger's seven-point plan

- *Physical make-up:* physical attributes such as ability to lift heavy loads or differentiate between colours.
- *Attainments:* educational or professional qualifications considered necessary for undertaking the work.
- *General intelligence:* ability to define and solve problems, and use initiative in dealing with issues that have arisen.
- *Special aptitudes:* skills, attributes or competencies that are specifically relevant to the particular job.
- *Interests:* both work-related and leisure pursuits that may be relevant to performance in the job.
- *Disposition:* attitudes to work and to other members of staff and customers, as well as friendliness and assertiveness.
- *Circumstances:* domestic commitments, mobility and family support.

Munro Fraser's five-point plan

- *Impact on others:* this covers much the same sort of issues as 'physical make-up' but it is more focused on impact on other employees and customers.
- *Acquired knowledge and qualifications:* see Rodger's second category above.
- *Innate abilities:* see 'general intelligence' above.
- *Motivation:* a person's desire to succeed in particular aspects of work and their commitment to achieve these goals.
- *Adjustment:* characteristics specifically related to the job, such as ability to cope with difficult customers or work well in a team.

168

Case studies of varied lengths and complexity give practical, real-life situations as a way of relating theory to practice. The case studies are taken from a wide range of organisations, including public, private and voluntary sectors, manufacturing and service industries and from various countries.

Questions accompanying case studies or tables are designed to assess students' understanding of the practical example or data and the underlying theory and concepts.

Figures and Tables are used to illustrate key concepts in a detailed and illustrative way to serve as memorable learning aids.

Activities provide self-test facilities for students, encouraging them to relate the topic under discussion to their own organisation or one with which they are familiar, or engaging aids for lecturers to use in a classroom situation or as a piece of assessed work.

HRM, Strategy and Performance

HRM, Strategy and the Global Context

CHAPTER 1

INTRODUCTION

HRM is now often seen as the major factor differentiating between successful and unsuccessful organisations, more important than technology or finance in achieving competitive advantage. This is particularly apparent in the service sector where workers are the primary source of contact with customers, either face-to-face in a service encounter or over the telephone or the Internet. Even in manufacturing firms the way in which human resources are managed is seen as an increasingly critical component in the production process, primarily in terms of quality and reliability. Much of this revolves around the extent to which workers are prepared to use their discretion to improve products and services.

In this argument a particular style of HRM is envisaged, one that can be broadly termed the 'high commitment' model. But HRM – as the management of employment – can take many forms in practice and it may vary between organisations and the occupational group that is targeted. There have been major debates about precisely what is meant by HRM, how it differs from personnel management and industrial relations, and in the extent to which it is seen to serve employer objectives alone rather than aiming to satisfy the expectations of other stakeholders. This means that HRM cannot be analysed in isolation from the wider strategic objectives of employers and measured against these, specifically the need to satisfy shareholders or (in the public sector) government and societal demands for efficiency and effectiveness. However, strategy itself is also a multidimensional concept and, despite common usage of the term, it is more complex than the simple military analogy implies. Strategies emerge within organisations rather than being set merely by senior managers (generals) and cascaded down the hierarchy by more junior managers to the workers (the troops). Moreover, as we show graphically in Chapters 1 and 2, strategies are also influenced by wider societal objectives, legislative and political frameworks, social and economic institutions, and a range of different stakeholder interests. This is most apparent when we analyse the way in which multinational companies (MNCs) operate in different countries and how the interplay between home- and host-country influences shapes HRM. In short, whilst this book is primarily about HRM, our discussion cannot be meaningful without some analysis of how it relates to organisational strategies and institutional forces. This chapter examines the first of these – the interplay between HRM, strategy and globalisation – while Chapter 2 reviews the wide range of influences that shape HRM at work.

By the end of this chapter, readers should be able to:

- **advise senior managers about how to recognise and respond to a wide range of stakeholder influences on business and HR strategies to enhance organisational and individual performance**

- **demonstrate an ethical and professional approach to HRM taking into account its multiple meanings**

- **contribute to recommendations about how organisations manage HR both in the UK and overseas.**

In addition, readers should understand and be able to explain:

■ the competing meanings of the term 'strategy', and their implications for HRM

■ the nature and importance of ethics, professionalism and diversity and their contribution to the business and moral case for HRM

■ the basis on which HR policies are established in multinational organisations due to the influence of home- and host-country factors.

THE MEANINGS OF HRM

HRM is a relatively new area of study that is seeking to gain credibility in comparison with more established academic disciplines. It is often contrasted with industrial relations and personnel management, with the former laying claim to represent the theoretical basis of the subject while the latter is viewed as the practical and prescriptive homeland for issues concerning the management of people. In addition, there are so many variants of HRM it is easy to find slippage in its use, especially when critics are comparing the apparent *rhetoric* of 'high commitment' HRM with the so-called *reality* of life in organisations that manage by fear and cost-cutting (Keenoy 1990; Caldwell 2003). As the remainder of the book explores these sorts of issues in depth, we focus here on a brief resume of the main strands of the subject. In the concluding section of the chapter we outline our own definition of HRM.

The origins of HRM

There is little doubt that the HRM terminology originated in the USA subsequent to the human relations movement. Two schools of thought predominate: Fombrun *et al*'s matching model and the Harvard framework.

The matching model (Fombrun *et al* 1984) emphasises the links between organisational strategy and HRM, dividing the latter into selection, development, appraisal and reward. The human resource cycle – as the four components are known – are tied together in terms of how effectively they deliver improved performance. In Devanna *et al*'s (1984, p41) words:

> Performance is a function of all the HR components: selecting people who are the best able to perform the jobs defined by the structure; appraising their performance to facilitate the equitable distribution of rewards; motivating employees by linking rewards to high levels of performance; and developing employees to enhance their current performance at work as well as to prepare them to perform in positions they may hold in the future.

The focus is on ensuring that there is a 'match' or 'fit' between the overall direction of the organisation and the way in which its people should be managed. The approach to rewards, for example, is expected to vary dependent on strategy; it is suggested that a single product firm would deal with this in an unsystematic and paternalistic manner while a diversified firm would operate through large bonuses based on profitability and subjective assessments about contribution to company performance. With regard to selection, the criteria used range from the subjective to the standardised and systematic depending on the strategy and structure of the firm (Devanna *et al* 1984, pp38–39). It is essentially a unitarist analysis of HRM whereby the management of people is 'read-off' from the broader objectives of the organisation. No account is taken of the interests of different stakeholders nor is there much room for strategic choice (Bratton and Gold 2003, p19).

By contrast, the Harvard framework (Beer *et al* 1985) consists of six basic components. These are:

1   *situational factors*, such as workforce characteristics, management philosophy and labour market conditions, which combine to shape the environment within which organisations operate

2   *stakeholder interests*, such as the compromises and tradeoffs that occur between the owners of the enterprise and its employees and the unions. This makes the Beer *et al* framework much less unitarist than some of the other models (Bratton and Gold 2003, p20).

3   *HRM policy choices*, in the areas of employee influence, HR flow, reward systems and work systems. Employee influence is seen as the most important of these four areas, again making this model somewhat different from some other versions of HRM.

4   *HR outcomes*, in terms of what are termed the '4Cs' – commitment, competence, cost effectiveness and congruence. This incorporates issues connected with trust, motivation and skills, and it is argued that greater employee influence in the affairs of the company is likely to foster greater congruence (Beer *et al* 1985, p37).

5   *long-term consequences*, such as individual well-being, organisational effectiveness and societal goals. Unlike many other models of HRM, this framework is explicit in recognising the role that employers play in helping to achieve wider societal goals such as employment and growth.

6   a *feedback loop*, which is the final component in the framework, demonstrating that it is not conceived as a simple, unilinear set of relationships between the different components.

Whilst acknowledging the role for alternative stakeholder interests – including government and the community – this framework still remains essentially positivist because it assumes a dominant direction of influence from broader situational and stakeholder interests through to HR outcomes and long-term consequences. In reality, the relationship is much more complex and fragmented as employers are unable to make policy choices in such a structured way, especially if they operate in networks of firms up and down supply chains or across national boundaries. Neither of the US frameworks pays much attention to the realities of work inside organisations and especially to the contested, contradictory and fragmented nature of the employment relationship.

Interest in HRM in the UK – both as an academic subject and a source of interest for practitioners – developed in the late 1980s, and contributions have come from a plurality of disciplinary backgrounds. Bach and Sisson (2000) identify three traditions. The first, the prescriptive tradition, was the dominant approach in the literature, stemming from the domain of personnel management, and it examined and prescibed the 'best' tools and techniques for use by practitioners. It was essentially vocational in character, although the universal prescriptions that were put forward had much greater resonance in large firms with well-staffed personnel functions. As with much of the US literature it was unitarist in its underpinning values, assuming that workers and employers could work together to achieve mutual gains within the framework of traditional hierarchical and capitalist relations. The second tradition, according to Bach and Sisson, was the labour process school, which contrasted sharply with the benevolent, yet paternalist, image of the prescriptive tradition. Whilst helping to introduce more critical accounts of HRM, and later providing a more nuanced and more subjective understanding of how organisations work, it tended to critique management for everything it did, in some cases assuming that managers' sole objective in life was to subjugate workers. The third tradition was from industrial relations, and here HRM was seen as 'part of a system of employment regulation in which internal and external influences shape the management of the employment relationship' (Bach and Sisson 2000, p8). Using both detailed case study and quantitative techniques, often from the Workplace Employee Relations Surveys, students have analysed HRM *in practice* in order to develop our understanding of the main elements of the employment relationship. Whilst crucially bringing in a pluralist perspective on HRM, this tended to focus on collective aspects of the employment relationship, and in particular view all forms of employment – including non-union firms – against the template of a unionised environment. To Bach and Sisson's three traditions, we can add a fourth, stemming from the work of organisational psychologists. Whilst common in the USA, this has become more significant in the UK as scholars analyse in more detail HR issues connected with selection, appraisal, learning and development, and the psychological contract. As we see throughout this book, this tradition has been at the forefront of studies examining the links between various aspects of HR strategy and practice and employee outcome measures such as commitment and satisfaction. In contradistinction to the industrial relations tradition, this approach tends to downplay notions of conflict and resistance, as well as overlook the realities of HRM at the workplace.

> Work in groups to compare these contrasting traditions in terms of their underlying assumptions, the HR practices on which they mainly focus and those they ignore or downplay.

The British debate initially focused on the distinction between 'hard' and 'soft' models of HRM (Storey 1989; Legge 1995). The 'hard' model – as with Fombrun *et al*'s approach – stresses the links between business and HR strategies and the crucial importance of a tight fit between the two. From this perspective, the human resource is seen as similar to all other resources – land and capital, for example – being used as management sees fit. Under this scenario, which stresses the 'resource' aspect of HRM, there is no pretence that labour has anything other than commodity status even though it may be treated well if the conditions are conducive, that is, when it is in short supply or it is central to the achievement of organisational objectives. Broadly, however, it would eschew the rules and procedures of industrial relations – such as procedures for dealing with redundancy – because they reduce employer flexibility to select on the basis of who they think is most valuable to the organisation.

By contrast, the 'soft' model focuses on the management of 'resourceful humans', assuming that employees are valued assets and a source of competitive advantage through their skills and abilities. Within this conception of HRM, there is one best way to manage staff, and this requires managers to engender commitment and loyalty in order to ensure high levels of performance. Storey (2001, p6) defines the soft version in the following way: 'HRM is a distinctive approach to employment management which seeks to achieve competitive advantage through the strategic deployment of a highly committed and capable workforce using an array of cultural, structural and personnel techniques.' Whereas the 'hard' model allows for a range of different styles, the 'soft' variant argues that one style is superior to all others in promoting levels of employee motivation, commitment and satisfaction that are necessary for excellent performance. In short, HRM can be viewed as a particular *style* of managing that is capable of being measured and defined, as well as compared against the template of an ideal model.

The soft/high commitment version of HRM has attracted most interest, especially in those seeking links between HRM and performance. Although important at the time, it also stimulated what might now be seen as a series of somewhat sterile debates about whether the management of employment equates more closely with HRM or with industrial relations and personnel management. For example, Guest (1987) differentiated personnel and HRM in terms of how they viewed the psychological contract, locus of control, employee relations, organising principles and policy goals. HRM was seen to incorporate a more organic, flexible, bottom-up and decentralised approach than personnel management which relied on mechanistic, formal rules delivered in a top-down and centralised manner. Storey (1992) compared HRM with personnel management and industrial relations, identifying 27 points of difference between the two in terms of beliefs and assumptions, strategic aspects, line management and key levers. Broadly, HRM – again seen as a distinct style – was regarded as less bureaucratic, more strategic, more integrated with business objectives, and substantially devolved to line managers; the key elements of the HRM model are outlined in

BOX 1   JOHN STOREY'S MODEL OF HRM

Beliefs and assumptions

- The human resource gives organisations a competitive edge.
- Employee commitment is more important than mere compliance.
- Careful selection and development are central to HRM.

Strategic qualities

- HR decisions are of strategic importance.
- Senior managers must be involved in HRM.
- HR policies need to be integrated into business strategy.

Critical role for line managers

- HR is too important to be left to personnel specialists alone.
- Line managers need to be closely involved as delivers and drivers of HR.
- The management of managers is critically important.

Key levers

- Managing culture is more important than procedures and systems.
- Horizontal integration between different HR practices is essential.
- Jobs need to be designed to allow devolved responsibility and empowerment.

Source: Adapted from Storey J. (ed), *Human Resource Management: A critical text*, 2nd edition. London, Thomson. 2001. p7

Box 1 (see page 7). Legge (1995) also compared HRM and personnel management in terms of how each related to strategy, to the role of line managers and to the contribution of the specialist function. There has been particular interest in the links between HRM and strategy, often however focusing solely on a particular version of strategy.

BUSINESS AND CORPORATE STRATEGIES

The classical perspective

Most definitions of strategy in the business and management field stem from the work of Chandler (1962), who argued that the structure of an organisation flowed from its growth strategy. Since then there have been major differences of opinion about the extent to which a strategy is deliberate or emergent, and about the extent to which organisations are able to determine strategies without taking into account wider societal trends and forces, and in particular the economic, legal and political frameworks within the countries in which they are located. Of course, some large multinational companies are able to exercise influence beyond national boundaries, and actually affect the development of policy within countries, but this amount of power is usually reserved for a small number of global players. The reality for most organisations is that strategic choices are shaped by forces beyond their immediate control. Nevertheless, organisations do have some room for manoeuvre to create their own strategies for the business.

Grant (1998, p3) notes that 'strategy is about winning ... [It] is not a detailed plan or programme of instructions; it is a unifying theme that gives coherence and direction to the actions and decisions of an individual or an organisation'. The leading British text on the subject (Johnson and Scholes 2002, p10) defines strategy as:

> the direction and scope of an organisation over the long term, which achieves competitive advantage for the organisation through its configuration of resources within a changing environment and to fulfil stakeholder expectations.

Drawing on these two definitions (Grant 1998, pp9–11; Johnson and Scholes 2002, pp5–9), the principal elements of 'strategy', in the classical sense of the word, are:

1   Establishing the *long-term* direction of the organisation, looking a number of years ahead and attempting to identify the product markets and geographical locations in which the business is most likely to survive and prosper. Goals need to be simple and consistent. The strategy that is adopted has clear implications for HR policy and practice, as well as for the types of workers needed in future. Of course, shocks to the system – such as major new inventions, political upheaval or changes in health and safety legislation – may disrupt strategic plans but without them organisations are likely to be rudderless.

2   Driving the organisation forward to achieve *sustained competitive advantage*. This may emerge through the creation of new products or services or in providing better value for money in a way that can be sustained even if competitors also take advantage of similar gains or move in other equally or more profitable directions. In HR terms this may lead to decisions about whether higher levels of performance are more likely from a quality enhancement or innovation route or one that focuses almost exclusively on cost reduction. However, as Boxall and Purcell (2003, p30) note, other

organisations do not stand still but also adapt continuously to achieve their own competitive advantage.

3   Determining the *scope* of the organisation's activities, in terms of whether it chooses to remain primarily in one sector and line of business or diversify into other areas. This can be done so as to spread risk by creating a balanced portfolio or seeking success from growing markets and higher profit margin products. Decisions are also required to determine geographical market coverage. Each of these different strategies has HR implications, for example in terms of the type of staff required or the extent to which services are provided by in-house personnel or subcontracted labour. Decisions concerning scope centre on the boundaries of organisations, and ultimately power differences between organisations up and down the supply chain, can have a significant impact on HR practices (Marchington *et al* 2004c).

4   *Matching* their internal resources and activities to the environments in which the organisation operates so as to achieve strategic fit. This requires an assessment of internal strengths and weaknesses as well as external opportunities and threats (SWOT) in order to decide how best to design the organisation to meet current and future needs. In HR terms, major problems can occur if enough adequately qualified and trained staff have not been employed to enable the organisation to meet its strategic objectives and satisfy customer demand. However, because other organisations are also trying to achieve this match, they may poach the best staff.

5   Recognising that top-level decisions have major implications for *operational* activities, especially when there is a merger or takeover, a joint venture or public–private partnership, or even a change in the organisation's strategic direction following a review of its activities. Grant (1998) particularly emphasises the need for effective implementation because if operational activities cannot adapt to new strategic goals, competitive advantage is hardly likely to flow. For example, deciding to grow the business through the creation of an IT-led customer service model will fail if there are not enough staff to receive calls or they are poorly trained. One of the biggest problems in any large organisation, especially one that operates across a number of different product areas, is determining the most appropriate structures and systems to put strategies into effect.

6   Appreciating that the *values and expectations* of senior decision-makers play a sizeable part in the development of strategy because it is how they choose to interpret advice about external and internal resources that ultimately shapes strategic decisions (Lovas and Ghoshal 2000). Although many organisations within the same market might choose to follow a similar path some may decide to differentiate themselves from the competition by adopting different strategies. This may or may not appear 'logical' from a rationalist perspective, but entrepreneurs typically want to mould organisations in line with their own style. In HR terms their attitudes towards trade unions or the employment of people with criminal records, for example, may set them apart from the rest of the market. There can be problems here as well, especially when a founder refuses to shift from their preferred position or a family-owned firm decides or is forced to bring in professional managers from outside.

Within this perspective, strategy is seen to operate at three levels. Corporate strategy relates to the overall scope of the organisation, its structures and financing, and the distribution of resources between its different constituent parts. Business or competitive strategy refers to how the organisation competes in a given market, its approaches to product development and to customers. Operational strategies are concerned with how the various subunits –

marketing, finance, manufacturing and so on – contribute to the higher level strategies. HRM would be seen as an element at this third level, although Johnson and Scholes (2002), in common with most writers on strategy, devote hardly any space to the human aspects of organisations.

This top-down perspective, in which it is assumed that strategies are formulated by boards of directors and then cascaded down the organisation, represents the dominant view of strategy in most published literature on the subject, and it is derived from military roots. Lundy and Cowling (1996, p16) note that the dictionary definition of strategy conveys this: 'the art of war, general-ship, especially the art of directing military movements so as to secure the most advantageous positions and combinations of forces'. Quinn (1988) suggests there are four dimensions to formal strategy:

- information, policies to guide or limit action, and action sequences to be accomplished

- the development of a few key concepts that need to be balanced and co-ordinated

- strength and flexibility to deal with uncertain events

- a supportive and cohesive hierarchy of mutually supporting strategies.

In short, the classical version of strategy relies upon an image of detached senior managers who determine the best plans for deploying workers to achieve victory over the competition.

Alternative perspectives on strategy

The 'classical' model is not the only way in which to look at strategy, however (Hussey 1998), and an alternative approach is put forward by writers such as Quinn and Mintzberg that treats strategies as *emergent* rather than deliberate. Quinn (1980, p58) regards the most effective strategies as those that tend to 'emerge step by step from an iterative process in which the organisation probes the future, experiments, and learns from a series of partial (incremental) commitments rather than through a global formulation of total strategies'. Quite rightly this casts doubt on the perspective that organisations make decisions on the basis of cold, clinical assessments in an 'objective' manner. Decisions are taken by people whose own subjective preferences and judgements clearly influence outcomes. Mistakes are made for a variety of reasons, and conditions change so as to render decisions that seemed sensible at the time totally inappropriate at a later date. Interpersonal political tensions and battles also play a major part in the outcome of decision-making processes within organisations. Mintzberg's (1987) notion of strategy being 'crafted' evokes ideas of skill and judgement, as well as people working together to make sense of confusing situations before reaching a conclusion that appears to offer a way forward. Of course, neither the classical nor the emergent perspective is correct in entirety. Mintzberg and his colleagues (1998, p11) have suggested that strategies are neither purely deliberate nor purely emergent as 'one means no learning, the other means no control. All real-world strategies need to mix these in some ways; to exercise some control while fostering learning.' Deliberate and emergent strategies form the poles of a continuum along which actual practice falls (Stiles 2001). Moreover, as we see below, strategy is sometimes used as a device for rationalising and legitimising decisions after they have been made. When people are subsequently asked to explain the rationale behind decisions which seemed messy and complex at the time, they often seem much more rational and clear cut in retrospect (Marchington *et al* 1993a).

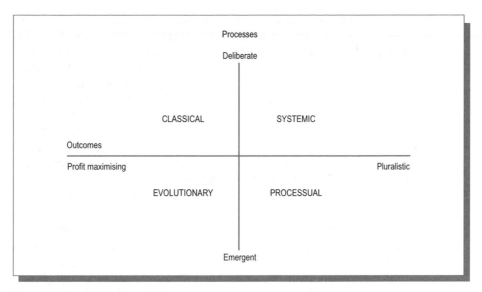

Figure 1 *Whittington's typology of strategy*

Source: Adapted from Whittington R. *What is Strategy and Does it Matter?* London, Routledge, 1993

Whittington's (1993) fourfold typology is extremely useful in helping us understand the complex and multidimensional nature of strategy. This is presented in Figure 1. It is based upon distinctions between the degree to which outcomes are perceived purely in either profit-maximising or pluralistic terms, and the extent to which strategy formulation is seen as either deliberate or emergent.

The four types are:

- *Classical* (profit-maximising, deliberate) – As we have seen, under this conception, strategy is portrayed as a rational process of deliberate calculation and analysis, undertaken by senior managers who survey the external environment searching for ways in which to maximise profits and gain competitive advantage. It is characterised as non-political, the product of honest endeavour by managers who have nothing but the organisation's interests at heart, and who are able to remain above the day-to-day skirmishes that typify life at lower levels in the hierarchy. In firms that have been dominated by engineering cultures, for example, senior managers like to portray themselves as independent professionals who make decisions in the best interests of all stakeholders. Using the military analogy by separating formulation from implementation, Whittington (1993, pp15–17) notes that 'plans are conceived in the general's tent, overlooking the battlefield but sufficiently detached for safety ... the actual carrying-out of orders is relatively unproblematic, assured by military discipline and obedience'. The classical view of strategy leaves little room for choice when devising HR plans, working on the assumption there is 'one-best way' to manage people and employment.

- *Evolutionary* (profit-maximising, emergent) – From this angle, strategy is seen as a product of market forces, in which the most efficient and productive organisations win through. Drawing on notions of population ecology, 'the most appropriate strategies within a given market emerge as competitive processes allow the relatively better performers to survive while the weaker performers are squeezed out and go to the wall' (Legge 1995, p99). For evolutionists 'strategy can be a dangerous delusion' (Whittington 1993, p20). Taken to its extreme, it could be argued there is little point in planning a deliberate strategy since winners and losers will be 'picked' by a process of natural selection that is beyond the influence of senior managers. They might, however, see some advantage in keeping their options open and learning how to adapt to changing customer demands, a process that Lovas and Ghoshal (2000) refer to as 'guided evolution'. Under this scenario, the maintenance of flexible systems, whether in HRM or elsewhere, is an important component of competitive advantage. Boxall and Purcell (2003) make a useful differentiation between the problem of viability (remaining in business) and the problem of sustained advantage (playing in the 'higher level tournament' through superior performance). Since so much of the debate about strategy focuses on the latter, this is a very useful corrective; we return to this point in Chapter 4.

■ *Processual* (pluralistic, emergent) – This view stems from an assumption that people are 'too limited in their understanding, wandering in their attention, and careless in their actions to unite around and then carry through a perfectly calculated plan' (Whittington 1993, p4). There are at least two essential features to this perspective. First, as Mintzberg (1978) argues, strategies tend to evolve through a process of discussion and disagreement that involves managers at different levels in an organisation, and in some cases it is impossible to specify what the strategy is until after the event. Indeed, actions may only come to be defined as strategies with the benefit of hindsight, by a process of post hoc rationalisation whereby stories are recounted that appear to be rational and carefully planned in retrospect. Quinn's (1980) notion of 'logical incrementalism', the idea that strategy emerges in a fragmented and largely intuitive manner, evolving from a combination of internal decisions and external events, fits well with this perspective. Second, the processual view takes a micropolitical perspective, acknowledging that organisations are beset with tensions and contradictions, with rivalries and conflicting goals, and with behaviours that seek to achieve personal or departmental objectives (Pettigrew 1973; Marchington *et al* 1993a). Strategic plans may be worth little in reality but they help to give some credibility to decisions, as well as a security blanket for decision-makers who operate with severely bounded knowledge about future events. From this perspective, strategy can never be perfect and, as Whittington (1993, p27) notes, it is 'by recognising and accommodating real world imperfections that managers can be most effective' rather than naively following a classical version of strategy that does not exist in practice.

■ *Systemic* (pluralistic, deliberate) – The final perspective follows Granovetter (1985) in suggesting that strategy is shaped by the social system in which it is embedded – factors such as class, gender, legal regulations and educational systems shape the way in which employers and workers behave. From this perspective, strategic choices are influenced not so much by the cognitive limitations of the actors involved but by the cultural and institutional interests of a broader society. For example, institutional forces in countries such as France and Germany have helped to shape HRM rather differently from Anglo-Saxon countries such as Britain and the USA (Lane 1989; Ferner and Quintanilla 1998; Rubery and Grimshaw 2003). Additionally, Whittington (1993, p30) argues that the very notion of 'strategy' may be culturally peculiar because it arose in the particular conditions of post-war North America. In other countries, the dominant perspective may be that the fate of organisations is pre-ordained and therefore unaffected by managerial actions, or it could based upon philosophies that regard the provision of work for local communities much more desirable than short-term gains for shareholders. A further advantage of viewing strategy from this perspective is that it enables us to appreciate how – under the classical approach – management actions are legitimised by reference to external forces, so cloaking 'managerial power in the culturally acceptable clothing of science and objectivity' (p37). Ultimately, the systemic perspective challenges the universality of any single model of strategy and demonstrates the importance of seeing organisational goals in the context of the countries and cultures in which they are located; 'strategy must be sociologically sensitive' (p39).

Discuss these competing versions of strategy with colleagues from other cultures or societies, and then try to take a fresh look at your original views.

This discussion of strategy has interesting implications for how we view its links with HRM. Under the classical perspective it can be seen as unproblematic, merely a matter of making the right decision and then cascading this through the managerial hierarchy to shop-floor or office workers, who then snap into action to meet organisational goals. The evolutionary view complicates the situation slightly, in that it puts a primacy upon market forces and the perceived need for organisations (which are seen in unitarist terms) to respond quickly and effectively to customer demands. This introduces notions of power and flexibility into the equation compared with notions of objectivity that underpins the classical perspective. The two pluralist perspectives highlight the contested nature of organisational life and demonstrate the barriers to fully fledged vertical integration in practice, whether this be due to tensions within management or to challenges which may be mounted by workers. The systemic perspective also forces us to look beyond the level of the employing organisation and be aware that employers are not totally free to determine their own strategies in many situations. Problems are bound to arise if critical social norms or cultural traditions are ignored or it is assumed that HR practices that work in one country can be automatically parachuted into others. Indeed, as Paauwe (2004, pp170–173) shows clearly in his study of a US firm operating in the USA and the Netherlands, planned change was typical in the former, whereas in the Dutch plants ample room was allowed for employee influence and for changes in the content of decisions during the process. These points need to be borne in mind in Chapter 4 because most of the models assume the predominance of classical perspectives on strategy.

STAKEHOLDERS, DIVERSITY AND CORPORATE RESPONSIBILITY

The balanced scorecard and human capital reporting

Strategy is not simply about financial returns to shareholders but also involves a rather wider base of stakeholders that includes customers, local communities, environmental issues, and of course workers. We take a similar line to Paauwe (2004) in stressing that HRM is different from other managerial functions because of its professional and moral base, and – in some countries more than others – its rejection of the simplistic view that HRM is merely a means to achieve greater corporate profits and shareholder returns. This is not to deny the importance of making an effective contribution to organisational goals but that trust and integrity are also critically important elements in how HRM is practised at work.

In a series of publications Kaplan and Norton (1996, 2001) argue that traditional approaches to management accounting have focused on short-term financial performance. This ignores the needs and expectations of other stakeholders and the way in which they are linked to organisational goals. They suggest (1996) that there should be a balance between four perspectives on business performance – financial, customers, internal business processes, and learning and growth – which can be combined to form the 'balanced scorecard'. Employees figure principally within the learning and growth perspective, although it is apparent that employee skills and satisfaction is identified as a critical factor only so far as this can enhance customer satisfaction and financial performance through their ability to support business strategy – not through any moral perspective. Kaplan and Norton (1996, p75) feel the scorecard enables 'companies to track financial results while simultaneously monitoring progress in building the capabilities and acquiring the intangible assets they would need for future growth. The scorecard wasn't a replacement for financial measures; it was their complement.' Evidence from an IRS survey (IRS Employment Review 796a 2004, p14) shows that only a minority of organisations make use of balanced scorecards but those that do seem to be enthusiasts, especially from amongst the HR community.

While accepting it is helpful to try and integrate 'key HR performance drivers into the strategic management framework', Boxall and Purcell (2003, p242) are concerned the balanced scorecard approach does not go far enough and it assumes certain HR practices are universally effective in promoting better performance. By contrast, they argue (p245) the way in which employer and employee interests might be aligned depends to a great extent on the circumstances and the institutional regimes within which organisations operate, and that what might appear highly appropriate in a US context (say, bonus systems) could well prove counterproductive in another. Moreover, it could be argued that the balanced scorecard approach includes additional processes merely in terms of their contribution to improved performance. It is very 'top-down' in its approach; for example, a key feature is communicating and educating the vision, HR processes that are seen as important in ensuring all employees understand the strategy and the 'critical objectives they have to meet if the strategy is to succeed' (Kaplan and Norton 1996, p80). Similarly some of the organisations they studied were solely interested in employee morale because of its links with customer satisfaction. Nothing is wrong with these objectives, but they are hardly 'alternative' in the sense of seeking to satisfy needs for equality at work or in addressing issues of corporate responsibility. Maltz et al (2003, p197) have attempted to rectify the lack of focus on the employee strand of the balanced scorecard by including a 'people development' dimension that explicitly recognises the critical role of employees in organisational success.

There have also been some attempts to develop HR scorecards as a means of measuring the return on investment in HR programmes, specifically in terms of the value created by deliverables and the control of costs through more efficient operations (Sparrow et al 2004, p170). These tend to rely on a similar range of metrics to those used in other approaches, basically relying on factors that impact directly on organisational performance – such as labour turnover, absence levels and productivity. An alternative – the real balanced HRM scorecard – is being developed by Paauwe (2004). This starts from the stance that HR specialists cannot focus solely on criteria such as efficiency, effectiveness and flexibility from an organisational standpoint, and that they should be prepared to risk unpopularity by questioning short-termist approaches that are so widespread. He argues (p184) that 'other appropriate criteria are those of fairness (in the exchange relationship between the individual and the organisation) and legitimacy (the relation between society and organisation)'. The 4logic HRM scorecard that Paauwe (pp194–208) develops consists of four components – strategic, professional, societal and delivery. The professional and societal logics comprise factors such as the following:

- providing assurance and trust about financial reporting of organisations
- maximising both tangible and intangible rewards to employees
- delivering reliable information to works council members
- offering information and individual help to employees
- safeguarding fairness in management–worker relations.

Recently there has been extensive interest in the idea of human capital reporting, stimulated by the Kingsmill Report, *Accounting for People* (2003a), and the requirement that by 2006 quoted companies will have to provide a 'high level, strategic commentary on a range of issues that includes the people dimension (IRS Employment Review 802 2004, p12). Not unusually for the UK, there were tensions between members on the Kingsmill Task Force about whether organisations should be allowed the flexibility to select from a wide menu of measures that reflected their own circumstances or prescribed a common core of areas in order to ensure rigour and comparability (Kingsmill 2003a, p14). Further work is to be done on this issue, but the Task Force did identify some areas that are likely to be relevant in the overwhelming majority of cases (p17). These relate to information about: (1) the size and composition of the workforce; (2) retention and motivation of employees; (3) training and the fit between skills and business needs; (4) remuneration and fair employment policies; and (5) leadership and succession planning. Some of the questions that directors might ask themselves in presenting this information are included in Box 2.

BOX 2   ACCOUNTING FOR PEOPLE: A SAMPLE OF THE KEY QUESTIONS

Information on the size and composition of the workforce

- What strategic trends are affecting the size of the workforce, either overall or in particular geographic areas or occupational groups?
- Are the age, gender and ethnic profiles of its workforce appropriate for the strategy it is pursuing?
- Is the balance between full-time and part-time workers relevant to its strategy?

Information on retention and motivation of employees

- Is the level of staff turnover 'efficient' in terms of the business strategy or it too high or too low to achieve the desired balance between new blood and experience?
- Do indicators of possible lack of engagement point to a lack of 'buy-in' to the organisation's strategy and what are the implications for the organisation's ability to pursue that strategy?
- What other intelligence is there on how far all sections of the workforce are engaged with its aims and values, for example through staff surveys, and do the directors understand the factors driving this?

Information on training and the fit between skills and business needs

- How does the skills base relate to current and future business needs?
- How do actual and planned training and development contribute?
- How does the organisation develop talent internally and how successful are the techniques it uses?

Information on remuneration and employment practices

■ What is the structure of remuneration and do the resulting differentials fit with the business strategy?

■ Is the balance between rewards for individual performance and rewards for team- or enterprise-based performance best suited to strategic needs?

■ How does the organisation satisfy itself that it does not discriminate unfairly in pay and employment?

Information on leadership and succession planning

■ What are the leadership skills and characteristics needed to implement the strategy the organisation is pursuing?

■ What is the role of external recruitment and what are the costs and benefits of recruiting in this way?

■ What initiatives does the organisation have to develop future leadership internally, and how successful are these?

Source: Adapted from *Accounting for People: Report of the Task Force on Human Capital Management*, presented to the Secretary of State for Trade and Industry, October 2003. pp17–19

Diversity at work

The management of diversity has now become the main avenue for addressing equal opportunities issues in employing organisations. This includes factors such as gender, age, ethnicity, disability and sexual orientation (Hicks-Clarke and Iles 2000), and it is recognised that 'people from different backgrounds bring fresh ideas and perceptions which make the way work is done more efficient and products and services better' (CIPD 1999). Typically this means the business case for equal opportunities is made in terms of benefits that might accrue to the organisation as a whole, rather than any assessment of how this might enhance the lives of workers. According to a number of sources (Cassell 2001; Anderson and Metcalf 2003; IRS Employment Review 785 2003), the business benefits include:

1 improved customer satisfaction and market penetration by employing a diverse workforce whose composition is similar to that of the local population

2 enhanced worker motivation and the use of skills from a diverse workforce

3 improved supply of labour because the organisation is seen as a 'good' employer

4 avoidance of costly discrimination cases because action has been taken to ensure the use of systematic and professional HR practices in selection and promotion.

Despite arguments in favour of employing a more diverse workforce, doubts remain about the durability and likely conversion of these potential benefits into everyday HR practice. The 'business case' can be fragile because it is so reliant on the specific circumstances confronting each organisation, as well as changes in the wider legal, political, economic and social context, which may lead employers to downgrade equality arguments if they are not seen to be of pressing concern. Other employers may have little interest in the long-term case for equality because they can gain substantially (in the short term, at least) from employing low-paid workers. Diversity may be accepted by employers in the case of professionals whose skill is scarce but ignored for casual or unskilled employees (Cassell

2001, p419). Moreover, despite national or corporate policies supporting equal opportunities, there can be pressure from existing staff who are male, white and able-bodied to protect their interests rather than those of disadvantaged groups. Furthermore, Dickens (1999) criticises the use of the business case to promoting equality because this excludes those external to employing organisations and it may actually increase disparities within groups – for example between white and ethnic minority women.

A new set of attitudes, beliefs and values is at the heart of effective equality provision, yet it is very difficult to change beliefs that may be deep-rooted, implicit and resistant to alternative ideas. Kandola and Fullerton (1998) argue that equality management needs to be systemic with a widespread and deep-rooted commitment to maximising the potential of the workforce, regardless of its age, gender or sexual orientation. It is only when 'women's or black issues' are recast as 'people's issues' that any real moves towards equality are likely, and diversity is recognised and commended – both in its own right and for its contribution to improved organisational performance.

> Make out a case for increasing diversity at your workplace or one with which you are familiar. To what extent would you draw upon the 'business case' to convince line managers of the value of equality provisions?

Goss (1994, p157) provides a two-dimensional categorisation for the form that equal opportunities policies and practices can take in organisations. First is the *depth* of management's commitment to equality, ranging from shallow and instrumental through to deep and principled. The second dimension, the *breadth* of its focus, ranges from a narrow list of practices driven largely by economic and legal expediency through to a broad set that includes a whole range of issues. This allows for four alternative agendas in practice. The short agenda is shallow and narrow, little more than a lip-service commitment to legal imperatives. The broad agenda combines a broad focus with a shallow commitment to equality. The focused agenda is built upon a narrow base, but at least has the advantage of a deep management commitment to achieve real change. Finally, the long agenda is broad and deep, essentially concerned with changing how the whole organisation is managed, and aiming to develop the talents of all employees.

Corporate responsibility

Corporate responsibility (CR) encompasses social, environmental and financial issues as well as legal compliance. Holme and Watts (2000, p9) define corporate responsibility as 'the commitment of business to contribute to sustainable economic development, working with employees, their families, the local community, and society at large to improve their quality of life'. It includes secondments to community work, charitable donations, responsible/fair trading, human rights and ethical investment. Internal workplace issues relate to the fair treatment of staff, diversity and environmental policies such as recycling and better use of chemicals, packaging and sourcing. It is a strategic issue because it involves fundamental issues about the purpose of business and what is required to remain in operation (CIPD 2003a, p7).

There has been much scepticism about corporate responsibility and it is not hard to see why given allegations of sleaze in public life, environmental catastrophes and continued global inequalities. Many continue to take Friedman's (1970) view that the only social responsibility of business is to maximise profits. This perspective is challenged by the stakeholder model that regards business as not just about profit but also about the well-being of individuals and society.

Awareness of CR is currently high on the corporate agenda, possibly as a reaction to major scandals (eg Bhopal, Brent Spar, Enron, Work Com, Union Carbide, Exxon, Nestle) and the lack of trust in business (Nijhof *et al* 2002, pp83–90). There is increasing legislative and regulatory pressure, in part recognising that ambitious social agendas – such as those set down at the UN Millennium Summit – cannot be achieved without the support of the business community. In 2000 the UN launched the Global Compact urging companies to comply with principles around human rights, labour standards, and environmental protection. In 2001 the EU Green paper on Corporate Social Responsibility was published to complement the EU Charter of Fundamental Rights and the Sustainability Strategy for Europe, in addition to the OECD guidelines and ILO labour standards. Aside from national legislation, pressure has also come from shareholders, with the Cadbury (1992), Greenbury (1995) and Hampel (1998) Reports giving guidance on best practice and there have been shareholder revolts over human rights abuses. Increases in the growth of socially responsible investment (SRI), as evidenced by FTSE4Good and the Dow Jones Sustainability Index (DJSI) (Tyrell 2003, p4), also provide incentives for employers to take CR seriously. The CSR Academy was launched in 2004 comprising members from a number of organisations including the DTI, the CIPD, the Association of Business Schools, the British Chambers of Commerce, and Business in the Community. At its heart is the creation of a competency framework, a template designed to help managers integrate CSR into their organisations.

Aside from legislation and policy initiatives, the motivation to adopt CR is diverse and overlapping (European Commission 2001, p3; DTI 2002a; IRS Employment Review 756 2002; Mullins 2004) although the business case and concern about loss of customers, investors and employees provides a major push. Sensitivity to criticism is especially noticeable when it is backed by boycotts that damage reputations, profits and prospects of longer term survival. The Co-operative Bank's research, for example, shows that 24 per cent of its profits are attributable to customers who cite ethics as their reason for being with the bank (Co-operative Bank 2002, p18). Requirements that suppliers comply with robust CR standards can also act as a powerful incentive, as Gap found when it was vilified for the labour practices of its suppliers (Lawrence 2002, p10). By contrast, just as with the high commitment HRM, some organisations view CR as a means of providing competitive advantage through differentiation.

> Bill Ford (Chairman of Ford) has stated that whilst 'a good company delivers excellent products and services, a great company delivers excellent products and services and strives to make the world a better place.' Do you agree with this statement? Discuss with your colleagues the idea that large organisations care about objectives other than making short-term profits.

However, there are a number of barriers. First, since CR necessitates systemic change and involves expensive adjustments, organisations competing on cost are unlikely to make the investment. Second, as with diversity management, it is argued that employer commitment to CR is superficial and used merely as a marketing ploy. Because there are problems with current reporting standards, verification systems and the confusing array of standards it is easy to use CR as window dressing (Belal 2002; Cerin 2002). Third, there are major problems in defining what is meant by ethical issues (Ackers 2001, p377) and ultimately this can boil down to considerations of which course of action might result in least harm. Sometimes, despite commitments from an organisation to stop using an unethical practice – such as the use of child labour to stitch footballs – work is subcontracted out to villages, thus making monitoring almost impossible (Legge 2000, p24). However, a report by Save the Children Fund found many children undertook this work in order to pay their school fees and worried that, if this was stopped, they would be forced into more risky work.

There are basically two sets of arguments in favour of establishing some code of international labour standards – social justice and human rights, and productivity – though both are intertwined (Rubery and Grimshaw 2003). The social justice argument assumes that some protections need to be universal – such as minimum standards of health and safety, rights to freedom of speech, and compensation in the event of an accident at work. Others however may be contingent as minimum standards – such as the level of a minimum wage or unemployment benefit – depend on the societal context and what is deemed fair in that situation. The productivity argument works on the assumption that higher skilled workers are generally more productive and committed than their counterparts who have not been trained properly. In addition their ability to use more efficient machinery or systems is higher as is the likelihood they will have fewer accidents at work.

For some market leaders, CR has become entwined with economic success, and is becoming more widespread. However, CR is unlikely to become more widespread without legislation, and unless this specifies rigorous standards of reporting and verification, those firms that use it as a veneer will continue to be able to do so.

INTERNATIONAL AND COMPARATIVE HRM

Although the principal focus in this book is on HRM in the UK, we need briefly to examine the issue of how HR practices might transfer across nation states and international boundaries. This can happen in a number of ways having a direct impact on workers in the UK but also on comparisons that may be made between their performance and those of others working at overseas locations within the same company, or indeed in firms up and down the international supply chain. As we have already argued, organisations are not independent entities that have total control over their own fate – or indeed their 'culture' – due to the shaping influences of legal, political, economic and institutional forces. At the same time, some organisations – especially those with significant financial power – are able to leave their 'footprints' on the nation states within which they operate. Before examining the role of multinational organisations in a little more detail, we need to analyse some of the assumptions that underpin international and comparative HRM.

The debate about convergence and divergence

Rubery and Grimshaw (2003), borrowing from Lane (1989), argue there are three broad schools of thought and theoretical frameworks that are adopted when examining HRM across international boundaries. Whilst acknowledging this simple distinction between the universalists, the culturalists and the institutionalists is inevitably oversimplified and overlapping, it does aid our analysis. In this section of the book we focus most attention on the culturalist perspective since the universalist perspective is addressed extensively in Chapter 3 and the insitutionalist perspective is central to the whole book.

The universalist perspective

This view suggests that whilst HRM may be at different stages of development in different countries, there is a gradual shift towards convergence – at least across developed nations. This comes about for a variety of reasons but principally because it is assumed there is 'one best way' of managing HR – and its associated practices such as job design, work organisation and quality control – which is permeating throughout the developed world. Convergence can occur, according to this approach, across nations as a whole (say, in the so-called modernisation of public services where 'new' practices are picked up both from the private sector and from the public sector in other countries) as well as across particular industries. Rubery and Grimshaw (2003, p31) feel that Womack *et al*'s view is the most explicit of these, being based on 'an unequivocal espousal of the notion of a new universalist best practice technique, based on the lean production model developed within the Japanese car industry'. According to Womack *et al* (1990, p278) the standard production model, with its associated HR practices, will make the world a much better place. The types of HR practice populating this model are primarily American in form, albeit with some influence from Japanese systems, in seeking to individualise the workforce through rewards for outstanding performance (Harris *et al* 2003, p56). The likelihood that these practices can be applied in non-Anglo-Saxon environments is limited, as we see below, and there are even doubts about their theoretical and empirical relevance on a universal basis in the UK (Marchington and Grugulis 2000).

The culturalist perspective

The culturalist perspective offers a welcome critique of universalist approaches, in particular in postulating that there are clear and unambiguous differences between nation states that are enduring and need to be recognised. This sort of thinking is implicit in TV adverts that stress the importance of knowing what particular gestures or mannerisms mean in different countries, and in academic terms it is best exemplified by the work of Hofstede (1980, 1991, 2001). His model, based on questionnaire responses from 117,000 IBM employees in 66 different countries, is exceptionally well-known and appears to carry enormous weight. Initially, it was argued there are four distinct factors across which national cultures vary:

1 *Power distance* – the extent to which societies accept that power in institutions and organisations is and should be distributed unequally.

2 *Uncertainty avoidance* – the degree to which societies feel threatened by ambiguous situations and the extent to which they try to avoid them.

3 *Individualism/collectivism* – the degree to which individuals are integrated into strong and cohesive groups or – conversely – have a quest for personal achievement.

4 *Masculinity/femininity* – the extent to which the dominant values are stereotypically 'male', such as assertiveness or focus on work as a central life interest.

Hofstede (1991) then produced rankings for different countries for each of these four factors, details of which are also provided in Harris *et al* (2003, pp21–26). For example, Britain is ranked towards the bottom of the list for power distance whereas most of the countries where this is most marked are in Asia or Latin America. On uncertainty avoidance, Britain is again towards the bottom (ie supposedly encouraging more diverse views) whereas the top-ranked include southern European countries such as Greece and Portugal. Britain is very high on individualism, along with a number of other Anglo-Saxon countries such as the USA and Australia, whilst many of the most collectivist (ie group-oriented) nations are in Latin America and Asia. Finally, masculinity is quite high in Britain, along with a mix of countries from all over the world, while Scandinavia is the most likely to espouse feminine values. A fifth factor – labelled 'Confucian dynamism' – was added later specifically for Chinese populations because uncertainty avoidance was not felt to be particularly appropriate. However, this has not been as widely used by researchers (McSweeney 2002).

Despite being well-known, the Hofstede approach has been roundly criticised (see for example, McSweeney 2002; Rubery and Grimshaw 2003). There are at least four sets of concerns.

- *Representativeness* – As the research was conducted solely on IBM employees, there are major doubts about the extent to which the results can be generalised to a wider population. Moreover, the respondents were principally from sales and marketing, further undermining the potential for generalisation. Even more worryingly, the sample sizes in some of the countries were very low – eg 37 on one of the surveys in Pakistan (McSweeney 2002, p94). A further question arises over the sponsorship and purpose behind the research because it was not independent of IBM and was used for development needs within the company (McSweeney 2002).

- *Perpetuation of national stereotypes* – The research assumes that cultures are longstanding and not subject to change, but this is clearly open to question when societies adapt through the influx of different communities and traditions that could alter the scores on each of the factors. Moreover, it ignores the existence of subcultures and profoundly different sets of values in different parts of a country; even in a relatively small country such as the UK, there are likely to be major differences between groups on the basis of factors such as social class, gender and region (Rubery and Grimshaw 2003, p36).

- *Explanatory power* – Even if we accept the culturalist data at face value, the models provided by people such as Hofstede do not seek to explain *why* these differences occur or why seemingly very different nations might appear at similar places in the rankings (Rubery and Grimshaw 2003, p35). This also limits the extent to which we can properly analyse how societies may change due to pressures from multinational companies or changes in religious traditions or demographic character. As Ferner and Quintanilla (1998, p713) note such 'approaches to differences between countries are inadequate, treating cultural variables such as "power distance" (themselves somewhat artifical constructs) in an ahistorical and static fashion as immanent properties of nations, rather than as dynamic and emerging characteristics linked to patterns of historical development and distinctive national institutions'.

- *Complexity* – While the decision to focus on workers from one organisation makes some sense from an experimental angle because it controls for one variable, it ignores the complexity and interaction between different factors in explaining how cultures might vary. For example, it is not plausible to assume no influence on these workers from IBM's corporate policies, which in themselves are the product of forces and tensions from different countries, a factor in itself which could weaken any concept of national culture. Moreover, there are likely to be different levels of access to training and other forms of development across the sample, based not just on national differences but also on personal attributes within workers from the same country. Indeed, research on ABB shows how similarities may depend upon technological and product market factors as much as they are on national culture (Martin and Beaumont 1998), and indeed how HR practices and cultures can vary significantly between plants in the same country (Bélanger *et al* 2003).

In summarising the evidence, McSweeney (2002, p112) argues that 'Hofstede's claims are excessive and unbalanced: excessive because they claim far more in terms of identifiable characteristics and consequences than is justified; unbalanced because there is too great a desire to "prove" his a priori convictions rather than evaluate the adequacy of his "findings"'.

The institutionalist perspective

This perspective accepts that there are differences between societies that need to be understood and recognised but that these are the product of a wide range of supportive and competing forces on HRM. It rejects the universalist approach for failing to acknowledge that HR practices emerging in certain countries and organisations have little meaning in quite different contexts due to institutional and societal forces. Equally the culturalist approach is rejected, not so much for its belief that convergence is unlikely but because it lacks a theoretical and explanatory basis for its views. Differences in HR practices between countries owes more to the institutional forces that are at play in that society than to any supposed national culture; forces such as the education and training system, the legal framework, and political, social and economic factors that impinge on and help to shape how employers deal with employment issues. It can also include other factors such as the organisation of family and support networks, the provision of health care and the informal economy (Rubery and Grimshaw 2003, p37). It is acknowledged that, while all societies might face similar pressures for change as a consequence of greater international integration and globalisation, 'these pressures will lead to modification and change of societal institutions, but the particular form of the response will reflect each country's own societal logic' (p39).

The institutionalist perspective is not without its shortcomings, and in particular there is a danger that, just like the culturalist perspective, it is static and deterministic in assuming that forces beyond the workplace are not open to influence. Rubery and Grimshaw (2003) recognise this potential problem and suggest a much more dynamic framework for analysing HRM. There is not the space here to examine this issue in detail but broadly it consists of four sets of interacting pressures: systems effects such as technology and global market structures; political systems effects felt through international trade and finance; international transmission of ideologies, tastes and fashions such as liberalism and deregulation; and the power of global corporations, for example through their pressure on nation states to provide attractive conditions for investing in new locations (pp43–50). We take up the final of these factors below.

HRM in multinational organisations

A number of typologies of multinational corporations (MNCs) have been developed to analyse how they conduct business as a whole, not just in HR terms. One of the most enduring is by Bartlett and Ghoshal (1989) who classified MNCs into four groups. First is the multidomestic company; this grows by diversification, setting up new subsidiaries that adapt to local conditions and are organised on a decentralised federal basis. Second is the international company, based on exploitation of the parent company's knowledge through professional managers as a co-ordinated federation. Third, the global corporation treats the world market as an integrated whole, operating as a centralised hub and only allowing limited delegation to local subsidiaries. Finally, the transnational corporation is expected to combine aspects of the first three categories, being both sensitive to local conditions and developing strategies at a global level. Since it is likely to have multiple centres, national units can make a distinctive and differentiated contribution to the company as a whole (Rubery and Grimshaw 2003, pp201–202). An alternative categorisation, by Adler and Ghadar (1990) relates the character of the organisation's development to phases in the product life cycle. Broadly companies become more global as they mature and seek to penetrate new markets. A third well-known categorisation, albeit of international HRM styles and cultures rather than broader business styles, was by Perlmutter (1969). This has implications for staffing decisions in the following way:

- *ethnocentric*, where the majority of managers are recruited from the home country
- *polycentric*, where local nationals are appointed
- *geocentric*, where managers are not appointed according to their country of origin but from countries other than the host or home country.

While each of these strategies can be beneficial, they can also generate problems due to a focus on one particular approach to the exclusion of others. Also, as with any ideal type, it is sometimes difficult to determine which of the approaches, if any, might suit organisational circumstances, and of course a lot depends on the availability of managers who possess the qualities to ensure high levels of performance. Readers wishing a more in-depth treatment of these issues are advised to look at Harris *et al* (2003), Rubery and Grimshaw (2003) and Sparrow *et al* (2004) amongst others.

The work by Ferner and Quintanilla (1998) is especially useful in helping us to track the complexities of HRM across international boundaries because they focus on the source of 'isomorphic pressures' on an organisation. Isomorphism refers to the degree of similarity in organisational practice produced by pressures to conform, such as through shared recipes of action for the same sector or through a process of mimicry by which organisations merely follow the lead of another firm in the same sector or country. It also relates to the institutional forces operating within a country (eg the legal framework) or sector (eg employers' organisations) that lead to similarity in 'choice' of HR practices. They distinguish between four different ways in which isomorphic pressures operate:

- *Local isomorphism*, in which the subsidiary behaves like any other organisation within the host-country environment and adopts policies and practices that are seen as appropriate in that context. In this case, the employer decides it is best to fit in with local norms and values even if they are contrary to those that are dominant in the home country or within the MNC more generally. A good example of this was IBM's decision many years ago to deal with unions at its Irish subsidiaries even though the company – drawing on its US roots – tended to operate, wherever possible, in a union-free environment. This happened because the company realised that the role of social partners in Ireland at the time meant it would have faced difficulty operating in any other way (Beaumont 1987). Of course, foreign-owned firms that fit in with prevailing traditions are rarely investigated by researchers precisely because they look similar to most other organisations in that country.

- *Cross-national isomorphism*, in which the subsidiary is expected to conform with home-country HR practices and approaches that are themselves embedded within the wider institutional structures in that country. In this case, HR practices are likely to be rather different from those of similar organisations in the host country, instead resembling those of similar firms in the home country. Once again, attitudes towards unions and collective employee relations are particularly significant, perhaps in terms of union-free arrangements in US firms abroad or the development of works councils in German companies. The debate has raged about whether the Japanese entrants to the UK in the 1980s adopted specific home- or host-country HR practices; indeed it was difficult to pinpoint the source of HR practices by companies such as Nissan as these comprised elements both of Japanese and UK approaches (Oliver and Wilkinson 1992) and the HR Director at the time merely referred to them as HR practices that made sense for Nissan in the context of entering the UK vehicles market (Wickens 1987).

■ *Corporate isomorphism*. This is where the MNC has a strong and essentially universal approach to HRM, to some extent free of both the home and the host country. In this case HR practices central to the MNC's corporate philosophy are regarded as so essential to its culture that they are transported into different countries and implemented in a way that pays little attention to either the host or home countries' institutional regimes or the HR practices of other organisations in the same product market. Of course it is difficult to disentangle where the motivation for such HR practices comes from – home country or MNC? Some large US firms introduced HR processes – such as prizes for the best team, a policy of wearing baseball caps at work, or calling their employees 'partners' – into their UK operations with mixed results (Marchington 1992). This makes for a potentially unique approach, although practices may well be copied by host-country firms in the same market segment if this is seen to offer advantages over existing techniques.

■ *Global intercorporate isomorphism*. This is the approach that would be expected if MNCs broke free totally from home-country institutional forces and adopted HR policies and practices similar to those of their major international competitors in the global market. According to Ferner and Quintanilla (1998, p713) this can be seen as a mimetic response by copying the HR practices used by leading international competitors and effectively adopting a position that is beyond national borders. Again, however, as with the previous category, it is hard for organisations to ignore their home country, provided they retain a strong core of employment there and continue to be influenced by home-country institutional pressures. Moreover, financial reporting mechanisms and shareholder expectations can be expected to reinforce the power of home country effects. On the other hand, the more these organisations are run by senior managers from different countries and institutional backgrounds, and the lower the proportion of staff employed in the home country, the easier it is to be influenced by a different set of institutional pressures – in this case, those operating at a global level.

Find out about two US multinational companies and analyse the extent to which their HR practices reflect the companies' US roots.

Useful though these ideal types are in providing a focus, in reality the situation is not so simple. Quintanilla and Ferner (2003, p364) argue that greater attention needs to be paid to how 'complex processes work themselves out in particular situations, often displaying elements of both convergence and divergence'. Moreover, they acknowledge that home or host country represents a relatively crude level of aggregation, and that we need to pay attention to sectoral levels of determination as well as management's strategic choices. This means there is always a tension between at least three potentially conflicting isomorphic pulls – from the home country, from the host country and from company-specific rules and operating processes. This leads to interaction between the different forces, such that on some occasions pressures exerted by forces in the home country outweigh those of the host country or the MNC, or vice versa. Moreover, this may even vary between plants owned by the same company in the same 'host' country, as we saw with ABB in Canada (Bélanger *et al* 2003). Nevertheless, we still need to remain alert to the fact that 'strategic choice' is always shaped by factors external to the organisation. In other situations, despite what appears at face value to be an acceptance of Anglo-Saxon business processes by German firms operating in the UK, Ferner and Quintanilla (1998, pp724–725) show how these were actually being adapted to provide a specifically German interpretation. For example, Daimler-Benz has been a major proponent of shareholder value but, unlike the British version of this philosophy, at its British plants the company was keen to emphasise medium- and long-term profitability. Similarly, German companies in the UK retained a strong commitment to their employees and to social responsibility in a way that would not figure highly in the Board-level statements of similar UK companies. How long this can be preserved is another matter, as the study by Gunnigle *et al* (2004) – summarised in Box 3 – suggests about US companies in Ireland. In essence this reinforces the fact that the relationship between home country, host country and MNC pressures is unstable, uneven and dynamic, and that reverse isomorphism can apply when national systems come under pressure to change because of influences from foreign-owned firms.

BOX 3 NEW APPROACHES TO HRM BY US COMPANIES IN IRELAND

In two of the case study firms examined by Gunnigle and his colleagues, both of which were US-owned, changes appeared to be taking place in their approach to HRM. Initially, both firms followed the Irish tradition of recognising trade unions, setting up post-entry closed shops and engaging in collective bargaining. This showed how the firms clearly aligned themselves with the prevailing trend amongst inward-investing companies in the host country at the time, and operated in contradistinction to their non-union stance in the home country.

In recent years, these companies have started to pay above the norm, as well as start to establish new plants on a non-union basis. Interestingly, the actual decision to do this was taken by the Irish management team, albeit in the knowledge that it accorded with the preferences of top management at the US corporate HQ. In one of the cases, the rationale for going non-union stemmed from a number of arguments: it was felt little opposition would be encountered to the decision; on balance it was felt a non-union plant would make management's task easier; and it was felt that the new workers – technicians and professionals/managerial grades – would not push for union membership. At the institutional level, the company felt that the Irish government would not want to challenge this stance because it was so keen to retain and get new foreign direct investment into the country. A critical factor in this is the high concentration of US firms that operate in Ireland.

In evaluating the dynamic between home and host country the authors suggest that this case shows how national business systems evolve in the context of management practices used by leading firms. It also shows how US firms are able to implement HR practices that are more in line with those operating in the home country and in the MNC more broadly.

Source: Adapted from Gunnigle P., Collings D. and Morley M. *Hosting the Multinational: Exploring the dynamics of industrial relations in US multinational subsidiaries in Ireland*. Employment Relations Research Unit Working Paper, University of Limerick. 2004

CONCLUSIONS

In this chapter, we have provided a brief analysis of the links between strategy and HRM, paying particular attention to the main arguments and debates in the subject area. Students need to be aware that HRM does not take place in a vacuum but operates within frameworks that tie it to the strategy of the firm, as well as through influences from the wider institutional framework within which organisations are located. The complexity of influences is greater still when HRM is analysed from an international and comparative perspective, as for example with foreign-owned firms located in the UK or in (often British-owned) MNCs that operate in other countries. The precise interplay of forces from the home country, the host country and from the MNC itself means it is impossible to identify a peculiarly British, European or global style of HRM in practice.

Before moving on to examine the forces that shape HRM at work, we need briefly to explain our view of the subject. Many of the frameworks and models tend to assume there is a specific model of HRM – the universalist, high commitment, 'best practice' model that we explore in detail in Chapter 3. Conversely, if we assume that HRM is a field of study rather than a distinct style, it is then possible to examine how the management of employment may vary between organisations and workplaces, as well as over time, because it can be shaped by the range of influences we examine in Chapter 2. This approach also allows us to examine the extent to which factors external to the workplace – such as legislative, political and economic changes – can impact differentially depending upon management choice, management–employee relations and worker attitudes and behaviours. Working with this conception of the subject area means that HRM can exist just as easily in a small owner-managed sweatshop as it can in a large and sophisticated high-tech organisation.

HRM can therefore be defined as 'the management of employment', so incorporating individual and collective relations, the whole range of HR practices and processes, line management activities and those of HR specialists, managerial and non-managerial actors. It is more than just another version of the 'hard' model because it assumes management styles depend not only on business goals but also on influences from a range of different stakeholder interests. Accordingly, HRM may include a role for unions, the development of so-called leading-edge HR practices, a commitment to employment security and have line managers at the helm of organisational change. Conversely, HRM may be individualised, HR policies can rely on cost reduction and rationalisation, and there is no provision for an internal HR function. Irrespective of the approach adopted, employers will probably be keen to enhance the contribution of HR practices to performance.

In addition to academic interest in defining HRM, not surprisingly there has also been a keen practitioner and professional interest, principally through the CIPD. Its Professional Development Scheme (PDS) was launched in 2001 and the Leadership and Management Standards (what was Core Management) followed in 2005. Key features of the PDS are that it is positioned at M(Masters)-level, it is based around the concept of the 'thinking performer' and the completion of a management report is now a requirement for entry into the CIPD. The twin elements of the 'thinking performer' concept are that graduates of the CIPD should be professionally competent – in terms of being able to 'do' HR through the development of a range of skills – and academically capable – in terms of being able to critically analyse situations, make independent judgements about HRM and know where and how to search for updated information. A requirement to intrepret findings from contemporary research, from refereed journals and from the CIPD, is seen as essential for the future development of the profession. Box 4 illustrates the 10 key elements in the 'thinking performer' role.

BOX 4   THE CIPD NOTION OF THE 'THINKING PERFORMER'

1	Personal drive and effectiveness	Sets out own professional objectives with a prioritised plan for managing time and service delivery
2	People management and leadership	Demonstrates a level of knowledge and understanding about managing people and leadership that meets the CIPD Professional Development Scheme Standards
3	Business understanding	Demonstrates an understanding of the business needs and issues of various types of organisation
4	Professional and ethical competence	Meets a defined range of the CIPD's professional standards
5	Added value	Identifies opportunities for adding value and makes appropriate recommendations
6	Continuing learning	Adopts a considered approach to continuing learning and professional personal development
7	Analytical and intuitive/ creative thinking	Demonstrates use of a range of analytical, intuitive and creative abilities, tools and processes
8	Customer focus	Shows empathy for and responsiveness to customers of the P&D function(s) and of employing organisations generally
9	Strategic capabilities	Understands the concept of strategy and the required contributions to it at all levels
10	Communication, persuasion and interpersonal skills	Uses 'active listening' with feedback; communicates clearly and positively; generates empathy with others

Source: Chartered Institute of Personnel and Development. Professional Development Scheme Standards

The rationale underpinning the PDS and the People Management and Development (PM&D) Standards specifies clearly the importance of acquiring a sound professional base for activities in the area, irrespective of the precise role that is occupied or the type of organisation for which a person works. The skills, knowledge and understanding that are developed are also appropriate for individuals who are not part of an internal HR function, but are employed as consultants, academics or line managers. It is now increasingly common for practitioners to move between functions and organisations throughout their working lives, as well as between different forms of employment status. As a consequence it is important that all HR practitioners are aware not only of their own area of specialist expertise but also of the wider contribution which HRM can make to organisational success and employee engagement. They need to be able to justify how they contribute to improved performance and to understand the integration of HRM with other organisational activities. In addition, specialists in discrete areas – staffing and resourcing, learning and development, reward management, and employee relations – need to understand how their own activities fit in with other elements of HRM, and the extent to which they may support or conflict with overall strategies. The need to realise that a range of stakeholder interests, and not just short-term financial gain, is a key component of professionalism (Paauwe 2004).

Four key points are central to our understanding of HRM, and these recur throughout the remainder of this book as well as in practice.

1   Defining the *subject matter* of HRM – We regard this as those aspects of people management that need to be understood by all HR managers. Using Torrington's (1998) medical analogy these are the subjects the 'general practitioner' needs to understand, and which remain important for the specialist consultant even though he or she is not explicitly aware they are being used. The categorisation of these varies from one author to the next but we have chosen to use the CIPD distinction between the four generalist areas of resourcing, development, relations and reward that are central to the PM&D standards. They also have a logic in that all aspects of HRM are covered by these four areas despite inevitable overlaps between specific topics.

2   *Integration* is at the heart of HRM – This takes two forms: *vertical integration*, which refers to the links between HRM and both wider business strategies and the political, economic, social and legal forces that shape (and to some extent are shaped by) organisations; and *horizontal integration*, which refers to the 'fit' between different HR policies and practices, and the degree to which they support or contradict one another. Readers will find similar topics being addressed at a number of places in this book but this should be recognised as a positive sign of complementarity, integration and reinforcement rather than unnecessary repetition. We assume that both vertical and horizontal integration probably need to be strengthened in order to maximise the HR contribution, as well as minimise the likelihood of conflicting messages.

3   *Line manager involvement* – Irrespective of the role played by an internal HR function or by external agencies that provide HR support, line managers are central to the delivery of HRM at the workplace. If they are to be effective, HR specialists need to gain line management commitment to and buy-in for their proposals and recommendations. It matters little that a course of action impresses other HR specialists if it fails to convince line managers – the people who have to put most policies into effect. This is not to say that HR specialists should become the servants of line managers, merely recommending what the line managers want to hear in order to gain 'customer' approval. It does mean however that HR specialists have to be acutely aware of their audience, of the purpose of HR policies and their contribution to organisational success. On some occasions the views of line managers will need to be challenged and the basis for their perspectives questioned, while on others their needs can be satisfied with clear professional judgement and sound practical advice.

4 *Ambiguity and tension* – Although there are increasing pressures to demonstrate added value to the organisation, as we saw earlier HRM is often in an ambiguous position within employing organisations. The HR function is sometimes criticised for occupying the middle ground between management and workers, because it is dealing with issues for which it is difficult to identify a simple best option. For example, there can be conflicting and often equally strong arguments in favour of the dramatically different approaches an employer can take in relation to trade unions – partnership or arms'-length relations – or to the development of skills – internal or external supply. In HRM, perhaps more than in any other area of management, the choices that are made can have significant implications for the future and lead an organisation down a path that is difficult to alter without lots of effort. Because the employment relationship is incomplete, ambiguous and contested, this means that HRM can never be a simple technical exercise, whereby answers are read off according to some scientific formula, and implemented without problem. HR professionals have to become accustomed to the fact – especially as they reach the higher echelons of the occupation – that their work is going to be fraught with tensions and contradictions, and with situations that are characterised by uncertainty, indeterminacy and competing perspectives.

USEFUL READING

GUEST D. *and* KING Z. 'Power, innovation and problem-solving: the personnel managers' three steps to heaven?', *Journal of Management Studies*, Vol. 41, No. 3, 2004. pp401–423.

JOHNSON G. *and* SCHOLES K. *Exploring Corporate Strategy*. London, Prentice Hall. 2002.

KINGSMILL D. *Accounting for People: Report of the Task Force on Human Capital Management*, presented to the Secretary of State for Trade and Industry. October 2003a.

MARCHINGTON M., GRIMSHAW D., RUBERY J. *and* WILLMOTT H. (eds), *Fragmenting Work: Blurring organisational boundaries and disordering hierarchies*. Oxford, Oxford University Press. 2004a. Chapter 12

PAAUWE J. *HRM and Performance: Achieving long term viability*. Oxford, Oxford University Press. 2004. Chapter 9

QUINTANILLA J. *and* FERNER A. 'Multinationals and human resource management: between global convergence and national identity', *International Journal of Human Resource Management*, Vol. 14, No. 3, 2003. pp363–368.

RUBERY J. *and* GRIMSHAW D. *The Organisation of Employment: An international perspective*. London, Palgrave. 2003. Chapters 8–10

SPARROW P., BREWSTER C. *and* HARRIS H. *Globalizing Human Resource Management*. London, Routledge. 2004. Chapter 2

WHITTINGTON R. *What is Strategy and Does It Matter?* London, Routledge. 1993.

Forces Shaping HRM at Work

INTRODUCTION

In the previous chapter we examined the role of strategy and its implications for managing people, as well as considering the different meanings of HRM, both in theory and its international and comparative context. The focus was primarily at the level of the organisation. Whilst it is clearly crucial to examine the ways in which internal factors influence and shape HRM, this often overlooks the fact that employers also operate within a wider institutional framework that comprises patterns of work and employment, organisational networks, and legal and political forces. To some extent these set limits on the choices employers can make about how to manage people at work, but they can also provide frameworks and structures that can aid effective HRM – for example, by setting limits on working hours that reduce the likelihood of accidents at work or in providing support for training initiatives that help to enhance workforce skills. We do not see these factors as determining and proscribing management choice, but more as shaping the decisions employers make in order to develop effective HR practice. Accordingly, rather than treating the material in this chapter as organisational 'context', and therefore beyond the influence of employers, we argue that it is the relationship between institutional forces and management choice that shapes HR policies and practices. Although the influence of such shaping factors is undoubtedly less in the UK than in many other European countries (Rubery and Grimshaw 2003), this does not mean it can be ignored. Indeed, in some industries – such as chemicals – employer choice is significantly influenced and shaped by the activities of employers' associations and trade unions, as well as by legal regulation (Marchington and Vincent 2004).

The remainder of the chapter proceeds as follows. First we examine the changing nature of work, acknowledging that it is contested, uncertain and ambiguous because workers are not like any other factor of production due to their independent will. Second we review data on labour markets and patterns of employment, focusing in particular on the sectoral distribution of labour, levels of employment, and unemployment and working patterns. Third, we discuss flexibility, emphasising in particular that fragmenting patterns of work and organisations clearly shape how employers manage HRM across organisational boundaries. Fourth, we consider legal issues, both from a UK and an EU perspective, showing how the myriad of changes has affected employers; this section of the chapter is one where readers are strongly advised to seek clarification from specialist law texts and legal bulletins such as IRS. Finally, we analyse a range of institutions that also influence and help to shape HRM at work, as well as provide details of websites and reports from which readers can access up-to-date information. Whilst this text provides a good grounding in these issues, it is critically important that readers consult specialist sources as a matter of routine. For example, the CIPD undertakes a range of surveys annually, *Labour Market Trends* appears monthly and other reports appear regularly in a wide variety of publications.

By the end of this chapter, readers should be able to:

■ **implement HR policies and practices that take into account influences from networks and institutional forces relevant to the organisation**

■ **supply accurate and timely advice about legislation in the area of HRM, in particular guiding people to sources of specialist information**

■ **access, use and interpret data from a range of internal and published sources in preparing and presenting reports about employment issues.**

In addition, readers should understand and be able to explain:

■ **the implications for HRM arising from the changing nature of work, employment and organisational structures**

■ **the role of legislation and institutions in shaping HRM at work**

■ **the relationship between employing organisations and the economic, societal and institutional frameworks within which they operate.**

WORK IN ITS CONTEMPORARY CONTEXT

The contested nature of work

Most writers on industrial relations and organisational behaviour see the employment relationship as comprising a mix of conflict and co-operation (see, for example, Noon and Blyton 2002; Thompson and McHugh 2002; Blyton and Turnbull 2004). Both of these are present to differing degrees in different workplaces at any one time, and the balance between them varies over time and between different countries. By contrast, it is rare for texts on other aspects of HRM (eg recruitment and selection, learning and development, reward management) to conceive explicitly of the employment relationship in such terms. Instead, discussion of motivation or commitment only tends to consider conflict in terms of management's failure to engender employee attachment to the organisation. In other words, the notion of conflict between the buyers and sellers of labour typically tends to be compartmentalised as an employee relations issue.

Issues of conflict and co-operation clearly come to the fore during industrial action or in collective bargaining between employers and trade unions. But these issues also pervade other aspects of HRM as well. For example, decisions to recruit new staff who are prepared to demonstrate loyalty and commitment, as well as work effectively with a minimum of supervision, implicitly assume that workers are willing to co-operate with employers – something that is far from guaranteed. As we see in Chapter 6, alternative paradigms of the selection process question the so-called 'objectivity' and scientific justification for psychometric approaches. Similarly, the attitude of workers towards training and their willingness to take on extra skills and responsibilities to help meet organisational goals assumes a mindset in which both parties to the employment relationship see mutual benefits from working together. As we see in Chapters 8 and 9, assessments of who gains most from training, both in the short- and the long-term, focus specifically on the contested nature of the employment relationship (see also Marchington et al 2004b). Furthermore, as we see clearly in Chapters 12 and 13, reward management manifestly focuses on subjects that go right to the heart of the employment relationship, concerning equity and fairness, harmonisation, and internal and external differentials. Too often, however, these issues are treated in straightforward technical terms, for example in how to choose a selection technique, design a training programme or install a new pay system. It is important to recognise that all aspects of HRM deal with how the employment relationship is constructed and developed, and discussions of conflict should not shunted off into an employee relations branch line.

There are many different perspectives on the employment relationship. Some of the early labour process writers (for example, Braverman 1974; R. Edwards 1979) saw it solely as a struggle for control between managers and workers. According to this viewpoint, what is good for employers (capital) is inevitably bad for workers (labour) because surplus value – which is required in order to finance and reward capital – can only be achieved through the exploitation of labour. Therefore, workers who co-operated with employers – say, through participation schemes – effectively became de-skilled or did themselves out of jobs by helping organisations to become more efficient. By contrast, other writers have been more interested in the balance between conflict and co-operation. For example, when introducing new technology, employees have shared interests with employers – such as in the development of new skills and the greater employment security that may derive from a more successful business in the longer term. Of course there are also potential conflicts between the parties caused by disputes between management and labour about the level of rewards for taking on new responsibilities. P. Edwards (2003a, p17) regards the employer–employee relationship as characterised by 'structured antagonism' which is created by the indeterminacy of the employment relationship. This relationship can never be constructed precisely enough to specify every aspect of an individual's work, and it relies upon both employer and employee to show some degree of trust and discretion for it to be discharged effectively. Because of this, he sees the employment relationship as both contradictory and antagonistic. It is contradictory because managers not only have to exercise control but also learn how to tap into and release creativity, and it is antagonistic because workers offer the only opportunity by which employers can realise surplus value. Whilst employees may have much to gain from co-operating with employers, the fact remains that employers need to maximise employee efforts to gain competitive advantage. It also needs stressing, particularly given the low levels of strike action in recent times, that an absence of overt conflict does not guarantee co-operation, nor does a bout of industrial action necessarily indicate a fundamental breakdown in the employment relationship.

> Debate with your colleagues the proposition that 'conflict is now a thing of the past in the UK'.

Given the incompleteness of the employment contract (Cooke *et al* 2004a) it should be clear that all workers possess some 'tacit skills'. This refers to the knowledge and understanding that workers accumulate throughout their lives, and in many cases it is extremely difficult for this to be codified, written down and copied. Tacit skills can be seen in many areas of paid and unpaid employment, such as in the ability to hear from the sound of a machine or a car engine that a problem is lurking. Thompson and McHugh (2002, p187) itemise over 20 detailed activities undertaken by a waiter when taking an order, but even these overlook the more hidden interactive skills that are crucial for the effective completion of this task. Increasingly, tacit skills are evident in interpersonal relations used by customer service agents in a call centre to ensure good service. Certain skills can be copied by watching other people or reading manuals, but others have to be 'learned' through practice or by doing similar jobs, sometimes outside of work. The key thing, however, is that many people fail to realise these skills and attributes are actually more than 'simple common sense'.

Tacit skills can be used in a variety of ways (Marchington 1992). First, they can be employed as a potential weapon against employers, either as part of a collective dispute or as an individual response to managerial domination. Tacit skills can be deployed overtly by refusals to 'work beyond contract' or covertly in order to undermine a management instruction, perhaps through sabotage. In these cases workers are using tacit skills in order to 'get back' at management, channelling creative energies into opposing, rather than co-operating with, employer objectives (Blyton and Turnbull 2004). Secondly, tacit skills can be used to make time at work more tolerable, but with no intention of offering employers any more than the basic minimum required to 'get by' at work; this can be seen when workers devise games to keep their minds occupied whilst at work (Burawoy 1979, pp81–82). This might include thinking up names for customers, producing a certain number of components in a 30-minute period, or dreaming about how to spend £1 million won on a TV quiz programme. In some cases, this may actually improve performance as workers set themselves targets, and by appearing to consent to management rules on the surface, low levels of attachment do not surface until they are expected to do extra work. Since their major life interests are fulfilled outside of work, they resent what is seen as an intrusion into their private lives (Thompson and McHugh 2002). Finally, workers may use tacit skills to contribute actively to the achievement of employer goals by 'getting on' at work. This can take several forms, such as working hard to gain promotion, taking on extra responsibilities to ensure that the organisation manages to satisfy customer orders or in working hard because this is seen as the 'right' thing to do. The idea of doing a 'good job' – turning out high-quality work, resolving difficult problems at work or providing superior customer service – is central to much of our socialisation, and also to much of the activity we undertake outside of paid employment (Ackers and Preston 1997). To some extent feelings of self-worth are reinforced by 'getting on' at work, perhaps by helping a customer or just clearing the in-tray.

Think about three different types of job that you have either done or about which you have some knowledge. What was the mix of 'getting back', 'getting by' and 'getting on' in these jobs, and what might have been done to increase the likelihood of workers wanting to 'get on'?

Job satisfaction, the psychological contract and work intensification

In analysing what motivates workers a number of classic studies, such as those by Maslow (1943) and Herzberg (1966), point to factors intrinsic to work, motivators such as interesting and varied work, the opportunity to develop, to be recognised for doing a good job, and so on. The current thinking on work motivation is summarised by Steers et al (2004). Other studies (eg Goldthorpe et al 1968) suggest that factors such as job security and decent wages, which were seen as hygiene factors by Herzberg, are important, especially for people who do not regard work as of central life interest. Yet other studies – making use of the so-called 'lottery question' – find that a substantial majority of people state that they would continue to work even if they won sufficient money to keep them comfortably off for the rest of their working lives. More recent research by Rose (2003, pp507–508) suggests that extrinsic factors (such as employment security, pay and promotion prospects) are slightly more important than intrinsic factors (such as the work itself, good relations with their manager and opportunity to use initiative) in explaining what workers get out of work as well as what would propel them to look for other jobs. Moreover, Rose (2000, p12) also suggests that aspirations in relation to intrinsic factors tend to be lower than those for extrinsic factors. Guest and Conway (2002, p17) asked a sample of 1000 workers how important work was to their lives in general; the results are outlined in Table 1 (see page 34), and from this it can be seen that people's personal goals and major satisfaction come from areas outside of work. Readers

Table 1   *The importance of work*

Statement	Strongly disagree (%)	Disagree (%)	Agree (%)	Strongly agree (%)
My personal life goals are work-related	23	40	27	10
The major satisfaction in my life comes from work	30	42	20	7
What happens at work isn't really important to me	21	38	27	14

Source: Adapted from Guest D. and Conway N. *Pressure at Work and the Psychological Contract: Research report.* London, CIPD. 2002. p17

who would like a more extensive treatment of the issues examined in this section of the book in more detail should look at sources such as Noon and Blyton (2002), Thompson and McHugh (2002) and Mullins (2004).

Much of the literature now examines satisfaction and motivation at work through the lens of the psychological contract, a concept first described by Schein (1978) and developed by people such as Rousseau (1995). Herriot (1998, p106) defines this as 'the beliefs of each of the parties to the employment relationship, the individual and the organisation, as to what their mutual obligations are'. In broad terms the contract can either be transactional – that is narrowly defined and closely monitored – or relational, in which case it is more open-ended and diffuse in character. It is implicit rather than explicitly written down, being based on a series of assumptions about the relationship between employer and worker. These relate to concepts such as fairness and honesty, security and certainty, recognition and opportunities for fulfilment (Mayo 1995, p48).

It is now widely argued that, whilst such reciprocal arrangements may have been present in organisations up until the 1980s, they have now disappeared (Herriot and Pemberton 1997; Rousseau 1995). The last two decades have been characterised by instrumentality and uncertainty, an imbalance in what is offered by the individual compared with that offered by the employer. Consequently, in contemporary Britain, Herriot (1998) argues, the individual offers flexibility, accountability and long hours, and if they are fortunate get a good job with a high salary – although many workers do not even get this.

Guest and Conway's surveys on the psychological contract were carried out from the mid-1990s, and the most recent report – at the time of going to press – was published in 2002. Readers are encouraged to get results from subsequent surveys themselves in order to trace changes over a longer period of time. Table 2 presents data on the degree to which promises are made and kept by employers according to this group of respondents.

From this it can be seen that the vast majority of employers made promises about equality and fairness of treatment, information and consultation with staff, and security and pay.

Table 2   *Promises made by the employer and how far they were kept*

Organisation has promised or committed itself to:	Promise made (% of all employees)	Promise fully kept (% of all those that made promises)	Promise not kept (% of all those that made promises)
Provide me with a reasonably secure job	75	82	1
Provide me with fair pay for the work I do	75	74	5
Provide me with a career	58	75	2
Provide me with interesting work	54	66	2
Ensure fair treatment by managers	82	65	4
Ensure equality of treatment	85	73	4
Keep me fully informed about changes affecting me	82	65	6
Involve and consult me about changes affecting me	77	62	5

Source: Adapted from Guest D. and Conway N. *Pressure at Work and the Psychological Contract: Research report*. London, CIPD. 2002. p21

Hardly any workers felt that management did not keep their promises at all and a large proportion felt they kept them fully. This is apparent in relation to most of the promises made by employers, particularly regarding job security, pay, career and equality of treatment. This was rather more positive than for previous years, and it was also echoed in responses to questions about satisfaction with work and with life as a whole. For example, very few people reported low levels of satisfaction with these factors nor with the balance between work and life outside of work. Views tended to be relatively equally split between moderate and high levels of satisfaction. High levels of satisfaction were particularly marked for those in privileged positions in employment such as professional workers or managers (Guest and Conway 2002, p34). Similar findings could be found in relation to commitment, expressed through loyalty to their organisation or pride in telling others who they worked for. Research by Rose (2003) allows us to compare satisfaction rates between occupations, showing that

Table 3 *Overall job satisfaction levels in a sample of UK occupations*

High level of satisfaction	Medium level of satisfaction	Low level of satisfaction
Hairdressers	Nurses	Management consultants
Farm workers	Retail cash desk and check out operators	Laboratory technicians
Care assistants	Marketing and sales managers	Assembly line workers
Bank, building society and post office managers	Computer analysts and programmers	Postal workers
Personnel, training and industrial relations managers	Painters and decorators	Bus and coach drivers

Source: Adapted from Rose M. 'Good deal, bad deal? Job satisfaction in occupations', *Work, Employment and Society*, Vol. 17, No. 3, 2003. pp503–530

these vary dramatically. The most satisfied are in occupations such as child care, caretakers and hairdressers, and the least satisfied are bus and coach drivers, waiters and waitresses, and sewing machinists. Table 3 provides the results for a sample of occupations, broken down into high, medium and low levels of satisfaction, although this does need to be treated with some care given that changes are likely when major contextual events – such as a pay dispute or a redundancy – take place.

> Do you feel engaged at work or with your studies, do you feel satisfied with your work–life balance, and do you feel loyalty to or pride in the organisation for which you work or at which you are studying? Why is this?

The evidence reviewed above suggests that, with certain exceptions, British workers are relatively satisfied with their work. However, other data indicates that work is becoming more insecure and intensive and that people are routinely working longer hours as well (Nolan and Wood 2003, p169). The so-called 'insecurity thesis' (Heery and Salmon 2000, p1) includes at least three separate elements:

- Risk is being transferred to workers through the growth of temporary and precarious employment so as to increase insecurity.
- Insecurity is damaging to economic performance.
- This leads to severe consequences for individuals and the wider society.

As we see in the next section of this chapter, there have been sectoral and other shifts in patterns of employment, with greater numbers now working part-time, on temporary contracts or from home. Those employed on short-term contracts, as in call centres or up the supply chain producing goods for retailers, tend to suffer the worst consequences of insecure and unstable employment (Marchington *et al* 2004b). Those working from home, ostensibly freed from direct surveillance by managers in the office, often find they are not implicitly trusted to manage their own time and working patterns but are subject to a variety of overlapping but connected systems of monitoring and regulation (Felstead *et al* 2003). Although most respondents to the CIPD survey did not agree they were subject to constant observation or that their work was continually checked by managers, a slight majority did feel their work performance was constantly being measured (Guest and Conway 2002, p12).

Whilst many analysts (eg Hutton 1998) agree that work is now much more insecure than in the immediate past, exemplified in particular by the growth of non-standard jobs and the decline of the 'job for life', Doogan (2001) disagrees. He argues that, rather than becoming more insecure, there is now an even greater likelihood that people will remain in their existing employment than 20 years ago. Table 4 presents a selection of his evidence that is drawn from various Labour Force Survey sets.

Between 1992 and 1999, the proportion of workers with 10 or more years service in the same employment grew from less than 7.5 million to over 9 million, from 28.6 per cent of the

Table 4   *The rate of long-term employment – those in same employment for 10 years or more*

Category of worker	Rate of long-term employment	
	1992	**1999**
Manufacturing	32%	38%
Public administration	42%	52%
Mining	49%	43%
Utilities	56%	52%
Construction	30%	40%
Hotels and catering	12%	15%
Education	34%	37%
Health and social services	28%	32%
Full-time	*32%*	*36%*
Part-time	*19%*	*23%*
Managers	37%	42%
Technicians	29%	32%
Clerical	23%	30%
Craft	33%	41%
Elementary	22%	22%

Source: Adapted from tables in Doogan K. 'Insecurity and long-term unemployment', *Work, Employment and Society*, Vol. 15, No. 3. 2001. pp419–441

working population to 33 per cent (Doogan 2001, p423). The same picture emerged in relation both to women and men, and indeed the growth in long-term employment is considerably greater for women (21 to 29 per cent) than for men (35 to 37 per cent). This trend also holds across shrinking sectors of the economy such as manufacturing and public administration as it does for expanding sectors. Table 4 shows that the rate of long-term employment in manufacturing increased to 38 per cent in 1999 compared with 32 per cent in 1992 while the increase in construction was most marked of all – rising from 30 to 40 per cent of total employment. In declining sectors, there had been an absolute decline in the number of long-term employees, hardly surprisingly, alongside a rather slower decline in the rate of long-term employment. Contrary to expectations, part-timers were more likely to have a higher rate of long-term employment than they had at the beginning of the 1990s, and indeed the rate of increase was actually higher than for full-timers. This increase for part-timers, however, was almost totally confined to those over the age of 30, thus suggesting that younger workers bore the brunt of short-term and unstable work patterns. Finally, all categories of worker saw an increase in the long-term rate of employment, varying from the higher skill levels to a miniscule improvement for those in the most basic jobs.

Of course, this analysis does not examine statistics relating to the length of job tenure for those people who experience frequent job changes and move in and out of employment. As we saw earlier in this chapter, the increase in numbers engaged in temporary work alone indicates that this is potentially a major source of job insecurity. Moreover, focusing on job tenure alone only tells half the story, as workers may *feel* much more insecure without actually losing their jobs and, perhaps more crucially, find there are lessened opportunities for promotion and advancement. As Burchell *et al* (1999, p39) note, 'many of the employees we spoke to were not unduly worried about losing their job per se but were, nevertheless, extremely concerned about the loss of valued job features such as their status within the organisation or their opportunity for promotion'. This shows how job insecurity is multi-dimensional and driven by a number of different forces. Hudson (2002a, p81), drawing on the same survey data, notes how the vast majority of workers felt that they had increased their skill level, responsibility and task variety during the past few years but nevertheless did not have improved career and promotion prospects. She refers to this as 'broken ladders' and 'disappearing pathways'. This demonstrates that even though people may be secure in their jobs – in the sense that they are not made redundant – they find that longer term expectations have deteriorated considerably. Moreover, it is widely accepted that working hours in the UK are greater than in other parts of Europe. As we see later, this has implications for the role of employment law given that the proportion of people working at least 48 hours per week has increased over the last 20 years, but equally those people working less than 20 hours per week has also increased as well. Even more significantly, in 1977 just 12 per cent of households that were inhabited by people of working age had no-one working, a figure that had nearly doubled by 1998 (Green 2001, p59). In short, there has been an increasing bifurcation in patterns of working time, with some working very long hours while others work rather fewer hours, either because of choice or due to exclusion from the labour market.

The picture in relation to work intensification is rather more straightforward. People seem to be working harder, both in terms of the speed at which they work and in the amount of effort they feel is being put into work. For example, just under two-thirds of the employees interviewed by Burchell *et al* (1999, 30) felt they were working faster and more intensively, about a third felt that things had not changed over the last few years and a handful felt that work was less intense. The wider range of tasks undertaken, the extra effort that had been devoted and the responsibility they had shouldered had not been rewarded in their view. According to Burchell *et al* (p38), they felt 'under pressure from managers, colleagues and, above all, from the "sheer quantity of work"'. In his analysis, Green (2001) differentiated between 'discretionary effort' – work beyond that which is normally required – and 'constrained effort' – the work required merely to complete the job. He concludes, from analysis of various data sets covering the last 20 years, that work has been intensified, both in terms of discretionary and constrained effort (p67). Other studies support this conclusion. For example, the 1998 Workplace Employee Relations Survey (WERS; Cully *et al* 1999) showed that 60 per cent of worker representatives felt that effort had increased a lot at their establishment during the past five years, with a further 20 per cent saying that it had increased a little. Managers were less convinced about the extent of the increased effort, but nevertheless 39 per cent of them felt it had gone up a lot and 37 per cent a little. Very few of either group felt effort levels had decreased. The implications of this degree of work intensification are considerable, and there is a long list of health problems that workers felt had been instigated or worsened by working so hard and to tighter deadlines. These include headaches, muscular problems, stomach-aches, stress, sleep problems and irritability (Giga *et al* 2003) As Hyman *et al* (2003, p237) note, this is particularly problematic for those in call centres, and indeed in the service sector more generally, who work fluctuating shift systems when there is no opportunity to establish a consistent routine in their working lives.

LABOUR MARKETS AND PATTERNS OF EMPLOYMENT

There has been a fundamental sectoral shift in employment away from manufacturing and the public sector – sectors that are renowned for more formalised HR systems, high levels of trade union membership, and larger employment units – towards the more informal, relatively union-free, and smaller employment units of the service sector. For example, the number of people employed in manufacturing halved over the last 25 years, and the proportion of staff working for the public sector declined significantly from about 30 per cent of all those employed in 1979. Much of this decline has been in the productive public sector (eg coal) and to privatisations of what were previously public service sector employers (eg gas, water, electricity and telecommunications). In addition, there has been widespread contracting-out of ancillary services to the private sector from healthcare and local government.

The principal growth area has been the service sector. As a whole, including both public and private services, this grew from around 10 million in the late 1970s to well over 20 million now. Indeed, numbers employed across the economy as a whole increased over the last decade and stands at over 28 million in 2004 (*Labour Market Trends* July 2004). The largest growth areas have been in finance and business services, but others – such as distribution, hotels and restaurants, transport and communications and public administration, education and health – also grew. The industries that declined the most over this period were agriculture and fishing, and energy and water. Although there has been a major shift to the service sector, there are other trends – such as moving call centre work overseas – and it is important to keep up-to-date by referring to *Labour Market Trends* for the latest figures. The changing nature of employment has major implications for HR practice, and the growth of 'new' firms is particularly significant as they typically to adopt quite different practices than their 'older' counterparts (Machin 2003).

Much of the growth is due to the increased participation rate of women in the economy. Table 5 shows that well over 3 million more women were employed in 2004 than had been in 1985, compared with a growth rate for men of 1.3 million. Nevertheless, the employment rate

Table 5   *Men and women in employment (millions) between 1985 and 2004*

	1985	1995	2000	2004
Women aged 16–59				
In employment	9.73	11.12	11.92	13.03
Full-time	5.58	6.34	6.77	7.25
Part-time	4.15	4.78	5.15	5.78
Employment rate (%)	59.7	65.6	68.9	70.0
ILO* rate of unemployment (%)	11.0	7.0	4.9	4.5
Men aged 16–64				
In employment	13.96	14.11	15.05	15.28
Full-time	13.46	13.13	13.83	13.67
Part-time	0.50	0.98	1.22	1.61
Employment rate (%)	77.9	76.1	79.1	79.3
ILO rate of unemployment (%)	11.7	10.2	6.1	5.3

*International Labour Organisation.
Source: Adapted from *Labour Market Trends* February 2001 and April 2004. Derived from Labour Force Surveys in Spring 1985 to Spring 2004

(number in employment divided by number in the 16–59 age group) for women remained below that for men at just under 70 per cent compared with a little below 80 per cent for men in the 16–64 age group (*Labour Market Trends*, July 2004). Women now comprise just over half of the potential workforce. However, the labour market remains heavily segmented with many more women than men working part-time, and with women concentrated in the service sector and in jobs with lower pay and lower status. In 2003, 82 per cent of the 6.3 million part-time workers in the UK were women, with almost half of these working part-time because of care responsibilities (IRS Employment Review 774a 2003). Women working full-time earn 82 per cent of the equivalent male rate – a pay gap of 18 per cent – and those working part-time earn 61 per cent of the male full-time wage (Kingsmill 2003a, p20). The UK has one of the widest pay gaps in the 15 EU member states, and this has led to increasing numbers of cases being referred to tribunals and courts. Only 34 per cent of managers and administrators are women compared with 64 per cent of men, women rarely make up more than 25 per cent of senior management teams, and only 10 women sit as executive directors on the boards of FTSE100 companies (Kingsmill 2003a, p34).

Associated with the growth in female participation in the labour market has been a major shift in the distribution of employment between full-time and part-time work, as well as some changes to the number of people working on temporary contracts or self-employed. Although the number of people who stated that they were employed on full-time contracts grew by about 10 per cent (approximately 1.4 million) between 1985 and 2004, part-time employment increased by over half (about 2.7 million) over the same period (*Labour Market Trends* July 2004). Depending on the measures used, the proportion of people working part-time is between 25 and 30 per cent. This is a higher proportion than most other EU countries (except the Netherlands where it is over 40 per cent) and it is significantly higher than Greece, Italy or Spain (European Foundation for the Improvement of Living and Working Conditions 2004). Part-time work is encouraged by EU employment guidelines as it facilitates better work–life balance, as well as making it easier for workers to enter or retire from the labour market, and so ease problems of unemployment. It is interesting to note that the growth in part-time work may be due more to sectoral change, and the emergence of new firms in the service sector that are more likely to employ part-timers, than to the extension of part-time working at 'continuing' workplaces (Millward *et al* 2000, p44). Employers tend to regard part-timers as providing more flexibility – and even being harder working – than full-timers and it also helps them to retain skills that might otherwise be lost (IRS Employment Review 735 2001).

Temporary employment has grown over the last 25 years from less than 5 per cent of the working population (excluding the self-employed), peaking in 2001 at about 7 per cent before slipping back to just over 6 per cent in 2004 – a growth that has been more marked amongst those in full-time jobs than in part-time employment (*Labour Market Trends* November 2001 and July 2004). Nevertheless, this still comprises a fairly small proportion of full-time jobs (about one in 20) whereas it is a much larger percentage of those in part-time employment at 15 per cent (Robinson 1999, p32). Britain has rather more temporary workers than the USA, but many less than our main European competitors; for example, in Germany and France, temporary workers comprise 11.5 per cent and 12.2 per cent of the total workforce respectively, and in Spain approximately one quarter of the workforce is on temporary contracts (Hudson 2002b, p41).

There has also been substantial and continuous growth in the people who are classified as self-employed compared with 25 years ago. In 1979, just over 1.8 million people were self-employed, a figure that rose to over 3.2 million in the spring of 2004 (*Labour Market Trends* July 2004). Many of the self-employed are people who have been made redundant and decide to set up their own businesses due to the relative scarcity of 'standard' employment opportunities. Recent rises in the banking, finance and insurance fields, as well as the proportion of professionals might be explained by City job losses (*Labour Market Trends* September 2003). Unfortunately, many of these businesses go bankrupt or their owners make only limited financial returns. Proportionately, part-time self-employment figures are seeing the largest rises whereas the proportion who are self-employed full-time has fallen below 10 per cent of all those in employment (Nolan and Wood 2003, p169). The number of part-time self-employed includes people who already work full-time but supplement their income through self-employment.

The number of agency workers from private recruitment bureaux more than trebled during the 1990s (Druker and Stanworth 2001) and grew by almost one third in a three year period from 2000 (White *et al* 2004, p21).

Similarly the numbers working from home have increased rapidly, with about a quarter claiming to do this. However, this includes not only those who work mainly from home, but also those who partially or sometimes work from home. Work by Felstead *et al* (2001), using Labour Force Surveys (LFS), show that the numbers working *mainly* at home rose from 1.5 per cent in 1981 to 2.5 per cent in 1998, and in Spring 1998 those *partially* working at home made up 3.5 per cent of the employed workforce. Their research highlights the complexities and nuances behind the statistics.

> Whilst workers on temporary contracts may offer advantages in terms of cost savings and flexibility, do they add other costs for the employer (in terms of quality, productivity or commitment, for example)? What do temporary workers gain from this form of employment, if anything?

Although the employed segment of the labour force changed significantly over the last 25 years, unemployment levels remained high for much of this period, only falling back around the turn of the century. Back in the 1960s, unemployment typically stood at about three per cent (around 600,000 people) before a variety of world-wide shocks pushed the figure steadily up beyond 1 million and to over 5 per cent by 1979. Since then numerous changes in the way in which unemployment is defined have made it difficult to make precise comparisons, but by the International Labour Office (ILO) definition it has oscillated between about 1.5 and 3.5 million over this period. In percentage terms, the figure has varied from about 5 to 12 per cent. Even at the lower levels this is higher than would have been considered reasonable in the 1960s. By the end of 2004, the (ILO-defined) unemployment rate stood at a little over 1.4 million, just under 5 per cent of the potential workforce (*Labour Market Trends* July 2004). Of course such statistics mask wide regional variations, and pockets of high unemployment persist, chiefly among young people in inner-city areas.

Discrimination affects ethnic minority groups, disabled, and older people, as well as women in terms of employment rates and pay gaps, despite legislation. Unemployment tends to be higher among ethnic groups, with young people aged under 25 particularly badly affected. The picture is relatively complicated and is heavily influenced by the specific group, as well as between women and men, and by age. Young black African men, Pakistani men and women, Black Caribbean men and women have unemployment rates in excess of 20 per cent, compared with 12 per cent for young White British men and 9 per cent for young White British women (www.statistics.gov.uk).

There are more than 6.2 million disabled adults in the UK, but only 1.27 million are in, or actively seeking, work (CIPD 2003b), something the government is currently working to address. As a result of the Disability Discrimination Act (DDA) 1995 employers are acting on access issues although many report confusion over the definitions under the act, as well as conflict between the DDA and sickness absence policies (Earnshaw *et al* 2002c; IRS Employment Review 762 2002).

Ageism has been cited as a cause of discrimination in a third of all cases (Smethurst 2004, p10), but the relevant legislation (EU Directive on Equal Treatment) will not be enacted in the UK until 2006. In the mean time many retired people are finding that they have to return to the labour market because stockmarket falls have affected their pensions. With this in mind, the government is attempting to introduce increased flexibility into patterns of retirement and pension provision. The next 25 years will see further pressures on the labour market due to an ageing population combined with attempts to lift the retirement age beyond 65. In Britain, for example, the ratio of pensioners to the working population is currently about 1:3, a ratio that could rise – on current projections – to over 2:5 by 2030. This is not just a British problem either, with estimates for Germany of over 3:5 by 2030, and for Italy of 7:10.

Table 6   *Yearly average for stoppages in progress in the UK, 1980–2003*

Years	Working days lost (000s)	Working days lost per 1000 employees	Workers involved (000s)	Stoppages	Stoppages involving the loss of 100,000 working days or more
1980–84	10,864	457	1,298	1,363	36
1985–89	3,940	170	685	894	23
1990–94	824	37	223	334	6
1995–99	476	23	201	213	2
2000–03	687	27	365	171	4

Sources: Davies J. 'Labour disputes in 2000', *Labour Market Trends*, Vol. 109, No. 6, June 2001. p302; Monger, J. 'Labour disputes in 2003', *Labour Market Trends*, Vol. 112, No. 6, June 2004. p 236

The extent of strike action also illustrates the degree to which UK labour markets have changed over the last 25 years. Table 6 (derived from *Labour Market Trends* July 2004) shows how the nature and extent of stoppages varied over time. The number of working days lost to industrial action has fallen sharply from an average of about 10 million in the first half of the 1980s to a little over half a million now. The number of workers involved in stoppages also fell dramatically, and the typical figure now is about 350,000 per annum compared with well over a million in the early 1980s. The number of recorded stoppages has also dropped by similar proportions, from nearly 1400 per annum in the early 1980s to under 200 now. Yet more notable are the length of stoppages, with the last three years recording just four strikes that accounted for 100,000 working days or more, a figure that was typically achieved in a single year during the 1980s (Monger 2004). In short, despite the occasional major strike – such as the firefighters in 2002–03 – industrial action has become a much rarer phenomenon in the UK. When it does occur it is often short term in nature, designed to achieve maximum effect without having to suffer long-term losses in earnings.

It can be seen that employment patterns have gone through some fundamental adjustments during the last 25 years, and the 'old' image of work – principally male, full-time and permanent – has had to be revised. Similarly, the extent of sectoral shifts in employment, away from manufacturing and to the service sector, has had major implications for HRM and for the role of HR professionals.

FLEXIBILITY AND FRAGMENTATION AT WORK

Popular and managerial interest in workforce and organisational flexibility grew following the publication of Atkinson's work on the flexible firm in the mid-1980s (Atkinson 1984, 1987; Atkinson and Meager 1986). Since then other writers have taken up the idea, notably Handy (1991) with the terminology of a 'shamrock organisation'. Both make distinctions between a core and a peripheral workforce, albeit in slightly different ways and with different foci, but Atkinson's is still widely referred to in other research. There have been some refinements to

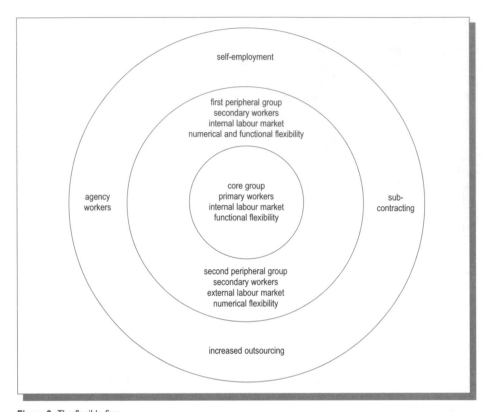

Figure 2 *The flexible firm*

Source: Adapted from Atkinson J. 'Manpower strategies for the flexible organisation', *Personnel Management*, August 1984. p29

the 'model' in the last 20 years, notably by Ackroyd and Procter (1998), as well as criticisms (Marchington *et al* 2004c), but the essential framework remains the same. A straightforward graphical representation of flexibility is provided in Figure 2.

The core comprises workers drawn from the primary labour market, who have greater security through 'permanent' (ie not fixed-term) contracts and whose skills are likely to be valued by the employer. In return, these core employees are expected to be functionally flexible by applying their skills across a wide range of tasks. Flexibility can be both vertical and horizontal. Vertical flexibility refers to employees who take on tasks that are at a higher or lower skill level than that for which they have been recruited. A good example would be craft workers undertaking labouring duties – such as sweeping-up – or semi-skilled employees assuming responsibility for certain skilled tasks, such as making minor repairs to keep production lines running. Horizontal flexibility refers to employees who undertake a wider range of tasks at the same broad skill level, as for example in the case of craft workers who operate across previous skill boundaries by doing both mechanical and electrical work. Workers may be both vertically and horizontally flexible if they are responsible for a complete task, such as teams of process workers in chemical plants (Frobel and Marchington 2005).

The periphery can be subdivided into several segments. The first peripheral group comprises workers from the secondary labour market but who are still internal to the organisation in the sense that they are employed on contracts that have some degree of permanence. They are typically full-time (though some part-timers could also be included in this category), but due to their lower level of skills these workers cannot expect similar degrees of security as their colleagues from the 'core'. They may display some functional flexibility, but typically their work is characterised by lower levels of responsibility and discretion. They are also numerically flexible as they can be laid off relatively easily since applicants with similar skills can be hired quickly. The second peripheral group comprises individuals who find it hard to break into internal labour markets and whose employment experiences tend to be precarious. This group includes individuals with little prospect of employment security. Many part-timers and temporary workers fit into this category, and for some a move into the internal labour market is a possibility, provided work continues and they are seen to do a good job and 'fit' with the organisational culture. Whilst the number of part-timers and temporaries has increased many of those on fixed-term contracts have little prospect that their employment will extend beyond the end of their current contract.

Beyond the second peripheral group are those individuals who are clearly external to the host organisation, that is, employed by another employer or in self-employment. The size of this group has also expanded significantly, especially where work has been subcontracted to other organisations. Agency workers fit into this category, which ranges from secretaries to accountants, nurses, teachers and lecturers (Druker and Stanworth 2001; Ward *et al* 2001; Grimshaw *et al* 2003). Ward *et al* (2001, p9) put forward a number of reasons why host organisations recruit temporary workers through specialist agencies, most of which relate to numerical flexibility and the shifting of risk to agencies and the temporaries themselves. Some employers vet temporaries to see whether or not they may be suitable for appointment to permanent positions at later dates (Forde 2001). In other words, elements of recruitment and selection thus transfer to an agency, leading in some cases, to the development of quasi-internal labour markets that may be advantageous both to the host employer and the agency (Rubery *et al* 2004). Whereas the Atkinson model views this group as very much within the secondary labour market, and at a major disadvantage to those in the primary internal labour market, some of these workers may be in a relatively powerful position. More highly skilled workers – such as consultants – who are in high demand, may choose to remain outside of mainstream organisational life in order to maintain greater control over their own lives, as well as earn larger amounts of money. Saloniemi *et al*'s research (2004) in Finland also demonstrates that poor psychosocial conditions are not an inevitable feature of fixed-term contracts.

Organisations have developed more flexible employment policies and practices through the increased use of part-timers and in the growth of subcontracting and self-employment. The public sector in particular health trusts and local authorities – has been at the forefront of these developments, with government requirements to extend outsourcing through a range of means in recent times. The move to compulsory competitive tendering (CCT), best value and public–private partnerships has increased extensiveness of fixed-term contracts (Colling 1999; Marchington *et al* 2003a) and the use of Transfer of Undertakings (Protection of Employment) Regulations (TUPE) transfers of employment have become commonplace (Cooke *et al* 2004a). Despite lots of publicity, there remain doubts about the extensiveness of the 'flexible firm' in reality, and some scepticism about whether or not such new organisational forms are the product of strategic thinking or muddling through. There are at least four sets of issues here:

1 *The concept*. There are doubts about the conceptual standing of the terminology. Publications on the subject seem to veer between *descriptions* of flexibility, *predictions* that the flexible firm is the design of the future and *prescriptions* that organizations should use the model to become more successful. At times it is difficult to tell which is

being used, and it has led to allegations that flexibility has been 'talked up' in order to support successive governments' ideological stance on market deregulation and 'lean' organisations (Legge 1995, p172). It is also argued that, despite its obvious intuitive appeal, the model itself lacks clarity in terms of the core–periphery distinction. For example, rather than viewing part-timers as peripheral, it is clear that some part-time workers may be critical to organisational success given the closeness of their contact with customers or their contribution to business goals. Questions arise therefore as to whether these workers should be classified as core because they interface with customers, or peripheral because they are part-timers (Rubery *et al* 2002, 2004).

2   *Extensiveness*. There are questions about the extensiveness of flexibility in practice and the reasons for its growth. Robinson (1999, p90) suggests that the more dramatic assertions about the impact of the core–periphery model are not really backed up by the data. The 1998 WERS survey data (Cully *et al* 1999, p35) shows there has been growth in so-called 'non-standard' employment. It appears that subcontracting is well established in both public and private sectors, as is the use of fixed-term contracts for staff in the public sector. Temporary agency workers are used in about a quarter of all workplaces and freelancers by one in eight, though rarely in the public sector. Despite the popular media interest in these forms of employment, homeworkers and zero-hours contract workers are relatively underused if one ignores those who work at home in addition to or instead of their normal workplace (Felstead *et al* 2001) and therefore can not really be classified as homeworkers in the traditional sense. Most workplaces make some use of non-standard labour, although it is hard to establish just how many workers in these organizations are employed on these sorts of contract and impossible to determine whether employers make use of 'atypical' work as part of a strategic HR initiative. It is also suggested that the rate of increase in flexible employment may now be slowing down if not actually hitting a ceiling (White *et al* 2004, pp31–32).

3   *Costs and benefits*. There is disagreement about the costs and benefits of flexibility. It is widely assumed that the flexible firm is naturally and automatically more efficient than its 'inflexible' counterpart, and that part-time workers, temporaries and subcontractors offer employers advantages over secure and permanent staff. It is difficult to estimate whether part-time workers are more productive than their full-time colleagues or whether they are more costly due to differing levels of absenteeism, commitment and quality (Hunter *et al* 1993, p398). There have been continuing concerns about levels of quality, for example, in work that has been subcontracted from the NHS and local authorities to the private sector (Colling 1999; Marchington *et al* 2003a). There are also questions about whether core workers maintain previous levels of commitment when many of their colleagues lose jobs through rationalisation due to fears for their own future security (Redman and Wilkinson 2001; Hebson *et al* 2003). However, it is also clear that some workers prefer to be able to work part-time and would not want to move into full-time employment for various reasons (Thompson and McHugh 2002, p161). The increased number of students in part-time and temporary jobs clearly influences these figures (Curtis and Lucas 2001), but even amongst people with a long-term presence on the labour market, there are often good reasons for wanting part-time work – especially from those with care responsibilities (Hogarth *et al* 2001, pp371–373; Dex 2003).

Who do you think gains most from flexible working, and why? Put together lists for workers and employers in relation to functional and numerical flexibility before making a judgement.

4   *Single employer.* The flexible firm model is limited because it focuses on a single firm and its HR practices, rather than taking into account interorganisational relations (Rubery *et al* 2002; Marchington *et al* 2004c). Most studies are predicated on the relationship between a single employing organisation and its employees even though this is no longer an entirely accurate characterisation of HRM. A series of changes – such as increasingly globalised capital markets, unstable and flexible labour markets, and breakdowns and fragmentation in the world of work – have brought about major adjustments to this picture. Many of the most significant employment changes have been stimulated by adaptations in ownership patterns and state policies that have changed the shape of both private and public sector organisations. Spin-off companies, joint ventures and strategic alliances have redrawn the boundaries between organisations in the private sector, especially in the high technology sector. The public–private divide has become increasingly blurred through a range of initiatives such as compulsory competitive tendering, Private Finance Initiative (PFI), 'Best Value' and Public–Private Partnerships (PPPs), and the associated transfer of staff. Multi-employer sites have become much more common in the service sector in particular, with the expansion of firms to cover activities such as postal services and banking, often through franchising, or in call centres or other workplaces increasingly staffed by agency workers. Other developments in interfirm collaboration that are less visible but equally significant are also increasing through supply chain linkages, through exchanges of staff, and through joint problem solving and new relational links.

It is apparent from research undertaken by Marchington *et al* (2004c) that work is becoming increasingly fragmented, that boundaries between organisations are becoming blurred and that existing hierarchies are being disordered. In order to meet performance targets, organisations are fragmenting and traditional divisions are breaking down. In many cases work has become more pressurised and controlled rather than liberated and empowered. So-called 'old' notions of skill, career and learning – that worked on the assumption of extended time horizons – are being replaced by new visions that rely increasingly on short-term and superficial levels of training and development where discontinuities are the norm and workers are increasingly bearing the risk for their own career development. Simultaneously, trade unions are finding their role, already under threat, is further marginalised as systems of worker representation are weakened following transfers of workers to other organisations. Boundaries are becoming increasingly blurred as organisations break-up and re-form, change their names and areas of activity, and place additional responsibilities on more junior staff. The boundaries within organisations are also becoming more blurred, both in terms of managerial relations and the traditional gender segregation of jobs. Shifting boundaries may open up new opportunities, but they also create more insecurity and confusion for people, and often fail to deliver the improved performance expectations that are promised to customers or clients. The growth of interorganisational relations also leads to a disordering of hierarchies as responsibility for the management and control of staff is diffused, and customers are increasingly seen to influence the management of employment, for example when powerful clients specifically ask for certain staff to be utilised on 'their' contracts, or where workers are rebuked following a customer-feedback survey. The increased use of agency staff, often a permanent feature at call centres, means that the responsibility for managing staff who have direct contact with customers is split between different organisations (Rubery *et al* 2003, 2004). White *et al* (2004, p31), in noting that almost half of all workplaces had 'non-employees' working on site, found that in a substantial minority of cases the managers were not able to estimate their number. This shows, yet again, the fragmentation and disordering of work.

In other words, models based around the concept of a flexible firm may no longer be adequate to analyse changes within and between different organisations that are tied together with a variety of commercial contracts. For example, a professional who works at the site of a client for long periods of time may be a peripheral worker so far as the client is concerned but a core worker for the management consultancy by whom she is employed. Equally, how can the self-employed person who routinely sells his services to an agency be classified: as self-employed, as a core agency worker, or as a peripheral contract worker? Even greater confusions can occur in circumstances where several employers operate from the same site. Box 5 gives a flavour of these new organisational forms.

BOX 5   FRAGMENTING WORK ACROSS ORGANISATIONAL BOUNDARIES

Research conducted over the last few years by Marchington *et al* (2004c) analyses the management of employment in a wide range of organisational networks. Each of these took on quite different forms in practice but several features were common across the case studies.

The influence of clients over HRM at a supplier's workplace was clear in a number of cases, either through external signs – wearing the client's uniform or answering the phone using its name – or through more hidden forces – such as attempts to influence which worker was assigned to a particular contract or questioning the level and type of training offered (Rubery *et al* 2004).

Many workers were confused about who was actually their employer and legal cases have shown doubts about this are widespread. For example the supply teachers in the study found certain aspects of their employment (say, pay) were determined by the agency while day-to-day control of their working patterns was overseen by the Head Teacher in the school where they were based (Earnshaw *et al* 2002c)

Even if there were no doubts about the status of the employer, staff transferred from the public to the private sector found difficulty in identifying where their loyalties lay – to their old employer (the NHS), to their new private sector employer, to their colleagues, to their union, to the patients or even to some wider societal goal of better health care (Hebson *et al* 2003).

Divisions within and between the workforce were also common, especially when workers were on different rates of pay depending on which business contract they were employed, when they were recruited, and which bonus system they were tied into. This also carried over into the opportunities for expressing worker voice and solidarity (Rubery *et al* 2003).

Each of these cases raises interesting HR issues relating to control and discipline, identity and commitment, recruitment and training, performance management and reward, as well as voice and representation.

THE LEGAL FRAMEWORK FOR HRM

This section provides a brief overview of how employment law, both in the UK and from the European Union (EU), shapes HRM at work. In the space available we cannot hope to offer a systematic and detailed analysis of the law, and readers are strongly advised to seek specific interpretations from employment law books (such as those by Lewis and Sargeant 2004 or Pitt 2004) or from employment relations texts (such as those by P. Edwards, 2003b or Gennard and Judge 2005). These texts, particularly the law books, are updated regularly to take account of recent legal changes.

UK and EU influences on HRM

In Britain employment law has traditionally played a minor role compared with many other countries, the system having been moulded by employers and trade unions rather than by legal enactment. 'Voluntarism' has been the prevailing philosophy with 'collective laissez-faire' (Kahn-Freund 1959, p224) seen as the best way to resolve problems in employment relations; in effect, the law has been seen only as a mechanism of last resort to be used when voluntary means fail. However, this ignores the critical role played by the law in shaping the expectations of employers and employees to make use of agreed rules rather than going to court to seek legal redress. Accordingly, the impact of legal intervention needs to be assessed not only against its desirability but also against the likelihood of attaining its objectives. As we know with any area of legal intervention (eg speed limits, smoking bans or limits on noise), the more this is accepted as appropriate behaviour by citizens, the more successful – and less interventionist – the law needs to be.

According to Kahn-Freund (1965, p302), the law performs a number of different roles in the rule-making process. Firstly, there is the *auxiliary* role through which the state provides a statutory framework of what is called 'organised persuasion'. This provides benefits – financial or otherwise – for those who observe agreements and a number of pressures are applied against those who do not. A good illustration of this is Acas, which provides services such as conciliation, mediation and arbitration. Secondly, the law has a *restrictive* role whereby it lays down sets of rules that stipulate what is allowed and what is forbidden in the conduct of industrial relations – for example in relation to strikes or picketing. Thirdly, the law has a *regulatory* role whereby it sets a 'floor of employment rights' for employees. This dates back to Victorian times when laws were introduced to provide protection in industries such as mining, and over issues such as pay in sweatshops. In the 1970s the employment protection legislation took on a wider remit, incorporating all employees rather than just those in particular industries or working under particularly harsh conditions. It has been extended further since Labour came to power in 1997. Apart from actively intervening in HR issues, the law also has a wider impact; for example, the unfair dismissal legislation has led to changes in the way people are recruited and selected, the formalisation of disciplinary procedures and the keeping of records. The law is not simply influential in directing what is required to be done but in shaping ideas about good practice, as well as potentially stimulating new ways of doing things. Various surveys have shown that employers still view the law as a major trigger for change (IRS Employment Review 740 2001).

Voluntarism came under attack in the 1960s and 1970s due to the poor performance of the British economy, leading the state to intervene more directly both through economic policies and legislation. For example, the Industrial Relations Act 1971 attempted to replace voluntarism with a more American-style system of legal regulation (Dickens and Hall 2003). Despite its failure, it did signify increasing concern over what were seen as the costs of voluntarism. The Conservative Party, elected in 1979, saw industrial relations as a major component of the 'British disease', and intervened with a step-by-step dismantling of union protections, ostensibly designed to free up the labour market. During the period from 1979 to 1997, the market was used to regulate labour standards; this included privatisation of nationalised industries and the use of contracting-out to remove large parts of the public sector – through compulsory competitive tendering and best value in local government and market testing in central government. Initiatives were taken to lessen the influence of collective bargaining and reduce trade union power, at the same time as reducing or removing the regulatory burden on employers (Ewing 2003). Most commentators agree the law played a significant part in shifting the balance of power after 1979 – a watershed in industrial relations, according to Gospel and Wood (2003a, p3). However, it would be unwise to overestimate the impact of the law on HRM compared with other factors, such as high levels of unemployment, technological change and increasingly competitive product markets.

In 1997 the election of Labour led to some adaptation in policy (Gennard 2002; Blyton and Turnbull 2004), though there are contrasting views about how much the Blair government really broke with the Thatcherite legacy (Dickens 2002; Howell 2004). Its approach has been concerned with general economic well-being, and not only the rights of workers in employment. There is both a renewed commitment to trade union recognition and an expansion in individual rights legislation. The contract of employment remains the cornerstone of the employment relationship, but this is a contract that, for most workers, is now regulated by legislation rather than by collective bargaining (Ewing 2003) – a point we take up again in Chapter 10. There have also been shifts in the law to refer to 'workers' rather than 'employees', a distinction that is extremely important for those people employed on agency contracts or where identifying the employer proves elusive due to chains of subcontracting (Earnshaw *et al* 2002c).

The Labour government's policy since 1997 has been based on five pillars. These are encouraging employment flexibility, protecting minimum employment standards in the workplace, promoting family-friendly policies at work, supporting partnership at work, and supporting union recognition. This has principally been via legal enactment and signing up to the EU Social Chapter (Bercusson 2002; Cressey 2003). The 'new deal' on employee relations incorporates support for a flexible labour market, underpinned by an extended but limited range of legal protections at work, largely for individuals but also, to a lesser degree, for trade unions (Farnham 2000). Yet it is noteworthy that many aspects of the legislation – for example on the closed shop, picketing, secondary and unofficial action, and trade union elections – have remained in place. In addition, financial sanctions are still imposed on unions (Smith and Morton 2001, p121).

Economically, the prevailing view of the Organisation for Economic Cooperation and Development (OECD) and the International Monetary Fund (IMF) has been that labour market flexibility – provided by weak employment protection legislation, low union power, low levels of and/or short-lived unemployment benefits and a low minimum wage floor – is one of the keys to economic success as well as lower unemployment rates – including the employment of marginalised workers who are less skilled, educated and experienced. The US, and to a lesser extent, the UK, provides an example of a flexible labour market, whereas France and Germany provide examples of more rigid economies. However research evidence from Baker *et al* (2004) and Schmitt and Wadsworth (2004) show that flexible labour markets fare no better than more rigid labour markets.

> To what extent do you think the state should intervene in employment issues? Discuss this question with colleagues on your course, and consider whether the 'new deal' has just benefited workers or have employers gained as well.

Many of the recent initiatives have come through the EU following the decision by the UK government to sign up to the Social Chapter; these include the national minimum wage, equal pay for work of equal value, the protection of employees' rights in the event of a transfer of an undertaking, and the introduction of information and consultation machinery for a variety of situations. More recently a number of EU decisions have helped to strengthen the position of British workers, especially those who no longer have support from trade unions to protect their rights at work. The influence of European law is more complicated than that resulting from domestic legislation because most EU employment and social legislation typically comes in one of three forms (Gennard and Judge 2002, p134):

- *regulations*, which take immediate effect, comprising detailed instructions that are directly binding on all member states
- *directives*, which are binding but require appropriate legislation from each member state within a set period of time to comply with the objectives of the directive. These are formulated in broad terms, allowing member states flexibility to interpret specific provisions
- *directions*, which affect only the parties involved in a specific case.

In addition, the Commission also issues a series of softer instruments such as recommendations, declarations and communications. Cases are heard at the European Court of Justice (ECJ), which is responsible for interpreting European legislation and for providing preliminary rulings on disputed or unclear points of law. These then have to be incorporated into domestic law.

EU social policy has evolved over time. The Treaty of Rome in 1957, which founded the European Economic Community (EEC), had a commitment to common action on economic and social progress as well as opening up barriers to the movement of goods (including workers) between member states. Two factors accelerated the development of EU social legislation. First, in the 1970s, the case law of the European Court of Justice began to grow significantly especially in the field of equal opportunities. Secondly, with growing trade between member states and the increased mobility of workers and organisations across national borders, there was pressure to add a social dimension to the 'economic' community and to incorporate adequate protection of workers so that the interests of owners and other stakeholders were balanced. This led to legislative developments in the areas of employment protection and workplace health and safety (Gennard and Judge 2002).

The Single European Act (1987) extended legislation to include social policy and employment, and also increased the use of qualified majority voting for measures designed to increase harmonisation of the internal market. While unanimity was required in relation to employment issues, qualified majority voting (QMV) could be used for health and safety – this was particularly important given the Conservative Government's opposition to working life legislation in the 1980s (Pitt 2004). Gennard and Judge (2002, p127) reckon the health and safety 'fast track' has been used lavishly since then, and has been the basis for the Working Time Directive, 1998 (IRS Employment Review 797a 2004). Box 6 (page 52) shows which issues are subject to QMV or unanimity.

The scope of EU social policy has widened since the adoption of the Social Chapter through the Treaty of the European Union in 1993 – and its incorporation, along with the 1989 Social Charter – into the 1999 Treaty of Amsterdam (Gennard and Judge 2002). The decision by the UK government to opt into the agreement on social policy is important for a number of

BOX 6 THE SOCIAL CHAPTER: BASIS ON WHICH ISSUES CAN BE DECIDED

Qualified majority voting

1 Health and safety
2 Working conditions
3 Informing and consulting workers
4 Equal treatment and equal opportunities for men and women
5 Integration of those excluded from the labour market

Unanimous voting

1 Social security and worker protection
2 Protection of workers where employment is terminated
3 Representation of workers and employers, including co-determination
4 Financial contributions for the promotion of employment and job creation

Excluded issues

1 Pay
2 The right of association
3 Right to strike
4 Right to lock out

Source: Gennard J. and Judge G. *Employee Relations*, 3rd edition. London, CIPD. 2002. p142

reasons according to Gennard and Judge (p129), not least because it promoted a joint commitment to achieving high levels of employment across the EU. It can be seen that the UK labour market is increasingly shaped by legislation adopted at EU level, and UK employers have expanded operations into other member states, which has increased the range of experiences and influences on HR managers. The new social model advocated by the Commission seeks to 'balance the employer's demand for flexibility with the employee's hopes for security. Equally important, education and training are increasingly seen not only as a way of helping individuals to become more adaptable in their present employment, but also of providing opportunities to acquire knowledge and skills so that they can find alternative employment should the number of jobs be reduced in their present workplace' (Bach and Sisson 2000, p34).

The Treaty of Amsterdam introduced a number of amendments to the original Treaty of Rome. The equal pay provisions were amended to include a direct reference to the principle of equal treatment, which provided private sector employees with the same rights as those currently enjoyed by employees of the state to rely on principles of European law in national courts and tribunals. The Treaty of Amsterdam also introduced a provision enabling the EU to take action against any form of discrimination, whether based on sex, racial or ethnic origin, religion or belief, disability, age or sexual orientation. In deciding the basis of social policy, the EU can utilise the ideas behind the Social Charter. This provides a wide floor of rights in areas such as employment and remuneration, improvement of living and working conditions, freedom of association and collective bargaining, vocational training, equal treatment for men and women, information, consultation and participation for workers, and health and safety at the workplace. As Gennard (2000, p120) notes:

> **The EU is about a lot more than beef bans. For employees the EU has given minimum standards in the fields of working time, hours of work, holiday entitlement, information and consultation in pan-European companies, in redundancies and transfer of businesses and parental leave. These are protections UK governments have been less than enthusiastic to give. The EU is an integral part of the UK employee relations system and not something entirely external to it.**

As we have seen, between 1997 and 2004 the Labour government took on board – sometimes reluctantly – many new legal provisions emanating from the EU. However, at the 2004 European elections the UK Independence Party (UKIP) stood on a ticket that was highly sceptical about EU membership, and there may well be attempts to weaken European influences on employment relations. Consider the merits and shortcomings of reverting to a more isolationist UK stance in the HR area.

The new framework of EU social policy-making includes provision for the European social partners – the European Trade Union Confederation (ETUC), the Union of Industrial and Employers' Confederations of Europe (UNICE) and the European Centre of Enterprises with Public Participation – to be consulted about both direction and the content of EU legislation in the social field. They can also negotiate framework agreements as a substitute for legislation. The social partners may also engage in negotiations (social dialogue) at their own initiative, as happened in relation to accident prevention and working conditions. Framework agreements have been negotiated on parental leave, part time work and fixed term work contracts. In some other areas – for example information and consultation – the social partners decided not to negotiate, so the Commission submitted its legislative proposal through the normal decision-making procedures.

The legal basis for proposals can be challenged. For example, the 1993 Working Time Directive came into force in the UK under the Working Time Regulations in 1998 covering not just management working hours but holidays and rest periods (Bone 2002; IRS Employment Review 797a 2004). It was considered by the UK government as an issue of working conditions, not a health and safety issue as put forward by the Commission. This was because health and safety was then subject to QMV, while working conditions were subject to unanimity, and therefore susceptible to a UK veto. The UK Government took its case to the ECJ but lost (Reid 2000; Gennard and Judge 2002). Box 7 on page 54 shows how disagreements remain over the working time proposals.

Find out the latest position on working time by looking at *People Management* or other publications that provide such information. Read the paper by Barnard C., Deakin S. and Hobbs R. 'Opting out of the 48 hour week: employer necessity or individual choice?', *Industrial Law Journal*, Vol. 32, No. 4, 2003. pp223–252.

BOX 7   BATTLES OVER WORKING TIME

The 1998 Working Time Regulations provide that a worker's working time (including overtime) should not exceed an average of 48 hours per week over a 17-week period. The UK took advantage of an opt-out allowing workers to agree with their employers that the 48-hour ceiling should not apply to them. A DTI study (2002b) estimated that about one million workers worked sustained long hours whilst about 20% occasionally worked more than 48 hours in a week. The social partners (ETUC and UNICE) have been trying to hammer out a deal on this, but it is apparent the European Commission is running out of patience with their failure to reach an agreement. By the middle of 2004, the social partners were some way apart from each other. This may result in the Commission issuing a Directive that could signal the end of the opt-out, although the UK government is still keen for this to be retained because, in its view, it enhances flexibility.

A whole host of issues relate to this case, many of which have little to do with the law. It is acknowledged there are major consequences from the pursuit of a long-hours culture, such as increased stress at work, potentially increased numbers of accidents due to tired workers, and a reliance on using inefficient labour practices rather than investing in technology, and reduced productivity (Jones 2004). On the other hand, the UK has always operated with higher working time than other parts of the EU, and it has helped to provide a decent level of income for many workers while allowing employers an easy route to meeting extra demand, especially in the short term. Two groups of people – managers and manual workers – are particularly prone to working long hours, although the reasons for doing so are generally very different. Research by Barnard et al (2003) has shown that many workers are keen on retaining the opportunity to work long hours and it has been rare for employers to pressure them into overtime. As they suggest, much of the problem has come about because UK businesses have been allowed a high degree of autonomy, and high amounts of overtime have therefore become institutionalised.

Although a majority of those who work more than 48 hours per week choose to do so, 30 per cent feel *compelled* to do so (CIPD 2004a). Although UK workers get more time off than workers in the US, they get less time than those in many other countries (IRS Employment Review 783 2003). More than 25 per cent work more than 48 hours per week (up from 10 per cent in 1998) and more than one in eleven works over 60 hours per week (CIPD 2003b). According to Taylor (2002a, p8) 'overwork in our society is seen as a primary cause of growing ill health, both physical and mental'.

The Employment Act 2002 requires employers to 'seriously consider' requests for flexible working hours from employees with children under the age of six or disabled children under 18 unless there are clear business reasons for not granting it (IRS Employment Review 797a 2004). In theory flexible work arrangements accord the same rights and status as full-time, but a *People Management* survey (CIPD 2002d) showed that 73 per cent of HR practitioners thought that working part-time meant fewer promotion opportunities and Houston and Marks' (2003, p212) research showed that part-time workers experienced a drop in status of their post. Too many workers cannot afford to take up basic rights (for example for unpaid maternity leave), similarly it is often difficult for small firms to accommodate flexible work arrangements.

Other European developments that affect the UK include directives on race and ethnicity, equal treatment on a whole variety of grounds including religion or belief, disability, age and sexual orientation. The Human Rights Act 1998, which came into force in 2000, incorporates into UK law certain rights and freedoms set out in the European Convention on Human Rights. According to Lewis and Sergeant (2004, pp201–204), the key sections of the Human Rights Act likely to affect UK employment issues are as follows.

- *Article 8 – the right to privacy.* This could apply if employers were to interfere with communications, such as intercepting staff telephone calls or e-mails. This also ties in with the Data Protection Act.
- *Article 9 – freedom of thought, conscience and religion.* Cases have arisen relating to dress code, religious observance and the expression of political views.
- *Article 10 – freedom of expression.* Cases have arisen in relation to the leaking of confidential information and regulations preventing senior local government officers participating in political activities.
- *Article 11 – the right to freedom of assembly and association, including joining a trade union.* This was tested in relation to the rights of workers at Government Communications Headquarters (GCHQ).

The current system of employment law is thus a synthesis of competing values and traditions. On the one hand, it accepts a great deal of the Thatcher inheritance, especially in relation to collective issues, but it has also been shaped to accommodate new values. For example, there are rights to trade union recognition where there is a prescribed level of support, but tight restrictions on trade union government and on industrial action. There is now a stronger emphasis on a more comprehensive role for legislation rather than treating collective bargaining as the basis for setting minimum standards (Ewing 2003). The provision of minimum standards has been seen as important not only to promote improved competitiveness but also to enhance workplace democracy and provide greater 'fairness' in the employment relationship. At the same time, Labour has been keen to avoid excessive regulation and promote flexibility by active labour market policies, often linked to employability and new skills (Gennard 2002).

So, how does this leave the current legal system? One view is that the period since 1997 has been a balancing act (Dickens and Hall 2003, p148), trying simultaneously to appease employers and trade unions/workers, by tackling the worst excesses of employer behaviour (in relation to pay and discrimination, for example) while not burdening employers with too much regulation. Far from satisfying employers and unions, some would suggest that the government has actually managed to annoy both (Gennard 2002, p593). The whole approach could be criticised because it lacks coherence and is little more than a ragbag of initiatives. Indeed, it may be more accurate to see the first few years of the Labour government as 'a policy adaptation specific to centre-left governments in weakly co-ordinated liberal market economies' rather than a distinctive 'third way' (Howell 2004, p19). On the other hand, rather than viewing the law as a constraint on business and a cost to be borne, employment regulation could be seen more positively as providing a framework of social justice that guarantees workers some minimum level of security which allows them to contribute to economic success (Dickens and Hall 2003, p148). These comments show how much the law is influenced by wider political events – such as a change of government – that might slow down or even derail the gradual Europeanisation of HRM.

Individual rights at work

Employer–worker relations are organised principally around the concept of the employment contract, the main terms of which are outlined in texts such as Lewis and Sargeant (2004, pp11–33) or Pitt (2004, pp89–115). It is important to clarify the difference between the employment contract and the statement of terms and conditions. The contract may or may not be written, and in practice the parties enter into a contract after the stages of advertisement, interview, offer and acceptance. In most cases employers provide a statement of the main terms and conditions of employment or a written contract, but a contract is still formed even if no written material changes hands. It is also important to know that a breach of contract, which can lead to an action for wrongful dismissal, is different from a claim for unfair dismissal. Not only is each case typically dealt with through different channels (wrongful dismissal through the court system, and unfair dismissal through the employment tribunals), they each cover different issues (Lewis and Sargeant 2004, p140; Pitt 2004, p200). There are several sources of contractual terms.

Express agreement between employer and employee

These are the terms that are spelled out, either in writing or orally. These may include points in the advertisement, oral terms outlined at interview, or a written contract provided after the interview, either at the time the individual starts work or some time thereafter. The express terms may differ from what is contained in a job advertisement, but are clearly laid down as part of the individual contract or are expressly incorporated from a collective agreement (Lewis and Sargeant 2004, p12)

Terms implied by common law

These are the terms inferred from the courts as inherent in all contracts of employment. They can arise in two sorts of way. First, they may be based upon the presumed intention of the parties, either through 'the officious bystander' test – which means that a term is so obvious that it need not be stated – or 'the business efficacy' test, in which it can be presumed that this was the clear intention of both parties. The second influence of common law is that certain terms are implied in every contract (Lewis and Sargeant 2004, p4; Pitt 2004, pp21–25). Under this, the employer has a duty to:

- pay wages if an employee is available for work unless there is an express term limiting this

- provide work in certain circumstances, such as when an employee's earnings are dependent upon work being provided, when lack of work could affect their reputation, or when the employee needs to practise their skills continuously

- co-operate with the employee, so as not to destroy any mutual trust and confidence upon which co-operation is built, say by requiring contractual obligations which are impossible to comply with or persistently varying conditions of service

- take reasonable care for the worker by providing safe premises and working environment, and avoiding risks which are reasonably foreseeable.

In return, the employee also has obligations under common law. These are to:

- co-operate with the employer, by obeying lawful and reasonable instructions so as not to impede the employer's business. Complications arise when workers are asked to take on duties falling outside the scope of their contract (see Lewis and Sargeant 2004, pp25–26 or Pitt 2004, p108 for further details)

- be faithful to the employer, and not engage in actions which cause a conflict of interest with the employer, say by disclosing confidential information which may be of benefit to a competitor or some other third party

- take reasonable care in the performance of their duties by not putting themselves or other employees at risk.

Collective agreements

Terms may be derived from collective agreements as well as being individually negotiated, either by express provision or by implication. Pay and conditions of service are routinely incorporated into an individual's contract of employment if there is an express provision that the contract is subject to the terms of a particular collective agreement.

Works rules

These can be incorporated into the contract in two ways. First, if employees are required to sign an acknowledgement at the time of entering employment that works rules will form part of the contract. Second, if 'reasonable notice' is given by the employer that works rules are to form part of the contract. Questions then need to be asked about how much the contract is to be varied, as well as how prominently the rules have been displayed.

Custom and practice

In the absence of express terms, custom and practice may help to define what constitutes the employment contract provided it is 'reasonable, certain and notorious'. It is 'reasonable' if it fits with norms in the industry in question, and would be interpreted in this way by a court. Custom and practice is 'certain' if it is capable of precise definition and not open to substantially different interpretations. It is 'notorious' if the custom is well-known by all those to whom it relates. The requirement to provide written statements probably limits the scope for there to be customary terms in the contract (Pitt 2004, p99).

Statute

These are terms Parliament has decreed will be put into all contracts of employment. As we have seen, employment legislation regarding employer–worker relations has expanded considerably over the last 30 years. These cover just about every aspect of the employment relationship, and specific aspects of the law are dealt with in later chapters.

Employees can ask for a written statement of particulars when they have been employed for one month, and there is a time limit within which the employer has to provide this. The statement should include the following items or indicate clearly where they can be found (see Box 8 on page 58).

Employers are allowed to collect and hold information on workers but there is an issue over misuse of information, and various Data Protection provisions have provided some protection for workers. This now applies to manual records as well as computerised information. Employers have a duty to ensure that personal data is only obtained for specified, lawful purposes and is used only for those purposes. The information kept must be accurate, up-to-date, relevant and not excessive – suggesting that personnel records should regularly be culled of old and irrelevant information. The Act contains strict limitations on the processing of such information, which includes its disclosure. For more information see Lewis and Sergeant (2004, pp204–208).

BOX 8   WRITTEN STATEMENT OF FURTHER PARTICULARS

- Identity of employer and employee
- Date on which the period of continuous employment commenced
- Rate of remuneration, and the interval at which it is to be paid
- Terms and conditions relating to hours of work, holidays and holiday pay, and sick pay
- Terms relating to pensions arrangements
- Length of notice that employees are required to receive and obliged to provide
- Title of the job
- Name of persons to whom the individual employee can apply in the event of a grievance or dissatisfaction with a disciplinary decision
- Place(s) of work at which the employee is required or allowed to work
- Details regarding collective agreements that directly affect the employee's terms and conditions of employment.
- Where the employment is temporary, the period for which it is expected to continue or, if it is for a fixed term, the date when it is to end
- Arrangements where the employee is required to work outside the UK for more than a month

Collective rights at work

We have already seen that the period between 1979 and 1997 saw a piecemeal and gradual reform of employer–union relations, albeit driven by a central objective to weaken the power of trade unions, both by limiting their ability to engage in industrial action, and by making it harder for trade union leaders to gain mandates from the membership. Not many employers have actually taken out injunctions to delay industrial action, and even fewer have gone beyond the injunction stage to seek damages against trade unions because of the potential detrimental effect on employee relations (Farnham 2000, pp394–400). On the other hand, the potential threat of the law has probably constrained union leaders and members, and may well have prevented some deep-seated conflicts from being translated into strike action.

For many years, public policy in Britain encouraged the support and development of collective bargaining and emphasised voluntarism. For example, up until the early 1990s Acas had a general duty to 'encourage the extension of collective bargaining', although there were no formal powers to impose changes on employers or employees. The period from 1979 to 1997 saw a gradual erosion of collectivist principles in employment law, and was seen as a move to enhance individual freedom, free employers from the abuses of union power, and improve efficiency and competitiveness. Since 1997, Labour has added new statutory provisions covering information and consultation, recognition and representation whilst largely leaving the previous Conservative regime in place (Dickens and Hall 2003, pp137–138). Public policy has promoted partnership as a more sensible and co-operative way forward for employers and workers, and we deal with voice and representation in Chapter 10. As with individual employment rights, there has been a whole raft of legislation in the area of collective employment relations since the early 1980s that has affected issues concerned with the closed shop, picketing and industrial action, and union recognition.

Efforts to dismantle the closed shop – where employment was conditional on union membership to be a condition of employment, were at the forefront of the legislation, and, with some exceptions, this is now more or less complete. Progressively, it has been made more difficult for unions to organise workers at the workplace due to restrictions on check off or DOCAS arrangements (deductions of contributions at source) and the requirements for members to reiterate their commitment to unions. There has been a shift to get members to pay subscriptions by direct debit, but the 1998 WERS survey showed that DOCAS remained the predominant method of collection at almost two-thirds of workplaces (Cully *et al* 1998, p89).

The legislation on strikes and picketing has followed a similar gradualist route, to the point where it is now extremely difficult for trade unions to organise industrial action. Prior to the Employment Act 1980, picketing was allowed at any place other than an individual's home. In 1980 it was effectively restricted solely to a person's place of work, although there were exceptions for individuals with no fixed workplace. A Code of Practice issued by the Employment Department also recommended an upper limit of six pickets, although this has not been rigorously applied by the police who have preferred to control picket lines via the use of public order offences. There were several moves to restrict strike activity in the 1980s and early 1990s, falling broadly into three categories:

- Definitions of a lawful trade dispute have been narrowed progressively. Interunion disputes are excluded from immunity, as are those deemed to be of a 'political character', that is, wider than those concerned wholly or mainly with conditions of employment. Secondary industrial action (ie that which relates to disputes beyond the initial employer–employee dispute) is now outlawed in effect.

- The dismissal of strikers has been made easier. This prevented individuals who were dismissed during a lawful dispute from claiming unfair dismissal if all strikers at a workplace had been dismissed and none had been re-engaged within three months. The selective dismissal of strikers engaged in unofficial action is now allowed.

- The requirement to hold ballots of members before taking industrial action was extended, initially on a voluntary 'auxiliary' basis by providing public funds to pay for postal ballots and through the removal of immunity if ballots were not held. At first unions were allowed to hold workplace ballots but this is now restricted to postal ballots alone. The wording on the ballot paper has been specified more precisely, there are now time limits regulating the use of industrial action after a ballot, and notice has to be given to an employer that a ballot is to be held. All of this makes it much harder for trade unions to organise strikes and much easier for employers to counter them.

There have been some changes since 1997 in the area of collective rights, in particular regarding union recognition which is dealt with in Chapter 10 but this does not apply to small workplaces. Basically, recognition can come about through agreement, with the help of Acas or through an application to the Central Arbitration Committee (CAC), which might order a ballot to be held. In this area, as with other aspects of collective rights, use of the law is never easy and there are concerns that employers who are hostile to recognition can still find ways to undermine the union's case whilst the procedure is taking place (Wood *et al* 2003, p142).

> What do you think about the current position of the law in relation to trade unions? Do existing restrictions make it easier or harder for HR practitioners to develop co-operative relations at work?

THE INSTITUTIONAL FRAMEWORK FOR HRM
Trade Unions and the Trades Union Congress (TUC)

The British trade union movement has a long and proud history, stretching back at least to the early part of the nineteenth century. It has helped to shape HR practice not just at those organisations where unions are – or have been – recognised but also through its influence on employment law and government policy. Moreover, some well-known non-union employers have introduced superior terms and conditions of employment primarily to prevent unions from gaining a foothold. Trade unions can be categorised in two ways: craft, general and industrial; or open and closed (Turner 1962). Readers who wish to find out more about the union movement are advised to consult one of the specialist texts on employment relations or trade unions (such as Waddington and Hoffman 2000; P. Edwards 2003b; Blyton and Turnbull 2004).

The earliest unions were for crafts*men* (sic) who experienced high levels of autonomy in their work, and sought to maintain and extend job control by preventing a dilution of their skills. These craft unions were based on single trades – such as printing, carpentry and milling – and they were organised typically at a local and regional level, with no real attempt to form national federations until later. Each trade union jealously guarded its own specialist field, both against other craft unions and against encroachment by unskilled workers. Union strength came from the ability to regulate entry to a particular set of jobs by maintaining strict controls over numbers. This meant that unskilled and semi-skilled workers had to form their own bodies – the general unions – which are very different from those of their craft-based colleagues in a number of ways. They were established in the 1880s and 1890s at national level and adopted a more overtly political stance. The final category is industrial unions, formed to represent a wide range of workers in a particular industry or sector. These unions varied somewhat in structure and orientation, but prominent among the industrial unions were those for workers in coal mining and the railways. Merger activity over the last 20 years has rendered the old craft/general/industrial classification increasingly obsolete and the emergence of more 'super unions' makes it even less appropriate as an instrument of categorisation.

The alternative classification – open and closed – has the benefit of focusing on the recruitment methods of the union, and the extent to which it seeks to expand or restrict membership. Examples of closed unions include those originally formed for craft workers or in some industrial sectors, but technological change has accelerated mergers of what were once closed unions. The open unions, by contrast, seek to expand membership in order to increase their strength and influence. Trade unions can thus be categorised in terms of the degree to which they are open or closed in nature.

The overall number of unions has declined consistently from nearly 1400 in 1920 to under 200 now. Membership has become more concentrated as well, with the 15 unions whose membership is in excess of 100,000 accounting for nearly 85 per cent of all trade union members (Certification Officer 2004, p56). Multi-unionism has diminished markedly. According to WERS in 1998, 55 per cent of workplaces employing 25 or more employees did not recognise trade unions; of those that did, the largest proportion (43 per cent) recognised only a single trade union, and just 23 per cent recognised more than three (Cully *et al* 1999, p91). Union mergers have contributed to the reduction in multi-unionism y*et al*so to the greater heterogeneity of membership of some of the larger unions. It has long been an aim of the TUC to create a small number of super unions that can work together rather than, as on

Table 7 *Numbers of members in the largest British unions in 2003*

UNISON	1,289,000
Amicus	1,061,551
Transport and General Workers' Union	835,351
GMB	703,970
Royal College of Nursing of the UK	359,739
National Union of Teachers	331,910
Union of Shop Distributive and Allied Workers	321,151
Public and Commercial Services Union	285,582
Communication Workers Union	266,067
National Association of School Masters and Union of Women Teachers	265,219

Source: Certification Officer. *Annual Report of the Certification Officer, 2003–4*. London, Certification Office for Trade Unions and Employers' Associations. 2004. p56

some occasions, wasting resource by battling with one another. The 10 largest unions are shown in Table 7.

The changing sectoral nature of employment, outlined earlier in this chapter, has had significant implications for the trade unions. Less than 30 per cent of those in employment are union members, a dramatic decline since the zenith of 1979 when it stood at approximately 55 per cent of all employees. Union density increases with workplace size, organization size and workplace age (Cully *et al* 1999, p237). The shifts have been:

- higher union density in the 'old' declining industrial regions of Britain, and lower density in 'new' areas of employment growth
- decline in large units of employment and an increase in the number of smaller establishments
- higher union density in the contracting sectors of employment and lower density in the expanding sectors
- contraction in manual occupations and an increase in non-manual occupations.

What is the level of union membership in your organisation (or one with which you are familiar)? To what extent has this changed recently, and what are the reasons for this?

Unlike most other Western European countries, Britain has only one main union confederation – the TUC – whose affiliates constitute the vast majority of union members. The TUC has no direct role in collective bargaining and cannot implement industrial action, largely because British unions have generally been too jealous of their own autonomy to allow it such powers. Instead, the TUC's primary role has been to lobby governments although its political influence is now much less than in the past (Marchington *et al* 2004b). The return of the Labour Party in

1997 presaged a more fruitful role for the TUC as a social partner with government, though this has been much more distant than in the past. The TUC has also played an important role in trying to regulate interunion relations (Waddington 2003). It has occasionally become involved in trying to settle industrial disputes by putting pressure on strike leaders or in attempting to widen the dispute by encouraging other unions to become involved, typically through moral and financial support. In interunion disputes, the TUC has applied the Bridlington Principles to encourage unions to take care before trying to recruit members from another union or in an organisation where another union had representation or bargaining rights. The TUC has been a keen advocate of partnership at work through its role in the Involvement and Participation Association, the Partnership Fund and its own Partnership Institute (see Chapter 10). Moreover, the adoption of a more continental European-style approach, ie pressing for broader statutory rights for *all* employees (including non-unionised), has questioned the old voluntarist philosophy (Marchington *et al* 2004b). There has also been a greater willingness to accept new unions as affiliates, most notably when the Association of Teachers and Lecturers joined the TUC in 1997. The only large union still outside the TUC is the Royal College of Nursing (Waddington 2003, p233).

As well as promoting the partnership model, the TUC also sought to stem membership decline via more effective recruitment strategies and set up an Organising Academy to train a new generation of union organisers (Heery 1998). The need to prioritise recruitment of new members led some unions to focus on broader services to individual members, and to adopt models closer to customer 'servicing' than to the traditional fraternalist ideals and collective consciousness. The servicing model focused on links with union officials external to the workplace and on the provision to members of financial products such as credit card facilities, cheap loans, and independent legal advice. The 'organising' model takes a different approach (Blyton and Turnbull 2004, pp164–168) and focuses on the provision of support to workplace representatives who receive training, guidance and advice from their unions in how to recruit and retain members. Heery *et al*'s (2000, p413) analysis of the first two years of the Organising Academy's work concluded there had been a number of problems, not least in the lack of support from some large private sector unions. On the other hand, it was felt that sufficient successful outcomes resulted from the experiment – in terms of new union members being recruited – to ensure its continuation.

Employers' associations

Organisations of employers have a history as long as the trade union movement, but in recent times their prominence and influence over employment issues has also declined. Employers' associations can be defined as 'any organisation of employers, individual proprietors, or constituent organisations of employers whose principal purpose includes the regulation of relations between employers and workers or between employers and trade unions' (Farnham 2000, p42). Their numbers have declined in much the same way as have trade unions, from well over 1000 in the mid-1960s to under 100 now (Certification Officer 2004, p64). In the early 1980s, about one-quarter of all workplaces were in organisations that were members of a relevant employers' association, a figure that has since halved (Cully *et al* 1999, p228; Millward *et al* 2000, p75).

Employers' associations differ widely in their structure and organisation, and can be categorised into three broad groupings (Salamon 2000, p271). First, there are national associations or federations with local branches or affiliates, such as the Engineering Employers' Federation (EEF) which has about a dozen regional affiliate organisations or the Chemical Industries Association, both of which retain a key role in their respective industries.

Second, there are specialist bodies that represent a distinct segment of an industry, such as in printing where there are a number of different bodies for newspaper printing, book publishing and general printing. Others would include the England and Wales Cricket Board or the National Hairdressers Federation. Finally, there are small local associations such as the Lancaster Morecambe and South Lakeland Master Plumbers Association (see the annual report of the Certification Officer for the entire list).

Historically, employers' associations played an important part in shaping the British voluntarist system of employment. Initially at local level and then (more importantly) at national level they brought together and acted as representatives for employers in each industry, reaching agreements with unions over recognition, disputes procedures and the substantive terms and conditions to apply in member companies. They tended to shift the determination of basic wages, hours and other employment conditions beyond the level of individual companies. Since that time, their membership and influence has declined considerably, although they still play an important role in shaping employment relations activities at the workplace, especially in single industry firms and in specialist sectors (Marchington *et al* 2004b).

Employers' associations have traditionally offered four major sets of services to members:

1 *Collective bargaining with trade unions* – This role was central for many years, and is still particularly important if any collective bargaining takes place at industry level. In a small number of industries, agreements are comprehensive in scope and coverage, specifying wage rates and other terms and conditions of employment that apply broadly at each establishment. As Cully *et al* (1999, p228) noted in the late 1990s, multi-employer bargaining covered 47 per cent of all employees in the public sector, 25 per cent in manufacturing and just 12 per cent in the private services sector, figures way down from 1980. Despite lessened influence, nationally negotiated rates of pay – and perhaps more importantly patterns of working time – still help to shape employment relations at workplace level. For conglomerates whose interests span many different industries, the collective bargaining role does not offer any advantages. Conversely, for employers with a single industry focus and intense labour market competition in a specific region or area, a useful role can be fulfilled.

2 *Assisting in the resolution of disputes* – To some extent, this is linked with the previous role, in that employers' associations and trade unions agree to abide by joint grievance, disputes, and disciplinary procedures if there is a 'failure to agree' at establishment or firm level. The major purpose of these procedures is to allow for an independent view, by individuals who have a good knowledge of the industry, and so assist the parties to reach an agreement. It also has the advantage of encouraging the parties to use procedures rather than taking unilateral action – such as going on strike or dismissing a worker without appeal. The use of employers' associations for this role has declined as employers have chosen to appoint their own appeals body, or seek external advice from lawyers or Acas.

3 *Providing general advice to members* – This can range from seminars for member companies on the impact of new legislation through to informal assistance in the event of a query. An IRS survey (IRS Employment Review 748 2002, p8), viewed this as the most widely used service, in particular for advice on health and safety, training and education, industrial relations and employment law. Overall, however, Millward *et al* (2000, pp72–73) report a reduced reliance on the use of employers' associations as a major source of external advice with lawyers the most popular source of advice, followed by Acas and other government agencies, and management consultants.

4 *Representing members' views* – This role takes two forms: first, employers' associations, and in particular the Confederation of British Industry (CBI), acts as a pressure group for employers generally, both in relation to national government and with the European Commission (IRS Employment Review 748 2002, p9). In some industries they play a major role in raising the awareness of the general public, say in relation to the employment consequences of tax increases on alcohol or on the value of attracting inward investment to a particular region. Second, employers' associations also provide specialist representation for member firms at employment tribunals, although some employers now prefer to use lawyers or consultants instead.

> Choose an industry-based employers' association and find out how it serves its members nowadays in terms of the four roles discussed above. In particular, assess the extent to which it shapes HR practice in the workplace.

The peak body for employers is the CBI. Its membership includes individual employers as well as employers' and trade associations. Indirectly, it can claim to articulate the views of up to 250,000 organisations with a combined employment of approximately 10 million people (Salamon 2000, p276). Its objectives, according to Farnham (2000, p45), are to:

■ provide a voice for British industry and influence general industrial and economic policy, and to act as a national point of reference for those seeking industry's views

■ develop the contribution of British industry to the national economy

■ encourage the efficiency and competitive power of British industry

■ provide information and advice to members.

In addition to the CBI, other organisations that speak for employer interests include the Institute of Directors, the Institute of Management and the CIPD. We look at the CIPD in Chapter 5.

Third party agencies

Third party involvement has been a prominent feature of the British employment relations scene. For most of the twentieth century, services such as arbitration and conciliation were provided by the state, but once Acas was set up in 1975, it brought together a number of duties previously handled by government departments. *Acas* is truly a tripartite body as its Council comprises members drawn from employers' organisations (not just the CBI), employees' organisations (not just the TUC), and independent members such as lawyers and academics. Acas is independent of government, and this is seen as vital in maintaining its reputation as a genuine third party agency which can help resolve problems at work, both of a collective and an individual nature. Acas is charged with the general duty of promoting the improvement of industrial relations (Lewis and Sergeant 2004, p6). Much of the information outlined below is drawn from the Acas Annual Report for 2003/2004; readers should update their knowledge by looking at the most recent report – available free (www.acas.org.uk).

Acas is keen to promote workplace effectiveness and productivity, and its model forms the basis of advice and training on good practice. According to Acas, effective workplaces should have:

1 goals and plans that employees understand

2 managers who genuinely listen

3 workers who feel valued so that they can talk confidently about their work and learn from success and mistakes

4 equality and diversity – everyone is treated fairly and differences are values

5 understanding that workers have commitments and interests outside of work

6 a pay and reward system that is clear, fair, and consistent

7 a safe and healthy place to work

8 as much employment security as is possible.

9 a culture that promotes learning and skill development

10 a good working relationship between management and employee representatives

11 procedures for dealing with grievances, disputes and disciplinary matters that managers and employees know about and use fairly.

Acas services cover six main areas:

1 *Resolving collective disputes.* This is where Acas provides assistance through its officers generally at the request of either party to a dispute, and the parties are encouraged to use their own internally agreed procedures to resolve disputes. On some occasions the intervention of Acas makes headline news, but generally the collective conciliation work is done quietly and unobtrusively, proactively but necessarily 'unsung' (Goodman 2000, p64). Acas was involved in 1245 disputes in 2003/2004, most of which related to pay and recognition cases. As Goodman (p38) notes, the conciliator's role is 'to facilitate a voluntary agreement', acting as an intermediary, maintaining communications, clarifying issues, eroding unrealistic expectations, establishing common ground and pointing out the costs and disadvantages of not settling the dispute.

2 *Arbitrating and mediating disputes.* This aspect of its work is not actually conducted by Acas officials themselves, but by appointed independent experts – such as academics – who investigate the issue and make an award that the parties agree to accept in advance. Some disputes procedures provide for Acas arbitration following the exhaustion of internal procedures, including conventional practice of reaching a compromise through to pendulum arbitration. In 2003/2004, there were about 70 cases under this heading.

3 *Building better employment relations.* Advisory work is undertaken by Acas in order to help the parties prevent problems arising in the first place: this is perhaps best viewed as 'fire prevention', rather than fire fighting which takes place following a breakdown in negotiations or after a contested dismissal. This aspect of Acas' work focuses on the processes of employment relations, getting the parties to work together more effectively (Purcell 2000). The principal issues are collective bargaining, employee involvement and change management. In 2003/2004, over 400 projects were completed.

4 *Settling complaints about employee rights.* Unlike the situation with collective conciliation, the area of individual conciliation is a statutory part of Acas' activity, as a prelude to consideration by an employment tribunal. In sheer volume terms, this represents one of the major aspects of Acas' work, with over 100,000 cases in 2003/2004, of which only 24 per cent went to hearing. This is probably the area in which HR practitioners have greatest contact with the service, and, as with other

areas of its work, this generally receives very positive feedback from users. The Employment Rights (Dispute Resolution) Act 1998 allowed Acas to set up an arbitration scheme to enable parties to submit their dispute to arbitration instead of going to employment tribunal, but this has not generated many cases.

5   *Providing impartial information and advice.* Enquiries are the fifth broad aspect of the Acas workload, and in 2003/2004 over three-quarters of a million calls were answered by the national helpline. The range of topics is very broad, although many questions are about the law, particularly on flexible working provisions. Acas's own surveys show very high levels of satisfaction with the quality of these services.

6   *Promoting good practice.* There are two aspects to this area of work: events to promote good practice such as conferences and seminars; and the issuing of Codes of Practice that contain practical guidance on how to improve employment relations. The former of these activities involved over 2500 separate events around the country. Acas has issued a number of Codes of Practice; the one on disciplinary practice and procedures in employment has been widely used leading to major changes over the last thirty years in HR policy and practice.

> Get hold of a copy of the most recent Acas Annual Report, and assess whether or not your organisation (or one with which you are familiar) is getting maximum benefit from its services.

The *Central Arbitration Committee* (CAC), like Acas, is not subject to ministerial direction. It is a permanent independent body whose main function, under the Employment Relations Act 1999, is to adjudicate on applications relating to the statutory recognition and derecognition of trade unions for collective bargaining purposes (see Chapter 10 for more details). The CAC receives applications for recognition and supervises the process – including ballots – before deciding whether or not recognition should be granted. In addition, the CAC has a statutory role in determining disputes about disclosure of information for collective bargaining purposes, and regarding the establishment and operation of European Works Councils. Its work is almost entirely concerned with applications for trade union recognition for collective bargaining. In 2003–4, 106 applications for recognition were received; it received six complaints under the disclosure of information provisions; and no applications on the establishment and operation of European Works Councils (CAC 2004).

The importance of its role cannot be estimated solely from the relatively small number of cases with which it deals, but from its influence on employers and employees in reaching settlements regarding union recognition that may not otherwise have been achieved. It is also clear that some lessons have been learned from the government's previous attempt to create a statutory framework for union recognition in the late 1970s, in particular in relation to the balloting provisions (Wood 2000, p142). The Chairman of the CAC, in reviewing the first few years of its work, suggested that three themes underlay its approach: adopting a problem-solving and constructive stance to issues; being aware of the responsibilities that accrue from having the ultimate power to make decisions; learning and adjusting their approach as necessary (Burton 2002, p618).

The *Certification Officer* has the following areas of responsibility:

■   maintaining a list of trade unions, and determining whether or not they can be classified as independent, ie able to continue in existence without support from the employer

- recording trade union political activities, mergers, and transfer of engagements, as well as complaints about how these have been handled

- ensuring that trade unions keep up-to-date membership returns for election purposes, and investigating complaints from members about the administration of elections

- dealing with complaints from members about breaches of the union's own rules relating, for example, to ballots and the operation of the executive committee (see Lewis and Sargeant 2004, p8).

The *Equal Opportunities Commission* (EOC) was established under the Sex Discrimination Act 1975 with the general duties of working towards the elimination of discrimination, promoting equality of opportunity between men and women, and reviewing the operation of the relevant legislation – such as sex discrimination and on equal pay. The EOC is able to bring proceedings under the various pieces of legislation, carry out formal investigations on its own initiative and publish reports and recommendations. Since the 1990s, there has been a large increase in the number of equal opportunities issues taken to employment tribunals. The EOC has issued a Code of Practice on how to eliminate discrimination in employment, as did the CIPD, and it can issue 'non-discrimination' notices. Despite good business reasons for employers tackling pay inequality, many organisations do not check whether their systems are guilty of perpetuating pay-gaps. According to the EOC (2001) inequalities persists because of pay discrimination, occupational segregation, and the continuing unequal impact of family responsibilities on women (IRS Employment Review 774a 2003).

The *Commission for Racial Equality* (CRE) was established under the Race Relations Act 1976, with similar general duties to the EOC, but with an added requirement to promote good relations between persons of different racial groups. The CRE has three principal functions: to conduct formal investigations into a discriminatory matter, and (like the EOC) issue non-discrimination notices; to institute legal proceedings in the case of persistent discrimination and in relation to advertisements; and to assist individual complainants in taking their case to an employment tribunal. Like the EOC, it has produced a Code of Practice on how to eliminate discrimination in employment; this can be used in evidence at a tribunal.

The *Disability Rights Commission* (DRC) was set up in 1999, with functions similar to those of the EOC and CRE. Breaches of the Act's requirements can be enforced through individual complaints to an employment tribunal and the Disability Rights Commission can conduct formal investigations and issue non-discrimination notices (Pitt 2004, p13). Disabled workers are defined as those with a mental or physical impairment that has lasted or is likely to last at least 12 months and that has a substantial adverse effect on their ability to carry out normal day-to-day activities.

The government proposes to merge the EOC, CRE and DRC to form a Commission for Equality and Human Rights, possibly by early 2007. However, there is fundamental opposition to this from CRE (Wintour 2004, p11)

The *Health and Safety Commission* (HSC) operates with an independent chair and a council composed of part-time members drawn from a variety of backgrounds, but broadly representative of both sides of industry and commerce. The Health and Safety at Work Act (HASAWA) 1974 brought together the myriad different bodies which had previously held responsibility for safety and health issues, thus providing the HSE with a unified and integrated set of powers. The general duties of the HSC are:

- to assist and encourage people to secure the health, safety and welfare of persons at work, and protect those not at work
- to undertake and encourage research, to publish findings, and to train and education people in relation to the purposes of the legislation
- to provide an advisory and information service
- to make proposals for regulations.

The HSC therefore has a wide remit, including more obvious safety issues – such as the wearing of protective clothing and investigation of accidents – through to less obvious, but equally important, areas concerned with health at work. Recently this has involved issues connected with stress-related illnesses and the provision of management support for employees who are under intolerable pressures at work.

Vocational Education and Training (VET)

The VET infrastructure is seen as critical to increasing skill levels and thereby ensuring the future prosperity of the country. Over the last few decades all of the VET institutions have been frequently revised, and attempts made to persuade employers to increase training although to date the voluntarist approach persists. The major institutions which the government uses to increase demand for skills are the Learning and Skills Councils and 'Skills for Business' – the collective name for the Sector Skills Development Agency (SSDA) and the Sector Skills Councils (SSCs). Chapter 8 examines VET provision in greater detail.

The *Learning and Skills Council* (LSC) and its nine regional Councils were established in 2001 to replace the Training and Enterprise Councils (TECs) and the Further Education Funding Council. The LSC is responsible for funding and planning education and training for post-16 year olds in England (other than in universities). Its remit covers further education, work-based training and young people, school sixth forms, workforce development, adult and community learning, information, advice and guidance for adults, and education business links. Each of the nine regional councils works to national learning targets, but is given some freedom, and a proportion of their budget, to meet local needs and to pump prime innovation. Their key tasks are to:

- raise participation and achievement by young people
- increase demand for learning
- raise skill levels
- improve the quality of education and training delivery
- improve effectiveness and efficiency.

This is the first time that all planning and funding of post-16 education and training has been integrated into a single system (LSC 2004).

The *SSDA* (www.ssda.org.uk) is responsible for the delivery of the government's Skill Strategy through the development and funding of the SSCs. These are owned and run by employers, but work in partnership with trade unions, professional bodies and other stakeholders in each sector. Their specific aims are to:

- produce intelligence and analysis of future sector skill needs
- reduce skill gaps and shortages by influencing the planning and funding of education and training
- improve productivity
- develop occupational standards for skills in their sector
- increase opportunities for everyone in work to boost skills.

The SSDA fills gaps not covered by the SSCs; ensures quality and consistency across sectors; and facilitates communications between sectors and major stakeholders. Eventually 23 SSCs will be established covering 90 per cent of the UK workforce.

By 2004 four sectors had analysed future skills needs and drawn up Sector Skills Agreements (SSAs) with educational/training suppliers. Eventually every SSC will develop and implement an SSA, ensuring that employers' wishes are reflected through the education and training systems. Their work will be overseen by a Skills Alliance, and by working with the key partners (RDAs, LSCs, Business Link and JobCentre Plus) it is hoped that there will be a joined-up approach to adult learning and skills. Cross Sector Boards will focus on management and leadership, IT skills, employability, and 'Golden Threads', which covers a wide range of social issues. A small part of the workforce (perhaps 10 per cent) will remain outside of the network. There is already concern that the SSCs were slow to get started, with blame placed with the 'pedestrian' SSDA and concerns that they will be no more effective than the National Training Organisation framework they replaced (Merrick 2003, p16).

CONCLUSIONS

This chapter has reviewed the myriad of external forces and institutional factors that impinge on HRM. It should now be clear that employers do not have a totally free rein in sorting out their HR practices due to inter-relationships with a wide range of institutions such as trade unions and employers' organisations, Acas and other third party agencies, and the VET system. Equally, EU and UK law provides a framework within which employers operate, both in terms of ensuring compliance and in shaping good employment practice. Moreover, given that workers differ from all other factors of production, their wants and needs at work influence how employers seek to gain the most out of the employment relationship. While keeping wages or conditions of employment at or below minimum levels may represent a cheap option for employers, as an HR strategy this can also store up problems – in terms of recruitment, training and involvement, or indeed persuading workers not to restrict their effort. All these forces help to shape the employment relationship and the types of HR practice that employers adopt. In the next chapter we move on to consider one specific approach to motivate employees – the high commitment model.

USEFUL READING

DICKENS L. and HALL M. 'Labour law and industrial relations: a new settlement', in P. EDWARDS (ed), *Industrial Relations*, 2nd edition. Oxford, Blackwell. 2003.

GRUGULIS, I. 'The contribution of National Vocational Qualifications to the growth of skills in the UK', *British Journal of Industrial Relations*, Vol. 41, No. 3, 2003. pp457–475.

GUEST D. and CONWAY N. *Pressure at Work and the Psychological Contract: Research report.* London, CIPD. 2002.

LEWIS D. and SARGEANT M. *Essentials of Employment Law*, 8th edition. London, CIPD. 2004.

MARCHINGTON M., GRIMSHAW D., RUBERY J. *and* WILLMOTT H. (eds), *Fragmenting Work: Blurring organisational boundaries and disordering hierarchies*. Oxford, Oxford University Press. 2004c.

NOON M. *and* BLYTON P. *The Realities of Work*. London, Macmillan Business. 2002.

PITT G. *Employment Law*, 4th edition. London, Sweet & Maxwell. 2004.

ROSE M. 'Good deal, bad deal? Job satisfaction in occupations', *Work, Employment and Society*, Vol. 17, No. 3, 2003. pp503–530.

RUBERY J., CARROLL M., COOKE F. L., GRUGULIS I. *and* EARNSHAW J. 'Human resource management and the permeable organisation: the case of the multi-client call centre', *Journal of Management Studies*, Vol. 41, No. 7, 2004. pp1199–1222.

High Commitment HRM and Performance

INTRODUCTION

There have been a significant number of studies over the last decade investigating the links between HRM and organisational performance. These have focused on the extent to which – if at all – high commitment or best practice HRM may lead to improvements in worker or organisational performance. This was stimulated initially by the work of a number of US academics but it has been developed more recently by people in Britain as well. Basically, the idea is that a particular bundle of HR practices has the potential to contribute improved employee attitudes and behaviours, lower levels of absenteeism and labour turnover, and higher levels of productivity, quality and customer service. This, it is argued, has the ultimate effect of generating higher levels of profitability. Since the HR practices that supposedly contribute to an improved bottom line performance are generally perceived as 'good' for workers – for example, employment security, training and development, information and consultation, and higher levels of pay – this looks like an attractive scenario for employers and workers alike.

However, not all the studies report such glowing and positive links between best practice HRM and performance, and there are some doubts about the precise sorts of HR practices that comprise the high commitment bundle, about their supposed synergy with one another, about their attractiveness to workers and employers, and about their universal applicability. Even if an association is found between high commitment HRM and performance, questions remain about directions of causality and about the processes that underpin and drive these linkages; recent research sponsored by the CIPD, undertaken by John Purcell and his colleagues, provides further analysis of the make-up of this so-called 'black box'. This chapter reviews these debates and presents evidence about the value of best practice HRM to workers and organisations. We use 'best practice'/'high commitment' HRM interchangeably.

By the end of this chapter, readers should be able to:

- **contribute to the implementation of appropriate HR policies that maximise the contribution of people to organisational objectives**

- **convince other managers of the business benefits to be gained from adopting 'best practice' HRM**

- **benchmark their own organisation's HR practices against those of competitors.**

In addition, readers should understand and be able to explain:

- **the meaning of 'best practice'/high commitment HRM, and the ways in which bundles of HR practice may be combined together**

- **the contribution of HR policies and practices to improvements in organisational performance**

- **the theoretical, methodological and empirical concerns about claims that 'best practice' HRM can be applied universally in all organisations.**

DEFINING AND MEASURING HIGH COMMITMENT HRM

In recent years, there has been much interest in the notion of 'best practice' human resource management (HRM). Sometimes this is referred to as 'high performance work systems' (Berg 1999; Appelbaum *et al* 2000), 'high commitment' HRM (Walton 1985; Guest 2001a, 2001b) or 'high involvement' HRM (Wood 1999a). Whatever the terminology, the idea is that a particular set (or number) of HR practices has the potential to bring about improved organisational performance for all organisations. Since the 1990s, a number of US publications have explored the links between HRM and performance (eg Arthur 1994; Pfeffer 1994; Huselid 1995; MacDuffie 1995; Delaney and Huselid 1996; Delery and Doty 1996; Huselid and Becker 1996; Youndt *et al* 1996; Ichniowski *et al* 1997; Pfeffer 1998; Appelbaum *et al* 2000; Cappelli and Neumark 2001; Batt *et al* 2002; Bartell 2004). This has been supplemented by an increasing number of studies in Britain (eg Wood 1995; Wood and Albanese 1995; Patterson *et al* 1997; Guest and Conway 1998; Wood and de Menezes 1998; Wood 1999b; Guest *et al* 2000a, 2000b, 2003; Purcell *et al* 2003), several of which have been published by the CIPD.

Despite this substantial and growing output, it is still difficult to draw generalised conclusions from these studies for a number of reasons. Some of the principal differences between the studies are:

- the nature and type of HR practices examined
- the proxies developed for each of these practices
- the measures of performance used
- the sectors in which the studies have taken place
- the methods of data collection
- the respondents from whom information has been sought.

Guest (1997, p263) argued some time ago that there is 'little additive value in these and whilst statistically sophisticated, they lack theoretical rigour'. Despite a plea for more theoretical models to underpin empirical research, this has not prevented even more of these sorts of studies taking place, and there remains concern about the strength of the conclusions that can be drawn from them. There are also more serious and deep-seated disagreements about the extent to which high commitment HRM is something all employers might wish or be able to implement, and to what extent the precise mix of practices varies between countries and types of employer, as well as whether or not it is equally attractive to workers. These issues are taken up later in the chapter.

Rather than review all of the studies mentioned above – which would be lengthy and repetitive – we have decided instead to focus on the list of high commitment HR practices outlined by Pfeffer (1998), and adapt these for a UK/European context. For example, our analysis makes use of a wider definition of employee involvement and information sharing that incorporates the notion of employee voice (Marchington and Grugulis 2000; Dundon *et al* 2004). Box 9 outlines this list of HR practices.

BOX 9   COMPONENTS OF 'BEST PRACTICE'/HIGH COMMITMENT HRM

- Employment security and internal labour markets
- Selective hiring and sophisticated selection
- Extensive training, learning and development
- Employee involvement, information sharing and worker voice
- Self-managed teams/teamworking
- High compensation contingent on performance
- Reduction of status differentials/harmonisation

Source: Adapted from Pfeffer J. *The Human Equation: Building profits by putting people first*. Boston, Harvard Business School Press. 1998

Employment security and internal labour markets

Pfeffer (1998) regards employment security as fundamentally underpinning the other six HR practices, principally because it is regarded as unrealistic to ask employees to offer their ideas, hard work and commitment without some expectation of employment security and concern for their future careers. The contribution a positive psychological contract makes to open and trusting employment relationships (Holman *et al* 2003), and the notion of mutuality that is seen as a key component in partnership agreements both relate to this. For example, whilst the partnership agreement at Borg Warner does not contain an explicit statement about employment security, both managers and shop stewards from the company recognise that the plant could not have stayed open without employee support (Suff and Williams 2003, p39).

There are obviously limits to how much employment security can be guaranteed. It does not mean that employees are necessarily able to stay in the same job for life, nor does it prevent the dismissal of staff who fail to perform to the required level. Similarly, a major collapse in the product market that necessitates reductions in the labour force should not be seen as undermining this principle. The most significant point about including employment security as one of the high commitment HR practices is that it asserts that job reductions will be avoided wherever possible, and that employees should expect to maintain their employment with the organisation – if appropriate through internal transfers. Employment security can be enhanced by well-devised and forward-looking systems of human resource planning (see Chapter 6) and an understanding of how organisations may be structured to achieve flexibility (Chapter 2). It is perhaps best summed up by the view that workers should be treated not as a variable cost but as a critical asset in the long-term viability and success of the organisation. Indeed, there is also a business case for employment security. As Pfeffer (1998, p66) notes, laying people off too readily 'constitutes a cost for firms that have done a good job selecting, training and developing their workforce ... layoffs put important strategic assets on the street for the competition to employ'.

The definition and measurement of employment security has varied considerably, to a large extent depending on whether information is sought about policy or practice. For example, Wood and Albanese (1995) include three measures in reaching their assessment of employment security: a policy of no compulsory redundancy; the use of temporaries primarily to protect the core workforce; and an expectation on the part of senior managers that new employees will stay with the firm until retirement. Delaney and Huselid (1996) asked managerial respondents about 'filling vacancies from within and creating opportunities for internal promotion' as a proxy for employment security. Guest *et al* (2000a) use the presence or absence of a 'job security guarantee for non-managerial employees', finding that this is only reported by a very small number of workplaces – 5 per cent in the private sector, 15 per cent in the public. Guest *et al* (2003) ask a mix of questions about internal labour markets and organisational commitment to employment security, as well as enquiring about whether or not compulsory or voluntary redundancies have occurred in the last three years. Over half of these organisations acknowledged that compulsory redundancies had taken place during this period. Box 10 provides information on employment security at different organisations.

BOX 10   EMPLOYMENT SECURITY PROVISIONS

Inland Revenue
'The Inland Revenue is committed to avoiding compulsory redundancies except as a very last resort, and one which it will do its utmost to avoid.'

The Co-operative Bank
'to jointly recognise that effective use of the revised organisational change process (agreed with UNIFI) will require continued commitment to maintain an approach which keeps the number of redundancies to a minimum and achieves redundancies on a voluntary basis, as far as possible.'

Welsh Water
'Partnership gives employment security – in these days of rapid change it is impossible to give a guarantee of job security – that is, doing the same job at the same location doing the same things. But it does mean that permanent staff who want to continue working for the company can continue to do so providing they understand their obligations – to share responsibility for continual improvements in meeting business objectives and providing the highest levels of customer service.'

BMW Hams Hall
'The company and the trade union officers ... both seek to establish a productive and harmonious relationship between the parties. Job security, prosperity and development depend upon the company continuing to grow and be successful. Both parties recognise the objective is to achieve long-term prosperity.'

Source: Adapted from various publications by the Involvement and Participation Association

After reading Box 10, to what extent do you think that employment security is an important aspect of work and does it give an indication to workers that they are being treated properly by employers?

Pfeffer (1998, p183) reckons that compulsory lay-offs and downsizing undermine employment security, and sees the following as alternatives: (1) proportionately reducing working hours to 'spread the pain' of reduced employment costs across the entire workforce; (2) reducing wages to reduce the labour costs; (3) freezing recruitment to prevent overstaffing; and (4) putting production workers into sales to build up demand.

This is some way short of full-blown employment security, and it is clear that employment security is not expected to reduce corporate profits. The employer's financial flexibility is maintained by increasing employee workloads and by ensuring that salaries are related to organisational performance in the event of a downturn in demand.

Selective hiring and sophisticated selection

Recruiting and retaining outstanding people and 'capturing a stock of exceptional human talent' (Boxall 1996, p66–67) is seen as an effective way to achieve sustained competitive advantage. Even though employers have always wanted to recruit the best people available, this is nowadays more likely to be systematised through the use of sophisticated selection techniques and taking greater care when hiring. Increasingly, employers are looking for applicants who possess a range of social, interpersonal and teamworking skills in addition to technical ability. For example, Wood and de Menezes (1998) asked about the importance of social and teamworking skills as selection criteria, and Wood and Albanese (1995) found that two of the major facets sought by employers were trainability and commitment. Hoque's (1999) study of large hotels also identified trainability as a major selection criterion. Indeed, in a growing number of situations, it would appear that employers feel that they can provide technical training for people so long as they have the 'right' social skills, attitudes and commitment (Sturdy et al 2001; Callaghan and Thompson, 2002; Marchington et al 2003b).

The proxies used to measure 'selective hiring' vary widely. They include the following:

- the number of applicants per position (Delaney and Huselid 1996) or as many good applicants as the organisation needs (Guest et al 2003)
- the proportion administered an employment test prior to hiring (Huselid 1995; Guest et al 2003)
- the sophistication of (selection) processes, such as the use of psychometric tests (Patterson et al 1997) and realistic job previews (Hoque 1999; Guest et al 2000b, 2003).

These measures capture quite different components of the selection process and on whether the focus is on the overall approach taken by employers or the precise techniques they use. Moreover some of them emphasise inputs rather than outputs in terms of the quality of those eventually recruited. For example, attracting a large number of applicants for a position may indicate poor HR procedures due to failures to define the job and the field adequately prior to advertising. As we see in Chapter 6, it is also possible that selective hiring, especially when it focuses on how well new recruits might fit with the prevailing organisational culture, can lead to under-represented groups being excluded from employment. Moreover, an excessive 'cloning' of employees could be problematic if the organisation is keen to promote initiative and diversity, and counterproductive if business needs and markets change. On the other hand, there may be situations where it is impossible to attract sufficient applicants due to skills shortages – as with some professional jobs in the health and education sectors – where the emphasis shifts to generating a pool of potential recruits rather than finding more sophisticated ways to choose between them.

Recruiting high quality, committed staff is seen as central to 'best practice' HRM, and the use of psychometric tests, structured interviews and work sampling is likely to increase the validity of selection decisions. Competencies to be sought at the selection stage include trainability, flexibility, commitment, drive and persistence, and initiative. The key point about 'best practice' selection is that it should be integrated and systematic, making use of the techniques which are appropriate for the position and the organisation, and administered by individuals who have themselves been trained.

Extensive training, learning and development

Having recruited 'outstanding human talent', employers need to ensure that these people remain at the forefront of their field, not only in terms of professional expertise and product knowledge but also through working in teams or in interpersonal relations. Boxall (1996, p67) views this as one element in 'organisational process advantage', the idea that employers aim to synergise the contribution of talented and exceptional employees. There is little doubt that there has been a growing recognition of the importance of individual and organisational learning as a source of sustained competitive advantage as employers introduce more skills-specific forms of training and experience continuing skills shortages in some areas.

Wright and Gardner (2003, p312) note this is one of the most widely quoted and important elements of high commitment HRM. The use of the word 'learning' is crucial as it demonstrates employer willingness to encourage and facilitate employee development rather than just providing specific training to cover short-term crises. Different types of measure have been used here: fully fledged 'learning companies' (Hoque 1999), employee development and assessment programmes or task-based and interpersonal skills training (see Chapter 9). The time and effort devoted to learning opportunities is also important. A range of proxies have been used here – such as the number of days' training received by all workers, the proportion of workers who have been trained, the budget set aside for training, or the establishment of agreed training targets over a two-year period. The WERS survey used a simple absence/presence distinction in relation to induction training and formal job training, finding that well over half of all workplaces engaged in this. Training was provided at fewer workplaces in the private sector than the public sector. The CIPD survey (Guest *et al* 2000a, p15) reports, quite surprisingly, that almost one-quarter of respondents claimed to offer at least one month's training per annum to their staff, although 13 per cent admitted that they provided none at all. West *et al* (2002) used several measures for assessing training in their study of NHS hospitals, each of which related to the amount of money spent, whilst Guest *et al* (2003) focused instead on the amount of training received by workers.

Of course, there are problems in trying to measure and evaluate the concentration of training and learning. While it is clearly important to establish how much time and resources employers invest in formal training, and whether or not this covers the entire workforce, it is also crucial to identify the type of training which is provided and who has responsibility for managing this. Quite a number of the studies have looked solely at the financial or quantitative aspects – in terms of money or time invested in training – and ignored the quality or relevance of training and learning that is provided. It is now widely acknowledged that most workers are overqualified for the jobs they do (Grugulis 2003), and as such extra training may add little to organisational performance or worker skills. Even where training opportunities are provided, there is often 'no explicit aim within the training of increasing the individuals' skill base or broadening their experience' (Truss *et al* 1997, p61). Similarly, questions need to be asked about whether or not longer term budget safeguards are established so as to protect training provision (Wood and Albanese 1995) or if training is tied in to 'increased promotability within the organisation' (Delery and Doty 1996). The quality of training, both in terms of its focus and its delivery, is clearly more important than a simple count of the amount provided. These issues are taken up again in Chapters 8 and 9.

> How much time has been devoted to training in your organisation – or one with which you are familiar – and what sort of training has been available? To what extent has it been worthwhile?

Employee involvement (EI), information sharing and worker voice

There are a number of reasons why EI is an essential component of the high commitment paradigm (Marchington and Wilkinson 2005). First, open communications about financial performance, strategy and operational matters not only ensures workers are informed about organisational issues, it also conveys a symbolic and substantive message that they are to be trusted and treated in an open and positive manner. Second, for teamworking to be successful workers require information in order to provide a basis from which to offer their suggestions and contribute to improvements in organisational performance. Third, participation can provide management with some legitimacy for its actions on the grounds that ideas have been put forward by workers and/or at least considered by them before decisions are ultimately made. As we argue throughout this book, even if management has more power at its disposal than do workers, the employment relationship is not complete and legally defined in detail but open to interpretation and disagreement over how it is enforced on a daily basis. Of course there are also arguments that workers have a moral right to participation and involvement, but these are considered elsewhere in the book, particularly in Chapters 10 and 11.

Information sharing or EI appears in just about every description of, or prescription for, 'best practice' or high commitment HRM. EI can include downward communications, upward problem-solving groups and project teams, all of which are designed to increase the involvement of individual employees in their workplace. The precise mix of EI techniques depends upon the circumstances, but the range of measures used and the 'flexible' definition of involvement are potentially confusing. Many of the studies restrict this to downward communications from management to employees which measure the frequency of information disclosure (Patterson *et al* 1997), the regularity of teambriefing or quality circles (Wood and Albanese 1995) or the extent to which workers are informed or consulted about business operations or performance (Guest *et al* 2003). The regularity of attitude surveys also features strongly in many of the studies (eg Huselid 1995; Hoque 1999; Guest *et al* 2000a). Some go further and enquire about the percentage of employees who receive training in group problem-solving (Arthur 1994) or the level at which a range of decisions is made (Delaney and Huselid 1996). The WERS survey analysis only included briefing in its estimates if at least 25 per cent of the time at the meeting was devoted to employee questions and discussion (Guest *et al* 2000a, p16), something that happens at about half the workplaces.

Again, the range of proxies used is so wide that it is difficult to compare results across these studies and arrive at any firm conclusions about the importance of information sharing and EI to high commitment HRM. The fact that EI is often little more than a cascade of information from management means that any meaningful worker contribution is unlikely. Indeed, one of the objectives of schemes such as team briefing is to reinforce the supervisor as an information disseminator who adapts messages to suit specific operational requirements. This one-way version of information sharing – rather than being seen as educative, empowering and liberating as the terminology might imply – could more easily be interpreted instead as indoctrinating, emasculating and controlling (Marchington and Wilkinson 2005).

Although only a relatively small number of authors (eg Huselid 1995; Roche 1999; Batt *et al* 2002; Dundon *et al* 2004) specifically include voice as an aspect of high commitment HRM, it seems essential that workers should have the opportunity to express their grievances openly and independently, in addition to being able to contribute to management decision-making on task-related issues. Employee voice may be achieved through trade union representation and collective bargaining as well as through formally established grievance and disputes procedures, but in addition it could be through speak-up schemes, which offer employees protection if their complaints are taken badly by managers (Marchington *et al* 2001). In their study of telecommunications, Batt *et al* (2002, p589) regarded direct participation and union representation as 'complementary vehicles for employee voice at work'.

Self-managed teams/teamworking

This practice has become more prevalent over the last decade for a variety of reasons, not least as a way of pooling ideas and improving work processes in response to Japanese competition. It has been identified by many employers as a fundamental component of organisational success (Marchington 1999). It is also one of the key attributes that employers look for in new recruits, something asked for in references, and it even plays a part in courses organised for school students. Teamwork is typically seen as leading to better decision-making and the achievement of more creative solutions (Pfeffer 1998, p76). Evidence suggests that employees who work in teams generally report higher levels of satisfaction than their counterparts working under more 'traditional' regimes, although they also report working hard as well (Wilkinson *et al* 1997; Edwards and Wright 1998; Geary and Dobbins 2001; Batt and Doellgast 2003).

The range of measures used by researchers to assess teamworking has been rather narrower than those used to assess many of the other 'best practices'. Generally, it refers to the proportion of workers in teams (MacDuffie 1995; West *et al* 2002; Guest *et al* 2003), the use of formal teams (Patterson *et al* 1997; Guest *et al* 2000a) or the deliberate design of jobs to make use of workers' abilities (Hoque 1999). However, such measures can not tell us whether or not these teams actually are self-managed or act as autonomous groups, and much depends upon decisions concerning, inter alia, the choice of team leader, responsibility for organising work schedules, and control over quality (Frobel and Marchington 2005). A distinction is also made between off-line teams – such as quality circles – and on-line teams where workers are involved in daily decisions about work organisation (Batt 2004). Regarding the latter, WERS showed that whilst 65 per cent of workplaces claim to have teamworking, just 5 per cent of these could actually be categorised as autonomous groups where team members have responsibility for managing their own time and appoint their own leaders (Cully *et al* 1999, p43).

In contrast, there is a less optimistic perspective on self-managed teams, which suggests that they are intrusive and difficult to implement in practice, and that they serve to strengthen – rather than weaken – management control. It may also be impossible to introduce any realistic version of teamworking when workers are unable to enlarge their jobs to embrace higher level skills or where there are legal, technical or safety reasons that prevent workers from making certain types of decision. Moreover, the prospect of teamworking is limited where the rotation of a range of low-level jobs means that one boring job is merely swapped for another boring job on a regular basis. In situations such as these, teamworking may only serve to make work more stressful and intrusive, and add nothing to the skills or initiative that workers are able to deploy. While these criticisms of self-managed teams can be seen as failures of implementation, some analysts see this form of organisation as potentially flawed because it gives the impression of control without devolving any real power or influence. Barker (1993, p408), for example, suggests that self-managing teams produce 'a form of control more powerful, less apparent, and more difficult to resist than that of the former bureaucracy' because it shifts the locus of control from management to workers – what he terms 'concertive control'. The consequence of this is that peer pressure and rational rules combine to 'create a new iron cage whose bars are almost invisible to the workers it incarcerates' (p435). The negative impact of teamworking may be especially problematic for lower skilled workers (Bacon and Blyton 2003).

What is your experience of working in teams? Do you think that peer pressure is more likely to generate better performance than supervisory control? Is teamworking automatically 'positive' in your view?

High compensation contingent on performance

Pfeffer (1998) reckons that there are two elements to this practice – higher than average compensation and performance-related reward – although both send a signal to employees that they deserve to be rewarded for superior contributions. To be effective, this needs to be at a level in excess of that for comparable workers in other organisations so as to attract and retain high-quality labour. In addition, according to this scenario, rewards should reflect different levels of worker contribution, perhaps being paid as a regular bonus or through profit sharing schemes. Despite the extensive criticisms of performance-related pay (see Chapter 12), it is included in most lists of 'best practice', particularly those conducted in the USA. Given that research in the UK is much more critical about the value of incentive pay, it might be better to include the entire reward package in this HR practice so that it is not restricted to pay alone, and it can then relate to employee contributions to organisational performance – whether this is on an individual, team, departmental or establishment-wide basis.

Huselid (1995) includes two measures for this factor: the proportion of the workforce who have access to company incentive schemes and the proportion whose performance appraisals are used to determine their compensation. MacDuffie (1995) refers to contingent compensation. The UK studies also focus on merit or performance pay. Wood and de Menezes (1998) enquired about merit pay and profit sharing, Guest et al (2000a) included performance related pay for non-managerial staff, whereas Hoque (1999) asked about merit pay and appraisal schemes for all staff and West et al (2002) and Guest et al (2003) focused on appraisal as the key factor. Indeed, in West et al's study, appraisal had an extremely significant impact on performance, as we see later in the chapter. Not surprisingly, the proportion of workplaces covered by performance-related reward was rather less widespread in the public sector than in the private (Guest et al 2000a, p16). However, equally surprisingly, given the degree of practitioner interest in incentive pay schemes, about two-thirds of the respondents to the CIPD survey (Guest et al 2000b, p16) said that their organisations did not make use of individual performance related pay for their non-managerial employees.

Reduction of status differences/harmonisation

Symbolic manifestations of egalitarianism seen in the HR practices of some Japanese companies are meant to convey messages to manual workers and lower grade office staff that they are valuable assets who deserve to be treated in a similar way to their more senior colleagues. It is also seen as a way to encourage employees to offer ideas within an 'open' management culture. This can be seen through egalitarian symbols, such as staff uniforms, shared canteen and car-parking facilities, but it is also underpinned by the harmonisation of many terms and conditions of employment – such as holidays, sick-pay schemes, pensions, and hours of work (IRS Employment Review 784a 2003). The principal point behind moves to single status and harmonisation, as we see in Chapter 13, is that it seeks to break down artificial barriers between different groups of staff, thus encouraging and supporting teamworking and flexibility. Extending employee share ownership to the workforce as a whole is a further way in which status differences can be reduced, typically through schemes whereby staff are allocated shares according to some predetermined formula. Pfeffer (1998, p38) argues that 'employee ownership, effectively implemented, can align the interests of employees with those of shareholders by making employees shareholders too'. Firms with high shareholder returns also often have some form of employee ownership.

The proxies used for harmonisation and the reduction of status differentials are also wide and variable. For example, Wood and de Menezes (1998) ask about whether or not any employees have to 'clock in' to work, and about the existence of employee share schemes and welfare facilities/fringe benefits. Hoque's (1999) questions relate very broadly to harmonisation and single status. Guest et al's (2000a, 2000b, 2003) questions vary between the highly specific (harmonised holiday entitlements for all staff) through to whether or not the organisation has a formal commitment to achieving single status. Over 80 per cent of the organisations in the CIPD survey (Guest et al 2000b) claimed to have harmonised holidays and just under half reckoned to have a formal commitment to single status.

Table 8 shows how widespread these sorts of HR practices are in UK organisations. For example, a significant proportion of workplaces surveyed for WERS (Guest et al 2000a) have grievance procedures in place, make extensive use of appraisals for a large percentage of their non-managerial staff, and have a standard induction programme for all recruits. These features are especially marked in the public sector. Around half of all workplaces use performance tests, provide some degree of formal training, engage in teamworking and administer attitude surveys. On the other hand, hardly any offer job security guarantees, only a small number have problem-solving groups for a sizeable proportion of the workforce, and not many of the private sector firms have a family-friendly policy or an all-employee share ownership scheme. The CIPD survey by Guest et al (2000b, p37) reports different figures, but the conclusion is much the same, that is 'human resource practices are not well embedded in a majority of workplaces'. Moreover, few of these workplaces 'have put in place a coherent range of practices of the sort commonly associated with "high commitment" or "high performance" HRM' (p37).

This is disturbing for the proponents of high commitment HRM because it appears to offer the prospect of a more pleasant and stimulating working environment than would be experienced in traditional, Taylorist regimes. For example, the provision of employment security is attractive, the opportunity to earn above average wages and to be rewarded for performance may be enticing, and the chance to gain extensive levels of training can be highly desirable. Most attitude surveys have shown that employees would like to have more information about their organisation and a chance to contribute to and influence decisions that affect their working lives, as well as remove status differences between separate categories of workers.

Table 8   *The extent of high commitment HRM in the public and private sectors*

Human resource practice	% of workplaces with this practice in place	
	Public sector	**Private sector**
Use of performance test for selection	58	44
Preference for internal candidates in selection	16	30
Standard induction programme for new recruits	80	76
40% or more received formal job training in last year	68	37
Employees have a lot of variety in their work	52	41
40% or more work in formally designated teams	54	40
At least 25% of time at meetings devoted to employee questions	63	49
40% or more take part in problem-solving group	28	16
Attitude survey in last three years	54	40
Formal appraisals for 40% or more of non-managerial staff	77	87
Formal grievance procedure in place	100	90
Job security guarantee	15	5
Performance related pay for non-managerial staff	20	38
All employee share ownership scheme	n/a	25

Source: Guest D., Michie J., Sheehan M. and Conway N. *Employment Relations, HRM and Business Performance: An analysis of the 1998 workplace employee relations survey.* London, CIPD. 2000a. p16

Selective hiring is less obvious as a source of direct benefit to employees, although it might reduce the likelihood of having to work alongside what might be seen as incapable or ineffective co-workers. In addition, delaying recruitment or using temporaries might enhance the employment security of those permanent staff in the event of a downturn – although there is also evidence that temporary staff may be used in order to reduce wages and put pressure on so-called permanent staff (Rubery *et al* 2003). Put together – especially in comparison with the 'bleak house' policies described by a number of authors – high commitment HRM seems very attractive. However, as we have also seen, digging beneath the surface implies that some of these 'best practices' may not be quite as appealing in reality.

Look at Table 8. Do any of these figures come as a surprise to you, either in terms of how extensive or rare they are? Why/why not? If you work for an organisation, develop a business case for increasing the number of high commitment practices used at your workplace.

BUNDLES OF HUMAN RESOURCE PRACTICES

It should be clear from the previous section that there are often links between these high commitment HR practices. For example, workers are more likely to welcome EI and information sharing if they have employment security and their workplace is relatively status-free. Equally, they are more likely to show an interest in teamworking if their efforts are rewarded with performance-related incentives, share ownership, and access to training opportunities. Similarly, if sufficient care has been taken at the recruitment and selection stage, new recruits are more likely to adopt flexible working practices and welcome teamworking, as well as be striving for internal promotion in the future. In isolation, or without the support of a strong organisational culture, each of these practices can easily be dismissed as nothing more than a short-term fad or fashion. Conversely the more that HR practices form a coherent and synergistic bundle of related practices, it is argued organisations are more likely to enjoy success due to the fact that the high commitment paradigm is more deeply embedded into the culture of the workplace. Benson and Lawler (2003, p157) note that 'research at the work unit level confirms the importance of viewing practices as complementary' and that the high commitment model (in general) out-performed more traditional control-oriented work systems despite the fact that the exact combination of practices is uncertain and may be industry-specific.

There is certainly theoretical support for the notion that HR practices should operate more effectively when combined together. For example, it could be argued that extensive training is essential for self-managed teams to run effectively, or that higher than average rewards are likely to have a positive impact on numbers of applications for jobs. An employer may feel more inclined to promise employment security if selective hiring has taken place, self-managed teams are extensive throughout the organisation, and rewards are contingent upon performance. Wood and de Menezes (1998, p485) find an 'identifiable pattern to the use of high commitment HR practices' and confirm that they are being used in conjunction with each other. Similarly, despite finding a low take-up of the high commitment model across his sample of Irish workplaces, Roche (1999, p669) notes that 'organisations with a relatively high degree of integration of human resource strategy into business strategy are very much more likely to adopt commitment-oriented bundles of HRM practices'.

Guest (1997, p271) categorises previous attempts to examine internal fit across HR practices into three distinct groups. First, there are criterion-specific studies, such as that by Pfeffer, which outline a number of 'best practices' and suggest that the closer organisations get to this list the better their performance is likely to be. The danger with such universalist approaches is that they ignore potentially significant differences between organisations, sectors and countries, and posit a particular model – in this case, the US model – as the one to be followed. With this approach, the principal job is to detect the bundle that seems to work and then get all organisations to apply this without deviation. Second, there are two sets of criterion-free categories, 'fit as gestalt' and 'fit as bundles'. In the case of the former, it is assumed that the synergies are achievable only with the adoption of all these practices, and that if one is missing the whole effect will be lost. These approaches are termed 'multiplicative', and it is assumed that the whole is greater than the sum of its parts. In this scenario, an organisation that adopted a majority of the practices would be no better off than one that adopted none of them because the chain tying together the different elements of HRM would be broken.

By contrast, bundles are 'additive'. Generally speaking the more practices that are in place the better, so long as some distinctive core exists. In other words, it may be possible to adopt a large number of high commitment HR practices and ignore others, but still gain from the interactive effects of those that are in place. Questions then arise as to how many practices are needed to make a difference, from what areas of HRM these are to be drawn and whether certain practices are fundamental to make the synergies work. As we see in the section on HRM and performance later in this chapter, much of Guest *et al*'s recent work has differentiated between organisations on the basis of how many HR practices they use. Their analysis of the WERS data led them to conclude that 'despite trying a variety of approaches and combinations, we could not find any coherent pattern of bundles of practices in the private or the public sectors. The only combination that made any sense was a straightforward count of all the practices' (Guest *et al* 2000a, p15). Provided a certain minimum number of practices are in place, it is likely (though not automatic) that high commitment HRM will be found in a range of different areas of practice – such as selection, training, EI and harmonisation.

It is assumed that contradictions between 'best practice' in one area and 'worst practice' in another will undermine the package as a whole. Workers, it is argued, soon notice differences between employment practices, and are quick to spot inconsistencies between policy statements and workplace practice. There have certainly been many occasions when a high-profile cultural change programme, for example, which majors on learning and development as a key principle, has been undermined by the announcement of massive redundancies. Similarly, it has not been unknown for an organisation to introduce a new set of EI policies without first consulting employees about its shape. Inconsistencies between different HR practices are likely to be even more apparent in situations where several employers operate at the same workplace or clients have a direct or indirect influence over the work of supplier organisations, either through short-term secondments of staff or through employers exercising joint responsibility for the completion of work tasks (Marchington *et al* 2004c).

Even in the context of the single employer–employee relationship, Wood and de Menezes (1998, p487) note that most studies indicate a lack of consistency, reporting fragmentation, a 'pick and mix' approach to managing human resources, ad hocism, pragmatism and short-termism, rather than the deployment of consistent, integrated and long-term packages of HRM. Truss *et al* (1997, pp66–67) sum this up by stating that their research 'found little evidence of any deliberate or realised coherence between HR activities. For instance, one HR Officer commented that the firm could be recruiting someone in one department and laying-off someone with a similar profile in another.' Moreover, they saw no evidence of any coherence among HR activities in different parts of the organisation, and whilst the language of the soft HRM model was in evidence so too was that of the hard model – emphasising financial control. More seriously, while Caldwell (2003) shows from a survey of about 100 major organisations that significant progress has been made in the adoption of HR practices, unfortunately most has been made in implementing those practices that are regarded as least important, and least progress with those that are most important. His respondents recognised the value of bundling but found the linkages extremely difficult to achieve for a number of reasons: it was felt there was no universal or magic formula; the size, complexity and multidivisional structure of their organisation impeded co-ordination; devolution to line managers tended to increase fragmentation; and the difficulty the HR function experienced in breaking out of its operational requirement to provide administrative efficiency rather than strategic vision (p203). Perhaps the lack of any sizeable take-up of these HR practices should not surprise us. As Pfeffer suggests, even smart organisations often do 'dumb things', failing to learn from other examples or being driven by criteria which are ultimately wide of the mark.

Does it matter if there are contradictions between different components of the HR bundle? After all, the employment relationship is characterised by conflict and co-operation, so why should these additional tensions cause any problems?

Although the principle of bundling together HR practices may appear sound, what happens if the achievement of one of these practices contradicts with or undermines (some of) the others? For example, employers may make employment security conditional on an agreement that pay rates can be reduced in order to maintain the guarantee through lean times. Selective hiring on the basis of future potential rather than immediate contribution may require existing staff to work harder and longer in order to induct new staff. This may be acceptable at the margins, but if the profit-sharing or performance-related component of rewards is a significant proportion of overall income, then it could be problematic to existing staff – as well as to customers who may have to wait longer to be served. Equally, if staff are routinely expected to work long hours, their own quality of life can be adversely affected and their own safety and that of others may be affected. Presumably, there is a point at which the value of employment security is outweighed by the need for a certain minimum salary or work–life balance.

One of the many advantages of self-managed teams, according to Pfeffer (1998, p77), is that they can remove a supervisory level from the hierarchy: 'eliminating layers of management by instituting self-managing teams saves money. Self-managed teams can also take on tasks previously done by specialised staff, thus eliminating excess personnel.' It is not self-evident that the personnel who are 'eliminated' are actually found other jobs, so the implementation of self-managed teams – even if it does empower certain groups of workers – may result in others losing their employment security. There are further potential contradictions between the different practices. For example, teamworking may be undermined by the use of individual performance-related pay or by the HR practices of other firms in a network that cut across internal organisational coherence (Scarbrough and Kinnie 2003). Similarly, Cordery (2003) quotes a number of studies in which teamworking took place against a background of increased numbers of lay-offs and reduced levels of pay. It is also hard to square the notion of an organisation without major status differentials with one where senior managers are able to collect substantial bonuses because their pay is linked with company performance. In other words, while there is strong support for bundling – in one form or another – it is also clear contradictions and tensions may arise between the different HR practices in the bundle. Indeed, Boxall and Purcell (2003, p57) do not see this as surprising as any notion of organisational coherence inevitably 'oversimplifies the paradoxical elements involved in managing people'.

HRM AND PERFORMANCE

Analysing the links between high commitment HRM and performance is now a major area of interest for research and policy. Originally, this stemmed from work in the USA, but there have now been several studies in the UK, most notably by David Guest and his colleagues. Before reviewing some of this work in more detail, it is worth reminding readers of some of the earlier studies that claimed to establish a link between HRM and performance. Huselid (1995) drew his conclusions from a survey of nearly 1000 US organisations. He divided high commitment work practices into two broad groupings: employee skills and organisational structures, and employee motivation. The former included items concerned with the proportion of workers taking part in attitude surveys, the number of hours training received in the previous year and the proportion of workers required to take an employment test as part of the selection process. The latter included items such as the proportion of the workforce with performance appraisals linked to compensation and the number of applicants for those posts where recruitment took place most frequently. Output measures included labour turnover, productivity and corporate financial performance. Huselid (p667) concludes that 'the magnitude of the returns for investments in [what he calls] high performance work practices is substantial. A one per cent standard deviation increase in such practices is associated with a 7.05 per cent decrease in labour turnover and, on a per employee basis, 27,044 US dollars more in sales and 18,641 US dollars and 3,814 US dollars more in market value and profits respectively.' Appelbaum and her colleagues (2000) also argued that high performance work systems paid off. Their research was conducted in a number of different industries (steel, apparel and medical electronic instrument), and in each they were 'large enough to be important to the companies in our study but not so large as to strain credulity' (p19). Importantly, they also found (p20) that high performance work practices increased workers' trust, job satisfaction and commitment, and notably no evidence of 'speed up' (work intensification) and higher levels of stress. A key factor, as we see later when we look at the work of Purcell et al (2003), is that having the opportunity to participate enhances workers' discretion and effort.

The results from the survey by Patterson et al (1997) published by the Institute of Personnel and Development (now CIPD), were quoted widely by the media and put forward as evidence for the importance of HRM as a driver of, and contributor to, improved performance. The research was based on longitudinal studies of 67 UK manufacturing that were predominantly single site and single product operations. It has been claimed – on the basis of this research – that HRM had a greater impact on productivity and profits than a range of other factors including strategy, R&D and quality. For example, it was argued that 17 per cent of the variation in company profitability could be explained by HRM practices and job design, as opposed to just 8 per cent from research and development, 2 per cent from strategy and 1 per cent from both quality and technology. Similar results were indicated for productivity.

Below we examine in more detail four of the studies undertaken in the UK – by Guest et al (2000a, 2000b), West et al (2002), Guest et al (2003) and Purcell et al (2003) – and we draw on some in-depth reviews of the HRM–performance link. Some of the best-known studies are outlined in Table 9 (see pages 86–7).

On the basis of these studies some forceful claims have been made about the impact of high commitment HRM on performance. Two CIPD reports (2001a, 2001b) argued that the economic and business case for good people management has now been proved. One notes (2001a, p4) that 'more than 30 studies carried out in the UK and the US since the early 1990s leave no room to doubt that there is a correlation between people management and business performance, that the relationship is positive, and that it is cumulative'. Since, it is argued, senior personnel practitioners now agree that the case for HRM impacting on organisational performance is not in dispute, the key question is how to make it happen (Caulkin 2001). From a US perspective, Pfeffer (1998, p306) agrees that best practice HRM has the potential to have a positive impact on all organisations, irrespective of sector, size or country. Organisations only need leaders possessing both insight and courage to generate the large economic returns that are available from high commitment HRM. Many of the studies have focused on manufacturing but Batt and Doellgast (2003, p306) also suggest that 'a growing number of studies show that collaborative forms of work organisation predict better performance in the service sector'.

Table 9   *Some of the major studies examining links between HRM and performance*

Empirical studies	Sample	Nature of study
Arthur (1994)	USA: 30 mini-mills in the steel industry	Cross-sectional study
Huselid (1995)	USA: 968 US-owned firms with more than 100 employees	Cross-sectional study
MacDuffie (1995)	USA: 62 automotive plants	Cross-sectional study
Delery and Doty (1996)	USA: 114 banks	Cross-sectional study
Youndt et al (1996)	USA: 97 manufacturing plants	Longitudinal study
Patterson et al (1997)	UK: 67 manufacturing firms employing less than 1000	Longitudinal study
Wood and de Menezes (1998)	UK: use of data from WERS (1990) and Employers' Manpower and Skills Practice Survey – approximately 2000 workplaces with more than 25 employees, all sectors	Cross-sectional study
Guest et al (2000a)	UK: use of data from WERS (1998) – approximately 2000 workplaces with more than 25 employees, all sectors	Cross-sectional study
Guest et al (2000b)	UK: 835 private sector companies with more than 50 employees, interviews with HR professionals and CEOs	Cross-sectional study
Appelbaum et al (2000)	USA: 40 manufacturing plants in steel, apparel and medical electronics and imaging	Cross-sectional study
West et al (2002)	UK: 61 NHS acute hospital trusts, interviews and questionnaires mainly with HR Directors	Cross-sectional study

Table 9   *continued*

Empirical studies	Sample	Nature of study
Guest *et al* (2003)	UK: 610 private sector companies both from services and manufacturing, telephone interviews with Head of HR.	Longitudinal study

Review articles	Source	
Wood (1999a)	*International Journal of Management Reviews*, Vol. 1, No. 4	
Wright and Gardner (2003)	Holman *et al* (eds), *The New Workplace: A guide to the human impact of modern working practices.* London, Wiley	
Godard (2004)	*British Journal of Industrial Relations*, Vol. 42, No. 2	

These sorts of claims have also led to a stronger policy thrust from government. As we saw in Chapter 1, *Accounting for People* (2003) notes that one way to increase the potential impact of workers on performance was to encourage better HCM reporting. Whilst acknowledging there was no single widely accepted 'best practice' approach, the report nevertheless argued (p3) that 'there is a growing consensus that high performance is linked with high quality in practice in such areas as recruitment, skill development. and training, remuneration, job design and organisational culture'. Ultimately, the Task Force decided to recommend a consultative approach to encourage human capital reporting (and approaches) through the setting-up of Standards Board which would bring together leading employers, professional bodies and other relevant stakeholders to develop guidelines and to report back to government within two years of its formation.

We now turn to look at four of the UK studies in more detail in order to address a number of key points about this material. First, as will be apparent from Table 9, David Guest and his colleagues published the results analysing two separate data sets on the links between HRM/employment relations and performance during 2000. Both these are useful as they focus on slightly different issues, and the CIPD survey – unlike WERS – makes some estimate of whether or not HR practices are effective. Although it varies slightly between the publications and with the detailed analyses, the broad theoretical framework guiding the analysis is outlined in Figure 3 (Guest *et al* 2000b, p5; see page 88). Broadly, this proposes a path model linking together business and HR strategies on the left-hand side of the diagram (the input in positivist terms) with performance outcomes on the right-hand side. These include indicators such as financial performance, quality and productivity, as well as employee outcomes in terms of competence, commitment and flexibility. The overall framework is glued together by a number of HR practices covering all the usual areas of HRM, as well as by HR effectiveness. The HR practices include job security, recruitment and selection, induction, appraisal, training and development, EI and teamwork, pay and rewards, harmonisation and equal opportunities. The inclusion of a factor assessing effectiveness is particularly important because this allows us to evaluate how well the practices are working, in addition to whether or not they are present. In the CIPD survey, to some extent in

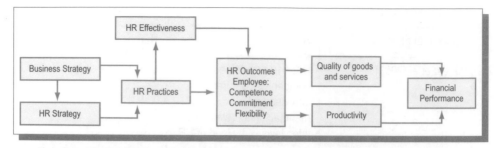

Figure 3 *Model of the link between HRM and performance*
Source: Guest D., Michie J., Sheehan M., Conway N. and Metochi M. *Effective People Management: Initial findings of the Future of Work study*. London, CIPD. 2000b. p5

contradiction to the findings of Patterson *et al* (1997), it was revealing that whilst 70 per cent of the chief executives felt that their business strategy relied a lot on people as a source of competitive advantage, considerably less than half felt that 'people issues' were more important than financial or marketing issues (Guest *et al* 2000b, p14).

A critically important finding of the study by Guest *et al* (2000a) is that a very small proportion of organisations actually use more than three quarters of the HR practices outlined. At the other extreme, an equally small proportion use less than a quarter. In general, those organisations in the public sector and with trade union involvement utilise more practices than those in the private sector and non-union firms, and indeed nearly 60 per cent reported using less than half of the whole list of HR practices. We can see from the data in Table 8 that certain practices are extremely widespread in the public sector – such as a formal grievance procedure, a written equal opportunities policy, and a standard contract. The private sector typically shows lower levels of extensiveness, but the same sorts of HR practices emerge as most widespread apart from the fact that appraisal appears to be used in more organisations. The least extensive HR practices from the list are job security guarantees, the use of quality circles and preference being given to internal candidates when filling vacancies. What the data is unable to tell us, given that it relies on a straight number count, is whether or not specific HR practices are essential for the HR bundle to work.

Even if organisations employ a wide range of HR practices, this does not mean that they are applied effectively or that they have any impact on workers or managers. For example, while it is important to know whether or not an employer makes use of regular appraisals or provides information about performance targets, this gives us no clue as to whether the appraisals make any difference or the information is supplied in a meaningful and timely fashion. This is why measures of effectiveness are so useful. In the CIPD survey (Guest *et al* 2000b), Managing Directors and HR professionals were asked to assess the effectiveness of each practice area, and in most cases they were judged to be either slightly or highly effective. The results are outlined in Table 10. It can be seen that there are relatively small differences between the respondents, with the HR professionals being slightly more circumspect about the effectiveness of the practices. The most positive responses were in relation to employment security, which is strange bearing in mind the fact that over half of the sample had made compulsory redundancies during the last three years. The HR practices deemed to be least effective were those related to financial flexibility, job design and appraisal, and it is notable that the HR professionals felt they were less effective (Guest *et al* 2000b, pp18–19). HR effectiveness – both of the practices themselves and of the personnel department – increases the strength of the relationship between HRM and performance,

Table 10 *The effectiveness of HR practices according to Managing Directors and HR professionals*

Assessment of HR practice	Managing Directors		HR professionals	
	Quite effective	Highly effective	Quite effective	Highly effective
Recruitment and selection	41	13	41	12
Training and development	40	17	39	17
Appraisal/performance management	34	14	27	11
Job design	31	7	27	4
Communication, consultation, EI	43	23	39	12
Financial flexibility	24	9	22	6
Harmonisation	32	20	34	17
Employment security/labour market practices	39	23	45	26

Source: Guest D., Michie J., Sheehan M., Conway N. and Metochi M. *Effective People Management: Initial findings of the Future of Work study.* London: CIPD. 2000b. p19

again because of its impact on employee commitment, contribution and flexibility (Guest *et al* 2000b, p31). In short, the more HR practices that are used, and the more effectively they appear to be used in enhancing organisational performance.

The research by West *et al* (2002) investigated the links between particular HR practices and performance in the NHS, based on interviews/questionnaires with HR managers in 61 separate Trusts. They found that three particular HR practices – training, teamworking and appraisal – had a particularly strong impact on performance. A number of measures were used to assess these practices as we have already indicated earlier in the chapter. Measures of performance included information about mortality rates, waiting times, complaints and financial outcomes. This data was gathered by different researchers so as to prevent any possibility of conscious or subconscious influence on the conclusions. The analysis 'reveals a strong relationship between HRM practices and mortality' (2002, p1305), with appraisal having the strongest influence of all. These results have been widely quoted because of the massive potential impact on policy but also because of the finding that 'better' HRM might lead to lower mortality rates. Drawing on this and other research, West *et al* (2002, p1309) suggest that 'it may be possible to influence hospital performance significantly by implementing sophisticated and extensive training and appraisal systems, and encouraging a high percentage of employees to work in teams'. However, the authors do urge caution in assuming any direction of causality, and agree that it could be argued there is less pressure on staff when the hospital is already achieving low mortality rates – and so more time can be devoted to investments in high commitment HRM (West *et al* 2002, p1308).

Subsequent work by David Guest and his colleagues has provided a further twist to the debate (Guest *et al* 2003). We have already described the data (both HR practices and performance measures) on which this research is based earlier in this chapter. The major conclusion (2003, p307) is that 'the results are very mixed and on balance predominantly negative. The tests of association show a positive relationship between the use of more HR practices and lower labour turnover and higher profitability, but show no association between HR and productivity. The test of whether the presence of more HR practices results in a change in performance shows no significant results.' Moreover, they conclude (Guest *et al* 2003, p311) that despite showing some strong evidence there are links between high commitment HRM and performance, their study 'fails to provide any convincing indication that greater application of HRM is likely to result in improved corporate performance'. The key point is that the methods used have a major impact on the results. When subjective performance measures are used, there is a consistently positive message, whereas the associations are less strong and consistent if objective measures of performance are employed. This leads them to suggest, contrary to some of their earlier conclusions, that reverse causality is actually quite likely; that is, rather than seeing HRM as leading to better performance, it could be that profitable organisations have the scope to introduce more high commitment HR policies than their less successful counterparts – a point to which we return later in the chapter.

One of the problems with survey research is that, while it may be possible to demonstrate links between HRM and performance, it is unable to explain in any detail why this might happen. Research by John Purcell and his colleagues (Hutchinson and Purcell 2003; Purcell *et al* 2003) has sought to open up this 'black box', and we briefly review some of the major findings here that relate to high commitment HRM and performance; discussion on the role of line managers is covered more extensively in Chapter 5. The Purcell study was undertaken over a 30-month period in 10 organisations drawn from different sectors and comprising quite a wide range of employment contexts; the sample included household names such as Tesco, PricewaterhouseCoopers, Selfridges, Jaguar, Siemens and the Royal United Hospital at Bath. Interviews were conducted with HR and line managers, as well as non-managerial staff, in these organisations, generally on two separate occasions during the research period. The research also involved close liaison with these organisations.

There are a number of significant findings that confirm, overturn or extend previous work investigating the links between high commitment HRM and performance. First, the researchers used the AMO model, which argues that in order for people to perform better, they must:

■ have the *ability* and necessary knowledge and skills, including how to work with other people (A)

■ be *motivated* to work and want to do it well (M)

■ be given the *opportunity* to deploy their skills both in the job and more broadly contributing to work group and organisational success (O).

Second, each of the case study organisations was recognised to be operating with a 'big idea', a feature or way of working that served to glue together all the different attempts to make the organisation successful. The 'big idea' was embedded within the organisation connecting together different activities, it was seen as enduring, and it was collectively shared. Moreover, one way or another, performance against or progress towards the big idea was measured and managed in an ongoing basis (p13). Third, line managers were identified as critically important for the achievement of high performance working as they provide the principal point of contact with non-managerial staff and they are in a position to strengthen, ignore or even undermine the messages conveyed through the big idea. Finally, measures of performance were adapted so they were particularly relevant for the organisation concerned; for example, at Tesco these included data on queue lengths, stock availability, theft and stock errors as well as financial data relating to the store (pp53–54). The decision to collect this data at unit level makes considerable sense, and it is a much more meaningful measure of how workers might be able to contribute to improved performance than some distant measure of profitability over which most workers have little influence. Indeed, it could be argued that it also makes sense to vary the measures of high commitment HRM depending on the workplace because workers are likely to stress different practices depending on their occupational status, age or gender for example.

Find a copy of one or more these surveys – or any others that are available – and analyse the links between high commitment HRM and performance. Prepare a presentation on the benefits that can be gained from investing in high commitment HRM.

RAISING QUESTIONS ABOUT THE HRM–PERFORMANCE LINK

Persuasive as they might appear, and attractive as they might be to HR professionals, studies that argue high commitment HRM leads to improved levels of performance have not escaped criticism, including – as we have seen – some by the authors themselves. Drawing on a number of sources (eg Holman *et al* 2003: Wright and Gardner, 2003; Godard, 2004), some of the major concerns are outlined below.

Questions about the direction of causality and the 'black box'

It will be apparent from the earlier discussion that this is a major issue, and much depends on the theoretical framework adopted by the researcher. Conceptually, it is equally likely that the use of a strong bundle of high commitment HR practices could lead to improved performance, at least at workplace level, as it is that high commitment HRM is made possible and paid for by high levels of organisational performance. As we saw earlier in the chapter, questions will remain until there is more longitudinal research and greater efforts have been made to open up the 'black box' by tracking organisational changes via case studies.

Little consistency in the HR practices included in the bundle

The number of HR practices in each of the lists varies substantially (from as few as six or seven to twenty or more) as does the inclusion or exclusion of specific techniques. For example, despite the importance attached to employment security by Pfeffer, this is not included in several of the lists (eg Delaney and Huselid 1996; Patterson *et al* 1997; Wood and de Menezes 1998). Similarly, while some authors include measures of employee voice other than that achieved through self-managed teams and employee involvement, Pfeffer does not. Perhaps this does not matter if we are clear as to why certain HR practices should be included, but that does not seem to be the case. As Wood (2003, p280) argues, it is much more important to focus on an underlying orientation for integrated management or high commitment HRM that may be reflected in slightly different types of practice rather than spending time trying to identify a set of practices that might be appropriate across all workplaces. However, far too often, the lists seem to be developed on the basis of individual preference, by looking at what other researchers have used or by constructing groupings of practices on the basis of factor analysis, and then attempting to impose some theoretical justification for this ex-post facto. Of those that do have a theoretical model to underpin their approach, even then it is not always clear why certain practices are included and others are not. For example, Huselid (1995, pp645–647) uses two groups of practices, entitled 'employee skills and organisational structures' – which includes job design, enhanced selectivity, formal training, various forms of participation, and profit sharing – and 'employee motivation' – which comprises performance appraisal linked to compensation and a focus on merit in promotion decisions. It seems strange that participation and profit sharing should be in the first grouping rather than the second given the supposed importance of these as techniques that enhance employee motivation. Patterson *et al* (1997) also emerge with two groups of practices, subtitled 'acquisition and development of employee skills' and 'job design', and on this occasion, participation and teamworking find their way into the second grouping rather than the first. In short, a simple count of how many HR practices are used tells us little of any theoretical value.

Variations in the proxies used to measure high commitment HRM

The studies use a range of different proxies for the same HR practice. For example, some are straight yes/no or absence/presence type measures whereas others ask for the percentage of the workforce covered by a particular aspect of HRM – such as performance-related pay. In some cases, the proportions vary between studies with, say 25 per cent in one and 90 per cent in another. Worse still, they can vary within a particular study between different items. Differences in the way in which practices are counted as present or absent have a major effect on the construction of the overall bundle, and it is rare for there to be an explicit discussion as to why certain levels have been set. Notably, Guest *et al* (2000b) do openly explain why they went for a figure of 90 per cent in some of their questions. More seriously, the mere absence or presence of a practice is irrelevant because what matters is how this is used and what impact it has on the people employed and on organisational performance. Take the example of grievance procedures; these are almost universally employed in organisations, so a proxy based around absence or presence tells us nothing about how people take up grievances, how many they take up, and whether they regard the processes as open and reasonable – arguably more important as a differentiator. A similar point arises in relation to days spent on training. Knowing that the typical employee is trained for about five days per annum is hardly evidence of high commitment HRM if they are trained merely in how to conform to strict rules and procedures – as sometimes happens in call centres (Sturdy *et al* 2001). Moreover, potential problems also arise when compiling scores of high commitment HRM in deciding whether or not each practice should be weighted equally. This is clearly a problem where there are more measures of a particular item than others, for example as often occurs with EI. It is possible in this situation that the overall measure gives too much weight to one factor compared with others. Moreover, what happens when, as in the WERS analysis, one practice is widely used – such as a formal statement on equal opportunities – and another, such as job security, is rarely provided? Do these deserve to be equally weighted or is the use of a relatively rare practice something that differentiates organisations from their competitors.

Variations in the proxies used to measure performance

One of the major problems is the different types of performance measure that are used, in particular whether they are based on objective or subjective assessments. Many of the studies have focused on the former, using measures of organisational performance such as profitability that have very little obvious linkage with the efforts of individual workers, even though ultimately this is what matters to organisations. This is clearly problematic in multiplant organisations within the same industry, and even more complicated in conglomerates that operate across a range of sectors and countries, as well as in public–private partnerships and interorganisational networks where it is hard to establish identifiable boundaries between them. Questions can also be raised about the appropriateness of the measures used to assess performance; in the West *et al* (2002) study, for example, one measure was the number of deaths following hip surgery. Clearly, death during surgery is a major problem – not least to the patient – but a more appropriate measure of success could be how well the person felt a few months later or whether the new hip actually provided them with a better quality of life. Other studies have asked HR managers or managing directors to estimate how well their organisation is performing compared with others in the same sector. Although there is some research that shows consistency between objective and subjective assessments (Wall *et al* 2004), others are less convinced, and indeed Guest *et al* (2003) found no association between them. Analysis of some of the WERS data shows that managers consistently overestimate the performance of their organisation in relation to competitors. Some of the intermediate employee outcome measures are simple to quantify but less easy to interpret. For example, it may be important for an organisation to have low labour turnover or absence levels compared with the average for the industry as a whole, but there are questions about whether or not a zero figure is actually indicative of good employment relations. In the case of labour turnover, work may be so pleasant and relaxed that very few people ever want to leave but if productivity levels are poor, then this is hardly evidence of effective HRM. Similarly, absence levels may be low because people are scared to take a day off for fear of reprisal or because they have so much work to do they feel that it is impossible to stay at home even when they are ill. Clearly, what appears initially as technical measurement problems actually obscure rather more serious conceptual weaknesses.

Dangers in relying on self-report scores from HR managers

Differences can arise depending on the expertise of the person who completes the questionnaire for an organisation. For obvious reasons, questions used in telephone surveys tend to be those that are capable of an immediate answer that can be coded easily. As Purcell (1999) notes, this may not get us very far in establishing what factors really make a difference to employee commitment or organisational performance. Further problems arise because personnel specialists, who are often the respondents in these surveys, often lack detailed knowledge about the competitive strategies utilised by their organisations and the proportion of sales derived from these strategies. At least the Guest *et al* study did overcome a number of these shortcomings by including managing directors and HR professionals in their sample, but they were unable to get opinions from employees themselves. This is particularly problematic if worker perceptions are not even included in studies when the focus is on 'objective' measures of performance. Anxieties such as these mean that considerable caution is needed when interpreting conclusions from these quantitative studies, and one suggestion (Wall *et al* 2004) is that a team of independent experts could assess how schemes were working rather than relying on internal evaluations alone. For example, someone with a deep knowledge of EI could compare and contrast how these schemes were working across a range of different organisations.

Doubts about how much autonomy organisations have in decision-making

It is implicitly assumed that organisations are free agents that are able to choose precisely which HR practices they wish to employ without considering any forces beyond their own organisational boundaries. As we have seen from Chapter 2, any organisation is subject to forces that shape its HR policies, in terms of legal and institutional arrangements or through the pressure exerted by clients or industry bodies. This is most apparent in how the high commitment HRM package might be applied in different countries, and we should not assume the Anglo-Saxon model (based principally on North American and UK research) is easily applicable to other countries. Boselie *et al* (2001, p1122) make it clear that 12 out of Pfeffer's original list of 16 practices are common in the Netherlands, whereas very few UK organisations could boast anything like this many. Because of the legal, political and social infrastructure, certain HR practices are deemed necessary there. However, the same situation could occur within certain industries in the UK whereby Codes of Practice or industry norms are regarded as part of the 'way we do things around here'. Moreover there are also assumptions that, once the link is proven, all employers will see the benefit of adopting the high commitment paradigm as opposed to a low-cost or bleak house philosophy, and this is far from assured. For companies that are competing against cheap foreign imports or have no interest in having committed, enthusiastic workers who wish to exercise their discretion to improve performance, the high commitment model offers few advantages. Indeed, even amongst those organisations that adopt the high commitment model in relation to their own employees, higher profits may be made at the expense of subcontractors whose low profit margins mean there is little chance to invest in best practice HRM even if they wanted to (Marchington *et al* 2004c)

In addition to the points made above, there is also a more radical critique that questions whether or not the findings actually support a link between high commitment practices and performance, as the interpretation of this material takes for granted. Ramsay *et al* (2000) propose an alternative, labour process explanation that suggests that higher levels of organisational performance are achieved not through 'progressive' employment practices but instead through work intensification. Basically, both the high commitment and the labour process versions agree that a distinctive set of HR practices may well contribute to improved levels of organisational performance. However, as Ramsay *et al* (p505) argue, 'it is at this point that the two approaches part company. The labour process critique holds that, while high performance work systems practices may provide enhancements in discretion, these come to employees at the expense of stress, work intensification and job strain, the latter being a key explanatory factor in improved organisational performance'. This interpretation is quite different therefore, mirroring the discussion about competing versions of teamworking.

In order to test their proposition, Ramsay *et al* (2000) used the 1998 WERS survey material, focusing in particular on employee outcomes. They also included other factors in their analysis related to job strain and work intensification – measured by questions about the lack of time to complete work, worrying about work outside working hours, and changes in productivity (p527). Their conclusions are at odds with those of the high commitment school, in the sense that they find little support for the notion that positive performance outcomes flow from positive employee outcomes. They suggest that the high commitment approach has been adopted without sufficient analysis of whether or not employees really do prefer such regimes. At the same time, however, they find little support for the labour process interpretation either. While acknowledging that lack of support for either model may be due to problems with the methodology, they conclude instead that neither bears much resemblance to reality. This is due to the inability of senior managers to implement strategic thinking – either to treat workers as resourceful humans or as costs to be minimised (p522). This conclusion leads Godard (2004, p350) to conclude that state support is probably required to ensure the high commitment paradigm takes root.

What do you think workers want from their employment, and does this equate with the high commitment bundle of practices considered here?

THE UNIVERSAL APPLICATION OF BEST PRACTICE HRM

One key aspect of the celebratory literature is that 'best practice' HRM is capable of being used in any organisation, irrespective of product market situation, industry, or workforce. Pfeffer (1998, pp33–34) produces evidence from many industries and studies which he claims demonstrates the case for 'putting people first'. These include 'relatively low technology settings such as apparel manufacture to very high technology manufacturing processes. The results seem to hold for manufacturing and for service firms. Nothing in the available evidence suggests that the results are country-specific. The effects of high performance management practices are real, economically significant, and general – and thus should be adopted by your organisation.' Support for this argument comes from several other studies. For example, Huselid (1995, p644) states that 'all else being equal, the use of High Performance Work Practices and good internal fit should lead to positive outcomes for all types of firms'. Delery and Doty (1996, p828) find 'relatively strong support' for the universalistic argument and some support for other perspectives, and suggest that 'some human resource practices *always* [our emphasis] have a positive effect on performance'; these were profit sharing, results-oriented appraisals and employment security. There is support from a non-US study as well, with Wood and Albanese (1995, p242) agreeing that certain HR practices have a universal effect.

There are criticisms of this view, ranging from minor adjustments through to downright rejection of the case that 'progressive' HR practices can always provide sustained competitive advantage. Youndt *et al* (1996, p837) suggest that 'the universal approach helps researchers to document the benefits of HR across all contexts, ceteris paribus, [while] the contingency perspective helps us to look more deeply into organisational phenomena to derive more situationally-specific theories and prescriptions for management practice'. Purcell (1999, p36) is particularly sceptical of the claims for universalism, which lead us, he argues, 'down a utopian cul-de-sac'. He stresses the need to identify 'the circumstances of where and when it [high commitment management; HCM] is applied, why some organisations do and some do not adopt HCM, and how some firms seem to have more appropriate human resource systems than others'.

At a conceptual and empirical level, however, there are a number of reasons to doubt that high commitment HRM is universally applicable (Marchington and Grugulis 2000). First, it is apparent that the 'best practice' works on the assumption that employers have the luxury of taking a long-term perspective or that, with a bit of foresight, they could do so. For example, they are encouraged to hire during the lean times when labour markets are less tight rather than seek to recruit when they have a pressing demand for staff and it is harder to attract the type of applicant desired (and desirable). Similarly, employers are advised to invest in employees with non-specific skills that will offer most over the longer term rather than seek to fill posts with staff who can solve immediate needs. It is suggested that employees should be retained during downturns because it will only cost more to rehire them when the market improves, a practice that also ties in with employment security guarantees. Similarly, instead of cutting back on training when times get tough or cash is in short supply, employers are urged to spend more money on training during the lean times because it is easier to release employees from other duties when production schedules are less tight. There are good economic and labour market reasons for employers to do all of these things, but they all depend, to a greater or lesser extent, upon the luxury of a long-term perspective and the prospect of future market growth. Of course, institutional forces beyond the level of the organisation may serve to shape HRM more significantly in some countries than they do in others. As Boselie *et al* (2003) note, employers in some countries may take for granted what in the UK is seen as 'best practice' offered by just a few organisations.

Second, it is rather easier to engage in high commitment HRM when labour costs form a low proportion of controllable costs. In capital intensive operations, it makes little sense to cut back on essential staff who have highly specific and much-needed skills – say, in a pharmaceutical or chemical plant or with research scientists. When labour costs represent a major cost compared with other factors, as in many service sector organisations for example, it is much more difficult for managers persuade financiers that there are long-term benefits from investments in human capital. It is unlikely, given their previous behaviour, that bankers and lenders in Britain will perceive the benefits of taking a strategic perspective on human resources and sacrifice short-term gains for longer term accumulation. In contrast, it is immensely difficult to persuade employers to adopt a 'best practice' approach if they operate in situations where labour costs are sizeable, and where it is difficult to increase pay rates or offer training when resources are constrained. Moreover, it is unlikely that customers or users will accept inferior levels of service even if it is helping to develop talent over the longer term (eg in the health service, pubs and restaurants). Furthermore, given an emphasis on contracting and recontracting up and down the supply chain, there is often little incentive for employers to invest in high commitment HRM if their contracts are of limited length and they are expected to compete on the basis of reduced costs (Marchington *et al* 2004c). Cappelli and Neumark (2001) report that, while high commitment HRM actually does increase worker output, it also raises labour costs and employee rewards. This leads Godard (2004, p355) to argue that the proponents of high commitment HRM 'overestimate the positive effects of high levels of adoption of these practices, but also underestimate the costs'. The end result is likely to be little overall gain in productivity.

> Bearing in mind some of the recent furore about contracting out manufacturing or call centres to low wage economies, discuss whether or not customers really do gain from 'best practice' HRM or whether they would prefer to buy cheaper goods no matter how they are produced.

Third, so much depends upon which categories of staff employers are trying to recruit. MacDuffie (1995, p199) is often quoted as someone whose research is supportive of the universality argument, but it is apparent from his studies that high commitment HRM may actually be situationally specific. He suggests:

> **Innovative human resource practices are likely to contribute to improved economic performance *only when* [our emphasis] three conditions are met: when employees possess knowledge and skills that managers lack; when employees are motivated to apply this skill and knowledge through discretionary effort; and when the firm's business or production strategy can only be achieved when employees contribute such discretionary effort.**

This seems to indicate clearly that the circumstances under which 'best practice' HRM will make a difference are quite specific. For example, it makes sense for the employer to encourage discretionary behaviour in order to achieve organisational goals – such as in high technology industries where work systems and processes can not be easily codified or overseen by managers, and qualified workers are in short supply and there may be strong arguments for hoarding labour. In many other situations, the time taken to train new staff is relatively short, work performance can be assessed simply and speedily, and there is a supply of substitutable labour readily available. The rationale for employers adopting the high commitment paradigm in these circumstances is hard to sustain. In addition, some jobs are so boring or unpleasant that it is inconceivable that many people would see employment security, basic training or information sharing – for example – as any kind of benefit. On the contrary, these workers would probably resent being expected to take an interest in their organisation beyond routine work performance, and find it stressful and intrusive. In short, the best practice model may not be attractive or appropriate for all groups of workers or employers.

Finally, the growth in 'non-standard' contracts has led many commentators to question if 'flexible' employment is compatible with 'best practice' HRM, and whether or not the latter can be applied to all employees in an organisation irrespective of their occupational status or labour market value (Kinnie *et al* 2004). As we saw in Chapter 2, the changing nature of the psychological contract has led to worries that employment insecurity is now widespread, and evidence shows that between the 1970s and the 1990s, the proportion of people who had experienced a spell of unemployment almost trebled from 7 per cent to approximately 20 per cent of the population (Gallie *et al* 1998, p124). Other data reinforces case study and anecdotal evidence that employees now feel rather more insecure than they did 20 years ago. However, some groups of employees appear to be gaining more from 'best practice' HRM than others, especially those who remain working for the same employer for many years. This suggests distinctions could be arising between long-serving workers, whom employers might wish to nurture, and short-term contract staff or subcontracted workers (Purcell 1999).

CONCLUSIONS

The focus in this chapter has been on high commitment HRM, and we have examined the way in which HR policies and practices may be used to provide coherent and comprehensive human resource bundles. This has led to suggestions that there is one best way in which HRM should be delivered, and moreover that this has a positive impact on organisational performance. There is currently a good deal of interest in the high commitment HRM–performance link, and to ideas that a specific bundle of human resource policies and practices is inherently superior and capable of making a major contribution to organisational success in all workplaces. There is also policy interest in this approach through the notion of HCM reporting. We have reviewed this argument in the chapter, pointing to alternative and competing interpretations of the research findings, as well as calling for greater reflection on whether or not best practice HRM really can make a difference to bottom line performance in all workplaces. Holman *et al* (2003, pp422–424) summarise the scale of the research task that is needed to move the debate on, and include many of the points that have been raised in this chapter. The high commitment model is appealing as it supports the case for implementing 'good' people management practices on business grounds. However, there is also a strong theoretical and empirical basis for arguing that high commitment models cannot be – and are not being – applied in all workplaces and to all groups of staff. Having considered the 'best practice' perspective in this chapter, we are now in a position to analyse the alternative – 'best fit' – scenario in Chapter 4.

USEFUL READING

Boxall P. *and* Purcell J. *Strategy and Human Resource Management*. Basingstoke, Palgrave Macmillan. 2003.

Godard J. 'A critical assessment of the high performance paradigm', *British Journal of Industrial Relations*, Vol. 42, No. 2, 2004. pp349–378.

Guest D., Michie J., Conway, N. *and* Sheehan M. 'Human resource management and performance', *British Journal of Industrial Relations*, Vol. 41, No. 2, 2003. pp291–314.

Guest D., Michie J., Sheehan M., Conway N. *and* Metochi M. *Effective People Management: Initial findings of the Future of Work study.* London, CIPD. 2000b.

Holman D., Wall T., Clegg C., Sparrow P. *and* Howard A. *The New Workplace: A guide to the human impact of modern working practices.* London, Wiley. 2003. The chapters by Wood, Batt and Doellgast, Wright and Gardner, and Legge are particularly useful

Marchington M. *and* Grugulis I. '"Best practice" human resource management: perfect opportunity or dangerous illusion?', *International Journal of Human Resource Management*, Vol. 11, No. 6, 2000. pp905–925.

Pfeffer J. *The Human Equation: Building profits by putting people first.* Boston, Harvard Business School Press. 1998.

Purcell J. 'The search for best practice and best fit in human resource management: chimera or cul-de-sac?', *Human Resource Management Journal*, Vol. 9, No. 3, 1999. pp26–41.

Purcell J., Kinnie N., Hutchinson S., Rayton B. *and* Swart J. *Understanding the People and Performance Link: Unlocking the black box.* London, CIPD. 2003.

Ramsay H., Scholarios D. *and* Harley B. 'Employees and high-performance work systems: testing inside the black box', *British Journal of Industrial Relations*, Vol. 38, No. 4, 2000. pp501–531.

West M., Borrill C., Dawson J., Scully J., Carter M., Anelay S., Patterson M. *and* Waring J. 'The link between the management of employees and patient mortality in acute hospitals', *International Journal of Human Resource Management*, Vol. 13, No. 8, 2002. pp1299–1310.

Designing HRM to Fit Organisational Goals

CHAPTER 4

INTRODUCTION

We saw in the previous chapter that it has become commonplace for management gurus to extol the virtues of investing in human capital and treating workers as the vital component in the achievement of competitive advantage. At one level it obviously makes good business sense for workers to use their discretionary behaviour to improve performance. Other things being equal, it is likely that committed and motivated employees will provide higher levels of customer service that lead to increased productivity and improved quality. However, there is not a lot that committed and excellent staff can do if the organisation has low-quality products, poor designs and an insufficient investment in technology, or if there are unstable exchange rates, collapsed economies or political upheavals. Equally, even if senior managers believe in the high commitment model, this does not guarantee that supervisors have either the skills or the motivation to put it into effect. It should have been apparent from Chapter 3 that 'best practice' HRM may not be appropriate for all situations and that, despite the claims, other approaches to people management may have greater success in generating high levels of performance (Hoque 2000; Boxall and Purcell 2003). This brings us neatly onto an analysis of 'best fit' (or contingency and configurational analyses) as an alternative way of looking at HRM and assessing the extent to which there is vertical integration (external fit) with business strategy. This chapter also takes up issues raised in Chapter 1, and it will be apparent that most of the models rely on 'classical' versions of strategy.

In this chapter, we analyse three different contingency/configurational frameworks – life cycle models, Schuler's adaptation of Porter, and Delery and Doty's extension of Miles and Snow – so as to examine the links between strategy and HRM. This is followed by a consideration of resource-based views of HRM and strategy, as well as a critique that brings to the fore the importance of using ideas developed from the institutionalist perspective. We also present material showing that employing organisations are beset by political rivalries, departmental splits and functional conflicts that make it difficult to translate broad corporate goals into specific workplace practices. To complicate matters yet further, strategies do not emerge in a simple, unilinear top-down direction, but are complex, multifaceted phenomena. In other words, we need to consider the inter-relationship between business strategy and HRM rather than viewing this solely from a top-down perspective.

By the end of this chapter, readers should be able to:

■ **contribute to the choice of appropriate HR policies that can lead to enhanced organisational and individual performance**

■ **benchmark their own employer's approach to HRM against those of other organisations**

■ **recognise and overcome barriers to the effective implementation of HR strategies.**

In addition, readers should understand and be able to explain:

- **the nature of the relationship between business strategy and HRM at work**

- **the value of analysing the links between HRM and organisational goals from the resource-based and institutionalist perspectives**

- **the range of barriers that obstruct the conversion of HR strategy into practice.**

'BEST FIT' HRM: CONTINGENCY AND CONFIGURATIONAL IDEAS

There have been a number of attempts to develop categorisations linking HRM with business strategy, competitive circumstances or national business systems. Many of these are developed from the notion of 'external fit' (Baird and Meshoulam 1988), and as Boxall and Purcell (2003, p51) note, 'the basic recipe for HRM involves bringing HR strategy into line with the firm's chosen path in its product market (more accurately this entails matching HR practices to the competitive strategy of a business unit)'. The models used include product or organisational life cycles, the Boston Consulting Group (BCG) matrix, derivations from Porter's ideas on competitive advantage, strategic behaviour and organisational flexibility. These include: Thomason (1984), Kochan and Barocci (1985), Streeck (1987), Lengnick Hall and Lengnick Hall (1988), Purcell (1989), Schuler (1989), Marchington and Parker (1990), Storey and Sisson (1993), Purcell and Ahlstrand (1994), Delery and Doty (1996), Sisson and Storey (2000), and Boxall and Purcell (2003). For the purposes of this book, we will focus on three of the most important: life-cycle models (Kochan and Barocci); competitive advantage (Schuler); and strategic configurations (Delery and Doty). The different models are outlined first, followed by a general critique of contingency approaches.

Life-cycle models

A number of US researchers (for example, Kochan and Barocci 1985; Lengnick Hall and Lengnick Hall 1988) have attempted to apply business and product life-cycle models of strategy to HRM in an effort to explain why employers adopt different policies from one another. Leung (2003) and Rutherford *et al* (2003) have applied this to small businesses, and Boxall and Purcell (2003) work on the basis of three stages to the life cycle. For this book, however, we will use four stages – start-up, growth, maturity and decline – since this has been applied to a UK context by Sisson and Storey (2000).

Start-up

During the early stages of business growth, it is felt that flexibility is necessary to enable the organisation (or subunit) to grow and develop, with a strong commitment to entrepreneurialism and organisational flexibility. The ability to recruit and retain staff with the motivation to work long hours and engage in self-development is the key to this stage being successful. Employers aim to gain employee commitment to the business, and while there may be some return in the form of highly competitive salaries in some circumstances, it is more likely that employees will be encouraged to see the potential benefits as part of a long-term investment. There is likely to be little or nothing in the way of formalised practices, for example in relation to learning and development or structured performance management systems. In the most unlikely event that trade unions are present, their role will probably be minor. It is unlikely that a specialist HR manager would be employed, so this role would either be combined with other managerial tasks or it may be more cost-effective to employ consultants instead.

One of the problems with this characterisation is that it seems to assume start-up only relates to small businesses. In a quite different context, any organisation that opens a new outlet faces the problems of start-up, although in the case of larger firms (such as Nissan when it first came to the UK in the 1980s) existing systems may provide a much more systematic and comprehensive base from which to build, and the critical role of HR might be recognised from the outset.

Growth

As the organisation – or subunit – grows beyond a certain size, formal and systematic HR policies and procedures are needed to build upon earlier successes, as well as retain expertise and ensure that earlier levels of commitment are maintained. For example, in order to recruit staff, it is likely that managers will make use of more sophisticated methods for recruitment and selection, management development, training, appraisal, pay and reward and organisation development. In employee relations, priorities become the maintenance of peace, and the retention of employee motivation and morale (Kochan and Barocci 1985, p104). As the need for specialist expertise becomes apparent throughout the business as a whole, so too is the pressure for professional HR services internal to the organisation. If HR policies remain informal and ad hoc, there is a danger that problems will emerge because grievance and discipline procedures, pay systems and performance management are not adopted consistently.

However, the entrepreneurs who first set up the organisation may resist any shift to greater formalisation. This is a common occurrence, even in large firms such as Starbucks, where the original founder bemoans the way in which the organisation has lost – what he sees as – its informal culture as the company has grown in size and geographical spread, and that workers consider turning to trade unions to represent them in dealings with management.

Maturlty

As markets begin to mature, and surpluses level out, the business needs to take stock of its activities and shift priorities so as to cope with much lower levels of growth – and even a complete flattening out of performance. By this stage there is likely to be a range of formalised procedures, covering everything from HRM to purchasing. In the early period of this stage, it is likely the organisations will operate with a range of high commitment HR policies of the sort outlined in Chapter 3, and indeed many publications implicitly refer to this 'golden age' where effective compromises are reached because weak competitive pressures allow employers to offer win–win solutions to problems. Even during this period, relative calm and stability may be punctured by crises – such as new global pressures in the sector, political turmoil in product markets or a hostile takeover bid – which cause a rethink of existing practices.

As this stage progresses, however, there is an increasing focus on the control of labour costs, something that is often hard to achieve given that employees have become accustomed to enjoying the continuing fruits of prosperity. Staff replacements are no longer automatic, training and development programmes may become harder to justify, and the overall wage bill is kept firmly under control. Union representatives, if they are present, are likely to find that previously good relationships may start to become strained. This is the time at which all parties start to worry about employment security and doubts emerge about management's ability to sustain a positive psychological contract. Staff may be encouraged to leave the organisation or become more mobile around the business, as efforts are made to improve productivity against a backcloth of worsening competitive prospects.

Decline (and renewal?)

The process of decline brings to a head many of the problems that become apparent in the previous phase, as the business struggles to survive. In this stage the emphasis shifts to rationalisation and redundancy, with obvious implications for HR philosophy. Many of the HR policies developed through previous years are reconsidered, and indeed may be ditched as the employer seeks desperately to reduce costs. The specialist HR function could well be disbanded, there may be pay cuts, training opportunities become focused on re-skilling and outplacement counselling, and there is a tendency to contract-out even more services. The culture can become tense and difficult, and trade unions may find that they are marginalised or de-recognised.

This pattern was apparent in many manufacturing firms that have struggled to survive over the last 20 years, often characterised by successive plant closures, an increased tendency to use coercive comparisons between establishments to get higher levels of productivity, and increasingly soured employment relations. Of course, not all organisations continue on the path to terminal decline, and some – such as Ford – bounced back by re-engineering and a genuine shift to more participative management for those workers that remained with the new slimmed-down company (Boxall and Purcell 2003, p200). If this sort of strategy is successful, organisations re-enter the life cycle at one of the earlier stages. Box 11 provides an analysis of how the life-cycle model can be applied to small firms.

BOX 11 CHANGES IN HRM DURING THE LIFE CYCLE OF SMALL FIRMS

There have not been many empirical studies examining how HRM might change during the organisational life cycle – in order to test the general theories advanced in this section of the chapter. Some work in the USA has examined the interplay of organisational life cycle and various firm characteristics in a sample of nearly 3000 small and medium-sized enterprises so as to test the hypothesis that the principal HR problems would change as the firm develops. It was suggested that recruitment problems would be greatest during the birth stage, issues to do with development would be most prominent during the growth stage and retention would become a principal concern once the firm reaches maturity. As a by-product the study also examined whether or not a four-stage model was appropriate.

The results were quite varied, and there was only partial support for the proposition that HR problems would change in the way suggested above. The four-stage model received support from this study, although the age of the firm was much less important as a contextual influence than its size. Indeed variations in the rate of growth proved to the most critical factor explaining the emergence of HR problems. The highest growth firms reported the greatest problems in dealing with development issues, something which is to be expected as small businesses grapple with how to formalise their HR practices. In contrast high growth firms reported few retention problems, presumably because existing staff enjoyed the challenge of meeting fresh targets. The moderate growth firms reported the biggest problems with retention as workers left because they had few opportunities to meet new challenges and became bored with organisational routines. Low growth firms reported few problems with either training or recruitment. Paradoxically, firms that were experiencing no growth (and presumably did not have to recruit many staff) found that recruitment was the most difficult problem they had to face, perhaps because they were unable to attract sufficient high quality recruits in the first place.

Source: Adapted from Rutherford M., Buller P. and McMullen P. 'Human resource management over the life cycle of small to medium sized firms', *Human Resource Management*, Vol. 42, No. 4, 2003. pp321–335

On the basis of the research in Box 11, what HR advice would you offer to a small to medium-sized business? Justify your answer with the use of examples and evidence from other types of organisation.

Table 11   *Competitive strategies and HRM*

HR practices	Competitive strategy		
	Cost reduction	**Quality enhancement**	**Innovation**
Resourcing	Ad hoc methods predominate, use of agencies/ subcontractors Tight performance management	Sophisticated methods of recruitment and selection Comprehensive induction and socialisation	Focus on core competencies and transferable skills Agreed performance outcomes
Learning and development	Poor or non-existent training in specific immediate skills	Extensive and long-term focus Focused on learning and career development	Provided if necessary Personal responsibility for learning
Employee relations	Little EI or communications Non-union workplace or unions tolerated	Well-developed systems for employee voice Partnership arrangements	Preference for informal communication systems Professional associations
Reward management	Low pay levels No additional benefits	Competitive pay and benefits package Harmonisation	Cafeteria reward system Share ownership/ profit-sharing
HR function	Slimmed down Lacking in influence	Work closely with line managers Potentially large influence	Advice and support to employees Potentially some influence

Source: Adapted from Sisson K. and Storey J. *The Realities of Human Resource Management*. Milton Keynes, Open University Press. 2000

Competitive advantage models

These seek to apply Porter's ideas on competitive strategy to HRM. Porter (1985) argues that employers have three basic strategic options in order to gain competitive advantage: cost reduction, quality enhancement and innovation. Schuler and Jackson (1987) draw out the HR implications of these strategies, and in a later work Schuler (1989) attempts to combine this with life-cycle models. The original paper has also been developed by Sisson and Storey (2000; see Table 11 on page 103) and Kelliher and Perrett (2001).

The 'cost reduction' employer seeks to produce goods and services cheaper than the competition, with no frills and an emphasis on minimising costs at all stages in the process – including people management. The HR implications are similar to the 'bleak house' or 'black hole' employer (Guest 2001b), with no systems for independent worker voice and no evidence of high commitment HRM. Recruitment and selection is likely to be ad hoc, especially for low-grade tasks, and the employer may well use agencies or subcontractors to perform much of the work (Marchington *et al* 2004c). Training is likely to be poor or non-existent, with no recognition that employees should be provided with opportunities for learning and development. Pay levels are unlikely to be much above the minimum wage, and may well be less if the employer can get away with it. There are likely to be minimum health and safety standards, tight performance monitoring, little emphasis on employee involvement and communications, and little empathy with staff experiencing problems. Non-unionism is likely, although if unions do make an approach they are ignored or tolerated provided they are not seen as problematic. If a specialist HR function exists, it is likely to be slim and have little influence.

The cost reducer category is undoubtedly the most common form in Britain, largely because so many people work for small firms that have neither the resources nor the commitment to develop their staff. Reports by The Low Pay Commission on the operation of the national minimum wage inevitably focus on these kinds of employers, drawn from industries such as retailing, hospitality, cleaning and security, and social care. For example, studies completed for the Low Pay Commission by people such as Grimshaw and Carroll (2002), highlight the HR problems experienced by employers. For example, one care home said 'there's a new retail park going to be built in the local area ... How the hell am I going to keep our employees when they do that? I haven't the faintest idea because they will pay them a damn sight more' (Low Pay Commission 2003, p91). However, despite particular problems in social care that probably require policy intervention, as a general point the Commission reported (2003, p110) that 'in each of the sectors we have looked at we conclude that the minimum wage and the 2001 up-rating have been absorbed without significant adverse impact on employment'.

> How can 'cost reducers' continue to recruit and retain staff if their conditions are so much worse than other employers in the same labour market?

The 'quality enhancement' employer operates with a set of HR practices that are the exact opposite of the cost reducer because the goal is to produce goods and services of the highest quality possible in order to differentiate itself from the competition. HRM in this situation is likely to resonate with the 'best practice' model analysed in the previous chapter. This includes: systematic recruitment and selection; comprehensive induction programmes; empowerment and high-discretion jobs; high levels of EI; extensive and continuous training and development; harmonisation; highly competitive pay and benefits packages; and a key role for performance appraisal. There is no mention of unions in the Schuler model, but if they are recognised it is probable that both parties are keen to maintain co-operative relations and a de facto (or de jure) partnership arrangement would be in place. The HR function is likely to be well staffed and highly proactive in helping to shape organisational cultures and change programmes. Close co-operation between HR and line managers would be desired so that competitive advantage could be sustained.

A growing number of large organisations are likely to aspire to this model, and offer the more favourable employment package that this implies if only to attract and retain key staff at times of labour market shortage. As we saw in Chapter 3, there are problems ensuring that HR policy is actually converted into 'real' practices at workplace level and that commitments to employment security or to equal opportunities are not jettisoned if problems arise. Also, the extent to which high commitment HRM is sustainable during downturn and recession is open to question, as too is the ability to apply these HR practices across the entire workforce over time. Of course, some employers may be able to maintain a quality enhancement approach with their own staff by imposing tightly specified business contracts on suppliers that lead to inferior terms and conditions for their workers (Marchington *et al* 2004c).

The 'innovation' category of the Schuler framework is likely to be the least widespread of the three. Here, it is assumed that groups of highly trained specialists work closely together to design and produce complex and rapidly changing/adaptable products and services. The consequences for HR policy are similar in many respects to the quality enhancement model outlined above, but there is much greater emphasis on informality, problem-solving groups, a commitment to broadly defined goals, and flexibility. Employee development is likely to be seen as a personal responsibility rather than the employer's obligation, and basic pay rates are likely to be supplemented by access to share ownership schemes that enable employees to link their fortunes to that of the employer. Schuler does not mention unions, but given an emphasis on individualism they are unlikely to figure prominently. Box 12 provides an example of how the link between strategy and HRM might be more complex than some of the models imply.

BOX 12   HRM IN A DESIGNER RESTAURANT

Much of the literature on hotels and catering quite rightly places this sector in the cost reduction category, largely because of the highly competitive environment in which these organisations operate and the fact that one of the major sources of cost savings comes from relatively low rates of pay for staff. While the majority of staff are not particularly well-paid and probably fit well with the cost reduction model, leading chefs may be hired in order to provide a very strong and identifiable product. Although segmenting the workforce may make sense from a certain angle, it is also potentially short-sighted as customer satisfaction with an excellent product may be jeopardised through poor service. Nowhere does this come more to the fore than in designer restaurants. These tend to be characterised as innovative, providing high quality, sophisticated food in an environment that is informal and offers a relaxed style of service. They also tend to be at the more expensive end of the market.

A string of adjectives described the company investigated by Kelliher and Perrett, and give some idea of the business strategy: internationally renowned; up-market; trendy yet affordable; innovative. The HR practices illustrated a well-planned system for HR as a whole, including a strong emphasis on recruiting the right kind of people, systematic performance appraisal, a high commitment to training and development, pay levels at or above that of competitors, and informal staff–management relations. However, although it was agreed the restaurants were pursuing an innovation strategy, there was little evidence that the HR strategy had been aligned, nor was it clear that human resources were seen as a source of competitive advantage. In other words this raises questions about whether or not the restaurants were achieving maximum organisational effectiveness. From an HR perspective, the cues sent to employees about their (lack of) importance to business success could be regarded as impeding the performance of the restaurants. However, the case also highlights the point that integration between HR and business goals may be hard to achieve in practice, and that researchers and practitioners ought to recognise more explicitly the fundamental tensions and contradictions in the employment relationship. As such, searching for an ideal 'best fit' may be a wasted exercise.

Source: Adapted from Kelliher C. and Perrett G. 'Business strategy and approaches to HRM: a case study of new developments in the UK restaurant industry', *Personnel Review*, Vol. 30, No. 4, 2001. pp421–437

Since it is unlikely that entire organisations will be located in the 'innovation' category, it is possible this set of HR practices may be preserved for small groups of highly qualified staff or those engaged in 'leading-edge' activities. This opens up the possibility that different groups of staff may be employed on quite different terms and conditions from one another. One way to insulate these workers from others employed by the same organisation is to locate them on a different site or in a division set up specifically to develop new ideas and products, perhaps ultimately being spun-off as a separate company.

Strategic configurations

Traditional, bivariate contingency theory is criticised for oversimplifying reality by seeking to relate one dominant variable external to the organisation (say, product market position) to an internal variable (say, HRM) in a deterministic manner. For example, it is assumed that HR style can be 'read-off' from product market circumstances or position in the product life cycle. The choice of an alternative external factor (say, labour market circumstances) might indicate that the employer should adopt a different style altogether, and it is at this point that contingency models are found wanting. Delery and Doty (1996) propose the notion of configurational perspectives in an attempt to overcome this problem, by identifying ideal-type categories of both the HR system and the organisation's strategy. The principal point about this perspective is that it seeks to derive an internally consistent set of HR practices that maximise horizontal integration (internal fit) and then link these to alternative strategic configurations to maximise vertical integration (external fit). Delery and Doty (p809) do this by linking an 'internal' employment system with Miles and Snow's (1978) 'defender' strategy and a 'market-type' employment system with their 'prospector' category (Table 12).

Defenders concentrate on efficiency in current products and markets, on narrow product ranges, and have a centralised organisation structure. They tend to 'build' their portfolios and extend their activities slowly and carefully. As such, an internal employment system offers the most appropriate fit with the strategic goals and capabilities of such an organisation, and it allows for the derivation of a bundle of HR practices that support each other. Recruitment, wherever possible, is through specific ports of entry and employees are promoted internally

Table 12 *Strategic configurations and HRM*

HR practices	Strategic configuration	
	Defenders – internal employment system	**Prospectors – market employment system**
Resourcing	Great care over recruitment and selection Well-developed internal labour markets	Buying-in of labour to undertake specific tasks Tight performance standards and expectations
Learning and development	Extensive and long-term focus Well-defined career ladders	Likely to be extensive Personal responsibility for learning and development
Employee relations	Emphasis on co-operation and involvement Voice through grievance procedures and trade unions	Emphasis on responsibility and performance Little attention paid to voice
Reward management	Clear grading structures and transparent pay systems Employee share ownership	Pay determined by external market comparisons Bonus and incentive payments
HR function	Well-established Potentially large influence	Limited role Managing external contracts

Source: Adapted from Delery J. and Doty H. 'Modes of theorising in strategic human resource management: tests of universalistic, contingency and configurational performance predictions', *Academy of Management Journal*, Vol. 39, No. 4, 1996. pp802–835

as appropriate to fill other positions. Career ladders are well defined, training and development activities are extensive, and socialisation into the dominant organisational culture is high on the managerial agenda, both through formal induction programmes and through day-to-day reinforcement. Appraisals are principally for developmental purposes, and the reward structure is geared up to long-term employment with the organisation, for example through clear grading structures and increments, as well as via employee share ownership. Employment security is likely to be high for those who make it through probationary periods, and there are plenty of opportunities for employees to exercise their voice through grievance procedures, problem-solving groups and (where recognised) trade unions. The HR function is likely to be well established and may be encouraged to play a major part in management decision-making because of specific expertise about HRM in the particular industry and sector. Moreover, senior HR managers are likely to be active in wider industry bodies concerned with training and development or health and safety, or in pay clubs that share information about compensation levels and practices. Furthermore, defender organisations are keen not only on their own survival and performance but also on how well the industry as a whole fares over the long-term since this fits their own interests.

By contrast, *prospector*s are inclined to change and adaptability, exploring new product markets and business opportunities, and therefore less reliant on existing skills and abilities. Consequently, their HR strategies are less internally oriented, and they search the external labour market so as to 'buy in' staff rather than 'build' them as do the defenders. Recruitment tends to be from the external labour market and there is little use of internal career ladders, other than for a specialist core group of staff who have a range of transferable skills that might be appropriate in different environments. Given the emphasis on external recruitment to meet new demands, training is likely to be much less extensive than at defender firms and typically related to short-term needs rather than long-term learning and development. Appraisals are likely to be results-oriented, and incentive pay systems – such as performance-related pay – tend to be prominent, as do other short-term financial incentives. Participation and voice are unlikely to be given a high profile, and unions tolerated rather than encouraged. The role of the HR function in such organisations may be limited to administration and support rather than acting as a strategic business partner unless this is as an expert in managing external contracts, interpreting the legal situation and leading on rationalisation and change. Given that HR is not providing industry-specific expertise, these organisations may well contract-out these services to specialist firms such as Capita or PwC.

Research by Rodriguez and Ventura (2003) sought to examine whether the Miles and Snow model could be applied to HRM. Their results were mixed, although it is always hard to generalise on the basis of one project given its location (Spain), its sample size (5 per cent return) and the other problems associated with survey results – such as the reliance on a single respondent and the type of proxies used for each of the practices. Broadly, the authors found that an internal HR system (defender) was related to low levels of labour turnover and superior firm performance, but that reward practices had a negative relationship with productivity. They also note that, while they found greater support for the universalistic approach (best practice) than for contingency perspectives, both could well be important in helping to define appropriate HR strategies and practices. As we suggest elsewhere in the book, there may well be a certain minimum stock of HR practices that are essential for organisational survival and continued viability, while others that combine in more particularistic ways to enhance sustained competitive advantage.

LIMITATIONS OF 'BEST FIT' MODELS

There are clear similarities between these models, and parallels can be drawn between HR practices in some of the different categorisations, eg cost reducer and start-up, or quality enhancer and internal employment system. There are also at least six general shortcomings:

1   The models are deterministic and top-down in orientation. Each of the models is overtly deterministic, making the assumption it is possible to 'read off' a preferred HR from an understanding of business strategy or competitive prospects. There are several problems with this assumption. Many organisations do not have clear business strategies, and it is impossible to claim there are links with HRM if no strategy exists (Boxall and Purcell 2000, p187). In addition, the contingency

approaches adopt the classical perspective on strategy, in which logical, rational decision-making takes place in an ordered and sequential manner between non-political actors. We have already seen that such an assumption is unrealistic. Drawing on research with companies in the oil and chemicals industries, Ritson (1999, p170) argues that the relationship between HRM and strategy is much more interactive than the classical models suggest. One problem is the assumption that HRM is owned by and undertaken in specialist departments rather than being integrated into the line management of the organisation, and thus inseparable from all other managerial functions and activities. Moreover, these models are normative, relying on 'what ought to be' rather than 'what is', assuming there is one best way to manage people in particular situations. There is enough empirical evidence from looking at organisations to see that styles vary even for organisations in similar product market or competitive circumstances, each of which may be equally successful at the same or different periods of time. Also, we need to be aware there is a danger in analysing organisations merely in terms of existing practice because, had managers made different decisions, performance might have been even better or worse. Moreover, senior managers do make mistakes in assessing the most appropriate approach.

2   There are multiple influences on organisations in a pluralistic system. Each of the models puts a primacy on a single – albeit different – contextual factor and assumes that these determine patterns of HRM. Even if we accept that a particular set of product market circumstances is related theoretically to a particular HR style, problems then arise if different factors external to the organisation suggest the adoption of different types of HR strategy, or that different parts of a business operate in quite different market circumstances. For example, a tight and competitive product market situation might imply the organisation needs to reduce labour costs wherever possible. On the other hand, a tight labour market for particular grades of worker who are essential to the process might suggest great care needs to be taken in recruiting, developing, involving and rewarding these staff for fear they will leave. In such circumstances, employee retention becomes a dominant HR concern. Moreover, as we suggested above, the rationale for decisions about HR style in each of these models is primarily influenced by factors beyond the employment relationship. While acknowledging that employment issues are lower down the management decision-making hierarchy than financial or customer-driven goals, neglecting labour relations is problematic if workers have a substantial influence over the ultimate quality of the product or customer service. In service sector organisations in particular, the daily interactions between front-line staff – who may often be amongst the lowest paid in the organisation – and customers can have a substantial impact on sales and customer satisfaction in highly competitive markets (Sturdy *et al* 2001). Similarly, employers in relatively high-skill sectors – such as health and education – have faced persistent problems recruiting staff solely from within the UK. Even though some of the work of nurses and teachers is now being done by less-well qualified assistants, retention has remained a major concern. In other words, as Boxall and Purcell (2003, p54) note, we do need to recognise that 'the strategic goals of HRM are plural. While they do involve supporting the firm's competitive objectives, they also involve meeting employee needs and complying with social requirements for labour management ... The firm after all is a network of stakeholders.'

3   Managers do not have complete control over workers. Each of the models follow traditional scientific management principles in assuming managers are omniscient

(all-knowing) and omnipotent (all-powerful) in their dealings with those lower down the hierarchy. The concept of 'bounded rationality' tells us it is impossible for anyone to retain sufficient information in their head to make judgements that take into account all possible effects and scenarios. Moreover, the models also assume that once a preferred strategy has been identified, there is no problem putting it into effect. While accepting that employers typically have greater bargaining power than employees, it is unrealistic to pretend that no thought needs to be given to how to meet the 'baseline needs of employees whose skills are crucial to the firm's survival' (Boxall and Purcell 2000, p187). Even in workplaces that utilise computer technology to monitor performance – such as call centres – it is clear that there are strict limits to the extent to which managers are able to fully control the activities of their staff (Taylor and Bain 1999; Kinnie *et al* 2000; Taylor *et al* 2002). Employer goals and visions are not determined in a vacuum, but emerge through negotiated processes within the managerial hierarchy and with employees/trade unions, as well as being shaped by governmental and institutional forces. Moreover, it is no longer accurate to assume that senior managers within one organisation are free to make decisions without influence from other parts of the supply chain; work on a call centre undertaken by Rubery *et al* (2004) shows the multiple influences on both managers and workers in this particular setting. Even though workers were employed at the same location, they were supplied from a range of sources, worked on different contracts and had quite diverse terms and conditions of employment.

4   The models are static and do not focus on the processes of change. All of the models seek to relate two sets of variables together (eg life cycle and HRM) in a static way that takes no account of the processes involved. Evidence suggests that, for example, organisations do not travel in the direction indicated by the life-cycle model, but instead move through a series of recurrent crises as they grow and develop (Legge 1995; Hussey 1998). Assumptions also tend to be made about the size, shape and structure of organisations in each of the phases and categories, so that a start-up business is typically assumed to be small and a mature business large. It is difficult to gauge when an organisation moves from one stage of the life cycle to the next, and at what point there might be a change in HR practice to reflect – or drive – this change. In addition, even if one were able to identify the precise moment when an organisation moved from one stage to the next, it would be a major task to adjust the terms and conditions of staff in order to realign the business and HR strategies. Such a change may also lead to a worsening of management–employee relations. Accordingly, there needs to be a clearer focus on the way in which change takes place, on the major influences over and obstacles to change, and of course on the actual processes of decision-making. One of the problems with this is that organisations are not keen in having independent observers watch their internal debates, and we are typically reliant on post-facto assessments of which factors shaped events as well as necessarily subjective estimates of how and why changes occurred. The problem with historical accounts of organisational change is that they focus more on observed and so-called rational elements rather than on how power relations, tacit agreements or even mistakes, influence the eventual outcome.

5   There is neglect of how institutional forces shape HRM. As with much research on business strategy, the principal focus is at the level of the individual organisation and an assumption is made that employers are free agents who are able to make decisions based merely on their own assessment of the situation. While this may be a more

accurate statement for organisations operating under relatively unregulated Anglo-Saxon systems of employment in the UK or the USA than it would be for firms operating on the European mainland, this is still a gross oversimplification of how decisions are made (Marchington and Vincent 2004). Notwithstanding the increasing role that European legal decisions have over employment relations in the UK, for example in relation to information and consultation, working time and parental leave, in some industries the regulatory system has always been more significant than in others. For example in chemicals, the health and safety legislation has had a major impact on HR practices, while in education and health there have been highly enforced standards and expectations in relation to minimum qualifications. As we saw in Chapter 3, the list of what might be regarded as 'best practice' HRM in the UK, and therefore undertaken by a minority of employers, is standard practice in the Netherlands due to its long history of social partnership and positive support for how national-level institutions shape employment relations (Boselie *et al* 2001). Rubery and Grimshaw (2003, p39) show clearly how institutional factors have shaped HRM in different ways in different countries, largely influenced by societal logics and trajectories. Perhaps this is best summed up by Boxall and Purcell (2003, p61) who remind us that 'firms are "embedded" in societies which regulate and influence them while also providing social capital of varying quality. The firm can never be the complete author of its own HRM.' As we saw in Chapter 1, research on multinationals comparing the effect of home country versus host country has shown how there is a deeply interactive relationship between firm-level and societal-level factors (Quintanilla and Ferner 2003).

6   The categorisation of 'real' organisations can be difficult. Crawshaw *et al* (1994) showed with their analysis of Sainsbury's 'good food costs less' slogan that the company could be seen to be stuck in the middle, neither a quality enhancer nor a cost reducer. The differences in HR practices between organisations as diverse as a research-led pharmaceutical company and a service-oriented fast-food chain are probably apparent to most observers, but it is more problematic to assess differences between two organisations in separate – or even the same – segments of the same broad product market. Why, for example, has General Motors developed its HR policies in a certain way while Ford has taken a quite different stance (Mueller 1994), or why did Tesco choose to work closely with trade unions while Sainsbury's preferred to minimise union involvement? Bird and Beechler (1995, p40) did find that organisational performance (in a sample of Japanese companies in the USA) was higher when there was a match between their business and HR strategies than when there was a mismatch. However, they did suggest that a more holistic approach was needed in which strategies in other functional areas – such as production, sales and R&D – was considered as well. As we saw in Box 12, Kelliher and Perrett (2001) found problems applying the models in their examination of the strategy–HRM links in 'designer restaurants'. Since these establishments stress the importance of a quality experience and adopt an 'innovation' strategy, application of contingency approaches would imply that a similar HR strategy would emerge, but there was little evidence that any alignment had taken place. The dominant HR practices were hard-nosed and short-term, relying on the use of a transient workforce, particularly at the front-of-house, that received only average levels of pay and few other benefits (p433). However, it was apparent that certain 'key' groups of staff – notably in the kitchens – did receive an employment package that was more in line with the strategy. Box 13 (page 112) provides another example of how it is sometimes difficult to apply 'best fit' models to real organisations.

BOX 13   BUSINESS STRATEGY AND HRM IN SPAIN

This study is based on questionnaire returns from a sample of 200 firms in South East Spain. Over half employed less than 50 staff, and a large number had been in operation for at least 20 years and were under family control. The researchers used factor analysis to develop a series of clusters that approximated to the model outlined above which differentiated between quality enhancement, cost reduction and innovation. A range of HR practices were investigated, including recruitment and selection, type of employment contract offered (temporary or permanent), training and development, reward and compensation, and appraisal. A number of statistical differences were found between the categories for business strategy, and these were broadly supportive of the Schuler predictions. Namely, the cost reduction firms were the least likely to invest in human resources, compared with the other two categories. The most important differences between the firms were:

1   Lower levels of training, teamwork, internal labour markets, employee participation and pay were found – as might be expected – at the firms with cost reduction strategies.

2   Higher levels of teamwork, temporary contracts and promotion plans were found at the innovative companies.

3   Higher levels of hierarchy in payment systems operated at the companies with a quality enhancement strategy. A number of other HR practices – such as training, promotion plans, pay and employee participation – were found at the firms with innovation strategies.

4   Despite the statistical differences between these categories, only a minority offered temporary contracts. There were similar levels of training offered compared to sales turnover, pay levels were reportedly above the sector average, and all firms said that they engaged in employee participation.

The authors note that these results should be treated with caution for a number of reasons. On average, the firms were much smaller than in most other studies and the HR function was more developed at the quality enhancement and innovation firms than at the cost reducers. In addition, the research was dependent on management interpretations of issues, and it is well known – on productivity comparisons for example – that respondents typically overestimate their own organisation's performance. Moreover, some HR issues – such as voice, trade union representation or employment security – were not examined in this study. Furthermore, there are also questions about the ability to generalise from results derived from analysis in different countries. Nevertheless, this does provide an empirical test of, and some support for, the Schuler categorisation.

Source: Adapted from Sanz-Valle R., Sabater-Sanchez R. and Aragon-Sanchez A. 'Human resource management and business strategy links: an empirical study', *International Journal of Human Resource Management*, Vol. 10, No. 4, 1999. pp655–671

Criticisms such as these indicate that is not sufficient to focus on one particular factor – say competitive strategy – and ignore the effect of others in shaping HR practice. This is not to say that contingency approaches are useless, but that the principal factors may vary in importance over time. Additionally, it is the mix of factors that is critical. Moreover, within a large, diversified company, some HR practices may appear inappropriate for certain businesses while being in line with those for others. Preferred HR styles may also vary from one country to another.

On the other hand, these models are useful for at least two sets of reasons, especially if they are used as a tool for guidance rather than a prescriptive technique. First, each model attempts to predict appropriate HR strategies from an analysis of business strategies. At the polar extremes this may fit quite well. For example, it may explain why so many British manufacturing companies that failed to move out of mature markets suffered so badly in the 1980s, with such disastrous consequences for employment. Equally, it is easy to see how the HR activities of new firms can be aligned with start-up or innovation business strategies. In short, it causes us to question the prescription that all employers should adopt 'best practice' HRM policies irrespective of their market fortunes or business strategies. Second, these kinds of analysis should encourage HR practitioners to think more carefully about how they can contribute to business goals, and in particular frame proposals in ways that can be 'sold' to senior managers. The case for a new HR initiative might have a better chance of success if it is seen to 'fit' with business strategy and it can be justified through a business case.

> Do you think the 'best fit' models can be of any practical use for employing organisations, and how might you use them if you were an HR practitioner?

RESOURCE-BASED AND INSTITUTIONALIST VIEWS

In a recent review of theory and research in strategic management, Hoskisson *et al* (1999, p417) conclude that the resource-based view (RBV) of the firm has now become the dominant framework in the area. Drawing on Penrose (1959), they argue that a focus on the internal resources at the disposal of the firm (and its agents) has produced a useful corrective from earlier paradigms that analysed performance in terms of external competitive forces. In simple terms, while theories of best fit take an 'outside-in' approach, those from the RBV perspective analyse strategy from the 'inside-out' (Paauwe and Boselie 2003, p58). In best fit studies it was assumed that internal decisions – such as those about recruitment or training – were unproblematic operational concerns. By contrast, these are precisely the sorts of issues that RBV regards as strategic because they can and do influence performance (Boxall and Purcell 2003, p73). Of course RBV can be criticised for failing to take sufficient notice of forces external to the organisation, both in terms of competitive strategies and institutional forces, as we see later, but it is now widely accepted that this approach constitutes the third dominant strand in strategic HRM – along with best practice and best fit. It is the mix of resources, including human resources, that gives each firm its unique character and may lead to differences in performance (Rugman and Verbeke 2002).

In its most recent manifestation, the notion of the RBV was rediscovered by Wernerfelt (1984) and developed into a more meaningful set of concepts by Barney (1991). According to Barney (pp105–106), the potential for sustained competitive advantage requires four firm-specific attributes – value, rarity, imperfect imitability and a lack of substitutes. *Value* means that the resource must be capable of making a difference to the organisation in the sense that it adds value in some way. *Rarity* means that there must be a shortage of these particular resources in the market to the extent that there are insufficient to go around all organisations. *Imperfect imitability* refers to the idea that it is very difficult, if not impossible, for other employers to imitate (copy) these specific rare and valuable resources, even if there were sufficient available in the market as a whole. Finally, these resources must not be easily *substitutable* by other factors so that they are rendered obsolete or unnecessary. It is the combination of these resources (human and non-human) that provides an organisation with the opportunity to gain sustained competitive advantage.

Most often the analysis turns on barriers to imitation. There are three sets of reasons for imperfect imitability (Barney, 1991, pp107–111). First, unique historical conditions make it difficult for a competitor to copy another firm's resources, even if it knows what they are, because of its particular path through history. Entering the field later in the day means that initial learning has been lost and extra efforts have to be made in order to catch up with market leaders, although poaching key individuals could be one way to do this. Secondly, due to causal ambiguity, it is difficult to understand the precise nature and mix of the resources that provide competitive advantage due to the fact that much knowledge is tacit – that is, not open to public scrutiny and often not apparent to those involved because it is held subconsciously. Third, a firm's resources 'may be very complex social phenomena [and] beyond the ability of firms to systematically manage and influence' (p110). For example, the web of interpersonal relations that develops in an organisation, or the firm's reputation in the local labour market or the industry as a whole, is often highly complex. Informal routines are deeply embedded in the organisation's social architecture (Boxall and Purcell 2003, p77).

While the RBV approach is potentially very useful in helping us understand why differences exist between firms in the same industry, it tends to neglect forces for similarity between organisations in the same industry. A paper by Oliver (1997) deals with this issue well. She suggests that the potential for applying the RBV is limited because it focuses on internal resources and does not examine the social context within which resource selection decisions take place. She advocates combining the RBV with the new institutionalism of organisation theory (DiMaggio and Powell 1983). Oliver (p701) sees firms as being influenced by powerful forces for difference *and* for similarity. While internal history, culture and politics inevitably create some idiosyncrasy, pressures for similarity within industries (DiMaggio and Powell 1983) include a mixture of external forces (for example, regulation), mimicking other successful organisations and normative traditions (for example, professional networks). These forces can be formal and informal, as well as explicit and implicit, codified and uncodified.

In a similar vein, Deephouse (1999) proposes what he terms 'strategic balance' theory, whereby firms aim to achieve a balance between differentiation and conformity. While the RBV focuses on how firms seek competitive advantage through differentiation, firms that are too different from the rest of the industry face legitimacy challenges since they do not represent what customers expect or want (p154). He argues that an attractive niche 'is one that is different from other firms' niches yet similar enough to be rational and understandable. In sum, the need for legitimacy limits the firm's ability to differentiate into specialised niches' (p162). Moreover, not all organisations aspire to be market leaders, a factor that is especially noticeable in the small firm sector and in family-owned businesses where long-run survival that generates sufficient profit to reinvest for future generations is deemed a goal in itself (Gray 1992; Hunt 1995). For further criticisms of RBV, readers are referred to Barney (2001) and Priem and Butler (2001).

Wright *et al* (1994) made the first major attempt to apply Barney's (1991) ideas on the RBV to the field of HRM. Human resources are deemed to be *valuable* because they are generally heterogeneous in both supply and demand (people vary in the skills they offer and firms vary in the jobs they offer). High-quality human resources are also *rare* because of the well-known spread in human cognitive abilities. On *inimitability*, the issue is rather less clear: human resources are potentially highly mobile, but then there are often substantial costs involved in moving from one workplace to another, and the more that skills become firm-specific the harder this is likely to become. Wright *et al* (p311) argue that it is through the 'combination of social complexity, causal ambiguity and unique historical circumstances with imperfect mobility that the value created by human resources is accrued by the firm'. Human resources are seen as *non-substitutable*, even by technology ultimately, because 'they have the potential (a) not to become obsolete and (b) to be transferable across a variety of technologies, products and markets' (p312). Accordingly, the contribution of human resources to competitive advantage is felt to be just as significant as, if not more than, other firm resources (p313). In the strategy and strategic HRM literatures, Barney's (1991) four conditions are now commonly supplemented by a fifth: *appropriability*. Theorists such as Kamoche (1996) and Coff (1997) have argued convincingly that it is important to ensure that shareholders appropriate a healthy share of the profits generated by valuable resources. Superior sources of profitability attract interest from inside and outside the firm. It is not an easy thing to ensure a good return to shareholders because key value creators are often well placed to exploit their special knowledge or negotiate for themselves.

At least five important issues have emerged from the application of RBV ideas to HRM:

- managers or workers as the key resource
- focus on people, practices or processes
- the importance of path dependency
- tackling the neglect of institutional forces and networks beyond the firm
- viability and industry leadership.

We will now discuss each of these in turn.

Managers or workers as the key resource
There are questions about whether the RBV relates to the entire human capital pool or just to senior managers who are not only likely to be rarer in quantity but also have the potential to exert greater influence over organisational performance. Wright *et al* (1994, p314) are clear it is the former because employees as a whole are directly involved in making products or delivering a service, and are typically less mobile (although that is open to question) and less able to claim excessive wages for their efforts. Mueller (1996, p757) is even more convinced that it is the 'social architecture' (cf. Barney's 1991 'social complexity') that resides in an organisation; this means that value can be dispersed throughout the organisation. This has clear implications for HR policy and practice, and organisations that are truly keen to encourage discretionary behaviour and reward good performance might seek to promote an organisational culture that is conducive to that. Workers need to know how their own activities can contribute to organisational performance and see a clear link between their efforts (as individuals or as part of a team) and rewards (either on an individual or group basis). This suggests that specific HR practices – such as performance management or employee involvement – are critically important to organisational success. It also shows the limits of trying to adopt HR practices that have been used successfully elsewhere without analysing how well they might work in different situations.

Focus on people, practices or processes
Questions have been raised as to whether the RBV relates to human resources/human capital or to the HR practices or processes that employers use to manage employment. Boxall (1996, 1998) makes the distinction between 'human capital advantage' (a stock of

exceptional human talent latent with productive possibilities) and 'organisational process advantage' (causally ambiguous, socially complex, historically evolved processes – such as learning and co-operation – that emerge and are difficult to imitate). Combined together, they form 'human resource advantage', the idea that competitive advantage can be achieved by employing better people and using better HR processes. Each element is therefore important, whether it be an individual's inherent ability to learn or their manual dexterity, or the policies and practices that are implemented in order to 'secure, nurture, retain and deploy human resources' (Kamoche 1996, p216). It is therefore clear that the employment of highly qualified and talented people can be useless without effective processes to ensure that they work well in teams and are keen to contribute to organisational goals (Wright *et al* 1994, p320). The interdependence of people and processes, the complete bundle of HR practices that combine together, and the integration with other managerial systems is illustrated graphically by Leonard (1998, pp15–16):

> **Competitively advantageous equipment can be designed and constantly improved only if the workforce is highly skilled. Continuous education is attractive only if employees are carefully selected for their willingness to learn. Sending workers throughout the world to garner ideas is cost-effective only if they are empowered to apply what they have learned to production problems.**

This simple distinction suggests important roles for HR strategy and practice, as well as for the management of culture by executive leaders. One of the biggest problems with the 'best practice' literature is that it does not really differentiate between the extent to which organisational performance is potentially improved by HR practices or by workers. For example, most of this literature focuses on HR practices (such as sophisticated selection, employment security, learning and development), which are then assumed to ensure the recruitment, retention and motivation of the best possible workers. But it should be recalled that perfectly executed HR practices – say in terms of selection – still cannot guarantee the appointment of staff who will perform at a high level, and high-quality and appropriate recruits may still be taken on with poorly executed HR practices.

The importance of path dependency

Third, RBV provides a particularly useful framework for analysing HRM because it recognises the importance of historical conditions and the different paths taken in organisations over time, as well as industry movements (Boxall 1996, p65). A number of major studies in the area have demonstrated the importance of processes, as well as procedures and outcomes, for understanding the nature of the employment relationship. This is particularly apposite in relation to the degree of trust (or lack of it) that develops over time between different organisational actors (see, for example, Purcell 1980). The informal relations that emerge at workplace level are especially difficult to imitate. This is often referred to as 'the way we do things around here' or the corporate glue that holds an organisation and its people together. The HR policies adopted may look no different from many other workplaces, on the surface at least, but they seem to combine well together to produce high levels of organisational performance and committed staff who are keen to work hard and effectively. To some extent this relates to workers' prior expectations, as well as the degree to which they believe managers are genuine in their actions. Research shows us that, irrespective of the systems in place – say, for employee involvement – the informal styles used by first-line managers has a major influence on the attitudes and behaviour of workers (Marchington 2005). It is also apparent in change programmes that employee reactions are heavily influenced by their previous experiences.

Tackling the neglect of institutional forces and networks beyond the firm

We have already noted that RBV approaches focus at the organisational level, and therefore downplays the significance of institutional arrangements at national, industry and network level beyond the workplace. As Boxall and Purcell (2003, p87) note, some firms have an immediate advantage in international competition because they are located in societies that have much better educational and technical infrastructure than do others. This reminds us that choices about HRM are shaped not just by managers but by external forces. Boselie *et al* (2003) argue that strong institutional mechanisms decrease the impact of HRM on performance because it is less likely that organisations will be able to differentiate themselves from the rest of the competition if HR practices are embedded in wider institutional norms and are therefore routinely adopted by organisations. Their work was undertaken in three settings in the Netherlands and the results showed the effects of high commitment practices were much greater in the private sector hotels than in public sector hospitals and local government. Taking this further, Paauwe and Boselie (2003, pp62–63) suggest that there is an increased degree of homogeneity across organisations in terms of their HR practices in the following situations:

■ The wide application of blueprints, introduced by consultants, which impact on HRM; in the UK context this could include the use of psychometric tests, Investors in People and partnership agreements.

■ The extent to which formalised professional education and subsequent membership of professional bodies impacts on HRM; the increasing numbers studying HRM at universities, the growth in membership of the CIPD, and the influence of professional bodies and employers' organisations over legal developments.

■ The degree to which legislation and directives at international and national level impact on HRM: these have already been discussed in Chapter 2, but include the national minimum wage, parental leave, and the information and consultation directive. The impact of the legislation on unfair dismissal shows clearly how much the law has changed HR procedures since it was first introduced.

A further area where the RBV needs development is in acknowledging the individual organisation has only a limited amount of autonomy in determining its future – much less than an 'inside-out' theory would imply. Theoretically and practically, this means that HRM, industrial relations and employment law need to be defined not solely in terms of the single employer–employee relationship, given that networks of suppliers, customers and subcontractors can influence HR practice within other firms in the network. This is particularly apparent when people are employed by agencies working at the site of another employer, but it can also take place behind the scenes when powerful customers influence the actions of suppliers – in terms of hours of work, levels of pay and trade union membership for example. Research has shown that several different employers can influence the work of staff operating in call centres (Rubery *et al* 2004) or in knowledge-intensive firms (Swart and Kinnie 2003).

Viability and industry leadership

As with the strategic management literature on the RBV, in HRM there has also been a tendency to focus almost exclusively on industry leadership and competitive advantage. Boxall and Purcell (2000, p15) suggest that 'caution is needed before we get too carried away with the idea of differentiation. It is easy under the RBV to exaggerate the differences between firms in the same sector. All viable firms in a sector need some similar resources in order to establish their identity and secure some legitimacy.' It is suggested that a set of minimum human resource investments is necessary merely to 'play the competitive game' in any industry. These are sometimes termed 'table stakes' (Hamel and Prahalad 1994, p226; Boxall and Purcell 2000, p195) or 'enabling capabilities' (Leonard 1998, p4). Rather than viewing these resources as necessary for a firm to gain competitive advantage, as a classic RBV position would, the argument is that they are critical for the firm just to remain in business and maintain a presence in its industry. In other words, firm resources that are valuable, rare, imperfectly imitable and non-substitutable may well be needed merely in order to survive and achieve satisfactory performance. In industries where significant numbers of firms go out of business, as is the case with small firms, this may be a more appropriate way to apply the ideas of the RBV than to focus on the 'differentiation' route alone (Boxall and Steeneveld 1999).

Although there have been a number of publications examining the RBV, there have been few field studies using it as a framework. To some extent, this may be down to methodological problems and the difficulty of analysing concepts that are hard to observe. The use of case studies probably offers the best way forward, although one of the earliest attempts to use the RBV in the area of HRM used questionnaires (Koch and McGrath 1996). The authors asked executives in charge of business units a series of questions about their HR practices in areas such as recruitment, development and planning. It was noted that the uncertainty associated with hiring decisions needed to be reduced in order to increase the likelihood that 'highly productive people' – who are relatively rare and difficult to imitate – would be recruited. Koch and McGrath (p339) argue that 'the better an employer "knows" the labour market, in terms of workers' supply and skills distribution, for example, the better informed its hiring choices will be'.

Probably the best RBV-informed, longitudinal, case-based study is that conducted by Boxall and Steeneveld (1999) who examined a strategic group of firms in the engineering consultancy sector in New Zealand. Five firms were studied in two rounds of data gathering over a three-year period. One of these firms went out of business during the 1987 share market crash but remained a research subject because staff in the surviving firms regularly drew comparisons with it. Of those that remained in the industry, there were many common elements in their approach to managing employment. In particular, certain key staff ('rainmakers') who generated significant business opportunities were critical to continued viability. In their analysis, Boxall and Steeneveld make a distinction between the notion of HRM for 'credible membership in the industry' and HRM for 'industry leadership' (pp456–459). In relation to the former, it is apparent that all the firms need to recruit and retain a suitable group of 'rainmakers' merely to remain in business. They conclude that their study, among other things, 'affirms the point that successful firms enact those HR strategies which enable them to survive as credible members of their industry or sector ... First and foremost, HRM must support the viability of the firm as it faces the challenges of stable operation and radical change in its sector. Those firms which fail to adequately resolve this complex of problems are doomed, sooner or later, to receivership or to take-over by better managed companies' (p459). The second, and more difficult, task is to enact those HR strategies necessary for industry leadership. How to do this is neither obvious nor easy, and it is a strategic opportunity that not all firms choose to embrace. Marchington *et al* (2003a) also demonstrated the critical importance of survival – as opposed to industry leadership – in their study of small firms in the road haulage sector. In this situation, drivers were rare due to skills shortages, valuable because they were needed to drive trucks, and not substitutable unless the firm moved into a different area of transportation. The key to attracting and holding on to staff lay in the distinctiveness of the HR practices the firms used and the degree to which their managerial systems and approaches were incapable of being imitated. Box 14 provides more detail on this.

BOX 14   HRM IN THE ROAD HAULAGE INDUSTRY

This study was undertaken in the highly competitive 'hire and reward' sector of the British road haulage industry. As with most of the firms in this sector, those studied for this project were relatively small – employing on average about 50 drivers – and the majority had been in business for several generations. Aside from major problems with the cost of fuel, a major constraint on continued growth of these firms was the shortage of good drivers.

In RBV terms, the drivers were *valuable* in that they made a difference to these organisations, not only in allowing the firm to put more trucks on the road but also in the way that they interacted with customers. Drivers were seen as a critical factor for survival, let alone success. Drivers were *rare* even though many more people were trained to LGV level than the industry needed, but had left for other jobs with more money and better working hours. There was great reluctance to use agencies to supply drivers for fear that they would damage customer relations, crash the trucks (which were expensive) or just not turn up for work. There were no obvious *substitutes* for drivers unless the company chose to move out of the 'hire and reward' market and set up an alternative transport organisation, using other forms of travel such as railways. However, these do not take away the need for some form of road transport for at least some stage of the journey. Finally, in an effort to keep staff, the firms tried to engage in HR practices that were felt to differentiate them from the rest of the market – imperfect imitability. They used 'word of mouth' recruitment to attract suitably qualified staff, they tried to offer them working conditions that might retain the better drivers, and they made efforts to make the environment preferable to that at other haulage firms. Some sought to offer additional incentives for drivers with longer service, others tried to organise social events and offer opportunities for greater involvement in the business, and some set up internal promotion ladders for drivers. But, this was not easy in the face of competition from other companies, reductions in pricing for contracts, and tighter performance specifications from the firms for which these hauliers worked. Ultimately, staying in business was as much as many of them could expect. The firms also took advantage of a wider institutional system for training drivers, as well as industry bodies and local networks that helped to support their activities and embed them in a wider framework.

This study is useful given its application to SMEs as well as to a business sector that is typically in a highly dependent product market position. Moreover, the industry is not renowned – unlike some of the 'best practice' organisations in pharmaceuticals – for its progressive HR practices. The research also illustrated well the distinction made by Boxall between the 'table stakes' that are necessary for viability and survival – moderate performance – and the HR processes that can catapult a firm into a dominant market position and sustained competitive advantage.

Source: Adapted from Marchington M., Carroll M. and Boxall P. 'Labour scarcity and the survival of small firms: a resource-based view of the road haulage industry', *Human Resource Management Journal*, Vol. 13, No. 4, 2003a. pp5–22

After reading Box 14, does it come as a surprise to you to find that not all organisations either want or expect to be market leaders? Think of examples from your own experience where this might be the case or of organisations that had a corporate goal to be the market leader when in fact you knew this was unlikely to be achieved. What impact did this have on HR practices?

CONVERTING HR STRATEGY INTO PRACTICE: BLOCKAGES AND BARRIERS

Much of the management literature is based on classical versions of strategy that presuppose its unproblematic conversion into practice. Once the plans have been laid, therefore, individual managers from different functions and departments are expected to follow the senior management line. Because of this, training and development for managers focuses on tools and techniques rather than on underlying values and behaviour. However, if we reject such superficial assumptions about organisations, it is possible to appreciate how senior management strategies may not be put into effect. In this section, we consider the blockages and barriers inherent within management circles – Chapter 10 covers employee and trade union resistance to management initiatives.

A useful starting point for discussion is Brewster *et al*'s (1983) distinction between espoused and operational policies. *Espoused* policy is a 'summation of the proposals, objectives and standards that top-level management hold and/or state they hold for establishing the organisation's approach to its employees' (p63). These may or may not be committed to paper, and in many cases they are little more than broad philosophical statements about how senior management feel towards staff – such as those exhibited in a mission statement that states 'employees are a key and valued resource'. Obviously, the phraseology used in these documents is very general, and is capable of interpretation in different ways depending on the circumstances. In contrast, *operational* policy describes 'the way senior management are seen to order industrial relations (and human resource) priorities vis-à-vis those of other policies' (p64). This may well be done subconsciously, as well as with intent, since it is reflected in managerial value systems and is clearly moulded by issues arising on a daily basis. If two policies are seen to be in conflict – say, a commitment to staff development and to be customer-responsive – then, it is argued, HR policies typically take a lower priority. There are many examples from different industries illustrating the way in which espoused policies are ignored, amended or downgraded in the face of conflicting pressures on organisations.

In order to put strategies into effect, 'champions' are required within organisations. Champions are managers who have the energy and the ability to lead new initiatives, to ensure that others are persuaded of their merits, and are prepared to commit themselves to ensuring that strategies are embedded in the workplace. By their nature, however, champions tend to be mobile and career-oriented, often moving to new positions soon after introducing fresh initiatives. As Ahlstrand (1990, p23) notes, in relation to a succession of productivity deals at Esso's Fawley refinery, each initiative received a high-profile launch and commanded powerful symbolic significance within the company. The champions made great use of what Barlow (1989) calls 'impression management', making their activities visible to more senior managers, with the result that they were often promoted soon after implementing a new deal. In short, soon after making an impression, champions move on to other posts, either within the organisation or elsewhere. Those left with responsibility for maintaining these new initiatives feel little ownership of them, are less committed to making them work, and in any event want to introduce their own ideas in order to gain promotion themselves. A cycle is set in motion, with the inevitable consequence of fads and fashions, cynicism and short-termism (Marchington *et al* 1993a; Marchington 2005).

Which of the following statements do you think is more accurate, and why?

1 'Champions are necessary to achieve organisational change.'

2 'Champions are ultimately the major cause of failure to achieve change in organisations.'

Conflicts and contradictions can occur within the ranks of management both on a hierarchical and a functional basis. In this chapter we deal with the former, given that this relates to questions of vertical integration and the conversion of strategy into practice. The question of interdepartmental conflicts is considered in Chapter 5 as part of the discussion about horizontal integration and links between line managers and their HR colleagues. Broadly, there are five separate sets of reasons why middle managers and supervisors might not implement HR strategies in the way desired by their senior colleagues.

- lack of identification with employer goals
- problems of work overload
- limited investment in training and development
- the value of retaining some flexibility at workplace level
- failure to apply organisational rules.

Each of these is discussed below.

Lack of identification with employer goals

Many middle managers and supervisors do not identify closely with employer goals, but instead view themselves as distinct from senior management (Thompson and McHugh 2002, pp94–96). There are several parts to this argument. Scase and Goffee's (1989, p186) conceptualisation of 'reluctant managers' sees persisting class divisions within British employing organisations as the reason why supervisors fail to share senior management views. First-line managers might feel that they have escaped from the working class, but are not accepted into the managerial class, to some extent stuck in the middle and unable or unwilling to align themselves either with workers or managers. They may also have doubts about the validity of senior management's ideas, especially those philosophies that espouse employee involvement and use the language of 'resourceful humans', regarding attempts to empower workers as akin to soft management (Marchington *et al* 1993a; Denham *et al* 1997; Heller *et al* 1998; Dundon *et al* 2004). The language of teamworking and empowerment, for example, while potentially attractive to more senior managers, sometimes appears threatening and problematic to first-line managers whose authority has been built on technical expertise and the restriction of information to the shop floor (Marchington 2001, p241). They are often cynical about the value and potential life span of new management initiatives, arguing that they 'have seen all this before' (Yong and Wilkinson 1999).

Feelings of role ambiguity and insecurity are reinforced if supervisors and middle managers lose their jobs or find their existing skills are no longer appropriate for modern working practices. Though written some time ago, Scase and Goffee's (1989, p191) conclusion is still very apposite: 'corporations may succeed in cultivating "cultures of excellence" and introducing more flexible organisational forms, but predominant practice in Britain will tend, we suspect, to lead mainly to the compliance of reluctant managers'. Supervisors often receive little genuine support from senior managers, and they are often left to fend for themselves when things go wrong or even disciplined when their attempts to maintain production or customer service misfire. Anxieties are fuelled as their own job security is lessened and they find little attempt to 'involve' them in management decisions (Rubery *et al* 2003). It is rare for line managers and supervisors to be involved and given responsibility and authority during change programmes even though this makes sense (Fenton O'Creevy, 2001, p37).

Problems of work overload

Line managers and supervisors already suffer from work overload, conflicting requirements from senior management, and a lack of explicit rewards for undertaking the HR aspects of their jobs. Like most staff, they are being asked to take on extra duties and find it difficult to squeeze yet more into their working hours. Fenton O'Creevy (2001, p36) found that de-layering and job loss put even greater pressures on line managers by reducing the time available for implementing new initiatives. However, rather then seeing negative attitudes as the problem, and therefore regarding supervisors as scapegoats, Fenton O'Creevy (p37) reckons that management systems are to blame. He questions whether or not existing reward and appraisal mechanisms encourage positive behaviours or if there is sufficient time left in the working day to devote to staff development. It is hardly surprising if line managers concentrate on achieving targets they know will be used to assess their performance at appraisal (Bach 2000). If meeting production deadlines, having zero defects or reducing queue lengths gains a higher priority when they are appraised than does regular team briefings, staff development or low levels of absenteeism, then they are bound to focus on the former set of goals. First-line managers pick up signals from their more senior colleagues about the ordering of priorities irrespective of what is contained within the formal mission statement and, understandably, aim to meet these demands rather than more ephemeral, 'soft' HR goals. In other words, the heavier the workload, the more difficult it is for line managers to satisfy HR objectives. Even at the 'leading edge' organisations studied by Gratton *et al* (1999), it was clear that a series of pressures led the line managers to place a low premium on HR activities at work. In a separate paper (McGovern *et al* 1997, p26), they conclude that:

- there are limited institutional pressures to reinforce the importance of carrying out HR activities
- the short-term nature of managerial work leads them to put greater emphasis on the achievement of numbers per se rather than the achievement of numbers through people
- downsizing and de-layering limits the time that line managers can allow for HR activities.

Limited investment in training and development

Given the prominence accorded in mission statements to 'investing in employees', it might be expected that considerable time and effort would be expended on developing first-line managers. The reality, however, is rather different, and training in people management has tended to be a low priority. Yet more worrying is the feeling that line managers and supervisors may not have sufficient interpersonal skills to cope with the responsibilities required to lead change programmes at workplace level (Cunningham and Hyman 1995; Marchington *et al* 2001). Too often, insufficient time is allocated to the training of first-line managers because senior managers are keen to implement new initiatives with a minimum of delay. This has been particularly apparent from our own studies of employee involvement. Training in how to run a quality circle, for example, could consist of little more than a half-hour session on 'how not to communicate' followed by an amusing video illustrating how things went wrong elsewhere. Occasionally, a speaker may be invited from another organisation to explain their approach and answer questions, but there is little attempt to give supervisors the chance to practise their skills (Marchington and Wilkinson 2005). At one of the banks studied by Marchington *et al* (2001, p56), there was an explicit recognition that 'we haven't done enough training to support our line managers in how to hold team meetings ... certainly the style of managing in an organisation as big as ours is always going to be a problem'.

The value of retaining some flexibility at workplace level

First-line managers do not generally like to be too constrained by instructions from above, but wish to retain some flexibility to adapt rules at the workplace. This aspect of behaviour – termed 'management by commission' by Brown (1973) – allows supervisors to vary the application of rules, to provide themselves with leeway so as to reward, ignore or discipline workers on a selective basis. This can work not only to reinforce managerial control over recalcitrant employees, but also as a way of showing leniency or providing a negotiating counter as appropriate. This notion of 'deal-making' (Klein 1984) gives supervisors discretion in dealing with employees, by allowing staff some flexibility (say, in taking time off) in return for an expectation they will work harder or stay later in order to complete a rush job. In a sense, this allows supervisors to be seen as independent from the more oppressive face of management. In each of these cases, employers gain from a limited degree of rule-bending. However, this can also work to the detriment of their plans or policies, such as when unacceptable precedents are set in relation to disciplinary issues or custom and practice leads to limitations on worker performance (Earnshaw *et al* 2000). This notion of flexibility becomes even more complicated when organisational boundaries are blurred across networks of suppliers or where traditional hierarchies are disordered through interventions by clients (Marchington *et al* 2004c).

Failure to apply organisational rules

A final reason why it may be difficult to achieve vertical integration is that managers can be unaware that they are breaking or not following organisational rules, and in the process creating precedents that may run counter to employer goals: Brown (1973) terms this 'management by omission'. In these situations, first-line managers may not realise that rules are being broken, as for example with workers who appear to comply with health and safety instructions but deliberately flout them when the supervisor is elsewhere. Equally, senior managers may agree to requests from staff that undermine previous agreements made by a line manager, so creating awkward precedents. This is particularly problematic in the employee relations area when an agreement in one department may be used as a bargaining counter by workers elsewhere in efforts to improve their pay and conditions. What makes acts of omission so hard to manage is that they are often not noticed until a later date, perhaps when being used to support a case against disciplinary action (Earnshaw *et al* 2000).

> Some might see this discussion as being unduly pessimistic because it assumes that supervisors are unlikely to support senior management actions. What could be done to encourage supervisors to support management?

CONCLUSIONS

This chapter has reviewed material examining the way in which HR strategies might be aligned with wider organisational goals. 'Best fit' HRM is the idea that HR practice should and does vary between organisations depending on business strategy or product market circumstances – as we said earlier these are 'outside-in' theories. This approach is useful not only for countering the more simplistic versions of 'best practice' HRM, but also because it appears to reflect organisational reality – at least at a broad level. The notion that HRM in a leading pharmaceuticals firm may differ from that in a small textiles factory, or that a local authority may manage its staff differently from a restaurant, can be explained to some extent by the best fit analyses. However, greater problems emerge when we attempt to explain differences between two firms in a similar market position. The difficulty is that the models used are top-down and deterministic, driven by classical theories of strategy, whereas it is clear that a range of factors can influence HRM at work. Amongst the most important of these are the style and philosophy of senior management and the differing ways in which organisations seek to achieve competitive advantage. By contrast, the resource-based view of the firm is especially helpful as it focuses on internal resources ('inside-out') and the specific, sometimes unique, factors that enable organisations to remain viable in the market as well as achieve sustained competitive advantage. Ultimately, any analysis of HRM has to take into account the role institutional forces and internal politics play in shaping managerial actions. In particular, employer goals may be adapted, ignored or resisted by managers at lower levels in the hierarchy or in different departments. To conceive of management as a cohesive, omnipotent and omniscient entity is clearly unrealistic as different managerial functions typically fight for influence within organisations.

USEFUL READING

BOXALL P. *and* PURCELL J. *Strategy and Human Resource Management*. London, Palgrave Macmillan. 2003.

COFF R. 'Human assets and management dilemmas: coping with hazards on the road to resource-based theory', *Academy of Management Review*, Vol. 22, No. 2, 1997. pp374–402.

DELERY J. *and* DOTY H. 'Modes of theorising in strategic human resource management: tests of universalistic, contingency and configurational performance predictions', *Academy of Management Journal*, Vol. 39, No. 4, 1996. pp802–835.

FENTON O'CREEVY M. 'Employee involvement and the middle manager: saboteur or scapegoat?' *Human Resource Management Journal*, Vol. 11, No. 1, 2001. pp24–40.

MARCHINGTON M., CARROLL M. *and* BOXALL P. 'Labour scarcity and the survival of small firms: a resource-based view of the road haulage industry', *Human Resource Management Journal*, Vol. 13, No. 4, 2003a. pp5–22.

OLIVER C. 'Sustainable competitive advantage: combining institutional and resource-based views', *Strategic Management Journal*, Vol. 18, No. 9, 1997. pp697–713.

PAAUWE J. *and* BOSELIE P. 'Challenging "strategic HRM" and the relevance of the institutional setting', *Human Resource Management Journal*, Vol. 13, No. 3, 2003. pp56–70.

PURCELL J. 'The search for best practice and best fit in human resource management: chimera or cul-de-sac?', *Human Resource Management Journal*, Vol. 9, No. 3, 1999. pp26–41.

RUTHERFORD M., BULLER P. *and* McMULLEN P. 'Human resource management over the life cycle of small to medium sized firms', *Human Resource Management*, Vol. 42, No. 4, 2003. pp321–335.

Sisson K. *and* Storey J. *The Realities of Human Resource Management*. Milton Keynes, Open University Press. 2000.

Changing Responsibilities for HRM

INTRODUCTION

HRM had its origins in activities designed, in part at least, to ameliorate the worst effects of industrial capitalism, and its pioneers were individuals with a strong social conscience – such as Seebohm Rowntree and Jesse Boot. On occasions, the HR function has been regarded as the conscience of employers, there to ensure that in the pursuit of more productive and efficient work the human dimension is not overlooked. The ethical and professional perspective is demonstrated by what some would see as obsession with rules, compliance with legal standards or the maintenance of employee voice. But professionalism should also relate to how organisations can achieve greater productivity and efficiency through the adoption of up-to-date and proven HR practices, as well as making a contribution to societal goals and the interests of all stakeholders. Accordingly, consideration of how the HR function can be structured to offer the best possible service to its customers – line managers, individual members of staff, the organisation and society as a whole – is also a key consideration. In recent times there has been lots of interest in alternative forms of organisation, typically involving the outsourcing of HR administration and processes to specialist firms or the setting up of shared service centres to cover the organisation as a whole or to provide HR services to more than one organisation. At the same time, many aspects of HR work have been devolved to line managers, and HR specialists act as advisors to support them in achieving organisational goals. In this vein, efforts to persuade line managers to implement 'best practice' HRM is a clear sign of professionalism, in much the same way that engineers would be expected to disseminate new ideas on the latest technology. Finally, however organisations choose to deliver HRM – through an internal HR function, an outsourced facility or a shared service centre – it is increasingly expected that this is seen to add value. This has led to interest in the measurement of how adequately HRM is being delivered, and concern for ways in which its services might be provided more effectively through what are sometimes referred to as 'HR metrics'.

A key feature of this chapter is the recognition that HRM is ambiguous and beset with tensions between what Legge (1995, p10) calls 'two potentially incompatible orientations' – the 'caring' and the 'control' elements of the role. Both of these were apparent in the early days of the welfare role, whereby employees were given assistance at work, largely – though not exclusively – to ensure their contribution could be enhanced. It is also illustrated by the dual usage of the term 'counselling': it is either a non-directive activity helping staff come to terms with anxieties or shorthand for the preliminary stages of disciplinary proceedings. In addition, HR practitioners are often seen as intermediaries between managers and employees, ready to listen to both but on the side of neither, and applicants for HR positions sometimes mistakenly think that they want to go into personnel because they 'like working with people' or they see themselves conciliating between warring factions. In reality HR specialists are expected to contribute directly or indirectly to the achievement of employer objectives, something that is reinforced by increased interest in metrics, measurement and quantification.

By the end of this chapter, readers should be able to:

■ **identify the most appropriate roles for the HR function in different types of organisation**

■ **work in partnership with other stakeholders to overcome blockages and barriers to change**

■ **make recommendations about the advantages and disadvantage of outsourcing some or all elements of HRM and adopting new models of service delivery.**

In addition, they should understand and be able to explain:

■ **the different models available for analysing the role of the HR function**

■ **the implementation of HRM by line managers, HR specialists and consultants, and how these interact with each other**

■ **the contribution that HRM can make to organisational success and the measures used to illustrate this.**

THE DEVELOPMENT OF HR AS A SPECIALIST FUNCTION

The emergence of the personnel function

Several books provide potted histories of how HRM emerged: some describe the major changes from its early roots in Victorian Britain (see, for example, Crichton 1968; Farnham 1990), while others present a sociological critique of the occupation (Watson 1977; Legge 1995). Both approaches make it clear that a wide range of activities is included within the boundaries of HRM. The early roots were in welfare, championed by social reformers who displayed a genuine paternalistic concern for their workers. Often driven by strong religious motivations, such as Quakerism and non-conformism, they were keen to improve working conditions and provide their employees with assistance should they fall on hard times. Nevertheless, reforms were implemented within a clear business framework, in which tight controls were maintained in relation to discipline, time-keeping, and output (Crichton 1968, p15). Many of the earliest welfare workers were women, especially in munitions factories during the First World War, and these specialists were brought in to make work more tolerable for the female workers who worked on the production lines. Some of the first companies to invest in personnel are still well-known names: Boots, Cadbury's, Lever Brothers, and Rowntree (now owned by Nestlé). There are alternative interpretations about how the subject and the specialist function developed since then. Its history can be viewed sequentially, with different aspects of the subject coming to the fore in different time periods, or it can be seen in a summative fashion, with each new set of activities representing an addition to the HR portfolio (Torrington 1998). The other themes are:

■ *Administration* – This comprises what is now seen as the transactional aspects of HR work, including duties such as dealing with job applications, organising induction programmes and maintaining employee records. These sorts of activity have formed a central part of the role since the 1940s, and are now important as a support and trigger mechanism within a computerised personnel information system (Taylor 2002c).

■ *Negotiation* – This aspect of HRM became more prominent in the 1960s and 1970s, as employers responded to growing trade union influence and the rise of workplace bargaining. It is most apparent in pay negotiations although it is also used when managers try to introduce new working practices or deal with grievances, and it requires different skills from many other elements of HR work (Gennard and Judge 2002).

■ *Legal expertise* – Once employment legislation became more prominent in Britain from the 1960s, there has been an increased need for people with specialist expertise in this area. This has led to substantial procedural reform in HR practices and now most HR professionals will have some working knowledge of the law and be aware of when to ask for expert advice (see Lewis and Sargeant 2004).

■ *Organisation development* – Although there was some interest in this area from a few large companies during the late 1960s and early 1970s, this has become more central during the last decade. It is often connected with ideas on change management, learning and organisation culture, and is portrayed in terms such as empowerment, capabilities and knowledge management (Whittington and Mayer 2002).

■ *Business partner* – Many of these aspects are now pulled together under the banner of strategic human resource management in which the HR function is prominent at the most senior levels in the organisation. The style varies depending on whether the emphasis is on 'human *resource* management' or the 'management of *resourceful humans*'. The notion of business partner (Ulrich 1998) is examined more fully in the next section.

Tensions can also occur between different elements of the HR function, especially if it is highly specialised and differentiated. For example, employee relations specialists are typically more inclined to recognise the ambiguity and tensions inherent in the employment relationship than their colleagues elsewhere in the HR function and believe more in the value of structures as a key aspect of HRM. Similarly, issues may fall within the province both of personnel and other management functions. For example, corporate communications may be the responsibility of specialist functions such as sales and marketing, public relations or planning, as well as HR. Given contrasting traditions and backgrounds, it is highly likely that different management functions will devise alternative 'solutions' for these issues.

How many of these aspects of HRM are evident at your place of work or one with which you are familiar? Are some more prominent than others?

The development of the professional body

The first seeds for a professional body for personnel practitioners were sown in 1913 when Seebohm Rowntree invited firms to send representatives to a conference of welfare workers in York. The 48 people present decided to form an Association of Employers 'interested in industrial betterment and of welfare workers engaged by them' (Niven 1967, p36). The Welfare Workers' Association, as it became known, joined with the North Western Area Industrial Association six years later to form the Welfare Workers' Institute, with a membership of 700 (Farnham 1990, p22). After the First World War membership fell as the welfare tradition lost ground, and the association was renamed the Institute of Labour Management in 1931, a name it kept until after the Second World War. During this time the type of duties undertaken by practitioners in the field broadened to include wages, employment, joint consultation, health and safety, employee services and welfare, as well as education and training (pp22–23). In 1946 the Institute of Personnel Management (IPM) was formed, thus reflecting this broader orientation, and it remained in existence until 1994 when

Table 13   *Membership of the professional body – selected years since 1913*

Year	Number of members
1913	48
1919	700
1939	760
1956	3,980
1971	14,260
1981	22,620
1990	41,000
1994	75,500
2001	110,015
2004	120,713

the IPM joined with the Institute of Training and Development (ITD) to form the Institute of Personnel and Development (IPD). Chartered status was granted in 2000 when the name was changed to the Chartered Institute of Personnel and Development (CIPD).

Since 1913 membership has grown dramatically, and Table 13 illustrates how numbers have increased substantially during certain periods, often in the earlier days following mergers and rebadging. The merger between the IPM and the ITD added about 20,000 to the membership of the IPM, so the vast amount of this growth has been due to new members, with membership almost trebling over the last 15 years, although the period since 2001 has seen a less dramatic rate of increase.

The CIPD is Europe's largest professional body for individuals specialising in HRM. It operates a series of committees at national and local level, as well as having a sizeable number of staff at its London headquarters – including a library service. It has national committees, such as membership and education or employment relations, comprising members from the branches, as well as HQ staff and ex-officio members. It is at local level that most CIPD members have the initial opportunity to be more involved in the work of the Institute, and this is a critical part of the whole structure, with approximately 50 branches across the country. The CIPD's mission is to:

- lead in the development and promotion of good practice in the field of the management and development of people, for application both by professional members and by their organisational colleagues
- serve the professional interests of members
- uphold the highest ideals in the management and development of people.

To what extent does the CIPD fulfil criteria typically associated with a professional body, and do its members deserve the title 'professional'? Freidson (1973, p22) defines professionalisation as:

> ❛ a process by which an organised occupation, usually but not always by virtue of making a claim to special esoteric competence and to concern for the quality of its work and its benefits to society, obtains the exclusive right to perform a particular kind of work, control training for and access to it, and control the right of determining and evaluating the way their work is performed. ❜

The CIPD meets several elements in Freidson's definition well. The Professional Development Scheme (PDS) lays down a set of standards (in the form of performance indicators) to be met by all aspiring members, and these have to be updated by Continuing Professional Development (CPD) on a regular basis. CPD is particularly important when it comes to upgrading decisions, and members have to demonstrate not only what they have done but also indicate the impact this has had on their employing organisations and the broader specialist community. Standards for the majority of new entrants are maintained by a formal coursework and examination assessment scheme, overseen by the CIPD Vice President and Director for Membership and Education, as well as by Chief Examiners appointed for their expertise in the area. Graduate membership can be gained through other routes as well – for example through exempted courses or by the professional assessment, Accreditation of Prior Certificated Learning or NVQ/SVQ routes. CIPD standards are monitored by external examiners and professional advisers and are subject to regular re-accreditation – typically on a five-year basis. The Chief Moderator–Standards, introduced along with the new PDS in 2001, plays a central role in maintaining comparable standards across the whole range of entry routes (Whittaker 2001).

All members of the CIPD are expected to comply with the Code of Professional Conduct, which can be downloaded from the CIPD website. Its principal elements are:

- endeavouring to enhance the standing and good name of the profession
- continually seeking to improve performance and update skills and knowledge
- seeking to achieve the fullest possible development of people
- adopting HR processes and structures that enable their employer to achieve its goals
- maintaining fair and reasonable standards in the treatment of people
- promoting policies that remove unfair discrimination for any reason
- respecting the legitimate needs and requirements for confidentiality
- using due diligence and timely, accurate and appropriate standards of advice
- recognising the limitations of their own knowledge and ability.

A failure to follow the Code of Professional Conduct could lead, ultimately, to expulsion from the Institute, as of course would a failure to pay subscriptions. In terms of qualifications structure, research and influence, therefore the CIPD satisfies many of Freidson's criteria.

However, despite its size the CIPD is not able to claim exclusivity in the performance of HR work because managers in the field are not required to gain professional qualifications before being able to practise – unlike professions such as law, medicine or dentistry. Many organisations do not employ specialist HR professionals and many of those undertaking HR work are not members of the CIPD. Not surprisingly, HR specialists are more likely to be found in larger organisations and workplaces, as well as in foreign-owned firms, the public sector and in industries such as financial services, gas, electricity and water (Cully *et al* 1999, pp51–52). HR in the public sector comes in for particular criticism, although Lupton and Shaw (2001) suggest this is based on mythical stereotypes. All line managers have some responsibility for HRM at work. However, while line managers may actually implement HR practice, it is typical for HR specialists to have designed the policies and procedures governing this work. Moreover, even if an employer does not employ a dedicated specialist, 'good practice' in the field may well have been developed initially by experts in the function – either through research or the experiences of other employing organisations that do possess specialist expertise. Apart from accountancy, however, the CIPD is in a much stronger position than most management bodies, and its research activity influences government and industry. The PKI (professional knowledge and information) group at CIPD produces a wide range of publications in the form of fact sheets, surveys and guides, as well as issuing papers covering topics such as recruitment and labour turnover, absence and learning and development.

ANALYSING THE ROLE OF THE HR FUNCTION

There have been many attempts to categorise the work of the HR function in order to analyse its variety, diversity and complexity. Some writers argue that it is possible to identify discrete roles that are logically distinct from one another, even if tied together by a single continuum. Others regard the different categories as cumulative, with each role building upon the previous one, resulting in categories of increasing complexity. Yet others argue that individuals or departments display multiple roles, so it is possible for more than one category to be in evidence at any organisation at the same time. Each of the categorisations explicitly or implicitly assesses how the HR function can best contribute to improved performance. See Table 14 (page 132) for a summary of some of the major categorisations.

One of the oldest, and arguably still one of the best, models was proposed by Karen Legge (1978) over 25 years ago. She argued personnel managers could adopt one of a series of strategies to gain power and influence within their organisations. The first is *conformist innovation* whereby HR managers attempt to relate their work clearly to the dominant values and norms in the organisation, aiming simply to satisfy the requirements of senior managers. An alternative approach is *deviant innovation*. Here, the personnel specialist subscribes to a quite different set of norms, gaining credibility and support for ideas driven by social values rather than strict economic criteria. This could include concerns about equal opportunities, long working hours or empowerment. Finally, there is a contingent role, that of *problem-solver*, in which the HR contribution is assessed through its ability to identify and resolve problems for the employer.

An alternative classification is Tyson and Fell's (1986) 'building site' analogy in which three roles are identified for the personnel function, differentiated along a continuum defined by factors such as the planning time for HR, the degree of discretion exercised by personnel and the extent to which it helps to create organisational culture. The role with least discretion is termed *clerk of the works*, where the HR system provides administrative and clerical support – now termed transactional work – to line managers. In the middle is the *contracts manager*, a role most likely in industries with a significant trade union presence, where systems and procedures are heavily formalised, and the underlying emphasis is on trouble-shooting. The final role – *the architect* – is the most sophisticated; it is concerned with grand designs at a

Table 14   *Models of the human resource function*

Author/date	Categories for the HR role	Reasons for differentiation
Legge (1978)	Conformist innovator Deviant innovator Problem-solver	Ways to gain power and influence
Tyson and Fell (1986)	Clerk of the works Contracts manager Architect	Time span for decision-making Degree of discretion Involvement of HR
Storey (1992) Caldwell (2003)	Handmaiden/service provider Regulator Adviser Change-maker	Level: strategic or tactical Degree of interventionism
Wilkinson and Marchington (1994) Procter and Currie (1999)	Facilitator Internal contractor Hidden persuader Change agent	Level in the hierarchy: senior or junior Profile: high or low
Ulrich (1998)	Administrative expert Employee champion Change agent Business partner	Level, focus and time frame Managing processes or people

senior level and the integration of HR into broader business plans. Architects are expected to take the lead in creating the 'right' culture for the organisation, operating as business manager first and personnel professional second (Caldwell 2001). Although it is tempting to do so, Tyson and Fell (1986, p24) reject the assumption that HR assumes greater maturity as it develops along the continuum. They argue that the choice of role is contingent upon organisational circumstances, and each variant may be found at each level in the hierarchy. Tyson and Fell's model has been refined by Monks (1993). Based on a sample of Irish organisations, she suggests it is possible to identify four categories rather than three, with an extra role in between the contracts manager and the architect. Monks (p36) also argues the roles are cumulative rather than discrete, such that in organisations where the architect-type role is present, so are the other three.

A further set of categorisations is based on ideal-types that differentiate between roles along two separate independent axes. The best known are: Storey (1992), recently re-examined and updated by Caldwell (2003); and Wilkinson and Marchington (1994) which has been re-tested by Procter and Currie (1999). Broadly each proposes a fourfold 'map' based on two cross-cutting dimensions: the degree to which HR is strategic or operational, and the extent

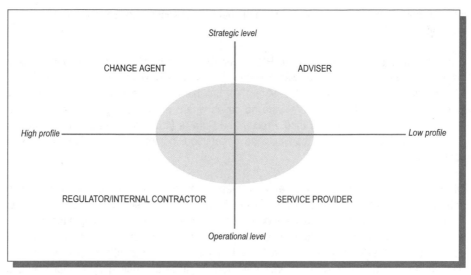

Figure 4 *Categorising the role of the HR function*

Sources: Adapted from Storey J. *Developments in the Management of Human Resources.* Oxford, Blackwell. 1992; Wilkinson A. and Marchington M. 'Total quality management: Instant pudding for the personal function?', *Human Resource Management Journal*, Vol. 5, No. 1, 1994. pp33–49; Caldwell R. 'The changing roles of personnel managers: old ambiguities, new uncertainties', *Journal of Management Studies*, Vol. 40, No. 4, 2003. pp983–1004.

to which it intervenes and has a high profile. The former dimension makes the simple distinction between policy and practice, long- and short-term time horizons, and the level in the hierarchy at which decision-making takes place. The latter dimension reflects continuing tensions about the contribution HR specialists make to organisational decision-making, and the extent to which it is possible to measure their contribution in quantitative or financial terms. The labels representing each of these four main types of HR specialist have been adapted from the different models for simplicity and it is presented in Figure 4.

The most significant role is that of *change agent*, a role that aims to establish new HR cultures, seeking ways in which to persuade the Board to adopt new HR initiatives and in eliciting employee commitment. Change agents can be proponents of either soft or hard HRM, and they gain credibility by framing their proposals in ways that are attractive to other senior managers. This role is likely to be particularly prominent when the organisation is going forward with a clear vision and, somewhat surprisingly, it was the second most common role identified by Caldwell's (2003, p1000) research. The most common role was that of *adviser*, with more than 80 per cent of his respondents claiming this was the main aspect of their work or one of the most important. Advisers operate at a strategic level but tend to work behind the scenes in helping to shape HR policies and practices, in a sense providing 'cabinet office' support for senior managers. Third, there is the *service provider* role (named 'handmaiden' by Storey and 'facilitator' by Wilkinson and Marchington), a low level operational role in which HR responds to routine problems raised by line managers, being driven almost totally by their needs and demands. In the Caldwell study, this was only rarely the main role occupied by HR specialists but it comprised a significant part of what rather more actually did at work (p994). Finally, the *regulator/internal contractor* also works at the operational level but is much more prominent either in dealings with trade unions or with other functions internal or external to the organisation – say, when large parts of the HR function is subcontracted. As the regulator has declined in significance since the time of Storey's initial categorisation, the internal contractor has become more prominent in response to shifting organisational demands.

It is also important to stress that the HR function at one site or one organisation typically plays more than one role. There was evidence of a service provider role at each of the 15 sites studied by Marchington *et al* (1993b, p36), but this was the only role observed at only four sites. Similarly, although there were no cases where all four categories were present, three roles were present at one third. Procter and Currie's (1999) study of the NHS supports the idea that the HR function can best be understood in terms of its multiple roles and contributions.

Of course, there are dangers with each of these roles as well. The change agent, while potentially the most influential because of its high profile and strategic contribution, also runs the risk of significant costs if problems occur with any interventions. By taking such a visible role, the HR function may create enemies within the organisation, and interventions therefore have to be successful in order to prevent the build-up of overt dissent from elsewhere. The problem for the adviser is almost entirely the opposite, since the managing director may use HR as a confidante precisely because of its assumed neutrality. Unfortunately, continued effectiveness is dependent upon sustained support from its champion, and the basic problem is that other managers may be unaware of this contribution. The service provider suffers in a similar way because the support HR provides to line managers is often hard to evaluate and is difficult to isolate from what is typically expected. This is not a problem for the regulator/internal contractor, due to its very public role and often the commitments made by the HR function to its internal customers. However, there is a risk that the function may be contracted-out if it fails to meet targets.

> Consider whether there are circumstances (internal and external to the organisation) under which each of these roles is more likely to occur. Is it possible for HR practitioners and departments to simply 'choose' a role – such as change agent – they like the best?

The final model is that developed by Ulrich (1997, 1998). He acknowledges that there is 'good reason for HR's beleaguered reputation. It is often ineffective, incompetent and costly; in a phrase, it is value-sapping' (Ulrich, 1998, p124). In order to overcome this reputation, he argues that HR needs to adopt four roles – see Figure 5. These are:

- *Business partner* – HR acts as a partner in strategy execution, not in the making of strategy, but in ensuring that it is developed and put into effect. HR defines the 'organisational architecture', carrying out audits and renovating those aspects of the organisation in need of repair. In short, the HR function plays a significant part in creating the systems and processes that help deliver organisational success.

- *Administrative expert* – HR acts as an expert in the way that work is organised and executed, and delivers administrative efficiency both in terms of its own function and for the whole organisation, typically through information technology. This happens in call centres and shared service operations that deal with the transactional aspects of work – such as salary administration and personnel records. Ulrich (1998, p129) argues that success in this role can help HR to gain higher status: 'improving efficiency will build HR's credibility which, in turn, will open the door for it to become a partner in executing strategy'.

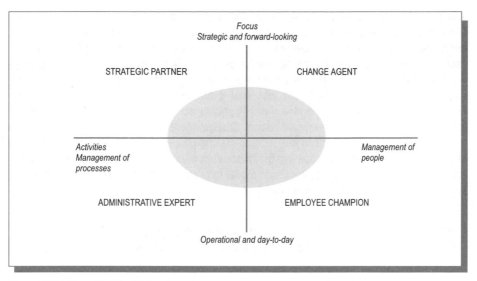

Figure 5 *Ulrich's model of the HR function*

Source: Developed from Ulrich D. 'A new mandate for human resources', *Harvard Business Review*, Jan–Feb 1998, pp125–134

- *Employee champion* – HR acts as a voice for employees both in representing their concerns to senior managers and in working to improve their contribution, their commitment and engagement. Ulrich suggests that the HR function should be held accountable for ensuring that employees are motivated and willing to work beyond contract. This envisages a major role for the HR function in assisting line managers to achieve employee engagement.

- *Change agent* – HR acts as 'an agent of continuous transformation, shaping processes and a culture that together improve the organisation's capacity for change' (Ulrich 1998, p125). He argues that the HR function needs to help the organisation embrace and capitalise on change, as well as transform vision statements into practical realities in the workplace.

Ulrich's contributions have certainly had a major impact on the HR profession, especially in how to achieve a position as business partner (Guest and King 2004, p419), as well as develop shared services and e-HR. What impact has it had on the ground? The respondents – typically senior HR managers – to Guest and King's study (p420) were somewhat reluctant to beat their way into the boardroom 'armed only with rhetoric about people as the key resource, somewhat ambiguous evidence about the impact of HRM on performance and a set of professional but widely un-welcomed bureaucratic procedures'. Caldwell (2003, p1003) echoes this sentiment, suggesting that 'Ulrich's prescriptive vision may promise more than HR professionals can ever really deliver.' A survey of HR professionals in 118 organisations (IRS Employment Review 795a 2004) found administrative work was still dominant and that, despite wanting more of a strategic role, it took up very little of the HR function's time. In a sense, the excitement about the Ulrich models is strange, given that they do not differ dramatically from those reviewed above. At least one of the dimensions (level/focus) used by Ulrich is similar to those that were employed by Storey. Tyson's architect has much in common with the business partner role, and his employee champion is not so different from Legge's deviant innovator. Moreover, his view that the HR function should adopt multiple roles tells us nothing more than Wilkinson and Marchington did. A more careful analysis of his vision suggests the roles may not be quite so influential after all. For example, the business partner is 'an architect within an already constructed building' – perhaps doing little more than choosing the right wallpaper! The administrative expert is responsible solely for the ways work is organised within the HR area and not work redesign throughout the organisation. The employee champion is tasked with jobs that trade unions ordinarily do in most large organisations in Britain, and the idea that HR should act as the workers' 'voice' smacks of paternalism rather than organisational justice. Change agents do not actually execute change themselves or play a major role in the decision-making process, but instead facilitate the work of other senior managers. In other words, rather than offering the vision of a new and more strategic role for HR managers, the Ulrich model may merely confirm their position as useful support staff rather than strategic masters.

> Read Dave Ulrich's paper in the *Harvard Business Review* (January–February 1998), and decide whether or not the business partner role is an achievable reality for the HR function.

CHANGING MODELS OF HR SERVICE DELIVERY

Much of the above discussion assumes that there is a specialist function internal to the organisation, based either at workplace or regional level, which deals with HR issues. Of course, apart from the subcontracting of certain aspects of work – such as specialist recruitment and selection, technical training and team development of senior members of staff – this was a pretty accurate picture. The last decade, however, has seen a more explicit move to assess whether or not there is any need for an internal HR function or at least for quite large elements of its work. For example, a PricewaterhouseCoopers survey in 2002 reported over 70 per cent of organisations outsourcing at least one aspect of their HR work compared with just under 50 per cent two years earlier. There have been many quoted examples – such as BP, BT and several local authorities – where organisations have chosen to subcontract their transactional work to an external provider through a dedicated call centre or even transfer all but core, strategic activity to a specialist firm. Consequently there has been a growth in these kinds of provider, firms such as Capita, Accenture and Exult taking large chunks of HR business. Some of these appear to have worked well, and contracts have been extended, while others have been terminated because the expected improvements have not been forthcoming. Numerous articles have appeared in *People Management*, suggesting there is 'outsourcing fever', an 'offshore boom' or (more recently) some questioning of the value of subcontracting (Pickard 2004). The example of Novo Nordisk is briefly outlined in Box 15.

A major problem with headline publications is that they tend to conflate all the different forms of alternative service delivery into one category. Outsourcing can take many forms; these include a shared service centre dedicated to the work of one organisation, a joint venture between organisations that combine HR resources, and a multiclient call centre providing HR services to several organisations (McEwen 2002; Cooke *et al* 2004b). In addition, shared service centres may be set up within a large organisation that is then floated off as a subsidiary designed, initially at least, to support the host company across all its sites in one country or wider, and then extended to become a profit centre in its own right which is expected to find work from elsewhere in addition to its internal role. The length of the contract between the organisations can also vary from one-off or relatively short periods of duration

BOX 15   OUTSOURCING PROVIDES THE RIGHT MEDICINE

This report examines the partnership between Novo Nordisk – a multinational medical products supplier with 18,000 employees worldwide and 250 in the UK and Ireland – and RebusHR. A decision was taken following a restructuring exercise in the company that left it with a severely imbalanced HR function across Europe, and it was reckoned that new staff of the right calibre were difficult to recruit. In November 2002 RebusHR took over responsibility for administration of items such as pay, pensions and maternity leave, staffed with two people. Two consultants covered most other areas – including employment law and performance issues. HR strategy remained in-house as did the UK training and development operation. Recruitment was outsourced to another agency. The contract with RebusHR was for three years.

RebusHR agreed to use its 'reasonable endeavours' to respond to any query to its helpdesk within three working hours, Monday 9am to Friday 5pm. More complex questions needing detailed research have a longer response time of one working day if at all possible. The Service Level Agreement also commits RebusHR to 12 visits per year, although in the early days the principal consultant spent two days a week at Novo Nordisk. This later fell to one day and attendance is now on an 'as and when' basis.

Novo Nordisk seems happy with the deal. Its director with overall responsibility for HR says the deal has saved the company up to £300k per annum, and feels it has been a really good partnership, which has produced excellent results and customer satisfaction ratings.

Source: Adapted from IRS Employment Review 787a. *Outsourcing HR at Novo Nordisk.* 7 November 2003. pp19–21

through to deals over a five- or seven-year period that are then renewed; the expectations of both parties and their commitment to meeting short- or long-term goals are bound to vary due to this. Moreover, the type of staff who are recruited to run the contract can also vary dramatically, with some organisations preferring agency workers with no HR qualification to staff their generalist support centre while others feel it is necessary to retain and strengthen the existing skills base with higher paid and experienced professionals (Xu 2003; Mellor-Clark 2004).

The type of work involved can also vary substantially, with different arrangements for different aspects of HRM. This 'balkanisation' (Adams 1991) of HR practice results in some areas being heavily outsourced – training and development, executive search and selection, recruiting temporary staff, and outplacement and redundancy counselling. Even in the case of training and development, however, it is clear no single category of consultancy is used exclusively and many organisations continue to use in-house services. Hall and Torrington (1998 p126) found that training and development, recruitment and selection, and outplacement were the most extensively outsourced activities, and this has been confirmed by more recent studies (Cooke *et al* 2004b). Research from the USA on nearly 500 organisations (Klaas *et al* 2001) noted similar trends but instead categorised this into HR generalist activities (such as performance appraisal) transactional work, human capital activities (for example, training), and recruiting and selecting. These authors also argued that reliance on outsourcing depended on a whole host of factors relating to organisational size and complexity, product market uncertainty and the importance of HR strategy to the organisation. One particularly interesting finding from this study is that firms utilising idiosyncratic or unique approaches to HRM were much less likely to outsource generalist and human capital activities, presumably because it is very hard for contractors to provide equivalent levels of support without a substantial investment in training up their staff (p132). Conversely firms whose future product market projections were uncertain were more likely to outsource generalist and transactional activities in order to reduce risk and future commitments to their own staff (p133).

The nature of consultants also varies sizeably. On the one hand, there are large strategy or specialist HR firms, often operating on a global scale, that can run the entire HR function or undertake specific projects on strategic aspects of HRM. At the other extreme, individuals can offer a total HR service to small firms on a regular and ongoing basis or engage in specialist work as it is needed. Other bodies – such as Acas, The Work Foundation (previously known as The Industrial Society) or the Involvement and Participation Association – also provide services in this area. In general terms, employers looking for consultants (on an individual or a wider basis) need to exercise great care in their choice because while some will be good, others lack expertise or are poor value for money.

We also need to examine the forces that guide employers when choosing whether or not to implement new forms of service delivery. These include cost savings, expertise and independence.

Cost savings

The outsourcing literature in general typically takes transaction costs as its starting point (Williamson 1975) in arguing that decisions about whether to 'make or buy' are governed by the relative costs involved. Outsourcing clearly incurs initial start-up costs as the contractor needs to learn what is involved and the time taken to resolve issues is higher during the learning period. On the other hand, a prime reason for outsourcing is to reduce existing costs, perhaps downsizing the current HR function and replacing high-paid staff with cheaper substitutes. Additionally, the employer can shift the associated costs of employment and the inherent risks in recruiting and retaining an in-house team to the contractor. Moreover, the actual costs of running the HR function – or the parts that have been subcontracted – is more transparent with an outsourced service and clauses can be written into the contract to stipulate no additional payments (Cooke et al 2004b). In theory, if senior managers are unhappy with the service provided, it is easier to dispense with their services than with in-house personnel.

However, depending on the size of the contract, the number of credible, alternative suppliers available and the importance of achieving cost reductions in relation to other benefits, it is not always easy to secure performance improvements once standards have started to slip and it may be costly to terminate a contract prematurely. Although intended to increase flexibility, outsourcing can sometimes add new costs and rigidities that are just as hard to eliminate (Greer et al 1999; Marchington et al 2004c). Furthermore, if employers do decide to use consultants on cost grounds, they need to be fully aware of the complete financial implications. This should include both direct and opportunity costs of internal management time in putting together the tender in the first place, as well as the costs of implementing recommendations and monitoring performance with a continuing contract. Any contract will require some specification of agreed performance indicators, and in many cases these are tightly specified – in terms of answering the telephone within five rings or responding to a letter within a certain number of days. When seen as part of a wider package, these indicators may not be problematic but when treated in isolation, there is a danger that HR activities become distorted in order to meet certain standards while neglecting others. Moreover, factors that can be measured tend to be relatively easy to define, and HR processes critical to the business can be very difficult to define precisely.

Expertise

Outsourcing can be used to take advantage of specialist expertise that is not available internally. The expertise may be in a particular subject (eg European Works Councils, executive reward or psychometric testing) or it may relate to process skills. In the former situation, assistance might be available from a specialist consulting firm or a leading academic. One of the respondents to the Greer *et al* (1999) study summed it up well by saying 'you outsource when someone else can perform the activity better than you'. Smaller firms may use an ex-HR manager who has plenty of experience but is no longer in full-time employment or perhaps someone from an interim management agency. In the case of process consultancy, senior managers may get help implementing a programme of cultural change or improving teamwork amongst Board members for example. This argument hinges around the idea that organisations should specialise in areas they regard as central to their mission and corporate goals, and consider commercial contracts for all other work. Consultancy firms have the resources to set up extensive databases of information, to offer benchmarking and – in the case of the large, multinational firms – provide support on a global basis (IRS Employment Trends 698 2000, p9; Sparrow *et al* 2004, p165). The most widely quoted examples of outsourcing have involved transactional work that relies heavily on expensive IT systems staffed by people who are not necessarily experts in HRM, and it is argued that subcontracting these activities frees internal HR professionals to engage in strategic decision-making (Ulrich 1998).

However, contracting-out HR to an external firm means that expertise is no longer retained in-house, and there is a loss of internal synergy if the entire function is outsourced. An in-house function provides an opportunity for benefits to be derived from internal teams learning across and within the organisation. Tacit skills that are difficult to codify and formalise are lost when outsourcing takes place (Klaas *et al* 2001, p128) and organisations then become dependent on external providers maintaining service quality and professional standards. While this may not be a problem in the early stages if experienced staff continue to work on the contract, there is no guarantee that this will continue, especially if the subcontractor does not consider it appropriate to provide continuing development or employs agency staff as a way of reducing costs. Having lost their own internal staff, the employer may find it hard to negotiate low prices at subsequent contract renewals or when the stock of quality providers is small. Additionally, one of the best ways to develop future directors is to plan their career development so that they are familiar with all aspects of HR and with the business as a whole. That opportunity is missed if routine activities are sub-contracted to an external consultancy (Hall and Torrington 1998, pp191–192). Indeed organisations such as Ciba Speciality Chemicals believe one of the best ways for HR staff to gain legitimacy is to move around between different functions and jobs during their working lives and gain expertise in a wide range of activities within the organisation (Morton and Wilson 2003). Immersing HR professionals in other aspects of the business can be beneficial for enhancing their contribution in the long term.

Independence

Consultants tend to be regarded as independent from the organisation and able to provide an expertise that is (theoretically) free from internal influence. This may be particularly useful in complex and multifaceted situations, as well as beneficial in providing an alternative and fresh perspective on issues, as an outsider's view of issues can help to resolve problems which had previously seemed insurmountable, and consultants are able to use the language of independence, objectivity and so-called 'rational' solutions (Baxter 1996). If attitude surveys are undertaken by independent consultants, this may help to increase its acceptability with a range of stakeholders and lead insiders to make decisions that seemed impossible before.

Being external to the organisation, however, is not a universal advantage, and it means there is less understanding of workplace culture and past traditions. While subcontractors may have access to wider streams of knowledge and contemporary developments, they do not know what has been tried before and failed, they lack insight into the politics that permeate any organisation, and they lack knowledge of organisational products and services. Much depends on what is acceptable to the parties involved, and this proved to be a major problem in BP's experience with outsourcing (Higginbottom 2001). There are limits to benchmarking against other organisations, and it is suggested that sometimes external consultants come along with 'solutions looking for problems' (Baxter 1996; Fincham and Evans 1999). In other words, HR practices that have worked effectively in other organisations tend to be recommended for quite different sectors and situations.

> Debate with your colleagues whether or not it makes sense to outsource the HR function. Make use of the arguments outlined here, as well as others, and find contemporary examples to support your case.

An alternative structure that makes use of some aspects of outsourcing but retains HR in-house is the shared service centre (Incomes Data Services 2003), an idea that had its roots within the finance function in the USA (Quinn et al 2000; Cooke et al 2004b). The model typically results in the creation of a small group of HR professionals at corporate level that help to drive the strategic vision of the organisation while a call centre is set up to give advice to line managers on administrative issues such as employee records, recruitment services and relocation. Several large multinational companies have gone down this route and if they operate globally the service can be available 24 hours per day in different parts of the world (Sparrow et al 2004, p66). The implications of adopting this model are considerable according to Reilly (2000): major gains include more efficient processes; higher customer satisfaction ratings; more integrated 'solutions' to problems; better management information; and a more strategic contribution from HR. In practice, shared service centre models have also hit problems – such as lower levels of customer satisfaction, less interesting work and reduced career opportunities for HR staff; higher than expected costs; and transfer of jobs from high wage to low wage economies (Reilly, 2000; Sparrow et al 2004). Box 16 provides an outline of a shared service centre.

BOX 16   USING THE LANGUAGE OF HR ACROSS THE GLOBE

USHRSC is an in-house service centre based in Southern England which is part of a large multinational organisation, providing support to a large number of managers and non-managerial staff (the customers) in 20 countries and 15 languages across Europe, the Middle East and Africa. The HR shared service centre is divided more or less equally numbers-wise into generalist and specialist support, although the former is predominantly staffed with agency workers rather than in-house personnel. The generalists are the first point of contact with customers, and the vast majority of their work is responding to straightforward questions about employee benefits or sickness reports. The average call time is six minutes. The rest of the queries are either dealt with initially by the HR generalists or handed on to a specialist immediately. If the specialists are unable to deal with the query it is passed on to a process specialist in the country concerned. The specialists also devote time each week to training the generalists and working with them to add knowledge and improve customer service

Interviews with staff at the call centre indicated they were given plenty of autonomy in dealing with queries and were encouraged to undertake further training if they wanted to. Nevertheless the majority of their work was relatively routine in terms of the range of HR queries that were raised. Some staff experienced difficulty with the range of languages they were expected to know, and even though every generalist was required to be at least bilingual, the size of the geographic areas they had to cover inevitably caused problems. A further problem is that with so many agency staff on site, it was difficult for USHRSC to increase motivation and commitment, and some of the staff felt they were being used as cheap and flexible labour.

Source: Adapted from Xu Z. 'It's a call centre but it's a strange call centre: HRM and employment practices in HR service centres'. Unpublished MSc dissertation, UMIST. 2003

DEVOLVING HRM TO LINE MANAGERS

Line managers are renowned for criticising the contribution HR specialists make to organisational performance. This broadly takes one or more of four forms. First, HR practitioners are regarded as out of touch with commercial realities, not really aware of how the business operates or its customer needs, but instead applying principles – such as welfare or employee rights – that may run counter to business goals. Second, HR is often seen to constrain the autonomy of line managers to make decisions they feel are in the best interests of the business. Frustration is most apparent in relation to what are seen as legal constraints or in having to negotiate and consult with union representatives. The third criticism is that HR managers are unresponsive and slow to act, always wanting to check options thoroughly rather taking action immediately (Cunningham and Hyman 1999, p17). Finally, HR practitioners are criticised for promoting policies that may be fine in theory but hard to put into effect, or inappropriate for their particular workplace. For example, while line managers may support the principle of appraisal they are often annoyed by the practical requirement to keep records of meetings. The HR function is caught in a cleft stick, criticised both for being too interventionist and too remote. In his classic book, Watson (1986, p204) sums this up well:

> ❝ **If personnel specialists are not passive administrative nobodies who pursue their social work, go-between and firefighting vocations with little care for business decisions and leadership, then they are clever, ambitious power-seekers who want to run organisations as a kind of self-indulgent personnel playground.** ❞

Legge (1995, pp27–28) terms this problem the 'vicious circle in personnel management'. Because senior managers do not involve the HR function at an early stage, this results in 'people' issues being ignored or downplayed during the decision-making process. Problems inevitably arise with new initiatives or with routine business issues because HR has not been involved – difficulties such as poor recruits, inadequately trained staff or stoppages of work. When this happens, HR is asked to help resolve the crisis and the short-term solutions they provide merely store up trouble for the future because they are rushed through. Accordingly HR gets the blame for not being able to resolve the problem, and so continues to be excluded from major decisions, thus completing the vicious circle.

Criticisms such as these have led to line managers taking even greater responsibility for HR activities – although in one sense this has always been the case because line managers operate at the workplace alongside the people they supervise (Lowe 1992). Rather than having to wait for an 'answer' from the HR department, they can resolve issues instantly. Moreover, line managers would regard their 'solutions' as more in tune with business realities, and therefore contribute more overtly to improved performance. Having ultimate responsibility is also likely to enhance line management ownership of these issues, and so increase their commitment to integrating HR with other objectives. Although there have been suggestions that HR should be disbanded altogether, a more realistic option is for line managers and HR professionals to work together as partners (Ulrich 1998, p129).

Successive surveys have shown that line managers now have far greater responsibility for HR issues, typically in conjunction with HR practitioners where they are employed. Storey (1992) found that line managers were at the forefront of various change initiatives in the early 1990s, as well as communicating with their staff through team briefings, appraising them for pay purposes and dealing directly with employees rather than channelling issues through trade union representatives. By the mid-1990s, Hutchinson and Wood (1995, p9) noted that most of the organisations in their sample reported greater line management involvement in personnel issues over the last five years. Hall and Torrington (1998, p50) argued that there were very few areas in which the HR function now makes a decision on its own, but that typically first-line managers make decisions in conjunction with HR specialists. The 1998 WERS survey (Cully *et al* 1999, p56) also found that supervisors were much more likely to play a part in HR-type decisions than they had previously, as did an IRS survey in 2000. Unfortunately, the latter survey did not differentiate between sole and shared responsibilities and was therefore only able to conclude that first line managers had a heavy involvement in decisions about HR issues relating to their own staff. More recent research (Purcell *et al* 2003; Renwick 2003) has confirmed the critical role that line managers now play in the implementation of HR issues, and it is no longer regarded as the novelty it appeared back in the 1990s. For example, IRS (IRS Employment Review 795a 2004) found that line managers and HR typically worked in conjunction to deal with issues such as industrial relations, staffing and performance appraisal while topics such as equal opportunities, training and pay determination tended to remain the preserve of HR. HR involvement tends to remain highest in policy formulation, where issues of consistency and specialist expertise are most important, and lowest when line managers are responsible for putting plans into effect (Hutchinson and Wood 1995; Hall and Torrington 1998; Hutchinson and Purcell 2003; Renwick 2003). Nevertheless, it is apparent that HR specialists and line managers tend to work in conjunction with each other across a wide range of issues.

Another IRS survey (IRS Employment Review 793a 2004) asked respondents in 62 organisations about the areas of responsibility typically held by first-line managers. The broad results are outlined below:

- *major responsibility* – teambriefing; performance appraisal; team and staff development; absence
- *shared responsibility* – induction and ongoing training; discipline; quality circles
- *little responsibility* – performance pay; recruitment; promotions; welfare.

Although practice varies between organisations, with some devolving much more responsibility to line managers than others, the overall conclusion confirms previous research in that many more activities were shared between HR and the line than were done solely by

BOX 17   HOW LINE MANAGERS CAN MAKE THE DIFFERENCE

The research that John Purcell and his colleagues undertook for the CIPD has major implications for the roles of line managers and HR specialists. Based on interviews with 608 workers in 12 organisations over a two-year period, including repeat interviews following the introduction of changes, they concluded that line managers could make a real difference to employee attitudes and behaviour. Managers who were good at 'front-line leadership' – things such as keeping people up-to-date and giving them a chance to comment on proposed changes, responding to suggestions, dealing with problems and treating employees fairly – also had team members with high levels of satisfaction, commitment, motivation and discretion. At the Royal United Hospital, Bath for example, there were marked improvements in employee attitudes in response to changes in HR policies and practices, such as in selection techniques, appraisal schemes and support and training for line managers. Specifically, there were major improvements to employee morale following the appointment of a new ward manager who was seen as very approachable and supportive of staff. At Selfridges similar changes occurred, with much higher levels of pride and loyalty reported subsequent to a new approach to how line managers were selected and evidence that the HR elements of their work – such as appraisals – now got done and staff were recognised for their contributions. The research at Tesco was slightly different in that four stores were examined, and it became clear that major differences in employee attitudes to HR and the company as a whole were due to differences in how store managers were viewed by staff. Not surprisingly, motivation levels and commitment were more positive at stores where staff felt they had more influence over their work, the chance to comment on changes and managers were responsive to suggestions. Given that Tesco has uniform, centralised HR policies this shows up well the influence that line managers can have at the workplace.

Source: Adapted from Purcell J., Kinnie N., Hutchinson S., Rayton B. and Swart J. *Understanding the People and Performance Link: Unlocking the black box.* London, CIPD. 2003

either party. The study undertaken for the CIPD by Hutchinson and Purcell (2003) takes this a stage further by analysing the relationship between first-line managers and HR activities in terms of the difference they make to performance and employee attitudes. Based on over 600 interviews with employees, as well as many others with managers, six activities seem to be particularly influential: performance appraisal; training, coaching and guidance; involvement and communication; openness (the ability to express grievances or raise concerns); work–life balance; recognition (p26). If these are done well, then positive benefits can accrue, but unfortunately the evidence shows that they are often done badly. For example, it was felt by employees that performance appraisals suffered due to lack of clarity in targets and measurements and system complexity, and tellingly that 'many of the problems could be directly linked to the behaviour of managers' (pp28–29). However, line managers can also make a major contribution as Box 17 on page 143 shows.

Much also depends on the respective power bases of the line managers and HR practitioners. A study by Lupton (2000) provides a useful corrective for any personnel specialists who believe that decisions about devolution rest solely with them. He examined the role played by personnel in the selection of doctors, and concluded that it was little more than 'pouring the coffee', acting as an administrative support while the consultants made decisions. In this situation, the HR professionals were on low grades and had little opportunity to influence the highly paid and very influential consultants who made it clear that they resented any interference from an external source. On occasions, the consultants short-circuited the formal procedures, as well as making it clear to candidates that they felt questions asked by the personnel officer were of little importance (p62).

If organisations are intending to devolve greater responsibility to line managers, a number of issues need to be addressed. The following are among the most important.

Lack of skills

A common complaint is that line managers do not possess the skills and competencies necessary to perform the HR aspects of their jobs effectively without specialist support and involvement (Gennard and Kelly 1997; IRS Employment Review 698 2000; Renwick 2003). Their knowledge of motivation theory and worker commitment or pay systems and employee involvement is typically based on experience or deeply held personal beliefs about what makes people tick at work. Given that so few line managers, especially those at the supervisory or departmental level, have undertaken any formal study in HRM, this is a potential problem. Indeed, McGovern et al (1997, p14) reckon that the low educational and technical base of line managers in Britain is a significant constraint on the effective devolution of HRM in Britain. Changes tend to occur so rapidly that training fails to be done properly or systematically, and line managers pick things up as they go along. Cunningham and Hyman (1999, p18) provide examples of insufficient training for line managers expected to take on extra responsibilities. The faddish nature of many management interventions helps to explain why line managers fail to take new ideas seriously because they expect these to be jettisoned when the next fashion appears. At the same time, some line managers do recognise that they need the support of HR practitioners if they are to do their jobs effectively. As one of the managers in Renwick's study (2003, p268) noted, grievance handling 'is done by the line manager but during all this you are getting advice, comment and support from personnel'. Another acknowledged that it was crucial to take on board HR's ideas because they had the training and the professional back-up. The senior managers in Whittaker and Marchington's (2003) study were much more open to this, and implicitly recognised that they needed to acquire more skills if they were to do the HR elements of their role satisfactorily. If partnerships are to be successful, line managers will not only have to be selected with greater care but also accept the need for more systematic induction training as well as regular updates as new initiatives are introduced.

Disdain for HR work

This is more problematic because we have already argued that line managers need further training and development in HRM if they are to be more effective. However, many line managers feel they do not actually need any training in HRM, a point that comes out strongly from Cunningham and Hyman's interviews. They note (1995, p18) that many supervisors and line managers feel that competence in the area is gained from a mixture of common sense and experience, and that training is unnecessary. Moreover they feel that they could do an HR job if they were put into one. As we have seen, some managers do acknowledge the value of working with HR, but many others are very negative about its contribution; as one manager said:

> **I'm the one who knows the individual team – I know what motivates them, I know what demotivates them, I know the personal pressures they are dealing with ... while I don't know everything about HR, I feel I know what's best for my team.**

This disdain for learning and development is very worrying as it contrasts sharply with what the line managers believe is needed to fulfil their own traditional work roles, especially if this is a technical area where knowledge and skills in science or engineering would be considered essential. By contrast it is often assumed that the skills held by HR specialists are either irrelevant – because this is all common sense – or inappropriate because they are derived from models of human behaviour that are seen as naïve and idealistic. This is very apparent in small organisations that do not have a specialist HR presence where personnel work is undertaken by people without any training and whose main responsibility is to ensure that wages are paid correctly and on time. The case of doctor recruitment mentioned above (Lupton 2000) is also a clear, albeit extreme, example of how the personnel presence can be marginalised in the workplace even if it is required as part of the organisation's policy. This showed how doctors refused to work with person specifications, feeling that they could 'spot a good doctor' when they saw one without any interference from personnel. Moreover, the consultants leading interview panels were quite explicit in undermining personnel officers who tried to prevent improper questions being asked of applicants (p56).

Competing priorities

Line managers have more pressing priorities than managing and developing the people who work for them. At the 'leading edge' organisations studied by Gratton *et al* (1999), line managers did not feel any institutional pressure – through their own performance criteria – to consider HRM issues seriously because they were low on their list of priorities. Even at these supposedly forward-looking organisations, issues to do with people management did not appear in formal or unwritten performance expectations. Line managers report frustration that they are not able to devote sufficient time to HR issues – such as appraisal – because 'harder' priorities tend to dominate (Cunningham and Hyman 1999, p25). A key finding from the IRS (IRS Employment Review 795a 2004) survey was that line managers felt over-burdened by having to do HR work in addition to their other tasks and this led to a reluctance to accept responsibility for these issues. In a sense, HR duties are often seen as 'an extra' beyond the main aspects of their role and any balancing between competing priorities leads to HR being ignored or left until later as it is regarded as less urgent (Whittaker and Marchington 2003; Renwick, 2003). Without explicit proactive support from senior managers, and recognition and rewards for their work in the HR area, it is easy to understand why line managers do not take this part of their job too seriously.

> How would you convince a line manager that it was important to take the HR aspects of her/his job seriously in the absence of any explicit performance criteria?

Inconsistencies in application

Without specialist HR support and clear procedures to follow, it is highly likely there will be inconsistencies in how staff are managed. This is most apparent in relation to compliance with employment legislation (IRS Employment Review 795a 2004) – although we believe this does little more than formalise 'good practice'. Earnshaw *et al*'s (2000) research on discipline and dismissal in small firms demonstrates clearly the potential problems that can occur. Dismissals arose after 'heated rows' at the workplace or due to personality clashes, without following any procedure whatsoever. Evidence, due process and the opportunity to appeal all tended to be lacking. Moreover, action taken on one occasion in relation to a particular member of staff is ignored on a subsequent occasion in relation to another worker who is liked or valued, and dismissals are deferred until after the completion of an urgent order or a replacement is available. Inconsistencies are also apparent in other HR activities as well, such as in team briefings, dealing with absence from work or performance appraisal. Some of these are taken up again in subsequent chapters but inconsistencies in relation to performance appraisal, especially if it is tied into reward, are particularly serious. As two managers said (Hutchinson and Purcell 2003, p29):

> **It seems rather subjective. There are concerns that if you've got problems and you raise them, you're perceived as being negative.**

> **The pay aspect is down to line manager discretion rather than based on actual information. It depends on how well you get on with your line manager.**

The fact that HR issues are increasingly dealt with by line managers has several implications for the work of HR professionals – not least in terms of how many are employed. New skills are also likely to become more important. For example, HR professionals might play a larger part in the formulation of HR policies and procedural frameworks – such as in recruitment or grievance handling – to ensure adherence to corporate policy and legal requirements. They might also provide expert advice and guidance on all HR matters perhaps through guidance manuals. Finally, there is likely to be an even greater demand to train line managers so that they have sufficient skills to enable them to devise a job description, conduct an interview, or harness employee commitment. This new role is likely to be strengthened by the effective use of information technology in areas such as absence monitoring, standard letter production, spreadsheets and personal records. Box 18 raises a number of questions about the interface between line managers and the HR function.

BOX 18   HOW CAN HR AND LINE MANAGERS WORK TOGETHER MORE EFFECTIVELY?

This case concerns the education department of a local authority, and it demonstrates clearly that major problems can arise without clear lines of accountability and a systematic framework for relations between different managers.

The organisation in question has a personnel presence both at corporate and at departmental level, with some element of dotted line relationships between the two. Broadly, however, the personnel function in each department is left to get on with its own work within a framework that applies to the council as a whole. The Head of HR for the Education Department has no previous personnel experience but had worked as a line manager in the service for many years and was well-known to staff there. The Chief Officer for the Education Department felt that one of his strengths was HR and was therefore keen to run this himself; indeed, he made a point of stressing that he wanted 'someone who knew the service, rather than an expert in human resources'. The other HR staff in the Department were on low grades and part way through their CIPD courses at the local college. Accordingly, they had little experience of HRM beyond their current jobs but they were aware of the main professional issues.

The department was run in a very hierarchical way, and all decisions had to be approved by senior managers. Line managers were allowed relatively little freedom to make decisions, and this often resulted in long delays. Many of the front-line staff in the department had been transferred in from other jobs in the council, as part of its employment security policy, and some were renowned around the authority for being difficult to manage. This led to a number of issues at workplace level, set within a context of an increasingly problematic employment relations agenda at national level.

During the past year, there have been problems with time-keeping, with poor performance and with fraudulent use of the council's property. In some cases, the evidence is clearly available while in others it is more difficult due to differing interpretations of the situation. The line managers have tried to address these issues, but on each occasion the matter has to be referred up the chain for a decision. It has not been unusual for there to be delays of several months as more senior managers work out what to do. As the Head of HR in the Education Department knows so many of the staff, and had worked there himself for so long, he finds difficulty in taking a hard line with disciplinary issues. This inertia is also reinforced by the fact that some of the senior managers are in a similar position.

The authority of the line managers is often undermined as long-serving front-line staff go directly to the senior manager if they have problems and effectively short-circuit the management chain. They also ensure that their views about line managers are made known. The Head of the Education Department always expects to be involved in HR decisions and this causes yet more problems. The junior HR staff – the only ones that have any professional training in the subject – are on low grades and find it difficult to impose their own views on the situation. Indeed, this lack of influence has led several of these staff to leave the organisation in frustration.

Clearly, the situation depicted in the education department in Box 18 is a mess. What would you do to address these issues, and what advice would you provide about (a) the organisation of the HR function, (b) the authority to be vested in line managers and (c) how relations between line managers and HR could be made more effective?

In order to convince line managers to take advice about HR more seriously, two sets of arguments seem relevant. Both of these demand that HR managers acquire better financial awareness and the ability to provide costings for their recommendations. The first set of arguments relates to the cost of getting things wrong and it is worthwhile estimating the financial implications of mistakes. Examples include the cost of a tribunal case for an unfair dismissal, a lapse in safety awareness resulting in an accident or the cost of lost orders due to a strike because an employee relations issue was badly handled. Organisations with a poor public relations profile can suffer costs at the recruitment stage through a lack of high quality applicants or because staff leave since the organisation has not met their expectations. Costs should also be viewed in 'softer' motivational terms reflected in low levels of productivity, unsatisfactory customer service and inadequate quality standards, or through poor levels of attendance and time-keeping, high levels of labour turnover, stress, and general dissatisfaction.

The second set of arguments is about the benefits of getting it right, many of which are the converse of those outlined above. Financial benefits can accrue through the higher value that is added from each well-motivated and productive employee while public relations benefits can improve the image of the employer and attract high-quality applicants. Moreover, 'softer' motivational benefits can flow from low levels of absenteeism, from the positive impact on customers, and from higher levels of productivity and quality associated with high commitment HRM.

MEASURING THE CONTRIBUTION OF THE HR FUNCTION

We have already noted the distinction between HR as a discrete function staffed by specialist managers and HR as an integral part of every line manager's job. Sometimes, this distinction is forgotten in evaluations of the impact of HR issues on organisational performance or the ambiguity causes problems in our attempts to assess whether or not HRM adds value. It also helps to explain why HR specialists appear to be so critical of their own contribution to organisational goals in a way that does not appear to concern other specialist functions (Torrington 1998). Guest and Hoque (1994a) suggest three reasons for this. First, as we have seen, the profession has always been in an ambiguous position, and on cost grounds alone there are questions about the need for an internal HR function. Second, doubts about the value of HR is reinforced by a UK national culture that puts a primacy on financial control and short-termism to the neglect of longer term considerations. Third, the contribution of HR specialists has always been hard to quantify because they work closely with line managers and are dependent on them to put policies into effect. Consequently, although 'we may be able to identify the impact of personnel decisions, we cannot always be sure whether the personnel specialists contributed towards them' (p41). In other words, while the philosophy and framework may be set by the HR function, line managers are responsible for delivery. Is it fair therefore to criticise the HR function for high levels of absence in a particular department when individual line managers may be ignoring policies designed to address this issue?

Some observers have concluded that the HR function has a minor impact on organisations, summed up well by Skinner's quote that the personnel function is just 'big hat and no cattle'

(Guest 1991). Fernie *et al* (1994, p12) concluded from the WERS database that 'workplaces with a personnel specialist and/or director responsible for personnel matters have very much worse relations than those without such workplace or board specialists'. However, detailed analysis of the responses to the WERS questions reveals severe methodological and conceptual problems, both in terms of the respondent base for their research and in the interpretation of the results. Since 93 per cent of the sample rated the employee relations climate at their workplace as good or better, and only 2 per cent considered it to be poor or very poor, their conclusion is perverse.

One way to raise awareness about HR issues is to have a specialist personnel presence on the Board. Millward *et al* (2000, p76) found that by the late 1990s, 64 per cent of workplaces in the private sector were in organisations where there was a specialist presence on the Board. In fact, this had declined since the mid-1980s when it stood at 76 per cent, but this was due to a change in the composition of workplaces between the surveys rather than organisations deciding to dispense with their HR directors (p77). Indeed, the proportion of workplaces in large multinationals having a HR Director remained constant, and in workplaces where trade unions were recognised it actually rose slightly. Despite using a less representative sample and focusing on organisations rather than workplaces, an IRS survey (IRS Employment Review 795a 2004) found 60 per cent had a director responsible for HR issues. Although most observers feel that a seat on the Board should mean HR issues are taken seriously, Hope-Hailey *et al* (1997) and Torrington (1998) warn that a formal place on the Board does little to increase influence and it is possible for HRM to be treated as a strategic issue without a specialist presence. However, this is only possible if the Chief Executive is convinced of the value of HRM and these values are embedded throughout the entire organisation via line managers.

Influence may depend more on how the Chief Executive views HR and on the career paths of HR Directors themselves. Drawing on interviews with HR and Managing Directors in 60 organisations, Kelly and Gennard (2000) identify three different routes to the Board. A very small number of HR Directors were 'parachuted' into the role, usually because the Chief Executive needed broader expertise. About one-third had taken what was termed a 'vertical' route through personnel, undertaking a range of generalist rather than specialist HR duties over their careers. The largest proportion however, had taken a 'zigzag' route spending periods of time in general or line management as well as in personnel. They felt that this had equipped them well for the wide range of skills needed to perform effectively at Board level. Three factors seemed to be important in selecting a specialist HR Board member: professional and technical competence, business focus and being a team player (see also Stiles 2001). While HR representation on the Board may help to ensure people management is given proper consideration, it would also appear that HR Directors are usually appointed because they can make a general contribution to the business (Caldwell 2001; Guest and King 2002); because they are 'a director first and an HR Director second'.

An alternative way to assess the effectiveness of HR is to ask key stakeholders and 'customers' – line managers, chief executives and non-managerial staff – what they think (Guest and Peccei 1994; Wilkinson and Marchington 1994). Mayo (1999, p33) believes that HR managers will gain influence by escaping from the balance sheet mentality and using their expertise to help other managers achieve their goals. For example, Tesco adopted a balanced scorecard approach by developing a 'steering wheel' with four quadrants – people, finance, customers and operations (IRS Employment Trends 703 2000). Moreover, the senior management team at store level – including the personnel manager – take it in turns to manage the store for about 20 per cent of their working time, thus providing ideal opportunities for the HR function to learn about other aspects of the business, and at the same time identify the services that other managers need to run the store.

The services and support valued by other managers varies depending upon their level in the hierarchy. Buyens and de Vos (2001) asked senior managers, line managers and HR managers to indicate (a) the value of various HR practices to the organisation and (b) the value that the HR function added to the organisation in general. Using Ulrich's model outlined earlier in this chapter, the senior managers in their study valued HR's role principally in the areas of change and transformation – such as balancing organisational and individual needs, and overcoming barriers to change. The line managers were not really bothered about HR as a strategic partner, but felt that added value came from administrative expertise, managing costs and delivering core HR services such as recruitment and training. The HR managers interestingly felt that the role of employee champion added the greatest value – either in terms of regarding employees as 'the heartbeat of the organisation' or providing a bridge between different interest groups. The HR managers were valued just as much for their ability to solve problems as for making a strategic contribution.

The assessments made by directors about the HR contribution are clearly very important if HR wants to make an impact. Guest and King (2002) interviewed 48 directors, drawn equally from Chief Executives, Operational Directors and HR Directors. Rather more were positive than negative about the contribution of the HR function, and indeed the most critical were the HR Directors themselves. Views were split on whether there should be an HR presence on the Board. One Chief Executive suggested that, without an HR presence on the Board, the message given out would be that people management is not as important as other activities. In contrast, one of the Operations Directors felt there was no need for specific HR representation on the Board because this was the responsibility of all members. If present, HR Directors were expected to operate as 'thinking partners'.

> Debate with your colleagues whether it is possible for the HR contribution to be effective without a specialist personnel presence on the Board?

Because there are few published surveys seeking the views of employees about the performance of the HR function, it is hard to assess what they think. Gibb's (2001) survey of over 2600 employees in 73 organisations found the HR function tended to do best in areas concerning interpersonal relations (such as being approachable, helpful and prompt) and professionalism and knowledge (such as confidentiality and advice). Although assessments were less positive in relation to HR practices such as recruitment, absence and appraisal, overall they seemed to 'indicate that employees have a favourable view of the work of specialist HR staff' (p330). Interestingly, HR staff were seen in a more positive light than HR practices.

There are two broad options available to HR professionals wanting to measure the effectiveness of their own function. First, use can be made of *external* benchmarking exercises through industry clubs, consultants and employers' organisations, involving processes to audit their processes and costs. A number of key statistics can be used but these are subject to some variation between organisations, regions and occupational group, as well as over time depending on the state of the external labour market. Drawing on a range of sources (Mayo 1995; Ulrich 1997; IRS Employment Trends 698 2000; IRS Employment Trends 754 2002), some of the most widely used measures are listed in Table 15.

Table 15   *Benchmarking the HR function*

HR measures	Extent to which sometimes or regularly used (%)	Degree of satisfaction (%)
Levels of labour turnover	98	76
Absence rates	96	74
Expenditure on training	88	18
Employee satisfaction	85	60
Employee relations indicators	81	26
Days spent on training	77	16
Cost to fill vacancies	75	11
Time to fill vacancies	66	8
HR costs as % of costs or profits	41	13
Time spent communicating with staff	35	16
Productivity	18	24

Source: Adapted from IRS Employment Review 754, *Measure for Measure*. 24 June 2002. pp8–13

From this it can be seen that hard measures – such as levels of labour turnover, days lost to absence and expenditure on training costs – are the most widely used, although soft measures such as employee satisfaction levels are not far behind. Productivity assessments are rarely employed according to this survey. The most effective of these are reckoned to be absence and labour turnover, once again followed by satisfaction. Other frequently used measures are:

- ratio of HR staff to full-time equivalent employees
- percentage of employees involved in training
- percentage of employees receiving formal appraisals
- ratio of salaries and wages to those of competitors
- speed and effectiveness of response to employee grievances.

However, great care needs to be exercised with benchmarking to make sure that the measures used are appropriate and accurately measured. For example, recruitment and training costs vary considerably between occupations, as does the amount of time that needs to be committed to these. Levels of absenteeism and labour turnover differ significantly across the economy and much depends on the nature of the external labour market. Equally, figures for absence levels can vary depending on whether or not all forms of absence are included. Levels of worker satisfaction show differences between countries, industries and occupations, as well as between men and women (Rose 1999, 2003). Even if we can be sure that the comparisons are valid, the problem remains that most of the measures relate to costs rather than value-added. Higher costs can be offset by, or contribute to, much higher levels of performance in the short or the long term. In addition, a single, blanket figure for the costs of replacing a member of staff assumes that all employees are worth retaining because they perform at or above expectations, while it may actually be cost-effective for people whose performance is not up to standard to leave the organisation. Complexities such as this make basic comparisons much less useful.

Pfeffer (1997, p360) questions whether or not benchmarking exercises have any value because 'what is easily measurable and what is important are often only loosely related'. For example, consider the ratio of number of permanent HR staff to number of employees. The IRS Guide to Benchmarking (IRS Employment Review 742 2001) shows this varies sizeably between industries as well as between organisations within the same industry. For example, in chemicals the ratio varies from 1:22 to 1:167, in finance from 1:45 to 1:200 and in public services from 1:16 to 1:610. It is difficult to draw firm conclusions from this information. If an organisation is above the average, does this justify a reduction in the number of HR staff without a consideration of how these people operate and some estimate of the value that is added by their contribution?

An alternative option is to focus on *internal* evaluations, perhaps by drawing up service-level agreements. These can cover a range of HR practices and processes such as payroll management, recruitment advertising and induction. Service-level agreements offer several advantages to employers, not least in enabling a more specific statement of service provision against which performance can be assessed (Mayo 1995). This approach has also been used by large multinational corporations such as Shell (Sparrow *et al* 2004, pp165–166). Although the precise list of items can obviously vary between organisations some of the more typical might be:

- preparing offer and contract letters within one day
- providing advice on disciplinary matters within two days
- advising staff on terms and conditions of employment within five days
- preparing, disseminating and analysing absence and labour turnover data to line managers on a monthly basis
- evaluating training provision on an annual basis.

There are also dangers with this approach as the HR function may find that in trying to satisfy the needs of internal customers, it becomes the servant of other people. As we saw earlier, allowing HRM to be defined by line managers downplays the judgement of professionals and focuses on the need to satisfy short-term cost-effectiveness to the neglect of longer term HR considerations (Sisson 2001, p94). Provided figures are used with sensitivity and discretion, they may help HR improve its service to stakeholders and its contribution to organisational success.

Write a short report for your manager outlining the limitations of benchmarking and service-level agreements, and explain what other measures might be used instead.

It is important to realise that by attempting to quantify its contribution, the HR function basically succumbs to the accountants' vision of how organisations are meant to operate. As Armstrong (1989, p160) cautioned many years ago, this cedes too much to 'the dominant accounting culture and may also, in the end, achieve little security for the personnel function'. Pfeffer (1997, pp363–364) argues that HR is unlikely ever to win the numbers game because other departments have much more experience of this – and they also set the rules! He warns that 'if all HR becomes is finance with a different set of measures and topic domains, then its future is indeed likely to be dim' (p364). Alternatively, Toulson and Dewe (2004, p88) offer an alternative view that HR managers need 'to become conversant with different accounting practices, experienced in using a range of analytic tools and capable of providing an alternative view'. As we suggested above, the focus on costs is too narrow, and it is better to direct attention to how the HR function can add value to the organisation as a whole.

CONCLUSIONS

In this chapter, we have reviewed the changing nature of the work undertaken by HR departments in Britain. There has been a great deal of interest in the notion that the function needs a presence on the board in order to make a contribution, and that this may be best achieved via a strategic partner role. There is little evidence that this has actually occurred in the vast majority of organisations, although it is clear that high commitment HRM is more likely in workplaces that have a personnel presence. On the contrary, the tendency to subcontract HR work to consultants, either in its entirety or in a piecemeal fashion, has become more extensive. Moreover, line managers have continued to take over activities that were once the preserve of the HR function. This has led to doubts about whether there will be a role for HR departments in the future. This situation is made worse by the increased tendency to seek quantitative assessments of HR work, sometimes using indicators that are inappropriate or too simplistic to allow a fundamental review of departmental performance. Although management is dominated by accountancy versions of performance, it is important for students and practitioners to be aware of the limitations of these sorts of model. The fact that they focus on easily measurable, cost-driven indicators does not sit easily with models resting upon the assumption that HRM – especially high commitment HRM – provides much greater benefits over the longer term and can add to enhanced levels of performance.

USEFUL READING

CALDWELL R. 'The changing roles of personnel managers: old ambiguities, new uncertainties', *Journal of Management Studies*, Vol. 40, No. 4, 2003. pp983–1004.

HUTCHINSON S. *and* PURCELL J. *Bringing Policies to Life: The vital role of front line managers in people management.* CIPD, London. 2003.

INCOMES DATA SERVICES. *HR Service Centres.* IDS Study 750. London, IDS. 2003.

IRS EMPLOYMENT REVIEW 793a. *Welcome the New Multi-tasking All-purpose Management Expert.* 6 February 2004. pp8–13.

KELLY J. *and* GENNARD J. 'Getting to the top: career paths of personnel directors', *Human Resource Management Journal*, Vol. 10, No. 3, 2000. pp22–37.

KLAAS B., McCLENDON J. *and* GAINEY, T. 'Outsourcing HR: the impact of organizational characteristics', *Human Resource Management*, Vol. 40, No. 2, 2001. pp125–138.

PFEFFER J. 'Pitfalls on the road to measurement: the dangerous liaison of human resources with the idea of accounting and finance', *Human Resource Management*, Vol. 36, No. 3, 1997. pp357–365.

PROCTER S. *and* CURRIE G. 'The role of the personnel function: roles, perceptions and processes in an NHS trust', *International Journal of Human Resource Management*, Vol. 10, No. 6, 1999. pp1077–1091.

ULRICH D. 'A new mandate for human resources', *Harvard Business Review*, Jan–Feb 1998. pp125–134.

WHITTAKER S. *and* MARCHINGTON M. 'Devolving HR responsibility to the line: threat, opportunity or partnership?', *Employee Relations*, Vol. 25, No. 3, 2003. pp245–261.

Resourcing

Staffing and Resourcing the Organisation

INTRODUCTION

Staffing and resourcing, and in particular recruitment and selection, is a crucial element of HRM in all organisations irrespective of their size, structure or sector. Over the last two decades, the literature on selection has become much more sophisticated as organisational psychologists have sought ways to improve the reliability and validity of selection decisions. This is important because new recruits provide managers with an opportunity to acquire new skills as well as amend organisational cultures. Too often, however, decisions are made in an ad hoc and reactive manner to fill vacancies without systematic analysis of whether specific jobs are needed. Moreover, other key areas of resourcing – concerned with HR planning, analyses of labour turnover, and recruitment – are often downplayed because attention is focused on how selection decisions can be improved by using 'new' or 'sophisticated' techniques. Yet, without a proper understanding of HR planning, of how jobs might be designed or of the best channels to use for attracting candidates, the selection decision can be worthless.

This chapter reviews all stages of the recruitment and selection cycle, from HR planning through to appointment. An initial analysis is needed to establish whether or not a particular post needs to be filled internally on a permanent, open-ended contract, on a temporary basis, or externally through an agency; in the final option, decisions about selection are made by a different employer and therefore greater care may need to go into selecting the agency with which to work rather than the individual workers (Marchington *et al* 2004c). If it is decided that the post should be filled internally, job descriptions and person specifications or accountability profiles should guide the process. Care should be taken at each stage to ensure that the organisation continues to convey the message it wants to the outside world. Once a suitable pool of candidates has been found, choices have to be made about selection methods, although it is generally advisable to employ multiple methods to increase the validity of selection decisions.

The implications of poor selection decisions can be catastrophic for the business as a whole. They may be expensive in terms of the management time required to deal with disciplinary cases, in retraining poor performers, and in having to recruit replacements for those individuals who have been wrongly selected and/or who quit soon after starting. The potential effects on customer service and product quality are also significant, whether workers are employed on a supermarket check-out, or in an engineering factory or a hotel. Problems can occur not only through the recruitment of someone who is underqualified or is unco-operative but also if new recruits are overqualified and/or soon become bored with their work. Selecting the *right* person for the task and for the organisation is what matters.

By the end of this chapter, readers should be able to:

- **undertake the main aspects of the recruitment and selection process**

- **implement, operate and evaluate cost-effective processes for recruiting and retaining the right calibre of staff in their own organisation**

- **contribute to the design, implementation and evaluation of selection decisions.**

In addition, readers should understand and be able to explain:

■ **the links between human resource planning, recruitment and selection and other aspects of HRM**

■ **the nature of the recruitment process and its principal components**

■ **the major advantages and disadvantages of the most important selection methods, and their contribution to organisational effectiveness.**

HR PLANNING, LABOUR TURNOVER AND RETENTION

At a time when world markets were much more stable and predictable, HR planning was prominent in HRM, personnel management and labour economics. There were many books on the subject, and large organisations put a lot of emphasis on planning their future employment needs, especially of managers. This has been referred to the 'golden age of manpower planning', and the techniques in favour at the time drew heavily upon statistical techniques (Bowey 1975; Bramham 1975, 1994; Walker 1992; Sisson and Timperley 1994). While some HRM texts discuss whether HR planning is still worthwhile and describe the principal techniques, very little attention is paid to analysing the methods used in HR planning, and typically texts rely on more general discussions of strategy or management control systems (Liff 2000; Iles 2001). In what are often characterised as 'new, flexible' organisations, the mention of HR planning conveys images of bureaucracy, rigidity, and a failure to comprehend the limitations of planning in an uncertain environment. It is sometimes implied that planning is irrelevant or misguided in a turbulent and increasingly insecure competitive environment.

Such a view, however, misunderstands the nature and uses of planning, and it can be used to justify 'ad-hocery' and reactive management. Planning remains critically important during turbulent times, if only to ensure that employers have staff of the right quality and quantity available at the right time (Taylor 2002c, p73). Compared with its international competitors, Britain has suffered from recurrent skill shortages both at a national and organisational level (Grugulis 2003) and it could be argued that long-term HR planning might have alleviated some of these problems. Indeed, current pressures to control labour costs and protect tighter profit margins demand an increasing – rather than decreasing – emphasis on HR planning. Similarly, employers faced with declining markets need to start planning well in advance for reductions in numbers employed, so as to maintain long-term employment security for as many staff as possible and minimise the need for compulsory redundancy. Forward planning provides an opportunity to consider alternative forms of contract or to subcontract work that is unpredictable in nature. Accordingly, long-term HR planning has potentially positive implications for many features of the psychological, as well as the legal, contract in organisations that plan ahead, although it may well lead to worsened conditions for those working for the subcontractor. It is difficult to get firm estimates about how many organisations engage in HR planning, but as Liff (2000, p125) notes, 'perhaps the most one can say with any certainty is that many UK companies continue to express a commitment to the idea of HR strategy and planning. How this translates into practice, however, is less clear.'

Do you believe HR planning is worthwhile in your organisation (or one with which you are familiar)? What do you see as the organisational benefits of spending time making plans about future employment projections?

HR planning can be regarded as important for at least four sets of reasons:

1 *It encourages employers to develop clear and explicit links between their business and HR plans, and so integrate the two more effectively* – There are two ways in which this linkage can be viewed. First it can be seen solely in terms of the degree of 'fit' between HR planning and broader strategic plans, and the ability of the HR function to deliver precisely what the business requires. Second, it can be viewed in terms of an interactive relationship between corporate and HR plans, with the latter contributing to the development of the former, and at least demonstrating that longer term business goals may not be achievable if there are problems with labour supply. Either way, HR planning can be viewed as a major facilitator of competitive advantage.

2 *It allows for better control over staffing costs and numbers employed* – It is important for employers to make projections about anticipated staffing needs, irrespective of whether a growth or decline in numbers is predicted, because this makes it easier for employers to match supply and demand, and therefore make decisions about recruiting from the external labour market, relocating staff, or preparing for reductions in numbers employed in order to achieve greater control over staffing costs (Taylor 2002c, pp75–76). For example, if future product market demand is uncertain or known to be highly variable, decisions can be made about whether or not to subcontract or use temporary contracts. This allows employers to shift the risk to agencies and workers other than their own staff (Cooke *et al* 2004a).

3 *It enables employers to make more informed judgements about the skills and attitude mix in the organisation, and prepare integrated HR strategies* – While it is important to ensure a match in numbers employed, it is also critical to achieve the right skills mix among the workforce. Choices about the skill mix can be linked to decisions about the future shape and nature of the business, and shifts can be planned in advance. For example, if an organisation is shifting to a more customer-oriented approach, decisions are required about whether existing staff can be retrained or new recruits are needed, or indeed whether the work might better be done by another firm.

4 *It provides a profile of current staff (in terms of age, gender, race and disability, for example), which is important for any organisation claiming to promote equal opportunities* – Without accurate and up-to-date figures on existing staff numbers and their breakdown by grade and position, it is impossible for employers to make decisions about how equality management can be achieved (Liff 2000, p103). In this and each area discussed above, new ICT provision makes this a more manageable task.

Several techniques have been used to derive 'hard' HR plans. Broadly these have been applied to three sets of issues: forecasts of future demand for labour; forecasts of internal supply; and forecasts of external supply. Each of these is considered below, although the greatest emphasis is on internal supply forecasts since this has traditionally been where HR has made the biggest contribution.

Forecasting future demand

Basically there are two types of method for assessing future demands for labour, the objective and the subjective. The former relies upon projection of past trends and, to be of any value, needs to take into account shifts brought about by changes in technology and organisational goals. Past ratios can be extrapolated to indicate how much or what type of

BOX 19 THE DEMAND FOR JOBS IN 2010

While many employers feel comfortable forecasting the internal supply of labour, trends for the overall market, broken down into sectors and occupations, remain more of a mystery. Research by the Institute for Employment Research and Cambridge Econometrics has produced forecasts for recruiters' needs up to the year 2010. This is worked out by adding or subtracting changes in the overall job levels from the underlying number of replacements required for staff that leave the particular labour market so as to calculate net demand. Overall, recruiters will have to fill over 13.5 million vacancies in the first decade of the twenty-first century in the main occupations in the UK. Five times as many will involve vacancies in existing jobs as will be newly created posts in expanding occupations and sectors.

The major areas where greater numbers of recruits will be required are:

Administrative and clerical occupations	1.34 million
Caring work below para-professional level	1.14 million
Sales assistants and cashiers	1.11 million
Teaching and research professionals	0.82 million
Business and public service associate professionals	0.79 million

The major areas of decline will be in the following:

Elementary occupations such as cleansing, security, sales and personal services	1.17 million
Managers in hospitality and leisure services, farming, horticulture, forestry and fishing	0.50 million
Elementary occupations in agriculture, construction, goods handling and storage	0.46 million
Plant and machine operatives, assemblers and construction workers	0.46 million
Skilled metal and electrical trades	0.45 million

Source: Adapted from a report in IRS Employment Review 732a. 'Think local: using jobcentres for recruitment', *IRS Employment Development Bulletin 139*, July 2001. pp12–16

labour is required in the future. For example, in education, norms may have been established for the number of full-time equivalent (FTE) students per member of staff, or class sizes deemed appropriate for effective learning to take place. Arguments for increases, decreases or replacements typically use established figures, and comparisons made with schools or departments in similar situations. However, technological change may lead to major shifts in demand for certain types of labour or political parties may shift the goalposts, so simple extrapolations are of little value in these circumstances.

Fears that 'objective' systems may be unresponsive to local needs have fuelled arguments that subjective methods are more appropriate. In their simplest form, these may be little more than managerial judgement about future needs and perhaps an excuse to speculate based on limited data. Subjective approaches can be either 'top-down' or 'bottom-up', or a mixture of both. A top-down approach relies heavily on estimates from senior managers, a group of people who ought to have a clear idea about the direction in which the organisation is moving. With the bottom-up method, conversely, departmental managers make estimates about future requirements based upon their experience and judgement (Walker 1992, p162), and is therefore susceptible to 'inflated' demands for fear of losing out. In reality, both methods are combined to arrive at meaningful estimates of future demand.

Forecasting demand relies on product market projections and its implications for the numbers and type of workers required. This is rarely a central task for HR specialists, being more likely to involve business planners, finance and marketing managers. It is much easier to forecast future demand in certain sectors than in others. For example, based upon past projections, reasonable assumptions can be made about *overall* levels of demand for health care, primary school education or food products in the next five years, thus allowing for relatively sensible estimates of future labour demand. However, even in these relatively simple cases it is rather more difficult to estimate the numbers of patients, schoolchildren or shoppers likely to attend a *specific* hospital, school or supermarket, given mobility patterns and, in principle, a wider degree of choice for consumers. Since classes at school are run in broad unit sizes (say, 30), problems arise if an extra 10 children are enrolled across two age groups. This can also lead to further questions about the need for more facilities, buildings and infrastructure. IRS Employment Review 732a (2001; see Box 19) provides a forecast for future job needs.

Examine the set of figures in Box 19, as well as other data, and prepare a brief paper outlining the implications of this for the following:

■ a recruitment agency specialising in secretarial and administrative work

■ government departments overseeing the training of health staff and teachers

■ a careers adviser who is providing advice to school leavers on future jobs.

Forecasting internal supply

Once forecasts have been made about the likely demand for labour, decisions can be made about the balance between external recruitment, internal staff development or workforce reductions. The principal techniques cover two sorts of estimate: wastage/labour turnover, and internal job and grade movements. Data about these issues can be used for a variety of purposes and highlight a range of organisational problems. High levels of labour turnover, for example, can indicate problems with just about any HR policy or practice – inappropriate recruitment and selection methods, poorly designed or uncompetitive pay systems, and ineffective grievance and disciplinary procedures. External factors, such as external competition for labour or poor public transport provision, also contribute to these problems.

Two schools of thought dominate research and practice on turnover: the labour market/economic and the psychological (Morrell *et al* 2001). The former focuses on factors external to the organisation – such as the level of unemployment, wage differentials and the availability of alternative jobs in the local, national or global economy. The latter focuses on individuals and their decisions to quit, relating labour turnover to factors such as job satisfaction and worker commitment (Tang *et al* 2000; Taplin *et al* 2003). Morrell *et al* (2001, p240) are clear that neither school is capable on its own of providing sufficiently good explanations or predictions of labour turnover.

Two measures are typically used to calculate rates of labour turnover. First is the *wastage* rate, which divides the number of staff leaving in a given period by the number of staff employed overall; the formula is presented in Figure 6. Both the numerator and the divisor can include different elements and be applied to different departments in the organisation. For example, leavers may refer solely to those who quit voluntarily, or it can include those made redundant, those at the end of fixed-term contracts or those dismissed, each of which inflates the numerator. The divisor can be calculated on the basis of the number employed at the beginning of the year, at the end, or the average of the two figures. Because comparisons of raw data are inevitably complicated by this, it is essential to know the basis on which the statistics were derived before making comparisons. Exit interviews may shed some light on the problem but people are often unwilling to provide an honest answer to explain their resignation. A more serious problem with these indices, however, is that they do not differentiate between leavers in terms of their length of service, grade or gender. As Morrell *et al* (2001, p222) note, 'this is because any single-figure measure of turnover will be inadequate in so far as it treats all those who leave as a homogenous group'.

The second measure is the *stability* index. Here, the number of staff with a certain minimum period of service (say, one year) at a certain date is divided by overall numbers employed at that date (Figure 6 also shows this calculation). Stability indices provide a good indicator of the proportion of long-term staff or conversely the extent to which the turnover problem is specific to new recruits. This latter phenomenon is referred to as the 'induction crisis' as it occurs within the first few months of employment; perhaps people find out the job is rather different from what they expected, or that their previous post may not have been that bad after all. It is broadly acknowledged that about 20 per cent of workers leave within the first 12 months, a further 12 per cent leave during the second year of their employment, and thereafter it falls to under 5 per cent per annum. In short, about one-third of people leave within the first two years of employment, at some cost to both parties. Of course, this is likely to vary between industries. Taplin *et al* (2003, p1044) found a turnover rate of 26.5 per cent in their study of the clothing industry, with 45 per cent leaving during the first three months of their employment and only one-third lasting beyond a year. The problem was most marked at smaller workplaces. Overall, they concluded that unless firms in this sector could find 'ways of incorporating workers into new routines and remunerating them appropriately, they will continue to be plagued by issues such as turnover as workers seek alternative employment'. The annual CIPD surveys are very useful for giving information about levels of turnover. This showed (CIPD 2004b, pp22–23) that all forms of turnover fell from above 25 per cent per

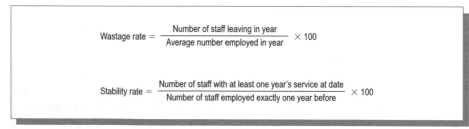

Figure 6 *Indices of labour turnover*

Table 16   *Labour turnover fact file*

Labour turnover for main occupational groups (2004)

Occupational group	%
Managers and professionals	12.5
Administrative, secretarial and technical	15.4
Services (customer, personal, protective and sales)	17.7
Manual/craft	15.7
Graduate trainees	1.6
All employees	16.1

n = 530: base = UK and Ireland

Labour turnover (voluntary and all leavers) for selected industry sectors (2004)

Industry sector	% all leavers	% voluntary turnover
Manufacturing and production	13.8	6.5
Voluntary, community and not for profit	15.5	10.4
Private sector services	20.5	12.9
Public sector services	12.4	7.5

n = 483: base = UK and Ireland

Estimated total costs of recruitment per individual employee (2004)

Occupational group	Cost (£)
Managers and professionals	5,000
Administrative, secretarial and technical	1,500
Services (customer, personal, protective and sales)	2,000
Manual/craft	750
Graduate trainees	900
All employees	2,500

n = 637: base = UK

Source: Chartered Institute of Personnel and Development. *Recruitment, Retention and Turnover: A survey of the UK and Ireland*. London, CIPD. 2004b

annum – that is, one in four staff – in 2000 to 16 per cent in 2003, although it must be noted that 2000 was a particularly high figure. More people left voluntarily than were forced to leave through the ending of a fixed-term contract, dismissal or redundancy, but the latter was still a substantial amount of the overall figure; once again, a reminder to check the basis on which ratios are derived. Table 16 on page 163 shows how rates of labour turnover vary significantly between industry sector and occupational group, as do the costs of recruitment. Most employers say they collect statistics on labour turnover, not without incurring sizeable problems to do with lack of data or software issues (IRS Employment Review 793b 2004). Many also conduct exit interviews, but both of these tasks are generally undertaken by the HR department rather than line managers. The information is used to improve HR practices – such as communication, induction, learning and development and selection – in an attempt to reduce turnover (CIPD 2004b, p31).

> How have labour turnover rates changed recently? What factors might help to explain this? You can find more information from CIPD or IRS surveys to update the figures quoted here.

Although estimating costs might be useful in emphasising how important recruitment and selection is to senior managers, this is necessarily limited because of the assumptions made in reaching such figures. Perhaps the most problematic is that all cases of labour turnover are treated in the same way, with no allowance for the performance levels and potential of the employees who leave compared with those who stay at the organisation. Clearly, managers may be relatively happy if a poor performer were to leave, and there are suggestions that employers actually encourage turnover if future demand is uncertain so they do not end up 'carrying' staff (Smith *et al* 2004, p375). On the other hand, if turnover was concentrated amongst high-flyers or those with vast amounts of experience, and those who remained were all poor performers or lacked ambition, this could have serious consequences for the organisation. However, if the objective is to trim back the workforce or reduce costs, a high rate of labour turnover could actually be advantageous (Sadhev *et al* 1999); alternatively, employers may decide to use temporary employment agencies rather than recruit their own staff and so shift the problem somewhere else (Rubery *et al* 2004; Smith *et al* 2004). Another question that arises repeatedly is whether there is an optimum level of labour turnover, just sufficient to 'churn' the internal labour market and keep new recruits coming in, or whether the costs of turnover make most cases expensive and unwanted (Glebbeek and Bax 2004). A range between 6 and 10 per cent has been quoted but it will be apparent from this discussion that it is not really sensible or worthwhile to rely on limited quantitative information without analysing the characteristics of leavers.

Forecasting external supply

Most texts on HR planning devote much less attention to forecasts of external supply and it probably explains why so many employers are shocked to discover there are skill shortages or a lack of suitably qualified staff when recruiting. The so-called 'demographic time-bomb' in the 1990s was a good illustration of this (Taylor 2002c). Due to a decline in the birth rate in the late 1970s, it was apparent that the number of school and college leavers entering the labour market in the early to mid-1990s would be significantly less than in previous years. This stimulated a spate of recruitment and advertising schemes designed to attract school leavers, but also the introduction of new policies to retain existing female and elderly staff, and the employment of individuals past the normal age of retirement.

A number of factors determine labour supply from the external labour market, both at a local and a national level. Obviously, local labour market information is important when recruiting manual or office workers whereas national and global trends and educational developments matter more for professionals. Broadly, the major factors influencing external labour supply *locally* include:

- levels of unemployment and qualified staff in the travel-to-work area
- opening or closure of other workplaces which compete for the same types of labour
- cost of housing and availability of transport to and from work
- reputation of the employer compared with that of others in the area, measured by such things as wage levels, working conditions, and general public relations image.

The major factors influencing labour supply at a *national* level, and by implication locally, include:

- levels of unemployment in general, and in particular occupations
- number of graduates in general, and in specific fields
- UK and EU legal frameworks governing issues such as working time, equal opportunities and employment protection
- government and industry-wide training schemes.

Take **two** occupational groups in an organisation with which you are familiar, and draw up a list of the factors influencing labour supply for each group. What can the organisation do to ensure there is an adequate supply of labour in each case?

JOB AND ROLE ANALYSIS

Job and role analysis is the second stage in recruitment and selection, and it is pivotal in identifying the tasks that new recruits are expected to undertake (Searle 2003, p23). In firms with relatively buoyant product markets and high levels of labour turnover, in which recruitment takes place on a frequent and continuing basis, it is probably not necessary to re-analyse jobs every time a vacancy occurs. However, it is useful to examine whether or not existing job descriptions, person specifications or competency profiles are appropriate for future needs. This may demonstrate there is no need for further recruitment or that the type of job and person required differs from expectations. Job analysis refers to 'the process of collecting, analysing and setting out information about the contents of jobs in order to provide the basis for a job description and data for recruitment, training, job evaluation and performance management' (Armstrong 1999, p190). The emphasis on gathering information differentiates job analysis from job descriptions, with the latter being seen as an output of the former. Role analysis is probably a more accurate and useful term to use as it focuses on the importance of the activity to the organisation (Pearn and Kandola 1993; Armstrong 1999), and emphasises the purpose of the role, as opposed to its individual components.

The methods used to analyse jobs and roles vary in terms of their sophistication, cost, convenience and acceptability, and these need to be borne in mind when deciding which method to employ. The issue of cost is particularly pertinent, as the benefits always need to be weighed up against the time, effort and money involved in its application. Similarly, the methods need to be acceptable to staff involved and be capable of gaining their agreement and commitment. No one method is inherently superior so choices should be made on the basis of the jobs to be analysed and the context in which the analysis takes place. For example, the use of sophisticated techniques is unlikely to be cost-effective if a small number of low skill jobs are to be analysed. Moreover, it may make more sense to use relatively simple methods rather than employ untrained or unqualified staff to undertake a sophisticated role analysis. A whole range of methods can be used but here we focus on four: observation, diaries, interviews, and questionnaires and checklists. The first three are relatively simple and are the most widely used. Each of the techniques is reviewed briefly below, but readers needing more detailed analysis should consult books such as Cook (1998), Cooper and Robertson (2002), Taylor (2002c), Cooper *et al* (2003) and Searle (2003).

- *Observation* is the most straightforward and readily available method, and it forms part of job analysis even if other techniques are employed. It is also one of the cheapest methods, and if there are any problems clarification can be sought direct from the job-holder. On the other hand, it may be difficult to interpret precisely what tasks are being undertaken, especially if there is a high intellectual or cognitive content to the job, and the fact that someone is being observed can impact on job behaviour.

- *Work diaries* are also commonly employed. These operate on the principle that job-holders record their activities over a period of time – say each hour over the course of a week, or every time they change the task on which they are engaged. To be effective this requires a high degree of commitment and co-operation from the job-holder, and a willingness to spend time explaining items in the diary. It is heavily reliant on job-holders keeping a comprehensive record of their activities, and not excluding items because they are deemed unimportant or common sense, or omitting items that are done frequently.

- *Interviews* are the third broad type of method employed, ranging from the relatively unstructured – in which job-holders are asked to describe their job while the interviewer probes to get more detail – through to the more standardised format where similar questions are asked of each job-holder. The major advantages of interviews are cost, convenience and the opportunity for interaction between interviewer and interviewee. The major disadvantages relate to bias and reliability, and interviewer skills. A rather more sophisticated technique involving interviews and focus groups is repertory grid analysis, although this requires analysts that are skilled at probing for further detail and do not take comments at face value (Searle 2003, pp36–39).

- *Questionnaires and checklists* are the most sophisticated of the methods used, often making use of computer packages to analyse data. There is a range of techniques, the best known and most widely used in the UK and the USA being the Position Analysis Questionnaire (PAQ) and the Work Profiling System (WPS). Readers wishing to see examples of these are referred to Searle (2003, pp39–41) where she shows how PAQ can be used to analyse the work of firefighters, and Cooper *et al* (2003, pp36–37) for WPS.

Cooper *et al* (2003, p33) argue that several techniques should be combined to ensure the development of a clear person specification. It is also acknowledged there are problems with job analysis, in particular regarding its stability over time, given that jobs change and its accuracy. Because of this there needs to be regular updating (Taylor 2002c, p103). Searle (2003, p53) has a wider concern, from a *social constructionist perspective* (Sandberg 2000), that because job analysis focuses specifically on what precisely people do at work, it tends to separate workers from the context in which they are doing the job – for example their role in teams – as well as assuming there is one best way to do each job.

JOB DESCRIPTIONS, PERSON SPECIFICATIONS AND COMPETENCY FRAMEWORKS

The results from job analysis provide the basis for some description or definition of the job(s) to be filled. This can be very specific or relatively broad in character, and the tendency in recent years has been to focus on the skills that employers need not just in the short-term but over a longer time frame, but it is clear that most organisations continue using job descriptions. They are particularly prevalent in large organisations and in the public sector. A job description typically includes the following:

1   *Job title*: a clear statement is all that is required, such as employee relations manager or wages clerk

2   *Location*: department, establishment, name of organisation

3   *Responsible to*: job title of supervisor to whom member of staff reports

4   *Responsible for*: job titles of members of staff who report directly into the job-holder, if any

5   *Main purpose of the job*: a short and unambiguous statement indicating precisely the overall objective and purpose of the job, such as 'assist and advise customers in a specific area', 'to drill metals in accordance with manufacturing policy'

6   *Responsibilities/duties*: a list of the main and subsidiary elements in the job, specifying in more or less detail what is required, such as maintaining records held on computer system or answering queries

7   *Working conditions*: a list of the major contractual agreements relating to the job, such as pay scales and fringe benefits, hours of work and holiday entitlement, and union membership if appropriate

8   *Other matters*: information such as geographical mobility and performance standards

9   *Any other duties* that may be assigned by the organisation.

Despite being widely used, job descriptions have been heavily criticised for being outmoded and increasingly irrelevant to modern conditions, symptomatic of what is seen as a collectivist, inflexible and more rules-oriented culture. It is argued that workers should not be concerned with the precise definition of 'standard' behaviour but rather with how 'value' can be added through personal initiative. Instead of 'working to contract' and abiding by explicit and published rules, staff should be encouraged to work 'beyond contract' under a regime of 'high-performance work systems' and 'blame-free cultures'. Consequently, highly specific job descriptions have been replaced by more generic and concise job profiles or accountability statements that are short – say, less than one page – and focused on the outcomes of the job rather than its process components (Beardwell and Wright 2004, p206). Another alternative is to use role definitions and 'key result area' statements (KRAs) that relate to the critical performance measures for the job (Armstrong 1999, p200). Examples of KRAs are: 'prepare marketing plans that support the achievement of corporate targets for profit and sales revenue'; or 'provide an accurate, speedy and helpful word-processing service to internal customers'.

Given the criticisms, it is surprising job descriptions or role profiles continue to be so widely used. However, they provide recruits with essential information about the organisation and their potential role, and without them people would apply for jobs without any form of realistic job preview. Having to outline critical results areas or accountability profiles can help managers decide whether or not it is necessary to fill a post, and if so in what form and at what level. On the other hand, vague and 'flexible' accounts of what is needed in a job may only store up trouble if there are subsequent concerns about performance and whether or not people are doing what is expected of them. There is a danger that commentators are seduced by the language of liberation and empowerment that articulates these ideas, without being mindful that some employers exploit their newfound freedom to redesign people's jobs without consultation or negotiation.

> Do job descriptions still exist in your organisation or one with which you are familiar? If they have been abandoned, has this led to greater autonomy or greater stress? If detailed job descriptions still exist, how well do these work?

BOX 20 A TRADITIONAL VIEW OF PERSON SPECIFICATIONS

Rodger's seven-point plan

- *Physical make-up*: physical attributes such as ability to lift heavy loads or differentiate between colours.
- *Attainments*: educational or professional qualifications considered necessary for undertaking the work.
- *General intelligence*: ability to define and solve problems, and use initiative in dealing with issues that have arisen.
- *Special aptitudes*: skills, attributes or competencies that are specifically relevant to the particular job.
- *Interests*: both work-related and leisure pursuits that may be relevant to performance in the job.
- *Disposition*: attitudes to work and to other members of staff and customers, as well as friendliness and assertiveness.
- *Circumstances*: domestic commitments, mobility and family support.

Fraser's five-point plan

- *Impact on others*: this covers much the same sort of issues as 'physical make-up' but it is more focused on impact on other employees and customers.
- *Acquired knowledge and qualifications*: see Rodger's second category above.
- *Innate abilities*: see 'general intelligence' above.
- *Motivation*: a person's desire to succeed in particular aspects of work and their commitment to achieve these goals.
- *Adjustment*: characteristics specifically related to the job, such as ability to cope with difficult customers or work well in a team.

Whereas *job descriptions* relate to the tasks to be undertaken, *person specifications* outline the human attributes seen as necessary to do the job. The best known are the seven-point plan (Rodger 1952) and its later adaptation by Fraser (1966) in the form of the five-point plan. These describe and categorise the principal features required for any job, with a differentiation between aspects that are essential to perform the job and those that, in an ideal world, are desirable. The two methods are outlined in Box 20.

Before moving on to the next part of this chapter, on competency frameworks, analyse the two plans in Box 20 in a little more detail. Focus in particular on the specifications that are used, explain what they are looking for and assess how easily and effectively these can be measured. What are the major shortcomings of these approaches?

Although both methods are now dated they are still used widely, albeit in an adapted form, and most texts (eg Newell and Shackleton 2000; Taylor 2002c; Beardwell and Wright 2004) focus on these methods, sometimes referring to other competency-based approaches as well. A major problem with the traditional methods is that they were devised at a time when it was considered acceptable to ask questions about an individual's domestic circumstances or private life. Although the broad framework may still be valid, it is now unethical, inappropriate and potentially discriminatory to probe too deeply into some of these areas. Moreover, except in specific cases where technical expertise is critical, it can make little business sense to restrict applications to people with specific qualifications or length of experience.

Both the Rodger and the Fraser frameworks rely heavily on personal judgement to specify the human qualities associated with successful performance (Newell and Shackleton 2000, p115). Accordingly, the traditional person specification is giving way to competency frameworks, the most significant advantage of these being that the focus is – or should be – on the *behaviours* of job applicants. There is therefore no need to make inferences about the personal qualities that might underpin behaviour (Newell and Shackleton 2001, p26). Job descriptions and person specifications often exist alongside competency-based approaches (Taylor 2002c), not least because they set a framework within which subsequent HR practices – such as performance management, training and development, and pay and grading – can be placed (Whiddett and Hollingforde 1999). In addition, the competencies can be related to specific performance outcomes rather than being concerned with potentially vague processes, such as disposition or interests outside of work. Moreover, these approaches eschew the use of criteria just because they are easy to measure – for example, educational qualifications or length of service – but might not relate closely with job effectiveness. According to IRS (IRS Employment Review 782 2003, p45) the most commonly used competencies are team orientation, communication, people management, customer focus, results orientation and problem-solving. Interestingly – or worryingly – ethical behaviour, responsibility, enthusiasm and listening are rarely used.

Roberts (1997, pp71–72) differentiates between four types of competency. These are:

1 *natural* competencies – made up by the 'big five' dimensions of personality: extraversion/intraversion, emotional stability, agreeableness, conscientiousness and openness to experience

2 *acquired* competencies – knowledge and skills acquired through work or other avenues

3   *adapting* competencies – the ability to adapt natural talents and acquired skills to a new situation

4   *performing* competencies – comprising observable behaviours and outputs.

Whiddett and Hollingforde (1999, p14) give an example of a three-level competency framework for a job that involves working with people, which covers three levels of activity: building relationships internally, building relationships externally and maintaining external networks. The behavioural indicators that are appropriate for each level can then be defined. For 'external networks', for example, these are:

1   Takes account of different cultural styles and values when dealing with external organisations.

2   Actively manages external contacts as a business network.

3   Identifies and makes use of events for developing external network.

These indicators tend to focus on 'softer' customer service skills rather than 'harder' technical skills, and employers are increasingly seeking attitudinal and behavioural skills; for example positive employee attitudes – such as a preparedness to work flexibly, a willingness to change and a responsiveness to customers (Morris *et al* 2000, p1053). Royle (1999) argues that McDonalds has been keen to recruit an acquiescent workforce unlikely to resist management control, and the target is therefore people who are in a weak labour market position with minimal work experience. In short, the strategy is to recruit on the basis of attitude and train staff subsequently in required technical skills (Callaghan and Thompson 2002). However, there must come a point by which customers find the soothing tones of the customer service operator do not compensate for the poor quality service provided by the train company, the food retailer or the hospital that is operating with poorly trained staff or suboptimal staffing levels merely to save costs (see also Taylor 2002c, p107). Box 21 provides an example of this.

BOX 21   LOOKS GOOD, SOUNDS RIGHT – LOUSY PRODUCT!

It has become part of modern business language that employers are now recruiting staff who have the right attitude or 'smile' down the telephone rather than have well-developed technical skills. A report by Warhurst and Nickson (2001) took this to an even higher level when they reported that workers are being selected on the basis of their looks or their voices. This is referred to as 'the commercial utility of aesthetic labour' where image and design pervade the new economy. This means that certain groups of workers – who are the wrong weight or speak in the wrong way – may be excluded from an increasing range of employment opportunities.

Source: Warhurst C. and Nickson D. *Looking Good, Sounding Right: Style counselling in the new economy*. London, The Industrial Society. 2001

After reading Box 21, talk this through with your colleagues and friends, drawing on your own personal experience. Do you think that it makes commercial sense to focus so much on attitudes rather than technical skills? If you are annoyed about a product do you feel that your irritation can be overcome just because someone listens attentively to your complaint? Is it ethically or morally right that people should be excluded from jobs in a clothes shop on the basis of their looks or from a call centre on the basis of their accent? Consider these issues in relation to person specifications and competency frameworks.

RECRUITMENT METHODS

Recruitment is typically regarded as the poor relation of selection, typically afforded limited space in most publications and with little evidence of theoretical underpinnings (Breaugh and Starke 2000). While selection has caught the attention of organisational psychologists keen to improve the reliability and validity of selection methods, recruitment has received scant attention. This is strange because, as Watson (1994, p203) argued cogently some time ago, 'recruitment provides the candidates for the selector to judge. Selection techniques cannot overcome failures in recruitment; they merely make them evident'. Important decisions have to be made about whether or not to recruit, from which sources, using which media, and at what cost. Moreover, the documentation used in the recruitment exercise has an impact beyond HRM in that it conveys images of the organisation, its products and its overall philosophy. Legal issues have to be borne in mind when recruiting, particularly in the design and wording of adverts and in online channels (Taylor 2002c). Furthermore, if the recruitment process generates insufficient applications, or too may unsuitable ones, it will prove expensive. Choosing a cost-effective recruitment method therefore depends on factors specific to each organisation and to different types of vacancy. However, rather than

Table 17   *Types of external recruitment methods used by employers*

Recruitment methods used by employers	% respondents used in	
	2004	**1999**
Closed searches		
Word-of-mouth	58*	53
Links to schools, colleges and universities	51	40
Recruitment agencies	81	60
Responsive methods		
Speculative applications	58*	69
Open searches		
Local newspaper adverts	87	82
Adverts in specialist press	75	91
National newspaper adverts	61	80
Job Centres/Employment Service/ONE	61	69
Employer's website	72	42
Radio or TV adverts	9	13

* The categories for word-of-mouth and speculative applications were combined in the 2004 survey.
Sources: Chartered Institute of Personnel Development. *Recruitment Report*. London, CIPD. 2001a; Chartered Institute of Personnel Development. *Recruitment, Retention and Turnover: A survey of the UK and Ireland*. London, CIPD. 2004

describing a long list of different methods, it is more sensible to categorise these into four groups depending on whether they are internal or external, closed or open in character. Figures for usage are provided in Table 17 (see page 171).

Internal recruitment

This is where the internal labour market is used for filling vacancies, something that is more popular during rationalisation than in periods of boom and expansion. Posts can be filled following a search of employee records, and then redeploying staff from one task or area to another. At its best this can be seen as a form of career development whereby people move around the organisation to make effective use of their skills and abilities as part of a wider HR plan. At its worst, as in situations where external recruitment is frozen, it may simply entail shifting staff from one department to another, resulting in untrained and/or demotivated employees. A slight alternative is where staff are transferred from temporary posts to open-ended contracts or from agency work onto the payroll. This provides employers with a form of quasi-internal labour market where they can observe people at work before committing to an offer of more secure employment (Rubery *et al* 2002, 2004). This form of recruitment is prevalent in small firms as managers 'take a "good hard look" at potential staff before deciding to offer direct employment' (Earnshaw *et al* 1998, p547) as well as at some call centres.

Closed searches

While using the external labour market, these methods are limited to those groups of worker the employer wants to hire and it is not open to general applications. It includes 'word-of-mouth' recruitment by existing staff who nominate potential recruits through their personal contacts or by managers recruiting people who have worked for another local firm. The CIPD survey showed that word-of-mouth recruitment remains widely used though it is sometimes hard to differentiate from speculative applications. Some organisations pay 'bounties' or referral payments to staff who recommend a friend who then remains in employment for more than a set period of time. The amount paid depends on the post but could be in the region of £250–£500, and in one case – Capital Consulting – all workers who have provided a referral have the opportunity to win a new car through a draw at the end of the year (IRS Employment Review 804 2004). A major advantage of referrals is the quality of candidates provided, as most employees are unlikely to recommend friends they deem to be unsuitable or someone who would not 'fit in' with the culture of the organisation. The Coventry Building Society filled nearly a quarter of all its posts through this method (IRS Employment Review 804 2004). All 40 of the firms investigated by Carroll *et al* (1999, p244) used this method, often in tandem with more formal approaches, and two-thirds had rehired former employees. As with internal recruitment, this is a cheap option in that recruits are readily available, are known to existing members of the workforce, and simple selection techniques can be used. On the other hand, organisations such as Acas, the EOC and the CRE are worried that such 'ring-fencing' may reinforce existing imbalances (gender, race and disability), thwarting attempts to encourage greater workforce diversity. Recruitment of managers follows similar routes in some respects because, although more open methods are used just as widely as agencies, the latter are felt to be much more effective where they are used in the private sector (IRS Employment Review 796b 2004).

> Debate with your colleagues the justification for employing 'word-of-mouth' recruitment methods. Consider both the performance and the ethical implications of this approach.

Closed searches also make use of external contacts (say, at schools, colleges or universities) to identify suitable candidates, especially if this has worked well previously. Obviously, this is especially appropriate for the recruitment of younger workers and graduates, and the CIPD survey found it was on a par with the organisation's own website in popularity. This was also seen as one of the most effective methods for recruiting graduates, especially through campus visits, sponsored and ex-placement students, although open methods – such as national adverts and company websites – were also seen as equally effective (IRS Employment Review 788a 2003). Similarly, headhunters are used for high-level appointments, particularly those that need to be handled sensitively or confidentially, or for those where the executive search agency has extensive contacts. This method is expensive, and is used much more in the private sector than for public or voluntary bodies.

Responsive methods

These differ from closed methods in that employers interview casual callers or former applicants whose names and addresses are on file. Employers often display notices of vacancies, and this can be a very good source of applicants. It is difficult to tell whether this has declined in popularity given the merging of this with word-of-mouth recruitment in the CIPD survey, but in the study by Carroll et al (1999) over half the sample of 40 SMEs made a point of contacting former applicants if there was a vacancy, and a similar proportion had offered work to casual callers. This method is more 'open' than the previous two categories because it relies on people actually making the effort to search for work rather than applying for a vacancy that is advertised in the press. Indeed, employers argued that this showed initiative and potential commitment by applicants, making them stand out from others in the field. In pubs, clubs and restaurants this can also help to create synergies between customers and workers that may well lead to improved performance.

Open searches

This covers the largest number of techniques. Advertisements in national and local papers are amongst the most widely used methods, and for specialist posts it is usual to advertise in the trade press (CIPD 2004b). By contrast, radio and TV adverts were rarely used, although there have been campaigns attempting to persuade people to undergo teacher training or nursing at times of shortage. E-recruitment has become a much more significant tool in the last few years, as Table 17 (on page 171) and Box 22 (see page 174) show, with usage increasing by about 70 per cent during the five years up to 2004. The advertising media used depends on the vacancies to be filled and the resources the employer is prepared to commit. The state of the external labour market is also important, and the most appropriate methods vary depending upon local and/or national levels of unemployment, on specific skill shortages, and on competition in the labour market. For example, a company seeking to recruit manual workers or clerical officers may target the local job centre and put advertisements in local newspapers at little cost. Conversely, recruitment for technical jobs is likely to require adverts in specialist trade magazines, schools and further education colleges to generate a suitable pool of applicants. We have already mentioned graduate recruitment but the costs involved are likely to be relatively high because potential future contribution is likely to be higher than for many other groups of applicants. Interestingly, research by Turban and Cable (2003, p746) demonstrates 'good' employers tend to receive a higher quantity and quality of applicants for posts.

It is likely that e-recruitment is set to grow. Do you feel that this is a positive trend? After reading Box 22, analyse the pros and cons of e-recruitment.

BOX 22   E-RECRUITMENT

The usage of e-recruitment continues to expand. According to IRS 90% of firms are using some form of electronic recruitment at some stage in the process and over 18 million people annually post their details on Monster.com. Some firms use job boards (websites with job advertisements), often together with portals through the corporate website. Vacancies tend to be wide-ranging and across all sectors, and not confined to graduate and IT recruitment.

The main advantages include:

- reduced costs
- improved corporate image
- reduced administration
- shortened recruitment cycle
- wider pool of applicants
- easier recruitment process for candidates
- improved overseas recruitment
- easing of recruitment problems.

The process is not without problems, and the IRS survey found that more than 25% of organisations met 'significant' problems with its use; for private sector service organisations this rose to almost 40%.

The main disadvantages include:

- too many unsuitable applicants
- technical problems
- shortage of applicants
- expense.

The CIPD also warns that exclusive use of e-recruitment may disadvantage certain groups (eg young black men are less likely to have access). In many cases use of self-selection tools can reduce the number of unsuitable applicants, and a number of organisations report successful use of e-learning – Marks and Spencer, British Gas, Bristol University.

From the point of view of the applicant, there is a different range of problems:

- slow feedback or follow-up
- not enough relevant jobs available on-line
- lack of essential information on the organisation's web pages
- concerns about security of personal information
- wish for human contact
- technical problems.

Sources: Feldman D. and Klaas B. 'Internet job hunting: a field study of applicant experiences with on-line recruiting', *Human Resource Management*, Vol. 41, No. 2, 2002. pp175–192; IRS Employment Review 792a. *Recruiters March in Step with Online Recruitment*. 23 January 2004. pp44–48; IRS Employment Review 799a. *Answering the Recruitment Call Online*. 7 May 2004. pp46–48

Employment agencies and job centres are also widely used, with the former particularly active in the field of professional, secretarial and administrative posts, and especially in the area of temporary employment (Druker and Stanworth 2001; Ward *et al* 2001). This is also evident in the provision of supply teachers (Grimshaw *et al* 2003). There are often concerns about the quality of provision and the extent to which agency workers are committed to organisational goals, and it has been argued (Ward *et al* 2001) that the use of temporary workers is not sustainable in the long term for a variety of reasons – high levels of labour turnover, limited career opportunities, differential rates of pay and other employment conditions. Agency workers may offer employers a short-term solution but there are worries about the consistency with which temporary labour is managed. Concerns about quality of provision were repeatedly made by the owner-managers in Carroll *et al*'s (1999) study of road haulage firms, with a majority very anxious about allowing temporary workers to drive 'expensive and potentially lethal trucks' without proper training. Research by Hebson *et al* (2003), Marchington *et al* (2003a) and Rubery *et al* (2004) in quite different contexts shows up the potential problems caused by a reliance on temporary workers.

CHOOSING THE RIGHT SELECTION METHOD

We now move on to review selection methods, examining interviews and tests in more detail. It is beyond the scope of this book to analyse the whole range of methods – such as references, application forms, work sampling, assessment centres and graphology – in greater depth. Readers needing more information on these techniques should consult sources such as Cook (1998), Taylor (2002c), Cooper *et al* (2003) and Searle (2003). It is worth stating at the outset that no single technique, regardless of how well it is designed and administered, is capable of producing perfect selection decisions that predict with certainty which individuals will perform well in a particular role. Employers are advised not to rely on one method, advice that appears to be needed in most cases. Interviews are used extensively in most organisations, along with application forms and references. Practice varies as to whether references are sought prior to or after interviews, whether they are consulted before or after interview, or merely sought as a final vetting device prior to making an appointment. Even when references are taken up, some practitioners are sceptical of their value while in others – particularly where public money is being used – references tend to be seen as a critical part of the whole process.

It is easy to gauge the popularity of different selection methods from the annual CIPD survey and the results are shown in Table 18 on page 176. This indicates that, across the sample of nearly 1000 employers, the most widely used techniques were traditional interviews, competency-based interviews and tests for specific skills. By contrast, online tests were only rarely used. Taken together it appears that interviews and tests are used by a similar proportion of these organisations, but it is also clear that usage varies greatly between sectors. As expected, the public sector and voluntary bodies are much more likely to use structured interviews while private sector firms tend to use traditional and critical incident interviews, as well as personality questionnaires. Though not widely used in total, telephone interviews are rather more common in the private service sector than anywhere else – presumably for customer service jobs. The use of different methods also varies between occupations: assessment centres and personality questionnaires are rarely used except for applications for managerial and professional positions, while there is little variation between occupations for the other methods. For example, even though they were applied less widely with manual workers, competency-based interviews were still used by about one-third of the sample.

Table 18   *The popularity of different selection methods by sector (% of organisations using each technique)*

Method used by organisations	Overall	Manufact-uring and produc-tion	Voluntary, comm-unity and not for profit	Private sector services	Public sector services
Traditional interview	66	79	52	71	42
Structured interview (eg critical incident)	38	41	18	45	20
Structured interview (panel)	55	46	88	45	82
Competency-based interview	62	63	49	66	57
Telephone interview	26	19	10	38	13
General ability tests	53	58	64	49	52
Literacy and/or numeracy tests	48	56	46	44	42
Tests for specific skills	60	62	72	55	63
Online tests (selection/self-selection)	6	4	3	9	4
Personality questionnaires	46	53	34	48	36
Assessment centres	43	41	34	44	48

Source: Chartered Institute of Personnel and Development. *Recruitment, Retention and Turnover: A survey of the UK and Ireland*. London, CIPD. 2004. p14

The use of specific selection techniques also varies in popularity between countries. Newell and Tansley (2001, p199) found that interviews are most widely used in Britain and North America, graphology in France (and French companies in other countries), and assessment centres in Britain, Germany and the Netherlands. Tests in general are more popular in France and Belgium, and although integrity tests are rarely used they are becoming more popular in the USA. There are clear societal, cultural and organisational effects on choices about which techniques to use and applicants from certain backgrounds – such as women and ethnic minorities – are known to have concerns about their legitimacy (Iles and Robertson 1997; Schmitt and Chan 1999; Searle 2003).

Robertson and Smith (2001) provide data (see Box 23) indicating that most techniques have very low levels of accuracy in terms of producing effective selection decisions. Of techniques used on their own, work sampling offers the highest likelihood of success, closely followed by intelligence tests and structured interviewing. References score fairly low on accuracy levels, and graphology is regarded by some (Cooper *et al* 2003, p152) as hardly better than random selection. Schmidt and Hunter (1998, p270) argue that it is not so much the characteristics of writing that leads to different estimates of people's abilities and personalities but its content, clearly quite a different attribute. It is also clear that combining techniques greatly increases accuracy; for example, the combination of intelligence tests with structured interviews, integrity tests or work sampling leads to a substantial improvement in validity (Schmidt and Hunter 1998, p272).

Because no single method offers a panacea for all situations, choosing the most appropriate selection techniques for each situation is what really matters. Interestingly, Wilk and Cappelli (2003, p122) note that despite the literature on selection being voluminous, 'virtually no research has been done on the determinants of the selection process itself, on the employer's choices'. They found that a greater number of more sophisticated methods were used when the complexity of work increased, presumably because more traditional methods were unable to capture the range of attributes that were being sought and different methods

BOX 23   ACCURACY OF SELECTION METHODS

1.0   perfect selection

0.65 intelligence tests and integrity tests

0.63 intelligence tests and structured interviews

0.60 intelligence tests and work sampling

0.54 work sample tests

0.51 intelligence tests

0.51 structured interviews

0.41 integrity tests

0.40 personality tests

0.37 assessment centres

0.35 biodata

0.26 references

0.18 years of job experience

0.10 years of education

0.02 graphology

0.0   selection with a pin

Source: Adapted from Robertson I. and Smith M. 'Personnel selection', *Journal of Occupational and Organizational Psychology*, Vol. 74, No. 4, 2001. pp441–472

were able to provide multiple perspectives on the ultimate choice. Moreover, failures with these groups of workers were also likely to be more serious for the organisation. However, choice can vary depending on the situation; for example, telephone screening may be highly appropriate in the selection of call centre operatives, work sample tests for secretarial staff, and presentations for management consultants or professional engineers. Various authors (Newell and Shackleton 2000; Taylor 2002c; Cooper *et al* 2003; Searle 2003) discuss in detail the criteria needed to assess the value of each method: practicability, sensitivity, reliability and validity.

- *Practicality*, according to Cooper *et al* (2003, p94), is one of the most important criteria. The method chosen has to be acceptable to all parties – managers, candidates and statutory bodies such as the EOC and CRE and professional organisations such as the CIPD and The British Psychological Society (BPS). It also has to be economical in terms of costs and benefits, the time that is required to administer the exercise, and within the capabilities of those running the selection process. The issue of cost is particularly critical. There is little point running a sophisticated and complex personality test if just one candidate applies or if it is for a temporary post.

- *Sensitivity* is a key feature in the choice of selection methods, as this represents the ability of any particular technique to discriminate between candidates in terms of their ability to do the job. Care is needed to ensure it is not simply a smokescreen for making employment decisions that disadvantage or exclude applicants on grounds of race, gender, age or disability.

- *Reliability* comprises several different elements, but refers essentially to 'the consistency of a method used to select individuals' (Newell and Shackleton 2000, p119). It should not be influenced too much by chance factors. Cooper *et al* (2003, pp50–52) outline various forms of reliability: between different raters, when the same technique is used on different occasions and between different methods. For example, inter-rater reliability is crucial if several interviewers are being used, as one might reject candidates others would have selected. Similarly, tests may prove to be unreliable if applicants are able to improve their performance over time.

- The final criterion is *validity* – the correctness of the inferences that can be drawn from the selection method. Newell and Shackleton (2000, p121) define this as 'the relationship between the predictors (the results from the selection method used) and the criterion (performance on the job)'. The competency debate revolves around this issue, as selectors attempt to define the key attributes and skills demonstrated by high (or satisfactory) performers and then use these as a benchmark against which to assess applicants. This is a difficult task to undertake, not least because it is hard to find proxies for characteristics such as effectiveness in leading teams or managing change. It is also hard to draw inferences about future job performance from statements made at interview or characteristics displayed during an assessment centre. Clearly, many factors influence subsequent job performance, some of which occur outside of work, and their effects may be unknown at the time of appointment. On the other hand, based on a review of existing research Salgado (2002) found there were correlations between the Big Five personality factors and subsequent levels of labour turnover and aspects such as theft and disciplinary problems.

Interviews

We have already seen that interviews are extremely widely used and surveys show they are regarded as the single most effective selection method for groups ranging from managers to semi- and unskilled workers (IRS Employment Review 791 2004). They are also the most roundly condemned, criticised in particular for unacceptable levels of reliability, poor predictive validity and low sensitivity, although they do have the advantage of being relatively cheap. Many legal issues surround the interview, in terms of bias and equal opportunities, data protection and confidentiality, as well as human rights (Leighton and Proctor 2001). However, the interview itself is often blamed whereas the real problem is that it has been conducted by untrained and inadequately prepared interviewers. One way to reduce this problem is to use interviews in conjunction with other methods. Nevertheless, there is a deeper question here about the purpose of the interview. To what extent is it seen as a two-way decision-making process involving choices both for the organisation and the applicant, or is it principally a technical exercise in which the employer seeks a perfect selection decision with high predictive validity?

> Consider **two** interviews – one you think was well handled and one that was poorly handled – in which you have taken part, either as an interviewer or as an applicant. Identify the reasons for the differences between them. What can you learn from this to improve the validity of interviews as a selection device?

Selection interviews can take a number of forms (Cook 1998; Taylor 2002c; Cooper *et al* 2003; Searle 2003). Firstly they can be between individuals on a *one-to-one* basis. These have the advantage of relative informality, of encouraging rapport, and potentially of generating more frank and open discussions. They also suffer from problems of interviewer bias (both the 'halo' and the 'satan' effects), low levels of reliability, and lack of coverage of the subject matter. This type of interview is particularly prone to the accusation that interviewers make up their minds about an applicant in the first few minutes, and then spend the rest of the interview finding reasons to justify their view. The sequential interview is a slight adaptation of this format, in that candidates are seen by a series of managers in one-to-one situations, with each probing for evidence about different aspects of the job.

The second type is the *small group* or tandem interview, where two or three people interview a candidate together, making their judgement on the basis of the same interaction. They may explore different aspects of the job or even take on specific roles during the interview. In the case of a supervisory appointment, for example, it makes sense for a line manager and an HR specialist to interview together to explore both the technical elements of the job and the applicant's management style. This has the benefit of allowing at least two people to observe the candidate first-hand and reach a joint decision.

The final type of interview is the *panel*, typically comprising between three and five interviewers drawn from different parts of the organisation, and fulfilling – if roles have been allocated beforehand – different duties. Panel interviews for senior academics may involve 12 or more people – in which case the interview really does become something of a ritual or trial, depending upon which side of the table one is sitting. The arguments in favour of using a panel are much the same as for the small group interview. It allows several people to see the candidate together, it minimises the potential for overt bias and it ensures – in theory at least – that decisions are made by those individuals most closely related to the post. The disadvantages are also well known. It is more difficult for interviewers to build up rapport with candidates, some interviewees may be extremely nervous about the prospect of facing a large number of people in a formal setting, and panel members often lack training in how to interview. Though not always apparent, bias can be a problem because some panel members exert a sizeable influence over the decision, yet this is often hidden and covert.

Most commentators agree that selection interviews are riddled with problems, some due to the nature of the interview process, others to the skills of interviewers. The major problem was clearly articulated by Plumbley (1991, p103) many years ago when he wrote that interviewing is 'an everyday occurrence and is the most widely used assessment technique. It is part of the popular vocabulary. It looks easy, and everyone is inclined to believe they are good at it. Therein lies the danger and the confusion.' Much of this can be explained by attribution theory, the view that applicants are defined as 'good' if they obey the rules of the interview set by the interviewer, and 'bad' if they do not comply (Cooper *et al* 2003, p104). Similarly, interviewers have a tendency to select candidates who display attributes that they regard as important, who behave – or even look – like others for whom they have positive feelings, or who say something early in the interview with which the interviewer agrees (Taylor 2002c). The converse also applies, but such 'halo' or 'satan' effects are not visible to other members of the panel, and sometimes not to the interviewers themselves, and are therefore almost impossible to take into account. A common problem is that interviewers have highly selective memories for what has been said, typically picking up on one point to support their predetermined opinion while being unaware of contraindications (Taylor 2002c, pp173–174). The rituals associated with the interview are more important than is often admitted and it is unusual for hiring decisions in Britain to be made without face-to-face contact, though this has happened with the recruitment of teachers and nurses from overseas.

Structured interviews are seen as a way of improving the validity and reliability of selection decisions (Cooper *et al* 2003, pp94–98). Several features differentiate them from traditional interviews: questions should be developed from the job analysis; each candidate should be asked standard, though not necessarily identical, questions; and a systematic scoring procedure should be used, preferably based upon a behaviourally anchored rating scale. Arguments in favour of the structured interview include:

1   It is tied into job analysis and competency profiles.
2   There is an increased focus on job-related questions.
3   Multiple interviewers tend to be used.

In some local authorities, as part of the drive to ensure that selection decisions are free from gender and race bias, applicants are asked precisely the same set of questions – which are agreed in advance – in the same order, and the answers are rated in a systematic manner. On the other hand structured interviews may not be acceptable to senior decision-makers because they prefer to avoid rigid, fixed and standardised processes. It is also acknowledged that the interview is not a one-way exercise (Cook 1998; Searle 2003). Structured interviews do improve reliability but problems remain with validity. For example, some individuals may be extremely good at impression management (Posthuma *et al* 2002, p11; Searle 2003, p120), articulating their achievements and plans with ease but poor at putting these into effect. Conversely, others may be very good at their jobs but fail to convey this at the interview.

A slight variant of the structured interview is the behavioural or situational interview where candidates are asked to describe how they have operated in previous situations or suggest how they would act if a particular situation were to arise. Barclay (2001, p88) cites evidence from a sample of organisations that used behavioural interviews; these appeared to produce better selection decisions due to improved quality of information, which more than offset additional training costs incurred for interviewers.

> Which selection techniques would you advise using for the appointment of (a) a worker in a call centre, (b) a manager in a restaurant and (c) a research scientist? Justify your answer.

Selection testing

Selection tests have become more popular over the last decade as employers have sought higher levels of validity in their selection decisions. We have already seen that tests are used in some form or another by a large number of organisations, although the types of test used varies according to occupational group. This section of the book aims to provide an insight into the major types of tests available, their principal merits and shortcomings, and their part in selection decisions. It must be stressed at the outset that it is *not* designed to enable readers to design, administer and interpret tests. It is crucial that HR practitioners recognise the limits of their own expertise and know when to seek advice on test usage, and from which suppliers. It must be realised that acting beyond their own professional competence can have severe consequences, not only for recruitment and selection and public relations but also on applicants. Readers needing more detailed analysis of these techniques are advised to consult Cook (1998), Taylor (2002c), Cooper *et al* (2003) and Searle (2003), as well as the CIPD and BPS.

Smith and Robertson (1993, p161) have defined psychological tests as: 'carefully chosen, systematic and standardised procedures for evoking a sample of responses from a candidate, which can be used to assess one or more of their psychological characteristics by comparing the results with those of a representative sample of an appropriate population'. This highlights several important features about tests: they should be chosen carefully and be appropriate for the situation; they should be applied systematically in a standard manner; and the results should be capable of comparison with norms for the particular group in question. The CIPD Quick Facts guidance on Psychological Testing stresses that tests must be supported by a body of evidence and statistical data that demonstrates their validity in an occupational setting before being used.

Cooper *et al* (2003, p126) distinguish between two broad categories of test. *Cognitive tests* are designed to measure mental ability, and take several different forms in practice. First, tests of achievement purport to measure the degree of knowledge and/or skill a person has acquired at the time the test is administered, such as school examinations. Second, tests of general intelligence are designed to assess 'the capacity for abstract thinking and reasoning within a range of different contexts and media' (Toplis *et al* 1994, p17), an example of which is Wechsler's Adult Intelligence Scale (WAIS). This category of tests also aims to assess what a person could learn (Cook 1998, p98). The third set of cognitive tests measure special aptitudes or abilities, such as assessment of verbal, numerical or spatial ability, and manual dexterity. These include tests for clerical speed and accuracy, computer aptitudes, or sales skills, which are sometimes compiled into batteries of tests for use in organisations. Some (Cook 1998, p135) argue that 'validity generalisation analysis has proved that tests of natural ability predict work performance very well. For a vast range of jobs, the more able worker is the better worker'. Stairs *et al* (2000, p28) are not totally convinced, suggesting that such techniques are most appropriate for testing managerial abilities.

The second broad grouping – *personality tests* – are based around 'trait' or 'type' theories, involving 'the identification of a number of fairly independent and enduring characteristics of behaviour which all people display but to differing degrees' (Toplis *et al* 1994, p28). The Big Five personality factors are agreed by the scientific community as generally applicable across all contexts but this does not mean that all five factors are applicable in all situations and for all occupations, nor does it mean that the correlations between these factors and performance is strong across the board (Cooper *et al* 2003, pp131–132). For example, Barrick *et al* (2001) show that conscientiousness and emotional stability seem to be relevant for selection decisions in all occupations, whereas other factors – agreeableness, extraversion and openness to experience – are more specific to particular jobs and situations; extraversion appears to be useful in predicting performance amongst managers.

> Can selection decisions ever be truly 'objective' tests of a person's suitability for employment?

Choosing the most appropriate test should be judged on the basis of existing evidence in similar situations and perceived organisational needs. There are many types of test on the market, some of which were designed and tested in the USA and therefore need to be treated with caution if they have not been validated in other countries. Amongst the most common types of personality questionnaire are Cattell's 16PF, the SHL Occupational Personality Questionnaire (OPQ), the Myers–Briggs Type Indicator and the Californian Psychological Inventory (CPI). In addition to personality questionnaires, there are also interest questionnaires (such as the Rothwell–Miller Interest Blank and a range of SHL questionnaires for different levels), values questionnaires, and work behaviour questionnaires. As so many of these are now available listing them alone would cover several pages, so further information can be obtained from the sources quoted previously.

Not surprisingly, increased usage has highlighted a number of problems, particularly in the choice of tests and in their deployment. The CIPD and the BPS are both concerned about the emergence of disreputable providers and untrained assessors who do not know how to interpret the results of tests. In addition, there are major anxieties that some tests could discriminate against particular groups of people, most notably ethnic minorities and women (Schmitt and Chan 1999; Newell and Shackleton 2000; Searle 2003). There are also occasions when financial or other pressures on organisations may encourage them to take short cuts in the use of tests, or there may be inconsistencies in their usage, and although HR managers may raise professional objections organisational politics can mean these are ignored (Baker and Cooper 2000, p78). Used in isolation, tests are not particularly good predictors of future job behaviour (Newell and Shackleton 2000, p127) because strong situational pressures lead to alternative solutions in practice. Moreover many jobs, especially those with discretionary potential, can be done perfectly well in a variety of different ways. Other problems arise if individuals fake their responses in order to present an image that increases their chances of being selected (Arthur *et al* 2001, pp665–666). Even more worrying is the case where applicants provide a 'true' answer to a question – say, about never having stolen anything – only to be penalised because this has been inserted to check on lying as it is assumed that everyone will have stolen something during their lives (p668).

Nevertheless, tests do have a useful role to play in selection decisions provided they are used properly, preferably in tandem with other tests or selection methods. Guidance has also been issued about points to bear in mind when choosing and using tests. Key points include:

■ Tests need to be reliable and valid, and have accompanying evidence that they do not unfairly disadvantage certain groups of people.

■ Tests should only be sold to qualified users, carried out under standard conditions, and only released after adequate research.

■ Candidates need to understand the place of tests in the selection process, see their relevance to the job in hand, and be convinced of their accuracy.

■ Test administrators must be qualified to use tests and be able to interpret the inferences that can be drawn from them, and candidates need to be reassured about this.

■ Candidates should not be coached for tests.

■ The results should be confidential and held with the full knowledge of those tested, and provision must be made to feed back results to candidates.

DIFFERING PARADIGMS OF SELECTION

The discussion throughout this chapter has intimated that there are competing definitions and paradigms operating within the field of selection – for the most part implicit rather than explicit. In this final section of the chapter, while acknowledging that the distinctions between them are not always clear-cut, we review four of these perspectives: social exchange; scientific rationality; socialisation; and socially constructed reality, knowledge and power.

Social exchange

For many HR managers, the selection process has typically revolved around the interview. As such, it is not unrealistic to view this as 'a controlled conversation with a purpose', the purpose being to 'collect information in order to predict how successfully the individual would perform in the job for which they have applied, measuring them against predetermined criteria' (Torrington et al 2002, p242). The idea of a conversation, albeit controlled, conjures up images of a pleasant chat to share experiences, and downplays the fact the selector is typically in a much more powerful position, especially at times of high unemployment. But, there is some substance to this view. After all, applicants make decisions about whether or not they want to work for an organisation, and at times of labour market shortage or in jobs where it is difficult to attract people because of competition, this can be a much more equal exchange. Potential applicants may decide after reading the literature from an organisation they will not bother applying. Similarly, candidates may decide not to attend an interview or turn down a job after it has been offered. Moreover, applicants 'may create and maintain impressions of themselves which they believe the assessor is looking for' (Newell and Shackleton 2001, p37), thus undermining the validity of the selection process. The same process can occur if selectors are keen to persuade someone to work for the organisation and give unrealistic job previews in order to tempt them. Issues like this reinforce the importance of minimising the possibility of 'contamination' in selection by using methods with higher validity and reliability.

Scientific rationality

This approach is associated with organisational and occupational psychologists searching for the 'perfect' selection device. The emphasis here is on ways of making selection more scientific by using structured interviews, tests and work sampling (Posthuma et al 2002). This psychometric perspective has dominated the field for some time (Newell and Shackleton 2001, p24), following a simple sequence of premises:

1   Excellent job performance can be identified and codified.

2   There is one best way to work.

3   Competencies can be derived and used to define the key characteristics of a post.

4   Selection techniques can be devised to assess these competencies.

5   Validity and reliability can be improved by sticking to pre-planned and determined methods..

Newell and Shackleton (2001, p32) term this the 'actuarial method' of selection because 'it is based purely on a numerical calculation of the collected data'. However, the semblance of rationality implicit in psychometric ideas is a myth 'because it is based on assumptions that there is one best way to do a job'. Moreover they claim (p42) that the 'psychological perspective simply hides behind a façade of objectivity so it remains easy to perpetuate discrimination while presenting the whole process as fair'. Confidence in the apparent objectivity of testing can be undermined by inappropriate and poorly applied tests. The idea that any selection technique can be 'objective' is problematic, as decisions have to be made that render the exercise open to management choice; for example, in terms of the choice of test, the items contained within it, the perceived validity for the job in question, as well as the cultural norms surrounding their use. The use of standard tests may also contribute to organisational cloning and limit the achievement of a 'diverse' workforce. Searle (2003, p263) is particularly scathing; she argues that 'the psychometric approach reflects a Western context, which is based on a capitalistic premise of the dominance of profit and the market place as regulator. Recruitment and selection processes are only useful where the organisation has more applicants than vacancies.'

Socialisation

The third paradigm regards selection as the first stage in a wider exercise in achieving person–job–organisation fit (Anderson and Ostroff 1997) rather than confined merely to a fit between the person and the job. It is suggested that 'selection and socialisation are more accurately conceived as stages in a single, longitudinal process of newcomer integration ... socialisation begins during selection as the applicant experiences the organisation's formal procedures for the first time' (p413). The socialisation aspects take a number of forms depending on the methods that are used. These are:

■ *information provision* – extent and accuracy of communications

■ *preference impact* – procedural and distributive justice and personal liking for methods

■ *expectational impact* – assumptions about organisational climate and psychological contract

■ *attitudinal impact* – degree of investment in the selection process

■ *behavioural impact* – the extent to which the selection methods create/affect subsequent behaviour.

Socially constructed reality

This sees the selection process as not enacted solely within organisations – and therefore principally affected by selectors – but taking place within a wider societal framework (Ramsay and Scholarios 1999). This notion considers issues concerning knowledge and power, and with social structures and expected norms within societies. Consequently, 'an integrated model of selection should accommodate the subjective, discursive, power-laden, contested, negotiated and transient nature of each aspect of the process' (p77). This approach contrasts starkly with the notion of scientific rationality and objective decisions, and it helps us to understand why choices about selection methods vary so much between countries and organisations. Ramsay and Scholarios (p81) describe the case of senior executive selection to illustrate their argument, suggesting that techniques regarded as highly appropriate for other positions – say, graduates – would be seen as totally unacceptable for appointments at this level. The whole process is managed sensitively and confidentially, it makes use of informal sources of information, and both parties expect to influence the final decision.

CONCLUSIONS

This chapter has reviewed the major elements in an organisation's staffing and resourcing policies and practices, and it has argued that HR planning and recruitment should not be treated as the poor relations of selection. Because of increasing sophistication in the field of selection, it is often forgotten that without effective recruitment practices there may be limited numbers of applicants from which to choose, and this can impact on performance at later stages of the employment contract. Conversely, using well-chosen multiple methods can increase the likelihood that staff who are appointed will be capable of meeting targets. This is one area of HRM where assistance might usefully be sought from external providers, especially in relation to recruitment advertising and psychometric testing, and being aware of the limits to one's expertise is just as important as knowing which techniques to use. Given that selection decisions are increasingly devolved to line managers, it is even more important that these processes are well organised, delivered and evaluated.

USEFUL READING

CHARTERED INSTITUTE OF PERSONNEL AND DEVELOPMENT. *Recruitment, Retention, and Turnover: A survey of the UK and Ireland.* London, CIPD. 2004b.

COOPER D., ROBERTSON I. *and* TINLINE G. *Recruitment and Selection: A framework for success.* London, Thomson. 2003.

GLEBBEEK A. *and* BAX E. 'Is high employee turnover really harmful? An empirical test using company records', *Academy of Management Journal*, Vol. 47, No. 2, 2004. pp277–286.

IRS EMPLOYMENT REVIEW 791. *Picking the Best from the Rest.* 23 January 2004. pp42–48.

MARCHINGTON M., CARROLL M. *and* BOXALL P. 'Labour scarcity and the survival of small firms: a resource-based view of the road haulage industry', *Human Resource Management Journal*, Vol. 13, No. 4, 2003. pp5–22.

MORRELL K., LOAN-CLARKE J. *and* WILKINSON A. 'Unweaving leaving: the use of models in the management of employee turnover', *International Journal of Management Reviews*, Vol. 3, No. 3, 2001. pp219–244.

RAMSAY H. *and* SCHOLARIOS D. 'Selective decisions: challenging orthodox analyses of the hiring process', *International Journal of Management Reviews*, Vol. 1, No. 4. 1999. pp63–89.

ROBERTSON I. *and* SMITH M. 'Personnel selection', *Journal of Occupational and Organizational Psychology*, Vol. 74, No. 4, 2001. pp441–472.

SEARLE R. *Selection and Recruitment: A critical text.* Milton Keynes, Open University Press. 2003.

Sмith C., Daskalaki M., Elger T. *and* Brown D. 'Labour turnover and management retention strategies in new manufacturing plants', *International Journal of Human Resource Management*, Vol. 15, No. 2, 2004. pp371–396.

Taylor S. *People Resourcing*. London, CIPD. 2002c.

Wilk S. *and* Cappelli P. 'Understanding the determinants of employer use of selection methods', *Personnel Psychology*, Vol. 56, No. 1, 2003. pp103–124.

Performance Management

CHAPTER 7

INTRODUCTION

It should now be clear that horizontal and vertical integration are key themes in HRM, and nowhere is the concept of integration more important than in the management of performance. As we see below, performance management (PM) aims directly to link together individual goals, departmental purpose, and organisational objectives. It incorporates issues that are central to many other elements of HRM, such as appraisal and employee development, performance-related pay and reward management, individualism and employee relations. Indeed, it has been argued that performance management is synonymous with the totality of day-to-day management activity because it is concerned with how work can be organised in order to achieve the best possible results.

In this chapter we stretch beyond conventional definitions of performance management to include other aspects of the employment relationship, starting with the *induction* of new staff. While it is crucial to select the right people, it is also imperative to ensure that, from the outset of their employment, employees understand not only the nature of their tasks but also how these fit into broader organisational cultures. These principles should be continuously reinforced both through the informal daily interactions between managers and their staff, and through systematic and formal *reviews of performance*. Even if great care has been taken with recruitment, selection and induction, individual performance standards may fall below expectations and decisions on how best to deal with such competency issues may be needed. Problems may arise due to events outside of work (for example, family issues) or within work (for example, career blockages or a change in management style). These can manifest themselves in a lack of interest in work, in psychological problems, poor performance, and/or poor attendance.

This brings us to the third stage of the performance management system (PMS), the phase of *reinforcing performance standards*. There are several possible issues that could be dealt with here, ranging from minor lapses through to a more serious and potentially long-term deterioration in standards. This could be expressed through problems with capability, either due to a lack of expertise or knowledge, a failure to cope with changes in the nature of work, or absenteeism. Incapability issues are all too often swept under the carpet for many reasons. Managers may hope that problems will disappear or that the employee concerned will leave. Sometimes, the problem becomes so severe that it explodes and the organisation is faced with a difficult situation, perhaps culminating in an application to employment tribunal.

Where there are problems, *counselling and support* should be provided to enable individuals to meet performance requirements. In some cases informal support from the line manager may be enough, in other cases professional help may be necessary using occupational health, or counselling services.

Like many well-known terms, performance management has a variety of meanings, and it has been used to describe just about any HR initiative. Lowry (2002, p129) sees it as 'the

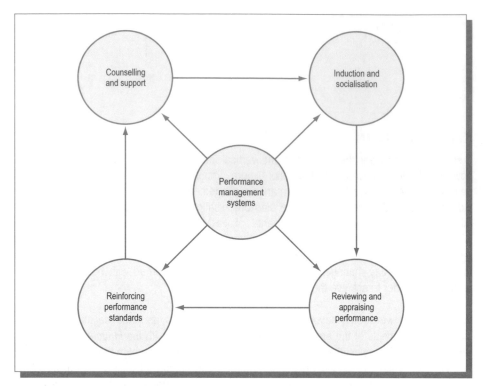

Figure 7 *The performance management process*

policies, procedures and practices that focus on employee performance as a means of fulfilling organisational goals and objectives'. Armstrong (2002, p373) defines PM as 'a means of getting better results from the organisation, teams and individuals. It is about the agreement of objectives, knowledge, skill and competence requirements, and work and personal development plans. The focus is on improvement, learning, development and motivation.' Performance management processes can be used as a means of distributing rewards – either through performance-related pay (PRP) schemes, or through promotion. Some differentiate between *basic* and *complex* PM practices (Pritchard and Payne 2003, p219). The former includes training and review, and the latter includes TQM, knowledge management, autonomous work groups, empowerment, and productivity measurement and enhancement. Since complex PM includes almost everything in HRM, we adhere to the more traditional 'basic' concept.

Most performance management systems are broadly similar, in that they each link together strategy and planning with employee socialisation, monitoring and review of progress, reinforcing performance standards and supporting individuals to achieve performance expectations. The principal components of the process are illustrated by Figure 7.

It is impossible to deal with every aspect of performance management in this single chapter. Related issues are examined elsewhere in the book – training (Chapter 9), disciplinary procedures (Chapter 11) and performance-related pay (Chapter 12).

By the end of this chapter, readers should be able to:

■ **design systematic induction programmes that provide a solid grounding for employees**

■ **advise line managers about the key issues involved in handling performance reviews**

■ **identify sources of information and expertise about counselling and support.**

In addition, readers should understand and be able to explain:

■ **the contribution that effective performance management systems can make to the achievement of organisational goals**

■ **the importance of tackling problems of poor performance as soon as they become apparent**

■ **the role that attendance management can play in a comprehensive HR strategy.**

INDUCTION AND EMPLOYEE SOCIALISATION

Most texts stress that induction is a process that starts with recruitment and leads into continuous development. New recruits are briefed about performance standards and expectations, with learning needs established, and attempts are made to socialise them into the organisation. Typically, this is expressed through mission statements that articulate organisational goals, which are transcribed into departmental/divisional objectives. Much of the literature on performance management assumes that this phase of the cycle/process is concerned with corporate communications, job descriptions and key accountabilities, each of which are considered elsewhere in this book. Induction training and initial socialisation into employment are rarely mentioned, but this is a critical time for establishing understanding about, and commitment to, wider corporate and departmental goals. A formal induction need not be expensive, and the huge benefits gained from a systematic process far outweigh the costs of recruiting new staff if large numbers of people leave at the time of the 'induction crisis' (Reid *et al* 2004, p224) and it is estimated (Taylor 2002c) that almost one in five new starters leave an organisation before the end of the first three months.

Irrespective of whether or not a structured programme is in place, all employees go through an induction phase. In many organisations, especially those that do not have a specialist HR function or manager, this may be little more than a rudimentary greeting before being shown to their place of work. New recruits may be told to ask questions if they need assistance and they are left to get on with the job, as it is assumed they have the required technical or administrative skills to cope. The rite of passage may consist of practical jokes (eg 'go and find a left-handed screwdriver') as the new recruit is socialised into the workplace norms. There may be little attempt to explain anything about the company mission, philosophy or policies. Even information about health and safety, disciplinary rules, and company procedures may be dealt with informally, despite their importance in setting the tone of the workplace and defining acceptable behaviours. The problems associated with such informality are obvious. Employees may feel isolated and confused, unaware of rules and procedures and they may struggle to learn how to do the job. Low morale and commitment are likely to result if they end up breaking safety or disciplinary rules, and they may leave. Each of these problems represents a cost to the employer, either in direct financial terms (poor-quality work, time spent on disciplinary issues, re-advertising jobs) or in public relations terms. In such circumstances, it is hardly surprising that employees question the depth of employers' commitments to people as their most important resource. It is worth remembering too that evidence of effective induction is required for a number of awards, such as Investors in People, ISO 9000 and the Management Charter Initiative.

Planning an induction programme

Planning an appropriate induction is a balancing act, and is not simple. Empathetic understanding of the stressful nature of being a new employee should lead to induction being accorded the priority status that it merits. Although there is a considerable amount of information to get across, new recruits do not want data overload, and they also want to settle into their personal workspace and be given meaningful tasks. In order to ensure interest and relevance, the induction programme needs to be individually tailored in recognition of the experience and job specification of the newcomer. This usually translates into a combination of group and one-to-one activity paced over a period of time. The line manager should play an important part in the process as building a positive relationship at this stage will set the scene for future interaction (Taylor 2002c, pp316–317). Others likely to be involved in induction include HR specialists, Health and Safety officers, IT staff, peer group, Chief Executive/MD and possibly trade union representatives (IRS Employment Review 772 2003, p34).

HR specialists typically maintain quality assurance standards and deliver parts of the induction programme – such as information about welfare, wage and salary administration, grievance and disciplinary procedures. Specialists can aid line managers by designing policies and training in conjunction with them, and monitoring their effectiveness. Data on labour turnover crisis points, on the results of exit interviews, on the degree to which all aspects of the induction checklist are being covered, and on evaluating the experiences of recent recruits should all feed back into the process.

In small groups work together to plan an induction programme for a particular individual and job role with which you are familiar. Be prepared to justify your scheme.

The content can be divided into three broad perspectives on the nature and purpose of the process. The first views it as an *administrative* exercise, in which the sole purpose is to impart information about the job, procedures and the organisation. The key point is what to include, when, so as to prevent information overload. CIPD Quick Facts suggests that the following would be included in a 'good' induction:

- physical orientation – where everything is located
- orientation – how the person fits into the structure
- health and safety information (required by law under the Health & Safety at Work Act 1974)
- terms and conditions of employment
- culture and history of the organisation
- job/role requirements.

Reid *et al* (2004, pp225–227) add to this list:

■ company rules and policies, eg disciplinary and grievance procedures, equal opportunities policies, site speed limits, energy conservation

■ employee development opportunities and sports and social amenities.

The second and third perspectives analyse the underlying philosophy of the process and its interpretation. The *social integration perspective* assumes that informal groupings have a powerful influence on how quickly a newcomer settles in and feels loyalty and commitment. Some organisations allocate a friend or mentor to help employees join in formal and informal social gatherings. In some cases contact is made before the employee starts work and this enables help and advice to be offered where appropriate, eg with relocation (Taylor 2002c, p119). Picking the right person for this is obviously important. There may be groups of workers for whom some cosseting is particularly appropriate, such as school-leavers, long-term unemployed or employees with disabilities (IRS Employment Review 772 2003).

The final perspective views induction as a hard-nosed business issue, in which employers make use of various techniques to 'educate' employees about the company values and ethos, aiming to integrate them with existing organisational cultures. This, the *cultural control perspective* is rarely to be found in mainstream HR publications, which view induction as a relatively value-free device. It is hardly acknowledged that induction can be a powerful device for integrating new employees, gaining their commitment and inculcating them with a sense of belonging and identity, which forms a basis for effective performance 'beyond contract'.

The cultural control perspective is one often associated with Japanese and US companies, exemplified by artefacts such as similar uniforms, badges, baseball caps and company credit cards. Japanese electronic and automotive firms have been intensively researched (Wickens

BOX 24   NIPPON CTV INDUCTION

At Nippon CTV, all new recruits receive a two-day induction, which lays down the company rules. The first person to speak was the personnel officer. Rather than enthusing about the company, she seemed cynical and often referred to the company as 'them'. She explained, 'we have to make sure you know the rules and things so that you can't say that you didn't know if you don't do something right … Nippon CTV is harsh and strict, but that is the rules. If you are away three times in three months then it may well be that we'll be letting you go', and 'procedures can be very short'. She advised people to come in if they felt unwell and see the doctor in work, 'don't be ill, it's easier that way' and 'people do get ill, though Nippon CTV doesn't believe it'. All calls are logged so that workers cannot allege that they have called in sick. After the session with the personnel officer, recruits were shown a video and given general information about the company. Throughout emphasis was placed on the company rules and who to turn to with problems – usually the individual's team leader. On day 2 of induction much of the talk concentrated on training and there was a talk by the chief union shop steward. He explained that the union had signed a no-strike deal and did not get involved in collective bargaining, but that it was useful in handling grievances.

Source: Adapted from Delbridge R. *Life on the Line in Contemporary Manufacturing: The workplace experience of lean production and the 'Japanese' model*. Oxford, Oxford University Press. 1998. pp46–51

1987; Delbridge 1998; Oliver and Wilkinson 1992) together with their 'intensive induction' during which new recruits are developed into loyal and trusting members of staff. More recently, Dundon *et al* (2001, pp445–446) describe a highly unusual approach taken at 'Consultancy UK' in which a full time 'culture manager' was appointed to promote 'having fun at work'. At interview, personality was valued above job competence ensuring that all staff fitted into this culture. Some argue that these tactics involve 'indoctrination' rather than induction. Clearly, there is a balance between getting across the cultural values (such as those of corporate responsibility) in order to increase workforce commitment without too much repetition or being accused of 'brainwashing' (see Box 24 on page 191).

> Do you think there is any substance to the view that induction can be interpreted as indoctrination?

PERFORMANCE REVIEW

Review is the second stage of the performance management process. As with other elements of HR, appraisal/review systems have become more widespread over the last decade, particularly in the public sector and there has been an increase in use with non-managerial staff. Armstrong and Baron's (2004) survey showed that 87 per cent of the respondents operated a formal performance management process, and of those that did not, 65 per cent planned to introduce a system over the next two years. The majority operated systems for *all* employees.

According to a recent IRS survey (IRS Employment Review 769a 2003, p8) the main reasons for appraisal are: to identify training/development needs (89 per cent), to evaluate individual performance (82 per cent), to identify and acknowledge good performance (32 per cent), to ensure managers and staff communicate (31 per cent), to help to make reward decisions (19 per cent), to identify and deal with poor performance (17 per cent), to increase productivity (9 per cent) and to measure the standard of people management (5 per cent).

There are many ways of conducting review, and these are dealt with in greater detail below. The main difference is whether the appraisal is top-down or encompasses an open discussion based on equality. In recognition of this, Armstrong (2002, pp374–375) differentiates between 'performance management' and 'traditional appraisal schemes'. He sees the former as:

- involving all employees as equals
- concerned with all aspects of performance including skills and competency levels
- based on agreements between managers and individuals/teams
- a continuous process which emphasises continual improvement of performance
- constructive and forward-looking
- encouraging self-management.

In the ideal process Armstrong describes, rewards may be included, although where they are present great care must be taken with rating systems to ensure transparency and equity. He emphasises the need for training to effectively deliver the system and suggests that *process* is given primacy. In comparison, traditional appraisal schemes are more concerned with setting and measuring objectives. Although Armstrong differentiates between 'appraisal' and 'performance management', we have chosen to use the term 'review' throughout.

Typically, formal review takes place on an annual or more frequent basis, with informal meetings taking place more frequently. The process should be continuous, but sadly, the ongoing and unsolicited support (such as the telephone call or the 'chance' conversation just to check that all is going well) is often overlooked. The 'review interview' then becomes the sole event when staff are praised or criticised, and when training and development needs are identified. Feedback also alerts an individual that aspects of their performance are not satisfactory, and again this is better if it takes place straight away rather than being left. Not that informal meetings should replace the formalised review at which adequate time is devoted to overview all performance issues in a structured and focused manner.

Ideally, the review should be an honest and open conversation between colleagues. It should summarise and draw conclusions from what has happened since the last review based on fact rather than opinion. Moreover, there should be no surprises, as issues should have been dealt with as they arose. Learning from mistakes and motivations arising from successes are both more likely if they are commented on immediately. The manager uses counselling skills to actively listen and to offer constructive feedback, as well as to agree on future aims, career and personal development plans. In terms of self-development, every phase should be joint between the individual concerned and the supervisor and it is most effective if it includes self-assessment. The interview may also give employees an opportunity to comment on leadership, support and guidance from their managers.

Who does it?

The most prevalent model in the past has been the individual performance review (IPR) – usually conducted by line managers, although others may be involved. Choices about who should appraise often depend upon prevailing organisational cultures and the group to be appraised. Options include: self-assessment, peer assessment (colleagues at the same grade/level), upward assessment (the appraisee's subordinates), external assessors (such as consultants or assessment centres), internal or external customers for the individual's services.

Reviews conducted by the immediate supervisor are particularly appropriate where reward is linked to performance, and where control is one of the aims of the process, although it is also prevalent where the aim is developmental. This method ideally results in strengthening relationships, but only where the relationship is already sound, and where the manager has the appropriate skills (Lowry 2002, pp135–136). If the aim is developmental, both the organisational culture and the managers' approach are critical, as a 'control' focus is likely to stifle open discussion. As Harrison (2002, p200) points out, it is the relationship between the parties that has the single most powerful influence on the success of the review, and is one of the major problems related to it. Disagreements may well arise with extreme cases ending with allegations of victimisation or discrimination. The process can quickly break down where neither party subscribes to the goals or philosophy of the system, or where mutual trust is lacking. It is inevitable where one of the aims of the review process is reward that the manager is balancing control/judgement and support/development while acting as both judge and helper.

In recent years there has been a shift away from relying predominantly on managers' appraisals, with increases in systems such as *360-degree appraisals*, which collate a number of perspectives and thereby act to increase employee involvement and reduce defensiveness (Fletcher 2004, p47).

Self-assessment is often combined with other forms of assessment. Research seems to indicate that most self-assessments are reasonably accurate, although there can be problems with overinflation and down-rating. Where rewards depend on review, it can be a powerful incentive to overinflate. On the other hand, research has shown that some groups (women in particular) tend to rate themselves lower than men (Lowry 2002, pp135–136; Fletcher 2004, p47) and further problems arise when cultural differences are involved (Fletcher 2004, pp141–144). *Peer assessment* involves colleagues, and is particularly suited to team review. When used outside of small teams it can lead to problems of selection. *Upward appraisal* is increasingly being adopted by UK companies (for example, W.H. Smith and The Body Shop). Employees comment on their manager's performance, usually by using an anonymous questionnaire, although this may be very threatening and/or undermining for managers. Moreover, they rely on employees not feeling intimidated, nor using the opportunity to register unjustified complaints against their supervisors, factors that may explain lack of widespread use in the UK (Redman 2001, pp64–65). An example of upward appraisal is given in Box 25.

BOX 25   TALKING OVER COFFEE: 180-DEGREE FEEDBACK

CoffeeCo carries out annual 'performance development reviews' for store managers. The managers are asked to select six employees who then complete a detailed questionnaire on their manager. They can elect to remain anonymous and the questionnaire is posted direct to the district manager. The information is used together with the store manager's self-appraisal, and the district manager's views as part of the annual performance review. The review is based 70% on behaviour, and 30% on financial factors and is used to determine the level of performance related pay.

Issues included in the questionnaire. Ability to:

- foster open communications with partners
- coach and develop
- motivate others
- lead courageously
- analyse issues
- manage execution, eg goal setting, health & safety
- establish plans, eg shift rosters, training plans etc
- build relationships at all levels in the company
- demonstrate adaptability.

Is there a performance management system (PMS) in your organisation? Could it be improved? If so, how? If your organisation does not have a PMS, what value might it add?

Customer appraisal is becoming more widespread, sometimes feeding into the setting of performance targets, especially if service guarantees involve compensation to customers. Customer surveys might include a wide variety of techniques, including electronic surveillance, and it is now common for call centres to record a random sample of conversations. A more controversial means is the use of individuals posing as customers or 'spies' to check quality of service.

360-degree performance review

Because of problems with other forms of appraisal, 360-degree performance reviews have been growing in popularity. They typically incorporate voluntary feedback from peers, subordinates and supervisors, and are particularly useful if customer feedback is included. They are usually confidential, self-determining and learning-oriented, rather than linked to assessment. However, there is a range of types and purposes for 360-degree feedback. Its use is based on two assumptions: first that self-awareness increases when feedback is based on a number of assessments and second, that self-awareness is a prerequisite for improved performance as well as an initial building block for leadership and management development programmes (Leopold 2002, p141).

There are a number of reasons why upward and 360-degree appraisals have recently become popular (Mabey 2001, p42; Leopold 2002, p142; IRS Employment Review 769a 2003; Fletcher 2004, pp60–61):

- It encourages self-awareness.
- It is multi-rater rather than single-rater assessments that provide greater validity, and therefore stands a better chance of acceptance.
- Information gathered can be used for strategic planning purposes.
- It facilitates open communications as people become used to giving and receiving feedback.
- It provides a framework for effective assessment and development of poor performers.

In addition, 360-degree performance review may be more appropriate for new organisational forms:

- It fosters the spirit of continuous improvement.
- It aligns with the shift from management-driven to employee-driven performance management processes. With flatter organisations and greater spans of control it is more difficult for any one manager to appraise a large number of staff with any degree of accuracy or knowledge.
- Involving staff in upward appraisals may well enhance their commitment to the organisation. Subordinates are often in closer contact with their managers than senior staff and are on the receiving end of his or her actions.
- An open system in which employees have access to their personal files lessens the likelihood of legal action.
- The concept fits well with notions of employee involvement and empowerment, and open organisational cultures.

> What do you see as the major problems with 360-degree review? How might problems be overcome?

Although it is assumed that one approach to appraisal will be used within any organisation, in practice managers may adopt a wide variety of approaches depending on circumstances. The balanced scorecard is one such alternative system. This approach emphasises four perspectives – the customer, internal processes, improvement and learning – and financial and some organisations have attempted to align review with this. Armstrong (2002, p395) uses the Halifax Bank as an example. The Bank uses the four perspectives of the customer, internal processes, business and financial for review and rewards. Managers have to meet their targets, but also must show that they have coached their staff, are rated by customer surveys and that their administration is effective.

According to Luthans and Peterson (2003), the drawbacks associated with 360-degree feedback are that an overwhelming amount of information is produced, and this may not be consistent, meaning that there is need for guidance in analysing the information. Their research found that effectiveness of 360-degree feedback systems was considerable enhanced by combining it with coaching on developing self-awareness and behaviour management. This resulted in increased satisfaction with the system as well as enhanced commitment. The researchers admitted that such a programme might prove prohibitively expensive in large organisations unless the feedback coaching was adapted for the web, and that there may have been a Hawthorne effect on the research results.

Performance review: General problems

The culture is not conducive to its introduction

A developmental framework for performance review will only be successful if it is introduced into an open culture of trust and it cannot be expected to provide a universal panacea, as the case study in Box 26 on page 197 demonstrates, for motivating the workforce. For example, employees who are disaffected or who have low levels of trust in their managers will not want to participate and those who feel themselves to be continuously observed will feel that 'trust' is a hollow term. The CIPD's eighth annual survey on the state of the employment relationship (Guest and Conway 2002) revealed that over half of the respondents felt their performance was being measured all the time, and more than a quarter were under constant supervision.

Conflicting aims

Where the primary purpose of the review is reward or potential, the employee is unlikely to openly discuss performance problems. Furthermore, review for reward tends to be backward facing, and development needs may be overlooked. Despite these problems, there is ample evidence that reviews commonly incorporate *both* developmental and reward aims, and many remain, at least partially, top-down.

Bureaucracy

Reviews are often seen as a bureaucratic, expensive, time-consuming and irksome exercise that is done solely to satisfy the personnel and development function. The event becomes debased and meaningless to all parties, but the paperwork is duly completed and filed. Where appraisal is not seen to 'add value', and appraisers are not rewarded for conducting appraisals on time, then the system will peter out. Conversely, where the system works well, managers will adopt review as a key contributor to a high-commitment performance-oriented culture. Many organisations have acted to reduce the bureaucracy, and most continually adjust systems (Armstrong 2002, p391).

Validity

Whatever the system, there are likely to be problems in terms of meaningfulness, objectivity, accuracy, validity and equity. What is meaningful may not be measurable. For example, advice that covers all angles – on the basis that the customer does not know what they do not know – may be difficult to measure. Whereas answering the telephone within five rings may be measurable, but not very meaningful. Clearly, it is more important to be doing the right thing, rather than doing the wrong thing well. Where surveys are used, questions may be poorly worded, or open to wide interpretation, for example, 'Does the manager deal with problems in a flexible manner?' Setting SMART (Specific, Measurable, Achievable, Realistic and Time bound) objectives is thought to ease measurement and eliminate some subjectivity, although this may be difficult. Behavioural traits that might prove difficult to measure are creativity, teamworking skills, perception and judgement, commitment and enthusiasm.

BOX 26   JANET AS APPRAISER AND APPRAISEE – A LOCAL AUTHORITY CASE STUDY

Janet was newly appointed to a local authority post, line managing 20 staff. She quickly discovered that there had been a long history of laissez-faire management, and that two previous women managers had left the post after lengthy periods of stress having tried to put some structure into the service.

Rose and Janet

Rose had worked with the authority for some years and was used to working in her own way. People at all levels of the organisation trod gently around her. She could work hard and well when she wanted to, but she seemed to have little interest in the aims of the organisation and refused all training. At about the same time as Janet was appointed new management systems were introduced, including performance review. Rose resented what she saw as an encroachment on her usual ways of working, and resented Janet's role. Janet initially tried to harness Rose's motivation by using positive feedback and giving her a high degree of autonomy, but Rose refused to change her work practices to accommodate changes in the service needs, and in review meetings she was sullen. Janet maintained an open style through review, but felt that she would eventually have to use the reviews to set targets based on control rather than equality.

Salina and Janet

Salina was a dynamic, self-motivated single parent who was keen to stretch herself by taking on responsibilities and training. Janet and Salina met regularly to discuss work issues. Notes were taken at the meetings and Salina's development was often discussed. Salina was on a clerical grade, but took on professional level responsibilities to cover when her line manager was absent for a long period. She enrolled on a part-time HNC, but since the authority would not help with this, she paid for the course herself and attended in the evenings in her own time. Annual review provided quality time to discuss issues that had been skated over in their more regular meetings.

Janet and John

John had been in the service for many years and line-managed Janet. Janet felt under constant pressure when she joined the service, mainly because of the laissez-faire management style she had inherited that had lead to entrenched staff attitudes. She took her problems to John and on one occasion said that she desperately needed proactive support. John responded by saying that he always gave support when he was asked for it, and suggested that Janet attend a stress management course. Janet did not think that this was the answer, and began to realise that unless she took her own solutions to the meetings, John would not be able to help. John never initiated meetings, and often neglected to produce records of the meetings that took place. The reviews became increasingly irregular and Janet put less effort into preparation for them.

Grint (1993, p63) describes a variety of 'distortions' that may occur in assessment. The 'halo' effect occurs when the appraiser notes desirable traits and allows these to spread to all other attributes. The 'horn' effect is the reverse and results in a lower assessment than might otherwise be expected. The 'crony' effect is caused by closeness of the personal relationship between appraiser and appraisee. The 'Veblen' effect results in central tendencies, so-named after the tutor's habit of giving all his students C grades irrespective of their quality. Finally, the 'doppelganger' effect occurs when appraisers reward similarities between themselves and appraisees, whereas differences lead to adverse ratings. There are clear equal opportunities implications of the 'doppelganger' given that, with top-down appraisals, women and ethnic minorities are usually at the base of organisations. Some evidence of this has come to light in local government research (Rana 2003, p11) in which senior managers' performance ratings of ethnic minority managers were lower than ratings given by peers or direct reports. Other distortions include the 'recency' effect where only events that have happened recently are remembered and commented on. Personal idiosyncrasies may feature too. For example, the manager who manipulates ratings for their own ends by downgrading graduates to 'show them that they didn't know everything' or gives high ratings in order to get rid of weak performers (Redman, 2001).

Line manager training and skills

Feedback is critical to performance management, yet not all managers are skilled and/or trained in its delivery. Managers may feel embarrassed about commenting on standards and broaching personal/behavioural traits may be particularly difficult. Where weak performance is the issue, and the consequences may lead to loss of earnings or even dismissal, avoidance is a typical response. Negative feedback needs to be handled with support and sensitivity, if it is not to result in demotivation. One result of this may be ratings drift, in which large proportions of staff end up with above-average ratings. Additionally, there may be personality conflicts, or difficulties arising from attempts to motivate people who, for whatever reason, are not committed to organisational goals. Difficult and 'bizarre' personalities are particularly difficult to deal with. Redman (2001, pp71–72) cites studies showing that appraisers are ill prepared, talk too much, base much of the discussion on third-party complaints and rely on 'gut feelings'. Other managers may find it difficult to hand over ownership of the process to the appraisee. The CIPD 2003 Survey (Armstrong and Baron 2004) reported that 62 per cent of line managers found performance management useful, but 22 per cent 'went through the motions', and 2 per cent were actively hostile.

Performance management review for control and manipulation

Redman (2001, p60) believes that control may be the aim of appraisal and that the 'harder' approach is increasing with a shift away from using appraisal for career planning and determining future potential to one of using it for improving performance and allocating rewards. He cites the example (p64) of Semco, a Brazilian company, in which managers are upwardly appraised regularly and are given a mark out of 100. The results are made public and those who regularly underperform eventually disappear. Within systems where customers, peers, subordinates and colleagues are potential appraisers, they become a tool for control and manipulation. Peer review systems are labelled as 'screw your buddy' and managers who 'fail' appraisal are dispensed with. Bach (2000, pp255–256) also discusses appraisal in the context of Foucault's concept of power, with appraisal seen as a 'form of disciplinary gaze'. However, there would appear to be a decline in such systems with a shift of emphasis towards developmental approaches at the expense of reward-driven systems (83 per cent of respondents to the 2003 CIPD survey agreed that the focus of performance management was developmental; Armstrong and Baron 2004).

Evidence of this working in practice

The process assumes that individuals will accept feedback and amend behaviour accordingly although Redman (2001, pp67–68) suggests that there is a dearth of evidence that this happens. Once again, citing the CIPD Survey (Armstrong and Baron 2004) 75 per cent of respondents believed that performance management resulted in increased motivation (with 22 per cent disagreeing).

The Acas *Advisory Handbook* (2004) suggests the following:

1   There should be wide-ranging consultation prior to the introduction of review.

2   Senior managers should be committed to the idea and ensure that time, training and resources are available.

3   The scheme should be kept as straightforward as possible.

4   Timetables should be agreed for implementation.

5   There should be adequate training of all involved.

6   A senior manager should take responsibility for ensuring that reviews are carried out.

7   The system should be monitored and modified accordingly.

It is clear that many of these practices are not adhered to. Respondents to the CIPD 2003 Survey (Armstrong and Baron 2004) would presumably be those organisations adopting best practice, yet only 23 per cent consulted all staff and only 34 per cent trained all staff. Finally, as Fletcher (2004, p51) comments, the success of the scheme lies with the attitudes and aims of those involved rather than the quality of the paperwork.

> Do you agree that the main aims of PM are to motivate and value workers? Was review an effective motivator for the people in the case study in Box 26?

The future of performance review

Despite problems, there is considerable evidence that performance management review is here to stay, probably because of its centrality to day-to-day management. Many problems have been resolved and 70 per cent of employees now use annual appraisal, although more than half in the recent IRS survey (IRS Employment Review 769a 2003, p14) had plans to improve the system, commonly by altering the documentation. Most respondents to the IRS survey thought that it was an essential management tool, so long as it was under continual review – a selection of their views of employee appraisal is given in Table 19 (see page 200). When performance review works well, it aids self-determination, personal development and growth, as well as increasing confidence and job satisfaction. Developmental review suits the current trends away from control to high performance, autonomous working and, as stressed in Chapter 10, under the new psychological contract employees expect such treatment.

However, review is not a management panacea. Just as we have individual learning styles, so too we each have different motivational styles and values. Not all workers are easily motivated and committed to organisational goals and others may have difficult personality traits that preclude effective social skills and teamworking. Although review might motivate committed, rational employees, it must be remembered that it is but one tool in the

Table 19   *General views on employee appraisal*

Organisation	Comments
TRW Aeronautical Systems	*'TRW has a well-established web-based approach that incorporates performance management and employee development.'*
Plymouth City Council	*'Feedback on under-performance must be timely – otherwise it might be too late for the organisation, and the individual.'*
North Tyneside Council	*'If carried out properly, the appraisal process is a valuable management tool. It can improve performance, morale and commitment ... Done badly and we have got problems.'*
Budgens Stores	*'The importance of quality one-to-one time is the key, and the skills of the individual managers to achieve open and honest conversations determines the effectiveness of the appraisal.'*
Warburtons	*'Valuable tool if fully integrated vertically with business strategy and cascaded appropriately.'*

Source: Adapted from IRS Employment Review 769a. *Time to Talk: How and why employers conduct appraisals.* 7 February 2003. p11

management kitbag, and may not produce the desired outcome with every individual, however well managed.

REINFORCING PERFORMANCE STANDARDS

Managing poor performance

Much of the literature on HRM describes situations in which workers have used initiative to work well beyond their contractual obligations. Examples include the secretary who redrafted a letter to incorporate new information while his boss was away, or the production worker who ignored instructions and changed a machine setting to override a fault. Although such examples are quoted regularly, they are probably less extensive than the number of cases where employees fall short of targets or, worse still, fail to turn up for work at all. Performance management generally tends to be seen in terms of positive reinforcement and identification of weaknesses to aid setting development targets. In contrast, relatively little has been written about the management of ineffective performance and those who are unable or unwilling to meet standards required, although reviews are bound to expose poor performance. Where this occurs, most of the literature emphasises the role of organisational inadequacies that may contribute to ineffective performance. Examples include problems relating to recruitment and selection, promotion, work conditions, inadequate job descriptions, poor managers, work overload, stress and work organisation, and lack of appropriate training and development. The issue of managing poor performance is considered below in relation to two issues: capability and ill-health. Then attendance/absence is discussed.

Capability

It is acknowledged that mistakes can be made at the initial interview, or when people are promoted. However, where the problem is capability, use of procedures leading to dismissal can be used. According to Lewis and Sargeant (2004, p155), 'capability' is assessed by reference to 'skill, aptitude, health or any other physical or mental quality' with inflexibility or lack of adaptability included under 'aptitude and mental qualities'. Stress is placed on the importance of early identification of problems as well as an investigation into the causes of poor performance. The *Acas Handbook* suggests that at interview or point of promotion it should be made clear what standards of work will be expected and any conditions attached to probationary periods should be explained. Where poor performance is identified it suggests the following:

- The employee should be asked for an explanation and the explanation checked.

- Where the reason is lack of the required skills, the employee should, wherever possible, be helped through training and given reasonable time to reach the required standards.

- Where the employee is then unable to reach the required standards, it should be considered whether alternative work could be found.

- Where alternative work is not available, the position should be explained to the employee before dismissal proceedings begin.

Workers should not normally be dismissed because of poor performance unless warnings and a chance to improve have been given. Moreover, if the main cause of poor performance is the changing nature of the job, employers should assess whether the situation should be dealt with through redundancy rather than capability (*Acas Handbook*). Where individuals are not prepared to work as required – as opposed to not being able to – the case is likely to be dealt with as misconduct.

In practice, many managers tend to avoid capability issues by ignoring or side-stepping the problems. This can include moving the person to another department or establishment as a damage limitation exercise, or having a quiet word about inadequate performance and the prospect of capability/disciplinary proceedings in the hope that the person will leave.

Recent research investigating best practice in relation to teacher capability (Earnshaw *et al* 2002a), suggests that there is increased willingness to tackle capability issues due to cultural changes, in particular, the introduction of performance indicators combined with a rigorous inspection regime making teachers 'performance aware'. Poor performance is no longer tolerated by management nor by peers. The research found that in just under half of the cases capability issues were resolved informally outside of procedures, although in some cases work on the problems had lasted several years. In most cases the capability procedures were genuinely supportive and gave the teachers opportunity to improve, with adequate resources deployed. However, many of the teachers found the stress of procedures too great and went off sick as a result, and many more went into denial and were unable to accept that they were lacking in capability. Since many of the teachers had been in the profession for decades without any system of assessment, it is hardly surprising that their initial reaction was to deny any shortcomings. Where capability issues were addressed at an early stage, there was a higher likelihood of improvement. Cases that dragged on simply prolonged the agony for all concerned, and were no more likely to produce a positive result. The research found that just under a quarter of the teachers improved. Of the rest, the majority resigned and a small proportion (under 5 per cent) was dismissed on capability or ill-health grounds (Earnshaw *et al* 2004, p146). Some of the most effective managers, upon identification of a problem, immediately triggered capability procedures in order to give maximum support to the individual and a framework for improvement. This ensured transparency and fairness throughout, and meant that the situation was resolved quickly, hopefully by improvement, but otherwise by quickly moving through the procedures.

> How are capability issues dealt with in your organisation (or one with which you are familiar)? How should such issues be addressed?

Ill-health

Where the problem relates to ill-health, the basic issue is whether the employer could be expected to wait any longer for the employee to recover, as well as whether the contract has been frustrated. In cases of long-term illness, the *Acas Handbook* recommends the following:

- The employee and employer should maintain regular contact.
- The employee should be kept informed if employment is at risk.
- The employee's GP/consultant should be asked when a return to work is likely and what sort of work the employee might be capable of.
- Using the GP's report, the employer should consider whether alternative work is available.
- The employer is not expected to create a special job, but to take action on the basis of the medical evidence.
- Where there is doubt about the ill-health, the employee should be asked if they are willing to be examined by a medical expert employed by the company.
- Where an employee refuses to co-operate in providing medical evidence or to be examined, the employee should be told in writing that a decision will be taken on the basis of the information available and that this could result in dismissal.
- Where the employee's job can no longer be kept open and no suitable alternative work is available the employee should be informed of the likelihood of dismissal.
- Where dismissal takes place, the employee should be given the period of notice to which they are entitled and informed of right of appeal.

When there are intermittent absences owing to ill health, the employer does not necessarily have to rely on medical evidence, but can overview the worker's employment history. This should take into account factors such as the type of illness and likelihood of recurrence, lengths of absence, the employer's need for that particular employee, the impact of the absences on the workforce and how far the employee was made aware of their position. In such cases dismissal may take place at a time when the employee is fit and in work (Lewis and Sargeant 2004, p158). Decisions to dismiss are based on individual circumstances. For example, where an employer cannot manage without the post-holder, a decision to dismiss may take place after a short space of time. However, if it is possible to arrange cover for the post-holder, the employer may wait for the employee's return. Critical questions suggested by Acas are whether the employee could return to work if they were given help in doing so, or if more suitable alternative employment was available.

The Disability Discrimination Act (DDA) 1995 has had a major impact on these issues. Under the Act employers will be found to have discriminated unlawfully if they do not make 'reasonable adjustments' for a disabled employee. Section 1(1) of the Act states 'A person has a disability if they have a physical and mental impairment which has a substantial and long-term adverse effect on their ability to carry out normal day-to-day activities.' There is no definition of physical or mental impairment, but mental illness is included where 'clinically well-recognised'. Torrington *et al* (2003, pp38–41) elaborates on these definitions and demonstrates ensuing confusion over what is covered by the DDA and what is not, with stress as a case in point. In the research on teacher capability procedures referred to above, most LEAs were extremely unsure how to progress, particularly as DfES (2004a, 2004b) guidance was contradictory (Marchington *et al* 2004a, p40).

There are also problems where employees insist on coming into work despite ill-health that adversely affects their performance (Taylor 2002c, p368). This is particularly complicated where mental ill-health or personality disorders are involved and the employee denies that there are problems. In such cases the employer may be unsure which procedures to trigger (capability, ill-health or misconduct).

Readers should note that this section merely provides merely a brief overview of these complex procedures. For further information refer to Lewis and Sargeant (2004), Taylor (2002c, pp364–368), and the *Acas Handbook*, as well as Chapter 11.

Managing attendance

Absence is a measure of corporate health as it may indicate low morale and conflict at work, and it is intrinsically linked with retention. So much so that the government's report on human capital (*Accounting for People*, 2003) suggested that people-based statistics should be included in the operating and financial reviews (OFRs) many organisations will soon have to produce. Employers are increasingly aware of their 'duty of care' for employees, with the threat of litigation as a key pressure and attendance is now seen as a major business risk. A recent European survey found that for UK business it was the third highest risk (IRS Employment Review 786 2003). Small wonder, when the Civil Service estimates that absence cost £370 million in 2002 (IRS Employment Review 792b 2004, p20) and the cost to UK employers is estimated as £11.6 billion in 2002 (Manocha 2004, p28). Financial costs are not the only factor in the management of attendance. There is evidence that managers see employee morale (low where workers have to cover for others whom they see as 'pulling a fast one'), their own credibility, and loss of efficiency as being of greater concern than the immediate financial costs (Dunn and Wilkinson 2002). The indirect costs of poor levels of attendance are seen in inadequate levels of customer service, cancelled commuter trains, unanswered telephone calls and overworked staff who cover for absent colleagues, only to run into problems when attempting to complete their own work on time.

> In an organisation with which you are familiar, how would you rank absence as a business risk? Why?

The UK has a particularly poor health record with more than one in four of working adults having a long-term health problem (IRS Employment Review 792c 2004, p17) and with long-term (particularly stress-related) absences rising (IRS Employment Review 784b 2003; IRS Employment Review 800 2004). A recent report for the Department for Work and Pensions showed that 2.6 per cent of employees become sick or disabled every three months and, after nine–twelve months, 13 per cent of these who come under the DDA have not returned to work (IRS Employment Review 774b 2003, p43). This equates to 2.7 million people of working age signed off sick and on incapacity benefits, and 22 million requests to GPs for sick notes each year – 9 million of which the GPs believe to be 'suspect' (Roberts 2004, pp10–11).

A summary of key statistics based on the CIPD Survey (2004c) follows. The average level of sickness absence among survey participants was 4 per cent or around nine working days per employee based on a working year of 228 days. The *public sector* has the highest average level of sickness absence at nearly 5 per cent, with the private services having the lowest rate at 3.4 per cent. Absence rates for smaller companies were lower than for larger companies. 61 per cent of absence was accounted for by spells of fewer than five days; absence of five days to four weeks accounted for one-fifth of absences; and long-term absences (over four weeks) accounted for 19 per cent of absence. 39 per cent of respondents reported a decrease in absence levels over the previous year, compared to 31 per cent reporting an increase. Tightening policies for reviewing attendance was the reason given for the decrease in absence rates, and alterations in the recording of absences; changes in workload and workforce composition were the most common reasons given for increases in absence levels. The average reported cost was £588 per employee per year.

Much of the research on absence management concentrates on what are seen as 'preventable' short-term absence. It is generally assumed that long-term absence is more likely to be genuine, although this is not always the case. The number of long-term absences are relatively small, but account for a disproportionate (30 per cent) amount of lost time (Edwards 2004, p35) with rises in stress-related illness pushing this up (CIPD 2004c, p35). In 2002 it was estimated that there were 1.46 million people claiming unemployment benefits, but 2.7 million were claiming long-term sickness and disability benefits (Roberts 2003a, p10). This is one of the worst rates in Europe and among the employed the UK has the third-highest rate of long-term health problems (20.4 per cent) (IRS Employment Review 792c 2004).

Although nearly 90 per cent of employers believed it was possible to reduce absence levels, only about half set targets for this. Within the public sector almost two-thirds set targets and larger organisations were also more likely to set targets. These usually involved a reduction to the percentage of working time lost with 3 per cent the most usual target (7 days per year). Nearly half of the respondents benchmarked their absence rates, and this was particularly common in the public sector. The CIPD survey showed that almost three-quarters had changed their approach to absence management in the previous two years. The majority (three-quarters) had introduced or revised their policies and/or procedures, half had introduced return to work interviews, approximately one-third involved Occupational Health professionals, and one-quarter had introduced Bradford points or similar triggering systems to identify persistent short-term absences. However, the CIPD surveys typically involve larger organisations employing HR professionals. In its survey (2004c), 17 per cent of employers did not have a policy, this compares with 47 per cent in an IRS survey of smaller manufacturing workplaces (IRS Employment Review 796c 2004, p18).

The first stage in addressing absence is to gather data that is accurate and consistent. This would seem simple, yet the CIPD survey (2004c) estimates that around one-fifth of employers do not know the level of sickness absence in their organisation and, according to a Work Foundation survey, only 43 per cent calculate the cost (IRS Employment Review 769b 2003).

The Work Foundation survey found that the main reasons given for not measuring the cost of absence were: absence is not a problem (23 per cent), too time consuming (43 per cent) or no computerised personnel system (29 per cent). Even those organisations that do calculate costs are likely to underestimate them in part because calculated costs are based on *reported* absences, and there is evidence that not all absences are reported (Dunn and Wilkinson 2002).

Once sickness absence figures are collected, it is possible to define the problem and to set up effective management systems. Absence measures do not normally include anticipated and legitimate spells away from work – such as holidays or jury service. Other forms of absence are divided between authorised and unauthorised. Broadly, the former deals with situations in which employees are genuinely unwell and have a valid medical certificate, whereas the latter typically refers to cases in which it is not clear if the employee is actually unwell or has an acceptable reason for being away from work. Self-certification and problems over GPs' sick notes (IRS Employment Review 786 2003, p22, and 796c 2004) have blurred the distinction between these two categories although they need to be treated in different ways. For example, if an employee has been absent for a series of single days over a specified period, a quiet word may lead to improved attendance patterns. Conversely, if an employee has been off with a serious health problem, different measures are needed.

The most commonly reported reason for both short- and long-term absences for both manual and non-manual employees was minor illness such as colds or flu. For absences of more than five days, stress was the main cause for non-manual staff, and back pain for manual workers. The actual causes of absence are difficult to ascertain, as workers are unlikely to report low morale, alcoholism, mental ill-health or personal problems as valid reasons for absence. Travel difficulties, family and home commitments all act to pull the employee away from work. Factors that push the employee away might include low morale, job insecurity, long hours and the work culture – including an entitlement view. Overlaid upon these are personality traits.

Strategies to deal with absence

The CIPD survey (2004c) found that disciplinary approaches are widely used (83 per cent for short term and 58 per cent for long term) despite the fact that its perceived effectiveness is relatively low (35 per cent for short term and 5 per cent for long term). Case study material, however, points to softer approaches being prevalent with line managers given a wide degree of discretion. Such approaches might include informal chats, counselling, return to work interviews, and the provision of medical support services (see Box 27 on page 206). Dunn and Wilkinson (2002) found only one example of the disciplinary approach and in this case, the stringent application of disciplinary rules resulted in the reduction of absence rates from 11 per cent to 2 per cent, but there were also concerns about the resulting reduction in morale within the workplace. Delbridge's work in Nippon CTV referred to in Box 24 also describes how absenteeism is not tolerated with workers told 'don't be ill, it's easier that way'. Alarmingly, he goes on to describe how one worker was brought in and propped up on the assembly line with a bucket placed nearby (Delbridge 1998, pp127–128). This is clearly far from ideal, but for those organisations determined to use the ultimate sanction, dismissals for sickness absence can be fair and reasonable in certain conditions and where procedures are followed.

The most common and the most effective tools for managing short- and long-term absence are detailed in Tables 20 and 21 (see pages 206–7).

BOX 27   ABSENCE MANAGEMENT STRATEGIES

The Royal Borough of Kensington and Chelsea has 2800 staff and a wage bill of £100m. It has now stopped paying staff for days taken off if they do not let their line manager know by 10am. This has cut the average number of days lost per employee from 10 to 8. If any member of staff is off for a total of more than 10 days in one year, they are called to an absence review meeting and subject to a three-month period of monitoring, with a warning of possible dismissal if there is no improvement.

West Midlands probation service had a target average of 9 days per annum. In 2000 all staff were absent for an average of 13.4 days, but for probation officers this rose to 21 days. In order to meet its targets, voluntary health assessments, absence warning procedures, return-to-work interviews and stress management assistance were introduced. There was a recognition that high absence rates were partly to do with the nature of the work and that redesign of jobs may help.

Source: Adapted from Broad M. 'Nailing the serial skivers', *The Sunday Times*, 20 January, 2002. p13

The return-to-work interview is perceived as the most effective way of managing short-term absence, and the fifth most effective tool for long-term absence. It provides the opportunity to enquire about the reasons for absence, to follow up any serious problems, to suggest further assistance if required. Where this is caused by caring or domestic emergencies, the employee may be willing to be honest about these where the employer offers flexible work arrangements (IRS Employment Review 799b 2004, p18). It also signals that the absence has been noticed, helping to generate an attendance culture in which genuine illness is acknowledged but malingering is dealt with severely. As with all people management issues, this message is important not only for the individual concerned but also for other workers, many of whom suffer the immediate consequences of colleagues' absence.

Restricting sick pay is also seen as an effective tool for addressing both short-term and long-term absence. Tesco has been in the news recently because of its pilot schemes to address short-term, unplanned, absences. In one of the pilot schemes (the one that drew press

Table 20   *Tools for short-term absence*

Top 6 tools	Top 6 most effective tools
Disciplinary procedures	Return to work interviews
Information to line managers	Disciplinary procedures
Line management involvement	Line management involvement
Return to work interviews	Use of trigger mechanisms
Use of trigger mechanisms	Restricting sick pay
Leave for family circumstances	Information to line managers

Source: Adapted from Chartered Institute of Personnel and Development. *Employee Absence 2004: A survey of management policy and practice*. London, CIPD. 2004c

Table 21   *Tools for long-term absence*

Top 6 tools	Top 6 most effective tools
Return to work interviews	Occupational Health involved
Information to line managers	Line management involvement
Line management involvement	Rehabilitation programme
Occupational Health involved	Return-to-work interviews
Use of trigger mechanism	Restricting sick pay
Disciplinary procedures	Changes to work patterns or environment

Source: Adapted from Chartered Institute of Personnel and Development. *Employee Absence 2004: A survey of management policy and practice.* London, CIPD. 2004c

comments), staff will not receive pay for the first three days of any sickness absence. Two other pilots are concentrating on incentives such as extra leave or store vouchers as rewards for good attendance. Staff who participate in the schemes do so voluntarily (Czerny 2004, p9).

Reporting of sickness absence information to line managers and involving line managers in absence management are also widely employed strategies. However, the CIPD survey (2004c) found that line managers had been trained in handling absence in less than half of the organisations surveyed, and few had a nominated case manager to take responsibility for individual cases. The work by Dunn and Wilkinson (2002) throws light on some of the problems faced by line managers. In the absence of clear procedures there can be confusion as to whether line managers or the HR function should take responsibility for dealing with absence and where line managers deal with the problems, they may use totally different approaches resulting in allegations of unfair treatment. In the Dunn and Wilkinson study, some managers did not have the time to carry out return-to-work interviews, or avoided confrontation because they were so relieved to have the person back to help with work pressures. Many managers felt that absenteeism was not an issue for them, particularly where staff 'struggled in' or made up time, and absences were often not recorded in such instances. Lack of training was relevant, but so was the need for line managers to preserve good working relations (Dunn and Wilkinson 2002).

Research by James *et al* (2002, p87) confirmed that line managers had the major role in absence management, and two-thirds of organisations had specific policies on long-term absence, but even where there were policies, these were often vague, meaning it was usually left to the manager's discretion. They found that two-thirds of their interviewees reported problems over the way that line managers dealt with cases, particularly failure to follow guidance. Typically HR staff were unaware of what was happening, and often had to take over management of cases. Time factors, a lack of awareness of policies because of lack of training, as well as an unwillingness to confront issues all contributed to problems.

> Look at the most recent CIPD survey on employee absence (2004c) and devise strategies for the management of short-term and long-term absence.

The research evidence is mixed on the practice of Occupational Health Services (OHS). James *et al* (2002) report favourably on them particularly where the service was newly introduced, or had recently been 'significantly improved'. However, they also found some criticism that OHS solely represented the employee's interests, mirroring the findings of other reports (Earnshaw *et al* 2002bc, pp92–93; IRS Employment Review 786 2003, p22). Despite criticism, OHSs will however be a key part of the government's strategy on occupational health (IRS Employment Review 792d 2004).

Rehabilitation and wellness, health management at work

The UK in the past has been particularly poor at supporting employees' return to work. Research by James *et al* (2002) found that most organisations did not offer occupational therapy, rehabilitation or home employment. Only 19 per cent used rehabilitation specialists with the majority using internal, non-specialists to support the return to work process – usually line managers or HR staff. There was often a lack of consultation with the individual, the union, and with personnel; and a lack of training on how best to make workplace adjustments, and no budget to support such arrangements. Other problems reported were reluctance by other departments to take on redeployed staff, and problems around the 'work habit' of those who had been absent for long periods. Some organisations signalled their willingness to pay for private treatment, because it would enable the person to get back to work more quickly. The IRS (IRS Employment Review 788b 2003) identifies a different range of barriers to rehabilitation. These include costs, and the adversarial nature of the employer liability system, which militates against early intervention which is seen as critical for successful rehabilitation. The UK government is now focusing on rehabilitation as part of its 'Strategy for workplace health and safety in Great Britain to 2010 and beyond' (HSE) and the Department for Work and Pensions is reviewing employers' liability compulsory insurance. The Department has signalled that employers that do not provide effective rehabilitation systems may find their insurance premiums rising (Edwards 2004, p36). Rehabilitation pilots and a job preparation premium of £20 a week for people on incapacity benefits who want to return to work have been established (Department for Work and Pensions 2003; Smithers 2004, p21). The emphasis is part of the overall plan to get people off welfare and into work (IRS Employment Review 774b 2003, p43) and in response to depressing statistics on the nation's health. In the 2001 Census, nearly 10 per cent said that their health was 'not good', and one-fifth suffer from stress at work (Manocha 2004, p27).

A more recent study examining barriers to rehabilitation (IRS Employment Review 796c 2004) revealed that, apart from the health condition of the person on sick leave, other major barriers were:

- the capacity of the NHS to provide fast access to appropriate services (eg physiotherapy)
- employees' resistance to rehabilitation, in part because of 'generous' company sick pay
- difficulties finding 'light duties' or other suitable work
- persuading line managers that rehabilitation is worth the effort

- having to wait for GPs' sick notes to expire before starting rehabilitation
- concern that the employee may come under the DDA.

GPs came in for much criticism as quotes from the IRS survey (IRS Employment Review 796c 2004, p22) reveal: 'doctors and consultants are reluctant to push people back to work via the rehabilitation route. It is easer and safer to say they will never get better', and 'too many GPs are relying on the word of the employee, which is not always true – employees do not mention our attempts to rehabilitate them to GPs'. At the same time, GPs are unhappy with their roles in issuing sick notes (IRS Employment Review 792d 2004).

Where rehabilitation relates to mental health, issues would appear to be even more complex. According to Almond and Healey (2003, p731) around one in six adults in private households suffer from a clinical neurotic disorder, with depression and anxiety being the most common complaints. Naturally such problems impact on attendance as well as productivity, and both can be relatively easily managed. However, with mental ill-health attitudes play a major role, and sufferers are therefore often reluctant to seek help.

There is much to be learned from countries that have successfully adopted a range of strategies that have proved to be effective in reducing absence by getting workers back to work quickly, thereby reducing the proportion of unemployed workers reliant on state sickness benefits. In Sweden employers must assess needs quickly and arrange rehabilitation. In the Netherlands employers must report to the social security agency within 13 weeks details of rehabilitation plans for employees who are incapacitated (James et al 2002).

Some employers (see Boxes 27, 28 and 29) are adopting the American concept of 'wellness management', or acting preventatively by putting in place a range of services to promote good health. This is seen as important because it forms part of the duty of care, it impacts on recruitment and retention, forms part of the psychological contract, and people in poor health are 20 per cent less productive (Manocha 2004).

BOX 28 TACKLING LONG-TERM ABSENCE: DONCASTER COUNCIL

Long-term absence cost Doncaster Council £3.3 million in 2001/2. HR spearheaded changes to promote a culture of good attendance, with ownership handed over to line managers, and a move away from the previous approach of monitoring and disciplinary action. Emphasis was placed on maximising attendance.

After a broad consultation exercise involving unions and managers at all levels, a good practice guide was produced and all line managers and union reps attended a one-day briefing on attitudes to attendance. The emphasis was on approaching attendance in a welfare-oriented way. Monitoring was streamlined and communications improved. Each directorate allocated a co-ordinator for record-keeping, communications and ensuring that line managers were carrying out the policy. Their responsibilities included:

- checking references from previous employment before confirming employment
- stressing the importance of attendance in induction

- monitoring attendance and performance in probationary periods
- checking the quarterly attendance reports
- carrying out return-to-work discussions whenever possible.

The long-term absence trigger was four weeks' continuous absence, although it could be triggered after two days if this was appropriate. Line managers were expected to quickly identify what might be a long-term absence and to act by discussing problems with the employee and involving OHS, which offered counselling, advice on harassment and ill-health conditions. If a return to the original job looks unlikely, consideration can be given to redeployment. HR is informed of all long-term absences in a quarterly report, and a proportion of these cases were reviewed. OHS and HR meet to review each case and suggestions made as to how best to aid the person back to work.

The Council felt that it was important for the line manager and the employee to make contact as soon as possible, so that the absence became a shared problem. Long-term absence figures improved by 10% in the first year of the new policy a spinoff is improved communications and their managers and increased trust.

Source: Adapted from IRS Employment Review 768. *Tackling Long-term Absence: Doncaster Council.* 24 January 2003. pp42–44

BOX 29   STANDARD LIFE HEALTHCARE

Standard Life Healthcare put in place a health and well-being programme in 2002. Employees can access confidential health and lifestyle screening via the web. They then receive advice on stress, exercise, sleep and other problems. Experts visit the workplace to offer seminars, testing and free advice. The canteen provides healthy foods with free fruit and nutrition bars given away on certain days. Exercise classes are run in meeting rooms. Since the programme's introduction, there has been a 22.5 per cent decrease in turnover, a 4.9 per cent cut in absence levels and a 5 per cent rise in 'self-perceived effectiveness'.

Source: Adapted from Manocha R. 'Well adjusted', *People Management*, 8 April 2004. p29

COUNSELLING AND SUPPORT

Informally most managers, although not trained in counselling, use listening skills as part of their daily work. In addition, a number of organisations have made available access to professional counselling services for more personal and/or deep-seated problems. The ethos of counselling is that people have the ability within themselves to resolve their own problems when enabled to do so using a professionally trained counsellor. It would be highly unusual (and poor practice) for a counsellor not to be accredited by the British Association for Counselling and Psychotherapy (BACP), which publishes strict codes of conduct. Services may be delivered face-to-face, by telephone, or by e-mail. Use of e-counselling is spreading, and is particularly useful in dispersed organisations. Additionally, some people, initially at least, prefer the more distanced relationship in order to open up discussion of problems.

Counselling provision is often the central plank of Employee Assistance Programmes (EAPs). The role of the EAP is to attempt to solve organisational and individual problems by integrating the programme into the management culture of the organisation, perhaps by using line managers for counselling and support. The Employee Assistance Professionals Association (EAPA) defines an EAP as 'a worksite-focused programme to assist in the identification and resolution of employee concerns which affect, or may affect, performance'. This can include personal matters related to issues such as health, relationships, family, financial, emotional, legal, mental ill-health and addictions as well as employment matters such as work demands, relationships, personal and interpersonal skills, and stress. The aim is to enhance individual performance in the workplace for the benefit of the individual and the organisation.

There has been a rise of 40 per cent in under a decade in stress-related illness according to the Health and Safety Executive (HSE Research Report 133 2004), a fact confirmed by recent IRS and CIPD reports. During 2001–2 it accounted for 13.4 million lost days (this is higher than the 12.3 million days lost due to musculoskeletal disorders). The HSE report found that three-quarters of those reporting stress blamed their job, with rates rising for those with more than 20 years' service. Managers, teachers and nurses were particularly prone, with manufacturing and construction having lowest rates. Smaller organisations were seen as less stressful places to work. The CIPD 2004c report found that the top factors contributing to stress were workload, management style/relationships at work, organisational change and pressure to meet targets.

With stress rates continuing to rise, more employers are establishing EAPs. Perhaps particularly so following a landmark stress judgement in February 2002 when the Court of Appeal ruled that an employer providing an EAP (including counselling and treatment services) was 'unlikely' to be found in breach of its duty of care. The employer would be deemed in breach of duty if they had not carried out a stress risk assessment (IRS Employment Review 769c 2003). Naturally, this calls into question the effectiveness of the EAP. Evaluation of EAPs suggests that they provide many benefits to the individuals concerned as well as to their employers. Individual employees find they are able to function more effectively both within and outside of work, to operate with reduced stress levels, to work better within teams and to produce better quality work if they are not worried about personal or work-related problems. Employers may benefit through lower levels of labour turnover, reduced absenteeism, higher productivity and better customer service. The BACP's research on the impact of EAPs and counselling at work (McLeod 2001) concluded that provision of workplace counselling more than covers its costs. Despite the worth of EAPs and counselling services, if the CIPD findings on the causes of stress at work are correct, then work organisation, better management and flexible work arrangements might be better able to address the problems at source.

CONCLUSIONS

Performance management systems are now much more widespread than they were 10 years ago, and in some cases they are seen as synonymous with 'new' ways of managing human resources. They revolve around four stages: defining performance standards, reviewing and appraising performance, reinforcing performance standards, and supporting individuals to meet performance expectations. Several of these issues are taken up in later chapters in the book, for example in our analysis of learning organisations and performance-related pay. Each stage of PM is important, but often too little attention is paid to the critical role which induction can play in creating the right cultural expectations amongst new recruits. Employers who are serious about PM need to realise that this stage of the cycle makes a significant contribution to the socialisation of new staff, and it is much more than a routine administrative exercise. PM systems also need to be designed so that performance that is below standard can be dealt with in an appropriate way – that is, through counselling and assistance if an employee has a genuine problem or through disciplinary procedures if the employee is unable or unwilling to meet performance standards.

USEFUL READING

ADVISORY CONCILIATION AND ARBITRATION SERVICE. *Handbook.*

ALMOND S. *and* HEALEY A. 'Mental health and absence from work: new evidence from the UK Quarterly Labour Force Survey', *Work, Employment and Society*, Vol. 17, No. 4, 2003. pp731–742.

ARMSTRONG M. *and* BARON A. *Performance Management: Action and impact.* London, CIPD. 2004.

CHARTERED INSTITUTE OF PERSONNEL AND DEVELOPMENT. *Employee Absence 2004: A survey of management policy and practice.* London, CIPD. 2004c.

DUNN C. *and* WILKINSON A. 'Wish you were here: managing absence'. *Personnel Review*, Vol. 31, No. 2, 2002. pp228–246.

EARNSHAW J., MARCHINGTON L., RITCHIE E. *and* TORRINGTON D. 'Neither fish nor foul? An assessment of teacher capability procedures', *Industrial Relations Journal*, Vol. 35, No. 2, 2004. pp139–152.

FLETCHER C. *Appraisal and Feedback: Making performance review work.* London, CIPD. 2004.

IRS EMPLOYMENT REVIEW 796c. *Managing Long-term Absence and Rehabilitation: Part 2.* 19 March 2004. pp18–24.

IRS EMPLOYMENT REVIEW 788b. *Rehabilitation is the Key to Employers' Liability Insurance.* 21 November 2003. pp20–21.

IRS EMPLOYMENT REVIEW 772. *Induction to Perfection: The start of a beautiful friendship.* 21 March 2003. pp34–40.

LEWIS D. *and* SARGEANT M. *Essentials of Employment Law*, 8th edition. London, CIPD. 2004.

LUTHANS F. *and* PETERSON S. '360-degree feedback with systematic coaching: empirical analysis suggests a winning combination', *Human Resource Management*, Vol. 42, No. 3, 2003. pp243–256.

PRITCHARD R. *and* PAYNE S. 'Performance management practices and motivation', in D. HOLMAN, T. WALL, C. CLEGG, P. SPARROW *and* A. HOWARD (eds), *The New Workplace: A guide to the human impact of modern working practices.* London, Wiley. 2003.

REID M., BARRINGTON H. and BROWN M. *Human Resource Development: Beyond training interventions.* London, CIPD. 2004.

Development

Vocational Education, Training and Skills

INTRODUCTION

This chapter examines the ways in which government intervention has shaped vocational education and training (VET) in the UK in order to maximise the skills and contributions of people. It makes comparisons with our major competitors, and reports on current government research on skill gaps and shortages. There is a section outlining some of the major recent changes to education and training and the major influences on workplace learning, namely National Vocational Qualifications (NVQs), Modern Apprenticeships, Investors in People (IiP) and the Trade Union Learning Representatives. Consideration is given to how far workplaces are moving towards the ideal of the learning organisation or using high performance working. The main thrust of the chapter analyses how far the government strategy of increasing skills is triggering a shift from the low-skills equilibrium to a high-skill economy and looks at ways in which the demand for training by employers could be increased. Brief details about the institutional framework of VET (ie Learning and Skills Councils and Sector Skills Development Agency and Sector Skills Development Councils) appear in Chapter 1.

By the end of this chapter, readers should be able to:

- **advise their organisations on the value of training initiatives such as NVQs, Modern Apprenticeships and IiP**

- **work with trade unions to encourage non-traditional learners to take advantage of training opportunities**

- **assess the contribution of VET to the enhancement of worker skills and organisational performance.**

In addition, readers should understand and be able to explain:

- **why the government is concerned to shift the economy from its low-skills equilibrium**

- **the way in which the government is influencing the provision of VET and its rationale**

- **the major problems preventing the contribution of VET to skill improvement.**

SKILLS IN THE UK: INTERNATIONAL COMPARISONS AND FUTURE PREDICTIONS

The UK has a poor record of investment in vocational education and training (VET) compared with our major competitors, and employers frequently bemoan the fact that the educational system does not provide the skills and knowledge they want. The UK schools system suffers from problems associated with low status, morale and pay, with particular difficulties in recruiting and retaining maths and science teachers. OECD statistics show that almost one-fifth of 16- to 19-year-olds in the UK are not attending school and are not employed (Harrison 2002, p425). Comparisons with other systems are unfavourable. If we look at Japan and Germany, both systems were largely rebuilt after the Second World War and are particularly successful in the fields of advanced maths, science and technical subjects. In adult education, the UK's track record in delivering level three vocational qualifications is particularly poor. Government research indicates that around 20 per cent of adults have poor basic skills: 36 per cent – 13 million people – are not qualified up to level 2 (the equivalent of five good GCSEs). This compares with 28 per cent in France and 17 per cent in German (1998 figures) respectively (Prime Minister's Strategy Unit 2001). Only a fifth of young people in UK go into apprenticeships, and a low proportion (between 40 and 50 per cent) complete them. In Germany two-thirds enter apprenticeships and most complete them successfully; in Denmark, around a third enter and around 90 per cent complete (Rana 2002, p36). At higher levels comparison with Europe is fine. The proportion of those with degree-level qualifications is roughly the same in UK as in France or Germany. However, in Germany, it is assumed that those without degrees will be vocationally trained, and it is not possible to quit youth training before the end, or to drop out of the off-the-job training element (Harrison 2002, p421). Increases in wages and career prospects are linked to training and qualifications, and young people are not as prone to be lured by the prospect of high pay in the short term.

The UK persists with VET based on voluntary arrangements with employers, whereas in competitor countries the cost is shared (Harrison 2002, pp423–424). Using Germany again as an example, Chambers of Commerce are central to training for all workers and all firms are required to be members of their local Chamber and to pay a membership fee. In comparison, the UK uses public funds for the Learning and Skills Councils and Small Business Service, but delivery is through private organisations or through colleges. Significantly, within the EU the social partnership model is more deeply embedded, with a tradition of strong trade union involvement in the decision-making process, and less profit is distributed to investors.

In terms of the demand for and usage of skills, UK employers remain in the low skills equilibrium (Finegold and Soskice 1988), relying on low prices, rather than high quality, for competitive advantage. The result is low demand for employees with high skills, under-employment of existing skills and low priority given to training and development (Green et al 2003). The prevailing view is that the UK must make the shift from the low-skills equilibrium position to high skills in order to compete internationally. The government believes that in order to this, skill levels must rise. However, the so-called 'training problem' has been with us for a very long time; all political parties acknowledge this and over the years there have been many attempts at developing a coherent national VET policy. Sadly, most have not proved particularly successful, and as a result there have been regular radical reviews and revisions. This chapter concentrates on recent developments.

Notwithstanding the fact that much of UK remains in the low-skills equilibrium, recent government reports provide evidence of skill gaps and skill shortages. Skill gaps are defined when employers believe that their employees are not fully proficient to carry out the requirements of the job role. Skill shortages are defined as a lack of applicants for vacant posts with the right skills and qualifications. Using the National Employer Skills Survey (NESS) 2003 (LSC 2003a), the 2002 Employers' Skill Survey (Hillage et al 2002), the Skills in England 2002 report (LSC 2003b), the Government's white paper 21st Century Skills: Realising our potential: individuals, employers, nation (DfEE 2003) and the Working Futures: Sectoral report 2003–04 (Skills Sector Development Agency 2004) chronic problems have been highlighted.

Nearly a quarter of establishments had *skill gaps* and over two million workers (around 10 per cent) lack the skills needed to do their job. One-fifth of job vacancies are not filled because of lack of skilled applicants. 40–45 per cent of all vacancies were hard to fill, and almost a half of these were skills related (ie 20 per cent of all vacancies). Skills gaps were found at intermediate, professional, apprenticeship and technician levels. Particular problems related to maths, and leadership and management skills, and sectorally, Retailing, 'Other Business Services' and Health and Social Work. The main causes were lack of experience (72 per cent), low staff motivation (33 per cent), failure to train staff (29 per cent), not keeping up with change (29 per cent), recruitment problems (27 per cent) and high staff turnover (23 per cent).

Skill shortages translated into around 250,000 hard-to-fill vacancies usually among professional staff (particularly in education), associate professionals (particularly in health and social care), and skilled trades (particularly in construction). Reasons cited for skill-shortage vacancies included lack of experience and lack of qualifications. The impact of skill shortages and gaps were evident in increased workloads, customer service difficulties, loss of business, the delay of new products, increased operating costs, quality problems, and difficulties introducing new working practices. Firms wishing to move from low-skills to high specification products and services felt constrained by skill gaps and shortages.

Lack of training is one contributory factor to skills gaps and shortages and work by Hogarth and Wilson (2003) demonstrates that employers who continuously train and develop workers experience fewer recruitment problems. NESS (LSC 2003a) showed that as a response to skills gaps, 81 per cent of employers provided further training, 43 per cent changed working practices, 20 per cent increased recruitment and 7 per cent took no action. Employers responded to skill shortage vacancies by:

- increasing recruitment/advertising spending (56 per cent)
- expanding channels of recruitment (49 per cent)
- increasing salaries (37 per cent)
- redefining existing jobs (36 per cent)
- increasing training given to existing workforce (35 per cent)
- increasing trainee programmes (28 per cent)
- and 10 per cent took no action.

Although 29 per cent of employers blamed skill gaps on lack of training, about one-third had no training budget. In comparison with OECD countries, UK is second lowest in terms of time spent in training. Other factors playing a signification role include lack of experience and low motivation.

> What strategies do you think firms should use to combat skill gaps and skill shortages?

The government estimates that there will be a need for an extra 800,000 level 3 associate professional workers such as teaching assistants and medical technicians by 2010 (Johnson 2003), and the Institute for Employment Research suggests that 80 per cent of the 1.7 million jobs created by 2010 will require degree-level qualifications (Baldwin and Halpin 2004). Early in 2004, the *Working Futures* report produced by SSDA showed that over 13 million job vacancies are likely to be created over the next 10 years, most of which will be in the service occupations, with demand for high-quality managers and professionals up by around 20 per cent. Sloman (2003, p5) quotes from Hamel and Prahalad's 1994 book *Competing for the Future* in saying that long-term success depends on 'creating unimagined, but soon to be essential, products and services'.

ESTABLISHING A CULTURE OF LIFELONG LEARNING IN THE WORKPLACE

The creation of future products and services is dependent on human capital and much of the literature cites examples of organisations responding to shortages by maximising the skills and contributions of people, in recognition of this fact. It is assumed that employees are required to have high levels of education and skills in order to meet increasingly rigorous demands. They are expected to be able to use IT; continuously learn and update skills; take responsibility for their own learning; understand their role in the organisation; be able to work autonomously; and have the ability to solve problems, change and anticipate the future. It is argued that training and development professionals have responded to this challenge and become involved with teaching people how to learn, and encouraging them to become lifelong learners, as part of a business strategy to retain competitive advantage (Stern and Sommerlad 1999, p xi; Keep and Rainbird 2000, p175; Ashton and Sung 2002).

In particular, this has attracted interest in the notion of a learning organisation (LO). The concept was initially articulated by academics such as Morgan (1986), Senge (1990) and Pedler *et al* (1991). It can be defined as, 'an organisation that aims to extend and to relate the learning and learning abilities of individuals, groups and the organisation as a whole in order to change continuously at all three levels in the direction of existing and possible wishes and needs of customers' (Simons *et al* 2003, p43). Nyhan *et al* (2004, p75) add that it is about 'changing the way that work is organised so that it is conducive to learning'. However, they conclude that the LO is a complex form, and as a result, it is unlikely that any organisation can be said to have fully met the criteria.

There is currently debate about the concept of the LO. Research shows a paucity of evidence that organisations are moving in the direction of becoming a LO, and within so-called high-skills sectors it is a minority of workers who are given access to learning, and there is evidence that many employers do not value the potential of their workforce (Keep 2000). Moreover, the LO assumes empowerment of workers, whereas evidence points to the continued existence of 'command and control' styles of management. As a result, it has been complemented by theories of knowledge management (KM) and high performance working (HPW).

Both KM and HPW presupposes workers are highly skilled, continually learning and work autonomously in an organisational context of high levels of trust, communications and involvement. Because knowledge workers become the central plank of the labour process, HRM takes up a critical role in appointing, retaining and harnessing their skills to the full (Scarbrough and Swan 1999; Purcell *et al* 2003, p5; Swart *et al* 2003). Research carried out by the Engineering Employers' Federation and CIPD (2003) suggests that HPW boosts both profits and productivity. Despite the rhetoric about these idealised forms of work organisation, it remains the case that in many workplaces, access to training and development remains inadequate and partial.

Government skills strategy and targets

Successive governments have attempted to pump prime the shift to high tech working with limited success. The current government is no exception, and it has instituted wholesale reform of the education and VET systems through centralising control. In July 2003, the Skills Strategy was launched with the White Paper *21st Century Skills: Realising our potential: Individuals, employers, nation* (DfES 2003). Its aim 'to ensure that employers have the right skills to support the success of their businesses, and individuals have the skills they need to be both employable and personally fulfilled'.

The main reforms included:

- free learning for any adult up to level 2 (5 GCSEs or equivalent)
- Information and Communication Technology (ICT) joins literacy and numeracy as an Adult Basic Skill (all of which remain free)
- opportunities for adults to gain qualifications in technician and higher craft and trade skills through a level 3 qualification (2 A levels or equivalent) in regional or sectoral skills shortage areas
- a means-tested grant of £30 a week for full-time adult learners in priority groups
- reforming adult information, advice and guidance services with free access for all
- expansion of the Sector Skills Network and each Sector Skills Council to develop agreement on the action that needs to be taken to tackle skills gaps (see Chapter 2)
- use of employer training pilots to develop national programmes (see Box 30 on page 220)
- qualifications more employer friendly and responsive to business needs.

The government backed its strategic push with targets – one of which is that by 2010 employers would not be able to say that education and training failed to meet its needs. More specific targets were getting 50 per cent of young people into university; reducing the number of adults with literacy or numeracy problems by 1½ million by 2007, and increase the numbers of young people taking modern apprenticeships to 35 per cent by 2010. A 'Skills Alliance' has been formed comprising government departments, employers and unions, with control remaining with the government.

The education system is the first building block for a culture of lifelong learning and skill enhancement. Those who have experienced success at school are more likely to be natural lifelong learners, and best able to take on board rapid changes. In the UK the divide between the knowledge-rich and the knowledge-poor starts and widens through school and the class system still has a major influence on access to higher levels of educational opportunities and qualifications, and therefore to those jobs and careers bringing additional learning opportunities. In comparison, those with poor experiences in the education system are most likely to be found in the low-pay, low-skill sector of the labour market without access to training and development, and most at risk from unemployment. The 2000 report from the Chief Inspector of Schools revealed that one in seven 16-year-olds leaves school without a basic level qualification in English and Maths and there was still concern that the education system did not meet the needs of the economy (DfEE 2000).

Since 1985 there have been continuous changes to the education system aimed at improving quality and coherence. These include the introduction of the national curriculum, SATs testing,

BOX 30   EMPLOYER TRAINING PILOTS

Employer training pilots (ETPs) provide small businesses with money to help train their staff (targeting those with low skills levels) and to compensate them for time taken off for training. They were set up in six areas from 2002 offering free and flexible training. By 2004, ETPs covered over a third of England with 3000 employers and over 20,000 employees involved. Over 90% of the firms were SMEs and over 70% had under 50 employees (www.lsc.gov.uk). To date, they have been successful in getting employers who had not previously been involved in government training to train their low-skilled employees. A substantial proportion of ETP learners are from the care sector, where there is a legislative requirement to increase the proportion of qualified staff. 55% had no qualifications, and 21% had a level 1 qualification. Most had been involved in some form of learning over the previous three years, and most had a positive attitude to learning. 90% were working towards NVQ level 2, and 10% were take basic skills.

Up to the one-year evaluation, drop out was 5% (long-term evaluation ends in 2005). Employers appreciated provision of free training (44%) followed by the flexibility (9%). Wage compensation was only regarded by 9% as the most important element. Over 90% appreciated the potential benefits of employees with better skills and self-confidence. The learners saw the benefits as: getting a qualification (80%), skills to do the job (80%), the chance to learn something new (70%) and increased self-confidence (over 65%). Over 70% felt that the training would help to improve the quality of their work. The 2004 spring budget allocated £190 million to the scheme (www.lsc.gov.uk).

Using the scheme, Greggs the bakers offers literacy and numeracy training after a confidential training needs analysis to identify potential employees. Most employees attend classes, but those who are too embarrassed access one-to-one tuition. Of the 90 employees identified, only eight have so far taken up the offer in the first six months, although it is hoped that this will spread. The drop-out rate has been significantly less than that of FE.

Source: Adapted from Pickard J. 'A clearer provision', *People Management,* 12 June 2003b. pp28–32

national literacy and numeracy strategies, local management of schools, naming and shaming schools with poor results, the replacement of failing schools with autonomous City Academies, a national system of inspection (OFSTED), and universal nursery provision. In addition, the Qualifications and Curriculum Authority (QCA) was established in 1997 to co-ordinate academic and vocational qualifications. Despite teacher complaints of initiative fatigue, in 2001 the Education Green Paper, *Schools: Building on success* (DfEE 2001b) heralded still further changes and the government also turned its attention to low morale in the profession, with plans to increase retention rates and improve the skills of trainee teachers (Harrison 2002, p35).

New examinations were introduced, including AS levels, Advanced Extension Awards for the more able A level students, and Vocational GCSEs and A levels, although OFSTED has already criticised vocational A levels on the basis that they were neither popular nor well-designed (Halpin 2004). Eventually a wide range of vocational qualifications will be accredited covering every industry sector and linked to occupational standards with the aim of increasing flexibility and take-up of vocational qualifications.

In 2003, 14–19 Pathfinders was launched with the aim of providing broader curricula for 14- to 16-year-olds, involving vocational and work-related learning. In the first year 25 pilots were set up. Some led to vocational GCSEs or to NVQs; others incorporated Modern Apprenticeships. Many targeted disaffected pupils, others high achievers. An evaluation of the first year (Higham *et al* 2004) showed that they had been popular with young people. From 2004, Entry to Employment (E2E) was promoted for 16- to 18-year-olds. It incorporated NVQ level 1 and/or vocational qualifications. The March 2004 budget also committed to providing every 16- to 18-year-old with an offer of training or education. Employees aged 16–17 and not in full-time education and not qualified to level 2 were already entitled to paid time off work for study. A national minimum wage for 16- to 17-year-olds was also introduced, although there was fear that this will encourage young people to leave education.

It remains to be seen whether the government strategies in schools, which start with nursery education, will impact on skills of school leavers, and whether the technical routes will eventually become as popular as the academic routes.

Recently the government has focused on Adult and Higher Education. In adult education, the target is the 7 million adult workers not qualified to NVQ level 2 and the Adult Learning Inspectorate has been established to assure quality. Emphasis was given to improving communications between Further Education (FE) and employers as it is currently estimated that 70 per cent of companies, especially smaller ones, do not use further education provision (Pickard 2003a).

In Higher Education (HE), although numbers of students rose from approximately 15 per cent at the beginning of the 1990s to 43 per cent in 2003, the social mix did not change significantly. With regard to skills, the number of applications for degrees seen as relevant for filling skill shortages (for example, physical, material and environmental sciences) was declining, and at the same time many graduates are unable to find appropriate jobs. The Dearing Report (1997) attempted to address problems including the funding crisis. Following intense debate, changes were announced in 2004 which it was hoped would secure adequate funding while increasing and widening participation, especially for students from poorer backgrounds. From 2006 there will be a system of deferred tuition fees and increased financial support for students from the poorest families, in the form of non-repayable grants. Other changes have been the development of Foundation Degrees (FDs) and £30 million was allocated for the period 2004–6 to pay for bursaries for students on FDs (Baldwin and Halpin 2004, p1). These are work-related qualifications developed in conjunction with employers and SSCs. The hope is that they will ensure that skills match employer demand and will lead to increased numbers qualified to higher technician and associate professional levels. Examples include a technology FD set up by BASF and Teesside University and a hospitality FD set up with Radisson Edwardian Hotels and Thames Valley. FDs will eventually replace HNDs. They will cover sectors not previously covered by HNDs, although there seems little difference between them in structure.

What can be done to increase the proportion of young people from poorer backgrounds going on to higher education? What can be done to encourage students to apply for courses that fill the longer term skills shortages (such as languages, science and engineering)?

Although many agree with the government target of getting 50 per cent of young people in HE, it has met criticism. Baldwin and Halpin (2004, p1) report on research shortly to be published by Brown and Hesketh (2004) suggesting that 'hundreds of thousands of graduates will not find jobs that repay their investment in HE'. Their research shows that 40 per cent of recent graduates are in jobs that do not require degree-level skills three years after finishing their courses and that 2003 salaries (average £12,659) were lower than the previous year. They point out that HE expansion has led to employers raising the barriers for entry, reinforcing bias towards students from older universities rather than those from new universities, and use of UCAS points as a screen. This is an obvious outcome, but it is likely to discriminate against students from state schools, who traditionally achieve more added value through university than public school students, but whose UCAS points will be lower.

GOVERNMENT INITIATIVES TO DEVELOP SKILLS

Three main planks of the government's attempts to get firms to increase training are the National Vocational Qualifications, Modern Apprenticeships, and Investors in People, and we examine each of these in turn.

National Vocational Qualifications and Scottish Vocational Qualifications

National Vocational Qualifications (NVQs) and the Scottish version (SVQs) were developed in the late 1980s with the aim of establishing a wide range of employer-led vocational qualifications with national accreditation. At this time, less than one-third of UK workers held vocational qualifications compared with two-thirds in Germany (Harrison 2002, p451). There was a need for qualifications that reflected workplace need and to extend into areas in which none existed.

NVQs are based on National Occupational Standards, which describe what competent people in a particular job are expected to be able to do. They cover all the main aspects of an occupation, including best practice and the ability to adapt to future requirements, as well as the knowledge and understanding that underpins competent performance. While NVQs may require employees to be trained to reach a set of standards, it is not a training programme, nor is there a prescribed learning method. The NVQ concept is based on four main principles: it is industry-led; it is based on performance on the job rather than entirely on knowledge; accessibility; and finally, the qualifications are flexible and transferable because they are unit-based and include Accreditation of Prior Learning (APL).

Refinements to the system were made following the 1996 Beaumont Report, although there remain criticisms. In particular, there is concern whether a competence gained in one context is transferable to another, and whether the ability to carry out a series of discrete tasks implies that the person can do a complete job. Grugulis (2000, pp95–96) believes that the relevance of competence-based qualifications is based on bureaucratisation and routinisation of what are often the less important elements of work. Using teachers as an example, emotional elements of the work, such as enthusing students and conveying ideas, are excluded and, consequently, the meaningful element of the work is lost. Many employers fail to see their relevance and continue to run traditional and NVQ systems in parallel, with obvious cost implications. LSC has asked for further research to be carried out from 2004, looking particularly at the differences between NVQs and National Occupational Standards, assessment and verification problems, and use of unit certification and Credit Accumulation and Transfer (CAT), and of Accreditation of Prior Experience and Learning (APEL).

Find out about NVQs/SVQs in an occupation of your choice, and assess how effective they are in providing an appropriate and relevant qualification structure for that occupation.

Modern Apprenticeships – Foundation and Advanced

Because there is lack of respect for the vocational route, many young people who choose the educational route drop out before qualifying (Fuller and Unwin 1998, pp153–154) and end up in low-paid, low-skill jobs (Gray and Morgan 1998, pp126–127). Prior to the introduction of modern apprenticeships in 1994, training for craft-workers had been in decline and restricted to a small number of occupational sectors. This compared unfavourably with the German system where the training curriculum is devised by a consortium of training bodies, trade unions and teachers. Qualified instructors – who are legally obliged to stay up-to-date – deliver on-the-job training and companies without excellent training facilities make use of training centres or other firms. Once the training has ended, trainees can progress to 'Meister' level that allows them to become trainers or to set up in business.

The aim of remarketing UK apprenticeships was to harness the high quality traditionally associated with the word, to extend training to sectors previously excluded, to give a viable alternative to the academic route, and to fill the intermediate skills gap. Foundation Modern Apprenticeship (FMA) takes at least 18 months and leads to NVQ level 2 (see http://www.realworkrealpay.info/). Since there are insufficient employers demanding apprentices, the FMAs do not guarantee employed-status. Progression is to the Advanced Modern Apprenticeship (AMA), which lasts at least 24 months and is planned to lead to NVQ level 3; trainees are employed. From 2004 the scheme was extended to include junior apprenticeships and pre-apprenticeship courses. The apprenticeships are open to those aged 16–24 (from 2004, the age limit will go up gradually, possibly sector by sector) and are no longer time-served. Key skills (numeracy, communication, IT, problem-solving and team-working) are included. The scheme now covers over 80 sectors, many of which have no prior experience of apprenticeships; it accounts for around one-fifth of those eligible in the 16–24 age range.

The modern apprenticeships have been subject to continuous criticism and refinement. From 2000 extra money was provided to raise entry requirements, improve completion rates, increase off-the-job training with the addition of technical certificates as well as NVQs, and to plan progression routes through to foundation degrees. Current major criticisms revolve around outcomes and completion rates, popularity, flexibility, and quality.

Only a fifth of young people go into Modern Apprenticeships, just under half the AMAs are completed, and 41 per cent complete FMAs (Rana 2002, p36). Approximately one-fifth of AMA leavers do not qualify to NVQ level 3 – the target qualification – and there are particular problems in those sectors with no prior experience of apprenticeship, for example Business Administration, Retailing and Customer Service, which make up a large proportion of those on AMAs (Fuller and Unwin 2003). Part of the problem remains that the more able young people take the academic route whereas the less academic are more likely to be persuaded to take the vocational route, but are also less likely to attain NVQ level 3. Low completion rates were accredited to poor initial assessment and induction, and a lack of key skills from the start. However, key skills tend to be unpopular with apprentices and employers, and are often omitted or latched on to the end of training.

There are also reports that many of those recorded as achieving NVQ level 3 already hold higher level qualifications. In one case reported by Fuller and Unwin (2003), a large insurance company was asked by a training provider to join the AMA. Seventeen young people from the company took up the offer, all were already employed and in their early twenties, and had good qualifications. The majority had GCSEs (A–C grades) and/or A levels, and some had degrees. Clearly, they did not need training to NVQ level 3, nor did the training enhance their occupational competence, and yet their achievement counted towards government targets. The fact that many of those recruited onto the programme are already in employment may contribute to drop out, as the employer and/or apprentice don't see any need to complete.

Because the government and its agencies are keen to meet targets, the initiative is pushed by offering training subsidies, while the employer pays the wage. Naturally, employers welcome training where the government subsidises it, but the result might be that they are not fully committed, merely becoming involved because of the subsidies. Merrick (2004) describes how Asda night-workers had been requesting externally accredited qualifications, but the company had refused to provide this because it felt that Modern Apprenticeships and NVQs were too bureaucratic. However, when the LSC offered £500,000 funding, the company stated that they believed that the Modern Apprenticeships would meet their needs, and they were provided. Hogarth and Hasluck (2003) estimate that the net costs of AMAs in engineering and construction (which last 3–3½ years) were £16,000 and £10,000 respectively. However, in other industries (such as hospitality, retailing, business administration), the costs are much lower because most of the training is on-the-job and trainees are immediately productive. Despite financial incentives, certain sectors are unhappy with the lack of flexibility and unpopularity of Modern Apprenticeships and there are question marks over the quality of provision. Both Skillsmart and e-Skills (the retail sector and IT Sector Skills Councils) are revamping the qualifications (Watkins 2003; IT Training 2004) and the Adult Learning Inspectorate's (ALI) first report in 2002 found that 60 per cent of work-based learning provision was inadequate (Rana 2002, p36).

There are additional problems with the image, and the necessity of committing to a specific career, combined with lack of information. Since the new range of apprenticeships develop generic, broad-based competences (for example, Business Administration), they tend not to be job specific in the way that traditional apprenticeships had been. On a fundamental level, Fuller and Unwin (2003) question whether such training needs are better met by academic or vocational courses.

Although Modern Apprenticeships are being marketed as a quality product, the government has produced a hybrid, including elements of the traditional craft skill apprenticeship, but also elements of the old youth training schemes, which were designed to upskill young people who would otherwise not have the offer of training or be unemployed. The scheme therefore helps the government to meet its social inclusion targets of 16- to 17-year-olds in training and is supply led. However, merging social concepts associated with youth training with the quality of traditional apprenticeships has exacerbated image problems. Fuller and Unwin (2003, p22) question whether public money should be used to support employers' training in such a way, or whether it should be targeted to those sectors with a need for skills at or beyond level 3. They believe that quality Modern Apprenticeships are best suited to sectors and firms with a *genuine* need for level 3 training and a history of apprenticeships with associated community of practice and institutional infrastructure. In some of the sectors with the largest numbers on the schemes (retailing, hospitality and business administration), there is little evidence of demand for NVQ level 3 and nor do they have a tradition of apprenticeship training. In these sectors workers are usually trained to level 2 and managed by those qualified to level 4 and beyond.

While the aims of providing more training for those traditionally denied it is laudable, it is clear that the hybrid aims of the 'modern' apprenticeships are failing to meet the conflicting demands made upon it. The government would do well to look at the European model which is highly successful in that it provides an equitable funding system based on social agreements between employers, unions, the government and educators with quality underpinned by legislation guaranteeing minimum criteria. Further, without addressing the demand side from employers, it is likely that the reputation of Modern Apprenticeships will continue to suffer.

> In order to fill the intermediate skills gap (at level 3) in the UK, vocational routes must become as attractive as academic routes to able young people. Do you agree with this statement? Do you think that Modern Apprenticeships will achieve this aim? If not why not?

Investors in People

The initiative that has probably had the greatest impact on cajoling employers to invest in training has been Investors in People (IiP; www.iipuk.co.uk). As the literature from IiP UK (2001) states:

> **The Standard provides a national framework for improving business performance and competitiveness, through a planned approach to setting and communicating business objectives and developing people to meet these objectives. The result is that what people can do and are motivated to do, matches what the organisation needs them to do. The process is cyclical and should engender the culture of continuous improvement.**

IiP is based on four key principles that incorporate a total of 12 assessment indicators against which organisations are measured. They must:

- be fully committed to developing people in order to achieve aims and objectives
- be clear about aims and objectives and what people need to do to achieve them
- develop people effectively in order to improve performance
- understand the impact of investment in people on performance.

Once the award has been made, there are regular reviews no more than three years apart. IiP Quality Centres are responsible for assessment and quality assurance with the LSCs responsible for advice and support. IiP UK commissions independent research periodically and respond to feedback. By 2004, 32,000 organisations had been accredited covering 27 per cent of the workforce with 87 per cent of organisations staying with the standard. Independent research for IiP among 2000 accredited organisations found that 80 per cent had increased customer satisfaction and 70 per cent had improved their competitive edge and productivity.

Several pieces of research conclude that the majority of organisations accredited benefit from the liP standard. For example, the 2001d CIPD survey of national training and development practices among its members found that 55 per cent had achieved the Standard and most respondents felt that liP had an impact on both organisational change and improving performance irrespective of either the size of the establishment or the industrial sector. Other research (Spilsbury et al 1995; Alberga et al 1997; Down and Smith 1998, p154) also indicated that, in general, accreditation would seem to lead to benefits such as increased productivity, better customer service, reduction in workforce turnover and improved employee motivation. Hoque (2003) concludes that 'on balance, training practice is better within workplaces with IIP accreditation than in those without'.

While there is evidence to suggest that the majority of those organisations committed to the standard reap benefits, there are a number of concerns. Firstly, there is the issue of uneven distribution. According to Cully et al (1999, p58) under a third of all workplaces employing 25 or more people are accredited. A further 16 per cent had applied but were unsuccessful, but slightly over half had never applied. Accreditation was very closely associated with size, with 62 per cent of the largest organisations accredited and those in the public sector were more likely to apply for the award. Hoque's research (2003) also highlighted imbalances between sectors with single independent workplaces, the private sector and workplaces with a personnel specialist *less* likely to have secured liP and manufacturing; electricity, gas and water; wholesale and retail, motor vehicle repair; hotels and restaurants; and financial institutions were more likely to have attained liP. Ram (2000) reported that only 4 per cent of small firms had attempted to achieve liP. Most small companies gain the standard in response to their clients' demands and they rushed through the paperwork with the result that liP made little difference to their operation. Attracting SMEs remains the major problem and a Small Firms Initiative has been set up to provide financial support for smaller organisations to attain the standard. Targets are for 45 per cent of the workforce to be employed by organisations with, or working towards liP and at least 40,000 small firms to have achieved, or be working towards the standard by 2007.

Spilsbury et al (1995), Hill and Stewart (1999), Ram (2000) and Hoque (2003) all believe that a large number of organisations, particularly those in the initial waves of accreditation, already had good HR systems and procedures in place, so gaining liP was nothing more than a 'badging' process. As Hoque (2003) says, 'all in all, it's just another plaque on the wall' and training reverts to what it had been in the past once the award had been achieved.

A further concern is the uneven spread of training throughout workplaces, and the emphasis on formal training. Grugulis and Bevitt's research (2002) took place in a NHS Trust where the workforce was already highly motivated and committed, and most of the best practice systems were in place. They commented that as the interests of employees and employers diverge, liP may in effect set a ceiling on skill development for unskilled and semi-skilled workers as well as downplaying the role of informal training. The liP audit emphasises formal qualifications and training methods, especially NVQ – an approach Grugulis and Bevitt criticise because of its 'narrow focus and lack of developmental opportunities' – whereas many employees prefer on-the-job training. Spilsbury et al (1995), Hill and Stewart (1999) and Ram (2000) agree that small firms take *informal* training seriously, but that the informal, reactive and ad hoc nature of training in small firms is not suited to liP. Grugulis and Bevitt conclude that 'if what is desired is really a general increase in the national skills base, as well as an increase in employee motivation and commitment, then focusing on employers' needs may not be the way to achieve it. A national system that emphasised individual needs as well as corporate ones could provide a more convincing step'. Rainbird and Munroe's (2003a, p36) research with the public sector found that lower paid staff were excluded from training, leading to one interviewee to comment, 'Investors in People is just false unless you're in management.' Bell *et al* (2002) also pick up the point that the 'hard, content-focused nature of the IiP framework' does not suit the ideal of the learning organisation in which informal communications and individual development are emphasised.

The link between IiP and profitability has also been questioned although IiP UK challenges the validity of these findings (Mahoney 2000). The link between productivity, profitability and training is notoriously hard to establish, in any case; most organisations do not sign up to IiP for these purposes, and employers usually did not quantify or recognise them (Down and Smith 1998)

Research also questions the links between IiP and motivation and morale, and whether there are benefits in reduced absenteeism, labour turnover and workforce injuries. Most studies seem to confirm that there are improvements in employee attitudes, particularly in terms of motivation and morale, but much of this relies on employers' responses rather than those of employees and tangible evidence is difficult to find (Grugulis and Bevitt 2002). Alberga *et al* (1997) concluded that using indicators such as absenteeism/sick leave, labour turnover and workplace accidents/injuries, the accredited companies are only marginally better than those that are not.

Is your own organisation IiP accredited? If yes, evaluate the advantages that it has brought. If not, do you feel that it should be, and can you list the potential advantages?

The question remains whether or not IiP is able to attract a broader church, particularly small businesses, without an element of compulsion or financial incentives. Unfortunately, the concern remains that for companies with accreditation, 'there is plenty of scope for these companies – should they choose to do so – to treat it as a paper exercise that will have no long-term effect on training once accreditation has been secured' (Hoque 2003, p567).

TRADE UNIONS, TRAINING AND LEARNING

Throughout the 1960s and 1970s Britain operated a model under which trade unions, employers, the government and educationalists were all involved in vocational education and

BOX 31   CLEANSING AND HIGHWAYS DEPARTMENT, LONDON BOROUGH OF BARKING & DAGENHAM

The Borough is in the bottom five nationally in terms of basic skills, and often has problems filling vacancies. Most employees in the Cleansing and Highways Department have no qualifications and many have literacy and numeracy problems. Using the Union Learning Fund a project co-ordinator was employed to design courses to embed basic skills in other types of training, such as health and safety. An initial course involved making Christmas cards using digital cameras and a computer and now all 90 employees are taking a number of courses, all in work time.

Source: Adapted from Margolis A. 'Licensed to skill', *People Management*, 26 June 2003. pp46–48

training. This disappeared during the Thatcher years. Since 1997 the UK government's position has moved closer to that of the EU social partnership model, something required by the 1997 Treaty of Amsterdam. Sutherland and Rainbird (2000, p189) state that 'strong co-operative relations between trade unions and management have been seen as central to the work modernisation agenda, both in managing processes of change in the workforce and in contributing to workers' employability in the wider labour market'.

In the UK, unions and government have a common interest in promoting learning to improve competitiveness and move towards a more equal society. The TUC established its 'Learning Service' in 1994 with the mission 'to represent all employee interests in securing the learning and skills they require to maintain their employability, enhance their career progression and guarantee social inclusion'. The aim was 'to create a learning culture in every workplace and for every worker to be a lifelong learner'. The Learning Service involves the establishment of the Union Learning Fund (ULF) and training union learning representatives (ULRs). Box 31 on page 227 gives an example of one organisation that has taken advantage of the ULF.

> How might trade union representatives be able to help with the training renaissance, especially for the 'skills poor'?

There is much research focusing on the difficulty in attracting non-traditional learners (NIACE). Since it is likely that employees are more willing to discuss basic skills problems with a colleague than with a manager (Rainbird 2003), ULRs play a significant role in giving employees confidence to return to learn. This is not a new concept, as UNISON has for many years run a 'Return to Learn' course for those with few qualifications, having negotiated opportunity for paid time off with public sector organisations. The government has welcomed union involvement and has described the TUC's strategy as 'an inexpensive source of advice for employers'. In recognition, the TUC was given a £9 million fillip for its Learning Fund in 2003. Every worker in a union-recognised workplace is entitled to have a ULR and ULRs are entitled to attend training courses and have time off work to complete training needs analysis, give advice and guidance and organise training/learning. By 2003 there were over 6500 ULRs with a target of 22,000 by 2010. There were 180 learning centres open and each year over 65,000 enrol on trade union education courses.

A survey by York Consulting for the TUC (2003) found that more than half of the ULRs had helped colleagues with little or no experience of learning, one in three had helped colleagues improve basic skills. The commonest activities were advice and guidance on learning (nearly 82 per cent) and promoting the value of learning (over 80 per cent). The commonest learning need identified was help with IT basic skills (84 per cent) followed by basic skills (64 per cent) and vocational qualifications (58 per cent). Its success has been attracting traditional non-participants – one-fifth have no qualifications, and 36 per cent had gained no qualifications since leaving school; 7 per cent had a physical or learning disability that affected work.

Almost 70 per cent of ULRs said that they faced barriers, with the most important being lack of time, followed by lack of interest/apathy from colleagues, lack of support from management and, finally, lack of resources although around one-third of employers gave paid time off for learning and 20 per cent of employers gave unpaid time off (Capizzi 2002). A major spin-off for the unions has been increased trade union membership – particularly among women, younger people and people from ethnic minorities.

Although the trade unions have played a very active role in the training renaissance in the workplace, almost a half of all workplaces with more than 25 employees are non-unionised and there is still difficulty in promoting training activity in SMEs, and with the self-employed.

ASSESSING THE CONTRIBUTION OF VET TO SKILL IMPROVEMENT

As stated earlier, there is a consensus that Britain has operated in a low-skills equilibrium and that for long-term economic progress a shift needs to be made to a high-skill, high-value-added system based on a more highly educated and flexible workforce. The government's research indicates that there are present and future skill gaps and shortages across most sectors and at almost every level.

The government's strategy has been to use a variety of means (short of legislation) to improve skill levels through the education system and to cajole companies to increase levels of training. A number of issues relating to this are discussed below.

Definition

It has been difficult to gain an accurate picture, as this is the first time that a coherent attempt has been made to evaluate sectoral skill levels and predict those needed for the future based on the opinions of employers. Keep (2002) believes that employers are often vague, confused and contradictory and since most organisations lack any HR planning, accuracy of definition of skills is difficult. As he says (p463), 'skill strategies and forecasts are only as good as the weakest data upon which they are founded'. There is also the issue of accurate definitions of 'skill'. Keep (2001) gives the example of shop workers who are now defined as 'skilled', whereas 20 years ago they would have been 'unskilled'. Questions arise about whether or not they really are more skilled, and whether we get a better service as a customer, or a service user. Warhurst and Thompson (1998, p5) cite examples in the financial sector in which 'knowledge workers' in call centres have to use 'standardised quality' responses so that their work is routinised, and lacks autonomy. Sturdy *et al* (2001, pp186–187) showed that Glasgow residents were not regarded as 'posh' enough for many of the jobs requiring aesthetic skills and 'style' jobs were being taken by students and suburban commuters to the exclusion of inner city youth.

Distribution

There is an uneven distribution, which concentrates on larger firms, young workers and those with qualifications (Cannell 2002). According to the DfEE (2001a) 91 per cent of larger firms offer training, but only 25 per cent of the smallest do. Forde and MacKenzie (2004) found that 92 per cent of firms in construction and civil engineering offer training to directly employed staff, but small firms (which are numerically dominant) were much less likely to offer formal training and apprenticeship opportunities. A quarter of those with degrees have typically been involved in training in the previous four weeks, compared to only 4 per cent of those with no qualifications (Prime Minister's Strategy Unit 2001) thereby perpetuating the gap between the training 'haves' and 'have-nots'. Perversely, those with more education and in higher social classes are more likely to receive training, but are also more likely to turn it down. The less qualified are offered fewer training opportunities, but are less likely to turn them down. Where firms offer training, there is debate over the amount, distribution and type available. Felstead *et al* (1997) concluded that although the number in training had increased, the length of training had decreased. There is also evidence (Lloyd 2002; Rainbird *et al* 2004b) that training tends to be ad hoc, short term and non-strategic, and much of this is in workplaces with IiP accreditation.

Three case studies illustrating the importance of work organisation and context to training are given in Box 32.

Exclusion from training

The deregulative approach in the UK and USA makes it easy to dispose of workers without qualifications and skills who find themselves at the edge of the labour market, drifting in and out of low-paid work. Yet one of the government aims for VET relates to social cohesion and inclusion, equal access to employment, particularly that offering training. Still many

---

BOX 32   THE IMPORTANCE OF WORK ORGANISATION AND CONTEXT TO TRAINING

NHS Sterilisation and Disinfection Unit

Workers in this unit were low skilled and low paid and there was little potential for skill development. Many had qualifications although none were required for the work – the women staff in particular had a range of skills that were not used in the job. Workers were typically attracted to the job because of flexibility in choice of hours (numbers and timing). There was no opportunity for formal training, nor career progression (except to supervision), and little opportunity to acquire skills that would be marketable outside the workplace.

The Housing Department

The housing department was responsible for the maintenance of housing stock and sheltered accommodation. Staff numbers had been radically cut and there were intense budgetary pressures. Work had been redesigned so that managers' jobs were generic. Each manager was responsible for all issues to do with 350 houses, often in sink estates. The work involved being in the front line and stresses were intense because of innate frustrations, dealing with irate tenants and the volume of work. Initial training had been essential into order for staff to take on generic roles. However, there were complaints that inadequate time was allocated to training, and it usually took place at the end of the day, or in slack periods. The training was specifically targeted at ability to do the job, rather than for personal development or training for future need. For all of these reasons, the training was viewed negatively, and morale was low.

The local government cook-freeze centre

This is a small factory unit contracted by Social Services. The work is 'repetitive, boring and low skilled'. Despite this, turnover was low, and workers said that they were proud to be able to help others. All were encouraged by management to train; they were given time off and, wherever possible, the opportunity to use the skills they learned. It was thought that management's support of staff taking external courses helped motivate and retain workers, even though most courses did not contribute to their work role.

Source: Adapted from Rainbird H., Munro A. and Holly L. 'Exploring the concept of employer demand for skills and qualifications: case studies from the public sector', in C. Warhurst, E. Keep and I. Grugulis (eds), *The Skills That Matter*. Basingstoke, Palgrave. 2004b

employees are never offered training by their employers – Lloyd (2002) and Rainbird *et al* (2004b) report considerable unmet demand from employees for training. The CIPD survey report *Who Learns at Work?* (2002a) found that although most employees thought that they were provided with enough training opportunities, a quarter did not think that they had enough. Of course, those employees requesting additional training are likely to be the most dynamic and motivated. Those most likely to be excluded are those in low-status occupations, the less well-qualified, flexible workers such as part-timers, those in SMEs, and older workers. Rainbird and Munro (2003a, p37) add to the list: women, manual staff and those whose work role is not understood, or who are isolated. In some cases, even if there is awareness of training need, there is confusion as to who the line manager is and who pays for training. The evidence that age, gender, ethnicity and educational background are all determinants of access to workplace learning (Keep and Rainbird 2000, p181) is worrying and this is compounded by the rise in demand for aesthetic skills. These factors accentuate polarisation, rather than ameliorate it and although many individuals take responsibility for their own training outside of work, the barriers – in terms of time and money – are all too often insurmountable for those in part-time, low-paid work, or with family commitments.

Types of training

Statistics from the DfEE (now DfES) Learning and Training at Work Survey 2000 (DfEE 2001a) showed that 70 per cent of on-the-job training related to health and safety, and 50 per cent was induction-related. Since around 15 per cent of semi-skilled and unskilled workers are asked to use new technology at work (Pickard 2003a), IT can be added to the list of essential training and the problem with these types of training is that they are unlikely to provide the impetus for transformation to a high-skill workplace.

Work organisation and context

The case studies examined by Rainbird *et al* (2004b; see Box 32) demonstrate the importance of work organisation and context. In the cook-freeze unit, the work was low-skill and boring, with little opportunity for change to this situation. Nonetheless, staff were encouraged to train for their personal development and motivation levels were high, with low turnover. In comparison, in the housing department, highly skilled workers were trained to cope with generic working but the training was job specific and other aspects of work organisation lead to extremely low morale. In the NHS example, the majority of employees' existing qualifications are not used and they were offered no opportunity for development. Such case studies amply demonstrate the conflict between individual and organisational training and development needs.

The issue of line management involvement and the profile of the work organisation are as important as the product specification in creating the opportunities for continuous learning within the organisation. Rainbird and Munroe (2003b) examine the situation in which 'the government is the employer, so we might expect to see a commitment to "high skills", exemplified in management processes and in approaches to HRM and training and development'. In some cases there is investment in training, but it is almost accidental rather than strategic.

Barriers

Lloyd (2002) identified a number of barriers that prevent firms from investing in training and development:

- Firms tend to cut down on training in times of recession.

- There is a lack of time – the job still has to be done, and this leads to lack of encouragement for off-the-job training.

- Managers hold onto good workers, and do not want them trained up in case they leave to take up other positions.

- Flatter organisations restrict career progression and this is a disincentive to employees to push for training.

- Training is concentrated on those with high-skill levels who would be hard to replace.

- Devolution to line managers results in inconsistency and unequal access.

A traditionally reported barrier to provision of training has been fear of poaching, yet in the case studies reported in Box 32 it was the most highly skilled people who left, or threatened to leave, those workplaces that did *not* train. Lloyd (2002) also noted that firms might under-invest because of inadequate information about the economic returns to training and a lack of strategic manpower planning. This links to research by Aragon-Sanchez *et al* (2003, p956), who concluded that a major reason why firms do not train was simply because they did not evaluate the impacts of training on company profit or company performance. Their research on impacts of training in European SMEs demonstrated that training helps companies' competitive advantage because of the human capital element locked in knowledge, skills and attitudes. However, because of a lack of research, firms did not link training with performance results.

The research of Rainbird *et al* (2004b) cited above shows how training has been edged out as a result of contract specification that led to work intensification, narrowly defined job roles and pressure to reduce costs. Training was often job-specific, and the main difficulty was allowing staff the time off for training. Increased resources were viewed as essential for providing a quality service, and also for the 'demand and utilisation of skills'.

Marginalisation

The historical and cultural influences on the infrastructure are also important. It remains the case that in the UK, training and development is still seen as a bolt-on, non-strategic activity, which is not fully integrated into the work of the firm. In comparison, Japanese managers place the development of their staff as one of the highest priorities (Keep and Rainbird 2000, p190).

It is doubtful whether companies will invest in adequate training (even those in high-skill industries) without pressure such as legal requirements to train or regulations through collective bargaining arrangements (Keep 2003a). As we saw earlier, the UK is unusual in leaving most decisions about who gets trained to employers; elsewhere firms are either legally required to train, or there are trade union agreements on training, or both. At governmental level, Keep believes (2003b) that the major barriers are the government's non-interventionist view, its refusal to look at alternative models (particularly European) and, finally, the government's wish to avoid conflict with employers. However, the Chancellor in the March 2004 budget intimated that the latest government initiatives are 'post-voluntary' with the threat of regulation if current strategies do not work.

How far is your organisation along the road to becoming a learning organisation and what more needs to be done to embed a culture of learning?

Impact, and the supply and demand for skills

More fundamentally, there are questions whether raising the supply of skills will give the fillip for the UK to move from its low-skill equilibrium based on the assumption that high-value-added production and services require a highly educated and skilled workforce. Nolan and Wood (2003) believe that the reality is more fragmented with considerable stability as well as change in the labour market. Others question whether boosting skills does in fact impact on productivity, particularly as the US (with similar skill levels) is more productive, in any case, as stated earlier, productivity does not necessarily lead to profitability – particularly in the service sector (Keep 2003a).

There is particular disagreement over the proportion of jobs demanding highly skilled workers as well as the speed at which these sectors are developing and generating demand. The ESRC Working in Britain Survey 2000 (Nolan and Wood 2003) shows that the proportion of the labour force in the professions, scientific and technical occupations only increased from 34 to 37 per cent from the 1990s, but the number of manual workers remained constant (p170). Felstead *et al* (2002) estimate that jobs requiring degrees rose from 10 per cent in 1986 to 17 per cent in 2001 but also that there are 6.5 million jobs that require no qualifications.

There are few high-skills export sectors in the UK, the main ones being information technology, pharmaceuticals, some branches of chemicals, aircraft manufacture and some aspects of insurance and finance, but together these account for a small proportion of UK exports. Even in these industries, highly skilled workers may only be required in R&D, design and product management roles, and training is frequently only available to a small number of employees who are difficult to replace. Lloyd's qualitative work (2002) in pharmaceuticals and aeronautical engineering demonstrated that many jobs required no qualification or skills. She believed that the UK's short-termist approach in which the reduced productivity as a result of underinvestment in training was offset 'by lower social costs and wages, longer hours, and working longer'. Brown *et al* (2001, p240) concur and describe the US and UK labour markets as characterised by 'enclaves of knowledge work alongside large swathes of low-waged, low-skilled jobs'. Brown (2003, p151) also dispels the myth that knowledge workers are protected from job loss, as demonstrated by recent redundancies in 'Silicon Valley'.

In most of the developed world, the main employers of highly educated and trained employees are in the public sector in health, education and welfare and in these sectors high-level skills are not needed by a majority of staff, nor are they exported. The work of Rainbird *et al* (2004a) in the public sector graphically portrays the fact that 'many jobs will continue to require few formal qualifications, with limited scope for job enlargement and greater use of skills'.

There is evidence that rising skill levels on the supply side (particularly the number of graduates entering the labour market) results in underutilisation of these skills and underemployment (Keep and Rainbird, 2000, p183; Crouch *et al* 2001; Ashton *et al* 2002, p63; Manocha 2003, p40; Brown and Hesketh 2004; Rainbird *et al* 2004b). According to Rainbird and Munro (2003a, pp32–33), this issue commonly applies to low-paid workers in the public sector – particularly women and part-time workers. The Government's report *Skills in England 2002* (LSC 2003b) refutes claims about overqualification and oversupply of graduates, although it agreed that this needs continuous monitoring.

Partial coverage

A final criticism of the government's emphasis on increasing the supply of skills, it that it is merely one element in the equation, and probably the easiest to tackle. Finegold (1999, p79) maintains that it is unlikely to work on its own without addressing other issues. He looks at the prerequisites for creating high-skill ecosystems in California, and although he admits that they cannot simply be transferred wholesale to the UK context, some elements might be. These include increased funding for basic research and pre-venture capital, more courses on starting up new businesses – especially for scientists and engineers – strategies to retain the talents of overseas students, and increased regional networks (including research universities) to promote sector clusters and sector networks. To this list Keep (2003a) adds increased investment in R&D and improved public infrastructures (such as transport). As we saw earlier, UK companies are prone to distribute a larger share of profits to investors leaving less for investment in R&D or training. Others include seeking protected markets, cost-cutting, or moving work overseas (Fuller *et al* 2004, p1). The Government is responding to such criticism, and in 2003 the DTI produced an Innovation Review, *Competing in the Global Economy: The innovation challenge*, announcing the aim to be the leading country in Europe for R&D within a decade through:

- the development of a national technology strategy to provide a structure and support for innovation

- £150 million including £90 million for nanotechnology

- new procurement guidelines to make the government a more 'intelligent customer' by encouraging innovation through the £109 billion it spends each year on products and services

- an increased role for the Small Business Service to promote innovation and knowledge transfer.

CONCLUSIONS

The government has embarked on a brave attempt to combat 'the training problem' by commissioning research and revolutionising the education and training system in the UK and by unilaterally financing generic training. Its stated aim is to meet the needs of employers, individuals and the nation, in order to combat social exclusion and push the economy from its low-skills equilibrium. Their hope is that increasing the *supply* of those skills will provide impetus for change. However, increasing the supply of skills is only one part of the solution – and possibly the easiest to effect. Rather more difficult is to ensure that firms *demand* and *utilise* skills, as well as providing the opportunity for continual learning for *all* of their workforce.

It would seem that this is not happening. Too many workers receive no training at all, even in the most basic forms of instruction about how to do their jobs, let alone in how to develop their skills or improve their contribution to organisational success. There is little point in training people, if they then find themselves in a workplace that neither values nor utilises such skills. Too few UK organisations live up to the image of the 'learning organisation' and although employers report skill gaps and shortages and identify training as a solution, one-third have no training budget. Where decisions are left to firms, training tends to be limited to the essentials, with great inequalities in access. Since many employers in the UK aim to achieve competitive advantage through a low-skill equilibrium, this makes short-term economic sense but perpetuates the cycle. Some of the larger organisations do think longer term, but a major challenge is to engage with SMEs (the SSCs are dominated by the larger employers). The issue of formal versus informal learning is related to this, and although the government prefers formal learning (presumably because of ease of measurement), informal learning is more likely to grow in recognition because it is flexible, and therefore more attractive to firms, particularly smaller ones.

The UK system remains far removed from the European model in which trade unions, employers and educationalists are actively involved in developing strategy and the cost of training is shared. Many believe that most employers will not train in the absence of regulation (Keep and Rainbird 2000, p173; Lloyd 2002), but will continue to poach or outsource, so reinforcing a short-term approach in which training is a cost rather than an investment. It remains to be seen whether the government will eventually have to relinquish the voluntarist approach to training and will be able to act to persuade employers that effective development and utilisation of skills necessitates fundamental changes in job design and the organisation of production. This has obvious implications for effective HRM.

USEFUL READING

DEPARTMENT FOR EDUCATION AND EMPLOYMENT. *Skills for All: Research for the National Skills Taskforce*. London, DfEE. 2000.

FELSTEAD A., GALLIE D. *and* GREEN F. *Work Skills in Britain 2001*. London, Department for Education and Skills. 2002.

FORDE C. *and* MACKENZIE R. 'Cementing skills: training and labour use in UK construction', *Human Resource Management Journal*, Vol. 14, No. 3, 2004. pp74–88.

HOQUE K. 'All in all, it's just another plaque on the wall', *Journal of Management Studies*, Vol. 40, No. 2, 2003. pp543–571.

INVESTORS IN PEOPLE UK. www.iipuk.co.uk.

KEEP E. 'The English vocational education and training debate – "fragile technologies" or opening the"black box": two competing visions of where we go next', *Journal of Education and Work*, Vol. 15, No. 4, 2002. pp457–479.

LEARNING AND SKILLS COUNCIL. *National Employer Skills Survey 2003: Key findings*. Available at: www.lsc.gov.uk. 2003a.

RAINBIRD H., FULLER A. *and* MUNRO A. *Workplace Learning in Context*. London, Routledge. 2004a

WARHURST C., KEEP E. *and* GRUGULIS I. (eds), *The Skills That Matter*. Basingstoke, Palgrave. 2004.

Learning and Development at Work

CHAPTER 9

INTRODUCTION

We have seen how the lack of training and development in most organisations is due to the short-termism so characteristic of British employers. But some is also due to an imperfect understanding of how adults learn, and many learners are themselves wary about further training and development opportunities, perhaps due to unsatisfactory experiences in formal educational settings. Equally, many line managers regard the provision of learning opportunities for manual workers or clerical staff as pampering the workforce, and as an unwarranted distraction from their departmental targets and duties. Traditionally, organisations used to employ specialists whose job was merely to instruct and teach people how to work more efficiently. However, changes are taking place with the strategic value of training becoming increasingly important, with emphasis on meeting current and future corporate objectives. Additionally, the emphasis is moving from training to learning, both from the standpoint of the individual and from the organisation. This is what Sloman (2003, p xiii) calls the new paradigm:

> **Interventions and activities that are intended to improve knowledge and skills in organisations will increasingly focus on the learner. Emphasis will shift to the individual learner (or the team), and he or she will be encouraged to take more responsibility for his or her learning. Efforts will be made to develop a climate that supports effective and appropriate learning. Such interventions and activities will form part of an integrated approach to creating competitive advantage though people in the organisation.**

Some organisations recognise the value in encouraging workers to enhance their skills and knowledge, and to foster their creativity and initiative as part of a drive for continuous improvement. This is not necessarily undertaken for philanthropic reasons, but in order to improve productivity, performance and knowledge development and as a strategy for retaining key staff in order to enable the organisation to thrive in a competitive environment. For individuals the potential benefits are increased personal competence, adaptability and the likelihood of continuous employability. The shift from training to learning and development is also emphasised by the CIPD through its Continuing Professional Development (CPD) Policy.

In this chapter we examine learning theories, the training process system – which involves identification of learner needs, devising learning plans, delivery and evaluation – as well as how the strategic role impacts on the promotion of learning. Current trends are analysed (coaching and e-learning) together with management development and continuing professional development.

By the end of this chapter, readers should be able to:

- **utilise appropriate information in order to identify training priorities**

- **design and deliver learning and training initiatives to support organisational goals**

- **evaluate the effectiveness of training and learning initiatives both for the organisation and for individuals.**

In addition, readers should understand and be able to explain:

- **the differences between education, training, learning, skills and competency**

- **the methods used to deliver training that are most appropriate to specific situations**

- **the ways in which specific methods (e-learning, coaching, management development and Continuing Professional Development) can contribute to a systematic and well-designed training strategy.**

DEFINITIONS AND TERMINOLOGY

Although terms such as training, learning and education are often used interchangeably, we need to be aware of the major distinctions between them, at least in their pure form. In reality, of course, distinctions are less clear cut, there is sometimes overlap between the concepts, and one may feed into the other. For example, the educational process ought to involve learning, hopefully leads to development, and may contain some training in specific techniques. As the use of NVQs spreads, the distinction between education and training is likely to become even more blurred.

Education is the system that aims to develop people's intellectual capability, conceptual and social understanding and work performance through the learning process. Training is a narrower concept defined as 'a process which is planned to facilitate learning so that people can become more effective in carrying out aspects of their work' (Bramley 2003, p4). It is just one way in which an organisation can promote learning. The differences between education and training are not always obvious, and just because a two-day course in negotiating skills takes place away from the employer's premises, this does not qualify as education unless it comprises part of a wider product, such as a professional qualification or an MBA. Similarly, full-time students on a Masters' programme in HRM who take part in an outdoor-based development programme undertake this as an element in their education even though the course may be run by trainers. Education and training typically refer – albeit implicitly – to the process by which an individual's attitudes, behaviour or performance is changed. Learning focuses explicitly on the changes which take place within the individual and on the process by which the learner acquires knowledge, develops a skill or undergoes a transition in attitudes. Examples of attitudes mediated through the learning process might include confidence-building, recognising and dealing with prejudices or adopting socially responsible mores. Formalised learning has to have some purpose, typically measured by a series of outcomes, as is evident from the standards for the CIPD Professional Development Scheme.

Skills are those aspects of behaviour which are practised in the work situation, and which individuals need to be able to perform at an acceptable level in order to do the job satisfactorily (see Chapter 8 for more on work skills). They comprise motor skills, manual dexterity, social and interpersonal skills, technical skills, analytical skills and so on. They are frequently seen in terms of a hierarchy, in which the lower levels are prerequisites for the higher levels; for example, Bloom's taxonomy (reproduced in Collin 2004, p284) views learning as a series of building-blocks:

1 *knowledge* – simple knowledge of facts, terms, theories etc
2 *comprehension* – understanding the meaning of this knowledge
3 *application* – ability to apply this knowledge and comprehension in new situations
4 *analysis* – breaking down material into constituent parts and seeing relationships between them
5 *synthesis* – reassembling the parts into a new and meaningful relationship
6 *evaluation* – the ability to judge the value of the material.

Understanding and knowledge, and the ability to explain things to other people are therefore incorporated within the term 'skill'. For most observers, however, skill has a commonsense, everyday meaning, typically connected with these lower levels, and seen in the application of motor skills rather than the powers of analysis, synthesis and evaluation.

Tacit skills are hard to define, and are frequently overlooked. These refer to the ability to perform a task without necessarily being aware of how it is done. For example, female catering workers and home-care staff often undervalue their acquired skills and knowledge, regarding them as instinctive and natural. Since this know-how is typically acquired through experience, rather than formal instruction, it can be hard to specify and quantify. Yet tacit skills can explain high performance in business and, because they are unique to the people of the particular organisation, they give competitive advantage (Harrison 2002, p231).

Do you think it is possible for people to learn without being aware they are learning? Do they need to consolidate this learning or relate it to abstract principles for learning to be effective?

Competency is a newer term than 'skill' and has grown in importance since the publication of *The Competent Manager* by Boyatsis in 1982, but there remains much confusion about the terminology. According to Whiddett and Hollyforde (2003, pp5–7), 'competencies are behaviours that individuals demonstrate when undertaking job-relevant tasks effectively within a given organisational context'. In other words, competency and competencies are concerned with the individual and their behaviour or how they do something. Competence, and competences, relate to the dimensions of a job or task, or what an individual has to achieve to be proficient in a particular job. Competences can be used to determine job descriptions and performance standards by establishing generic requirements of a particular job. Mumford and Gold (2004, p51) see management competences as 'descriptions of behaviours, attributes, skills needed to perform management work effectively and/or the outputs to be achieved from such work which can be assessed against performance criteria'. Such descriptions are not neutral, but are linked to organisational objectives (Mumford and Gold, 2004, p51; Salaman 2004).

Competency frameworks provide a set of performance criteria at organisation or individual levels and identify the expected outcomes of achieving those criteria. The Management Charter Initiative (MCI) Management Standards are a framework based on the management of activities; resources; people; information; energy; quality; projects (Mumford and Gold 2004, pp54–56). Most such frameworks include the following:

- breadth of awareness and strategic perspective
- oral and written communication
- leadership, decisiveness and assertiveness
- teamworking and ability to work with others
- analysis and judgement
- drive and persistence
- organisation and planning
- sensitivity to others' viewpoints
- self-confidence and persuasiveness
- flexibility and adaptability.

How adequately do you think this list relates to the personal characteristics that are required to perform satisfactorily in your particular job?

THE PROCESS OF LEARNING

The way in which people learn should be important for HR professionals, given its centrality to most aspects of organisational life. Here we present a brief overview of some of the different learning process theories, and readers wanting a fuller explanation of these theories are referred to McKenna (2000) or Stewart (2002).

The first category is the behaviourist approach based on the work of B. F. Skinner. This incorporates signal and stimulus–response learning. Signal learning is exemplified when a pet runs into the kitchen when it hears the sound of its dish being filled (Gagne 1977, p77), It was popularised by the Pavlovian dogs experiment, although it might also be found in the fixed smile that appears on a salesperson's face the moment a customer walks through the door. Conditioning can be either classical (whereby the stimulus automatically leads to a response) or operant, in which case a desired response is rewarded and reinforced after it has been delivered. In the latter case, behaviour may be natural and unconditioned, in the sense that it has not been trained into the individual, in which case appropriate behaviour is often learned by trial and error. In organisations, operant conditioning can be seen in the recognition shown by a line manager to high-quality performance by a new recruit – this acts as a powerful reinforcement for learning how to do the job well. Reinforcement must occur soon after the event for it to be meaningful, and without appropriate reinforcement learning soon becomes extinct.

Stimulus–response reinforcement paradigms have been extremely influential in psychology, but they fail to account for all types of learning. In particular, given that the experiments were originally conducted on animals, the paradigm does not give sufficient weight to the dynamic and interactive complexity of human beings. Also, given the range of stimuli in a work (as opposed to a laboratory) situation, it may prove difficult to determine the precise influence of one stimulus over a defined response. Behaviourist learning theories are useful in classroom situations, but the focus on 'correct' responses may not help employees deal with the range of new experiences that they are likely to encounter at work, and the implicit power relationship may curb discretionary behaviour (Reynolds *et al* 2002).

The second category of learning is cognitive, which is based not upon stimulus–response theories but upon stimulus–stimulus connections. The idea of insight – known as the 'aha' experience – is central to cognitive learning, although in many situations we take insights for granted. The pleasure of gaining an insight acts as a powerful reinforcer of learning and stimulus to memory. Good examples of this are case studies, which help link theories and practical applications, or group problem-solving, which can have a highly positive effect on team-building if properly structured. Whereas stimulus–response applications might be suitable for training in basic practical skills, cognitive learning is more appropriate for mental skills. These types of theory rely on learners connecting together different concepts or actions to form a chain of stimuli enabling him or her to arrive at the ultimate goal (McKenna 2000).

Cybernetics represents the third strand of theories that attempt to explain the process of learning. This approach regards learning as an information-processing system in which a signal containing information is passed along a communication channel (Collin 2004, p280). Stammers and Patrick (1975, pp27–35), drawing upon earlier work by Crossman, outline the essential elements of this communication process. Signals have to be encoded to enable them to be transmitted along the communication channel, and decoded before they can be received. All messages are subject to 'noise', which acts as an obstacle to learning – this does not mean just audible noises but also other factors that interfere with the transmission process. Learning may be hindered, therefore, by the presence of other stimuli, which interfere with the receipt of messages and cause them to be confused or imperfectly picked up (stress is a good example of this). There are also limits to the amount of information that can be transmitted along a channel. Feedback is an important aspect of these models. It may be intrinsic to the learning itself, in which case the individual is aware of this during the acquisition or application of the skill, or it may be extrinsic, in which case it becomes available at a later date and can influence future performance.

The final category is social learning theory, which works on the principle of learning by imitation (Bandura 1977). This means that individuals learn to do specific tasks by watching other people perform them before trying for themselves and generalising from this as appropriate. Long ridiculed as 'sitting next to Nellie', these forms of learning enable the transfer of 'tacit' skills from one worker to another. Many basic skills can be learned in this way, although reinforcement through doing (often repeatedly) is crucial to their success. Social and interpersonal skills are also learned through this process, and often acquired without the individual being aware that learning has actually taken place. One of the major problems with social learning which does not incorporate feedback or evaluation, is that people may learn inefficient ways of working or fail to decipher some of the tacit skills which are used by experienced workers. There are also dangers that individuals learn behaviour that is not welcomed by management or society by imitation – for example, bullying or aggressive behaviour, fiddles and scams, racism and sexism.

Keep a diary for a week noting all the times when you learned something new. Categorise these learning experiences according to the different theories outlined above. Make sure that you include all learning events, not just those taking place at work or in a formal situation.

The Cambridge Programme for Industry (Reynolds *et al* 2002) uses a similar categorisation: learning as behaviour, learning as understanding, learning as knowledge construction and learning as social practice. They suggest that no one approach is sufficient for understanding learning and a mix of approaches should be used in any programme of learning.

Much of the mainstream psychology literature has focused on what is seen as 'traditional' learning – the importance of building-blocks, hierarchies of skills, and reinforcing theory with examples. This may be particularly appropriate to formal educational situations and in child development, but it may be less so for adults who come to the situation with very different motivations, experiences, and perspectives. Carl Rogers (1969, p5) is the major proponent of experiential learning, which he sees as having the following components: personal involvement, self-initiation, pervasiveness and evaluation by the learner. The essence of experiential learning resides in its meaning to the learner. This makes it quite different from traditional learning, and potentially exciting for employees who left school early and feel threatened by the classroom situation. Because it puts the responsibility for learning on the individual employee it can also require skilful management of the learning situation by professional staff; as Mumford (1988, pp171–172) warns, experiential learning can be 'a very inefficient, hit-or-miss operation … guidance helps the process to be both quicker and easier'. The experiential approach is best known in the HR field through the work of Kolb and Honey and Mumford and it forms a centrepiece of the CIPD's guidance for Continuing Professional Development. Kolb, Osland and Rubin (1995, p49) view the learning process as both active and passive, concrete and abstract. This model is displayed in Figure 8.

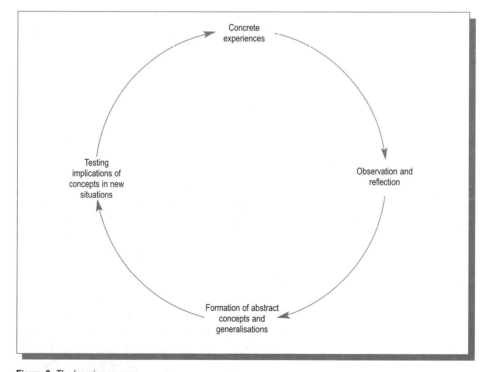

Figure 8 *The learning process*

Source: Kolb D., Osland J. and Rubin I. *Organisational Behaviour: An experiential approach*, 6th edition. New Jersey, Prentice Hall, 1995. p49

Kolb argues that effective learners rely on four different learning modes, and each individual has an orientation towards one or more of these: concrete experience, reflective observation, abstract conceptualisation and active experimentation. Honey and Mumford's learning styles classification (Mumford and Gold 2004, pp97–98) is similar:

- *Activists* – learn best by active involvement in concrete tasks, and from relatively short tasks such as business games and competitive teamwork exercises
- *Reflectors* – learn best by reviewing and reflecting upon what has happened in certain situations, where they are able to stand back, listen and observe
- *Theorists* – learn best when new information can be located within the context of concepts and theories, and who are able to absorb new ideas when they are distanced from real-life situations
- *Pragmatists* – learn best when they see a link between new information and real-life problems and issues, and from being exposed to techniques that can be applied immediately.

This focus on learning cycles and learning styles has major implications for the training and development process, and for the choice of methods, although there are doubts about the rigid use of learning styles questionnaires. Given that the four categories represent 'ideal types', it is unlikely that people conform totally or even principally to a single learning style, and they may be strong on two apparently dissimilar axes. The precise questions that are asked of individuals are also capable of differing interpretations, depending upon the context. For example, an individual may be a reflector in response to certain questions or situations, and a pragmatist in others. Moreover, the combination of people in a working group may lead individuals to adopt different styles than those in a formal learning situation. For example, a group of theorists may be cajoled into action, or a set of activists encouraged to reflect on their proposed course of action. Also people's preferred learning styles may alter over time rather than remaining static.

THE TRAINING PROCESS SYSTEM

The basis for most training remains the traditional training process system. This comprises four main steps: (1) identifying training and learning needs; (2) devising a learning plan; (3) delivering training; and (4) evaluating outcomes.

Harrison's (2002, pp269–273) 'learning event' is based on the training process system. She defines the 'learning event' as 'any learning activity that is formally designed in order to achieve specified learning objectives'. This typically involves the following: establishing needs; agreeing the overall purpose and objectives; identifying the profile of the intended learning population; selecting strategy, and agreeing on direction and management; selection of learners and producing a detailed specification; confirmation of strategy and design of the event; delivery; monitoring and evaluation.

There are clear advantages in using structured and sequential models for analysing the training process, especially if they establish a framework within which managers can operate. On the other hand, there is a feeling that these models represent an 'ideal' state of affairs rather than conveying an accurate and realistic picture of organisational practice. The idea that training and development regularly follows this logical and sequential cycle is open to question, and – as with other aspects of human resource development (HRD) – there is likely to be rather more ad hoc and reactive management of training than planned and proactive strategies (Reid *et al* 2004, p115). A more serious concern is that training and development often lapses into a 'closed' cycle, in which there are few, if any, links with other aspects of HR, let alone broader business plans and objectives. This can result in efficient rather than effective training. In other words, the effectiveness of training is assessed against the training needs identified by the trainers themselves, and not measured in relation to their contribution to business goals.

Identifying training and learning needs

The first stage of the training process system is identification of training and learning needs (ITN) which is often reviewed in conjunction with a training needs analysis (TNA). ITN detects and specifies training needs at an individual and organisational level, while TNA determines how needs might be met. A training need exists when there is a gap between the requirements of the job and the current capabilities of the incumbent.

We have to be certain, however, that training represents the best or the only solution to these problems, and that it is not being suggested as a panacea for all organisational ills. The problem may reside elsewhere, and there are dangers that employers prescribe training as a universal solution ('training is the answer irrespective of the question') without considering alternatives such as job redesign, better systems of communication and involvement, or adjustments to organisational cultures and structures. It may make sense to do nothing as there are dangers in providing too much training as there are in providing too little. Excessive levels of training cost money and use up valuable resources, and may even result in job dissatisfaction if employees are unable to practise their newfound skills back at the workplace or become frustrated by spending time on unnecessary training courses and then having to catch up on work left undone.

Training needs can be identified at three different levels – organisational, job/occupational and personal. ITN is regarded as the most important step in the effectiveness of training, and should be top-down and bottom-up (IRS Employment Review 761 2002, p7).

Organisational training needs

Most publications stress the importance of commencing with a review of organisational training needs in order to establish how specific training programmes may contribute to broader strategic goals – this forms a central plank of the IiP standard. The main methods of determining organisational training needs are outlined in Reid *et al* (2004, pp138–141). They might include a 'global' review in which the organisation's short- and longer term goals are examined to determine appropriate skills and knowledge needed to meet objectives. Each employee is then assessed against the skills and knowledge criteria. This is a time-consuming operation, and unsuited to organisations working with rapid change, or those that outsource. In effect this approach presumes that an organisation is the sum of its individuals and their skills, and this is a doubtful assumption. Reid *et al* (p138) believe that global review may be useful for some organisations, but is better when used with other methods. The second technique is 'competence and performance management approaches'. Job descriptions are used to draw up competences against which performance is measured. The line manager reviews performance using the competence framework and is expected to access appropriate training – typically NVQs, which are based upon the concept of competence. The third technique they call 'critical incident or priority problem analysis'. Using this method the focus is on prioritising the main problem areas within the organisation that require a training response. This fits with the concept of total quality management (TQM), in that training might be only one component when addressing problem areas.

Job/occupational training needs

The purpose of job or occupation analysis is to identify specific training needs. Harrison (2002, p269) terms this 'job-training analysis' in order to differentiate it clearly from its recruitment and selection counterpart. It is the 'process of identifying the purpose of a job and its component parts, and specifying what must be learned in order for there to be effective work performance'. A range of methods can be used including examination of job descriptions and job specifications, competences, role analysis, use of questionnaires, group discussions, observation of the task in hand, work diaries and even getting analysts to do the job themselves (Harrison 2002, pp269–279; Reid *et al* 2004, pp153–164). Interviews are particularly useful, not just with the job-holder, but also with line mangers, as well as with customers or clients. Self-observation is important here, and in some respects this is one of the best ways to determine precisely what the job entails. However, individuals may be too close to their jobs to identify training needs effectively, they may not keep an accurate record of events during the course of the day, and they may overemphasise certain aspects of the job they enjoy or dislike in order to gain training. There is also the problem that confusions arise between training needs which are identified for the job, irrespective of who undertakes it, and those which relate to the person who is currently in the post.

Personal training needs

Person-level analysis is the final stage and shares characteristics with the methods discussed above. This frequently involves the use of interviews and questionnaires, observation and work sampling, testing the knowledge of job-holders on specific issues, and performance appraisal and assessment centres. If employees are encouraged to acknowledge that areas of their work are not being performed at full capacity, or with inadequate knowledge or skills, then appraisal interviews help to identify training and development needs. However, where appraisal is linked to rewards, they are unlikely to unearth training needs (see Chapter 7 for more on appraisals).

It is generally assumed that all three levels can be integrated, although conflict is inevitable, particularly where learning is self-managed (Reid *et al* 2004, p136). All levels are important, and each feeds into the other so that organisational level strategy influences job and person-level analysis. A recent IRS survey (IRS Employment Review 807 2004, p12) shows that personal development plans, training needs analysis are the two most common means of planning learning and development.

Devising a learning plan

The traditional approach to devising training and learning plans focuses on the need to determine clear aims (why the learning event is taking place) and objectives specifying the attitudinal, behavioural or performance outcomes to be achieved (Harrison 2002, p284). Aims are expressions of general intent, such as 'to grasp the basic principles of x' or 'to be aware of the influence of y on z', and they make no attempt to specify measurable outcomes. Objectives, on the other hand, are more precise, giving a clear focus on learning outcomes in terms of competencies, abilities or understanding. Harrison (2002) and Reid *et al* (2004, pp179–180) suggest that the most helpful objectives are those which describe not only the kinds of behaviour to be achieved, but also the conditions under which that behaviour is expected to occur, and the standards to be reached in that behaviour. The clearer the objectives, the better the chance of success, as well as ease of evaluation.

A major consideration when devising plans is the characteristics of the trainees themselves, and the 'baggage' they bring with them to the learning event – their prior knowledge, skills, attitudes, motivations and expectations. Trainees are likely to differ in terms of their level of educational achievement, their attitudes towards learning, their ability to absorb new ideas or maintain concentration and their teamworking skills. They are likely to have very diverse reasons for being involved in the learning event. Some may be there under duress, determined to put little effort into the sessions, and keen to demonstrate their lack of interest at every possible opportunity. There may also be variations in the extent to which trainees have been briefed beforehand about the learning event or in the amount of preparation undertaken before the workshop gets under way.

Delivering learning and training

There are a multitude of methods that can be used to train and develop staff, both on- and off-the-job, ranging from the relatively unstructured and informal – such as 'sitting next to Nellie' – through to the carefully programmed and structured – such as the lecture. Most texts on the subject provide lists of different methods, their nature and meaning, their advantages and shortcomings (see, for example, Reid *et al* 2004, pp182–192).

While useful at one level, these lists are lacking in two respects. First, they are not organised into any coherent conceptual framework that differentiates between techniques according to learning principles or the characteristics of the learning situation. This makes it difficult for readers to 'locate' different methods within a structure, and to recall them. The second problem is that while the lists describe concisely the key features of different methods, as well as outlining their major advantages and disadvantages, there is little attempt to identify the conditions under which particular techniques may be appropriate for facilitating effective learning.

It is important to recognise therefore that no one method is inherently superior to any other, but that different methods are suitable for different sets of circumstances. Choosing when to employ the right methods, and why, is a much more critical consideration than being able to note the advantages and disadvantages of each method in the abstract. While the lecture may be inappropriate for most training situations, it may be the ideal technique for a newly appointed marketing director to open the annual sales conference. Conversely, e-learning can be very effective for reinforcing basic language skills but it offers rather less towards the development of teamworking and group problem-solving.

Rather than produce yet another list, here we review training methods in four distinct categories, differentiated according to the main approach that is adopted, and whether the training is individual or group-based. Snape *et al* (1994, p73) make the distinction between andragogical and pedagogical approaches to training and development. The former, more accurately titled 'auto-didactic', is essentially self-directed and participative, with the trainer providing a facilitative or supportive role. The latter, by contrast, is largely trainer-driven and allows little room for student input into the learning situation. The second distinction is between individual and group-based training. This categorisation is illustrated in Figure 9 (page 246), with an example of each type of training for illustrative purposes.

The top left-hand quadrant in Figure 9 includes methods that are principally pedagogically oriented and individually based, such as one-to-one instructional techniques and simulations. These are particularly useful for the acquisition of standard programmable skills, for the transfer of routine information and ways of working, but which also require practice and application in real-life situations. This can cover the extremes of the scale in terms of traditional job levels. At one extreme might be simulators for pilots in the early stages of

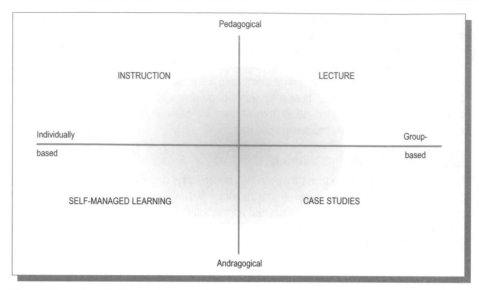

Figure 9 *Categories of training and learning methods*

training when they need to learn basic operating rules and principles. At the other extreme would be the basic stages of an assembly operation or the standard scripts used in call centres. The major point behind these techniques is that there is seen to be no room for discretion or creativity, or for employee input into the choice of how to speak to potential customers, fix together parts of a piece of equipment, or land planes safely. Of course, once employees actually start to do the work themselves and become more experienced there may be much more room for autonomy and use of initiative.

The basic principles of these kinds of training intervention are of the 'tell–show–do–review' variety, in which skills, knowledge and operating routines are transferred progressively to trainees until they have mastered the task. The trainer decides how quickly to move to a position of trust when he or she feels confident that the learner has acquired sufficient skills and knowledge, and has demonstrated competence in them so as to progress to the next stage of the instruction process. There is no room for vagueness or confusion in the instruction, especially if it relates to tasks that can have serious health or safety consequences. On the other hand, instructing staff to follow established routines may lead to motivational problems if the employees concerned feel that they already have the required skills or they do not share senior management's commitment to them. The top right-hand quadrant includes methods that are pedagogically and group-based, such as lectures, presentations and videos, and these are particularly appropriate in situations when a large number of people need to be given information at the same time, and/or it is cost-effective to deliver training in this way. Most learners have been subjected to lectures at some times during the lives, and are aware of the limits to the amount that can be retained during a session. Estimates vary, but it is reckoned that less than a quarter of what is said is recalled, and the maximum concentration span is typically less than 20 minutes. Given that many lecturers have not received professional training in lecturing, and many more seem incapable of conveying information or ideas, let alone enthusing their learners, it is to be wondered why this technique is still practised so widely. However, it is a cost-effective way of providing information, at least to the extent of class contact hours, although whether or not it represents a cost-effective way of learning is another matter. On the other hand, most of us will have listened to an individual speak for an hour or more, and been enthralled. Some management gurus are renowned for keeping audiences transfixed for a couple of hours using few, if any, visual aids. But for most lecturers it is essential to use overhead projections or slides, distribute short summaries of the lecture, and litter the talk with examples and anecdotes and even discussion in small groups, to ensure that some retention takes place. Enthusiasm and knowledge of the subject matter are also essential, as is an awareness of learner needs, an ability to present information in a clear and concise manner, and a recognition that tone and cadence need to vary to maintain attention.

One of the major problems with lectures and presentations is that they are often used inappropriately, transmitting information that can more easily be distributed electronically or as written documents or videos. These are now common as teaching aids, and can provide a useful interlude in the training programme to facilitate learning. But there are also dangers with these techniques. They have to be chosen carefully to ensure that they are specifically directed at the issue in hand, realistic and relevant, and contextualised in the programme with specific learning outcomes attached to them.

> Choose what you think has been a successful lecture, and someone whom you feel to be a good lecturer, and identify the attributes of both that led to that evaluation. Can these attributes be taught to other people? Why/why not?

The bottom right-hand quadrant is the andragogical/group-based category, which includes case studies, projects, group role-playing exercises (such as in a negotiating exercise) and business games, some of which are managed through the use of computerised models. The basic point about this set of techniques is that they are essentially team-oriented and allow the group to propose their own solutions and ideas to problems with a minimum of trainer intervention during the process. The job of the trainer is to support the team, help it to arrive at conclusions, and generally facilitate the process of learning through a sharing of ideas. In effect, learning should take place through a process of induction, in which examples and incidents are generalised to arrive at a better understanding of the principles and processes that underpin management issues. This set of methods allows for the development of the core competencies that are seen as central to any manager's job. These include decision-making, planning and time management, drive and persistence, ability to work under pressure, oral and written communication, flexibility and adaptability, self-confidence and persuasiveness. In the case of projects that are initiated during a formal training course, but which are then continued back at work, other skills may be developed as well, especially the ability to persuade senior managers that the project is worthy of time and effort.

Case studies provide a good avenue for 'real-life' problem-solving, for working out solutions in teams and for presenting recommendations to other people. Like any other training technique, they need to be well managed, have clear learning outcomes, and be relevant to the needs and abilities of the learners. They need to be of an appropriate length and degree of difficulty for the student group, as well as containing sufficient information and enough flexibility to allow for competing solutions between different teams. Problems associated with group-based training include the possibility of conflict, or one or more individuals dominating discussion in a way that excludes others, leading to unsatisfactory solutions. Some learners often feel dissatisfied with the amount of information provided by the trainer, either becoming stressed because they feel that there is too much to analyse in the time provided, or insecure because they reckon there is too little to make a recommendation.

The final set of methods is the individually based self-directed category. This group of techniques includes e-learning and use of language laboratories. Perhaps the principal point about these forms of training is that they are typically self-managed and can be undertaken at a pace, time and possibly location suitable for the individual concerned. With access to electronic media, both at work and at home, and new generations of computers that use artificial intelligence to interact with learners, the opportunities for this type of training are considerable. This set of techniques has the major advantage of being responsive to individual needs in a way that allows for a better fit between learning and domestic or work commitments. The self-management of learning is especially appropriate for the acquisition of impersonal techniques (such as accounting or computing), the development and reinforcement of basic language skills, and for gathering information for reports. Although these techniques have been used for interpersonal skills training, it is unlikely that their use will become extensive given the importance of face-to-face contact for improving these skills. In this sort of situation, role-playing (either with a colleague or friend/partner) offers a much better solution to learning how to cope, say with an aggressive senior manager or in counselling a poor performer.

Choice of method is determined by a range of factors including costs, benefits, likelihood of learning transfer to the work situation, profile of the learner group, applicability of method, as well as the culture of the organisation and its strategic goals.

It can be seen from Figure 10 that on-the-job training is regarded as the most effective way in which people learn at work, and also is the most common form of training (IRS Employment Review 807 2004, p12) presumably because research (Bramley 2003, p10) indicates that only 10–20 per cent of learning gained off-the-job results in changes in effectiveness at work. On-the-job training confers significant responsibility for learning and development onto the line manager, who can act as coach, mentor, appraiser and role model. It is increasingly acknowledged that where the line manager is committed, this has a major impact on learning and development. Reid *et al* (2004, p118) suggest that all managers should be responsible for the learning and training of their employees, but that in order to effect this it should be part of their job description, should form part of their reviews, with reward systems operating appropriately. This shift of responsibility onto the shoulders of line managers is relatively new, and there are many associated problems. Firstly, giving managers discretion can lead to equity issues, with wide differences in access to opportunities. Secondly, the responsibility for learning and development is onerous and it may be unrealistic to expect the line manager to assume such a role. Not all line managers are themselves competent, motivated, and confident learners, and they may see time taken out for learning as an unnecessary interruption. Lack of support from line managers was seen as the second most important barrier to learning at work. The main barrier was lack of time off (Crofts 2004) and where the line manager has control over time off for training these two factors are linked.

In-house programmes are usually devised by HRD professionals and still play a significant role, particularly for training on induction, legislative and regulatory updates, or IT training – all of which remain the most common forms of training offered. It is also important where an organisation adopts new policies that require embedding, such as corporate responsibility. In-house programmes do not necessarily imply one-way communications, they can incorporate participative techniques, and they may be consultative. Many organisations run their own qualification courses, particularly NVQs. Reid *et al* (2004, p186) suggest that internal training is more likely to result in learning transfer, especially where senior management signal their commitment by becoming involved.

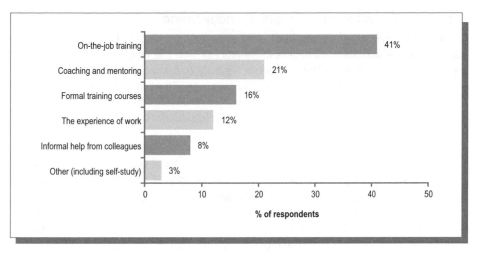

Figure 10 *The most effective ways in which people learn in organisations*
Source: Chartered Institute of Personnel and Development. *Training and Development Survey Report*. London, CIPD. 2004d. p16

External courses provide the advantages of exposure to those from other organisations, although learning transfer may not be as high as with internal provision, even when custom-built. Buying in external courses can be an easy option and, as with all types of learning provision, may not solve the problem. A good example is where the line manager sends employees on stress management courses when the problem lies with work organisation. To gain maximum advantage, the line manager needs to be involved in briefing and debriefing sessions to ensure any new ideas can be discussed and where appropriate learning is incorporated into work schedules.

> In a small group, brainstorm those factors that have facilitated and hindered learning for you. Compile the results and compare these with those presented by Mumford and Gold (2004, p109).

Self-managed learning fits with Sloman's new paradigm. Depending how far the organisation is down the road towards becoming a learning organisation (for more on this see Chapter 8), this may change emphasis within the role of the HRD specialist away from solely planning and delivering training, to one of facilitator, in particular, by supporting line managers. As David Slingo, Head of Learning at BT Academy says, 'We try to provide learners with a rich set of options in terms of the way they learn: some of them will take courses, but others will learn through communities of practice or through contact with professional bodies and universities. Others will simply draw on critical resources when they need them. We can't predict the situations they will all be in, so giving them flexibility is key' (Reynolds 2002, pp42–43).

Not all provision is work related, as with Ford's Employee Development and Assistance Programme (EDAP). Incidentally, the EDAP scheme recognised the support needed to enable workers to 'self-manage' their learning by buying in professional adult guidance workers. The resources invested in learning for personal goals (as opposed to departmental/organisational) are tied up with the psychological contract and interest in retaining and motivating key employees.

Evaluating the outcomes of training and learning

Whatever the method of training used, it is widely acknowledged that the evaluation of training is one of the most critical steps in the process, and one that is frequently not carried out in a comprehensive or systematic manner. Methods of evaluation commonly used include informal feedback from line managers and trainees rather than tests or formal evaluations conducted some time after the training had been completed. In other words, as with many other aspects of HRM, the extent of formal and systematic evaluation is limited, despite its known worth.

Bee and Bee (2003, p135) suggest it should be called 'learning evaluation' because this implies concern with the whole process, from identification of learning needs through to application. They suggest a practical definition adapted from Hamblin (1974), 'any attempt to obtain information (feedback) on the effects of the training/learning programme, and to assess the value of training/learning in the light of that information' (p135). The best time to plan evaluation is when analysing learning needs because this evaluation is necessary in order to improve the quality and effectiveness of training courses through feedback in terms of the design and relevance of the course in the achievement of individual learning objectives. It can enable organisations to establish whether training offers the most cost-effective and relevant solution to organisational problems and goals, instead of other HR actions such as recruitment or dismissal. It should also be part of the learning cycle, not only in causing trainees to reflect on what has been learned, but also in assisting them and their managers to identify future learning and development needs.

Once it is established why evaluation is being undertaken, it should then be possible to determine what should be evaluated, and when and how it might be done. Most ideas in this area stem from the work of Kirkpatrick (1967), who differentiated between four levels of evaluation: reaction, immediate, intermediate and ultimate. Although each of these is considered in turn, it is important to recognise that evaluation at all levels needs to be undertaken in order to form a full picture of training effectiveness. The most important level of evaluation may differ according to the circumstances and the needs of different stakeholders. For example, while trainers may be more interested in how well they are performing in front of the group, the finance director may be more concerned about the cost-effectiveness of training programmes, while the departmental manager may be keen to assess the precise impact of training on job performance.

Reaction level

This is most commonly used during or at the end of courses, and it is often termed the 'smile sheet' since it assesses the performance of trainers in both absolute and relative terms. This form of evaluation aims to establish the views of one stakeholder, the learners themselves. These views are useful to trainers, provided they see them as valuable and are prepared and able to act upon them. Concerns about 'smile sheets' include worries that students merely react to the quality of the performance, the lecturer's ability to maintain surface-level interest or tell jokes to the class. There are also doubts about the ability of learners to evaluate training in its wider context, as part of a broader educational programme, or for its relevance to future performance in work. Finally, research suggests that there is a very poor relationship between positive reaction-level assessments, learning, and changes in job performance and the transfer of learning into the workplace (IRS Employment Review 761 2002, p9; Bramley 2003, p114). Cunningham (2004, p38) cites the example of a leadership course that was highly rated, except for the input on coaching. One year on, it was the coaching skills that had stuck and been put into practice. Despite this, a recent IRS Survey (IRS Employment

Review 807 2004) reported that the 'smile sheet' remains the most common method of evaluation.

Immediate level

This attempts to measure the training objectives achieved, in terms of knowledge, skills and attitudes. Techniques include tests, examinations, projects, structured exercises and case studies, as well as discussion (Reid *et al* 2004, pp202–203). Questions could be true/false statements; forced-choice questions where the learner selects from three or four options; or a series of questions requiring short five-minute answers. The last of these options now forms part of the final examination assessment portfolio in the CIPD Professional Development Scheme. Forced-choice or true/false questions are seen by some to be superior to essays or more open questions, although there are problems with them. They guide the student towards an answer by providing signposts and parameters that are typically lacking in a management environment. In the work environment, open questions and problems are more common (for example, 'What should we do about X?'). It would be highly unusual for a manager to be confronted with forced-choice question.

Intermediate level

This refers to the impact of training on job performance and how effectively learning has been transferred back into the workplace. There is little point engaging in training if transfer does not take place, unless of course the objective is to keep employees away from work! Evaluation at this level is much less common than at the first two levels, both because it is harder to undertake and due to the problem of isolating the impact of training from the effect of other variables. Intermediate-level evaluation takes many forms, including interviews, self-report questionnaires, diaries and observation. For interpersonal skills a mixture of observation and self-reporting may be the most useful approach, given that part of the training objective is to encourage greater self-awareness of how relationships are handled. Successful evaluation is dependent on clear statements of objectives, consultation with all those involved, and a careful design and testing of assessment instruments.

Ultimate-level evaluation

This attempts to assess the impact of training on departmental or organisational performance, and on the individual's total job. The distinction between intermediate- and ultimate-level evaluation is somewhat blurred, but the former usually refers to performance in a particular task or set of tasks for which training has been provided, whereas the latter evaluates the impact of training on overall results. The best indicators for ultimate-level evaluation vary enormously depending upon what are deemed to be key performance criteria, but typical examples might include:

- number of customer complaints or rejects
- level of sales, turnover or productivity
- number of accidents or lost employment tribunal cases
- level of unauthorised absenteeism or labour turnover
- proportion of letters answered within two days.

As the name implies, ultimate-level evaluation is the most difficult to measure. In some situations there may be no clear and simple measures to employ, or data may not be collected in a form that allows for evaluation to take place. There are many factors other than training that could affect evaluation, especially at higher levels in the organisation when external influences can have a significant impact – for example, the influence of unemployment on labour turnover. In addition, only a small proportion of staff within a department or establishment might have been trained, and although their performance may have improved this may have relatively little overall effect. As we saw in the previous chapter, learning organisations attempt to satisfy organisational and personal demands at the same time, and organisations claiming to practise high commitment HRM look for links between training and other areas of people management, as well as assessing its impact on performance. This fuels the debate on the value of evaluation and whether it is worth spending on it in order to provide evidence of something that is not provable (IRS Employment Review 807 2004).

THE STRATEGIC DIMENSION

For effective learning to occur it is crucial that HR professionals gain agreement from key decision-takers and ensure that learning is located in the organisational context. Unfortunately, this political dimension is often overlooked. There are major issues in relation to gaining agreement and support from key managers, on dealing with negative reactions to training and on calculating the costs and benefits of training interventions. In other words, there is much more to training than choices about the most appropriate methods for establishing training needs or learning techniques. It can be seen from Box 33, the three most important ways in which organisations can promote learning are by ensuring the organisational culture is supportive, enabling managers to support and allowing employees time. A recent CIPD online poll (Crofts 2004) reported that the top two barriers to learning were time pressures (48 per cent) followed by lack of support from line managers (31 per cent). The findings of a recent IRS Survey (IRS Employment Review 807 2004, pp16–17) confirmed that allowing workers time off from the job was the biggest barrier (mentioned by 85 per cent of respondents), followed by cost (63 per cent) and administrative burden (44 per cent).

Being aware of costs and benefits is also important and it is not something for which HR practitioners are renowned. It is relatively easy to reel off a list of general benefits from training, especially those relating to other aspects of HR, but it is less easy to quantify them financially. Benefits might include:

- helping new staff to learn jobs more quickly and integrate into the organisation
- avoidance of costly errors or accidents at work
- an organisation with a good reputation for training may impact on recruitment and retention
- trained workers may be more flexible and able to undertake a range of jobs
- training can help improve productivity and performance.

It is hard to demonstrate unequivocally that training has a direct and measurable impact on organisational performance levels, although this does not stop people making the claim. For example, it could be argued that training led to an increase in market share from x to y, or it has ensured that 95 per cent of trains will arrive within five minutes of published time. Political skills might help the HR practitioner to identify measures seen as relevant to business objectives that may be accepted by senior management. But it might prove difficult to sell these solutions on more than one occasion, or to convince senior managers who want to have 'hard' estimates of costs and benefits.

BOX 33   LEARNING IN ORGANISATIONS

The 2004 CIPD Training and Development Survey asked about the ways in which organisations can promote learning. The most important activities in helping employees to learn effectively are produced below:

	% of respondents
Ensuring the organisational culture is supportive of learning and development	75
Ensuring managers are committed to, and are have the requisite skills for supporting learning and development	58
Providing employees with time to learn at work	33
Ensuring employees clearly understand the direction and strategy of the organisation and what this means in terms of their skills and development	32
Providing a variety of learning/training options to suit employees' learning styles	30
Providing employees with a work environment that is conducive to learning	28
Having innovative and committed HR/training professionals	20
Providing employees with advice on how to manage their learning	18
Understanding what motivates employees to learn	11
Rewarding employees who develop their skills and abilities	10

Source: Chartered Institute of Personnel and Development. *Training and Development Survey Report*. London, CIPD. 2004d. p14

Costs are easier to calculate than benefits, although much depends on the items to be included in the equation. First, there are fixed costs such as permanent accommodation or training equipment. Obviously these account for a much higher proportion of costs in an organisation with its own training centre than for one using external sources. The second item includes the salaries and on-costs of trainers and/or consultants and the cost of developing training materials and evaluation tools. Finally, there are direct or variable costs, which vary according to the amount of training undertaken, and include the costs of travel, and duplicated training materials. It is more difficult to decide whether or not to include the costs of delegates in the figures, either as a pro rata element of their wage and salary bill or the costs of replacements although these costs usually constitute the largest amount.

Calculating the opportunity costs of not training is rather more difficult. These costs may include items such as payments to employees when learning on-the-job, the costs of wasted materials or the time supervisors and other employees spend in dealing with problems caused by untrained staff. In other words, to consider the costs of training fully we need to be aware of the costs of not training, and of relying on informal, ad hoc and potentially inefficient methods for improving performance. It may also be useful to make comparisons with the amount spent by other organisations on training and development. We have already seen that employers in Britain spend relatively little on training compared with many of their foreign competitors, but comparisons should also be made with similar types of organisation in the same sector or area of the country. If figures are low, this information may prove helpful to HR professionals seeking to justify training expenditure, or if comparisons are favourable it may prove helpful in public relations terms. The judicious use of benchmarking is just as useful in the training field as it is in other areas of HR activity. For more information on cost–benefit analyses refer to Harrison (2002) or Reid *et al* (2004).

TRENDS AND DEVELOPMENTS IN LEARNING

As we saw above, time pressure is a major barrier to learning. In response, there has been increased emphasis on flexibility including coaching, e-learning and bite-sized provision (modular learning offered in shorter chunks of time). Cunningham's research (2004, p38) showed that people preferred 'just right learning' to meet individual needs at an appropriate time. We now turn to examine two types of learning that have currently experienced a doubling of provision – coaching and e-learning – as well as considering the role of management development and continuous professional development (CPD).

Coaching

As shown in Figure 10 on page 249, coaching and mentoring was used by over three-quarters of respondents to the 2004 CIPD survey with executive coaching particularly widespread. IRS (IRS Employment Review 787b 2003) defines it as 'personal assistance, generally offered on a one-to-one basis, that focuses on resourcefulness, interpersonal skills and emotional intelligence'. This is because of a widespread belief that coaching is an effective learning tool, impacts on the bottom line, and brings intangible benefits. It is seen as particularly useful for improving individual performance, tackling underperformance, and improving productivity as well as aiding with identification of personal learning needs.

Despite its popularity, there are significant problems. Few organisations have a policy on coaching so that it tends to be ad hoc with concentration on senior managers whose performance was seen as questionable (IRS Employment Review 795b 2004). Those who coach often lack training, and typically there is an absence of formal evaluation to assess its relative merits by undertaking a cost–benefit analysis for example. Additionally, there is confusion over the differences between coaching, mentoring and counselling (Mumford and Gold 2004, pp179–198). The skills needed for each are similar (particularly use of active listening, feedback and review) and line managers probably move imperceptibly between the three. Many issues relate to lack of professional regulation – almost three-quarters of those advertising as coaches are not members of any professional body (Rolph 2004). It is clearly important for coaching to become professionalised, and some of the main professional bodies are now working together to establish uniform standards.

E-learning

Sloman (2003, p49) defines e-learning as 'learning that is delivered, enabled, or mediated by electronic technology, for the explicit purpose of training in organisations'. The main advantages of e-learning are that it can be accessed at times and locations to suit learners who work at their own pace and the training is consistent and methodical and does not rely on variations between trainers. It is particularly useful for multinationals where new knowledge has to be quickly disseminated worldwide and/or across many sites. It accommodates employees who work shifts, who like to work alone or who prefer to learn in antisocial hours. It can be used for transfer of standard information as well as for rapidly changing complex information. Finally, it is ideally suited to learner-centred development.

E-learning has seen a rapid expansion over the few years, although this is not as great as many predicated. In the previous edition of this book, we quoted Tom Peters predicting that 90 per cent of all training should be delivered by new technology by 2003 (Sloman 2001). Of the examples cited, one was the development of UK e-university. However, this has just folded due to insufficient enrolments after an investment of £62 million (MacLeod 2004).

The take-up has not been as great as predicted for a number of reasons. According to a CIPD Survey (Sloman and Rolph 2003) these include lack of access to computers, as well as lack of familiarity. Support, which is usually required immediately, is a major issue, as is lack of a human interface. In order to overcome some of these problems, some organisations have set up learning centres, although these are not always well used. Some employees prefer to access materials through their desktops, although they are then unable to get away from frequent interruptions. There are also problems of cost since it is frequently additional to existing training methods. Hardware and development of software is expensive, and where generic materials are used they may not fit the need, although they can be used as a basis for developing in-house materials.

Despite drawbacks, most of the organisations surveyed by CIPD were sticking with e-learning and, as increasing numbers of workers become familiar with use of computers, the problem of unfamiliarity will ease. 'Blended learning' (combining e-learning with other forms of learning involving personal interaction) is addressing issues of support and lack of a human interface. This has been characterised as movement from 'stuff' to 'stir', where 'stuff' is the web-based learning objects, and 'stir' is the collaborative tools such as online discussions and virtual classrooms (Sloman and Rolph 2003, p2).

The CIPD survey asked about those factors that had the greatest impact on e-learning effectiveness; the top three factors were motivation, appropriate support and time to learn. On the question of evaluation, respondents reported it was extremely difficult to assess whether e-learning was more effective than face-to-face learning.

According to the CIPD, e-learning is most effectively used where:

- the content is largely concerned with knowledge, for example company procedures
- there is a long-term training need and thus a sufficient period in which to recoup the investment
- trainees are scattered geographically
- large numbers have to be trained in a relatively short time
- unusual, expensive or dangerous situations need to be simulated.

Situations in which it may not be appropriate include where:

- it is not the most cost-effective solution
- lead times are short
- learners are not comfortable using computers
- learning styles are more attuned to learning with others in groups
- it may not be suitable for teaching practical, hands-on skills.

How can e-learning be used to improve worker skills and organisational performance?

BA provides a good example of expedient use of e-learning for its 15,000 cabin crew, who typically use interpersonal rather than IT skills. The resource centre at Heathrow was opened for cabin crew to access essential training materials to keep them up-to-date (for example on health and safety issues). Open and flexible access proved popular and they are now hoping that the next stage will allow access from home or hotel rooms while on stopovers (Trapp 2003).

Management development

As we saw in Chapter 8, those higher up the organisational ladder are likely to receive more training than those at the bottom. It is certainly the case that there is a proliferation of management courses of various types and levels and a heightened awareness of the critical importance of management and leadership to both organisational and national economic success. Because of continuing concerns the Council for Excellence in Management and Leadership (CEML) has been established to 'ensure that the UK has the managers and leaders of the future to match the best in the world' (CEML 2002, p2).

In part the problems relating to management development (MD) revolve around definitions of 'management' and 'development'. Mumford and Gold's (2004, p2) define 'management' as a description of managers' activities, but this begs the question, what do managers do? There have been copious amounts written about this, and numerous attempts made to analyse managers' roles, but difficulties remain. A related issue that is hotly debated is whether management and leadership are separate functions. Mumford and Gold (p14) define MD as 'an attempt to improve managerial effectiveness through a learning process'.

MD is set in the context of the social and economic environment, within unique organisational settings, and is concerned with the individual development of managers, making a kaleidoscope of permutations. Overlaid on this is continuous and increasingly rapid change. MD is expected to respond, particularly as research (Burnes 2003) suggests that many change initiatives fail, in large part, because of failure of management. Additionally, MD covers a multitude of levels and situations – covering junior (graduate entry and self-grown) to senior management, the development of professionals (eg Professors or Doctors) as managers, SMEs and multinationals, as well as the issues involved in developing diversity within senior management structures.

Unsurprisingly, organisations differ in their approaches to MD. Burgoyne (1988, p41) suggests six levels of maturity of organisations' provision of MD:

1   *No systematic management development* – Reliance on natural, laissez-faire processes.

2   *Isolated tactical management development* – MD is ad hoc, structural and/or developmental, in response to problems or events.

3   *Integrated and co-ordinated structural and development tactics* – The use of career structure management, assisted learning, are integrated and co-ordinated.

4   *MD strategy implements corporate policy* – MD operates to implement corporate policies through HR planning, providing a strategic framework and direction for the tactics of career structure management and of learning, education and training.

5   *MD strategy input to corporate policy formation* – MD feeds information back into corporate policy decision-making on the strengths, weaknesses and potential of management, and helps with forecasting and analysis of manageability of proposed projects, ventures and changes.

6   *Strategic development of the management of corporate policy* – MD processes enhance the nature and quality of corporate policy-formation processes, which they help inform and implement.

As with all training/learning plans, MD should fit with the business aims of the company – for the present and for the future – as well as with its values and ethics. Mumford and Gold (2004, p28) present a sustaining model for MD in which organisational strategy is set in the external economic and social context; it provides guidance on managerial requirements; MD policy is used to develop MD delivery; and the outcomes are analysed and provide feedback to the organisational strategy. Burgoyne's (1988) model shows that the feedback loop from MD outcomes to strategy is absent from those at development stages 1–4, and this has been substantiated by more recent research (Kirkbride 2003; Mumford and Gold 2004).

The MD policy statement flows from corporate strategy, and involves allocating responsibility, deciding on beneficiaries, and choosing methods. Organisations with a formal policy are more likely to undertake more MD than those without (Thomson *et al* 2001). Mabey (2002, p1140) stressed 'the degree of priority accorded to MD (as against the formal but apparently less meaningful index of whether there is a written policy) and the usage of diagnostic and audit processes' are important thereby emphasising that merely writing a policy does not guarantee provision.

As with other forms of training, choice of the beneficiaries and defining needs may involve audits, development/assessment workshops, and appraisal systems. Competences are also often used although there is debate on their use with the development of skills such as intuition, emotional intelligence, and diplomacy (Rausch *et al* 2002; Hunt and Baruch 2003). The lead body for management is the Management Charter Initiative (MCI) with the Management Standards Centre establishing national standards of competence for managers at all levels.

The main methods used for management training include formal education and training such as the MBA or undergraduate management degrees; internal or externally provided training courses, outdoor MD, and coaching and mentoring. Outdoor MD remains a popular choice for team-building exercises and for development of problem-solving techniques, despite criticism that some providers include extreme and dangerous activities (Reid *et al* 2004, p239). Action learning is encompassed within many methods, and is influenced by the work of Revans (1982) who proposed that learning equals programmed knowledge plus the ability to ask good questions. This fits well with MD as well as with the model of the learning organisation.

BOX 34 TAPPING INTO MANAGEMENT DEVELOPMENT

Birmingham City Council

Birmingham City Council runs a senior management development programme that is largely work-based. Emphasis is on self-managed learning in recognition that taught courses date quickly and work-based learning is regarded as a better way of improving effectiveness at work.

The learning methods used for developing effective time management include:

- mentoring/coaching
- networking/teams/learning groups
- performance review
- 360-degree feedback
- buddying
- informal discussion
- observation/interviewing and questioning
- work shadowing
- deputising.

At the end of the programme, managers report back to the chief executive on their learning and its impact. One participant commented, 'I was initially uncertain and sceptical about the process, but I discovered that this style led to much deeper learning and had a greater impact on the workplace.'

Severn Trent Water

In 2001 company restructuring involved de-layering and the appointment of first-line managers most of whom had not received MD. External providers were asked to tender for the training of new managers. Roffey Park was awarded the contract and delivered three sets of three-day modules. The modules' content appears below:

- *Personal effectiveness*: personal communications; giving and receiving feedback; influencing others, influencing in groups; understanding and appreciating difference; personal power; managing self and time management
- *Developing individual performance*: performance management; performance feedback; motivating others; creating a motivational climate; adapting your management style to get results; delegation; managing conflict; coaching and managing geographically spread teams
- *Leadership*: the characteristics of effective leaders; leadership priorities; building an effective team; team roles; managing through change; inspiring a shared vision and overcoming resistance to change.

Some of the feedback identified incidental benefits such as mixing with others at the same level within the organisation but working in other functions and geographically dispersed.

Severn Trent believes that this will have a major impact on corporate performance.

Sources: Adapted from Cunningham I. 'Back to reality', *People Management,* 8 April 2004. pp37–38; IRS Employment Review 793c. *Management Skills on Tap.* 6 Feb 2004. p14

Action learning is also the most common approach used within SMEs, although the CEML (2002, p2) identified particular problems in relation to SMEs (and the professions). According to Storey (2004) this may be because the government tends to favour formal learning methods because they are easier to measure. Using coaching, feedback and performance review, managers are assisted to determine their own development needs. Two organisations that have tapped into MD are examined in Box 34.

The debates on MD are likely to continue as the skills and abilities required of managers grow, and as Reid *et al* (2004, p229) suggest, 'management is an art, not a science'. There remains dissatisfaction with provision (despite large amounts of money invested in it) partly because organisations remain unsure what is needed, and many managers remain unable to take up what training is on offer. The future is likely to see an extension of self-development generating demand for an ever-broader range of MD supply. As with other training provision, MD needs a high degree of flexibility in order to reconcile inherent tensions.

Choose an organisation with which you are familiar and investigate the ways in which it determines managers' training needs? How could this be improved?

Continuing professional development

Ideas about learning styles and learning cycles have influenced the growth of interest in continuous development. It is widely accepted that people learn in different ways and that learning can take place in a wide range of different settings – not just at work. Continuing professional development (CPD) enables the integration of learning (wherever and however acquired) with work in a way that should be meaningful and relevant to the individual, largely because it is self-directed and therefore relevant to an individual's own development needs. Learning undertaken in this way can become a habit, 'thinking positively about problems and viewing them as opportunities for learning' (Wood 1988, p12) and it is also important to stress that CPD is a process, not a technique.

In a world of rapid change, it is essential to ensure that skills, knowledge and experiences are regularly updated – this is relevant for all employees, but it is particularly pertinent for professionals. Emphasis on this is underpinned by terms such as 'learning to learn', 'reflective practitioners' and the 'learning organisation'. It is generally assumed that employees are motivated to learn in order to ensure employability and career development. This implies a narrow view of CPD as being undertaken for instrumental reasons, whereas CPD could mean 'continuing personal development' as it includes learning for individual motives – which may be somewhat different from organisational ones. Employers are aware of this and not all are enamoured by CPD because they feel that learning that is unrelated to the job in hand is a waste, and may lead to labour turnover. Since learning experiences can often lead to unanticipated and unplanned outcomes, labour turnover could result.

However, a growing number of professional bodies (such as The Law Society, the Royal Institute of British Architects and the General Social Care Council) are re-emphasising the importance of CPD, and looking for new ways in which to encourage its extension. For example, Glover (2001) noted that the interprofessional forum – covering over 50 bodies and chaired by the CIPD – led developments in making CPD a more user-friendly and effective process. It clearly confers a quality benchmark on the profession, and is often a prerequisite for charter status.

As mentioned earlier, it is usually the case that motivated professionals are keen to engage in CPD, although there may be barriers – particularly lack of time. Compulsion may be a way of providing impetus for individuals to get started, and some professional bodies refuse to upgrade those who do not comply, or at the extreme, even expel people from the profession. For the CIPD, it is policy that all members are expected to structure their learning and maintain a record of their CPD, and evidence is required for upgrading. A survey of CIPD members found that most were convinced of its long-term value (Sadler-Smith and Badger 1998, p74). Clearly, it is usually better to use encouragement by setting out the benefits (Stansfield 2002, p43). This may involve the establishment of support systems at work or at the educational institution where people are studying (Megginson 2001).

The essential principles of CPD are that it should:

- be continuous because professionals should always be seeking to improve performance
- be owned and managed by the individual learner
- be driven by the individual learner's needs and current state of development
- have clear learning outcomes that aim to satisfy individual and/or organisational needs
- evaluate learning rather than merely describe what has taken place
- be seen as an essential part of professional and personal life, not an optional extra.

BOX 35 BENEFITS OF CONTINUING PROFESSIONAL DEVELOPMENT FOR CIPD MEMBERS

Becoming a better learner	Developing reflection skills for now and in the future at work
Profiting from learning opportunities	Transferring ideas from courses to the workplace by understanding the principles of learning
Becoming a reflective practitioner	Developing the skills of being a 'thinking performer' by re-evaluating activities in relation to leading research findings
Managing self-development	Providing a template and a way of thinking to manage your own learning needs
Helping with career advancement	Compiling a list of achievements can help to focus your mind when deciding whether or not to apply for promotion
Upgrading CIPD membership	Keeping a record of achievement and a learning log makes it easier to apply for upgrading as soon as it is possible

Source: CIPD. *Requirements of the Applied Personnel and Development Standards*

This latter point is extremely important. Seeing CPD as an optional extra to be slotted into an already overflowing workload means it will never get done because it lacks priority. Obviously, this is facilitated by organisational support, but an emphasis on organisational benefits must be balanced against individual wants and needs. Many organisations recognise that benefits accrue in terms of increased motivation and commitment, as well as enhancing recruitment and retention. It has been observed that, even where CPD is unrelated to work, those undertaking it 'appear to be more engaged, less stressed, more interested in new opportunities and open to working with new colleagues' (Megginson and Whitaker 2003, p17). Megginson and Whitaker (p xiii) succinctly state that CPD is about recognising, releasing and realising potential, and as this benefits both the organisation and the individual its importance is likely to grow.

CPD is now a compulsory aspect of the Professional Development Scheme for all aspiring CIPD Graduates, and it is evaluated as part of the Applied Practitioner Standards along with the Management Report. The sort of activity that can be put forward as part of CPD breaks down into three broad areas. First there is evidence related to an ongoing qualification, such as research for course work, group activities and role-playing, and presentations. Second, there are work-related activities such as new projects or assignments, report-writing, attending training courses and secondments. Finally, there are personal development activities such as learning a new language, acting as a school governor, e-learning and organising sports or social events. A much longer and indicative list is available from CIPD, but the key point to stress is that CPD can be achieved via a range of different routes provided that learning takes place. The advantages of undertaking CPD are numerous as can be seen from Box 35.

There is no perfect way to compile a learning log, but the CIPD provides a number of templates that could be used. One option is to divide learning into development plans and development records, with the former indicating what is intended over the next year and the latter a record of what has been achieved.

CONCLUSIONS

In this chapter we have stressed the importance of having a systematic and well-organised structure for managing learning and development in organisations. Although there are a number of models and frameworks that can be used, each covers broadly the same cycle: identifying training/learning needs, devising learning plans, delivery and evaluation. It is worth reiterating that there is no single best approach to training interventions since the most suitable method depends on its purpose, its subject matter, the size of the audience, and the finance available. HR practitioners need to be able to choose the approach that is most appropriate for specific circumstances, while drawing on learning theories to inform their choice. At the same time, however, a thorough evaluation is critical, especially in assessing transfer back to the workplace. Perhaps most important of all, HR professionals must be at the forefront in establishing an organisational culture in which learning is allowed to flourish. As with other components of HRM, learning and development is changing rapidly, by becoming increasingly strategic, in changing emphasis from training to learning, and with responsibility being delegated to line managers and individuals. However, as we saw in Chapter 8, new ideas and methods are not growing so fast as some of the literature might lead us to believe, and traditional training methods still have an important part to play.

USEFUL READING

BRAMLEY P. *Evaluating Training*. London, CIPD. 2003.

BURNES B. 'Managing change and changing managers from ABC to XYZ', *Journal of Management Development*, Vol. 22, No. 7. 2003. pp627–642.

CHARTERED INSTITUTE OF PERSONNEL AND DEVELOPMENT. *Developing Managers for Business Performance*. London, CIPD. 2002c.

HARRISON R. *Learning and Development*. London, CIPD. 2002.

HUNT J. *and* BARUCH Y. 'Developing top managers: the impact of interpersonal skills training', *Journal of Management Development*, Vol. 22, No. 8, 2003. pp729–752.

IRS EMPLOYMENT REVIEW 807. *Learning and Development in the Workplace*. 3 September 2004. pp10–17.

MUMFORD A. *and* GOLD J. *Management Development: Strategies for action*. London, CIPD. 2004.

REID M., BARRINGTON H. *and* BROWN M. *Human Resource Development: Beyond training interventions*. London, CIPD. 2004.

REYNOLDS J., CALEY L. *and* MASON, R. *How Do People Learn?* Cambridge Programme for Industry research report. London, CIPD. 2002.

SLOMAN M. *Training in the Age of the Learner*. London, CIPD. 2003.

STOREY D. 'Exploring the link, among small firms, between management training and firm performance: a comparison between the UK and other OECD countries', *International Journal of Human Resource Management*, Vol. 15, No. 1. 2004. pp112–130.

Relations

Managing Worker Voice

INTRODUCTION

The management of employee relations is central to HRM. Different approaches have gained prominence in line with a variety of internal and external pressures on the employing organisation; these include the growth of trade unionism, changing product and employment market conditions, labour law and new technology (Blyton and Turnbull 2004).

During the 1970s employers were encouraged to recognise and work with trade unions, required to improve the floor of employment rights for workers, and prompted to conciliate with rather than confront staff. However, during the 1980s the climate became more hostile for unions and changes in the political and legal context removed much of their statutory support leaving many workers with little employment protection by continental standards. Moreover, the government encouraged employers to reassert their control, and high levels of unemployment in the United Kingdom contributed to the shift in the balance of power (Ackers and Wilkinson 2003; Gospel and Wood 2003b). Hence, some commentators talked of a 'new employee relations' and the transformation of the British workplace (Towers 2003, p18). Thus we note Farnham's view (2002, p69) that 'employee relations is the contemporary term for the field of study which analyses how the employment relationship between employers and employees is organised and practised'. The late 1990s marked a shift in the pattern of employee relations as the incoming Labour Government (re-elected in 2001) was more sympathetic to trade unions, and this is reflected in a statutory recognition procedure. The policy environment is also more animated with notions of employee rights (or in the EU case, citizenship) supported by new legal regulations (Gennard 2002; Ewing 2003). While the current government has remained committed to labour flexibility and considerable management 'choice' regarding employment practices, it has been prepared both to regulate independently on behalf of employees and to commit the UK to European Social Policy.

The decline in union membership has contributed significantly to the new employee relations terrain. Collective bargaining now has lower levels of coverage and scope than at any time since the 1930s, and trade unions have lost their national prominence and voice to an extent that would not have been thought possible in the 1970s. In addition the extent of industrial action has also fallen dramatically, with days lost through strikes at a very low level, and a whole generation of HR managers now unaccustomed to dealing with collective disputes at work.

There has been a major growth in legislation over the past 30 years, and lawyers have played an increasingly important role in setting the parameters within which employee relations is enacted. For the vast majority of employers, the most immediate and obvious influence on their activities, especially in the area of employment rights, comes from the employment tribunal system. But the employment tribunals are themselves overseen and explicitly influenced by the Employment Appeals Tribunal and higher level courts. Increasingly, this includes European legal institutions – such as the European Court of Justice – whose influence over the adjudication of employment rights has grown enormously over the last 20 years, and has led to major changes in employment law (see Chapter 2).

The purpose of this chapter is to examine management's role in employee relations focusing in particular on union recognition and the nature of union and non-union workplaces, as well as collective bargaining. Given its increasing prominence, the final part of the chapter analyses EI, consultation and social partnership.

By the end of the chapter, readers should be able to:

- **provide advice to management on employee relations objectives appropriate for their own organisation**

- **design an employee relations policy explaining how trade unions and collective bargaining will be dealt with, or how a non-union strategy will be effected**

- **provide advice on the appropriateness of adopting different forms of employee involvement within their organisation.**

In addition, they should understand and be able to explain:

- **the way in which effective employee relations can contribute to increased employee potential and commitment**

- **the processes of union recognition and derecognition**

- **the nature and meaning of collective bargaining and employee involvement and their place within the employee relations framework.**

MANAGEMENT'S ROLE IN EMPLOYEE RELATIONS

The centrepiece of employee relations is the relationship between employers and employees, with its common and divergent interests (Edwards 2003a). It is in neither party's interest for the organisation to perform poorly with consequent negative effects on profits (for the employer) or wages (for the employee). However, while there are clearly common goals there are also divergent interests. In simple terms, the employer is likely to wish to buy labour at the lowest possible price or cost so as to maximise profits, whereas employees wish to sell their labour at the highest possible price. This produces a conflict of interest, which not necessarily results in open conflict, but means that the arrangements reached may be unstable depending on relative bargaining power. Because employees are usually relatively weaker than employers, employees are likely to gain from organising themselves into trade unions so as to boost bargaining power.

Thus employee relations is characterised by both conflict and co-operation. Some people regard it as inextricably linked with conflict, since this is the only time employee relations obtains much media coverage. It is now accepted that the so-called 'British disease' of industrial conflict in the 1970s was largely a myth, as Britain had a record no worse than many other developed countries. Conflict may manifest itself through a strike or it may be contained or institutionalised through procedures (see Chapter 11).

Write **two** lists, one specifying the common interests of employers and employees, and the other the divergent interests. Apply this to an organisation you are familiar with and see if it helps you to evaluate the quality of employee relations there.

However, the notion of two sides is also too simplistic. Firstly, neither side is consistently unified and much bargaining and disagreement takes place within each party as well as between them. Within management there are likely to be conflicting objectives between different functions and between different levels; for example, the objectives of the sales team may conflict with those of the production function. Similarly, the demands placed upon line managers in terms of adherence to procedure agreements may cause conflict between them and the HR function. To some extent, though, the overriding objective of companies to secure profitability can help integrate the various subobjectives. On the union side matters are even more complex, with conflict between members in different departments and in different trade unions, as well as between different levels in the shop steward hierarchy. There may also be differences between different trade or interest groups or between the leadership and the ordinary rank and file members.

It is also inappropriate to conceive of only two parties in employee relations, because of third-party governmental intervention as we have noted earlier. This can take several different forms. For example, legislation on employee relations has developed considerably since the 1960s and it played a key role during the 1980s – legislation on the closed shop, industrial action and ballots, for example. The government has also played a role in pay regulation since the Second World War. This has been either through a formal mechanism – such as incomes policy during the 1960s and 1970s, or the imposition of cash limits for the public sector in the 1980s and the establishment of the minimum wage in 1998. In addition, via the agencies of independent tripartite bodies such as Acas, it has played a role in the resolution of disputes in both the public and private sectors. Furthermore, the Government is a key employer, with a managerial function.

Before looking at employee relations objectives, we need to remind ourselves of the nature of management itself, and especially the sharply differing contexts within which employee relations are enacted. Three aspects are worthy of mention. First, there is the distinction between different types of sectors (for example, manufacturing or service) and ownership (private or public). This leads to a categorisation of four types of employing organisation: private businesses, public corporations, public services and voluntary bodies (Farnham 2000). Second, there are major differences between employment in large, multi-establishment enterprises and small single-unit firms. Third, we need to be aware of the influence of employee relations decisions compared with other corporate-level issues (Sisson and Marginson 2003, pp176–182).

A number of writers in the USA have developed a 'strategic choice' model whereby employers are seen as the key movers of change, and industrial relations policies are seen as strategic in that they form part of a long-term plan (Kochan *et al* 1986). This is important in recognising both the element of choice management faces, and also the extent to which management is able to set the agenda to which other actors – eg trade unions – then react (Boxall and Purcell 2000).

It might be expected that employee relations objectives would be in line with corporate strategy, although this does assume that employers are proactive enough to have devised such strategies, and are not just muddling through. Even if we do assume that employers have some idea about what they are doing, and why they are doing it, their objectives may be implicit rather than explicit, and in many cases not committed to paper. In any event, employee relations objectives typically include the following:

- reducing unit labour costs, though not necessarily wages
- achieving greater stability in employee relations by channelling discontent through agreed procedures
- increasing productivity and the utilisation of labour
- increasing co-operation and commitment so as to increase the likely acceptance of change
- increasing control over the labour process
- minimising disruption at work and reducing the likelihood of overt conflict.

Some of these objectives do not make sense in isolation. For example, while management clearly wants to minimise disruption this should not be at the expense of high productivity. It could well be that the latter could be achieved in the long term by engineering a strike so as to confront inefficient working practices. Equally, some of these objectives may be more appropriate for certain stages in an organisation's development, or for some types of employer.

Think of examples of conflicts between different objectives that occur in your organisation. To what extent do objectives change over time?

Over the last 30 years a variety of bodies have argued that management must adopt a more strategic approach to employee relations, largely because firefighting was seen as leading to problems as short-term, ad hoc solutions merely stored up trouble for the future. In contrast, it was suggested that devising a strategy could provide a greater likelihood of success as this would increase consistency and harness commitment (Donovan 1968; Thurley and Wood 1983; Schuler *et al* 2001). However, research suggests that managers have adopted opportunistic and pragmatic approaches to managing employees rather than the strategic approaches extolled by the human resource management texts (Bach and Sisson 2000; Sisson and Marginson 2003). Companies tend to consider HR issues at the implementation stage of decisions, rather than at the point where initial decisions are being formulated.

To try to understand management's approach to employee relations, it is useful to draw upon the concepts of 'frames of reference' developed by Alan Fox (1966) in his research paper for the Donovan Commission. These embody the main selective influences that cause managers to supplement, omit and structure what they see. Thus, two people may see the same event in a completely different manner and may judge its meaning, significance and outcomes in contrasting ways. The unitary frame of reference sees the organisation as a team (like a football team), with all employees striving towards a common goal. All members of the team are assumed to work to the best of their ability, accept their place in the hierarchy, and follow their appointed leader. There is no room or reason for factions. Given that unions are unnecessary (since everyone is on the same side), conflict is seen as pathological or abnormal, the result of misunderstanding and trouble-makers. In contrast, pluralism conceives of the organisation as comprising varied interest groups with common and divergent interests, and management's job is to balance these competing demands. Trade unions may be seen as a natural reflection of varied interests, rather than a cause of conflict. Conflict is not regarded as illegitimate, but needs to be channelled or managed through rules and procedures (Ackers 2002a, 2002b).

In simple terms, the two frames of reference have different perspectives on management prerogatives (Bacon 2003). Managers with a unitary perspective would trust employees to make the 'correct' decision, and since everyone supposedly has the same interests there should be no conflict between what is the best for the company and what is the best decision for employees. In contrast, the pluralist, accepts the role of a union in the workplace and believes in a policy of gaining the support of unions and employees to achieve an 'acceptable' solution. Pluralists believe that shop stewards should be consulted about changes that may have a fundamental effect on employees. On many occasions the substantive outcome of joint decision-making may be little different from that which would have been achieved by direct management action. However, the procedural element is different and is critical.

Bacon (2001, p194) notes:

> **In the 1998 Workplace Employee Relations Survey [WERS 1998] most managers (54%) were "neutral" about union membership, whereas 29% were "in favour" with 17% 'not in favour' (Cully *et al* 1999, p87). However, when managers are asked more directly whether they prefer to manage employees directly or through unions then unitarist preferences emerge. For example, 72% of managers agreed with the statement "we would rather consult directly with employees than with unions", whereas only 13% disagreed (p88). Consequently, management approaches to industrial relations are often characterised as a mixing and matching between unitarism and pluralism in the "time-honoured British fashion".**

Individual managers may vary in their willingness to accept a curbing of managerial rights, to some extent depending on the subject matter under consideration. For example, managers may well be willing to negotiate on matters relating to payment methods, job design and work practices, but be unwilling to consult about matters such as investment and pricing policy, and product development. In any event, while management may be willing to consult, involve and even bargain, they will also insist that they have a 'prerogative' to make the final decision. Hence, in certain areas of employee relations – such as promotion and training – management prerogative is the norm. In organisations where unions are absent, management is more able to vary terms and conditions of employment at will.

THE EXTENT AND NATURE OF UNION RECOGNITION

The issue of union recognition lies at the very heart of employee relations, and policies and practices in this area have changed more than most in the last three decades. In the mid-1970s it was assumed that most employers would automatically recognise and deal with trade unions, support their activities in the workplace, and attempt to build close working relationships with senior shop stewards so as to lubricate relations at work and minimise the likelihood of disruption to business. By the 1990s many employers introduced new working patterns without even consulting, let alone negotiating with, union representatives. While derecognition has not been widespread, the lack of new recognition deals was seen as more significant (Cully *et al* 1998, p16). However, work by Gall and McKay (1999) showed there was a marked increase in new recognition agreements in the last few years. They put forward five possible explanations. Firstly, the number of companies likely to derecognise are becoming fewer as those that are likely to do this have done it. Secondly, notions of 'partnership' have been important in providing employers with a more positive view of unions. Thirdly, some companies were waiting to see what legislation was to be enacted and, as a result of the legislation, are now more likely to recognise unions. Fourthly, trade unions have put more resources into various campaigns to increase recognition. Finally, employers have adapted to the developments in European legislation in terms of consultation (see also Sargeant 2001).

Gall (2004) has argued that the 1999 Employment Relations Act marked a change in fortunes for the unions in terms of increasing recognition. They have many gains to be satisfied with under the tranche of new recognition agreements, even though they have not gained all of their demands and the majority of agreements are voluntary. The process and outcomes under post-recognition arrangements have delivered 'improvements for members'. Research by Wood *et al* (2003) also suggests that the legal procedures have had a great indirect effect. That is, there has been increased recognition agreements without the involvement of CAC, but as a reaction to the Act and the impetus that it created.

Until recently there was no legally enforceable route for unions and employers to follow in order to grant recognition. This made the British system different from those operating in many other industrialised countries in Europe and North America. In theory it meant that if they so desired, British employers could choose to grant recognition to a union with *no* members in the workplace. Indeed, this is precisely what happened at some of the greenfield sites when deals with a single union were signed before any employees were recruited, as at Nissan (Wickens 1987, pp129–137). Conversely, employers could choose not to recognise a union at a workplace where all employees are union members, although this is more of a hypothetical situation and in practice would be difficult to sustain. In other words, the ultimate decision to grant recognition remained the prerogative of management. The 1999 Employment Relations Act changed this by making legal provision for statutory trade union recognition but applied to only employers with at least 21 workers – hence excluding some 8 million workers (Smith and Morton 2001; Dickens and Hall 2003). It also provided some protection for workers taking industrial action in that it became automatically unfair to dismiss those taking part in lawfully organised action for eight weeks, although, if all reasonable steps are taken to resolve the dispute after this time, dismissal is likely to be fair (Anderman 2003). In addition ballots before action contain new wording explaining the new protection. Smith and Morton point out employers' freedom to dismiss workers has been regulated not abolished (2001, p130). Recognition can be achieved through several routes:

1   *Recognition by agreement* – In companies that employ 21 or more workers, an independent trade union can make a request to the employer for recognition. If there is no agreement after 28 days, Acas can be called on to intervene.

2   *Recognition from an application to the CAC* – If voluntary negotiations fail, the Central Arbitration Committee (CAC) assesses the extent to which a 'bargaining unit' exists for the purpose of recognition. The CAC is required to help both sides reach agreement about the bargaining unit and consider whether the trade union has majority support of workers within the defined unit. The CAC can then issue a declaration that the union is recognised for those workers. There is no agreed definition of a 'bargaining unit', although it should consistent with existing structures of

management, and ideally avoid small fragmented groups of workers within an undertaking.

3   *Recognition ballots* – The CAC has the discretion to conduct a ballot to assess the extent of support for trade union recognition if three conditions are met: (a) if it thinks this is in the interests of good industrial relations, (b) if a 'significant number' of employees within a bargaining unit inform the CAC they do not want trade union recognition or (c) if there is evidence that leads the CAC to conclude that a 'significant number' of union members do not want the trade union to bargain on their behalf. The employer is obliged to co-operate with the ballot and if at least 40 per cent of those eligible to vote support union recognition, the CAC will declare that the union is recognised (Farnham 2000, pp316–321; Dundon 2002a, pp252–254; Dickens and Hall 2003, pp138–139). For further information on CAC, refer to Chapter 1.

However, Dundon (2002a, pp253–254) notes the procedure has been criticised:

> **On one hand employers prefer the voluntary approach and view the law as impeding further regulation within the labour market. On the other hand, trade unions regard the 40% voting threshold as unworkable. They suggest it will be extremely difficult to achieve recognition for workers in those organisations for which the law was intended, particularly in smaller undertakings where membership is low (or non-existent) and employers are extremely hostile.**

Does the absence of strikes indicate that employees are content? How do employees show their discontent? How can discontent be monitored and handled?

In broad terms, there seems to be an increasing distinction between (a) those workplaces where unions have maintained a presence and where they appear to be supported by managements, (b) those where they are being edged out and are perhaps in danger of becoming extinct and (c) non-union workplaces. The critical importance of management attitudes is shown graphically by the WERS data. Unions were recognised in 45 per cent of workplaces overall, but in 94 per cent of workplaces where management had a favourable view of unions and in only 9 per cent of workplaces where management had an unfavourable view (Cully *et al* 1998, p15). This is shown in Table 22 (page 272).

We now examine these three options.

WORKING WITH THE UNIONS

The proportion of workplaces in Britain that recognise a union fell from 66 per cent in 1984 to 45 per cent in 1998, although there is still substantial sector variation (Cully *et al* 1998, p28; Millward *et al* 2000, p264). For example, 25 per cent of all private sector organisations recognise a trade union, whereas in the public sector this is 95 per cent. Union recognition appears to be a function of organisational size. Thus union recognition ranged from 33 per cent in the smallest workplaces to 76 per cent in the largest. It is also important to note that recognition is variable in both scope and depth (Brown *et al* 1998), such that employers

Table 22   *Indicators of union presence, by workplace size and management attitudes*

	% of employees who are members	% of workplaces	
		Any union members	Union recognition
Workplace size			
25–49 employees	23	46	39
50–99 employees	27	52	41
100–199 employees	32	66	57
200–499 employees	38	77	67
500 or more employees	48	86	78
All workplaces	36	53	45

Base: all workplaces with 25 or more employees.
Source: Cully M., Woodland S., O'Reilly A., Dix G., Millward N., Bryson A. and Forth, J. *The 1998 Workplace Employee Relations Survey: First findings.* London, Department of Trade and Industry. 1998. p15

recognise unions for specific activities, such as discipline, grievance or health and safety representation but not necessarily full-blown collective bargaining. For example at Sainsbury's, unions are recognised for individual grievance while at ICI unions are involved in business planning (Sisson and Storey 2000, p190). According to WERS, there are no union members at all in 47 per cent of workplaces compared with 36 per cent in 1990. The decline in the incidence of union recognition from 1980 was largely a private sector phenomenon and after 1990 entirely so (Millward *et al* 2000, p97).

Non-manual workers and women now constitute a much greater proportion of total union membership, and are as likely to be unionised as manual staff or men. At the same time, there remain differences between full-time workers (32 per cent) and part-timers (21 per cent), as well as between different age groups. Broadly, workers over the age of 30 are more likely to join unions than those who are younger. There are significant differences in density between industries. Private sector services have a lower union density than manufacturing and the public sector is much more unionised than the private. Regional variations are also very apparent, with the highest density in the 'old' industrial areas such as North East England, Northern Ireland and Wales, and the lowest in the South East, South West and East Anglia (IRS Employment Review 796d 2004). Finally, newer workplaces are much less likely to be unionised than those that were in existence before 1975 (Machin 2003, p16). However, it is interesting to note that a number of organisations, such as Vertex, which were initially avowedly non-union have now decided to recognise unions following changes in the law and the political climate (Walsh 2001).

There are a number of reasons why employers should choose to work with, rather than against, unions at the workplace:

1   Management may regard trade union representatives as an essential part of the communication process in larger workplaces. Rather than being forced to establish a system for dealing with all employees, or setting up a non-union representative forum, trade unions are seen as a channel that allows for the effective resolution of issues concerned with pay bargaining or grievance handling. Reaching agreement with union representatives, in contrast to imposing decisions, can provide decisions with a legitimacy which otherwise would be lacking. It can also lead to 'better' decisions as well. Even if this method of decision-making appears more time-consuming than the simple imposition of change, less time is spent in trying to correct mistakes or persuade employees after the event of the efficacy of management ideas.

2   Employers may decide that it is more important to achieve long-term stability in employee relations even though their power advantage might allow them to impose changes on the unions. It is argued that management is more able to persuade unions to observe procedures if they have also conformed to previous agreements. As a quid pro quo, employers have to be prepared to use procedures themselves for resolving differences at work, especially in the area of disciplinary matters. Indeed, it can be argued that 'responsible' workplace union organisation and 'responsive' management is mutually reinforcing.

3   Some employers have taken the view that unionisation is inevitable because of the nature of their workforce, the industry, and the region in which establishments are located. The new recognition procedure means that where there is sufficient support for a union, employers may feel it is far better to reach an agreement with a preferred union from the outset rather than suffer both poor employee relations and employee morale consequences in the process of defiance. This was the case at Airflight – a charter airline – which, in the context of having acquired a unionised company, and with imminent legislation on recognition, decided it made sense to recognise the pilots' union (Marchington *et al* 2001, p77).

4   Even if employers did wish to reduce the role of unions at the workplace, they may lack the power to carry through their intentions because of local constraints. For example, skill shortages may make wholesale dismissals unrealistic, as may fears that the tacit skills of workers will be lost, with the consequence of less effective and efficient organisations. Moreover it is often forgotten that trade unions perform a number of functions in the workplace that can assist the management of employee relations. In a non-union organisation following complete derecognition the onus falls upon management to perform an even greater range of tasks, and it may prove difficult to sustain alternative representation arrangements, as well as satisfy employee expectations. It is also important to keep the trade union issue in perspective. Employers have many concerns other than those relating to trade unions and, provided the latter do not present a major obstacle to the realisation of more important goals, a union presence can be tolerated or even promoted.

Most people join trade unions primarily for instrumental reasons – for example, for protection against arbitrary management decisions or for insurance against accidents (Charlwood 2003) – or peer-group pressure – and they may not necessarily believe in the notion of collective action. The predominantly instrumental attitude partially explains why participation increases considerably if there is a problem or employee relations issue (Waddington and Whitson 1997). It also explains why unions tend to be seen in local and economic terms. This 'local' perspective helps us understand why people agree that 'unions in general are too strong' and at the same time feel 'that unions at the [individual's] workplace are not strong'. However,

Millward *et al* (2000, p89) note that there has been a reduced willingness to become union members even in situations where the employer encourages unionism and there is a growing number of a newer generation who have never been union members or had any exposure to trade unions.

More recently, there has been a revival of interest in notions of 'partnership' (Involvement and Participation Association 1993; Ackers and Payne 1998; Guest and Peccei 2001; Ackers *et al* 2005). This refers to the situation in which management is prepared to support the activities of the trade union(s), and for their part employees are more likely to regard union membership as an important aspect of their employment conditions. A good example of this is the Involvement and Participation Association (IPA) report (*Towards Industrial Partnership* 1993), which is publicly endorsed by leading trade union and management representatives as well as a number of well-known academics. While not seeking to deny differences of opinions and goals, the report recognises the high degree of common interests shared by employers and unions, and stresses the need to accept the legitimacy of representative institutions. WERS provided a boost to collectivism by reporting that the combination of union recognition and high commitment management (HCM) practices had a significant positive effect on performance. As Cully *et al* (1999, p135) note: 'workplaces with a recognised union and a majority of the HCM practices ... did better than the average, and better than workplaces without recognition and a minority of these practices'.

EDGING OUT THE UNIONS

While some employers have sought to develop their relationship with unions, others have opted for marginalisation or derecognition. In these situations employers have decided that their objectives are more likely to be achieved by reducing or removing the union presence. In some workplaces there may have been disputes that slowed down or prevented changes in working practices, or managers may be concerned about whether or not they can work with trade unions. Others may simply have taken advantage of a superior power base to remove or restrict the activities of unions, to reduce wage costs, and enforce a stricter managerial regime, perhaps in line with some deep-seated antagonism among senior managers towards unions. Some of the reduction in union influence has occurred as part of a broader management strategy rather than an attack on unions as such, and the removal of the union is undertaken in conjunction with a shift to more direct methods of employee involvement (EI). For example, some employers place considerable emphasis on cultures stressing individualism and performance-related pay schemes rather than collectively negotiated rates. In short, management is seeking to deny, rather than legitimise, the unions. Take-up of 'new' management practices and EI schemes is illustrated in Table 23.

Even when trade unions are marginalised they retain a presence in the workplace, and in many cases maintain the right to collective bargaining. In these situations, even though the institutions of collective employee relations remain in place, they represent a much less important aspect of human resource policies and practices. A number of changes are typically associated with marginalisation:

- substantial reductions in the number of shop stewards at establishment level
- a severe tightening-up on access to time off for trade union activities and facilities for undertaking union-related work
- withdrawal of full-time shop steward positions, often subsequent to the dismissal (usually through redundancy or early retirement) of the existing role-holders

- lack of support for deduction of contributions at source (DOCAS) arrangements
- a lower priority accorded to collective bargaining with unions and the upgrading of consultative committees
- a greater emphasis on individualism and direct communications from line managers to all employees.

Certainly in recent years, as unions have become less able and willing to take industrial action, employers have pruned the collective bargaining agenda and relied more heavily on written and oral communications to all staff as opposed to going through union channels

Table 23   *Use of 'new' management practices and EI schemes*

	% of workplaces
Most employees work in formally designated teams	65
Workplace operates a system of team briefing for groups of employees	61
Most non-managerial employees have performance formally appraised	56
Staff attitude survey conducted in the last 5 years	45
Problem-solving groups (eg quality circles)	42
'Single status' between managers and non-managerial employees	41
Regular meetings of entire workforce	37
Profit-sharing scheme operated for non-managerial employees	30
Workplace-level joint consultative committee	28
Employee share ownership scheme for non-managerial employees	15
Guaranteed job security or no compulsory redundancies policy	14
Most employees receive minimum of 5 days training per year	12
Individual performance-related pay scheme for non-managerial employees	11
Workplace operates a just-in-time system of inventory control	29
Most supervisors trained in employee relations skills	27
Attitudinal test used before making appointments	22

Base: all workplaces with 25 or more employees.
Source: Cully M., Woodland S., O'Reilly A., Dix G., Millward N., Bryson A. and Forth, J. *The 1998 Workplace Employee Relations Survey: First findings*. London, Department of Trade and Industry. 1998. p10

alone. The production director at a carpet manufacturer reflected on recent changes. Ten years ago, managers would meet the shop steward who would then roll information out. 'We'd never dream of that now. It's crazy when you think back. We used to not talk to our employees, only through a union representative' (Marchington et al 2001, p64).

WERS 1998 confirmed that the trend to 'hollow out' collective agreements was continuing. Even where worker representatives were present, no negotiations occurred over any issues in half of these workplaces (Cully et al 1999, p110). In a further 13 per cent of workplaces negotiations only occurred on non-pay issues, in 17 per cent they only covered pay and in 22 per cent negotiations occurred over pay and one other issue. Managers in many workplaces appear to regard certain HR issues as 'off limits' to union representatives and do not even involve unions by providing information to them (Bacon 2001, p198).

Employers can take this strategy further and try to derecognise unions – an idea that entered the vocabulary of British employee relations only in the 1980s. It is important to appreciate at the outset that derecognition is not a homogeneous concept (Dundon 2002a). In its most straightforward form derecognition refers to the complete withdrawal of collective bargaining rights and trade union organisation for some or all employees at a workplace or throughout a complete employing organisation. In other words, no trade union is recognised for the employees involved, even though by law they retain the right to join unions of their choice. Alternatively, derecognition can mean the removal of bargaining rights for one or more unions in a multi-union environment, while allowing for, and even encouraging, the transfer of membership to other unions in the workplace. In this situation management might seek to simplify existing arrangements and reduce the number of unions with which it deals, and the end result could well be levels of union membership little different from before the derecognition. While one union loses, another gains.

The extent of union derecognition is difficult to gauge. WERS shows that the decline in union membership cannot be explained by the marginal rise in derecognition and is insignificant compared to other sources of membership decline – such as shifts in employment from areas of high to low union density. Furthermore, it is important to note that a number of problems often occur after derecognition, including increased workloads for line managers, particularly responsibility for communications and consultation.

> What are the advantages and disadvantages of union recognition for employers?

MANAGING WITHOUT UNIONS

As with derecognition, discussions of non-union firms did not receive much attention in publications prior to the 1980s. It was well known that there were large numbers of small, usually independent, companies which did not recognise or deal with trade unions, but they were generally labelled as 'traditionalist', 'unitarist' or 'sweatshop' employers, and castigated (usually quite rightly) for their poor treatment of staff. It was only with the growing awareness of what Beaumont (1987, p117) refers to as the 'household name' group – companies such as IBM, Marks & Spencer, Hewlett Packard – that academic and practitioner interest started to blossom (Colling 2003). These companies were praised for their employee relations policies, which were designed to offer employees more than could be achieved by trade unions through negotiations. At last it appeared that non-union firms could actually feel proud of their approach to employee relations, and these companies later began to be seen as fertile ground for the development of HRM in the UK.

Non-unionism is more extensive in certain parts of the country (such as the south-east of England) and in certain sectors of the economy (such as retailing, professional services, and hotels and catering) than in others. Younger and smaller establishments are also more likely to be non-union, and there has been some debate as to whether the high technology sector is adding to the stock of non-unionism (Farnham 2000, p183). But non-unionism can take many different forms, varying from the sophisticated, and arguably more pleasant, employment practices that characterise the 'household name' (eg Marks & Spencer's) groups through to the sweatshops and 'bleak houses' (Sisson 1993) of 'Dickensian' employers. One of the problems with studies of non-union firms has been the lack of differentiation between these highly contrasting forms of employee relations, which have little in common beyond the refusal by employers to recognise trade unions for collective bargaining. Guest and Hoque (1994a) argue that the term 'non-unionism' is actually limiting, in that firms are only analysed in relation to unionisation. They suggest a categorisation of non-union firms into the good, the bad, the ugly and the lucky – here we focus on the first three of these.

First, and most celebrated by commentators, are employers who are probably leaders in their product market, who would be classified by Guest and Hoque (1994b) as 'good'. These are often large employers, who have a clear strategy for managing people and operate with a wide range of human resource policies. These employers have tended to operate a 'union substitution' policy (Dundon 2002b; Blyton and Turnbull 2004) that offers a complete employment package intended to be seen by employees as an attractive alternative to trade union membership. Such an approach might include:

- a highly competitive pay and benefits package typically in excess of those offered by other firms in the same labour market

- a comprehensive battery of recruitment techniques (including psychometric tests) designed to select individuals who 'match' organisational norms and discard those who do not fit with the company profile (eg those with a history of union activism)

- a high priority accorded to induction programmes, which are geared up to socialising employees into the company ethos

- a stress on training and development opportunities, related both to the employees' work and more broadly to their role in the company and society (eg employee development and assistance programmes and career counselling)

- a focus on employee communications and information-sharing within the enterprise, such as through teambriefing

- a system (such as speak-up) enabling employee concerns and anxieties to be dealt with by management (rather than a union), as well as for contributing ideas which may help to improve organisational efficiency

- a commitment to providing secure and satisfying work while employed by the organisation, often involving regular moves to different types of job

- single status and harmonised employment policies between blue- and white-collar employees

- an individualised pay and appraisal system differentiating between staff in terms of previous performance and future potential, designed to reward those who contribute most to organisational success (eg performance-related or merit pay).

The HR practices used by these 'good' firms (see Chapter 3) certainly look attractive to employees. Do they represent a cost-effective alternative to trade unions?

However, such organisations have not escaped criticism. It could be argued that 'sophisticated' employment practices are merely an illusion designed to obscure the true nature of HRM regimes, or that workers are merely 'conned' by their overt appeal into working harder, not for their own benefit but for that of the company. Similarly, it has been suggested that employers may continue to provide superior employment practices only under favourable economic and competitive conditions, and that product market problems will lead to their permanent or temporary withdrawal. In other words, the supposed employer commitment to employees as their 'most valuable resource' is both superficial and trite. In the case of a steel plant that widely publicised the introduction of a HRM approach and subsequently derecognised trade unions, employee gains proved illusory, with managerial strategy geared towards compliance, work intensification and the suppression of any counterbalancing trade union activity (Bacon 1999). Gollan's work (2002) on News International argues that attempts to have a substitution or union avoidance strategy with non-union representation structures failed as the body lacked legitimacy and power thus

Table 24 *Non-union management control approaches*

Non-union approach	Type of anti-union behaviour and control
Fear stuff[1]	Union suppression: Employer behaviour here includes blatant intimidation of workers, the objective to instil a 'fear' (real or otherwise) of managerial reprisals to possible unionisation.
Sweet stuff[1]	Union substitution: Management argue that unions are unnecessary, with better terms and conditions and sophisticated employee voice channels to resolve any grievances.
Evil stuff[1]	Ideological opposition to unions: Management articulates the view that unions are 'reds under the beds', and will be destructive to the company performance.
Fatal stuff[1]	Blatant refusal: Employer behaviour here includes refusal to recognise a union, or at best refusal to 'bargain in good faith'.
Awkward stuff[2]	Stonewalling: Managers create what appear to be legitimate obstacles to union recognition, effectively employing 'delaying' tactics.
Tame stuff[2]	Damage limitation: Employer behaviour can take the form of 'sweetheart' deals, partially recognising 'moderate' unions or creating internal (managerial controlled) staff associations.
Harm stuff[2]	By-passing: Employer behaviour seeks to effectively marginalise collective employee voice, often through specific non-union communication channels.

[1]Roy's (1980) original classification.
[2]Gall's (2001) additional typologies.
Source: Dundon T. 'Employer opposition and union avoidance in the UK', *Industrial Relations Journal*, Vol. 33, No. 3, 2002b. p236

leading to employee dissatisfaction. There is also an argument that these sophisticated non-union organisations offer good benefits only because of the previous and continuing efforts of trade unions across the economy as a whole.

The second type of non-union firm is the traditional, sweatshop employer, often a small independent single-site company operating as a supplier to one of the sophisticated non-union organisations analysed above. Managements deliberately depriving workers of their rights are categorised as 'ugly', whereas those offering poor terms and conditions without such manipulative intentions are referred to as 'bad'. The subordinate role many of these small suppliers have with a larger company – dependent, dominated and isolated – leaves them with little control over their own destiny and places a primacy on labour flexibility. These firms are under considerable pressure to control costs and enhance flexibility, goals many of these employers believe to be achievable only without what they see as interference by trade unions. In these circumstances pay rates are likely to be low, while formal fringe benefits and welfare arrangements would be virtually non-existent. The regime in these small firms tends to be highly personalised (Scott *et al* 1989, p42; Dundon and Wilkinson 2003; Scase 2003). Recruitment practices are also likely to reflect the owner/managers' deep distrust of unions. The lack of formal disciplinary procedures means that employee protection is haphazard and arbitrary at best, totally absent at worst (Wilkinson 1999). Guest and Conway (1999) termed firms without a union presence or high commitment HRM as 'a black hole', noting the lack of satisfaction and commitment and high propensity of employees to quit. In a study by Dundon *et al* (1999, pp258–262) a personnel manager took the view that 'communicating to employees can be a dangerous thing. The current system of withholding information is a strategy that has been built up over the years and is used to keep employees on their toes.' At the same firm, one of the employees noted that the 'the firm is run by "family-men". What they say goes. It's as simple as that … and I can't see them giving that control up'. The WERS study noted much lower levels of sanctions and dismissals in workplaces where unions were recognised suggesting unions' success in defending against arbitrary dismissal (Cully *et al* 1999, p28).

Non-union management approaches are summarised in Table 24.

COLLECTIVE BARGAINING

Collective bargaining was a significant component of British employee relations from the end of the First World War through to the 1980s. It was the principal method by which wages and conditions were determined for a majority of the workforce although it has been described as a 'hollow shell' (Hyman 1997). In addition, collective bargaining outcomes (in terms of wage levels, hours worked and holiday entitlements, for example) also influenced the terms and conditions of employees whose pay was determined by management alone. One reason why sophisticated paternalist employers offer terms and conditions of employment superior to those negotiated by trade unions is to ensure that they remain union-free. In recent years, however, the prominence of collective bargaining has declined. Collective bargaining is by no means restricted to formal confrontation. Indeed, the mass of negotiations take place continually between shop stewards, supervisors/line managers and personnel managers at workplace level, incorporating a wide range of matters concerned with working conditions, health and safety, discipline and grievance cases, and welfare/social concerns. It is an all-pervasive social process that may be overt or covert, and informal or formal (Gospel and Palmer 1993, p180). Thus, collective bargaining is a process occurring principally – in terms of the time involved and the number of issues dealt with – at workplace level through unwritten deals and custom and practice. Conversely, some of the more important and long-term decisions about pay and working conditions are the subject of infrequent company-wide or multi-employer negotiations.

Collective bargaining is concerned with both substantive (what is determined) and procedural issues (how decisions are made). Many of the blockages in bargaining occur not because of disputes about substantive matters (such as marginal increases in pay), but are due to disagreements about how employee relations are to be managed in the future – for example, over union derecognition. In short, collective bargaining is both an adversarial and a co-operative process, one in which employees not only oppose managerial plans with which they disagree but may also wish to improve management decisions that they feel are inadequate. In rare circumstances unions may unilaterally set the rules, the other side of the coin to management prerogative. This was seen historically with the craft societies, which imposed their own employment rules on employers, often insisting on a specific period of apprenticeship and requiring all new workers to have a union card. It is also evident today in professions, such as lawyers and accountants, whose bodies operate in a similarly restrictive fashion.

The extensiveness of formal collective bargaining can be estimated from the WERS data. This shows that the proportion of employees (in establishments which employ 25 or more people) with recognised unions whose terms and conditions are formally negotiated by collective bargaining fell from 70 per cent of all employees in 1984 to 41 per cent by 1998 (Cully et al 1999, pp241–242). Sweeping changes in the political and legal environment in the last 20 years together with changes in sectoral employment and unemployment have had a major impact on workplace union organisation. The distinctive British system of adversarial collective bargaining is no longer characteristic of the economy as a whole. As Millward et al (2000, pp234–235) note, 'the system of collective relations, based on the shared values of the legitimacy of representation by independent trade unions and on joint regulation, crumbled ... to such an extent that it no longer represents a dominant model'.

The shape and character of collective bargaining varies considerably between workplaces, particularly in relation to the level at which bargaining takes place and the size/structure of the unit of employees who are covered by any agreement. The concept of bargaining level refers to the point(s) at which collective bargaining takes place, and it can range from workplace/section through to establishment, division, company and industry/multi-employer at its most complex. In many cases terms and conditions are the subject of negotiation at more than one level in the hierarchy, as for example with the setting of holiday entitlements at industry level, pension arrangements at the company level, and wages and flexibility issues locally. In other words, bargaining can take place both on a multi- and a single-employer basis, as well as at a range of levels within a multi-establishment organisation. Since the 1980s managements have rediscovered their prerogative (Sisson and Storey 2000) and are more prepared to make use of their superior bargaining power. Multi-employer bargaining has been replaced by single-employer bargaining, and now decentralised unit-specific arrangements associated with organisation-based employment systems are more common. In these new systems the role of the union may be marginalised as the employer focuses on direct communication with individual employees and the implementation of HR practices, such as performance-related pay, which are managerially determined. In short, the scope of managerial prerogative has been extended (Tailby and Winchester 2000; Kessler and Purcell 2003).

> Find out how pay and working conditions are determined at an organisation of your choice, and whether it has changed in the last few years? Why has it changed or why has it not changed? Review your answer after completing this section.

For a large part of this century, and certainly until the 1950s, multi-employer bargaining was considered to be the norm in the UK, and in some industries there was very little difference between the nationally negotiated wage rate and an individual's actual pay (Brown *et al* 2003). Overall, the last 20 years has seen a significant reduction in the extent of multi-employer bargaining – from 60 per cent of workplaces in 1980 to 42 per cent in 1990 and 29 per cent in 1998. Inevitably, this has been influenced by pressures from increasingly competitive international product markets, the growth in large multidivisional corporations, with profit and cost centre management and means to develop internal labour markets (Sisson and Storey 2000, p197) and the fact that trade unions have been less able to resist moves to decentralise negotiations in recent years. Government policies have also provided triggers for the abolition of multi-employer arrangements. This has occurred following the privatisation of major utilities such as water and electricity, or indirectly through the encouragement of local deals that more closely reflect company or plant-specific problems, such as in the ports following the abolition of the National Dock Labour Scheme in the late 1980s. In the public sector, privatisation and contracting-out has shrunk the range of bargaining activities. In other parts of the sector – eg teaching, local government and health care – there has been reform and in some parts of the sector pressure to decentralise pay bargaining. Within the private sector as a whole, the decline has been rather more pronounced. Multi-employer agreements have all but disappeared, and pay has been set at enterprise level by managers rather than by joint regulation (Millward *et al* 2000, p221).

A second trend has seen shifts within organisations away from centralised bargaining arrangements towards a greater emphasis on site- and unit-level negotiations. The aim has been to encourage units to take decisions themselves reflecting devolved responsibility for financial control (Sisson and Marginson 2003) although Sisson and Storey (2000, p201) note that such control is often an illusion, as key issues of employment policy may be decided at high levels in the organisation. Interest in recent years has focused on increasing the width of bargaining units, especially at workplace or company level, and the supposed attractions of single-table bargaining (STB). It is apparent that both management and unions can gain from STB. For the unions, the advent of STB can prevent 'divide and rule' tactics on the part of management and, provided the unions have clear objectives, help to develop closer working relationships and reduce the likelihood of interunion disputes. The rationalisation of unions at establishment level, whereby some of the smaller unions (in terms of membership levels at the establishments involved) lose representative rights to larger unions, can also increase the effectiveness of union organisation and cohesiveness on the ground. There is a feeling that STB deals have prevented employer-driven single union arrangements, and they have gained a measure of TUC support.

FROM INDUSTRIAL DEMOCRACY TO EMPLOYEE INVOLVEMENT

Interest in the subject of employee participation has swung dramatically over the last 30 years. The 1970s model of participation reached its high point with the 1977 Bullock Report on 'Industrial Democracy', which addressed the question of how workers might be represented at board level. This emerged in a period of strong union bargaining power and the Labour government's 'Social Contract'. The Bullock Committee's approach to industrial participation had several distinctive features. It was partly union-initiated, through the Labour Party, and based on collectivist principles that saw trade unions playing a central part in future arrangements. In addition, it was wedded to the general principle of employee rights established on a statutory basis (Ackers *et al* 1992, p272).

In contrast, the last 20 years produced a quite different agenda for participation, retitled 'employee involvement' (EI; Marchington 2005). The context initially was reduced union power and an anti-corporatist Thatcher government, which resisted statutory blueprints and encouraged firms to evolve the arrangements which best suited them. This agenda differed from that of the 1970s in several ways. First, it was management-initiated, often from outside the industrial relations sphere, and with scant reference to trade unions. Second, EI was individualist, and stressed direct communications with individual employees. Third, it was driven by business criteria concerning economic performance and the 'bottom line', with an emphasis on employee motivation and commitment (Ackers and Wilkinson 2000). Dutiful compliance and following rules no longer described the 'good worker'. Instead, management demanded employee commitment, working beyond contract and exercising initiative (Smethurst 2003). The notion of high commitment practices (see Chapter 3) made the case even more forcefully that long-term competitive advantage could only be achieved through people (Marchington and Wilkinson 2005).

Unlike notions of industrial democracy, which are rooted in ideas about employee rights, EI stemmed from an economic efficiency argument. It is seen to make business sense to involve employees, as a committed workforce is likely to understand better what the organisation is trying to do and be more prepared to contribute to its efficient operation. But management decides whether or not employees are to be involved and how they will be involved. EI in its most limited forms could be characterised as a move away from 'you will do this' to 'this is why you will do this' (Wilkinson *et al* 1993, p28). There was a sizeable growth in direct EI and communications during the 1980s as management stepped up their communication with employees as a whole (Millward *et al* 1992, p175). The 1998 WERS confirmed the growth in EI and communication (Cully *et al* 1998). Teamworking was practised in 65 per cent of all workplaces, teambriefing in 61 per cent, staff attitude survey in 45 per cent, and problem-solving groups in 42 per cent. Regular meetings of the entire workforce occurred in 37 per cent of these workplaces and were more extensive than workplace-level consultative committees (see Table 23). As in all surveys, however, this tells us relatively little about the character of EI as experienced by ordinary employees.

EI takes a number of forms in practice:

- *Downward communication* from managers to employees, the principal purpose of which is to inform and 'educate' staff so that they accept management plans. This includes techniques such as teambriefing, informal and non-routinised communications between managers and their staff, formal written media such as employee reports, house journals or company newspapers, and videos used to convey messages to employees about the organisation's financial performance or to publicise some new managerial initiative. These techniques provide employees with greater amounts of information from managers than most enjoyed previously. In theory, employers gain because employees are 'educated' about the needs of the business and utilise their greater knowledge base to improve customer service or product quality, so helping to sustain competitive advantage.

- *Upward problem-solving*, which is designed to tap into employee knowledge and opinion, either at an individual level or through small groups. The objective of these techniques is to increase the stock of ideas within an organisation, to encourage co-operative relations at work, and to legitimise change. These include quality circles, or action teams, suggestion schemes and attitude surveys (Wilkinson 2002). In theory these schemes offer employees the prospect of greater opportunities to contribute to discussions about work-related issues, and employers the possibility of higher levels of productivity and quality (Geary 2003).

- *Task participation and teamworking*, in which employees are encouraged or expected to extend the range and type of tasks undertaken at work. As with the previous categories, these are also a form of direct EI of an individualist nature, some of which have their roots in earlier quality of working life experiments in the 1960s and 1970s (Procter and Mueller 2000). Examples of task participation are horizontal job redesign, job enrichment and teamworking, each of which has figured in a number of chemical and vehicle components companies that operate their production systems on a teamwork and relatively autonomous basis. Task-based participation is probably the most innovative method of EI, given that it is focused on the whole job rather than comprising a relatively small part of an employee's time at work. In addition, unlike teambriefing or quality circles, which can be viewed as additional or incidental to working arrangements, this is integral to work itself (Geary and Dobbins 2001).

- *Financial involvement*, which encompasses schemes designed to link part of an individual's reward to the success of the unit or enterprise as a whole, has been the object of much attention since the 1980s. This takes a variety of forms in practice, ranging from profit sharing and employee share ownership schemes through to ESOPs (employee share ownership plans), which emerged in Britain in the 1980s (Pendleton 2000). Financial involvement shares similar objectives to the techniques already discussed but also operates under an assumption that employees with a financial stake in the overall success of the unit/enterprise are more likely to work harder for its ultimate success.

Thus EI schemes can be seen as a rejection of the classical school of management which emphasised a strict division of labour, with workers as 'machine minders', carrying out fragmented and repetitive jobs (Wilkinson 1998). They imply a neo-unitarist, win–win approach, which is moralistic in tone, and is 'represented as squaring the circle of organisational needs for high levels of employee performance and employees' demands for autonomy and self-expression in work' (Claydon and Doyle 1996, p13).

An example of a company where EI has been successfully implemented is given in Box 36 on page 284.

There is a danger that these programmes are viewed solely in a positive and upbeat manner, so ignoring the more contested and mundane nature of much participation. For example, rather than leading to autonomy and self-management, it may merely produce greater work intensification, increased stress levels and redundancies (Wilkinson 2002). There is a fear that employers are exchanging strong union-centred forms of participation for EI initiatives that are 'weak on power'. As one HR manager noted in a recent study, 'there are plenty of vehicles for staff to have a voice, but the question is whether his voice is being heard and whether action is being taken as a result of this. And that's debatable' (Marchington *et al* 2001, p24).

BOX 36   MIDBANK

Midbank is a clearing bank with regional roots employing around 4000 staff in over 100 locations in the UK. Like most financial institutions, the company provides HR support from a centralised base although many HR processes have been devolved to line managers. The small size of the branches facilitates a more informal atmosphere than in the call centres. New performance management tools have recently been agreed with the union for the call centres and their introduction has provided better terms and conditions, and resulted in reduced turnover, increased productivity and improved career progression.

A single union has sole negotiating rights for staff and membership is well over 70 per cent. Union presence in the workplace is in the form of local representatives as well as one full-time seconded representative. National joint partnership meetings are held monthly, supported by local and departmental partnership forums between the union and management representatives. These local forums concentrate on resolving local business-related matters thereby enabling the national partnership team to concentrate on wider issues. A separate consultation forum is the company's Staff Council, which enables elected representatives from all areas of the business to meet with senior managers to discuss bank-wide business related matters. There is also a well-established quarterly company newspaper, to which staff are encouraged to contribute. Attitude surveys, focus groups and suggestion schemes – one member of staff recently received £25,000 – are also regular features. Midbank's partnership approach commits it to measuring and reporting on issues that staff themselves identify as important.

As a result, Midbank recently won a *Sunday Times* award for its commitment to best practice HRM and employee involvement.

What purpose do these different forms of EI serve? Identify ways in which this practice could be improved.

The rise of EI has coincided with the decline of indirect, representative participation such as joint consultative committees (JCCs), which were found in under a third of all workplaces in 1998, being especially prevalent in the public service sector (Millward *et al* 2000, p109). Unlike the methods of direct EI discussed in the previous section, JCCs are built upon the notion of indirect participation and worker representation in joint management–employee meetings. The scope of joint consultation is typically wider than collective bargaining – and may, for instance, include financial matters – although the issues discussed are not formally negotiated. For some, they represent a diluted form of collective bargaining, and the shift in interest towards consultation reflects a decline in collectivism. However, JCCs can take a number of forms, often contrasting sharply with each other in terms of their objectives, structures and processes. Some researchers suggest that joint consultation has been revitalised in order to cover issues traditionally dealt with through collective bargaining, and involve stewards more closely with management issues in order to convince them of the 'logic' of their decisions. Others have argued that the committees have largely been concerned with trivia and are thus marginal to the employee relations processes of the organisation. Consequently, in some organisations JCCs can act as a safety valve (ie an alternative to industrial action) through which to address more deep-seated employee grievances, while in others they can be used as a device to hinder the recognition of trade unions or undermine their activities in highly unionised workplaces. In yet others they may be irrelevant to management–employee relations, merely existing as a forum to debate various forms of trivia. The relationship between collective bargaining and joint consultation in unionised workplaces can be a source of tension, particularly if management is trying to 'edge out' the unions and there has been a failure to engage in meaningful consultations

EMPLOYEE VOICE AND SOCIAL PARTNERSHIP

Recent research by Dundon *et al* (2004) and Wilkinson *et al* (2004) examined worker 'voice' – this was the term used to describe a forum of two-way dialogue, in preference to other terminology such as 'consultation', 'communication' or 'say'. Voice potentially allows staff to influence events at work, and can bring together collective and individual techniques into one framework. HR managers typically play an important role in the choices made about employee voice, in identifying the options available, forming alliances with line managers and devising strategies for implementation. Generally a broad mix of factors shaped management choice. For some managers the idea of rational choice was often related to satisfying employee expectations, particularly when faced with tight labour markets. Other respondents equated choice with their own understanding of corporate and organisational objectives. In the smaller and family-run enterprises this related to the personal styles and characteristics of owner-managers. A further group of managers made the point that in reality they had no choice, either because employees demanded 'a say' or due to market pressures and new legislative requirements. On the whole, however, management decide whether or not workers have a voice, and it is managers rather than employees who decide what mechanisms to utilise. Box 37 (page 286) discusses three barriers to voice.

Different external influences shaped management choice, evident across both large and small as well as single- and multi-site organisations. Legislation for trade union recognition or the requirement to establish a European Works Council (EWC; see below) is one pressure, meaning that choices are made merely to comply with new or forthcoming legislation. However, in a broader context, the research found that external influences also open up new options for managers, and regulation seemed to encourage more creative managerial thinking about the choices available. Box 38 (page 287) shows examples of worker voice in one organisation.

The research by Dundon *et al* (2004) on employee voice also found that it could have a positive impact, in three general ways. The first is valuing employee contributions. This might lead to improved employee attitudes and behaviours, loyalty, commitment and co-operative relations. The second impact relates to improved performance, including productivity and individual performance, lower absenteeism and (in a few cases) new business arising from employee voice. The final impact relates to improved managerial systems. This incorporates the managerial benefits from tapping into employee ideas, the informative and educational role of voice along with improved relations with recognised trade unions.

Using the WERS data, Bryson (2004) finds that direct voice is associated with better employee perceptions of managerial responsiveness than an absence of all voice mechanisms and either non-union representative voice or union representation. However, the combination of direct and non-union representative voice has the strongest effects. Union voice is not associated generally with perceptions of managerial responsiveness, but direct voice mechanisms are associated with perceptions of greater managerial responsiveness

BOX 37   BARRIERS TO EMPLOYEE VOICE

CIPD research (Marchington *et al* 2001; Ackers *et al* 2005) identified three particular barriers to employee voice – a partial lack of employee enthusiasm, an absence of necessary skills, and issues concerning line managers. In a few of the case studies employees lacked enthusiasm to participate in voice arrangements. At some of the larger and multi-site organisations, managers noted that while employees demanded a greater say it was not always borne out in practice. At Airflight, management had to work hard to get representatives involved in the employee consultative forum, and at Midbank some staff council seats were unfilled. There was also an issue of low employee response rates to surveys in some organisations that made it difficult to interpret employee voice. Of course, much depends on managerial support for voice and the range of issues open to employees. Thus a lack of employee interest in voice may be to do with the specific mechanisms in place rather than a generalised disinterest in voice *per se*.

There was evidence that some managers lacked the necessary skills to implement and manage employee voice programmes, and this seems a more important barrier than a lack of employee enthusiasm. The view was expressed, mainly among larger and multi-site establishments, that voice needed to be built up gradually, as individuals' confidence and skills developed.

Related to the issue of available skills and competencies is the role of middle managers. In several organisations support for employee voice from the top was critical. In a majority of cases, middle managers acted as a blockage either through choice or ignorance. In several organisations line managers viewed HR issues as secondary to operational matters. However, unlike earlier studies on employee involvement, this report identifies a major cultural change over time. The generation of 'cops' and 'giving orders' had much diminished and the departure of the old guard through restructuring and redundancy was a feature at several sites. It was also apparent that the use of new technology and electronic forms of employee voice allowed employers to bypass middle managers more easily.

Source: Adapted from Ackers P., Marchington M., Wilkinson A. and Dundon T. 'Partnership and voice, with or without trade unions: changing UK management approaches to organisational participation', in M. Stuart and M. Martinez-Lucio (eds), *Partnership and Modernisation in Employment Relations*. London, Routledge. 2005

even among unionised workers. The negative union effects are strongest where the union representative is part-time, and Bryson suggests that union representation raises expectations but is unable to achieve their goals due to time constraints. The results are no different when the managerial responsiveness is analysed by separating information sharing and consultation on the one hand and on the other measuring grievance concerns. One might expect the HR practices such as direct voice to affect the first with unions more effective in the latter. However, in both cases direct voice tends to be positively associated with perceptions of managerial responsiveness, and part-time union representation tends to be negatively associated (Bryson 2004).

The public policy context has changed markedly in recent years through the development of social partnership, and this has led to a revival of representative participation. The European Union concept of social dialogue centres on partnership between employers and employees,

BOX 38   EI AND DELTA AIRLINES

Delta Airlines traditionally had an employment strategy focused on customer service and positive employment practices in order to foster co-operation through non-union relations. In the 1990s competitive pressures led to wage cuts and downsizing. Out of this crisis came an EI programme designed to provide pilots with a non-voting seat on the Board of Director in exchange for contract concessions. While EI had not been originally part of the paternalistic family model it became central to the new competitive strategy.

The new EI infrastructure has three main components:

1   At the top level is the Delta Board Council, which provides employee input at the Board and top executive level on the entire spectrum of business and HR issues facing the company.

2   The middle level is composed of five division-level employee councils. Each forum/council deals with issues that affect operations and employees of the specific division (such as on-board passenger service, work schedules for flight attendants, training requirements and engine overhaul cycle time for mechanics).

3   At the bottom of the organisational pyramid are two major EI groups. The first is over 100 small-scale 'continuous improvement teams', which are convened as needed by either management or employees. They are usually 6–10 people in size, and focus on work-process improvements. Team members volunteer and rotate on an informal basis. Complementing these, but with a broader focus and mandate, are employee councils at the individual base, station or hub facility.

The Delta EI programme is supplemented with a variety of other initiatives. For example, twice a year a large group – including 200 front-line employees – from around the world are invited to attend a 'State of the Company Leadership Meeting'. The President and the top executive team attend and are available to answer questions following presentations. Other important events include the monthly CEO forum at which eight employees get to talk to the President for 90 minutes; and a monthly presidential breakfast at which the President and CEO provide a company update and answers questions for 80 employees.

Source: Adapted from Kaufman B. 'High-level employee involvement in Delta Airlines, *Human Resource Management*, Vol. 42, No. 2, 2003. pp175–190

through representative bodies, such as trades unions and works councils. It also advocates participation as an extension of employee citizenship rights and not just business expedience. Ferner and Hyman (1998) suggest social partnership has three characteristics: it acknowledges that workers have different interests from managers, it encourages their representation and it believes such an approach can be effective in regulating work and the labour market. Partnership can also be viewed at different levels – for example, European, national state, sectoral and enterprise level – but the focus here is at enterprise level, because the UK lacks the institutional and legislative support afforded in most other Western European nations (Haynes and Allen 2001; Heery 2002; Terry 2003). Of course, the idea of 'enlightened' consensual relations and co-operation is not new, but draws from a long history of modernisation in British industrial relations (Coupar and Stevens 1998; Martinez-Lucio and Stuart 2002; McBride and Stirling 2002).

Of course, interest in partnership did not occur in a political vacuum. The election of New Labour in 1997 and their 'Third Way' principles supposedly represented an alternative to adversarialism, and there has also been more active engagement in European social policy (Ackers *et al* 2005). Despite the ongoing debate in policy and academic circles, views on partnership remain divided. Firms enter partnerships for a variety of reasons. These include: financial problems, to win public sector contracts, facilitate change, implement quality initiatives or harmonise terms and conditions (Brown 2000; Oxenbridge and Brown 2004). While proponents predict mutual gains for all stakeholders (most notably Kochan and Osterman 1994), critics suggest that the benefits are elusive at best. Advocates suggest that employers may benefit from employee commitment, input from a new cadre of representatives, improved relations with unions and the facilitation of change. In turn, unions may benefit from more influence, access to information, job security and interunion co-operation. Partnership may offer a more favourable terrain offering unions a new role as joint architects, in contrast to earlier attempts to ignore and erode unions. Employees are also argued to benefit from greater job security, training, quality jobs, good communication and a more effective voice (Kochan and Osterman 1994; TUC 1999; Guest and Peccei 2001). The TUC claim that unions have a significant value-adding role, contributing to improved organisational performance, facilitating change, improved decision-making and creating a more committed workforce. It is argued, for example, that partnership workplaces are one third more likely to have above average performance, as well as lower labour turnover and absenteeism, and higher sales and profits (TUC 2002). Business benefits are argued to include greater productivity and an indirect link between partnership practice and organisational performance (Guest and Peccei 2001). The British government has also begun to promote the link between workplace consultation, high performance workplaces etc and organisational performance and competitiveness (DTI 2002b). Figure 11 shows the benefits of a good working environment.

However, some commentators are more sceptical. It has been argued that some employers may view partnership as another union 'Trojan horse' and express a preference for free labour markets and individualisation of the employment relationship (Claydon 1998). Managers may also be concerned that partnership may slow down decision-making, incur extra costs, and challenge managerial prerogative. Some argue that partnership may be a pragmatic management decision rather than evidence of a commitment to working with unions, as managers decide to 'involve' unions but only within strictly defined parameters (Ackers *et al* 2005). Critics also suggest that the British business environment and structure of corporate governance focuses on short-term performance, meaning there is less incentive to engage in long-term partnerships (Deakin *et al* 2004). Equally, trade unionists may have concerns regarding becoming too close to management, being party to unpopular decisions, or having only limited influence over management decision-making. Blurring of the traditional union role may also create unease and some argue that a union moderation strategy may lead to an inability of union members to resist management (Johnstone *et al* 2004).

Despite this an increasing number of organisations responded to the new public policy framework, for example, Welsh Water, Blue Circle, Tesco, Legal & General, Aer Rianta and the Co-operative Bank all struck voluntary partnership deals with trade unions. Others, like the non-union Marks & Spencer, have had to accept EWCs. British Airways, following the 1997 industrial dispute, also issued a statement about the principles of partnership. By and large these agreements balance the EI agenda, with a greater emphasis on employment security and employee representation through consultative committees and trade unions. The price for the latter is to shun adversarial bargaining and reactive conflict for consultation and

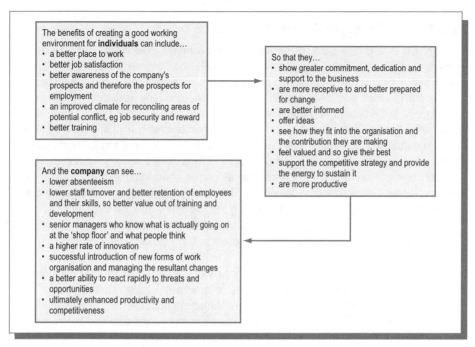

The benefits of creating a good working
environment for **individuals** can include...
- a better place to work
- better job satisfaction
- better awareness of the company's
  prospects and therefore the prospects for
  employment
- an improved climate for reconciling areas of
  potential conflict, eg job security and reward
- better training

So that they...
- show greater commitment, dedication and
  support to the business
- are more receptive to and better prepared
  for change
- are better informed
- offer ideas
- see how they fit into the organisation and
  the contribution they are making
- feel valued and so give their best
- support the competitive strategy and provide
  the energy to sustain it
- are more productive

And the **company** can see...
- lower absenteeism
- lower staff turnover and better retention of employees
  and their skills, so better value out of training and
  development
- senior managers who know what is actually going on
  at the 'shop floor' and what people think
- a higher rate of innovation
- successful introduction of new forms of work
  organisation and managing the resultant changes
- a better ability to react rapidly to threats and
  opportunities
- ultimately enhanced productivity and
  competitiveness

Figure 11 *Benefits of a good working environment*

Source: Department of Trade and Industry. *High Performance Workplaces: A discussion paper.* London, DTI. 2002b.
p16

proactive co-operation, following the trade union style of Scandinavia and Germany. The TUC
and the Involvement and Participation Association (IPA) have promoted a more positive-sum
relationship between trade unions and management which transcends 'arms-length
adversarialism' and connects representative and direct forms of participation based on trust
(Ackers and Wilkinson 2000; Guest and Peccei 2001; Dietz 2004). A practical manifestation
of this is the TUC's positive attitude to EWCs, despite their potentially non-union character
(see Monks 1998). Finally, according to work by Wood and Fenton O'Creevy (1999, p44),
multinationals that relied *only* on direct EI involved their employees less than those prepared
to also consult or negotiate. While the union was the channel for only a limited number of
issues, the overall level of involvement was still higher on average in unionised operations.
This may be because unions put managers under pressure to inform and consult via other
channels or because management involves staff in other channels in order to counter or
bypass the union. A third possibility is that management that is favourably inclined towards
unions is more likely to be well disposed to other forms of EI as well. In any case, employees
enjoyed more genuine participation when trade unions were present. Whether partnership will
provide the way forward remains to be seen. One company's experience of trade union
partnership is given in Box 39 on page 290.

In some cases unions have little alternative but to go along with partnership or face de facto
derecognition and exclusion (Haynes and Allen 2001; Ackers *et al* 2005). The work of
Danford *et al* (2003) concludes that there was little evidence of mutual gains, and suggests
that employees actually experienced work intensification, task accretion and increased job
insecurity. Kelly (2004) reports that these companies with partnership agreements shed jobs
faster in industries suffering decline while partnership firms in growth job industries created
jobs faster. Partnerships had no impact on wage settlements, annual holidays or union

BOX 39   PARTNERSHIP AT ENERGY CO

Energy Co is a British utility group serving over 3 million customers, and employing around 16,000 staff. Following privatisation in 1991 industrial relations in their highly unionised Generation Division were poor, characterised by antagonistic management–union relations, protracted pay negotiations and resistance to change. Employees in the division are predominantly male and power station-based, most have worked for Energy Co for over 20 years and union membership is high at around 90%. In 1995 a partnership agreement was signed between the division and the four recognised trade unions (GMB, EMA, AEEU and Unison). It was hailed as 'a new approach to relationships at work which recognises that all parties – management, staff and trade unions – have many common interests'. The founding principles of the agreement included explicit commitments to recognising the legitimate role of trade unions, and promoting issues such as employment security, information and consultation, flexibility, responsiveness to change, environmental awareness and employee development.

Management supported partnership in the hope that it might improve the beleaguered industrial relations climate, raise employee commitment, inform and educate the workforce and increase employee contribution. Management made clear that partnership was not, however, intended to facilitate joint-governance or power sharing. One manager suggested 'Partnership in its purest form within the business is a written agreement between unions and management about how we manage industrial relations, while in a broader sense it is about empowering staff, and how we work on a day-to-day basis'. In practice, the partnership combines direct employee involvement (EI) mechanisms such as teambriefing, problem-solving groups, newspapers and attitude surveys with representative participation through a formal partnership council system. Each site has a Local Partnership Council, consisting of management and union representatives which meets every two months. In addition, there is a business wide Generation Partnership Council which holds quarterly meetings and reports directly to the Company Council.

Management felt that, on balance, partnership has been successful, with benefits including improved industrial relations, quicker pay negotiations and increased legitimacy of decision-making. It was also suggested that there was a positive link – albeit indirect and intangible – with organisational performance. Union representatives thought that partnership was a success, citing benefits including greater access to information, greater influence, interunion co-operation, and more local decision-making. Employee views were heterogeneous. Supporters proposed that partnership had brought benefits including better decision-making, quicker pay negotiations, greater employee involvement and a more open management style. Critics suggested that feedback from the representatives was poor, union influence had been diluted, and that the partnership council only dealt with trivia.

Despite the generally positive assessments of most managers and union representatives, there were four main tensions evident within the partnership relationship. Firstly, employee apathy was a barrier with many employees unconvinced that their input would make a difference to final decisions. Secondly, management–representative relations were stressed, with evidence of a lack of trust and a failure to fully overcome traditional adversarial relationships and attitudes. Some managers admitted a personal preference for non-union employment relations, while most representatives expressed concern that

Energy Co was unwilling to expand partnership across the entire organisation. Thirdly, partnership created new tensions between representatives and employees, again highlighting the need for high levels of trust. In particular greater access to sensitive business information proved a double-edged sword for representatives. On the one hand, it was intended to allow them to be better informed with regard to business decisions, but the asymmetry of information led some employees to become suspicious of their representatives. Lastly, the role of full-time officers was significant with some FTOs believing they had been excluded since partnership, as the nature of the agreement meant that they were less involved in day-to-day issues, and had become a point of contact only when lay representatives had specific problems. From the union perspective, they may have lost visibility and a valuable marketing opportunity as a result.

Source: Johnstone S., Wilkinson A. and Ackers P. 'Partnership paradoxes: a case study of an energy company', *Employee Relations*, Vol. 26, No. 4, 2004. pp353–376

density and Kelly concludes they were unlikely to figure as a major component of union revitalisation. Guest and Peccei (2001) found that the balance of advantage in partnership was often skewed towards management. They concluded that a lack of trust between parties was often a barrier to effective partnership relationships. More positively, studies at Aer Rianta, Tesco and Legal & General have highlighted potential benefits for unions and employees (Haynes and Allen 2001; Roche and Geary 2002). Oxenbridge and Brown (2004), however, identified a continuum of potential employment relations outcomes, arguing that the consequences are less black-and-white than the polarised debate implies (Johnstone *et al* 2004).

An important contemporary issue is the European Works Council (EWC) Directive. The centralist philosophy underpinning this initiative is in sharp contrast to the voluntarist traditions that governed employee relations for many years. The EWC Directive requires employers to set up an EWC or equivalent information and consultation procedure if they have at least 1000 employees within the states covered by the directive (including at least 150 employees in at least two of these countries). There is scope for the negotiation of customised agreements, but in the event of failure to agree, a standard package will apply. In broad terms this provides a template for the composition of the EWC and its remit, as well as a stipulation that an annual meeting should take place. The EWC is informed and consulted about the enterprise's progress and prospects in a number of areas, including the broad financial and employment situation, as well as trends in employment and substantial changes in working methods.

The Directive seeks to ensure that employees in large and medium-sized multinational organisations are informed and consulted about the organisations where they work. Some see this Directive as one of the most far-reaching and important developments in European industrial relations, while others regard it as far too weak to make any substantial difference. On the positive side EWCs have been seen as an opportunity for management to communicate corporate strategy, to facilitate discussion of change, to encourage international contact, to facilitate employee identification with the company, build a 'European' culture and to enhance management–union partnerships. Trade unions and employee representatives in turn gain access to useful company information to facilitate collective bargaining (Cressey 1998). Trade union criticisms have centred on the limited capacity of EWCs to effectively influence managerial prerogative in multinational companies. Some research reports employers paying lip service to their EWCs – for example announcing major plant closures within days of a EWC meeting at which there was no discussion of such issues (Stirling and Fitzgerald 2001). Criticism from employers have been that EWCs have not added any value to their pre-existing employee involvement practices but have merely added another layer to the communication process. New EWCs in particular face a number of challenges to their effectiveness. They are being introduced in a very competitive and fast-moving marketplace with organisational restructuring involving mergers, acquisitions, joint ventures and divestments giving rise to problems of continuity for EWCs. EWC delegates also face difficulties in setting up effective communication and reporting back systems to inform those whom they represent about issues arising in discussions (Redman 2002, pp81–82; Hall *et al* 2003).

The Europeanisation of British industrial relations is set to continue as the Directive on Information and Consultation starts to be phased in from 2005. This provides employees with rights to be informed about the economic structures for the organisation, and informed and consulted with a view to reaching an agreement on decisions likely to lead to substantial changes in work organisations or contractual relations (Gollan and Perkins 2002). This would create a universal right to representation, which in turn creates opportunities for unions. At this stage, it is not clear whether this will provide the basis for a move towards comprehensive employee representation structures – such as through works councils – in the UK, and bring together the existing disparate range of EI mechanisms (Dickens and Hall 2003, p143).

> Do you think that employers have much to fear from the Information and Consultation Directive? What impact would the directive have on your organisation or one with which you are familiar?

CONCLUSIONS

It is important to reiterate that employee relations, like all aspects of HRM, is characterised by conflict and co-operation. At certain times, and in certain workplaces, one of these assumes predominance. This sometimes gives the misguided impression that employee relations at one site or at one point in time is solely about conflict, whereas at other establishments or times it is seen only in terms of co-operation. Furthermore, just because conflict is not expressed overtly, this does not mean that it is absent, and neither can it be assumed that the workplace is a haven of consent.

It would appear that employee relations is becoming increasingly bifurcated, not so much between union and non-union organisations, but within each of these broad categories. Given the degree to which labour markets have been deregulated over the last 20 years, employers now have greater flexibility in choosing appropriate styles and structures for managing employee relations, as well as a greater opportunity to integrate people management strategies with those affecting the business as a whole. To do this effectively, however, requires employers to embrace a more strategic and externally focused approach to the management of employee relations, to be aware of the techniques which are adopted by other employers, and to disregard the latest fads and fashions if these are inappropriate for their own workplace. How many do this, of course, is another question.

It should be clear from this chapter that the 'rules' of employee relations can be made and influenced in many ways. Although most analyses have focused on collective bargaining as the main rule-making institution, it must not be forgotten that some rules are made unilaterally by managements. The various WERS surveys clearly chart the decline in the collective institutions of joint regulation. However, these do not appear to have been replaced by any single new model of employee relations, but rather alternative approaches in different workplaces in different parts of the country.

Despite the decline in union influence, Cully *et al* (1999, p296) note that 'an engagement with a union presence is still part of the work experience for two out of three employees, even if only half that number are actually union members'. However, the representation gap identified by Towers (1997) has certainly increased since 1990. As Cully *et al* (p297) note there was an enormous gap between the percentage of workplace management who said they consulted employees about changes at the workplace (70 per cent) and the percentage of employees who agree with them (30 per cent). Millward *et al* (2000, p135) point out that while employees may not have lost their 'voice', the notion of voice had changed significantly. There has been a major shift from channels involving representatives – usually able to call upon the resources of independent trade unions – to channels where managers communicate directly with employees as and when they see fit. But they also note that 'the combined presence of a recognised trade union and union representation on a formal consultative committee was the only formulation to be independently associated with employees' perceptions of fair treatment by managers' (p137).

In this chapter we have sought to emphasise that patterns of collective bargaining vary greatly between workplaces and between organisations, and that HR managers are able to exercise some degree of choice and influence over their eventual shape. In order to do this, however, HR practitioners need to be aware of the different types of bargaining arrangement that exist, and their suitability for particular organisational contexts. It is important not to be seduced by the latest fads and fashions, but to make informed decisions about which bargaining levels and units are most appropriate for each employment situation. Similar options are also available for the mix of EI arrangements that might 'fit' with the needs of employers as well.

USEFUL READING

BACON N. 'Employee relations', in T. REDMAN *and* A. WILKINSON (eds), *Contemporary Human Resource Management*. London, Financial Times/Prentice Hall. 2001.

BLYTON P. *and* TURNBULL P. *The Dynamics of Employee Relations*, 3rd edition. London, Macmillan. 2004.

DIETZ, G. 'Partnership and the development of trust in British workplaces', *Human Resource Management Journal*, Vol. 14, No. 1, 2004. pp5–24.

DUNDON T., WILKINSON A., MARCHINGTON M. *and* ACKERS P. 'The meaning and purpose of employee voice', *International Journal of Human Resource Management*, Vol. 15, No. 6, 2004. pp1149–1170.

GENNARD J. *and* JUDGE G. *Employee Relations*, 3rd edition. London, CIPD. 2002.

GUEST D. *and* PECCEI R. 'Partnership at work: mutuality and the balance of advantage', *British Journal of Industrial Relations*, Vol. 39, No. 2, 2001. pp207–236.

MARCHINGTON M., WILKINSON A., ACKERS P. *and* DUNDON A. *Management Choice and Employee Voice*. London, CIPD. 2001.

SMETHURST S. 'Empowerment: blood and simple', *People Management*, 20 March 2003. pp42–44.

WILKINSON A. 'Empowerment', in T. REDMAN *and* A. WILKINSON (eds), *Contemporary Human Resource Management*. London, Financial Times/Pitman, 2001. pp336–352.

Procedures and Workplace Employee Relations

CHAPTER 11

INTRODUCTION

Policies and procedures are defined as 'formal, conscious statements' that support organisational goals. They are the official way companies disseminate their policies as the leitmotif of acceptable practice (Sisson and Storey 2000). However, there is a difference between a 'policy' and a 'procedure'. As Dundon (2002c, pp196–197) notes:

> Policies are written documents that outline defined rules, obligations and expectations for managers and employees. Typically, policy statements cover areas such as discipline, grievance, redundancy, reward, recruitment or promotion. The policy may be a statement of intent, such as "it is the policy of this company to promote and reward high achievers".
>
> Procedures outline the details of how to enact a policy. For example, having a policy of "rewarding high achievers" would require some guidance on how managers implement the policy, such as the criteria for promotion or how much they can reward an individual. Similarly, a discipline procedure would outline possible sanctions, areas of conduct and so on.

The scope and depth of HR policies and procedures can be used as a proxy for management style. The absence of policies and procedures can indicate an informal managerial approach, whereas very detailed policies and procedures could point to a formalised managerial style. Procedures are often seen as a product of the employee relations environment of the 1960s and 1970s in which there was a more explicit struggle for control at the workplace. This had two principal effects. First, it produced the need for clear procedures so that all employees were aware of works rules and the action that could be taken against them if these rules were flouted. Second, it made for greater clarity and consistency in management action.

In contrast, the environment today is one in which trade unions are weaker, and managers have greater freedom to avoid some of the so-called 'bureaucratic' rules which supposedly constrained their ability to manage. Moreover, as the principal activities of many HR practitioners have shifted away from employee relations to employee development, employee resourcing and employee reward, the main guides to management action are seen as business need, flexibility and commitment rather than adherence to rules and procedures (Storey 2001). Previous appeals to consistency, compromise and regulations have been displaced by a new language of competitiveness, customers and commitment. Storey's classic research (1992, p178) highlighted the following criticisms of procedures:

> From the hard side of [HRM] comes the criticism that the long drawn out appeals and referrals are simply inappropriate in a fiercely competitive and fast-changing climate. From the soft side ... the regulator's arguments about due process and about honouring agreements and observing custom and practice are anathema.

However, this interpretation contains a number of problems. It is by no means obvious that an emphasis on rules and procedures is outdated. Indeed, a belief in consistency and fairness is central to gaining the commitment of employees in any organisation (Bott 2003). Indeed, what may appear as flexibility to managers may seem unfair and arbitrary treatment to an employee. As Renwick and Gennard (2001, p168) observe:

> That there *are* [original emphasis] issues surrounding grievance and discipline handling in the workplace is a logical consequence of the employment relationship itself. Not all the interests of both employers and employees necessarily coincide, and inappropriate actions and transgressions on either side raise the issue of the satisfactory resolution of those differences within the parameters of both the organisational context and the law. These interests are expressed in both parties' rights and responsibilities to each other in legal contracts of employment.

In both hard and soft approaches to HRM, there is a case for using procedures to ensure consistency, equity and fairness. These take different forms (Bott 2003, p309):

- Those which are jointly entered into by management and employee representatives, often called 'procedural agreements'. Examples include negotiating procedures, recognition agreements and procedures designed to avoid or resolve collective disputes.
- Those created and imposed by management unilaterally. Examples may include equal opportunities, discipline and grievance handling and managing redundancies.
- Those prescribed by legislation, or guidance contained in Codes of Practice, and case law. Examples include statutory union recognition, disclosure of information and health and safety matters.

This chapter examines the role of procedures in the management of HR, provides guidance on assessment and looks at how procedures are designed and operated.

By the end of the chapter, readers should be able to:

- **devise procedures that help to achieve fairness and consistency at work**
- **advise line managers on how to handle disciplinary and grievance cases**
- **work in partnership with other managers during the collective bargaining process.**

In addition readers should understand and be able to explain:

■ **the value of procedures in helping to create a positive psychological contract**

■ **the principal components of, and differences between, disciplinary and grievance procedures**

■ **the way in which HR specialists may provide support for line managers in operating procedures.**

THE NATURE AND EXTENT OF PROCEDURES

A government social survey in 1969 found only 8 per cent of the establishments operated a formal disciplinary and dismissal procedure. The Donovan Commission (1968, p30) took up the cause of procedural reform, wanting 'procedures which are clear where the present procedures are vague, comprehensive where the present procedures are fragmented, speedy where the present procedures are protracted, and effective where the present procedures are fruitless'. It was felt that a lack of proper procedures was a major cause of industrial disputes and the procedures – if followed – would stabilise employee relations (Scott *et al* 1989, p97; Marlow 2002; Dundon and Wilkinson 2003).

There is evidence that procedural reform has taken place, at least formally. 'The 1970s saw a massive spread of formal disciplinary and dismissal procedures across British industry and commerce', so that by the 1980s they had become 'almost universal in all but the smallest workplaces' (Millward *et al* 1992, p212). Over 90 per cent of workplaces have disciplinary and grievance procedures. Even in smaller workplaces (25–49 employees) 88 per cent have a disciplinary procedure and 87 per cent have a grievance procedure (Cully *et al* 1998, p14). Part of this growth has been caused by the increasing involvement of the law. The Industrial Relations Act 1971 first introduced the notion of unfair dismissal, since then there has been considerable formalisation, largely due to the growth in cases being taken to employment tribunals. Earnshaw *et al* (2000) note that research in the 1970s and 1980s reported considerable employer hostility to procedures among small business owners. However, this was much less apparent by the end of the 1990s. They conclude that the unfair dismissal legislation – now in operation for over 30 years – as well as the emphasis given by tribunals to procedural matters have helped bring about attitudinal change. There are now frequent references made to the benefits such procedures have for managers (such as clarifying authority, indicating processes to be followed) and greater managerial acceptance.

A procedure agreement can be defined as 'a set of rules whose purpose is to influence the behaviour of management, employees and trade union representatives in a defined situation. The rules are, in effect, an agreed code of voluntary restraints on the use of power' (Hawkins 1979, p132). Procedures can be adopted in a number of different areas:

■ *Recognition* – specifying the rights of unions to recruit, organise and represent defined groups of staff in the workplace. Details may be included covering bargaining units and the facilities for, and duties of, shop stewards.

■ *Disputes* – indicating the route to be followed in the event of a collective or departmental issue, including reference to agreements between employers' organisations and trade unions.

■ *Grievance* – indicating what is to be done in the event of an individual issue or complaint.

- *Disciplinary* – setting the standards of conduct expected from employees, specifying what is to be done following behaviour or conduct that is deemed unsatisfactory.

- *Redundancy* – specifying the organisation's approach to consultation about redundancy, methods of selection, compensation and assistance in finding other employment.

- *Equal opportunities* – outlining the organisation's commitment to, and provision of, equal opportunities regardless of gender, race or disability.

Of course, this list is not exhaustive but merely indicative of the most common procedure agreements (see also Farnham 2000, pp76–81). The main objective of any procedure is to establish an agreed set of rules so as to channel any discussion or discontent through the appropriate mechanisms for its resolution. However, it is important to remember what procedures cannot do. Thomson and Murray (1976, p84) note that a procedure 'cannot solve the underlying causes of conflict ... it is very limited in the extent to which it can institutionalise conflict if there is not a basic consensus about the legitimacy of the roles of the parties. It cannot itself make up for deficiencies in the structure of the relationship.'

> Write down three procedures operating at your workplace and explain their purpose. How successful are they in meeting their purpose?

In relation to equal opportunities, the WERS data (Cully *et al* 1998, p13) is enlightening. 'One way in which employers may strive to give practical effect to these laws is by establishing policies and practices designed to combat discrimination and promote equal treatment.' Some two-thirds of workplaces (64 per cent) are covered by formal written equal opportunity policies addressing equality of treatment or discrimination. The areas covered by such policies include sex (98 per cent), race (98 per cent), disability (93 per cent), religion (84 per cent), marital status (73 per cent) and age (67 per cent). Of the workplaces without a formal written policy, half claimed that they had one, but that it was not written down or that they were aiming to be an equal opportunity employer. In a third of workplaces without a policy, managers saw them as unnecessary. A further 2 per cent said that they did not need a policy as their workplace employed few or no people from disadvantaged groups! There is also a relationship with size – workplaces without a policy were predominantly small. Larger units increase the complexity of the management task and 'The more complex the management task, the greater the need for rules and procedures to achieve consistency of behaviour on the part of individual managers. The greater the need for rules and procedures, the greater the need for workers and workers' representatives to accept this legitimacy' (p14). In Table 25, Cully *et al* compare practices employed at workplaces with and without a policy. It is clear that those workplaces with a *formal* equal opportunities policy are much more likely to have a range of procedures and practices to support equal treatment.

Small firms are less likely to have formal policies in place. Owners rarely possess the specialist knowledge to construct such policies or the inclination/resources to employ professionals for this task. The owner is likely to work alongside or in close proximity to employees as well as actually managing the employment relationship (Ram 1994). This is advantageous in creating an environment of 'teamwork' (Goss 1991) but the team analogy is vulnerable when ownership authority must be reinforced. Evidence would indicate that, rather than risk disrupting the 'team' environment, small firm owners resist using formal policy or practice, preferring instead a negotiated solution to employment-related issues, which avoids overt conflict or workplace dissonance (Marlow 2002). This informality is now being tested by

Table 25 *Equal treatment practices, by formal equal opportunities policy*

	% of workplaces	
	Formal equal opportunities policy	No policy
Keep employee records with ethnic origin identified	48	13
Collect statistics on posts held by men and women	43	13
Monitor promotions by gender and ethnicity	23	2
Review selection procedures to identify indirect discrimination	35	5
Review the relative pay rates of different groups	17	15
Make adjustments to accommodate disabled employees	42	16
None of these	27	67

Base: all workplaces with 25 or more employees.
Source: Cully M., Woodland S., O'Reilly A., Dix G., Millward N., Bryson A. and Forth, J. *The 1998 Workplace Employee Relations Survey: First findings*. London, Department of Trade and Industry. 1998. p13

European Directives and recent employment legislation that challenges the way the typical small firm manages its labour (Marlow 2002, p27).

THE CASE FOR PROCEDURES

There are a number of reasons why employers implement employee relations procedures (Bott 2003). These are:

- They help to clarify the relationship between the two parties and recognise explicitly the right of employees to raise grievances. This helps to focus conflict within agreed mechanisms and facilitates its resolution. In short, it can create a framework for good employee relations.

- They provide a mechanism for resolution by identifying the individuals or post-holders to whom the issue should be taken initially, and by specifying the route to be followed should there be a failure to agree at that level.

- They act as a safety-valve and provide time within which to assess the issue that has been raised. It can consequently 'take the heat out of the situation' by providing time to reflect.

- They help to ensure greater consistency within the organisation. They can reduce reliance on word of mouth or custom and practice, and minimise arbitrary treatment.

- They lead to more systematic record-keeping, and consequently to improved management control and information systems.

- If written down, applied appropriately, and meet the criteria of natural justice, they are important in employment tribunal cases.

■ The process of drawing up procedures involves both parties working together to decide on the agreed mechanisms. Thus, joint ownership of the procedure may indicate a willingness to make the agreed procedure work.

As with all lists, this must be read with caution, for the potential advantages may not operate in all situations and at all times. It is also likely that different levels of management have conflicting perspectives about the need for operating such procedures. For example, line managers may regard procedures as little more than red tape and bureaucracy, seeing all procedures as detracting from their main role of production or service. Equally, they may feel that the disciplinary process is long-winded, for example by taking too much time to get rid of unsatisfactory employees. It is up to senior managers, and especially HR professionals, to train line managers in how to use procedures and explain their value. For example, it can be stressed that arbitrary or hasty action can lead to unfair dismissal claims, and damages existing notions of the psychological contract in the organisation.

For procedure agreements to be of value, the parties have to be willing to use them rather than settling their differences through other means (such as strike action) before procedures have been exhausted. If managers, for example, continually flout the spirit of a procedure (perhaps by making unilateral changes to working practices), then it would not be a surprise if union representatives adopted a similar attitude. In short, if procedures are to be successful they require a degree of normative agreement as to their utility. In general terms, procedures have to reflect current practice. Where practice diverges significantly from the formal procedures, it is likely that they will fall into disuse and issues will be resolved in an arbitrary manner. Because of this it is not surprising that the language of procedures tends to be broad and general, and the duties and obligations that are placed on the parties remain imprecise.

This accords with the views of Marsh and McCarthy (1968, p3). They assess procedural adequacy by reference to acceptability and appropriateness. Firstly, for a procedure to operate effectively it needs to be broadly *acceptable* to all parties. Clearly, it is unlikely to operate to the complete satisfaction of each party since there may well be differing expectations. For example, managers may be more interested in 'the consistency of decisions' and for the procedures to filter out 'local' matters so enabling the more important issues to move upwards. However, unions and employees may desire speedy resolutions to problems as well as the opportunity to participate in the operation of procedures. Secondly, a procedure has to be *appropriate* to the structure of the industry and group within which it operates, and has to be related to the levels of decision-making within such a group. Thus, it may not be sensible for organisations always to impose a uniform procedure on departments or subsidiaries with a wide range of differing contexts. Indeed, it may well be that in such circumstances – where the procedure is seen as inappropriate within a particular context – the procedure itself becomes a cause of conflict.

Ultimately, however, the procedure is not an end in itself, and there may be times when it is sensible to short-circuit the procedure to sort out a pressing problem. For example, some stages may be missed out or employee representatives involved even before line managers are formally involved in resolving grievances. Similarly, procedures might be avoided altogether, or trade union or employers' association officials involved at an early stage.

While procedures reflect circumstances that are appropriate for different organisations and workplaces, there remains a remarkable similarity in terms of the main components. These relate to the spirit in which they are introduced, the role of the HR function and third-party involvement.

The preamble and 'spirit' behind agreements

Most procedures contain an introduction or preamble outlining the principles behind the scheme and the spirit in which it is to operate. For example, some refer to the agreement being in the mutual interests of both parties while others emphasise the need for a speedy resolution of differences. Some procedures make specific reference to the stage at which industrial action is allowed, and it is common to state that neither party should invoke sanctions prior to the exhaustion of procedures. While such provisions are not legally binding, the clause is in effect seen as a gentlemen's agreement. Management often accepts a mutual obligation to process issues through the relevant procedure as speedily as possible, within specified time limits to ensure that issues do not get bogged down, although, time limits can also be used as a stalling device by management.

Role of the HR function

HR specialists are often seen as the guardians or custodians of procedures. Grievances and disputes are usually seen as a line management responsibility but with personnel specialists available to provide advice and assistance when required. Given that the HR function may have been instrumental in designing the procedures, they usually have an influence over arrangements whether or not they have been formally involved at each stage.

> What should be the division of responsibility between line managers and HR specialists in relation to disciplinary practice and procedures? What factors should influence this and why?

It may be important that HR specialists are involved at an early stage if line managers lack human resource and legal skills. However, if line managers see HR only as providing information or interpreting procedures, this may not happen. Given this, HR specialists need to have a good idea of what is happening at ground level, a good relationship with line managers, as well as understanding the legislation and the customs and practices of a particular workplace. Where this is lacking, they may be excluded from decision-making and relegated to a back-seat role, with their involvement in issues of grievance or conflict resolution arising after rather than before the conflict has arisen. Their contribution to organisational effectiveness may then be perceived as limited. As we saw in Chapter 5, a common criticism of the HR function is that it 'always passes the buck' and is 'out of touch' with reality in the workplace.

Role of external third-party involvement

Some procedures provide an automatic role for third-party intervention from the Advisory, Conciliation and Arbitration Service (Acas), whereas others may be tied to an agreement between employers' organisations and trade unions. Yet others make use of an independent arbitrator on an ad hoc basis. Intervention by a third party can be in one of three forms: conciliation, mediation and arbitration. With conciliation and mediation, assistance is provided when the parties have reached an impasse but the parties themselves must resolve the issue. With conciliation, the third party must confine itself to facilitating discussion, while with mediation they can actually come up with specific recommendations. Arbitration involves the third party (such as Acas) coming up with a decision to resolve the issue. It should be noted that Acas should not be used as a substitute for the establishment of joint union–management procedures for dispute resolution as this allows the parties to avoid taking responsibility and employee relations can be damaged if commitment to agreed procedures withers away. (Refer to Chapter 1 for more information on Acas.)

DISCIPLINARY PROCEDURES

We have already noted that the concept of unfair dismissal was first introduced by the Industrial Relations Act 1971 and amended subsequently in the Employment Protection (Consolidation) Act 1978 (EPCA) and the Employment Rights Act (ERA) 1996. The ERA 1996 obliges employers to ensure the principal statement of employment conditions makes reference to rules, disciplinary and appeals procedures (Farnham 2000, p421). The Acas Code of Practice (Acas 2003c, p6) states: 'disciplinary procedures should not be seen primarily as a means of imposing sanctions but rather as a way of encouraging improvement amongst employees whose conduct or performance is unsatisfactory.' Minor misconduct is usually dealt with by informal warnings so being five minutes late, for example, is very unlikely to lead to dismissal. Clearly, actions must be appropriate to the circumstances. Managers should not look simply to punish employees but to counsel them, especially over inadequate performance. If performance is not up to standard, then management should investigate the reasons rather than just deal with the 'offence'. Employee performance may vary for reasons other than employee laziness or ineptitude. Lack of training, or problems at home need to be considered and employees should be supported to improve rather than simply be punished. As we saw in Chapter 7, counselling should be seen as a positive rather than punitive action.

Where employees feel that they have been dismissed unfairly, they can refer the case to an employment tribunal (provided that they have one year's continuous service), which determines whether or not the dismissal is fair or unfair. There are five potentially 'fair' reasons for dismissal within the Act:

- lack of capability (including health or qualifications) for performing work of the kind s/he was employed to do. The Disability Discrimination Act requires employers to make 'reasonable' adjustments to employment arrangement (Gennard and Judge 2002, pp363–364).
- misconduct
- redundancy
- duty or restriction imposed under or by a legal enactment
- some other substantial reason of a kind to justify the dismissal of an employee holding the position which that employee held (eg reorganisation of business).

Once the substantive case has been established, the question of whether the dismissal was fair or unfair can be determined, having regard to the reason shown by the employer. Fairness depends on whether in the circumstances – which include the size and administrative resources – the employer acted reasonably.

No question of 'reasonableness' arises, and no qualifying period is required, if dismissal is for an automatically unfair reason such as:

- pregnancy and/or maternity

- trade union involvement
- whistle-blowing (Public Interest Disclosure Act 1998)
- asserting a statutory right
- raising health and safety issues
- working in contravention of the Working Time Regulations 1998.

Although the legislation provides for unfairly dismissed employees to be reinstated or re-engaged, in practice they tend to be awarded compensation. This normally comprises a basic award of up to £8100 and a compensatory award of up to £55,000, although where dismissal is for whistle-blowing or raising health and safety issues, the compensatory award has no ceiling (Earnshaw 2002, pp262–263).

The Acas Code of Practice first appeared in 1977 and was most recently revised in 2003. While the code in itself is not binding, in the absence of other procedures, or poorly designed ones, it can be admissible in evidence to an employment tribunal that is attempting to determine the fairness of the dismissal. It recommends that disciplinary procedures should:

- be in writing
- specify to whom they apply
- provide for matters to be dealt with quickly
- indicate the disciplinary actions which may be taken
- specify the levels of management with the authority to take the various forms of disciplinary action, ensuring that immediate superiors do not normally have the power to dismiss without reference to senior management
- provide for individuals to be informed of the complaints against them and to be given an opportunity to state their case before decisions are reached
- give individuals the right to be accompanied by a trade union representative or by a fellow employee
- ensure that, except for gross misconduct, no employees are dismissed for a first breach of discipline
- ensure that disciplinary action is not taken until the case has been carefully investigated
- ensure that individuals are given an explanation for any penalty imposed
- provide a right of appeal and specify the procedure.

In addition, disciplinary procedures should:

- apply to all employees, irrespective of their length of service
- be non-discriminatory and applied irrespective of sex, marital status or race
- ensure that any period of suspension for investigation is with pay, and specify how pay is to be calculated during such a period (if, exceptionally, suspension is to be without pay, this should be provided for in the contract of employment)
- ensure that, where the facts are in dispute, no disciplinary penalty is imposed until the case has been carefully investigated and it is concluded on the balance of probability that the employee committed the act in question.

> Think of an attempt at disciplinary action by an employer that went wrong and explain why this occurred? What could have been done to stop this from going wrong?

It should also be recognised that indiscipline at work can have wider ramifications for the management of employee relations, as dismissal and other disciplinary measures can be a cause of strike action. It is important to appreciate that discipline at work also involves self-discipline and peer discipline as well as managerial discipline, and that the first two have been given greater attention in recent years (Edwards 2000; Dunn and Wilkinson 2002).

An IRS survey (IRS Employment Trends 727 2001) of 46 organisations found that the majority had rewritten their disciplinary procedures during the previous three years. This had been brought about by changes to the law specifically allowing for an employee to be accompanied by a fellow worker or a trade union representative, as well as to respond to the revised Acas Code of Practice. There were also 'internal' reasons for reviewing procedures, principally to ensure that required standards of conduct were communicated to employees, that the place of counselling and oral warnings were clarified, and that lists of the type of behaviour that constitute misconduct were provided.

The most common offences resulting in disciplinary action are outlined in Box 40. Absenteeism was ranked as the first or second most common reason by more than two-thirds of private sector firms and about half the public sector organisations. Poor performance, time-keeping problems and theft/fraud were also singled out by quite a number of organisations as a common reason for instigating disciplinary procedures. This tended to be more marked in the private than in the public sector. Generally though managers are reported to feel uncomfortable with the operation of disciplinary roles and procedures.

Research on teacher capability procedures indicates that in principle such procedures were accepted as appropriate to deal with sustained underperformance, and when operated effectively could generate a systematic approach to dealing with the problem in a supportive

BOX 40   THE MOST COMMON OFFENCES RESULTING IN DISCIPLINARY ACTION

1   absenteeism

2   performance

3   time-keeping

4   theft/fraud

5   refusal to obey instructions

6   aggression/verbal abuse

7   health and safety infringements

8   alcohol/drug abuse.

9   assault

10   sexual/racial harassment

Source: IRS Employment Review 727. 'Managing discipline at work', *IRS Employment Trends 727*, May 2001. p7

manner; in practice the procedures rarely operated efficiently and there were problems acting as barriers to their effective use. These included head-teachers' reluctance to trigger procedures stemming from fear of the law and unions, the resources likely to be involved – particularly the time commitment, and anticipated stress levels for all parties. Additionally, the concept of a capability process went against the teaching ethos with shortcomings in performance (other than misconduct) seen as individual misfortune and a management issue requiring assistance and support. This leads the authors to conclude that using informal means to secure improvement was much more likely to result in success, although when this approach failed rapid recourse to a formal procedures was needed (Earnshaw *et al* 2002a, pp234–235).

The Employment Act 2002 has made formal disciplinary procedures mandatory although as Earnshaw *et al* (2004) note there is little evidence that the existence of disciplinary procedures inhibit tribunal claims, although they may make them easier to defend.

The steps to be taken in dismissal, disciplinary and grievance procedures are outlined in Box 41.

BOX 41   STEPS IN DISMISSAL, DISCIPLINARY AND GRIEVANCE PROCEDURES

Dismissal and disciplinary procedures

Step one: Statement of grounds for action and invitation to a meeting

- The employer must set out in writing the employee's alleged conduct/ characteristics/other circumstances, which led the employer to contemplate dismissing or taking disciplinary action against an employee.
- A copy of the statement must be sent to the employee and they must be invited to attend a meeting to discuss the matter.

Step two: The meeting

- The meeting must take place before action is taken except in the case where the disciplinary action includes a suspension.
- The employee must take all reasonable steps to attend the meeting.
- After the meeting, the employer must inform the employee of their decision and notify the employee of their right to appeal against the decision.

Step three: Appeal

- If the employee wants to appeal, they must inform their employer.
- If the employee informs their employer of their wish to appeal, the employer must invite them to attend a further meeting.
- The employee must take all reasonable steps to attend the meeting.
- The appeal meeting need not take place before the dismissal or disciplinary action takes effect.
- After the appeal meeting, the employer must inform the employee of their final decision.

The procedure is, however, modified where an employee has been summarily dismissed for gross misconduct. In these circumstances the employer is required to set out in writing the employee's alleged misconduct which has led to dismissal and the employee's right to appeal against the dismissal, and send a copy of this to the employee. The provisions regarding appeals are identical to those contained in the standard procedure.

Grievance procedures

Step one: Statement of grievance

- The employee must set out the grievance in writing and send a copy to their employer.

Step two: The meeting

- The employer must invite the employee to at least one meeting to discuss the grievance.
- The employee must take all reasonable steps to attend the meeting.
- After the meeting, the employer must inform the employee of their response to the grievance and notify the employee of their right to appeal against that decision.

Step three: Appeal

- If the employee does want to appeal, they must inform their employer.
- If the employee informs their employer of the wish to appeal, the employer must invite the employee to attend a further meeting.
- The employee must take all reasonable steps to attend the meeting.
- After the appeal, the employer must inform the employee of their final decision.

The procedure is modified where the employee has already left the employment. In these circumstances, the employee is required to set out their grievance in writing and send a copy of it to their ex-employer. The employer is not required to convene a meeting, but must reply to the grievance in writing and send a copy of their response to the employee.

Source: Chartered Institute of Personnel and Development. *Guide to the Employment Act 2002*. London, CIPD. 2004e

TRIBUNALS

Before describing the tribunal system, it is important that readers are aware of the differences between criminal and civil law. Although the vast majority of HR issues are dealt with through the civil law, there are times when the criminal law comes into play, and individuals may be able to seek redress through either branch of the law. Criminal law is concerned with preventing breaches of society's rules, and with punishing offenders; cases are normally dealt with through the magistrates' courts or Crown courts. In contrast, civil law is concerned with settling disputes between private parties, such as between two individuals or between a worker and an employer. Although most employment issues are typically dealt with through the tribunal system, some may be routed through the County Court or High Court system, for example safety and accidents and dismissal due to a breach of contract.

The vast majority of HR practitioners who become embroiled in legal issues are likely to be involved in employment tribunals. Originally called industrial tribunals, these were set up under the Industrial Training Act 1964 to hear employers' appeals against levies, and their work was extended in 1965 to include redundancy payments issues. It was only after the Industrial Relations Act 1971 that tribunals started to play a major role in the HR area, largely in dealing with claims for unfair dismissal, but more recently an increasing proportion of their caseload has involved equal opportunities and redundancy payments. Over the years, the tribunal system has had a significant influence on the way in which management handles employment issues, and it has led to an increasing formalisation of procedures in employing organisations.

Employment tribunals are able to hear the following sorts of issues:

- unfair dismissal
- health and safety at work
- race discrimination
- equal pay, sex discrimination and maternity
- redundancy, reorganisation and transfers of undertakings
- pay and other terms of employment
- trade union membership and non-membership
- time off for public duties
- dismissal due to a breach of contract.

Individuals who have a complaint against an employer start the process by completing an originating application (IT1), typically, though not necessarily, after consulting with their trade union, the Citizens Advice Bureau, a friend or a solicitor. The application is received by the Employment Tribunal Office and a copy of the application is sent to the employer who has 21 days to respond. Copies of the employer's response are then sent to the employee or his or her representatives. At this point, Acas will contact the parties to see if a conciliated settlement can be achieved. Acas conciliation officers have the task of making speedy and informal contact with the parties, and a duty under the law to seek a conciliated settlement if either party requests it or if Acas believes there is a reasonable prospect that its intervention may be successful. Following conciliation, a substantial proportion of cases are settled, and in many cases this results in an out-of-court settlement to the applicant. It is rare for the individual to be reinstated or re-engaged, however.

The number of originating applications more than doubled since 1990 and the range of cases has broadened. Matters have been complicated yet further by the influence of European judgements on British employment relations. This led to what some see as a growing 'compensation culture' (Fairclough and Birkenshaw 2001, p4).

The legal pathway of cases through the criminal courts, and through the civil courts and tribunals, is illustrated graphically in Figure 12 on page 308.

Go to the library and find a recent copy of one of the specialist employment law publications – such as the Industrial Relations Law Report or IRS Employment Review. Choose a recent case, examine the details, and write a short report outlining any lessons to be learnt from the case.

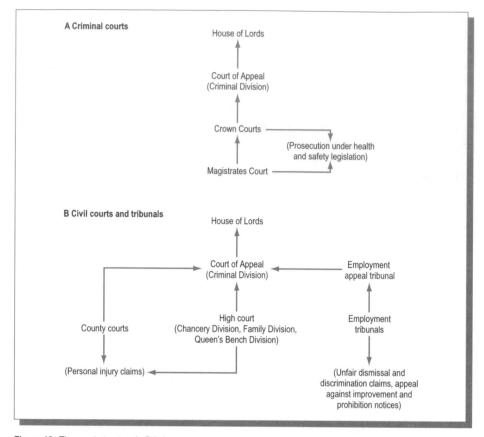

Figure 12 *The court structure in Britain*
Source: Reproduced from Earnshaw J. and Cooper C. *Stress and Employer Liability*. London, IPD. 1996

The Employment Rights (Disputes Resolutions) Act 1998 empowered Acas to draw up an arbitration scheme for individual disputes so as to reduce the load on tribunals, to minimise delay, and to contain demands on public expenditure.

Within the tribunal system itself there has been a continuing tension between its initial aim of providing a cheap, speedy and informal route to resolve employment rights problems, and the increasing tendency to legalism and reference to legal precedents. The latter is inevitable as the body of case law has built up and both parties (respondent and applicant) seek specialist representation at tribunal. In addition to the increasing likelihood that both parties will be represented by solicitors, employers' organisations and trade unions also provide specialist expertise, and some employers have their own legal experts to deal with these cases. Given that the costs of losing a case can be quite high for an employer, not just in terms of direct employment costs, but also in compensation, payment for representation, and negative public relations, the incentive to win becomes even greater. Many Tribunal Chairs attempt to retain informality by adopting a more inquisitorial approach, and assist unrepresented applicants or respondents with a line of questioning. The lay members of the tribunal provide knowledge and expertise from industry.

Appeals against tribunal decisions are made to the Employment Appeals Tribunal (EAT), a body with the same status as a High Court, which was established under the Employment

Protection Act 1975. It hears appeals on any question of law stemming from a tribunal decision. This relates to claims that the tribunal had misunderstood or misdirected itself as to the applicable law, where there is no evidence to support a particular finding, or where the tribunal has reached a perverse conclusion. Appeals can be remitted to the same or to a fresh tribunal for a rehearing if they are neither upheld nor dismissed. Appeals on a point of law are tightly circumscribed, and there have been repeated warnings that points of fact are not to be dressed up in the garb of points of law in order to bring an appeal. Appeals against EAT decisions can be made in certain circumstances to the Court of Appeal, then to the House of Lords and to the European Court of Justice (ECJ). In addition, individual employment tribunals can refer matters direct to the ECJ for interpretations of community law. The ECJ is becoming increasingly influential in several areas of employment law – for example, in relation to equal pay, maternity rights, sex discrimination, and health and safety.

GRIEVANCE PROCEDURES

A grievance is a complaint made by an employee about management behaviour (Gennard and Judge 2002). In the UK, grievances tend to be used widely and embrace both collective and individual issues reflecting the idea that the line between grievance (individual) and dispute (collective) can sometimes be a blurred one. However, in general, grievance procedures are used for handling individual issues, while collective issues are usually dealt with by disputes procedures. In practice some organisations have a combined procedure reflecting the fact that grievances are often likely to affect more than one employee, and others allow for grievances to be referred to the collective disputes procedure. A grievance procedure is a parallel mechanism to the disciplinary procedure (Rollinson 2002, pp98–99).

Problems can arise if agreements and rules are not written down because custom and practice is likely to produce ambiguity. Often it is possible to separate disputes of interest (what should be in the agreement) from disputes of right (what is in the agreement). During the 1960s and 1970s, grievance procedures were parts of national agreements and this led to problems because of the time it took to get a grievance to the end of the procedure. Consequently industrial action sometimes took place before the procedure had been exhausted. Nowadays, however, it is much more common to have local grievance procedures covering establishments or single employers. As Renwick and Gennard (2001, p171) observe, while a formal grievance procedure is not legally required, employers who do not have a formal grievance procedure can fall foul of the law. Furthermore, as Gennard and Judge (2002, p389) note, 'the benefits of having procedures for handling employee grievances are also clear from the case of Chris Metcalf Ltd v Maddocks (1985). The industrial tribunal ruled that a grievance procedure would have enabled employees to articulate their worries and anxieties, and would thus have prevented the problems occurring. An appeal by the firm against the decision failed.'

The aim of a grievance procedure is to prevent issues and disagreements leading to major conflict and to prevent employees leaving. Even if an employee's grievance is the result of a fellow employee's action – as in racial or sexual harassment – the grievance is taken against management for failing to provide protection. As with discipline, the spirit with which the grievance procedure is approached is significant. It may be easy for management simply to follow the letter of the procedure, making it a hollow sham, but once this is known employees will not bother to refer issues to the procedure. Consequently, it is important that HR professionals encourage the proper use of procedures to uncover any problems particularly where line managers wish to hide them because of fear that it shows them in a bad light.

Open-door systems operate in some organisations that allow workers to take up grievances with managers directly rather than follow a lengthy procedure. However, this relies on managers taking the system seriously and being prepared to devote time and effort to keep it going.

Disputes procedures specify how collective grievances should be dealt with. The chain of complaint may go from the supervisor, or immediate line manager, to the departmental manager or personnel manager to senior management. It may provide for matters to be referred to a third party such as Acas if matters are not resolved. It is also important that the procedure is efficient and relatively quick. Clearly there is a balance between the time needed to reflect on the issue at hand, while ensuring that it is not 'lost' in the process because of the length of time involved.

In WERS 1998 (Cully *et al* 1999), almost all workplaces (91 per cent) had a formal procedure for dealing with individual grievances raised by employees, only in stand-alone sites (74 per cent) was the incidence substantially below the average. Almost all the public sector workplaces had a procedure in place (99 per cent). Where workplaces operated without a procedure, managers were asked how problems were resolved. Typically, the answer was 'they come to me and we sort it out'. Employees were made aware of the existence and content of these procedures through the letter of appointment (47 per cent), a staff handbook (55 per cent) or via a notice board (19 per cent). In the small number of workplaces without a written procedure, it was claimed that employees were made aware of their rights either when they started work or at some other time by their line manager or supervisor. Thus, Cully *et al* (p77) noted that although most employees had access to a formal procedure for grievances, they might be reluctant to raise a grievance without some form of support. Consequently, relatively little use was made of grievance procedures. At workplaces with procedures, only a third (30 per cent) said that the procedure was utilised. The interpretation of this is complex: either employees had nothing to complain about, or the procedure was not seen as a particularly effective mechanism for resolving problems. Comments on the lack of usage included (pp77–78):

> **Because we are quite happy to listen to them at any time and deal with problems before they develop.**
>> **(Other business services, private sector, 500+ employees)**

> **It's not part of the culture of this company.**
>> **(Construction, private sector, 500+ employees)**

> **They haven't felt the need. If there is anything, they can usually sort it out without resorting to the procedure.**
>> **(Financial services, private sector, 50–100 employees)**

> **Probably because they imagine nothing will change – lack of confidence in the procedure.**
>> **(Health, private sector, 100–200 employees)**

Get a copy of **two** organisations' grievance procedures, and compare them. What are the major differences between them and why? How might they be improved?

The ERA 1999 provided for reasonable requests for accompaniment during hearings. A worker asked to attend a disciplinary or grievance hearing can now 'reasonably request' to be accompanied by a lay trade union official or a fellow worker. Although 'reasonable' is not defined, the Acas code suggests that it would not be reasonable to request someone who might prejudice the hearing or who might have a conflict of interest; or someone from a distant location when someone suitable is on site. The 'companion' does not act in the same way as a representative who may present the case. However, they can address the hearing – but not answer questions – and can confer with the worker. Aikin (2000) suggests that employers need to consider precise rules rather than leaving questions of reasonableness to individual managers who may well reach different conclusions. Given the introduction of the right to be accompanied, it is important for employers to be clear about particular stages in the disciplinary procedures and what constitutes counselling, coaching or an informal warning – where the right does not apply (Pitt 2000, p256). The Public Interest Disclosure Act 1998 amended the ERA 1996 to 'the opportunity for workers to raise concerns such as workplace malpractice, suspicion of criminal acts, miscarriages of justice, and dangers to health and safety' (Farnham 2000, p415) within the grievance procedure.

An IRS Survey (IRS Employment Trends 726 2001) of over 100 employers found that all but two had written grievance procedures – very much in line with the WERS results. Over half of the organisations first introduced these procedures more than 10 years ago. There was strong support for the argument that grievances should be dealt with quickly and fairly at the lowest possible level in the organisation, and this was best done informally between the worker and their immediate line manager. Although the number of stages in the procedure varied between organisations, three stages was the most common, and it was rare for there to be less than this. The most common causes of grievances are pay and grading issues, concerns about other terms and conditions of employment, and working practices and work allocation. Complaints about the handling of disciplinary cases and bullying were noted by quite a number of organisations, though grievances about sexual harassment were relatively rare.

The IRS respondents (Employment Trends 726 2001, p16) suggested six pieces of advice when designing and operating grievance procedures:

- emphasise quick and informal procedures
- keep policies simple
- liaise with and involve employee representatives
- communicate the policy to employees and managers
- provide training for line managers
- be consistent when applying procedures.

The Employment Act 2002 (Dispute Resolution) Regulations 2004 is based on the premise that the application of statutory procedures for the handling of disciplinary and grievance cases assists in the resolution of workplace disputes although merely following the minimum procedures will not necessarily ensure a dismissal is fair (Gaymer 2004, p17). All employers are obliged to follow a 'default' statutory dismissal and disciplinary procedure (unless the existing procedures exceed the requirements of the acts). The procedure is referred to in every employee's contract. There is both a standard and modified (shorter) procedure; the latter used in dismissals for gross misconduct. Employees must follow the statutory grievance procedure before applying to a tribunal. The Act states that failure by an employer to follow a procedure in the dismissal of an employee may not be regarded as unreasonable where the employer can show that dismissal would have resulted if the procedure had been followed. Failure to follow the procedure may result in the compensation award being increased or decreased (depending on which party is at fault).

LINE MANAGERS AND THE USE OF PROCEDURES

So far in this chapter we have discussed the importance of procedures, stressing the value of being proactive, taking the initiative and establishing/reinforcing their use. Management has been treated as if it were a unified group, sharing common interests and perspectives. However, in reality, there may well be conflict between the perspectives held by HR specialists and line managers. In practice operational pressures may take priority over HR considerations and directives from HR specialists tend to have less force than those coming from a production director. This helps to explain why line managers are often hostile to rules that emanate from the HR specialists who are often castigated for not 'living in the real world'. Thus, an HR policy that appears well formulated, embodies the basic rules of good management practice, and ensures uniformity and consistency may appear very differently when viewed from the position of the line manager. Under such circumstances, HR specialists need to be able to persuade line managers that procedures are valuable tools rather than millstones. One argument might be that the procedures are no more than the codification of good practice. So, for example, the disciplinary procedure represents a helpful prompt for managers, encouraging them to follow actions they should be taking in any case. Moreover, by not following procedure they potentially lay themselves and their employer open to the likelihood of appeals, time spent at an employment tribunal, and ultimately financial penalties. A second argument might be that, by breaking rules or condoning new custom and practice, this merely lays down the seeds of greater trouble. For example, if line managers concede demands to employees in exchange for greater co-operation to meet a production target, this can create an expectation that all extra effort will be so rewarded. Thirdly, the observance of procedures sets the tone for dealing with other issues in the workplace. If managers are seen to be fair and prepared to follow procedures, it is much more likely that employees will behave likewise if they are unhappy with some aspect of management behaviour. Rather than taking industrial action to settle differences, employees are encouraged to ensure that procedures are exhausted first. This allows employers to maintain production or services while resolving problems at work.

Procedures therefore have a role in giving line managers a clear perspective on the direction in which the organisation is moving, its objectives, and the general standards applied in relation to all aspects of the employment relationship. While line managers may not have the time to become experts in all these matters, they should know the broad parameters of actions, as well as where and when to look for advice. HR specialists clearly play a key role both in providing information and acting as a sounding board.

IRS research into managing discipline at work (IRS Employment Trends 727 2001) demonstrated that line managers were increasingly taking responsibility for disciplinary procedures. Over half of the 46 respondents (20 in the public sector and 26 in the private sector) reported that line managers spent up to 5 per cent of their time on disciplinary issues, and about one-fifth estimated that line mangers spent about 10 per cent of their time on disciplinary issues. Despite this, discipline still makes up a significant portion of the workload of HR staff. Over half of the respondents estimated that it took up 5 per cent, and approximately one-fifth that it took up 20 per cent or more of HR staff time.

How can HR practitioners convince line managers that it is worth using procedures and that they can make a contribution to organisational success? Renwick and Gennard (2001, p170) argue that all managers need to be trained properly to handle grievance and discipline cases so that they can draw a distinction between unjustified employee complaints and those that are justified under the organisation's procedure, collective agreement or works rule. Where a dismissal has occurred, in investigating whether or not the employee has a grievance against their employer, tribunals test the issues of fairness and reasonableness by asking whether procedures that are applied 'conform to the concepts of natural justice'.

THE CONTRIBUTION OF HR SPECIALISTS TO THE BARGAINING PROCESS

Gennard and Judge (2002, pp297–331) examine in detail the preparation for bargaining and in this section we outline the key elements relating to the roles of HR practitioners. Typically, a bargaining team includes three roles. These are leader (spokesperson and negotiator), note-taker (recording proposals, ensuring all issues are addressed) and strategist (monitor strategies and seek common ground). It is important for the team to maintain discipline throughout the process and not provide opportunities for the other side to exploit any lack of coherence. The HR function would normally take a key role in this process, and according to WERS over 90 per cent of HR/Personnel Managers have a responsibility for pay and conditions of employment (Millward *et al* 2000, p63). There are a number of stages in the bargaining process.

Analysis

This stage is concerned with collecting and analysing relevant information to support a claim/proposal. In preparing for this stage, managers are likely to gather a range of information from both internal and external sources. Many of these fall within the province of HR managers. Internal sources may cover issues such as:

- labour productivity trends
- profitability
- labour turnover
- absenteeism
- total sales
- investment
- pay changes
- orders pending
- cash flow position.

External sources include information from employers' associations (see Chapter 2), the trade press such as *People Management* and *Personnel Today*, as well as industry specific journals. UK government publications such as *Labour Market Trends*, *New Earnings Survey*,

Industrial Relations Services Employment Review and the *Incomes Data Services* are particularly helpful.

Identification of tradable items

Also important when preparing for negotiations, is identification of the key issues on which management may be prepared to trade. For example, changes in basic pay or to the working week may be ruled out, whereas variable pay such as bonuses and certain aspects of working conditions may be used as trade-offs. The team also needs to assess what they believe the other party may be willing to trade to see if there is any basis for agreement. Given that HR managers are more likely to spend time with worker representatives than most other managers, their assessment of the situation is likely to be very important.

Aims and strategy

Management should examine what it is seeking to achieve in terms of what is ideal, what is realistic, and what is the minimum acceptable. This can be done in relation to all the items on the 'shopping list' of each of the parties, and by putting these together they should be able to see if there is likely to be any basis for agreement. Key issues might include the following.

- Are employees willing to take industrial action?
- What is the degree of organisation and solidarity amongst employees?
- What is the quality of leadership amongst union representatives?
- Have employees imposed sanctions previously and, if so, what was the result?
- What type of industrial sanctions did they use? What tactics did they use?
- What is the degree of substitutability for products and services produced by employees?
- Can an alternative supply of labour be obtained?
- How crucial is the group of employees in the production/service supply process?
- How long will it take for industrial sanctions, if imposed, to have an adverse effect on the operation of the organisation?

Presenting proposals

The proposal should summarise briefly the main issues to be discussed and then present the case in detail along with supporting evidence. At this early stage management will set out its ideal position with an opening statement. There are advantages with opening from an extreme position in that it provides more room for movement in bargaining and it can lower expectations. The potential downside is it may not be treated seriously by the unions or it might trigger an equally extreme response. Much depends upon context and existing relationships.

Confirmation of common ground

Once the original presentations by both sides have been completed, it will be much clearer what the main sources of contention are. At this early stage there may be little common ground but through meeting, some common ground and possible agreement may be identified; enough to keep the momentum of the bargaining session going with difficult issues returned to later.

Adjournment

Apart from normal scheduled breaks, there are constructive uses for adjournments. Firstly, it gives parties a chance to withdraw and review progress. Secondly, it can provide a break if negotiations have reached an impasse. Thirdly, it provides an opportunity for one or two members from each side to talk informally with each other away from the negotiating table without any formal commitment.

Factors to consider in concluding the agreement

Management needs to be satisfied with the issues discussed and agreed and both sides need to understand and commit to what has been accepted. If this is not achieved or there is some ambiguity, problems may arise later as each party accuses the other of misapplying the agreement. Secondly, management has to convince the other party that the final offer is indeed the end of the process or it risks undermining credibility. Thirdly, management should not rush into concluding a final agreement. It is vital to have an adjournment to ensure they have all the information and have not missed any problems. Gennard and Judge (2002, pp329–330) note that once oral agreement has been reached the agreement can be written up in draft form stating:

- the names of the parties to the agreement
- the date on which the agreement was concluded
- the date upon which the agreement will become operative
- which groups/grades are covered by the agreement
- what are the exceptions (if any) to the agreement
- the contents (clauses) of the agreement
- the duration of the agreement
- whether the agreement can be reopened before this finish date, and, if so, in what circumstances
- whether the agreement can be terminated if it has no end date and, if so, how
- how disputes over its interpretation and application will be settled (will it be the existing grievance/disputes procedure?)
- which, if any, other agreements it replaces.

The written agreement should contain the signatures of representatives of the parties. Once both sides are happy with the wording, the agreement can be formally signed.

HR managers play an important role as policy actors and 'hidden persuaders' (Wilkinson and Marchington 1994) in the bargaining process (see Chapter 5). They are expected to interpret new employment regulations; to prepare the organisation for 'best practice' initiatives like Investors in People; to form alliances with general managers in search of recipes to enhance employee contribution; and to help line managers incorporate human resources dimensions into operational schemes such as teamworking. Increased regulation may therefore offer an important opportunity for the HR specialist. It provides them with opportunities to introduce new systems and processes into their organisations, as well as give them greater legitimacy as experts. The creation of a new institutional baseline of employee rights and a changed normative framework can provide management with an opportunity to exercise creativity. Without this framework, there is a danger that employees may choose instead to articulate their views through litigation or high labour turnover rather than through constructive internal channels.

CONCLUSIONS

In this chapter we have reviewed a number of the procedures that provide a framework for employee relations. In the current climate – where concepts of flexibility, empowerment and de-layering reign supreme – procedures are seen by some commentators as an anachronism, a legacy of the so-called 'old' collectivist and bureaucratic industrial relations of the 1970s. However, we need to remember why procedures were introduced in the first place, and the purposes they serve. One of the major rationales behind the emergence of unfair dismissal legislation was to reduce the likelihood of employees taking industrial action to protect fellow workers whom they felt had been badly treated by management. The procedures which were established as a result of this legal intervention helped to change attitudes and behaviour, and few HR managers (or their line management colleagues) would welcome a return to the days of industrial disputes. As Taylor (2002c, p5) notes, there has been an enormous growth of litigation and increased tendency on the part of workers to resort to tribunals. On the other hand, as we noted in Chapter 2, many employees now feel that the psychological contract is too one-sided. While they may lack the resources or the will to engage in industrial action, feelings of unfairness can easily translate into demotivation, a lack of interest in quality and customer care, and feelings of exclusion and powerlessness.

Procedures are an essential element of good employment relations and HR practice as they provide a clear framework within which issues can be resolved. In the absence of procedures, each new problem has to be tackled from first principles with managers and employee representatives spending considerable amounts of time trying to establish common ground rules before being able to resolve issues. Renwick and Gennard (2001, p169) suggest that the business case for procedures is that employee satisfaction would increase where they saw that discipline and grievance issues were handled properly, this would result in increased retention. Without procedures, there would be no incentive for managers or employees to attempt to resolve disputes in an orderly manner. The end result would be that both parties would seek to use their superior bargaining power to impose their own preferred solutions on the other. Procedures help create a positive psychological contract by emphasising the importance of fairness.

USEFUL READING

ADVISORY, CONCILIATION AND ARBITRATION SERVICE. *Acas Code of Practice Disciplinary Practice and Grievance Procedures.* London, HMSO. 2003c.

BOTT D. 'Employment relations procedures', in B. TOWERS (ed), *The Handbook of Employment Relations, Law and Practice*, 4th edition. London, Kogan Page. 2003.

EARNSHAW J., MARCHINGTON M. *and* GOODMAN J. 'Unfair to whom? Discipline and dismissal in small establishments', *Industrial Relations Journal*, Vol. 31, No. 1, 2000, pp62–73.

EARNSHAW J., MARCHINGTON L., RITCHIE E. *and* TORRINGTON D. 'Neither fish nor foul? An assessment of teacher capability procedures', *Industrial Relations Journal*, Vol. 35, No. 2, 2004. pp139–152.

EDWARDS P. 'Discipline: towards trust and self-discipline', in S. Bach and K. Sisson (eds), *Personnel Management*, 3rd edition. Oxford, Blackwell. 2000.

GAYMER, J. 'Making a molehill out of a mountain', *People Management*, 26 February 2004, p17.

GENNARD J. *and* JUDGE G. *Employee Relations*, 4th edition. London, CIPD. 2005.

IRS EMPLOYMENT REVIEW 778. *Discipline Procedures: Dawn of a new era?* June 2003. pp10–15.

MARLOW S. 'Regulating labour management in small firms', *Human Resource Management Journal*, Vol. 12, No. 3, 2002. pp1–25.

PRITCHARD H. 'Discrimination in employment', in B. TOWERS (ed), *The Handbook of Employment Relations, Law and Practice*, 4th edition. London, Kogan Page. 2003. pp47–67.

Reward

Motivation and Pay Systems

INTRODUCTION

The sight of employees sprinting away from the workplace at the end of the day suggests that well-motivated staff are not necessarily the norm in UK industry. Studies also show that even where labour turnover – one indicator of employee satisfaction – is limited, this may obscure deep-rooted discontent as employees feel they have little choice but to remain with their current employer because of the economic situation or their lack of transferable skills. The WERS survey found that all but 7 per cent of workplaces had some workers who were not satisfied with their jobs (Cully *et al* 1999, p298).

Given the increased emphasis in recent years on people as a key source of competitive advantage, it is not surprising to see corporate initiatives introduced to 'buy' employee commitment. But how successful are such campaigns, and on what assumptions are they based? It seems sensible to take a step back and try to understand the complexities of motivating people at work. This is important at three levels. First, for management, who need to know and understand what motivates people as it affects work performance, recruitment and retention. Second, employees need to think through what expectations they have of work and whether they are happy with their lot. Finally, for HR professionals, issues such as these influence the design and implementation of reward structures and systems which they implement or monitor (Gratton 2004).

Certainly money is a factor that can motivate people at work, but even here things are not straightforward. Many people are motivated to work hard regardless of financial reward, and for some the level of monetary reward is important symbolically – as recognition of worth. Clearly, there are other benefits from being at work as well as money – such as activity, variety, status and social contacts. In recent years there has been a growing emphasis in the literature that reward should be utilised as a strategic tool to manage corporate performance and to influence corporate values and beliefs (Lawler 2000a; Armstrong 2002; Kessler 2003) rather than just as a technique to recruit, retain and motivate staff. Armstrong and Brown (2001, p5) define reward strategy as 'a business focused statement of the intentions of the organisation concerning the development of future reward processes and practices, which are aligned to the business and human resource strategies of the organisation, its culture and the environment in which it operates'. This is very much a phenomenon of the last 20 years with an associated upbeat rhetoric, and it is often set against an alleged backcloth of earlier approaches criticised for being inflexible and bureaucratic.

Reward management is a key element in the strategic approach to HRM for a number of reasons. First, it is a mechanism by which employers aim to elicit effort and performance; second, the actual payment system may require adjustment to develop motivation; and third, it is often a significant part of the employer's financial strategy (Hendry 1994, p343). Such an approach ties in well with the HRM ideal, which sees policies designed around strategic choices rather than simply reflecting environmental pressures. This means that there is unlikely to be a state-of-the-art, 'one size fits all' set of practices suitable for all organisations, and managers need to develop a 'fit' between remuneration policies and the strategic objectives of the organisation (Brown 2001). However, the extent to which remuneration is used as a strategic tool in practice is more open to doubt. Management tend to assess or reassess one part of the remuneration package but often fail to analyse the whole system. The notion of 'total reward' (Thompson 2002) is more myth and hype than reality. Furthermore, management tends to have a whole host of objectives for remuneration policy but these sometimes contradict one another, and their wider implications are not always clearly thought through.

In this chapter we examine the varieties of reward system and the different elements in the reward package as well as the different type of pay schemes that can be implemented. It is important that the reward philosophy and policy reflects the overall objectives of the employer, and that the different elements of the package send a clear and consistent message to employees. Moreover, as organisations become flatter and promotion opportunities are reduced, this places even greater emphasis on the recognition and reward elements of the pay system.

By the end of this chapter, readers should be able to:

- **provide advice about how to motivate and reward people so as to maximise employee contributions to organisational performance**

- **advise management on the circumstances under which different payment systems may be appropriate for their organisation**

- **outline the case for and against the introduction of performance-related pay and specify the conditions under which it is appropriate.**

In addition, readers should understand and be able to explain:

- **the principal differences between types of pay scheme**

- **the importance of linking the pay system to wider organisational goals and other HR strategies**

- **how effective reward management practice can contribute to enhanced employee motivation and satisfaction at work.**

THEORIES OF MOTIVATION AND REWARDS

Most texts on social psychology divide theories of motivation into content and process theories. The former focus on what are seen as fundamental human needs (for example, physiological, food and safety needs), while the latter try to understand the psychological processes involved in motivation (Bowey and Thorpe 2000; Mullins 2001).

F. W. Taylor, the father of scientific management, viewed employees as rational and economic in their approach but basically lazy and having to be motivated by management through the pay system. Given that employees were motivated primarily by money, it was important to ensure that the jobs they were doing were capable of providing the opportunity to maximise earnings. Because of this, jobs needed to be examined scientifically through time and motion studies, broken down into their constituent parts, and then put back together in the most efficient manner. This 'best' method was devised by observing the 'best' workers on each particular task. Once the 'best' method had been established, it could then be taught to other workers, who could be retrained if necessary. His approach has been widely criticised, in particular for his tendency to equate people with machines, and his assumptions that there was one universal best method, and that the individual incentive to earn money is the primary motivating factor at work (Rose 1978, p62). His conception of rational–economic person led to a self-fulfilling prophecy in that if employees are expected to be only motivated by economic incentives, the management approach used to deal with them are likely to train them to behave in exactly this way.

The human relations movement emerged by the 1920s, presenting a picture of 'social man' against the 'economic man' of the scientific management school. This idea developed originally from research (known as the Hawthorne experiments) on fatigue and its link with productivity. The groups at the plants under investigation were studied over a period of time and changes were introduced relating to alterations in rest periods, refreshments, starting and finishing times, payment schemes and environmental conditions such as lighting. However, in contrast with the prevailing wisdom, variations in these conditions did not appear to correlate with productivity. Even when the experiment ended and conditions returned to their original state, production was some 30 per cent higher than at the start. These results were then interpreted as resulting from increased worker satisfaction through being given special attention, working as a close-knit group, and being involved in decision-making. It was clear that workers did not always respond to incentive schemes as managers had expected, often having their own goals (as a group) that acted against management objectives. As with scientific management, the human relations school has been criticised for its unitarist philosophy, its 'one best way' approach and for its methodology. The implications of this approach for reward strategy are not that payments are irrelevant, but that new payment schemes may have a once and for all Hawthorne effect which may increase productivity. This school of thought suggests that rewards need to be seen in a broader work context, one in which employee objectives, other than the simple maximisation of earnings, are important.

By the 1940s Maslow had developed the 'hierarchy of needs' approach to motivation. To some extent this incorporated the previous two theories of motivation, and rather than identifying a single source of motivation it suggested an ascending hierarchy of needs. The theory suggests that people are motivated by a number of factors at work, aiming to satisfy one particular need before moving on to attempt to satisfy the next in the hierarchy. Thus, basic security needs such as food, jobs and housing have to be achieved before individuals begin to consider their social and affiliative needs. Once these needs are satisfied they can then look to satisfy their personal needs for ego satisfaction and self-actualisation. One implication of the 'hierarchy of needs' approach is that for those on low wages, and consequently operating at the lower end of the hierarchy, money may loom more important than for those earning considerably more. The latter have satisfied their basic needs, and may move on to higher level needs. However, the ongoing controversy over executive rewards – which led to the Cadbury (1992) and Greenbury (1995) Reports – might appear to contradict this notion (see Box 42 on page 324). There is little research evidence supporting the notion of a universal hierarchy of needs. It is also apparent that, on the same day, employees may demand not only more money but also more satisfying work, and are thus operating at more than one level of hierarchy at one time. Maslow's work is also reflected to some extent in McGregor's (1960) distinction between theory X and theory Y managers. Theory X managers believe workers are lazy and uninterested in their work, and therefore needed to be highly controlled and offered incentives to get them to work harder. In contrast, theory Y managers believe workers can be motivated by goals of self-esteem and the desire to do a good job; consequently, management's role is to facilitate this.

BOX 42   FAT CATS STILL GET THE CREAM

The 2004 annual *Guardian* survey (Treanor *et al* 2004) revealed that the eight directors of Tesco earned £26m between them during 2003/4. This was nearly five times more than the £5.8m average for a top 100 board member. In total 187 executives earned over £1m in 2003, just below the figure of 190 for the previous year. The debate over 'fat cats' continues, as demonstrated by the outrage expressed by J. Sainsbury shareholders who refused to agree to Sir Peter Davis's payment of £2.3m at a time of declining sales and profits. He was subsequently removed from the board in advance of what would have been an embarrassing protest at the company's annual meeting.

According to Towers Perrin/*Business Week* (Denny 2000) American chief executive officers earn 475 times more than the average worker, while in Germany the ratio is 15:1, in the UK 24:1 (the biggest gap in Europe) and in Japan 11:1. However, the message that wage compression can help performance is not one of the lessons that British managers have been keen to promote! Of course this depends on the view one takes on what high pay is for.

According to Lazear (1998, p31):

> American CEOs have recently come under attack for their very high salaries, particularly in comparison to their European and Japanese counterparts. Whilst their salaries may be too high, focusing on their salaries alone misses the entire point of the compensation structure. The CEO's salary is there not so much to motivate the CEO as it is to motivate everyone under him [sic] to attempt to attain that job.

UK criticism (*The Guardian* 2001a) suggests that bosses all too easily downplay the performance link in favour of a self-serving market rate justification (Caulkin 2001). Concerns about high payments at troubled Marks & Spencers have kept the debate going (Finch and Treanor 2001) and at Railtrack the Chief Executive who resigned after the Hatfield crash received a £1.4m payoff. In 2002 the CE of GlaxoSmith Kline had a total package of £7 million but was reported as 'feeling underpaid' and needing 'more money to keep motivated' despite profits and shares both falling (Finch and Treanor 2002). A Top Management Compensation Report produced by consultancy Watson Wyatt showed that Top UK managers are among the highest earners in Europe, according to new research carried out across 17 western European countries; senior managers in Switzerland and the UK are the best paid with an average annual remuneration of around £260,000 (£181,278) (Roberts 2003b).

Herzberg's two-factor theory of motivation was very influential in the 1960s. His research (1966) found that satisfaction and dissatisfaction were not necessarily related, and that just because a person did not feel satisfied about a particular aspect of their work it did not mean that they were necessarily dissatisfied. Equally, if workers did not feel dissatisfied, this did not imply automatic satisfaction. The motivators that tended to be identified with good feelings included factors such as achievement, responsibility, recognition, advancement and the work itself. The so-called 'hygiene' factors – associated with bad feelings – included company policy, working conditions, supervision and pay. Thus, if an employee spoke about feeling good, it was related to having achieved something or having been granted recognition. Conversely, when speaking about feeling bad, this referred to factors such as poor supervision or insufficient pay. The key point here is that unless the hygiene factors are satisfied, motivators are of little use, and Herzberg felt that many firms did not satisfy the hygiene factors. If this theory holds true then it has similar implications to Maslow's work, in that pay is only significant as a 'hygiene' factor and that an appropriate level needs to be found which meets employee expectations. However, there will be no motivating effect by paying above this level. The theory also has implications in relation to the need to restructure or enrich jobs to provide satisfying work, as 'true' motivation is seen to derive from factors associated with the job itself and opportunity for achievement, involvement and recognition. We return to this concept in the next chapter when we deal with non-financial rewards and recognition. Bowey and Thorpe (2000, p84) observe that much of this literature was written from an 'upstream' position focusing on the potential for these ideas; there are few 'downstream evaluations' of what has actually happened to organisations following the implementation of a particular theory or idea.

Later literature has posited the existence of people as complex animals. This does not provide us with any automatically universal picture of the employee, for as Rollinson *et al* (1998, p184) note 'the needs and values of individuals are highly diverse and the organisations in which people work are very different'. Goldthorpe *et al* (1968) describe a group of manual workers – whom they termed 'instrumental' – who appeared to want little else from work other than enough money to enable them to enjoy life to the full outside the workplace. Few of the respondents seemed particularly satisfied with their work but neither were they dissatisfied; as a priority in their lives, work was unimportant. They came to work for purely instrumental reasons and their attachment to workmates, company and union was of a similar order. Other workers – while valuing their pay – also stressed the importance of the work group and the sense of achievement in their work.

In contrast to the content approaches, the process approach explores the psychological processes that are involved. Expectancy theory is based on the expectations that people bring with them to the work situation, and the context and way in which these expectations are satisfied (Vroom 1964). This is not a static model, and there may well be different sets of expectations at different times. Expectancy theory implies that management need to demonstrate to employees that effort will be recognised and rewarded, in both financial and non-financial terms. The importance of this theory is that the onus is on management to establish schemes to reward the behaviour it wants. Moreover, it helps to explain why employees do not always respond in the desired way. For example, they may not believe management's word that co-operation with the introduction of new technology will not lead to job losses.

Three concepts are central to this theory. First, performance–outcome expectancy: this means that employees believe that if they act in a particular way, there are foreseeable consequences. For example, employees might believe that if they exceed work quotas they will get bonuses, or if the target is not met pay will be docked. Second, the concept of valence, which refers to the value to the employee of an outcome deriving from behaviour. For example, one employee might value being promoted, while another would prefer to continue working doing the same job within the same department because of the strong value they place on friendship at work. Third, there is effort–performance expectancy, which is the employee's perception of the likelihood of achieving the desired objective. For example, if an employee believes it is impossible to meet a sales target because the product is of poor quality or that it is simply unrealistic, they probably will not try. In simple terms, employees focus on three questions:

- Can I perform at this level if I try?
- If I do manage to perform at the set level, what are the consequences?
- What do I feel about the consequences of that action?

The theory implies that low motivation will be the product of jobs where there is little worker control. Nadler and Lawler (1979) deduced some of these. They felt that management need to:

- discover what outcomes/rewards are valued (have higher valence) for each employee, for example whether it is monetary reward or recognition
- design tasks and jobs so that employees can satisfy needs through work
- individualise reward systems, including work organisation and benefits, possibly using a cafeteria-style approach
- be specific about the desired behaviours
- ensure that performance targets are attainable
- ensure there is a direct, clear and explicit link between desired performance and rewards; if staff value intrinsic rewards, such as interesting work, then management can concentrate on redesigning jobs rather than increasing pay
- check that there are no conflicting expectations
- ensure changes in reward/outcome are significant, for as Nadler and Lawler (p227) put it, 'trivial rewards will result in trivial amounts of effort and thus trivial improvements in performance', or, in more popular language, 'if you pay peanuts you get monkeys'
- check that everyone is treated fairly by the system.

BOX 43   AN OLD JEWISH FABLE

It seems that bigots were eager to rid their town of a Jewish man who had opened a tailor shop on Main Street, so they sent a group of rowdies to harass the tailor.

Each day, the ruffians would show up to jeer. The situation was grim, but the tailor was ingenious. One day when the hoodlums arrived, he gave each one of them a dime for their efforts. Delighted, they shouted their insults and moved on. The next day they returned to shout, expecting their dime. But the tailor said he could only afford a nickel and proceeded to hand a nickel to each of them. Well, they were a bit disappointed, but a nickel after all is a nickel, so they took it, did their jeering, and left.

The next day, they returned once again and the tailor said he had only a penny for them and held out his hand. Indignant, the young toughs sneered and proclaimed that they would certainly not spend their time jeering at him for a measly penny. So they didn't. And all was well for the tailor.

Source: Deci E. and Flaste R. *Why We Do What We Do: The dynamics of personal autonomy*. New York, Penguin. 1996. p26

A central concept of expectancy theory is the view that other approaches to motivation – such as advocated by Taylor, Mayo or Maslow – are based on the assumption that all employees are alike, motivated by money, recognition or whatever and all situations are alike. Hence there is one best way to motivate employees (Rollinson *et al* 1998, pp145–184). Contemporary thinking about motivation suggests we need an understanding of a range of theories given the wide variations in factors coming into play (Whiddett 2003; see also Box 43).

> Do you think that workers are (or should be) prepared to put up with dull, boring jobs if they are paid high wages?

REWARD MANAGEMENT IN CONTEXT

When trying to understand the strategic choices made by management about reward policies, the broader *political and economic context* is important. In the 1960s and 1970s the main reason for the introduction of incentive schemes was to provide a way of giving workers pay increases at a time of government restraints (Bowey *et al* 1982, pp37–53). Because of the lack of long-term strategic intent, few employers achieved reduced costs and less than half increased output. In the 1980s and 1990s the Conservative government's free-market philosophy and its attempt to cultivate an 'enterprise culture' influenced remuneration policies. This produced an ideological shift in ideas towards the concept of paying people for their performance rather than their attendance. At the time changes made to taxation policy – such as lower rates of income tax and new fiscal incentives for share ownership – also had a direct impact. In terms of the economic context, lower levels of inflation in the last few years have reduced the significance of general cost-of-living pay rises, and hence provided greater scope for the individualisation of annual pay increases. Product market developments also provided an impetus for change, especially with the intensification of international competition, privatisation, deregulation, and competitive restructuring.

There are several factors with an influence on salary and wage levels. Firstly, job 'size' has traditionally been the main determinant of pay. This includes factors such as responsibility, level in the organisational hierarchy, required knowledge, skills or competencies, external contacts, complexity and decision-making. Hence, the individual's hierarchical position in large organisations has been central to the design of internal pay structures, with performance rewarded by promotion. However, job size is now seen as less important than individual contribution. In other words, having a large staff or control of larger budgets does not in itself indicate a significant contribution that merits extra reward. Secondly, individual characteristics – such as age, experience, qualifications and special skills, contribution and performance – are also significant factors. Thirdly, labour market factors – such as the supply and demand of particular skills both locally and the 'going rate' in the particular labour market – are important. Fourthly, product market conditions and the employer's cost structure – such as its position in the market, profitability and market ambitions and strategies – have a major influence on pay strategy. Finally, the remuneration philosophy of the organisation also has an influence on wage and salary levels. An organisation with the reputation for being a 'good employer', and wishing to attract the most able staff, is likely to offer higher wages than one where staff are valued less positively.

Reward systems can influence a number of HR processes and practices, which in turn impact on organisational performance (Lawler 2000a), as follows.

1   Rewards influence recruitment and retention. High wages attract more applicants,

which allows greater choice over selection and hiring decisions, which in turn may reduce labour turnover. In addition, better performers generally need to be rewarded more highly than poor performers. The type of payment system – not just the level of rewards – also has an effect on recruitment and retention, so performance-based systems are more likely to attract high performers.

2   Employees see reward systems as signalling the importance the employer places on various activities or behaviours. Hence, reward systems have a motivational impact and need to be integrated with the corporate behaviour being sought. A key strategic issue is how to use the reward system to overcome the tendency towards short-termism. If rewards are tied too closely to annual performance, managers may not devote time and energy to long-term objectives and may 'mortgage the future for present performance'.

3   The way in which employees are rewarded has a major influence on corporate culture. For example, reward systems that provide benefits to long-serving staff are likely to shape the existing culture into one where loyalty is seen as central to the corporate ideology. In contrast, a system that rewards innovative behaviour is more likely to help create a creative and innovative culture.

4   Cost is a key factor in reward systems, and for service-sector organisations labour costs are a significant proportion of their overall costs. The employer might wish to achieve flexibility so that labour costs can be brought down if the organisation is under financial pressure. Having a lower cost ratio than competitors might be another aim. However, lower wages do not always lead to reduced labour costs because productivity may be lower whereas the cost of paying higher wages may be more than offset by higher levels of performance (Pfeffer 1998, pp195–202).

Integration or contradiction in reward structures

The fact that management aims may conflict with or contradict each other is a particular danger if those responsible for remuneration policy are unclear about its specific objectives. For example Armstrong (2002, p14) lists a number of possible management objectives:

- ensuring that firms can attract, retain and motivate the appropriate quantity and quality of staff
- communicating organisational values
- underpinning organisational change
- providing value for money
- supporting the realisation of key values
- encouraging behaviour to achieve organisations' objectives.

Another potential problem is that there may well be differences in the expectations of different groups of workers from the payment system, as we saw from the discussion on expectancy theory earlier in this chapter. While much of the literature discusses the functional and dysfunctional role of reward systems, it is not always matched by discussion of the strategic role of such systems. It is usual to regard the reward system as dependent on the business strategy and the management style of the organisation concerned. However, as we have seen from the previous section, existing human resources and reward systems may also exercise a constraint on corporate strategy, so the relationship is not simply one way.

The 'New Pay' is Lawler's term for an approach that asserts the need for an understanding of the organisation's goals, values and culture and the challenges of a global economy when formulating reward strategy. This has now become the orthodoxy in pay ideas (Schuster and Zingheim 1992; Lawler 2000a). The business strategy of the organisation determines the behaviours employees need to demonstrate in order to ensure that goals may be implemented effectively. These behaviours may, in part, be effected through the reward strategy (Lewis 2001). However, Lewis (p102) points out that there a number of assumptions underlying the model. First it assumes business strategy is a rational top-down process and that HR goals can be simply matched to this (see Chapter 4). Second, the model is 'essentially unitarist' in that it assumes employees will endorse business strategy and demonstrate the behaviours it implies. Third, it is deterministic – assuming that an effective reward strategy will have a direct impact upon organisational performance. Fourthly, it assumes pay will motivate employees to behave in a way in which they may not otherwise do. As Lewis (p102) observes:

> **Clearly, caution needs to be exercised in assuming that the implementation of strategic reward management will lead to a reward strategy that will automatically change employee behaviours in line with the organisation's business strategy. There are far too many variables which may conspire against such a straightforward cause–effect relationship. However, it would be foolish to abandon the possibility that reward strategy may play a role in contributing to organisational change.**

There are two dimensions to consider in the strategic design of reward systems (Lawler 2000a). First there is a structural content dimension (formal procedures and practices) and second there is a process dimension (communication and decision process parts). In relation to the *structural decisions*, there are several issues to address:

- *Basis for rewards* – Are people to be paid for the jobs they do (ie through job evaluation techniques) or for their skills or competencies? Skills-based pay is seen as more appropriate for those organisations that have a flexible, relatively permanent workforce that is oriented towards learning.

- *Pay for performance* – Should staff be paid on the basis of seniority or performance? Because of the problems in implementing performance-based schemes, some believe individual pay should be based on seniority, as in Japan, with motivation to be achieved through other means (such as personal growth or recognition). If management decides to pursue the performance route, then decisions need to be made on the behaviours to be rewarded and how they should be rewarded (for example, by individual or group plans).

- *Market position* – The market position and stance of an organisation will influence organisational climate. If management feels it is important to be a leading player with pay levels set above those of competitors, there is likely to be a different reward system from one in which staff are seen as less critical to business success.

- *Internal–external pay comparisons* – Management needs to decide the extent to which it values internal equity – someone doing similar work is paid the same even if they may be in different regions or in different businesses – or external equity, which focuses on the labour market as the key determinant of levels of pay. This issue depends on the extent to which the organisation wishes to have an overall corporate identity (eg everyone working for a multinational chemical company to have similar conditions of service) or product market differentiation (bulk chemicals and pharmaceuticals to be seen as distinct business or product lines).

- *Centralised–decentralised reward strategy* – Organisations with a centralised strategy usually have a corporate HR department that develops standardised pay and wage guidelines. This creates a feeling of internal equity and shared values. In decentralised organisations flexibility allows for local options.

- *Degree of hierarchy* – Management can choose whether it employs a hierarchical approach to reward – where people are rewarded according to their position in the hierarchy and are often also provided with symbols of their status – or a more egalitarian approach where the climate is more team-based and there are fewer status symbols.

- *Reward mix* – This refers to the type of rewards given to individuals (benefits, status symbols etc) or indeed the choice employees are given through a cafeteria-style approach where individuals can make up their own package (see Chapter 13). Again, the form of rewards should reflect the culture or climate the employer wishes to create and reinforce.

The Acas guidelines to selecting and installing a pay system are given in Box 44.

BOX 44 SELECTING AND INSTALLING A PAY SYSTEM: ACAS GUIDELINES

- Accept that there will inevitably be a cost involved.
- Avoid most potential problems with a systematic, well-timed and carefully planned approach.
- Re-examine the reasons for change and take advice both inside and outside the organisation. Obtain expert help if needed.
- Identify what the new system is required to do – how does it relate to the organisation's overall objectives?
- Look at possible new systems and consider which might best suit the particular organisation, with or without alteration.
- Don't just discard the existing system – take stock through discussions to enable the organisation to keep the good and change the less good.
- Involve the workforce, or its representatives, as much as possible, perhaps through a joint working party.
- Build in as much time as possible for proper discussion and consultation with the workforce and their representatives.
- New systems should be kept simple.
- Look out for any changes to differentials and relativities. Be careful the system does not directly or indirectly discriminate between men and women.
- Document the system and if possible run it for a trial period.
- Make arrangements for maintenance, monitoring and evaluation. Review the system regularly to ensure it is performing as required.

Source: Advisory Conciliation and Arbitration Service. *Pay Systems*. London, Acas. 2003a. pp5–6

Examine the strategic reward system of an organisation with which you are familiar and assess where the organisation fits with regard to the structural issues raised by Lawler. Do they support or contradict one another? How might greater horizontal and vertical integration be achieved?

In relation to the *process dimensions* of reward systems there are two key issues:

- *Communication policy* – How far the employer wants to have an open or closed policy on rewards depends on its philosophy. In some organisations disclosure of salary is a dismissible offence. The CIPD Reward Management Survey (2004f) revealed that as many as a third of employers asked their staff not to talk about pay and benefits with co-workers.

- *Decision-making practices* – The issue here is whether or not to involve employees in system design and administration. Involvement can lead to important issues being raised and expertise being provided, which is not always the case if a top-down approach is taken. Moreover, involving employees and their representatives helps the acceptance of any changes since there is a greater sense of legitimacy bestowed on decisions. Cox (2000, p363) presents the argument for involvement in pay scheme design as follows:

> Seeking information from employees may provide a fuller perspective on whatever problems exist in the operation of the current pay scheme, thus increasing the chance that they will be resolved in the design of the new system. Furthermore, this may also ensure that the rewards offered are commensurate in timing and kind with the rewards employees desire. Full explanations of the reasons for changing the system may make employees more likely to accept the new system. The consultation process may allow the opportunity to identify any individuals or groups likely to be adversely and unfairly affected and to take action to prevent this before the scheme is implemented. Some authors argue that the process itself of involving as many parties as possible in the development of a new scheme makes them more committed to its success.

There is no right or wrong approach, so what matters is choosing a position which supports the culture and systems, and which produces the behaviour necessary to enhance organisational effectiveness.

Moreover, reward systems need to fit with the HR system as a whole. Unless 'fit' exists, the organisation will be replete with conflicts and, to a degree, the reward system practices will potentially be cancelled out by the practices in other areas. In short, a contingency approach – which takes into account particular organisational and environmental factors – is likely to be superior to an off-the-shelf solution that reflects current fads and fashions (Brown 2001).

Much of the literature in the field tends to be prescriptive. We are told how management should tackle the subject of reward management but not what actually happens in practice. Kessler (2003) states that the overwhelming impression was one of incremental change in approaches to pay. Changes in reward policy appear to have been driven by short-term cost considerations and the need to respond to immediate labour market pressures rather than any strategic intent. A major concern is that few managements attempt to evaluate their pay schemes in any real depth. They appear not to have clear criteria against which the schemes can be evaluated, but rather tend to rely on a 'gut feel' assessment that, for example, because of its performance emphasis, a performance-related pay (PRP) system must be conducive to good performance (Sisson and Storey 2000). Conversely, any contraindications or problems are dismissed as mere 'teething problems' relating to issues of implementation.

TYPES OF PAYMENT SCHEME

According to Torrington *et al* (2002, p562), since the 1940s arrangements for payment have had one or two underlying philosophies. First the *service* philosophy, which emphasises the acquisition of experience, implying that people become more effective as they remain in a job so that their service is rewarded through incremental pay scales. These scales are typically of five to eight points, encouraging people to continue in the post for several years as there is still some headroom for salary growth. Second is the *fairness* philosophy, which emphasises getting the right structure of differentials. The progressive spread of job evaluation from the 1960s onwards was an attempt to cope with the problems of relative pay levels that were generated by increasing organisation size and job complexity. Legislation on equal value in the 1970s gave further impetus to this approach.

Accompanying the growth of pay systems emphasising service and fairness, was a steady decline in incentive schemes. These had been developed almost entirely for manual workers from the early part of this century until the late 1960s, but declined due to years of battling with union representatives, employees using their ingenuity in outwitting the work study officer, and changes in production technology. More recently there has been a return to the incentive idea and a new performance philosophy has arisen. Length of service is useful, fairness is necessary, but what really matters is the *performance* of the employee (Torrington *et al* 2002).

It is important that HR professionals see the payment system not solely as something in its own right, but also see the links with organisation strategy and other human resource practices. Simply adopting a policy of selecting a scheme because it is seen as the latest thing to do is likely to be a recipe for failure. Nor should management regard the adoption of a payment system as the complete and final solution to problems of pay policy. Indeed, there is a view that every scheme which is implemented, however satisfactory, contains the seeds of its own destruction (Watson 1986, pp182–183). As individuals or groups bring their own interests to bear on the system, this means that subsequently it becomes very difficult to manage as interests become embedded, and the system serves certain groups rather than the organisation as a whole. Furthermore, as technology, business objectives, work organisation and labour supply alter, systems may need to be re-evaluated. In short pay systems never last forever (Sisson and Storey 2000, p141).

> Describe the payment systems that exist in organisations with which you are familiar. Try to explain their rationale.

It is also crucial to understand that the choice of payment system depends on the particular circumstances of the organisation, the technology, the characteristics of the labour market and employee attitudes. Accordingly, managers need to think carefully about the conditions under which a scheme will operate and the messages it will send to various audiences. A contingency approach, in which managers pick a scheme appropriate to their organisational needs, is more likely to be successful (Taylor 2000a, pp15–18). For example, an employer who stresses the importance of quality is likely to undermine this philosophy by the introduction or maintenance of a payment-by-results scheme (such as piecework), sending a message that output is the key aim of the employer. Equally, an organisation which is not doing well financially may find it difficult to introduce a system of PRP as employees are likely to see few benefits for themselves. Indeed, research suggests that PRP schemes need to be well managed in order to facilitate a trouble-free introduction. Moreover, the paucity of systematic evidence on the incentive effects of various payment systems should urge us to be wary of swallowing a consultant's line that their package will improve performance where other schemes or strategies have failed.

Time rates

These are usually expressed as an hourly rate, a weekly or monthly wage, or an annual salary. Some three-quarters of British employees are paid on pure time rates, although in some cases a payment by results component may be added. There are two forms of time rate. The first is a flat rate per period of time, while the second incorporates fixed scales, with increases based on length of service (Lynch 2000, p275). Such schemes are simple and cheap to administer, are easily understood by employees and are unlikely to cause disputes in themselves. Having said that, they are limited in providing work incentives (Acas 2003a). Time rates are often found in managerial and white-collar work, although many managers put in more than their contractual hours, or in complex and process industries (such as in chemicals) where it is difficult to measure individual contributions to performance. With time-based systems, work effort and work quality has to be guaranteed by supervisory control or through well-established systems of custom and practice.

There has been a shift from simple wage systems, with a single rate attached to all jobs of the same description, to salary systems where there is a range of pay for each job grade. Salary systems with pay progression reflect a view that experience is important and should be rewarded; hence progression through salary scales is based on length of service or age (Thompson 2000, p127). However, there have been problems with traditional incremental systems – which in theory can provide both 'carrot and stick' by withholding or offering increments. In practice, the lack of a systematic appraisal system and high employee expectations means that automatic increments tend to be the norm. This means that staff bunch at the top of a grade, so making it expensive for employers to fund. While time rates should be simple, in practice additional payments for overtime add complexity. An additional problem with time-rate schemes is grade drift, whereby – over time – jobs bunch up in the higher ranks of the structure. Also there can be a proliferation of job grades, as new grades are used to 'buy' employee acceptance to a change in the job, which then requires restructuring every few years in order to simplify the structure. However, Brown and Walsh (1994, p454) argue that allowing grade drift in order to facilitate change – knowing there will be restructuring at a later period – is preferable to haggling over 'fair' cash shares from productivity improvements. In other words, one-off payments are granted in return for productivity improvements.

Payment by results

The philosophy with payment by results (PBR) is to establish a link between reward and effort as a motivational factor. Such schemes reflect the ideas of F. W. Taylor, the father of scientific management who, by standardising work processes through time and motion studies, laid the groundwork for such schemes to operate. As we saw earlier, views that workers are motivated solely by money led to payment schemes being designed to reflect this.

Individual PBR schemes vary in practice, and they can relate either to the whole of the employee's pay or be part of an overall pay package. They may involve payment varying according to output, or payment of a fixed sum on the achievement of a particular level of output. Most schemes have fallback rates and guarantee payments for downtime. The principal advantage of individual PBR schemes is that the incentive effect should be strong as workers can see a direct link between individual effort and earnings. By way of contrast, the major disadvantages of individual PBR are that they are expensive to install and maintain, often requiring a dedicated team to establish the system. Moreover, standards are often disputed and considerable effort is spent on both sides to apply the appropriate standards, or renegotiate in the light of any changes, such as new technology or problems with components supplied. Finally, there is often friction between employees because of the emphasis on personal performance as external factors are likely to impact on performance, but are not within their own control.

The most popular form of individual PBR is piecework. Such schemes have a long tradition in British industry, in particular in the textiles, footwear and engineering industries. They are based upon work-study methods whereby the employee is simply paid a specific rate or price per unit (ie piece) of output. Although piecework survives in some industries, such as clothing (Druker 2000, p115), few new schemes are being introduced and their importance has declined since the 1960s (Millward et al 2000, p213). Such schemes do not fit with the emphasis on team-based forms of work organisation, for example cellular manufacturing. Outside of the production arena, PBR was common in commission paid to sales staff in insurance and estate agencies. However, commission-based pay was badly hit by scandals over the mis-selling of pensions in the 1990s because this form of payment was seen as a major contributor to problems. More recently, this issue was evident deregulated telephone directory enquiries services, where the bonus system was based on reducing call time and it was reported that operators were providing wrong numbers so as to meet targets and receive bonus payments.

Three major issues need to be considered in relation to PBR schemes: control, erosion and complexity.

1 *Control* – It has been argued that under PBR, less personal or direct supervision is necessary as it is in the worker's own interest to be productive. The age-old problem of buying workers' time, but not their effort, is supposedly eliminated. On the other hand, the system encourages speed not quality (Druker 2000, p115), so supervisors need to watch for short-cuts that might lead to lower quality or to health and safety risks or hazards. With frequent changes in technology, management now need closer control over production, and hence individual PBR has become less popular.

2 *Erosion* – Schemes can degenerate through rate drift as a result of a learning curve, new technology (which does not always lead to remeasuring of jobs), and various worker fiddles that can hide slack rates.

3   *Complexity* – For PBR to operate properly, standards of performance need to be set. In the past, rate fixers who had expertise in the industry would set standard prices or times, but more recently standards are set by using work-study techniques. This requires both work-study and personnel maintenance, not to mention a quality department. However, changes in product, material, specification or method are likely to require a new set of standards, which in turn may stimulate a bargaining process that can lead to employee relations problems, especially when workers who have become proficient in a specific task resist new methods.

One other key issue relates to problems of leapfrogging and poor morale as a result of changes in rates that other workers then try to negotiate. PBR can rarely be applied uniformly to all employees in an organisation and hence may seem out of place in a harmonised environment.

A variation is group PBR, which is often used where the production process makes it difficult to attribute performance to any one individual, so it is based around the group. There are similarities with individual PBR. A group scheme is likely to be particularly effective if it harnesses group cohesion and solidarity. However, the motivational effect of group PBR schemes is likely to decline as group sizes increase, the group loses its ethos, and there is a greater distance between effort and earnings.

> Can you think of any jobs for which a form of PBR might be suitable? Why?

Plant/enterprise-based schemes

While PBR can be effective for particular industries or groups, it may do little for overall performance, especially if there is friction between different groups. Enterprise- or plant-wide bonus schemes (sometimes called *gainsharing*) encourage staff to identify more widely with the organisation as a whole, attempting to make work appear as a win–win situation with both employees and the organisation deriving direct financial success from the operation (Bowey 2000, p330; Ferrin and Dirks 2003). Gainsharing (a minority practice in the UK) differs from profit-sharing schemes in that it takes account of the fact that profits may be affected by external factors such as interest rates or increased price of raw material. It therefore recognises that profits may not be directly related to productivity gains. Employees are rewarded for their improved performance and this helps them to see the link between their efforts and the achievement of corporate objectives (Morley 2002a, pp93–94).

Scanlon plans are named after their inventor, an ex-union official who was responsible for a number of schemes in the US steel industry in the 1930s and 1940s. They are based on the ratio of total payroll costs to sales value of production. A norm is estimated from inspection of figures over a representative period prior to the introduction of the technique. The smaller the ratio, the higher the bonus. The payment aspect of Scanlon plans is supplemented by a participation element often incorporating both a suggestion scheme and some form of consultative structure at departmental and/or unit level.

The *Rucker plan* (and its UK variant, the *Bentley plan*) is similar in many respects, but the wage calculation is based on the ratio of payroll costs to production value added (PVA), that is the difference between the sales value of output and the cost of materials, services and supplies. It represents the commercial value of the process of conversion from raw (or bought-in) materials to the finished product, so that value added is then available for the payment of all potentially internally controlled costs such as wages, profits and investment. The amount that constitutes wages is a proportion of the value added, fixed at a rate determined after inspection of records over the preceding years. For example, assume that for every £1000 received for the sales value of output £500 is spent on the cost of materials, supplies and services. The £500 remaining is the production value added. An inspection of previous accounts suggests that labour's share of PVA is 40 per cent, that is wages have typically taken £200 of the £500 value added. Wages will then increase or decrease in future depending upon the absolute size of PVA, and this can be increased by greater sales value of output or lower costs of services, supplies and materials. Either of these will increase the amount available for distribution as wages, profits and investment. Increasing the sales value of output can be achieved by higher sales or prices, and costs of materials can be reduced – among other actions – by greater control over their usage, a higher proportion of output which is 'right first time', more efficient utilisation of energy and so on. The incentive for employees to improve these aspects of their work is recognised in an explicit manner and can be rewarded by higher payments; gainsharing is therefore institutionalised and becomes a non-negotiable bonus for the employee. In addition, so as to protect workers against loss-sharing, minimum wage levels are set, and a reserve account is set up to cope with this eventuality.

However, the payment element is only one part of the scheme. Central to the whole scheme is a structure enabling employee representatives to contribute to decision-making via a works council or Joint Consultative Committee (JCC) arrangement. IDS (1999) reports on a gain-sharing plan for workers at Philips Components in Durham where payment reflected local labour market rates, technical performance and an annual bonus. The plan operated as a production rather than team bonus linked to factors both team and plant based (Druker 2000, p16). Managers are charged with the responsibility of ensuring that employees understand the figures and with listening to worker suggestions about the operation of the system and its establishment. Thus a key feature of the scheme is formalising the relationship between employee participation in decision-making, organisational efficiency and individual reward.

In general such schemes have the advantage that employees see their contribution to the total effort of the enterprise and do not see themselves as individual units. In this way it can facilitate achievement of corporate identity. As this form of financial participation is often part of a wider consultation process, this can lead to a greater understanding of business issues as employees take more interest in the overall performance of the enterprise. There may be a greater willingness on the part of employees to accept and even push for change; managers may feel more able to discuss issues with workers; and greater productivity and efficiency can be achieved.

Set against the advantages, there are some potential disadvantages. Firstly, while gain-sharing plans are implemented on the assumption that employees can see the connection between their own efforts and the rewards generated by the scheme, in many cases they have little control over the size of the bonus. External factors – such as increased costs of raw materials or services – may limit the bonus, as may management decisions to delay an increase in prices due to competitive pressures. Secondly, rather than encouraging co-operation between different groups in the organisation, the schemes may increase intergroup hostility and recriminations if the bonus levels fail to meet employee expectations. Not only can this be problematic for employers and run counter to their objectives, it can also create conflicts within and between unions. Thirdly, some unions fear that gainsharing plans will lead to a progressive marginalisation of their role. This could occur because collective bargaining is likely to become less important in determining wage levels, or due to the fact that employees will develop greater commitment to the goals of the company and 'give away' hard-fought-for gains. Most important of all, some schemes may fail because managers are not prepared to accept a modified role, listen to employee suggestions for improvements, and act upon these ideas, and reassertion of managerial prerogatives is likely to undermine employee commitment to the scheme.

> Given the current vogue for empowerment and the gaining of employee commitment to organisational goals, why are establishment-wide incentive schemes not more popular?

Performance-related pay

The early 1990s have seen employers from both the private and the public sectors putting a much greater emphasis on 'paying for performance' and attempting to 'incentivise' remuneration in order to improve individual and organisational performance and create a new performance-based culture. (For more on performance management, refer to Chapter 7.) These schemes base pay on an assessment of the individual's job performance. While such schemes are not identical they provide 'individuals with financial rewards in the form of increases to basic pay or cash bonuses which are linked to an assessment of performance, usually in relation to agreed objectives' (Armstrong 2002, p261). Accordingly, pay is linked to performance measured by a number of specific objectives (for example, sales targets or customer satisfaction). This reflects a move towards rewarding output (rather than input), using qualitative (rather than quantitative) judgements in assessing performance, a focus on working objectives (rather than personal qualities) and an end to general annual across-the-board pay increases (Fowler 1988).

PRP became popular as a reflection of the 'enterprise culture' in the late 1980s but continues to find favour in two-thirds of organisations up to the present day particularly for managers and professional staff. In many sectors it has replaced traditions systems of reward that valued seniority and long service, but not performance. It has also become more widely used in the public sector (for example, local government, the NHS, the Civil Service and more recently teachers; see Box 45) where governments of both political complexions have promoted the concept.

BOX 45   TEACHERS AND PERFORMANCE-RELATED PAY

The teachers' case is interesting as it reflects the imposition of performance-related pay (PRP) on an unenthusiastic workforce. As part of a wider set of changes in the education sector designed to enhance skills, salaries have been raised 'substantially but selectively' by introducing a threshold (which is based on an application form with evidence of knowledge) on top of existing experience-related salary scales. Those who pass the threshold immediately receive £2000 and are able to enter a new pay range based on annual performance review that could take salaries up to £30,000 (Cooper 2000, p 11; Marsden 2000)

However, the scheme has been attacked by the NUT and NAS/UWT who claimed it would lead to jealousy and loss of morale. Academics such as David Guest stated that 'for performance related pay to work, you have to have a situation where the employee has control over the outcome. If they don't have control, the whole thing becomes a farce.' Guest noted though that teachers would be pragmatic and that 'most will overcome their distaste and see that the government is offering a free gift they might as well go for'. In research conducted at the London School of Economics, Marsden (2000) noted that as teachers are strongly attached to the principle that their pay should reflect job demands, there is a feeling that all teachers deserve a pay rise. Whatever the unfairness and inconsistencies of the old system it is suggested that the proposed link between pay and performance will do little to improve fairness. While the Government stressed the positive arguments for improving rewards and incentives, teachers' responses are likely to be conditioned by what they believe are its true objectives. There is general scepticism about the professed goal of raising pupil achievements, and a strong suspicion that there is a hidden agenda of minimising the cost of uprating teachers' salaries, and of getting more work out of them (Marsden 2000). The headlines and debates have continued as almost all teachers applying for the threshold bonus have been successful (only 3% of applications failed to qualify), and over £12 million has been spent on external assessors to verify that heads had correctly awarded bonuses (Cassidy 2001). Various studies have found little evidence to suggest payments had improved results or attracted more people into teaching. According to Professor Peter Dolton (2003) 'a bricklayer may lay more bricks if paid a bonus, but this does not apply to teachers, who are highly motivated professionals already working to maximum capacity'. It appears that the best features of the scheme were on the performance management side with staff given opportunities for personal development and many valued the opportunity to talk about their job with a mentor (Wragg et al 2004).

PRP is different from the types of incentive scheme that we have discussed so far in this chapter in that many traditional incentive schemes in manufacturing are collectively negotiated and based on standard formulae, whereas PRP is designed on an individual and personal basis. Accordingly, some workers do better than others – and some do worse – and it is this that makes PRP for manual workers a recent phenomenon. A common approach has been to have PRP on top of a general award, so that, say, 2 per cent is awarded to all employees to cover inflation, and additional payments are made to reward above-average performance. Alternatively, there may be no across-the-board increase but all pay increases are dependent on performance.

Typical PRP distribution is shown in Table 26.

Table 26   *Typical PRP distribution*

Rating	General increase/cost of living plus performance pay
Exceptional	General +5%
Highly effective	General +4%
Effective	General +2%
Less than effective	General
Unacceptable	No increase

According to Armstrong (2002, p271), PRP offers the following potential benefits:

- It motivates people and therefore improves individual and organisational performance.
- It acts as a lever for change.
- It delivers a message that performance generally or in specified areas is important and good performance is paid more than poor performance.
- It links reward to the achievement of specified results that support the achievement of organisational goals.
- It helps the organisation to attract and retain people through financial rewards and competitive pay, and reduces the 'golden handcuff' effect of poor performers staying with employers.
- It meets a basic human need – to be rewarded for achievement.

> What are the principal benefits that employer and employees gain from PRP? Does this general list correspond with experience in your own organisation?

It is hard to find definitive evidence to measure the achievements of PRP. Indeed, isolating one aspect of HR and linking it to performance is problematic. While PRP has been widely promoted and practitioners in particular seem to retain great faith in its merits, in recent years there has been a more cautious, and indeed critical, evaluation of the ideas behind PRP. Brown and Armstrong (1999) claimed that there are at least as many studies suggesting PRP can reinforce and contribute to organisational and individual performance as those suggesting that it cannot. The studies cited tend to be based on employer perceptions (often the personnel managers responsible for introducing the scheme) rather than employees (Hendry *et al* 2000). The best 'proxy' indicator is likely to be employee reactions. As Lewis (1998, p74) notes:

> **if employees are generally in agreement with both the principle and practice of PRP, then they will be motivated to better job performance and beneficial organisational outcomes will follow. Conversely, if they are not in agreement with either the principle or the practice of PRP, then they will not be motivated to perform more effectively in their jobs and such organisational outcomes will not follow.**

PRP is most commonly awarded on the basis of individual performance appraisal, by each employee's line manager, against pre-agreed objectives. Since the first performance pay schemes in the Inland Revenue in the late 1980s, appraisal has moved away from evaluation against a standard set of criteria for all employees, and towards setting individual objectives in line with those of the organisation as a whole (Marsden *et al* 2000).

The most comprehensive studies on the effects of performance-related pay on employee motivation and work behaviour have been conducted by Marsden *et al* (2000) looking at the public sector. They reported evidence of a clear incentive effect for those gaining above average PRP, but that it was likely that it was offset by a more widespread demotivating effect arising from difficulties of measuring performance fairly, although organisational commitment appeared to offset some of the negative effects of PRP (see Table 27 on page 340).

Table 27   *PRP – the good, the bad and the ugly*

	% agree	% disagree/ no view
PRP means good work is recognised and rewarded	33.3	66.7
PRP is a good principle	51.5	48.5
PRP has given me an incentive to work beyond my job requirements	16.6	83.4
PRP given me an incentive to show more initiative	17.9	82.1
PRP has made me more aware of the organisation's objectives	36.3	63.7
PRP causes jealousies among staff	66.8	33.2
PRP is bad for team working	46.5	53.5
Management operate a quota	61.3	38.7
PRP has made me less willing to co-operate with management	17.3	82.7

Source: Marsden D., French S. and Kubo K. *Why Does Performance Pay De-motivate? Financial incentives versus performance appraisal*. LSE Centre for Economic Performance Discussion Paper. London, LSE. 2000

The study confirms that PRP in British public services has had a positive incentive effect for significant numbers of employees, but that this depends on getting above-average additional financial reward, and even more importantly, on the quality of goal-setting and appraisal processes. Also evident are the corrosive effect on employee motivation of appraisals that employees feel are not a fair reflection of their performance. The problems associated with performance management are also covered in Chapter 7. Although discussions of PRP for top executives, sales and sports personnel have tended to focus on the incentive effect of additional rewards, the experience of ordinary public employees suggests that the strength of marginal financial incentives is weak compared with that of goal-setting and appraisal. Likewise, the damage done by poorly conducted appraisals outweighs the benefits of additional financial incentives and this puts the emphasis on the skills and motivation of line managers and suggests the need for them to have ownership of the process.

Where PRP motivated employees positively, their workplace performance, as judged by line managers, was better. Where it demotivated employees, line-manager judgements of workplace performance were less favourable.

It is difficult to grade performance in a way that staff find acceptable. One of the chief lessons from the work by Marsden *et al* (2000) is that the success of PRP is dependent upon the way that employees are allocated into different performance grades; wherever the line is drawn, it is likely to be controversial, especially when employees are suspicious of both management's intentions and its competence to appraise fairly. Finally, many staff felt that they were unable to improve their performance.

The experience at the Inland Revenue appears to have also been reflected in the public sector more generally (Marsden and French 1998). The Makinson Report (2000) examined the criticisms of PRP in the civil service and suggested replacing it with team bonuses, observing that while in theory performance incentives can improve productivity within the public sector, in practice 'most arrangements in place today are ineffective and discredited'. Makinson noted a 'stark contrast between the approval of the principle and the disenchantment with the practice of performance pay' (p2).

There are many other criticisms directed at PRP – the difficulty of formulating objectives, the risk of bias or perceived bias, the inevitable inflationary tendency, the high costs of administration, the dubious impact on performance, the problems associated with a focus on the individual and the difficulty of organising and delivering the necessary degree of managerial commitment (Harris 2001; Torrington *et al* 2002, pp604–605). Furthermore, performance pay stimulates high expectations. People respond to it because there is the prospect of more money, but it has to be significantly more money if it is to be attractive. Therefore, management often introduces the scheme by indicating how much one can expect. An enthusiastic, performance-enhancing response (which is the sole purpose of the exercise) will bring with it a widespread expectation of considerably more money. A theme echoed widely in the PRP literature is that people think it is a good practice in principle, and indeed it is difficult to object to the view that hardworking and effective employees should get more than those who are less hardworking or effective. However, they are likely to disagree with *how* the scheme operates in practice, a factor that may lead to continual changes to the schemes. Other concerns include the fact that managers are unhappy at marking staff below average, feeling that all their staff are above average. One way to prevent this is to allocate quotas for each category, to avoid ratings clustering at a central point, but this can seem arbitrary. As Purcell (2000, p41) notes:

> **most people in receipt of IPRP (Individual Performance Related Pay) are in the middle range of performance. We can expect 10% of staff to be in the top-performing bracket and 5% to be in the poor-performer category. The rest, all 85% of them, will get average awards that are similar to the going rate. Most of them have no prospect of getting into the top bracket next year, so the incentive is minimal. We could live with this if the outcome of the pay system was neutral, but often it is negative, costing more than any benefit achieved.**

In the performance assessment process, which lies at the heart of individual PRP, there are complaints about subjectivity and inconsistency (leading to accusations of favouritism). This is often compounded by lack of attention to the training of managers in carrying out appraisal and to the administrative procedures for monitoring arrangements. Furthermore, the links between performance and the level of pay are not always clear and effective. It is also apparent that individual PRP sits rather uneasily with a number of other policies that managers profess to be pursuing – especially the emphasis on teamwork.

There is a concern that PRP – with its emphasis on annual individual performance – leads to a short-termist approach whereby individuals look for quick returns from small-scale projects rather than addressing more fundamental problems. Of course, it is possible to argue that this simply suggests that care needs to be exercised in the choice of performance objectives. If sales targets are seen as the only real objective, then it is likely that long-term customer relationships, as well as management–staff relations, may be threatened. On the other hand, if the latter are highlighted as key priorities in the targets, the issue of measurement may be problematic.

Another key issue relates to equal opportunities. Armstrong (2002, p275) notes that there is ignorance of Danfors' 1989 ruling under the EC Equal Pay Directive, which states that 'The quality of work carried out by a worker may not be used as a criterion for pay increments where its application shows itself to be systematically unfavourable to women.' As Armstrong (p275) comments, 'there is a possibility that assessments made by managers (the majority of whom are still male) of their female staff could be biased'. Druker (2000, p123) also observes that 'payment "for the job" failed to deliver equal pay for women workers but, given a legacy of workplace gender discrimination, there is a risk that payment "for the person" will counter rather than advance the cause of pay equity'.

The damaging effects of poorly designed PRP in two organisations are outlined in Box 46.

BOX 46   THE DAMAGING EFFECT OF POORLY DESIGNED PRP

H. J. Heinz Company only paid a bonus to managers in individual areas if they managed to improve their profits on the previous year. In response to this plan, managers manipulated profits so that they could always show a year-on-year improvement. They did this by delaying or accelerating deliveries to customers, thus securing payment for activities that had not actually been performed yet. Although in this way the managers were able to secure a pay raise for themselves, it also meant that the future flexibility of the company was severely restricted, thus reducing long-term growth and compromising the value of the company.

At Sears, a badly designed compensation system had even more critical consequences. Mechanics working for the company's car repair operation were paid according to the profits earned on repairs requested by customers. With this incentive in mind, the mechanics talked customers – with some success – into commissioning unnecessary repairs. When this dishonesty was exposed, the Californian authorities threatened to close down all the Sears car repair shops in the state. The company abandoned this type of performance-related compensation.

Source: Adapted from Fry B. and Osterloh M. *Successful Management by Motivation*. Berlin, Springer-Verlag. 2002. p72

A dimension often neglected is a cultural one. Most research on PRP is based in the USA or UK. However, in more communitarian cultures, the Anglo-Saxon notion of pay for performance may be less popular. As Gannon (2000, p5) notes 'employers may not accept that individual members of the group should excel – a way that reveals the shortcomings of other members. An "outstanding individual" may be defined as one who benefits others. Customers in more communitarian cultures also take offence at a 'quick buck' mentality, preferring to build up and maintain relationships.

Another cultural insight is provided by Schneider and Barsoux (1997, p14):

> **While it would be unthinkable for most American managers to consider implementing a system at home where the amount that family members are given to eat is related to their contribution to the family income, at work the notion of pay for performance seems quite logical. In contrast, in many African societies a collective logic prevails; the principles applied to family members also apply to employees. One multinational, in an effort to improve the productivity of the workforce by providing nutritious lunches, met with resistance and the demand that the cost of the meal be paid directly to the workers so that they could feed their families. The attitude was one of "How can we eat while our families go hungry?"**

Although PRP is declining in popularity, it is still widely utilised. Cox (2000, p372) describes this as puzzling given negative findings, with PRP seen as 'almost universally condemned as unworkable and ineffective in the UK'. The concept of team reward is discussed in Box 47.

BOX 47   TEAM REWARD

Concerns regarding the potential limitations of individual performance related pay, combined with the shift towards a culture of team-working in many organisations, have led to extensive interest in the concept of team reward. Team reward is a broad term, used to refer to a wide range of schemes aiming to reward employees collectively on the basis of their performance, and in turn intending to increase employee contribution and improve productivity. A team may be defined as a small group of employees, all employees at a particular plant or location, or all employees in the organisation. Accordingly, specific schemes range from bonus rewards for small teams, to gainsharing and company- or plant-wide bonus schemes. Theoretically, team reward offers several advantages by providing an incentive to improve performance, encouraging teamwork and co-operation, clarifying team goals and aligning objectives of individual teams with the wider organisational strategy. It may also encourage low performers to improve to meet the team standards. Team reward may be introduced as part of a broader culture change programme. In practice, however, implementation and administration of team reward schemes may be difficult, and the use of team reward remains very much a minority practice. Firstly, it may be difficult to identify suitable teams. There is also the danger that individual contribution is overlooked, and this may demotivate the highest performing employees. Organisational flexibility may also be jeopardised if staff in high performing teams become reluctant to move. Competition may also lead to unco-operative behaviour and rivalry between teams. Developing fair and acceptable measures of team performance may also be problematic. Lastly, it is possible that the benefits of the scheme may fall once the scheme has been in operation for a few years. Ultimately, whether a team reward scheme will be successful within an organisation depends upon the specific culture and context, as well as the objectives of the initiative. In all cases, the introduction of team reward needs to be considered and planned very carefully, or else it could actually prove ineffective or even damaging.

Source: IRS Employment Review 732b. 'Whatever happened to team reward?', *Pay and Benefits Bulletin 524*, July 2001. pp2–7

Financial participation and employee share ownership

Since the 1980s there has been a substantial growth in the field of financial participation (sometimes termed people's capitalism) fuelled by a number of developments in the area. It included the Conservative government's interest in extending financial involvement on a voluntary basis as opposed to other more radical forms of participation. In addition the Social Chapter makes reference to employee participation in the capital or profits/losses of the European company. Unlike current British provisions, however, it goes further in requiring a scheme to be negotiated between the management board of the enterprise and the employees or their representatives. There are a number of objectives behind the introduction of financial involvement – such as education, motivation, recruitment and retention, performance and paternalistic ideas – although it is likely that several of these are combined (Hyman 2000, pp180–181; Gamble *et al* 2002, p10).

There was a major growth in employee share ownership schemes in the 1990s, which can be attributed partly to tax incentives in order to make them more attractive to companies. The WERS survey (Cully *et al* 1998) showed that over 40 per cent of employees received profit-related payments or bonuses and that nearly 30 per cent were entitled to Save As You Earn (SAYE) share options (Arthurs 2002b, p200). Such payments are on the increase in Europe with British companies leading the way (Pendleton and Brewster 2001) and there is some evidence suggesting that organisations in which employees have a financial stake perform better (Freeman 2001).

A number of problems are apparent in profit-sharing and employee share ownership schemes. Firstly, schemes do not usually provide any real control because employees are unable to influence to any great extent the level of profits or the quality of management decision-making within the enterprise. Secondly, investing savings in the firms for which they work can increase employee insecurity. If the employer goes out of business or suffers cutbacks, individuals not only stand to lose their jobs, they might also lose some or all of their savings (Heery 2000, p65). Marconi staff facing redundancy in 2002 found the values of shares held in the company reduced by 97 per cent over the previous 12 months (CIPD 2004g). The 2002 Enron scandal in the USA exemplifies this. A further major problem with financial involvement is that it does not link effort to reward in a clear and unambiguous manner, nor is the payout made at regular enough intervals to act as a motivator of staff. Because profits or share prices are affected by many factors other than employee performance, it is difficult to conceive of this as a reward for effort. Indeed, due to factors beyond the control of employees, an individual who has worked extra hard during the year may be 'rewarded' with a negligible profit share, or vice versa. Equally, by the time the share announcement is made, so much time has passed since the beginning of the financial year that it is difficult to recall how hard one had been working. All of these problems are especially marked in multidivisional businesses. This leads to the disembodiment of profit sharing from its alleged motivational base making shares/bonuses nothing more than an extra payment that leads to more or less satisfaction depending upon the amount. Some would argue that employers would be better advised using this money to reward specific individuals, rather than through a standardised, all-embracing system.

Can profit sharing make organisations more democratic?

New payment initiatives

Skills-based pay (sometimes referred to as competence-based pay or pay-for-knowledge) schemes have become more prominent in organisations (Hastings 2000; Acas 2003a). This approach emerged from the USA in the 1980s to provide incentives for technical staff. Core competencies or skills are built into the pay system, and rewarded according to the standard or level achieved, so inputs and outputs are considered rather than just the latter – which has become a criticism of PRP – and it is forward-looking rather than retrospective. Such an approach encourages skill development and should widen and deepen the skills base of the organisation. Furthermore, it may increase job satisfaction, break down rivalries between groups or units, and increase flexibility as well. This in turn could reduce the costs of absenteeism. Competence-based pay is actually wider than skills-based pay as it incorporates behaviour and attributes, rather than simply skills alone and some writers suggest that skills-based pay is suited to manual work, while competency pay suits white-collar work. In many respects this system represents a rejection of the concept of job evaluation as it evaluates the person rather than the job. There are potential problems with such systems, in that management needs to be thinking some years ahead about future skill requirements and it may create high and unfulfilled expectations among employees if they reach the top of the skills-based pay structure. As Lewis (2001, p108) notes:

> the more the approach moves from one where identifying discernable skills and outputs is possible, the more subjective the measurement process becomes. As yet, little empirical research has been done on the operation of competence-related pay but it would be surprising were it to uncover anything other than the same sort of employee dissatisfactions as PRP. However, the measurement criteria themselves may be more acceptable to employees than in the case of PRP. This is often because there is some form of employee involvement in the development of the competence statements, albeit that line managers are making the assessment of the extent to which they have been demonstrated. This is unlike PRP where it is usually the manager who defines the performance objectives and assesses performance.

Competency-based pay is seen as more applicable for organisations experiencing rapid technical change and where a high degree of involvement already exists, so that the new scheme can be introduced with the co-operation of employees and the exchange of information which is necessary (Cox 2000). There is little evidence of its impact in the UK, and it appears more written about than practised (Thompson 2000, p143). Furthermore as Druker (2000, p119) notes:

> **There are constraints as well as benefits in the use of skills-based pay. It requires a careful analysis of skill needs and a clear commitment to training opportunities. While skills-based payment systems seem to facilitate an open-ended commitment to upward mobility, employers are concerned with the application as much as with the acquisition of skill. There is a concern to avoid paying for skills that are not used. The scope for advancement through skills acquisition is likely to be inhibited both by the training budget and by employer willingness to accommodate increased wage costs, unless it is an integral and necessary aspect of organisational change.**

IN SEARCH OF THE HAPPY WORKPLACE

While there is considerable research on high performance workplaces the impact of HR practices on employee well-being is less well researched. According to work by Peccei, HR practices do have a significant effect on workforce well-being and the benefits were more positive than negative.

The characteristics of happy workplaces and the HR practices that emphasise them are listed in Box 48.

BOX 48   HAPPY WORKPLACES

Generally speaking, happy workplaces are ones where employees felt that they:

- have reasonable workloads and do not feel they have to work too hard
- have reasonable levels of control and variety of work, but where jobs are not felt to be too damaging
- have a good wage–effort bargain and feel that, on balance, they are well paid for what they do
- have reasonable job security
- are treated with consideration and respect by management and generally feel that management cares for their well-being and values their contribution at work.

The key question, then, is what are the main HR practices that help to sustain and underpin happy workplaces? Generally speaking, happy workplaces are more likely to be ones where:

- the workforce is employed on a more stable full-time basis, but where people do not necessarily have to work long hours or overtime. In other words, they are workplaces that make minimal use of peripheral workers on temporary and/or part-time contracts, but where hours of work are kept within reasonable bounds.
- considerable emphasis is put on multiskilling and where jobs, although individually paced, tend to be more loosely structured and defined. More generally, they are workplaces where management puts a reasonable emphasis on goal-setting and feedback, but where jobs are not particularly pressured and

where, on the whole, there is not a very strong emphasis on teamwork, on the systematic upgrading of skills and on the acquisition of new competences.

■ the workforce enjoys comparatively high rates of pay but where, at the same time, there is also a fair degree of internal dispersion in earnings and where, importantly, employees are provided with generous non-pay benefits, such as company health and pension plans and extra holiday and maternity leave entitlements.

■ management communicates extensively with employees through a variety of channels, and where there is systematic sharing.

Source: Peccei R. *Human Resource Management and the Search for the Happy Workplace*. Rotterdam, Erasmus Research Institute of Management. 2003

CONCLUSIONS

It is clear that there are fads and fashions in the reward area that are influenced by prevailing theories of motivation, as well as external and internal contingencies. In this chapter we reviewed the way in which dominant reward philosophies tend to reflect the views of leading management writers who make significantly different assumptions about what motivates workers. Accordingly, incentive schemes are typically founded upon the assumption that money is the sole motivating force, while time-based systems are more likely to reflect the view that employees have hierarchies of needs. By way of contrast, some of the process theorists argue that motivation is a highly personal concept, and therefore reward policies need to be flexible, allowing for cafeteria-style benefits and individualised packages. Factors external to the organisation – such as incomes policies, taxation systems, and the management of the economy and local labour market factors – also have an important influence over the choice of appropriate reward systems, as does the employer's overall business strategy and position in the product market.

We have reviewed a range of different payment systems, considering objectives and purpose, extensiveness, and advantages and disadvantages in practice. The point is that no one type of system is superior to the others, because so much depends upon the context in which the schemes are to function. In this respect, the history and traditions of the workplace, the industry and the local labour market are all critical, as too are the attitudes of management and employees. It is argued that the pay package represents a powerful potential lever in facilitating employee contributions to organisational success, but too often employers adopt pay systems without a full and systematic analysis of the available options. Rather than being commonplace, strategic reward management is a rarity, and all that seems to happen is that employers 'shuffle the pack' (Kessler 1994), moving from one scheme to another when deterioration sets in rather than develop a 'total reward scheme' (Zingheim and Schuster 2002). As the CIPD (2004f, p42) themselves note 'it seems that in their search for a magic bullet to solve their reward and recognition issues, people are overlooking the already extensive arsenal of total reward practices at their disposal never mind the intrinsic reward and regulation that can be derived from work itself'. Furthermore, pay is a double-edged sword given its centrality to the employment relationship. It *can* be seen as a lever for change but the importance of pay means the consequences of getting it wrong are serious (Kessler 2003). But we also need to recall that the reward package is somewhat more than the payment system alone, incorporating a range of financial and non-financial benefits; these are considered in the next chapter.

USEFUL READING

Advisory, Conciliation and Arbitration Service. *Pay Systems*. London, Acas. 2003a.

Advisory, Conciliation and Arbitration Service. *Appraisal Related Pay*. London, Acas. 2002.

Armstrong M. *Employee Reward*, 3rd edition. London, CIPD. 2002.

Arthur J. *and* Aiman-Smith L. 'Gainsharing and organizational learning: an analysis of employee suggestions over time', *Academy of Management Journal*, Vol. 44, No. 4, 2001. pp737–754.

Ferrin D. *and* Dirks K. 'The use of rewards to increase and decrease trust: mediating processes and differential effects', *Organizational Science*, Vol. 14, No. 1, 2003. pp18–31.

Gratton L. 'More than money', *People Management*, 29 January 2004. p23.

Hendry C., Woodward S., Bradley P. *and* Perkins S. 'Performance and rewards: cleaning out the stables', *Human Resource Management Journal*, Vol. 10, No. 3, 2000. pp46–62.

Kessler I. 'Reward system choices', in J. Storey (ed), *Human Resource Management*. London, Routledge. 2001.

Lawler E. *Rewarding Excellence: Pay strategies for the new economy*. New York, Jossey Bass. 2000a.

Lewis P. 'Reward management', in T. Redman *and* A. Wilkinson (eds), *Contemporary Human Resource Management*. London, Financial Times/Pearson. 2001.

Thompson P. *Total Reward*. London, CIPD. 2002.

Thorpe R. *and* Homan G (eds), *Strategic Reward Systems*. London, Financial Times/Prentice Hall. 2000.

White G. *and* Druker J. (eds), *Reward Management: A critical text*. London, Routledge. 2000.

Wright A. *Reward Management in Context*. London, CIPD. 2004.

Zingheim P. *and* Schuster J. 'Pay it forward', *People Management*, 2002. pp32–34.

Equity and Fairness in Reward Management

INTRODUCTION

In the previous chapter we examined a range of different types of payment systems and their relevance to particular organisational contexts. When examining the reward package as a whole, however, it is important to consider other benefits – financial and non-financial – that provide the total reward experience for employees. If we take into account the various schools of thought on motivation and reward (see Chapter 12) it is clear that pay is only one element of the total reward package and benefits are not usually seen in a strategic way but taken as 'givens'. Expectancy theory, however, suggests that a more contingent view needs to be taken, and that it may make sense to individualise rewards, a notion that has led to considerable interest in 'cafeteria' benefits.

In the reward management literature most attention has been focused on pay since this is often seen as a key lever of change, and much less attention has been devoted to benefits such as pensions and sick pay. Indeed, the other benefits have often been seen as fixed, despite the fact that many employers pay above the statutory minimum. The benefits package has itself been subject to fads and fashions, with many employers merely reacting by adjusting benefits to address short-term problems such as recruitment and retention, rather than adopting a long-term approach (Thompson 2002). In the field of pensions, probably the largest item in the benefits package, there has been an absence of strategic thinking (Smith 2000a), yet it should be apparent from our discussion of motivation that terms and conditions beyond pay can be very significant in the overall reward package.

The employment relationship assumes that employees will give their time to the organisation in return for a reward, which will certainly include money but may also include other factors such as status or job satisfaction. However, this is by no means a simple process as work is not precisely specified and/or different employees may expect different rewards. Because many factors are not specified in the contract – work intensity and supervision for example – the effort bargain can only be established over time by custom and practice. However, the effort bargain is potentially unstable because factors change, and the relationships may come to be perceived by one party as compromised. For example, at a time of recession managers may attempt to change working practices to increase productivity, whereas workers may perceive this as a breach of custom and practice, so leading to potential conflict (Baldamus 1961). The achievement of fairness is central to the issue of payment, and however well bonus schemes are devised it is unlikely to be effective if it is perceived to be unfair – see the discussion in Chapter 2 on the psychological contract. As Brown and Walsh (1994, p443) observe, 'the prudent personnel manager devotes far less time to devising new pay incentives than to tending old notions of fairness'. However, as they point out 'there is nothing absolute about fairness in pay', as it is 'a normative idea' based on comparison (p443). Equity theory suggests people will be better motivated if they feel they are treated equally and demotivated if they are treated unequally. This has been referred to as the 'felt-fair' principle (Armstrong 2002, p61).

When people compare wages, it tends to be with people close to themselves, rather than with football players or paupers. As a result much of the most intense rivalry is within organisations (and within families), although in many organisations salaries are kept secret. In families, it has been found that the more your spouse earns, the less satisfied you are with your own job. People are concerned about their relative income and not simply about its absolute level (Layard 2003, p8).

The remainder of this chapter is organised as follows: Firstly, we discuss job evaluation and equal value. Secondly, we look at benefits other than pay, examining pensions so as to illustrate our theme. Thirdly, we analyse the steps taken by employers to harmonise conditions, which includes benefits such as pensions and sick pay, but also the removal of barriers such as separate car parks, canteens or toilets. Fourthly, we discuss non-financial recognition, and the importance of involvement, autonomy and responsibility, before moving on to examine job redesign. Rewards are about more than promotion and benefits and individuals value other rewards as well.

By the end of this chapter, readers should be able to:

■ **prepare a case for introducing flexible benefits**

■ **assess the costs and benefits of implementing harmonisation between blue- and white-collar workers**

■ **advise management how job redesign can enrich jobs and motivate workers.**

In addition, readers should understand and be able to explain:

■ **the pros and cons of different methods of job evaluation**

■ **the nature of employee benefits and their contribution to the total reward package**

■ **the principal characteristics of non-financial rewards and their implications for HR practice.**

Before reading the remainder of this chapter, gather information about the pay levels for a sample of **five** occupations – for example, Member of Parliament, train driver, checkout operator, nurse, HR manager. Place these in rank order. Do you consider these pay levels to be fair in relation to each other. Why/why not? Discuss with your colleagues notions of fairness and differentials.

JOB EVALUATION

Job evaluation can be defined as a process whereby jobs are placed in a rank order according to overall demands placed upon the job-holder. It therefore provides a basis for a fair and orderly grading structure, but it is best regarded as a systematic rather than a scientific process. It is a method of establishing the relative position of jobs within a hierarchy, which is achieved by using criteria drawn from the content of the jobs (Acas 2003b). However, there is sometimes considerable confusion concerning the process. The process of writing job descriptions (which was dealt with in Chapter 6) is central to job evaluation, but this is not designed to evaluate the person or job-holder on his or her performance, or to establish the pay for the job. Job evaluation has existed since the 1920s but was given considerable impetus in the 1960s and 1970s because of government incomes policies. Job evaluation in some form is to be found and probably used in 50–75 per cent of organisations (Thompson and Milsome 2001, p9) and its incidence increases with establishment size. Job evaluation has a number of benefits. It provides a formula for dealing with grievances about pay, and decisions are likely to be more acceptable if there is a formal system rather than ad hoc ways of dealing with pay issues.

According to Arthurs (2002b, pp131–132), employers normally have some or all of the following objectives in seeking to introduce job evaluation:

- to establish a rational pay structure
- to create pay relationships between jobs, which are perceived as fair by employees
- to reduce the number of pay grievances and disputes
- to provide a basis for settling the pay rate of new or changed jobs
- to provide pay information in a form which enables meaningful comparisons with other organisations (see also Armstrong 2002, p107).

In broad terms job evaluations fall into two types of scheme – non-analytical and analytical. *Non-analytical schemes* use a simple ranking method, with jobs placed in rank order and no attempt is made to evaluate or compare parts of each job. They have declined in favour in recent years, as they are unlikely to be a defence in an equal value claim. There are various forms of non-analytical scheme.

Job ranking

Under this system, job descriptions or titles are placed in a rank order or hierarchy to provide a league table. It is a very simple method as the job is considered as a whole rather than broken down into constituent parts. It is usually seen as suitable for small organisations where the evaluation team is likely to know all the jobs. It is simple and cheap to implement but tends to be very subjective. Furthermore, while job Y can be identified as more difficult than job X, it is not clear how much more difficult it is (Duncan 1992, p277; Smith and Nethersell 2000, p219; Acas 2003b, p10). For example, Box 49 (page 352) shows a simple ranking system.

Paired comparison

This approach is similar to the above but more systematic in that each job is compared with every other job, and points are allocated depending on whether it is less than, equal to, or more than the other jobs. The points are added up to provide a league table. It is more objective than job ranking but can be time-consuming unless there is computer support, given the comparisons that need to be made (Acas 2003b, p10).

Job classification

This is the reverse of the above process in that, under this technique, the number of grades is first decided upon, and a detailed grade definition is then produced. Benchmark (representative) jobs are evaluated with non-benchmark jobs before being slotted in on the basis of the grade definitions. The main drawbacks are that complex jobs may be difficult to assess as they may stretch across grade boundaries, and given it works best in cohesive, stable and hierarchical organisations its appeal today is limited (Smith and Nethersell 2000, p219; Acas 2003b, pp10–11).

BOX 49   JOB GRADES

Grade 1   Supervised manual labour.

Grade 2   Unsupervised manual labour following prescribed procedures.

Grade 3   Tasks involving interpretation of procedures.

Grade 4   Tasks involving interpretation of procedures and responsibility for work groups.

The main drawback of these 'whole job' approaches is that they are highly subjective. Given that they are not analysed systematically, it is likely that implicit assumptions about the worth of jobs may be left unquestioned. Physical strength, for example, may be given extra weight and this has significant implications for equal opportunities, as 'women's' jobs may be rated lower than 'men's' jobs for historical reasons.

By contrast, *analytical schemes* involve a systematic analysis of jobs by breaking them down into constituent factors. There are two principal categories of analytical scheme.

Points rating

This is the most popular technique of all. It involves breaking down jobs into a number of factors, usually between 3 and 12, to include factors such as skill, judgement, knowledge, experience, effort, responsibility and pressure. Each factor receives weighting, which is then converted to points, with the total points determining the relative worth of a job. It is more objective than non-analytical methods, and by breaking down the jobs helps overcome the danger that people are assessed rather than jobs (Smith and Nethersell 2000, p220; Acas 2003b, pp11–12). However, it is a time-consuming process that is prone to grievances as small changes in job content can lead to regrading issues.

Factor comparison

This attempts to rank jobs and attach monetary values simultaneously. Jobs are analysed in terms of factors (mental and physical requirements, responsibility etc) and benchmark jobs are examined, one factor at a time, to produce a rank order of the job for each factor. The next step is to check how much of the wage is being paid for each factor. Where employees are shown to be overpaid for the job they do, the usual practice is red-circling, which protects the individual's pay in the post (sometimes for a set period of time), but a successor would be paid the newly evaluated (lower) rate. This system is not popular in Britain, partly because the allocation of cash values to factors is seen as too arbitrary and it assumes that a pay structure already exists. Factor comparison was the basis of the development of the Hay Guide chart profile method, the most widely used around the world (Smith and Nethersell 2000, p221).

Despite the growth of more 'scientific' forms of job evaluation, ultimately the process is subjective, as assumptions are made about the design of the scheme, the factors and weights chosen, as well as the judgement of those doing the evaluating. Because of this, employee involvement in the scheme is important to lend credibility to something that would otherwise be seen as management-driven.

Armstrong and Murlis (1998) suggest a number of reasons why job evaluation is in a transitional phase. Firstly, equal pay legislation has meant that it has been necessary to re-examine schemes to ensure they are analytical and gender-neutral. Secondly, new technology is changing roles, eliminating job differences and introducing new skills – for example, by reducing the emphasis on physical skills and increasing the relevance of more conceptual skills. Thirdly, there is now greater flexibility in working arrangements, and a growth in team-working, for example. Fourthly, de-layering meaning that decisions are being made by employees lower down the hierarchy. Hence, more is being demanded of employees, and their horizons may be narrowed rather than widened by job descriptions that define a single job. Fifthly, labour market pressures due to skill shortages can lead to comparisons based on external relativities rather than internal relativities. Finally, the notion of individual contribution is growing more important, a trend that is apparent in relation to performance-related pay schemes (see Chapter 12).

> What are the main strengths and weaknesses of analytical and non-analytical schemes of job evaluation?

Traditional criticisms of job evaluation have pointed to its costly and bureaucratic nature as well as its lack of flexibility (Lawler 2000b; Arthurs 2002a). It is argued that job descriptions assume stability and hierarchy in the world of work, a situation that no longer appears to exist and that job evaluation may not be compatible with employers' attempts to develop high performance workplaces (Rubery 1995). We have already noted that formal job evaluation processes began in the 1960s and 1970s, when, for many organisations, the main interest was in establishing internal equity, with a focus on jobs rather than on people. External labour markets were regarded as relatively homogeneous, and issues of individual performance and contribution were to a large degree optional extras, or accommodated by highly structured systems in which employees gained automatic progression. In addition, traditional job evaluation has difficulties in coping with jobs based on knowledge work and teamworking, as well as with flatter structures. Conventional job evaluation was seen as exaggerating small differences in skill and responsibility by the attachment of points in a way that impeded flexibility. Management stressed the need to evaluate employees and not just jobs. However, rather than abandoning job evaluation, it appears there is a movement to make it more flexible so as to reflect internal and external worth (CIPD 2004f).

There is some evidence that employers are developing simultaneously both more flexible forms of work organisation and systems of job evaluation (Kessler 2000). Strategies for doing this include the creation of generic job descriptions and broad bands; the development of career progression linked to attainment of key skills or competencies; the development of 'growth structures' involving clear career paths; and the integration of manual and non-manual structures. However, Whitfield and McNabb (2001) note that there is evidence that such schemes raise employee expectations and that the conflict between new forms of work organisation and job evaluation are not readily resolvable. Nevertheless, employers are pursuing flexibility with flatter structures and fewer grades, but with wider bands attached to each grade. Rather than abandoning job evaluation, it has provided the foundation for major changes to pay structure in the NHS and local government so as to deal with equal pay and single status issues (Thompson and Milsome 2001, p7). Work by Armstrong and Brown (2001) also concluded that the death of job evaluation had been greatly exaggerated, although they do acknowledge that new perspectives are evolving – such as competence-based job evaluation associated with broad banding. With de-layering and the growth of teamwork, employers appear to be attempting to value jobs in ways that fit with the need for operational and role flexibility. Hence there has been a growth of broadband or job–family pay structures, which reward people who adapt to new challenges and expand their roles (CIPD 2004f). An IRS employment survey (792e 2004) reported that few were abandoning job evaluation schemes and a substantial proportion of those who do not operate the system are planning to introduce it in the future.

Broadbanding involves the compression of a hierarchy of pay grades or salary ranges into a number of wider bands. Each of the bands normally span the pay opportunities previously covered by several separate grades and pay ranges (Lawler 2000a, pp114–116; Armstrong and Brown 2001, p55). They both suggest that broadbanding has not replaced analytical job evaluation as job evaluation can define band boundaries. Broadbanding is driven by twin pressures of the need to replace complex pay structures and organisational changes in structure and has now become the leading approach to pay structure (Thompson and Milsome 2001). Not all employees are likely to be enthusiastic because it adds uncertainty to pay determination, unlike the transparency and predictability of service related increments.

The key features of broadbanding, according to Armstrong and Brown (2001, p61), are:

- typically no more than five or six bands for all employees covered by the structure, although some organisations describe their structures as being broadbanded when they have as many as eight or nine grades

- wide pay spans, which can be 80 per cent or more above the minimum rate in the band

- emphasis on external relativities; market pricing may be used to define reference point or 'target rates' for roles in the band, and to place jobs in the band

- less reliance on conventional and rigidly applied analytical job evaluation schemes to govern internal relativities

- focus on lateral career development and competence growth

- increased devolution of pay decisions to line managers who can be given more freedom to manage the pay of their staff in accordance with policy guidelines and within their budgets by reference to information on market rates and relativities within their departments

- less emphasis on hierarchical labels for bands

- less concern for structure and rigid guidelines, and more concern for flexibility and paying for the person rather than the job.

Research also indicates that *competence-based factors* are being added to existing points factor schemes and/or replaced existing factors. Job descriptions are being replaced by generic role definitions setting out core competencies, a move that has been encouraged by the take-up of NVQs. If a role requires a particular level of competence, this can then be translated into a standard of competence performance for the individual in that role. 'A family' of closely related jobs – such as research scientists for example – can be constructed as a hierarchy of levels with employees paid according to the range and depth of their competencies (Armstrong 2002, pp197–199). However, management is interested in outputs such as bottom-line results or employee contributions, and not just inputs such as competency levels.

EQUAL VALUE CONSIDERATIONS

The Equal Pay Act 1970, which came fully into operation in 1975, gave men and women the right to equal treatment in contracts of employment, and was concerned with wages as well as with other terms and conditions. In simple terms, this meant that an employer was required to employ women and men doing the same work on the same terms and conditions. The Equal Pay Act did not originally provide for equal pay for work of equal value. It envisaged dealing with situations where men and women were doing the same or broadly similar work (which meant that the scope of comparison was narrow), where a voluntary job evaluation scheme had evaluated the work as equal, or where terms and conditions were laid down in collective agreements, employers' wage structures or statutory wage orders. While the earnings gap between men and women has narrowed since 1970, the Kingsmill Report (2001) found the earnings gap to be 18 per cent. The minimum wage may be expected to reduce the gap over time as women are disproportionately represented in the low pay sector.

The Equal Pay (Amendment) Regulations 1983 broadened the scope of the original 1970 Act. A woman or man is entitled to 'equal pay for work of equal value' (in terms of the demands made on a worker under various headings, for instance effort, skill, decision-making). Hence, if a woman is doing work of the same value as a man, even if it is a different job, she can claim equal pay (Equal Opportunities Commission 2000; see Box 50 on page 356). The change means that women performing jobs in which traditionally few men have been employed are now within the scope of the Act (or the reverse – the Act gives the same rights to men), whereas prior to this, women could not claim equal pay because they were doing jobs not done by men employed by the same employer. Equal value claims can be made across sites, provided employees are deemed to be in the same employment (that is, working for the same or an associated employer). This raises major questions when workers employed by several different employers are engaged in the same form of work – for example – at a call centre – but subject to different contractual arrangements (Earnshaw *et al* 2002c).

Equal pay regulations have far-reaching implications for organisations and their pay systems, and many employers have sought to introduce a new scheme or reassess their existing job evaluation system. Clearly job evaluation systems should reflect published objective criteria which can enable the employer to justify why particular rates are being paid to men and women. However, it is important to ensure that the scheme itself does not reflect discriminatory values, perhaps by overrating 'male' characteristics such as strength. In Bromley and Ors v H and J Quick Ltd (1988), the Court of Appeal held that paired comparisons in a whole job approach was inadequate, and a valid job evaluation scheme must be 'analytical'. It is believed that an integrated analysis job evaluation scheme (all employees) is the most defensible, and the case is helped if the system has been negotiated with a trade union and there is employee involvement in the operation of the scheme.

However, it has been argued that job evaluation may serve to reinforce existing hierarchies. This is partly the result of the aims of job evaluation, which tend to emphasise stability and acceptability, and hence do not disrupt established differentials (Armstrong 2002). Non-analytical schemes are particularly prone to bias because they produce a 'felt-fair' rank order that can be based on stereotypes. However, even with analytical schemes, problems can occur in factor choice and weighting. For example, tacit skills such as those involved in caring and human relations are often missed or misunderstood. Table 28 (pages 357–8) illustrates that the choice of different factors can produce quite a different rank order for the same jobs.

BOX 50   WORK, LIKE WORK AND WORK OF EQUAL VALUE

Like work comparisons that have succeeded in the particular circumstances of the case include:

■ male and female cleaners doing 'wet' and 'dry' cleaning in different locations at the same site

■ a woman cook preparing lunches for directors and a male chef doing breakfast, lunch and tea for employees.

Work rated as equivalent comparisons that have succeeded in the particular circumstances of the case include:

■ where a woman and a man had been placed in the same job evaluation grade, but the employer had refused to pay the woman (who had been evaluated as having fewer points) the rate for the grade.

Equal value comparisons that have succeeded in the particular circumstances of the case include:

■ cooks and carpenters

■ speech therapists and clinical psychologists

■ kitchen assistants and refuse workers.

Source: Equal Opportunities Commission. *Code of Practice on Equal Pay*. London, EOC. 2003

Arthurs (2003) has argued that job evaluation is a double-edged sword. On the one hand it has been used historically to legitimise the lower value accorded to women's jobs. On the other hand it could provide a tool for uncovering and correcting the bias that has contributed to the underpayment of women. It could help challenge the valuation of skills and knowledge, and also question some of the definitions and valuations placed upon such job evaluation factors as 'responsibility', 'effort' and 'working conditions'.

A model equal pay policy, suggested by the EOC, is given in Box 51 on pages 358–9.

An employer can justify differences in pay only where the variation between the terms and conditions is due to a 'material' (ie significant and relevant) factor, and not difference in gender. That is, even when 'like work' is proved, a woman has no right to equal pay if an employer can show there is a material difference (not based on sex) between the two employees, which justifies the differences in payment. Material factors held by case law to justify a difference in pay are market forces (for example, increasing the pay of a particular job to attract candidates) and 'red-circling' (ie where a job is downgraded but pay is not reduced) (Shaw and Clark 2000, pp211–212). Other material differences could be experience or a qualification. However, this is to be evaluated on a one-by-one basis, as experience may be deemed relevant in one instance but irrelevant in another. For example, if a man is being paid more than the comparator because of certain skills he has which the applicant does not, it needs to be shown that these are necessary for the job and do not represent, for example, a past pay agreement. The basis of comparison is each individual term of the contract. In Hayward v Cammell Laird, a cook claimed equal pay with a painter, joiner and insulation engineer. The report by the independent expert noted that her work was of equal value and

Table 28   *Is your job evaluation scheme free of gender bias? Job evaluation using discriminatory and non-discriminatory factors*

Factor		Maintenance fitter	Company nurse
Discriminatory factors			
Skill			
	experience in job	10	1
	training	5	7
Responsibility			
	for money	0	0
	for equipment and machinery	8	3
	for safety	3	6
	for work done by others	3	0
Effort			
	lifting requirement	4	2
	strength required	7	2
	sustained physical effort	5	1
Conditions			
	physical environment	6	0
	working position	6	0
	hazards	7	0
Total		64	22
Non-discriminatory factors			
Basic knowledge		6	8
Complexity of task		6	7
Training		5	7
Responsibility for people		3	8

Table 28   *continued*

Factor	Maintenance fitter	Company nurse
Responsibility for material and equipment	8	6
Mental effort	5	6
Visual attention	6	6
Physical activity	8	5
Working conditions	6	1
Total	53	54

Source: Equal Opportunities Commission. *Good Practice Guide: Job evaluation schemes free of sex bias.* Manchester, EOC. 2000

BOX 51   A MODEL EQUAL PAY POLICY

We are committed to the principles of equal pay for all our employees; we aim to eliminate any sex bias in our pay systems.

We understand that equal pay between men and women is a legal right under both domestic and European Law.

It is in the interest of the organisation to ensure that we have a fair and just pay system. It is important that employees have confidence in the process of eliminating sex bias and we are therefore committed to working in partnership with the recognised trade unions. As good business practice we are committed to working with trade union/employee representatives to take action to ensure that we provide equal pay.

We believe that in eliminating sex bias in our pay system we are sending a positive message to our staff and customers. It makes good business sense to have a fair, transparent reward system and it helps to us to control costs. We recognise that avoiding unfair discrimination will improve morale and enhance efficiency.

Our objectives are to:
- eliminate any unfair, unjust or unlawful practices that impact on pay
- take appropriate remedial action.

We will:
- implement an equal pay review in line with EOC guidance for all current staff and starting pay for new staff (including those on maternity leave, career breaks or non-standard contracts)

- plan and implement actions in partnership with trade union/employee representatives
- provide training and guidance for those involved in determining pay
- inform employees of how these practices work and how their own pay is determined
- respond to grievances on equal pay as a priority
- in conjunction with trade union/employee representatives, monitor pay statistics annually.

Source: Equal Opportunities Commission. *Code of Practice on Equal Pay*. London, EOC. 2003. p21

should be paid at the same rate. The argument that some of Hayward's terms and conditions were more favourable than those of the comparators, and therefore could offset the difference in pay rates was ultimately rejected by the House of Lords (Armstrong 2002, p140).

Equal value cases cannot be defended on the ground of implementation costs or of the impact on employee relations. Moreover, in North Yorkshire County Council v Ratcliffe, the House of Lords ruled that a local authority that paid female catering workers less than a group of male workers doing equivalent work – so that it could compete with a commercial firm for a tender – had not established that the difference in pay was due to a material factor other than gender.

The EOC has been recommending equal pay reviews as a method of ensuring that a pay system delivers equal pay. Reviewing and monitoring pay practice in collaboration with the workforce is seen as good practice (EOC 2003).

Some job titles that imply gender, leading to sex discrimination, are given in Table 29.

Table 29   *Job title variations that can result in sex discrimination*

Job title	
Male	**Female**
Salesman	Shop Assistant
Assistant Manager	Manager's Assistant
Technician	Operator
Office Manager	Typing Supervisor
Tailor	Seamstress
Personal Assistant	Secretary
Administrator	Secretary
Chef	Cook

Source: Equal Opportunities Commission. *Good Practice Guide: Job evaluation schemes free of sex bias*. Manchester, EOC. 2000

PENSIONS

Pensions can be seen as a form of deferred pay. They remain a widespread fringe benefit and the most costly element of the remuneration package especially for older workers, despite the fact that the reward management literature shows little interest in this area (Taylor 2000b). Occupational pensions were developed during the nineteenth century as part of a broader paternalistic-driven personnel policy in gas and public-service organisations, in conjunction with various other benefits such as paid leave, sickness and accident benefits. Paternalism was not simply the act of benevolent employers, but it was seen initially as a means of managing retirement, and later for attracting and retaining a good loyal labour force (Smith 2000a, pp154–156). After the Second World War, pension schemes began to develop as more employees became liable to tax, thus making the tax relief aspects of pensions especially attractive.

There are two main types of pension scheme: defined benefit (DB) schemes, where the level of pension is calculated as a percentage of the retiring individual's final salary, and defined contribution (DC) money-purchase schemes, where regular payments are made (by employee and employer) to a pension fund which are then invested – with the employee receiving a pension based on the value of the investment; these represent a minority of schemes. (See Table 30 for a comparison of these two schemes.) The result of the Social Security Acts 1985 and 1986 led to employees no longer being required to join a scheme, as well as reduced penalties for those leaving. Those who do leave can take their pension with them – hence the terminology of 'portable' pensions. The incentive to stay with a particular firm is reduced, although in practice final salary revaluation tends to result in a pension that is

Table 30   *Comparison of final salary and money purchase schemes*

Final salary or defined benefit schemes	Money purchase or defined contribution schemes
Benefits defined as a fraction of final pensionable pay	Benefits purchased by accumulation of contributions invested
Benefits do not depend on investment returns or annuity rates	Benefits dependent on investment returns, contributions and costs of annuities at retirement
Employer contributes necessary costs in excess of employee contributions	Employer contributions are fixed
Employer takes financial risk	Member takes financial risk
Early leavers often suffer a loss as benefits are broadly linked to prices rather than earnings	Early leavers generally do not suffer a loss because their account remains invested within the scheme
Benefits designed for long-serving employees with progressive increases in pensionable pay	Benefits designed for short-serving employees or those whose pensionable pay fluctuates

Source: Chartered Institute of Personnel and Development. *'Occupational pensions': Strategic issues.* London, CIPD. 2003c

less than they would have received if they had remained (Taylor 2000b). The view that pensions were a 'golden handcuff' because of poor transfer values when changing schemes now has less force. Employees can begin personal pension plans on which they receive a National Insurance rebate. Hence, it now seems that employers need to improve their schemes to ensure they have a retention/attraction value.

The European Court of Justice judgment in 1990 required employers to equalise pensions and is leading to the introduction of flexible pension ages, but this makes it more difficult for employers to use their schemes to determine the age at which employees retire. Furthermore, the net result will be a rise in the cost of pension provision, which may lead some managements to re-evaluate the aims of their funds. The pressures of an ageing population, greater flexibility in working patterns and retirement age, the decline in equity markets, the changing balance between private and public pension provision and increased pension regulation are all having an impact on traditional ideas about pension provision, and there is a clear shift towards DC and away from DB with a number of employees winding up their DB schemes. This is becoming a major HR issue with many organisations seeing a pension crisis, and the UK's first strike at Steel manufacturer Caparo in protest over closure of the company pension suggests growing employee concern (IRS Employment Review 759 2002).

The main objectives of occupational pension provisions are: retention, attracting new staff, improving employee relations and managing the time and manner in which employees retire (Taylor 2000b; Morley 2002b). Research suggests that senior management objectives rarely go beyond using pensions to attract new recruits, and many are not defined at all (Smith 2000a). Strategic intent is seen to be missing, thus reflecting the distinction between the management of remuneration, which is seen as strategic, and needing to be actively managed, and that of pensions, which is seen separately and related more to welfare.

Occupational or company schemes usually involve contributions from both the employer and the employee, although there are non-contributory schemes (that is, only the employer contributes), especially for managerial staff. The Inland Revenue approves schemes (for tax relief) and sets limits on the level of benefits payable – a maximum pension at two-thirds of the employee's final salary. In the UK annual contributions can add up to around 15–20 per cent of an employer's annual wage bill, and hence they represent a significant proportion of labour costs.

Changes in UK legislation in the late 1980s and 1990s and judgments of the European Court of Justice (for example, Barber v Guardian Royal Exchange) have each had important implications. In particular, it seems likely that the government will try to shift some of its current responsibility for old-age pension provision to the private sector. As individuals become more responsible for their old age, they may look more closely at employer provision in this area (Taylor 2000b). However, the research evidence suggests employees are either partially or wholly ignorant about the pension scheme provided by employers. There are also implications for HR professionals who may need to evaluate organisational objectives regarding pension schemes (Terry and White 1998). The Pensions Act (1995) also attempted to increase the involvement of employees (or pensioners) by giving them a right to nominate or select a number of trustees, and this establishes the need for an internal communications campaign to explain various details of the scheme. Because women have normally had shorter working lives, their pensions can be significantly lower than those of men and hence new legislation for sharing pensions was introduced by the Welfare Reform and Pensions Act 1999. The regulations allow for both private and state additional pensions to be shared by couples divorcing after 1 December 2000 (Morley 2002b, pp186–187). The decline in equity markets has reduced the size of many pensions funds so employers' contributions to these schemes has increased (Goodchild 2003). The CIPD Reward Management Survey (2004f) found that while 94 per cent of employees are contributing to the pension arrangements of their staff, they are restricting final salary schemes to existing staff with less than half offering them to new hires. A number of high profile companies such as BA, Safeways, Barclays, J. Sainsbury's, ICI and BT have all closed their schemes and opened money-purchase alternatives but HR issues such as the effect on motivation and productivity through damaging the psychological contract, reaction of employees and unions, and the impact on recruitment and retention suggest this decision should not have been taken lightly. Indeed some firms have made it clear that they are committed to continuing final salary provision (IRS Employment Review 759 2002) and those that are keeping them are resorting to increasing both the employer and employee contribution levels to guarantee the funding (IRS Employment Review 799c 2004). Very few employers update staff about their pension arrangements and it is clear that there is an HR role in bridging the communication gap between pension experts and staff (Upton 2004).

FLEXIBLE BENEFITS

There are many other benefits which employees may value – such as sick pay, company cars, health insurance and holidays, but there is not the space to review each of these here. Perhaps one of the most valued benefits in these uncertain times is job security. While few organisations today guarantee such benefits, some prescribe a lengthy process to be followed before redundancies are invoked, and this may provide some reassurance that terms will be fair and generous (for a wider discussion on benefits, see Armstrong 2002, pp401–415).

In recent years there has been great interest in the notion of 'cafeteria' and flexible benefits (CIPD 2002b; Tulip 2003b). The main reason for such an approach is to maximise flexibility and choice amongst a diverse workforce, particularly in the area of fringe benefits, which can make up a high proportion of the total remuneration package. Under this system staff are provided with 'core' benefits – including salary – and are offered a menu of other costed benefits (company car, health insurance, childcare, length of holiday entitlement etc) from which they can construct a package of benefits, up to a total value. The emphasis is on choice. Such schemes have been popular in the USA, but have not been widely taken up in the UK as a result of administrative complexity and taxation issues, as well as inertia within organisations. Smith (2000b, p385) argues that a preoccupation with simplicity and performance-related pay in Britain seems to act as a barrier to the lateral thinking required to evaluate flexible plans. Some of the ideas on 'cafeteria' benefits sit well with the motivation literature, which stresses that different individuals have different needs and expectations from work but studies suggest that only a small minority of organisations currently operate a flexible benefits package. Family friendly benefits (such as childcare vouchers, subsidised and crèche facilities, enhanced maternity/paternity leave) are a current trend, with more employers planning to introduce them than phase them out, according to the CIPD Reward Management Survey (2004f). Despite a cost-cutting environment this increase is not surprising in the light of difficulties in recruiting and retaining talented staff. So helping the staff achieve a work–life balance may be one of addressing this issue.

> Do you think 'cafeteria' benefits are a good idea? What would make an ideal package for you?

Organisations are introducing flexible benefits schemes as part of a wider move towards a more flexible working environment (CIPD 2004f). Such schemes increase the perceived value of the reward package offered to employees, with no additional cost to the organisation (in theory). While many organisations have always allowed a limited form of flexibility with just one or two benefits, it is only within the last five years that comprehensive flexible benefits schemes have started to become more common. They have often been avoided because of the cost of introducing and administering them but, with increasingly sophisticated computer programs, the administrative burden can be reduced and the number of organisations introducing them has increased (Tulip 2003b). Having said this the CIPD noted that while may employers have considered introducing such plans, few actually manage to implement it (CIPD 2004f, p32).

HARMONISATION

Recent years have seen considerable discussion about the advantages of harmonising benefits to remove status differentials – for example, separate pension or sick-pay provision – as this sends out a message that some employees are second-class citizens, with a different and inferior set of rights. Harmonisation is concerned with the process of reducing differences, normally between manual and non-manual workers – the major division identified by research on the manufacturing sector in the 1960s and 1970s. The ultimate aim is to eliminate differences based on the status of employees – hence the term 'single status', or sometimes 'staff status' (see Chapter 3).

Conditions of employment offering scope for harmonisation may include:

- payment systems and methods of payment
- overtime and hours of work
- shift premiums
- actual times of work
- clocking or other time recording procedures
- sick-pay schemes
- holiday entitlement and holiday pay
- pension arrangements
- period of notice (above the statutory minimum)
- redundancy terms
- lay-off/guaranteed week
- canteen facilities
- fringe benefits such as health insurance and company cars.

There are two dimensions to this: (a) economic returns in the form of pay and fringe benefits, and (b) aspects of discipline and labour control, notably in the area of time-keeping, working hours etc. Harmonisation is not just about fringe benefits.

What differences in terms and conditions still exist between groups of workers in your organisation or one with which you are familiar? Do you think that it is possible to justify these?

In the UK, fringe benefits have typically been dependent on the status of the employee, so reflecting class structure, and as such the status divide has proved to be especially resistant to change (Price and Price 1994, p527). During the industrial revolution in the nineteenth century it became impossible for the single entrepreneur to carry out all the management responsibilities, and so employees were brought in to take over some of these responsibilities. Two key features of this industrial bureaucracy emerged. Firstly, the hierarchy of control was associated with non-manual status, a division of brain from brawn (Arthurs 1985). Secondly, the number of controlling tiers of bureaucracy was associated with the idea of a 'career' with which loyal and good performance would be rewarded with promotion. At the same time, the application of scientific management principles was applied to the shop floor allowing workers little discretion, but highly specific work tasks, pay tied to output, and close discipline, all of which created a low-trust environment (Fox 1974). By contrast, in the civil service and local government, the greater size of the non-manual workforce, the absence of a manufacturing environment and the influence of a public sector ethos created less of a divide and, as a result, manual workers have tended to share better pension and sick-pay benefits.

Research in the late 1960s found particular disparities in relation to working hours, attendance, discipline and holidays. Manual workers had to operate according to stricter rules, and the penalties applied to them were more frequent and more severe. Manual workers were disadvantaged in a number of ways: a longer working week; shorter holidays; more likely to suffer deductions in pay; greater irregularity of earnings; pay linked to physical capacity; greater job insecurity; few promotions; stricter rules and discipline; and separate facilities such as canteens, toilets and car parks (Price and Price 1994).

As Sisson and Storey (2000, p128) argue, many of the differences 'cannot be justified and make little sense', and also make it difficult to win commitment and co-operation as demanded by HRM. While managers were keen to wax lyrical about the importance of people and the creation of a new corporate culture, demonstrating this in practice has proved to be somewhat more elusive. Where common interests are emphasised, it would seem somewhat odd if some groups of workers were treated differently. Important icons in the 1980s were high-profile Japanese implants such as Nissan, Komatsu and Toshiba, whose apparent success in achieving a committed and productive workforce made them leading-edge companies. The emphasis these companies placed on single status – with the removal of separate canteens, car parks and even different types of clothing – caught the headlines. The logic of treating people differently has never been obvious nor has the curious message about the value of different staff. As one union representative pointed out – does the fact that we get less bereavement leave than white-collar workers mean we grieve less or do managers believe we are a lesser breed of humanity? (Godfrey *et al* 1998).

Pfeffer (1994, p48) refers to such initiatives as 'symbolic egalitarianism' and suggests they have a role to play in reducing 'them and us' attitudes, and achieving competitive advantage through people. According to Morton (1994, p49), the demonstration of single status was a precondition for flexibility at Komatsu. He argues that if employees do not feel threatened by losing an employable skill, resistance will disappear. The strong emphasis on teamwork was also a significant factor, with employees recruited for their flexibility and team orientation. The work siren to start and end the shift was abandoned in favour of individual and supervisor responsibility. Demonstration by example was seen as central and described as 'wearing a hairshirt with sincerity'. This included all staff wearing the company uniform, using the same canteen and car park, working in open-plan offices and even all taking lunch at the same time (p82).

Table 31   *Entitlements to non-pay terms and conditions, by sector*

	Sector				All workplaces	
	Private		Public			
	% of workplaces		% of workplaces		% of workplaces	
	Managers	Employees	Managers	Employees	Managers	Employees
Employer pension scheme	78	62	93	93	82	71
Company car or car allowance	63	12	33	17	55	14
Private health insurance	61	22	7	2	46	16
Four weeks or more paid annual leave	91	81	96	95	92	85
Sick pay in excess of statutory requirements	83	64	77	76	81	67

Source: Cully M., Woodland S., O'Reilly A. and Dix G. *Britain at Work: As depicted by the 1998 Workplace Employee Relations Survey.* London, Routledge. 1999. p74

The 1980s witnessed an increase in harmonisation, inspired by the practices of Japanese new entrants, especially on greenfield sites where there was an acceptance among all parties that common terms and conditions were a good idea. At Nissan, Wickens (1987, p7) argues that single status is a misnomer – 'it is simply not possible for everyone to have the same status in an organisation – the plant manager has a different status to the supervisor to the line worker simply because of the position held ... what we can do however is to eliminate many of the differences in the way we treat people and end up with the same or similar employment packages. Thus the term "common terms and conditions of employment" is more accurate.' It is becoming increasingly difficult to present a coherent case for continuing distinctions between manual and non-manual workers in terms of separate car parks, toilets and canteens. The roots of such distinctions are deep and historically based, and in some cases the process of reform has been slow, although accelerated as a result of downsizing and restructuring over the last 20 years (Druker 2000). Harmonisation was also seen as a facet of employer initiatives to enhance high commitment on the shop floor, and WERS reported that single status was strongly associated with teamworking and job security (Cully *et al* 1998, p11; see Table 31).

Most employers have adopted a gradualist approach to change, but some have gone for fundamental reform with wide-ranging reviews of terms and conditions. The more extensive programmes are commonly found on greenfield sites, where great care is taken with the whole HR package so as to create an appropriate culture. At the Rolls Royce aircraft engine plant at Derby, harmonisation was implemented in several stages to take account of changes in the shift premium, the abolition of clocking off, and movement to staff terms for sickness. These were followed by consolidation of shift pay, reduction in the working week and flexible work hours (IDS 1998; Druker 2000, p120). When Price Waterhouse and Coopers and Lybrand merged in 1998 a commitment to harmonise conditions was central to the plan with a key feature being flexible benefits (Franks and Thompson 2000). This was seen as important as it recognised staff differences and diversity, it provided a good recruitment edge, and it facilitated alignment at the two existing arrangements. In some cases, as at BP Chemicals, single status has been part of a major change in management philosophy that has included continuous improvement and the rhetoric of individualising employment relations, through to non-union consultation schemes (Tuckman 1998).

A number of factors increase moves to harmonisation. Firstly, new technology cuts across existing demarcation lines (craft, skilled and semi-skilled), and status differentials tend to impede flexibility. Harmonisation is sometimes introduced as a way of 'buying-out' old work practices. The introduction of technology also increases demands and responsibilities on manual workers who are required to be more co-operative rather than compliant, taking on multiskilling and technician roles. In such circumstances harmonisation can play a key role in trying to make blue-collar workers part of the corporate team. Moreover, with such changes it may be difficult to make clear distinctions between blue-collar and white-collar (Sisson and Storey 2000, p128).

Secondly, the legislation on sex discrimination and equal pay has narrowed differences between blue- and white-collar workers and has also extended rights – such as maternity pay – to all workers who have sufficient length of service. Some employers used to provide these benefits solely to white-collar workers. Moreover, as the European Commission continues to press ahead in its moves to harmonise terms and conditions across Europe, the UK appears even more out of step if it maintains different conditions for different groups of workers. There is some evidence that firms attempting to individualise employment contracts also tend to standardise non-pay terms and conditions (see Brown *et al* 1998).

Thirdly, the growth in single-table bargaining and the recent spate of union mergers have also been important forces for change, as well as saving management time and reducing conflict between work groups. Fourthly, changes in employment structure in recent years have had an impact on lower level white-collar jobs, which have become increasingly routinised and de-skilled with fewer prospects for pay and promotion. A gap is now more apparent between clerical employees and professional workers, with little movement between the two. At the same time, many blue-collar jobs have been re-skilled due to technological demands which require additional training. As a result there is often little to distinguish manual from non-manual jobs. Similarly, now that many unions (such as UNISON) represent both manual and non-manual workers, it seems anachronistic to maintain status differentials between different groups of workers.

The WERS data provides an opportunity to assess how far harmonisation has actually progressed. Cully *et al* (1999, pp73–74) conclude that 41 per cent of workplaces were single status. Such workplaces were more common where there was a recognised trade union at the workplace (45 per cent), a personnel specialist (48 per cent) and where the workplace was covered by an integrated employee development plan (46 per cent). For more on single status, see Box 52.

BOX 52   SINGLE STATUS

In 1997 local authority employers and unions reached a national Single Status Agreement (SSA) to provide single status for manual and non-manual employees, equal pay for men and women for work of equal value, and increased flexibility with regard to pay and terms and conditions. The agreement provides for the harmonisation of working hours, but progress has been slow, and many have not completed the pay and grading review, especially the larger authorities. Job evaluation is an important component of single status agreements, ensuring equal pay for equal value, and fair and non-discriminatory pay structures. Again, progress has been slow with only 43 per cent of local authorities completing the process. The third part of the agreement covers issues such as weekend and public holiday working, training, and car allowances. National provisions may be modified locally subject to negotiation. Many authorities have not yet completed a review of these provisions.

It was argued that the SSA should reduce the possibility of equal pay claims, and encourage a shift towards equal opportunities through fairer structures. Research suggests, however, that progress in implementing all elements of the SSA has been slow and partial. The main obstacle is argued to be cost, both in terms of the costs associated with regrading staff as well as protecting staff downgraded as a result of the review. To cover costs, some authorities have made changes to allowance schemes or withdrawn bonus schemes. Others have staggered the introduction of new grading structures, introduced productivity initiatives, and reduced employee numbers. Additional obstacles include a lack of resources, the impact on staff morale, employee opposition and the overall complexity of the task, especially for the largest authorities. In short, the evidence suggests that there have been significant challenges introducing SSA in local government, with many authorities well behind schedule.

Source: IRS Employment Review 784a. *Councils Count the Cost of Fairer Terms and Conditions*. 19 September 2003. pp8–16

The largest harmonisation agreement took place in 1997 and covered 1.2 million council workers, merging the administrative, professional, technical, clerical and manual grades. While there was local flexibility there was a national pay spine (upon which council-level grading structures are based) and agreed terms on issues such as working time and leave. Overall, IRS Employment Review (710 2000, p10) concluded that progress had been slow and patchy because of the complexity of the task and cost pressures meant that few councils had instituted new pay and grading structures although most made significant changes in other areas – in particular the harmonisation of basic working hours.

Despite being part of the conventional wisdom of 'good employee relations' (Arthurs 1985, p17), there are a number of potential pitfalls to harmonisation. Firstly, cost. It may well be expensive to equalise notice periods, for example, especially in times where constant change puts an emphasis on flexibility. Although in the short run, costs may well increase, it is anticipated that the longer run offers more benefits. In local government progress on the implementation of single status has been slow partly as a result of costs (Hatchett 2001, p38). Secondly, workers may be unwilling to see cashless pay as a benefit, so making it necessary to 'buy out' cash payments. However, there could be cost savings in areas of capital costs (two different canteens replaced by a large one, for example), and reducing the administrative costs involved in operating two systems. Thirdly, as with many other management initiatives, supervisors and middle managers are often wary, partly because of confusion over what 'harmonisation' is designed to achieve and also because of insecurity and concern about their 'new' responsibilities and issues (Marchington and Wilkinson 2005).

A sceptical view was taken by McGovern and Hill (2003), who argue that there was limited evidence that the status divide is ending, with too much emphasis on high profile cases. Their work – based on two nationally representative samples – points to enduring divides both between and within blue- and white-collar employment. Significantly, they argue that the growth of white-collar employment (and the decline in manufacturing work) has not led to greater equality. In the area of fringe benefits, those holding higher managerial and professional positions tend to have the most fringe benefits while those in semi-skilled and routine manual jobs have the least. In 1992, 90 per cent of the former held an occupational pension scheme, beyond the basic state scheme and 77 per cent had a sick-pay scheme beyond that provided by the state. By contrast, only 52 per cent of semi-skilled and routine manual workers held an occupational pension scheme and 45 per cent had a sick pay scheme. Indeed the percentage holding such benefits declines steadily as one proceeds down the organisational hierarchy. Their research also reveals that the availability of these benefits is strongly influenced by a number of key variables such as economic sector, workplace size, unionisation and the proportion of non-standard employees. Employees in the public sector, as well as those in large organisations, or workplaces where trade unions are present are much more likely to have access to a range of fringe benefits. By contrast, those in workplaces where there is a high proportion of part-time staff are less likely to have these conditions. With regard to change over time, they found no significant trend towards a decline in the status divide between 1992 and 2000. The percentage of higher managers and professionals holding an occupational pension moved from 90 per cent in 1992 to 87 per cent in 2000 while those having access to a sick pay scheme remained stable at 77 per cent. At the same time, 52 per cent of routine manual staff held pensions and 58 per cent had a sick pay scheme in 1992 while the corresponding figures were 45 per cent and 51 per cent in 2000. To take another example, 23 per cent of intermediate workers had private health scheme in 1992 and 19 per cent in 2000, while only 12 per cent of the semi-skilled had such in 1992 and 9 per cent in 2000. If anything, employees generally may be experiencing some loss of benefits. There was no evidence of the status divided declining during the 1990s, a period when employers were supposedly introducing waves of harmonisation and Japanisation influenced single-status policies.

NON-FINANCIAL REWARDS AND RECOGNITION

According to Herzberg (1987, p30), 'managers do not motivate employees by giving them higher wages, more benefits, or new status symbols. Rather, employees are motivated by their own inherent need to succeed at a challenging task. The manager's job, then, is not to motivate people to get them to achieve; instead, the manager should provide opportunities for people to achieve so they will become motivated.'

Read Lynda Gratton's article in *People Management*, 29 January 2004, and answer the following questions: Why do we come to work? When we are at work, what influences our behaviour and performance?

It is important to consider the role which non-financial rewards and recognition play in motivating staff and in this section we examine a number of these. Having said that there is often 'lip service' to their significance. Semler's (1993) story of his company and management style in Brazil is a good example of how employees accept responsibility when they are treated in such a way that they are obviously valued. The desire of many individuals to seek opportunities for personal growth through their work is very powerful (Lewis 2001). Gratton (2004) argues that reward themes should emphasise both monetary and non-monetary rewards and the latter would include opportunity to participate in decisions about where and when they work as well as job design. This fits with the notion of 'total reward' where managers are urged to address the whole psychological contract to produce optimum results (Thompson 2002, p41).

How do job characteristics combine to motivate, reward and recognise good employee performance? According to Ford (1969), 'perhaps they have the effect of a shotgun blast; it is the whole charge that brings the beast down' (quoted in Robertson *et al* 1992, p62). A 'job characteristics model', developed by Hackman and Oldham (1976), incorporates the five core job characteristics they believe are involved in job satisfaction and motivation. These characteristics are:

- *skill variety* – the range of skills and talents required
- *task identity* – the extent to which the completion of a whole piece of work is required
- *task significance* – the impact of the task on others
- *autonomy* – freedom and discretion in selecting methods and hours of work
- *feedback* – clear information provided on performance.

According to these writers, if jobs are designed in a way that maximises these core dimensions, three psychological states can occur:

- *experienced meaningfulness at work* – the result of skill variety, task identity and task significance
- *experienced responsibility for work outcomes* – the result of autonomy
- *knowledge of results of work activities* – the result of feedback.

If these do occur then work motivation and job satisfaction will be high and other behavioural outputs – such as attendance – may also be positively affected (Rollinson *et al* 1998, pp244–246). Equally, employees with high 'growth-need strength' are more likely to experience changes in their critical psychological state when core job dimensions are improved. It is also important to realise that simply having a highly motivated employee does not necessarily equate with good job performance. Employees also need the necessary skills, tools and materials to do a good job. Obviously, a motivated but unskilled employee is unlikely to do a job to the required standard, but neither is a motivated and skilled employee who has had inadequate training or is provided with inappropriate raw materials.

Today it is perhaps more appropriate to take a less universalistic approach when considering motivation at work. Management needs to try to assess the subjective priorities of its employees, rather than assume and enforce a particular view. It is also the case that attitudes and priorities may change over time and hence managers need to be flexible.

There are two common themes relating to non-financial reward and motivation: first, recognition and feedback, and second, involvement, autonomy and responsibility.

Recognition and feedback

Employees' work needs to be valued by employers and hence recognised by them, a line taken up by a number of the TQM gurus such as Crosby and Deming. According to Crosby (1980, p218), 'people really don't work for money. They go to work for it, but once the salary has been established, their concern is appreciation. Recognise their contribution publicly and noisily, but don't demean them by applying a price tag to everything.' He argues that it is much more important to recognise achievements through symbolic awards and prizes. However, Kohn (1993, p55) argues that research shows that tangible rewards, as well as praise, can actually lower the level of performance, particularly in jobs requiring creativity. According to him, studies show that intrinsic interest in a task (the sense that it is worth doing for its own sake) tends to decline when the individual concerned is given an external reason for doing it. Extrinsic motivations are not only less effective than intrinsic motivations, they can also corrode intrinsic motivation. People who work in order to get a reward tend to be less interested in the task than those who are not expecting to be rewarded. According to Kohn (p55), when we are led to do something in order to get a prize, we feel that the goal of the prize controls our behaviour and this deprivation of self-determination makes tasks seem less enjoyable. Moreover, the offer of an inducement sends a message that the task cannot be very interesting, otherwise it would not be necessary to bribe us to do it.

As Pfeffer notes (1998, p217):

> All this is not to say that pay is unimportant to people. If individuals are not treated fairly, pay becomes a symbol of the unfairness and a source of discontent. If the job, or the organization, or both, are basically unpleasant, boring, or unchallenging, then pay may be the only source of satisfaction or motivation in the work environment. But, creating a fun, challenging, and empowered work environment in which individuals are able to use their abilities to do meaningful jobs for which they are shown appreciation is likely to be a more certain way to enhance motivation and performance – even though creating such an environment may be more difficult and take more time than merely turning the reward lever.

Others have argued that providing praise for good work, rather than criticism for poor work, is important. Managers should 'catch staff doing it right'. Token prizes/awards can also play a role as they have symbolic worth even if they are low in financial value (Crosby 1980, p218; see also Box 53). There has been growing interest in this field in recent years and some employers have moved beyond seeing non-financial recognition solely as the watch or clock presented on retirement (Hilton 1992). Thames Water for example has a Values in Practice (VIP) award designed to celebrate outstanding achievements (Trapp 2001). These are seen as being more motivating than cash, and can provide important feedback. Feedback itself needs to be regular, timely and relevant based on the principle of positive reinforcement. In other words, employees need to be given feedback more than once a year in a formal

BOX 53   TOTAL REWARD PACKAGES

When in a heat wave, staff at Volkswagen Group, UK were invited to cool down with refreshments morning and afternoon – it was different each day – watermelon and ice cream were among the treats. The Head of HR pointed out that 'it was inexpensive and didn't take a lot of time to prepare but it went down well with staff because it showed we were thinking about them as people and not just a resource'. But VW doesn't suggest that the more formal reward is unimportant, and are in the upper quartile when it comes to pay. However, they suggest that young workers want flexible working, sabbaticals and green policies.

The Head of Reward of Hay Group puts VW's policy in perspective by comparing it to the Bank of England when a memo granted permission to remove their jackets if temperatures went over 80°F for three days or more, pointing out that by the time the memo was received, temperatures had dropped!

Source: Adapted from Carrington L. 'Just desserts', *People Management*, 29 January 2004. pp38–40

appraisal. As far as possible it should relate to a recently completed task and it should also be directly relevant to the employee's work effort/output figures (the establishment as a whole may be too removed from the individual employee).

Stredwick (2002, pp208–209) identifies two types of formal recognition scheme. The first was developed from long established suggestion schemes. He sees key aspects of such schemes as:

- encouragement to employees to participate by inculcating a culture of 'continuous improvement' so employees think about how the work processes could be improved
- training for employees in putting forward their proposals
- committees drawn from all levels and activities in the company who will help to sift major ideas and encourage participation in their areas.
- swiftness in decision-taking, including instant awards and a guaranteed response for all ideas
- worthwhile awards, which can include a proportion of the saving and the opportunity to be entered in draws for various events
- encouragement to teams to apply themselves so that an idea can represent the thinking of a number of people in an area
- good publicity and recognition on success through company magazines
- campaigns that integrate with company strategy over issues such as health and safety, quality social responsibility and environmental issues.

The second type is where there are tokens as a result of staff going beyond the call of duty. Prizes are limited in value eg vouchers, badges. Recognition can also be through holidays, and day trips to other organisations that supply raw materials or market finished goods. The absolute cost of these sorts of reward is likely to be small, but they have a powerful symbolic significance (IRS Employment Review 792f 2004).

An example of an organisation with a range of HR initiatives is given in Box 54 (page 372).

BOX 54   CLARIDGE'S HOTEL

Senior management at Claridge's Hotel recently introduced a range of HR initiatives in order to reinforce the importance of valuing and involving employees. The policies aimed to improve various aspects of working practices including leadership, communication, and recruitment and selection processes. In addition, two employee recognition schemes were introduced: 'Employee of the Month' and 'Going for Gold'. The employee of the month scheme enables staff to nominate colleagues whom they believe deserve to be recognised for their outstanding effort or achievements in a particular month. Nominations are then reviewed by the Executive Committee, which makes the final decision. The winner receives vouchers and their photo is displayed on the wall. In addition, the 12 monthly winners have a chance of becoming 'employee of the year' with prizes such as a Caribbean cruise worth over £5000. The Going for Gold initiative involves the opportunity to take a 'lucky dip' in a pot of gold prize envelopes kept in the HR director's office. Again, staff can nominate colleagues whom they believe are worthy of the reward. There are various prizes available, ranging from a free make-over in the hotel's beauty salon to a night in the hotel's top suite. Management suggest that the schemes have been very successful and are highly valued by the hotel staff.

Source: IRS Employment Review 792f. *Thank You Goes a Long Way*. 23 January 2004. pp32–36

Involvement, autonomy and responsibility

Research linking participation to higher levels of satisfaction and increased productivity can be found in the social science literature (Pfeffer 1994, p42). People value the ability to influence their work. Much HRM literature endorses this, arguing that employees come to work motivated and interested but are soon alienated by the web of rules and constraints that govern their working lives. If only management could find ways to release and tap employees' creativity – for example, via employee involvement (EI) – their commitment to organisational goals would follow. It works upon the assumption that common interests are achievable in organisations, although most management fail to capture the interest of their staff, partly because of ineffective communications but also because contributions are not welcomed. HRM literature stresses that employees should have the opportunity to satisfy their needs for involvement, autonomy and responsibility through work, perhaps through participation in quality circles or merely by increasing involvement in day-to-day matters. When they agree policy and practice, they are likely to be more positive about implementation. Obviously, management styles are critical to this.

How might these states be achieved? Some of these aspects of management can be integrated into day-to-day management activity, and recognition and feedback can be made part of the corporate culture. However, to illustrate the variety of ways an employer might achieve such goals, we examine the practice of *job redesign*. Job redesign is concerned with the allocation of task functions among organisational roles, and has been defined as 'any attempt to alter jobs with the intent of increasing the quality of work experience and productivity' (Wilson 1999, p13). While early work in this area was largely concerned with matters of efficiency and rationalising work, breaking it down into tiny components in line with Taylor's ideas, modern job redesign has broader aims and looks to balance efficiency and job-satisfaction goals. As there has been increasing recognition that extrinsic rewards (such as pay) are insufficient on their own to motivate employees, more emphasis has been put on intrinsic factors such as job content. Drawing on expectancy theory, the aim is to design jobs that satisfy employee needs so that the work can be performed to a high standard, hence enabling both employee and organisational goals to be satisfied (Buchanan and Huczynski 2004, pp253–254). Job redesign can take a wide variety of forms in practice.

Job rotation

This is perhaps the most basic type of job redesign. It involves workers moving from job to job (with similar levels of skill) in an attempt to alleviate boredom. In a supermarket, for example, it might involve shelf-stacking, checkout-operating and counting boxes in the warehouse. A common criticism is that job rotation is little more than swapping one boring job for another and it can actually be demotivating if it affects a bonus pattern, or breaks up a work group.

Job enlargement

This involves widening a job so that one or more related tasks are added to the existing one at a similar level of responsibility. This can reduce the repetitiveness of performing jobs of short-cycle operations and may add to motivation for employees if they can see their contribution to the final product or service. Herzberg (1968, p18) sees this as 'enlarging the meaninglessness of the job', and it can add to work intensification. It has also been suggested that, while a worker can 'switch off' from one boring job, doing a number of different relatively mundane tasks requires concentration, which is resented if the job is monotonous.

Job enrichment

This is more radical. New responsibilities are added, such as production workers taking on responsibility for maintenance or taking on decision-making roles concerning work scheduling. In some cases employees acquire a complete job so that they can see the purpose to what they are doing.

Autonomous work groups

These extend job enrichment in that not only is there a wider range of operative/production skills but *groups* of employees also acquire responsibility for management tasks such as choosing work methods, regulating the pace of work, and allocating and scheduling work. Self-supervision is stressed which encourages autonomy. In some cases, groups may even take responsibility for training and recruitment.

Teamworking

This is perhaps the most recent manifestation of job redesign and involves a group of multicapable workers who switch between tasks, organise and allocate work, and are responsible for all aspects of production, including quality (Proctor and Mueller 2000). High-performance work teams operate without supervision and have wide-ranging responsibilities for production and maintenance. Other changes may also take place to support team-working, including open layout, flexitime, the removal of clocking and a new open management style. This raises a central issue about the extent to which such initiatives might need to be supported by changes in management style and HR practices (Marchington and Wilkinson 2005).

One company that has used reward initiatives strategically, with an emphasis on teamwork, is depicted in Box 55 on page 374.

Do you think that job redesign makes work more satisfying by rewarding and recognising employee contributions, or has it just made work more intensive and stressful?

BOX 55   USING REWARD STRATEGICALLY

Richer Sounds, a specialist hi-fi separates retailer in the UK, sees customer service as the driving philosophy behind the company. Employees are encouraged to help the customer buy rather than go for the 'hard sell'. The company's basic principles are quality products and branded names, value for money and customer service. While the first two can be controlled by head office, the latter is very much in the hands of branch employees or 'colleagues' as they are known.

The company sees reward as including both payment and recognition. Pay is above average for the industry with a basic rate supplemented by commission, profit-share and a customer service bonus. A customer service index is calculated, with individuals being assessed on several indicators, the main one being customer feedback. Each customer receipt includes a freepost questionnaire, with the customer invited to assess the level of service provided by the salesperson, who is identified by payroll number on the form.

The individual's bonus is related to the feedback. Thus, if a customer ticks 'excellent', the sales assistant receives an extra £3, if 'poor', a deduction of £3 takes place. These are totalled up at the end of each month and a bonus is paid. The company is at pains to point out that any deductions are far outweighed by the bonuses. Indeed, it is unlikely that anyone with a stream of negative feedback would actually retain their job, although management reports a relatively high voluntary turnover of new staff, some of whom find that they are uncomfortable with this approach. The peer group is seen as crucial in encouraging good performance, and managers are provided with the results on each individual's performance. While many of the incentives focus on the performance of the individual, and staff wear name badges to encourage greater individual responsibility, company performance is also rewarded with a profit-sharing scheme.

The company also believes non-financial recognition is important in motivating staff and has an array of initiatives designed to make working for the company satisfying and enjoyable. Staff performing above and beyond the call of duty receive gold aeroplanes as recognition of their achievement, while wooden spoons are given to staff for acts of amazing stupidity. A suggestion scheme does have a small financial component from between £5 and £25 but the key element is a dinner or other non-monetary award for the best two suggestions each quarter. The company receives 20 suggestions per employee per year – the highest number in the UK. Branches and departments compete in the 'Richer Way League'. This is based on customer service standards and profit, and provides the use of a Rolls-Royce or a Bentley for a week as the prize for the top performing branch. Thus, team-work is emphasised, and branch staff are encouraged to socialise outside the workplace as a way of consolidating the team identity.

Source: Adapted from Golzen G. 'Award scheme comeback', *The Times*, 13 April 2000. p19; Marchington M., Wilkinson A., Ackers P. and Dundon A. *Management Choice and Employee Voice*. London, CIPD. 2001

CONCLUSIONS

When reviewing reward systems, care needs to be taken not only with the choice of suitable payment schemes and benefits packages, but also with the processes by which they are implemented. Management needs to take into account a number of key factors when implementing reward systems. This is based on the view that a careful systematic analysis, which addresses potential problems, is more likely to succeed than an ad hoc approach. Firstly, it is important to analyse what is wrong with the existing reward system and separate out symptoms from causes, and establish whether or not the scheme is fundamentally flawed or just plagued by implementation problems. Secondly, it is essential to involve employees and their representatives in the process of change because they may add useful knowledge on the issues which affect them and about which management is unaware. It also allows management to sound out employee opinion and hence assess the feasibility of their plans, while employees who have been involved are more likely to accept and understand the system rather than reject it as an arbitrary management imposition. For example, with job evaluation, working parties or panels are usually set up to conduct the actual process of evaluation, ensuring a greater legitimacy to the decisions, subjective as they are. Thirdly, it is important to prepare the way by communicating the system, taking care to explain how it is intended to work, and the implications for each group of workers. Finally, it is not enough simply to install the system. It needs to be monitored and reviewed to ensure that it operates in the way that was intended, and that it is judged against established criteria. Given that all reward systems tend to have unintended consequences and decay over time, regular review is critical. There is no such thing as an ideal scheme that can operate for many years without modification (Thorpe *et al* 2000, pp247–273).

At times when it is difficult for employers to fund pay increases above the rate of inflation and provide a range of generous financial benefits (such as pensions and sick-pay arrangements), attention may need to turn to non-financial recognition and reward. This includes the harmonisation of certain terms and conditions such as clocking on and off, single canteens and car-parking arrangements, none of which is likely to be as expensive as financial rewards. It could also include initiatives designed to make work more satisfying and fulfilling, and increase variety, involvement, autonomy and responsibility through job redesign and total quality management. The gains to be made from these can be extensive and contribute directly to the achievement of organisational success.

For employees, it is important that reward systems should be fair and equitable and overall benefits and payments should be consistent with what is perceived as the quality of the individual's contribution, in comparison with other people, both internal and external to the organisation. The debate about the reward packages of top managers and executives sums this up well. Most manual and non-manual workers would deem it reasonable that these people should earn more than they do themselves, although there is disagreement about the ratio. It is seen as totally unfair that such individuals are not subject to an open regulatory system, that they are able to benefit from well-designed share option schemes, and gain excessive perks, especially if their organisations are not performing well.

USEFUL READING

ADVISORY, CONCILIATION AND ARBITRATION SERVICE. *Job Evaluation: An introduction*. London, Acas. 2003b.

ARMSTRONG M. *Employee Reward*, 3rd edition. London, CIPD. 2002.

CHARTERED INSTITUTE OF PERSONNEL AND DEVELOPMENT. *'Reward Management': A survey of policy and practice*. London, CIPD. 2004f.

EQUAL OPPORTUNITIES COMMISSION. *Code of Practice on Equal Pay*. London, EOC. 2003.

EQUAL OPPORTUNITIES COMMISSION. *Good Practice Guide: Job evaluation schemes free of sex bias*. Manchester, EOC. 2000.

HALES, C. *and* GOUGH, O. 'Employee evaluations of company occupational pensions: HR implications', *Personnel Review*, Vol. 32, No. 3, 2003. pp319–340.

IRS EMPLOYMENT REVIEW 799c. *Pay the Strategic Way*. 7 May 2004. pp10–13.

IRS EMPLOYMENT REVIEW 792e. *Putting Job Evaluation to Work: Tips from the front line*. 23 January 2004. pp8–15.

IRS EMPLOYMENT REVIEW 792f. *Thank You Goes a Long Way*. 23 January 2004. pp32–36.

REMERY C., VAN DOORNE-HUISKES A. *and* SCHIPPERS J. 'Family-friendly policies in the Netherlands: the tripartite involvement', *Personnel Review*, Vol. 32, No. 4, 2003. pp456–473.

SMITH P. 'Job evaluation', in R. THORPE *and* G. HOMAN (eds), *Strategic Reward Systems*. London, Financial Times/Prentice Hall. 2000c. pp217–231.

TULIP S. 'Just rewards', *People Management*, 10 July 2003b. pp42–46.

Research and Change Management Skills

PART

6

Research and Change Management Skills

INTRODUCTION

HR specialists are often involved in project work with other managers and achieving outcomes through the actions of other people. The skills needed in order to do this include interviewing, communication, presentation, assertiveness, time management, negotiating, influencing and persuading. In addition to these general transferable skills, for any project work to be successful a wide range of analytical skills need to be deployed. These include identifying key issues, planning and organising work individually or in teams, information search and retrieval, and data analysis. Project work forms a critical part of the HR manager's job, and provides the means by which HR impacts on broader management agendas.

Anderson (2004, p6) defines research in HR as 'finding out things in a systematic way in order to increase knowledge about people and processes involved in the management of work organisation'.

This chapter looks at good practice in carrying out a research project and introducing change into organisations. We examine research design and method, structure and layout, as well as considering the role of the HR manager and the skills required to implement projects. This chapter is somewhat different from the rest of the book, as it provides guidance on producing a research project and implementing recommendations. Naturally, this will be particularly helpful to those who have limited experience, but it should also be a useful reminder for more experienced practitioners. The word 'researcher' is used throughout but this also covers 'project manager', 'student' and 'change management specialist' as well.

By the end of this chapter, readers should be able to:

- **contribute effectively to the planning, design and implementation of projects**

- **make appropriate and correct use of different techniques in gathering data for a management project**

- **draw realistic conclusions from research and present these in a logical and systematic manner.**

In addition readers should understand and be able to explain:

- **the role of research and change management skills in organisations**

- **the advantages and disadvantages of different research methods and their relevance to different situations**

- **the structure and contents of a management report.**

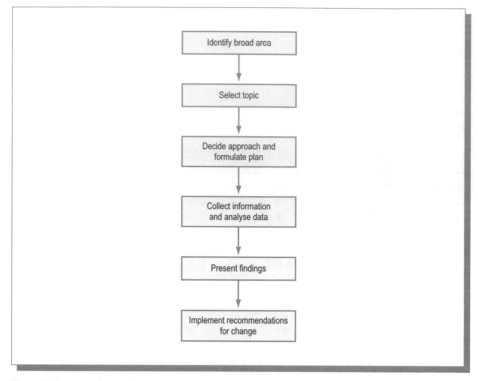

Figure 13 *Sequence for a project*

Source: Adapted from Howard K., Sharp J. and Peters J. *The Management of a Student Research Project*, 3rd edition. Gower, Open University. 2002

When planning projects a sequence proposed by Howard, Sharp and Peters (2002) is commonly used. This is illustrated in Figure 13 and is used as a framework for the remainder of the chapter. We have added to this an implementation stage (incorporating change management) – something that would be required of the HR manager.

Each step in the sequence should be given sufficient attention if time is to be saved in the longer term. A common error is to give insufficient attention to defining clearly the topic to be investigated (Gill and Johnson 1997, p3). This is similar to answering the wrong question in an examination – still the most common reason for failure. As a result the project may be too broad, take up too much time, and the recommendations be difficult to justify or do not flow from the content of the report.

IDENTIFYING THE BROAD TOPIC AREA

A number of issues are important when identifying the broad area. These include terms of reference, access and collaboration. The terms of reference indicate what the researcher is being asked to do and what access and budget are provided. If the report is a CIPD Management Report, the terms of reference will normally be a part of the brief. Clarifying the terms of reference shows what the report is about – and what it is not about. In short, it delineates the boundaries of the report (Johns 1996).

The prospect of gaining access and the type of access are very important issues (Saunders *et al* 2002, pp114–128). Topics concerned with, for example, redundancy, competitive product markets or managerial stress – although potentially interesting and useful research areas – may be difficult to study (Gill and Johnson 1997, p13). Similarly topics that are politically sensitive – such as executive pay for senior managers – may make access to information difficult. For those already employed in the HR function, access to the organisation itself may not be a problem but access to data and people may be more difficult. For researchers who are starting 'cold', one common approach is to send a project proposal (no more than two pages) to targeted organisations, and then follow this up with further letters or telephone calls. It is often difficult to gain access, and luck tends to play a large part in this.

The next issue is collaboration and research partners. As projects often depend heavily on working closely with prospective respondents and practitioners, it might be useful to involve them in the definition and management of research. This very often brings an immediate relevance to the work (practitioners are likely to have many 'hot' topics they need researching) and the findings can be disseminated quickly across user networks. However, work must be theoretically grounded in a way that makes its contribution to knowledge obvious and this cannot be traded off in the interests of 'practical utility'. If working within an employing organisation, it is similarly important to ensure that the needs of the researcher match organisational needs; otherwise it is possible to end up doing two quite different projects. Additionally, there are confidentiality and ethical issues. As Brewerton and Millward (2001, p4) note:

> **The researcher must be conscious of and respect any ethical issues raised. Research projects involving participants of any kind are likely to raise expectations, or have other implications for the organization or the participants involved. Confidential information gained from whatever source must remain confidential, and the researcher must retain a high degree of integrity in conducting research within a "live" setting.**

SELECTING A TOPIC FOR THE PROJECT

The choice and definition of topic is determined by a number of issues, including the amount of time available as well as the personal capabilities and interests of the researcher (Anderson 2004, pp33–37). Amongst the questions that need to be addressed are the following:

- What is the purpose of the project and how realistic is it to investigate?
- Will it usefully add to the existing store of knowledge?
- Will the subject chosen for investigation be manageable and not be too open-ended?

Further considerations are presented in Box 56 on page 382.

The general purpose of the project needs to be clear. It is important to have several ideas and be flexible over the choice and treatment of the research topic. Where possible, it is important to choose something interesting with enough depth, without it being too broad. For example, 'what impact does organisational change have on the everyday life of employees?' is far too vague, whereas 'what is organisational change?' needs a clearer definition in terms

BOX 56   CHECKLIST OF ATTRIBUTES OF A GOOD RESEARCH TOPIC

1 Does the topic fit the specifications and meet the standards set by the examining institution?

2 Is the topic something with which you are really fascinated?

3 Does your research topic contain issues that have a clear link to theory?

4 Do you have, or can you develop within the project time frame, the necessary research skills to undertake the topic?

5 Is the research topic achievable within the available time?

6 Is the research topic achievable within the financial resources?

7 Are you reasonably certain of being able to gain access to the required data?

8 Are you able to state your research question(s) and objectives clearly?

9 Will your proposed research be able to provide fresh insights on this topic?

10 Does your research topic relate clearly to the idea you have been given (perhaps by an organisation)?

11 Are the findings for this research topic likely to be symmetrical, that is of similar value whatever the outcome?

12 Does the research topic match your career goals?

13 To what extent does your research match the characteristics of a good project?

Source: Adapted from Saunders M., Lewis P. and Thornhill A. *Research Methods for Business Students*, 3rd edition. London, Financial Times/Prentice Hall. 2003. p16

of strategy, structure and culture (Thietart *et al* 2001, pp44–45). In short the topic should be manageable, precise and achievable in the time period. It is better to say a lot about a relatively specific problem, than a little about a very broad issue. Another trap is what Silverman (1993) terms 'tourism', that is only examining innovative and novel aspects and ignoring routine issues.

Time management is a crucial consideration. With limited time available there may be a temptation to select a topic before doing the preliminary groundwork. This is short-sighted as time will not be saved in the long run. It is generally the case that the time taken to accomplish a piece of research is underestimated. This can be lengthened by delays, illness or job pressures (Gill and Johnson 1997, p14). External factors may have a bearing on the time needed, especially when relying on the goodwill of others who may prove difficult to pin down in practice. Additionally, there may be unforeseen organisational changes that make it difficult to carry out the original project.

A *research plan* showing the phases of the research and dates for completion can assist in the management of unforeseen delays. It is useful to keep a research diary including targets, progress and ideas, and to review these regularly. In the business and management world it is often very difficult to plan ahead precisely, but that does not mean such planning should be avoided. Few research projects are as elegant and unproblematic as their eventual published form suggests. Companies may drop out, people go on holiday and circumstances change – this is part of the normal process of research. There is a danger of assuming all research projects are undertaken with fully articulated objectives at the commencement of the study, an error compounded by the rational and logical way in which results are written up after the event! As Pettigrew (1985, p222) honestly admits, 'it is more easily characterised in the language of muddling through, incrementalism, and political process' rather than a rationally contrived act. Similarly, access is often assumed to be unproblematic, with researchers having total freedom to inquire into the exact details in the precise location where their theoretical preconceptions lead them. Unfortunately, reality rests more on good fortune and opportunism; for example, making contact at a time when the 'gatekeeper' in the organisation wants outside intervention, or in not 'losing' sites through closure or takeover. As Buchanan *et al* (1988, p53) observe:

> Fieldwork is permeated with the conflict between what is theoretically desirable on the one hand and what is practically possible on the other. It is desirable to ensure representativeness in the sample, uniformity of interview procedures, adequate data collection across the range of topics to be explored, and so on. But the members of the organisations block access to information, constrain the time allowed for interviews, lose your questionnaires, go on holiday, and join other organisations in the middle of your unfinished study. In the conflict between desirable and the possible, the possible always wins.

Gill and Johnson (1997, p15) point out that a researcher with strong capabilities in the behavioural sciences but low numeracy skills should hesitate before choosing a topic involving complex statistical analysis. Similarly, a researcher with poor analytical and writing skills might be unwise to embark on an ethnographic study. If possible, projects should make use of existing skills, and of course, it helps greatly if the topic is of particular interest to the researcher. Finally, the value of the project is important. Gill and Johnson (p16) suggest that 'motivation and interest is higher if the work is clearly making a contribution to the solution of a significant problem'.

There are a number of techniques used to generate and refine research ideas. Some of these are shown in Box 57.

DECIDING ON THE APPROACH AND FORMULATING THE PLAN

Writing a project proposal is an important first step, whether it is going before a managerial meeting, a research committee, or a student's tutor. It is a process that repays very careful attention (Saunders *et al* 2002, p28). For example, writing can be a good way of clarifying thoughts and ideas, and it can also help organise ideas into a coherent statement of research intent. The proposal must convince the audience that the objectives are achievable in the timeframe allowed. If asked to carry out a project for a client or one's own organisation, researchers need a clear proposal to submit for approval. Acceptance of the proposal by the client forms part of the contract, and implies that the proposal is satisfactory (Saunders *et al* 2002, pp28–29).

BOX 57   FREQUENTLY USED TECHNIQUES FOR GENERATING AND REFINING RESEARCH IDEAS

Rational thinking	Creative thinking
Examining your own strengths and interests	Keeping a notebook of ideas
Looking at past projects	Exploring personal preferences
Discussion	Using past projects
Searching the literature	Relevance trees
	Brainstorming

Source: Saunders M., Lewis P. and Thornhill A. *Research Methods for Business Students*, 3rd edition. London, Financial Times/Prentice Hall. 2003. p.17

The struggle to finish on time often comes about because ideas were not focused at the earliest stage or the viability was not thoroughly investigated. A proposal should have the following:

- *Title* – should reflect the content of the proposal, even if this title is provisional.

- *Rationale* – why the research is important and worth the effort.

- *Objectives* – A precise statement of what is hoped to achieve.

- *Themes/issues* – The ideas that will be used to guide the project research and a statement of what will be investigated and why. If it is expected that the research will prove or disprove hypotheses, then these should be stated.

- *Existing literature* – A brief discussion of existing work on the topic, demonstrating how the proposed research will fit in.

- *Methodology* – A brief account of how the work might be carried out, an indication of the proposed sources of information, the research approach and methods (justified in the light of project objectives) and an indication of analytical or statistical tools to be used. The research design and data collection phases are both important. The latter is more concerned with detail of how the data is collected (for example, how many interviews are to be carried out and their length).

- *Proposed timetable* – A provisional outline of how the research will be completed over a period of time, suggesting how many days/weeks will be spent on each of the various stages involved – always assume it will take longer than you first think.

- *Potential problems* – An indication of any problems the researcher is likely to meet. Resources may be an issue here: to what extent does one have the resources, time, money, assistance in collecting data, software packages etc to carry out the project? Another key issue relates to access. If you are suggesting interviewing every Personnel Director in all the major competitors in the region you might want to think whether this is viable.

Think about a potential (or actual) project that you are doing. Write down **four** key questions that the project seeks to address. Which of these is the central question?

You might find the framework in Figure 14 useful in crafting research projects.

The project needs to be mapped out into clear stages eg planning and preparation, project design, project implementation, data analysis/interpretation, report and various substages.

What? What puzzles/intrigues me? What do I want to know more about/understand better? What are my key questions?	**Why?** Why will this be of enough interest to others to be published as a thesis, book, paper, guide to practitioners or policy-makers? Can the research be justified as a 'contribution to knowledge'.
How – conceptually? What models, concepts and theories can I draw on/develop to answer my research questions? How can these be brought together into a basic conceptual framework to guide my investigation?	**How – practically?** What investigative style and techniques shall I use to apply my conceptual framework (to both gather material and analyse it?) How shall I gain and maintain access to information sources?

Figure 14 *The process – a 'what, why and how' framework for crafting research*

Source: Watson T. 'Managing, crafting and rearching: words, skill and imagination in shaping management research', *British Journal of Management*, Vol. 5, Special issue, June 1994. p80

This might include meeting with contacts, seeking feedback on methods, acquiring ethical approval, and agreeing logistics. In addition measurable milestones need to be provided, although it is sensible to build in contingency times (Brewerton and Millward 2001, pp23–24). There are different ways of documenting the time-planning, but one of the best is by using a Gantt chart as shown in Figure 15.

Methodology is about choosing the most appropriate methods of research to fit the aims and projected outcomes. It provides a rationale for the particular methods utilised. Methods are the practical techniques used by researchers to test their methodological and theoretical assumptions (Ackroyd and Hughes 1992). A distinction is often made between quantitative and qualitative research with the former concerned with figures and the latter with words (Miles and Huberman 1984).

Quantitative research refers to studies concerned with measurement and quantification of data to answer research questions. To be useful data needs to be analysed and interpreted using quantitative analysis techniques. The archetypal approach is the application of a formula: a statement or hypothesis to be tested; an account of sampling and methods; and,

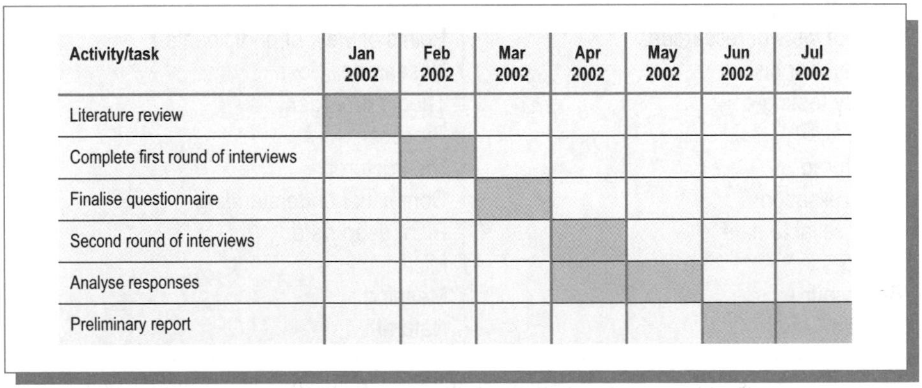

Figure 15 *Gantt chart*

finally, a description of results and a discussion of the implications. With quantitative work, the process of data collection becomes distinct from analysis (Easterby-Smith *et al* 1996, p116).

Qualitative research is more fashionable than in the past when there was greater stress on 'objectivity' and 'reliability' and an attempt to impose scientific use of theory. Qualitative research puts emphasis on individuals' interpretation of behaviour and their environment. The emphasis tends to be on understanding what is going on in organisations in participants' own terms rather than those of the researcher. As Fineman and Mangham (1983, p296) observe: 'if behaviour is viewed as situationally specific, idiosyncratic, multi-variate or holistic, then a "richer", more descriptive analysis may well be taken to be worthwhile'. The scientific model has been criticised on the grounds that research in the real world does not fit the textbook model. In contrast, qualitative research tends to generate data in a non-standard fashion and hence has been described as 'an attractive nuisance' (Miles 1979, p590).

In practice the differences between quantitative and qualitative approaches can be exaggerated, and both can be equally useful. Qualitative material can be generated from quantitative data – for example, interviews and surveys can incorporate open-ended questions that allow for qualitative analysis to be used (Easterby-Smith *et al* 1996, p116). Both approaches are frequently used together. For example, recent research into best practice in teacher capability procedures involved quantitative research (analysis of questionnaires sent to head-teachers) as well as qualitative data (analysis of interviews with head-teachers). The conclusions and recommendations resulting from the research were informed by both sets of data (Earnshaw *et al* 2002b).

Some common contrasts between quantitative and qualitative research are listed in Table 32.

Glaser and Strauss (1967) have emphasised the evolutionary nature of research, especially in the fieldwork phase. They stress the limitations of sticking to a prescribed research plan when events unfold that highlight different issues which are much more important than those originally identified. Mintzberg (1979, p587) is particularly critical of quantitative researchers who never 'go near the water' or collect data from a distance 'without anecdote to support them'. He argues that this may lead to 'difficulty explaining interesting relationships'. His focus

Table 32   *Some common contrasts between quantitative and qualitative research*

Quantitative	Qualitative
Numbers	Words
Point of view of researcher	Points of view of participants
Researcher distant	Researcher close
Theory testing	Theory emergent
Static	Process
Structured	Unstructured
Generalisation	Contextual understanding
Hard, reliable data	Rich, deep data
Macro	Micro
Behaviour	Meaning
Artificial	Natural

Source: Bryman A. and Bell E. *Business Research Methods*. Oxford, Oxford University Press. 2003. p302

on inductive research comprises two parts. Firstly, there is detective work, which involves tracking down patterns and seeing how pieces fit together. Secondly, there is the 'creative leap', which effectively requires researchers to generalise beyond their data in order to describe something new. However, he warns that this kind of research can tend to be haphazard and harder to plan than testing simple hypotheses in the relative security of the laboratory.

An understanding of theory and related research is an essential part of a good project and it is important to present the theoretical background to a project. This is the sum of what is already known about a subject area, and its related problems, in general terms. It should outline and provide a critique of the generally accepted models on which general understanding is based. This may provide a rationale for the proposed project, where it supplements existing theory, or fills a gap in theoretical knowledge. A critical review of other researchers' published work can be included as a part of a discussion of the general theoretical background. In most projects it is necessary to make comparisons with similar studies or similar problems in some detail. It is necessary to identify and discuss the key studies in the field, so their implications can be considered in the choice of research approach and method, and their results and conclusions can be compared.

There are generally accepted methods for choosing research sites, making data observations, collection, and analysis. Usually they depend upon on some common consensus held by a research community about what they think they know, and what constitutes a subject area, as well as appropriate research styles and approaches. It is important to take care over the sources of data and literature to identify the studies closest to the project. The research should relate to these studies, and if different findings emerge, explanations need to be found. Sometimes, however, it happens that there are competing schools of thought, or different research and theoretical traditions, so it is important to establish the state of knowledge. The perspective to be adopted in the project and an explanation about how the research fits into the general picture need to be provided. The research should then be designed with research methods to match this. It is important to state the reasons for the choice of approach and later, perhaps in the project discussion, state something about the validity of methods (Witcher and Wilkinson 2002).

> Critically assess the research approach, sample and methods used in a project that has been carried out in your organisation or in a paper in one of the main academic journals.

Research hypotheses are necessary to guide and direct the research process. Often, however, they do much more than this; they dictate quite precisely the nature of the research process itself. Many accounts of how to carry out research suggest the following process:

1   Read other people's work.
2   Construct a general model.
3   Propose hypotheses.
4   Design a survey and/or questionnaire to operationalise the hypothesis.
5   Process the results to see if the hypothesis is confirmed.
6   Assess the results in terms of implications for the usefulness of the model.

The role and purpose of different research styles, and the methodologies they suggest, constitute a major subject area in itself and would take too long to outline here. However, it is important to note that while, in principle, this general approach is correct, in practice it can often prove too simplistic. Research is often messy and plans continually change, perhaps because of unforeseen changes in the organisation being studied. Perfection and planning are difficult to achieve in practice, and the researcher should be aware that while taking a systematic approach is important, analytical quality in a project is also crucial. It can be difficult in management and organisational studies to prove or disprove hypotheses. The level of required theoretical abstraction is often too high, and the results are too specific to be meaningful for statements of theory that have a general application. Research in organisations is typically exploratory as well as investigative in its nature. Often, it is based around 'solving' a practical and clearly defined problem. Solving a problem or issue in one particular case means that the emphasis is on achieving insights rather than about formulating general theoretical statements. Where hypothesis-directed research is going to be used in its narrow and strict sense, such as to prove or disprove ideas, it needs to be clear

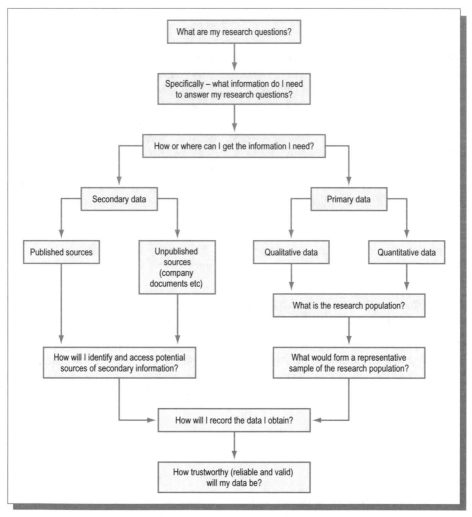

Figure 16 *Planning the methodology*

Source: Andersen V. *Research Methods in Human Resource Management*. London, CIPD. 2004. p113

how the research hypotheses will be operationalised in terms of data collection and quantitative analysis (Witcher and Wilkinson 2002).

The flow chart in Figure 16 will help you plan your methodology.

COLLECTING INFORMATION AND ANALYSING DATA

Literature search and review

Data that has already been collected is normally referred to as secondary data. There is always a huge amount of secondary data available from newspapers, government departments, trade organisations and professional bodies. They publish a huge volume of information, statistics, and official reports, much of which is available on the web. For example, the CIPD website has continuously updated material on a wide range of issues, written from an HR perspective. Some data is held by companies and is not always accessible. Basic factual data on companies is easily available through annual reports and web sites but some data – such as company minutes and reports – may be much more difficult to access. Redman and Wilkinson (2002, pp272–276) for a list of useful websites on HR issues and Saunders *et al* (2002, pp42–83) for advice on identifying literature and information. When carrying out the literature search, it is useful to look for work that has used theory and methods similar to those identified for the project. Classification of sources of organisational evidence is given in Table 33 on page 390.

The *literature review* has been referred to as 'a means of thought organisation' (Brewerton and Millward 2001, p36) and the most common approach is to start broad and then narrow down when a more specific focus is achieved (Anderson 2004, p68). It is important to be reflective and think critically. For example, if investigating a new topic, say knowledge management, one can look exclusively at books covering this subject. However, if examining the management of quality, this is by no means new and could be traced back to the building of the pyramids. Rather than assume a so-called 'hot topic' is new it may make sense to contextualise it by looking at other relevant literature rather than to restrict focus at the start. Reinventing wheels can be a needless task. Today, literature searches can be undertaken much more quickly and efficiently using computerised databases – such as AB Inform – that provide considerable detail on management topics. It is important to keep a good list of references and also to try to write up notes before the box files of material become too large. Writing notes helps to make sense of the material gathered and how it fits together rather than simply collecting it in an unfocused way. The danger otherwise is 'mountains of facts piled up on plains of human ignorance'. The literature should generate issues and questions to help choose the main objective. Once the main objective has been decided, it may then be possible to derive more specific questions.

RESEARCH APPROACHES

There is no one single model for project research, but a number of different approaches. Here we briefly examine three: the experiment, the case study and the survey. Each has its own advantages and disadvantages and it is important to identify what is most appropriate for the project. All three can be used for exploratory, descriptive or explanatory research (Yin 1984, p14). The type of research question (ie who, what, where, how, why) influences the choice of strategy. A survey may be the best approach for 'what'-type questions, whereas 'how' and 'why' questions are more appropriately addressed through exploratory and case study research. Table 34 (page 391) outlines these different research strategies and the types of questions they are designed to address.

Table 33 *Different sources of organisational evidence*

Primary sources		Secondary sources
Examples of evidence produced internally for internal use	Examples of evidence produced internally for external use	Examples of evidence produced externally using internal sources of evidence
Administrative sources: ■ personnel records ■ safety records ■ production/service records	Organisational Internet site(s)	Newspaper cuttings
Business records: ■ agendas ■ notes from meetings ■ progress reports ■ project proposals	Corporate brochure(s) (for clients/potential investors etc)	TV/radio transcripts/ recordings
Operational records: ■ letters ■ memos ■ e-mails ■ handwritten note	Corporate video/DVD (for PR purposes)	Books and journal articles featuring the organisation
Policy documents and procedures: ■ HR ■ purchasing and supply ■ finance and accounting ■ marketing	Marketing information	
Other internal 'artefacts': ■ briefing notes ■ induction presentations ■ corporate videos (for staff and associates) ■ maps, plans and drawings ■ process diagrams	Published diaries/memoirs of key people	

Source: Andersen V. *Research Methods in Human Resource Management*. London, CIPD. 2004. p113

The experiment

This is the common 'classical' approach in the physical sciences (Saunders *et al* 2002, pp91–92). The researcher sets up a project in a laboratory with a number of variables (usually controllable) and conducts the experiment by altering one variable at a time, so they can study the relationship between the different variables (Bryman and Bell 2003, p39). The

Table 34   *Relevant situations for different research strategies*

Strategy	Form of research question	Requires control over behavioural events?
Experiment	how why	yes
Survey	who what* where how many how much	no
Case study	how why	no

*'What' questions, when asked as part of an exploratory study, pertain to all strategies.

Source: Adapted from Yin R. *Case Study Research: Design and methods*. London, Sage. 1984. p.7

researcher controls the independent (or input) variables while measuring the effect on the dependent (or output) variables and keeping intervening factors constant (Bennett 1983). The social experiment takes place in a field setting where the researcher follows the above pattern by treating different groups of people in different ways. For example, evaluating the effect of a training course on a group of managers will involve measurement of knowledge or attitudes before and after the course and a comparison of their responses with a group of similar managers who did not attend the course. This assumes nothing 'happens' to the 'control' group (those not on the course). Easterby-Smith *et al* (1996, pp37–38) note that this is naïve and provide the example of a course which they evaluated. While the course was ongoing those not on the course (the control group) took the opportunity to improve relationships with their bosses and strengthen their political standing – in effect shutting out some of those who were absent because they were on the course. This meant that the original topic – assessing the impact of a course – was rendered meaningless by changes elsewhere in the organisation.

To what extent is it possible to draw meaningful conclusions from studies that have used laboratory experiments – for example, on sleep patterns of students in order to predict the effects of shiftwork on long-term health?

Case studies

Here research is carried out in an organisation to examine a particular topic or event (Bryman and Bell 2003, p53). Case studies have formed an essential plank of research in a variety of disciplines, from medicine and psychology through to political science. According to Yin (1981, p59) the case study is an attempt to 'examine a contemporary phenomenon within its real life context; when the boundaries between phenomenon and context are not clearly evident; and in which multiple sources of evidence are used'. Mitchell (1983, p191) describes the case study as 'a detailed examination of an event (or series of related events) which the analyst believes exhibits (or exhibit) the operation of some identified general theoretical principle'. In short, the case study method tries to capture the whole, is intensive in nature, and is open-ended and flexible at all stages of the research process. A comparative case approach could involve the researcher in examining a particular topic via visits to several different organisations to interview staff and collect data. For example, this approach could be used to examine the impact of a particular pay system on employees in different organisational contexts. It has been argued that the technique utilised by case study researchers can lead to bias in the results, either via the inherent limitations of any single method (Denzin 1970, p13) or due to the effect of the researcher on the situation itself (see discussion on interviews below).

Survey

This is also one of the most widely adopted approaches in social science and business and management research and HR projects are no exception (Anderson 2004, p208). Surveys are cheap, quick to administer, and provide a much wider coverage than say an experiment or case study (Bennett 1983). The main method of data collection is via the questionnaire (see below) although other survey methods include structured observation. The main aim of the survey is to collect information from, or about, a defined group or 'population' (Easterby-Smith *et al* 1996, p122). The data is standardised so allows for comparison. Saunders *et al* (2002, p92) note that the data is less wide ranging than that collected by qualitative methods as there is a limit to the number of questions that can be asked. An example of this would be WERS surveys that collected data from a representative sample of 2000 workplaces on various aspects of employee relations (Cully *et al* 1999).

METHODS OF RESEARCH

Whatever the broad approach adopted, researchers may use a number of different techniques to collect data. This is particularly apparent in case study research.

Observation

According to Ackroyd and Hughes (1992, p127) 'the most well-known of the observational methods is participant observation, which requires researchers to involve themselves in the lives of those being studied – looking, listening, enquiring, recording, and so on'. Observations are directed towards an understanding of how interaction patterns are linked – with symbols and meanings used to understand behaviour – rather than the frequency and distribution of events. Participant observation, according to Denzin's wider meaning of the term, is a method of qualitative analysis that requires observer submersion in the data and uses analytical induction and theoretical sampling as the main strategies of analysis and discovery. A major advantage is that it allows the 'simultaneous generation and verification of theory' since the researcher tries to share his/her life with those being studied (Denzin 1978, p187). There are four variants of participant observation:

- *Complete participant* – In this role the researcher aims to become an ordinary member of the group and their full intent is not revealed. Perhaps the researcher may need to collect information without revealing their identity for fear that this would either undermine access or affect the results. An example of this might be a study looking at the extent to which companies observe minimum wage or health and safety legislation.

■ *Participant as observer* – The role of observer is made clear to the research subjects. Although the researcher undertakes the same tasks as the people being observed – as in the work on assembly lines undertaken by Delbridge (1998) – their reason for being there is made explicit.

■ *Observer as participant* – In this role the contact is brief and tends to take the form of interviews with no attempt to create a longer term relationship. This is probably the most typical of research situations in the HR area.

■ *Complete observer* – The researcher is removed completely from interaction with his/her subjects, and merely administers questionnaires or observes their behaviour – perhaps through a one-way mirror as in some psychology research.

A balance between involvement and distance is needed. The researcher needs to get close enough to the subjects in order to empathise with them, but maintain enough distance to retain a theoretically informed and detached viewpoint (Pettigrew 1985, p228) and avoid 'going native'.

Interviews

Interviews have been defined by Ackroyd and Hughes (1992, p100) as 'encounters between a researcher and a respondent in which the latter is asked a series of questions relevant to the subject of the research. The respondent's answers constitute the raw data analysed at a later point in time'. It is based on the assumption that the answers offered by respondents are valid indicators of the subject under investigation, and these answers provide access to observable and reportable behaviour. Put another way, the information collected is 'presentational data' – based upon symbolic projections and appearances – rather than 'operational data', which is behaviour actually observed by the researcher. This analytical distinction is critically important for interpretation, since there is a danger that 'the presentational data will literally swamp the operational data, thus masking the difference between fact and fiction in the findings' (van Maanen 1979, pp542–543). Questions asking line managers how they have handled grievance and disciplinary cases is presentational data, whereas, with operational data, their handling of actual cases would be observed. By using multiple triangulation (see next section) and longitudinal research, as well as a degree of common sense, researchers can remain aware of any potential shortcomings in their analysis and interpretation of results, and can minimise this by using a range of techniques.

The interview may be classified into three major forms/types, according to the degree of standardisation or structuring (Brewerton and Millward 2001, pp70–71; Bryman and Bell 2003, p119; Saunders *et al* 2002, p246). The most rigid and formalised is *the schedule or standardised form*, in which there is strict adherence to a prearranged schedule both in terms of the wording of the questions and the order in which questions are put to respondents. In addition, other features of the situation are also standardised across different interviews, such as location, in order to minimise the possibility of variance between responses (Ackroyd and Hughes 1992, p103). Rigidity is relaxed in the second type, the *non-schedule standardised or semi-structured interview*. In this type, the researcher aims to elicit certain information from all respondents, but the phrasing of questions and their order is varied in order to allow for the special characteristics of each respondent, and to maintain rapport throughout the interaction. However, the same sorts of questions are posed to each interviewee. Finally, there is the *non-standardised (unstructured) interview*, which is sometimes compared with a conversation (Denzin 1970, p126; Ackroyd and Hughes 1992, p103). In this situation the interviewer can work from a list of topics, indicating broad areas in which issues are to be pursued, or the interaction can be totally free of prearranged sets of questions. The principal advantage of this latter type of interview is that it does not attempt to fit respondents into predetermined categories, and so enables the interviewer to explore issues as they arise. The interviewer is free to adopt whatever mode of behaviour seems appropriate in the circumstances in order to elicit information from the respondent. This type of interview is particularly useful at the commencement of the research, and with more senior managers who could amplify their views with examples, especially when the researcher 'plays dumb' (Denzin 1970, p131). It may be less effective in situations where the respondents felt less at ease in the interviews, or where the range of their experiences (in relation to the research) was more limited.

One of the principal criticisms of the interview, and especially the non-standardised variety given its less rigid and more open structure, is that bias can invalidate the results from the research process. Bias can enter into the process at a number of stages:

- in the construction of interview questions, their precise order and wording and the context in which they are posed (Ackroyd and Hughes 1992, pp110–120; Brewerton and Millward 2001, p71) and in the extent to which the interviewer poses leading or bland questions

- due to physical characteristics of the interviewer, such as age, gender, class and colour, which cannot usually be removed in the typical research programme. Other factors – such as mode of dress or gestures – are more easily controlled, although it should be remembered that whatever the interviewer's characteristics, these always create some impression with the respondents (Denzin 1970, pp140–141).

- through respondents not conforming with the rules governing the interview – for example by telling lies or by providing answers that they imagine the researcher wants to hear

- the situation in which the interview takes place, its location and timing, and the way in which this may limit or facilitate rapport in the interaction. It is often assumed that good rapport is an essential precondition of a successful interview, to the extent that the researcher must communicate trust, avoid technical language, and adapt to the type of interviewee (Brewerton and Millward 2001, p71). However, while good rapport may be a necessary requirement for successful interviews in most cases, it is not sufficient to guarantee such an outcome. Indeed, it may actually be counterproductive in some instances, leading to overidentification between researcher and respondent

- in the recording and interpretation of results. Data from the interview can either be recorded by hand, relying upon rough notes taken verbatim by the interviewer(s), or by tape recording the proceedings and later transcribing the findings. Tape recording has been used in a variety of research studies and has the principal advantage of ensuring that everything the respondent says is noted, so that the transcript can be reanalysed to tease out the meanings and subtleties in the interviewee's responses. Of course, it also has the associated disadvantages that transcription takes a considerable amount of time and the presence of a tape recorder may inhibit the respondent from providing open answers. Taking notes during the interview is a more manageable process, and can ensure relatively full accounts of the interview, particularly if the notes are written up very soon after the interaction, and the notes are kept in case they need to be re-examined. It is possible to recall with some precision the words used by respondents, so that these can be used as verbatim quotes to supplement the argument of the research report. Nonetheless, there is still the danger that the interviewer consciously – or more likely unconsciously – fails to report accurately the respondents' words or nuances in the write-up, thus introducing another source of bias into the process.

> Assess what can be done to minimise the effect of bias on the results gathered from a set of interviews.

Focus groups are a specific form of interview that simultaneously uses multiple respondents to generate data. It is used to get close to participants' understanding and perspectives of issues and more appropriate as a technique for generating ideas rather than testing hypotheses (Brewerton and Millward 2001, pp80–81). It can either be used as a self-contained means of data collection or a supplementary approach. However, results must be interpreted in the context of group dynamics.

Documentary data

In addition to the techniques described above, data can be collected via the inspection of documentary information produced by individuals within the organisation involved. Personnel departments can provide a range of statistics and information to go alongside the material that emerges from the use of other techniques. Minutes of meetings can also be inspected. However, it is foolhardy to rely too heavily upon such data for a number of reasons. They do not provide a detailed account of meetings; they are not sensitive enough to capture the nuances which generally lie behind specific items; and they tend to represent one version of reality – that of management as they are usually responsible for their completion. However, recognising these limitations, minutes are of some value in that they can help the researcher appreciate the kind of issues that have arisen over time, and the arena in which they were raised, as well as the manner in which they were subsequently formally resolved. If combined with observation of current-day meetings, the adequacy or comprehensiveness of previously recorded minutes can also be assessed, and their worth evaluated with a little more precision.

Questionnaires

Questionnaires are perhaps the most widely used research tool in social sciences and management studies. They are attractive as they require minimal resources, do not cost much but can provide a large sample. However, Saunders *et al* (2002, pp281–286) warn that questionnaires are not easy to design, administer and interpret. One needs to ensure that precise data can be collected to answer the specific research questions and it is not usually easy to go back to respondents if one realises the questionnaire is badly designed or inappropriate. Broadly speaking three types of data can be collected. Firstly, demographic or background data, secondly, behavioural data and thirdly, attitudinal data (Brewerton and Millward 2001, pp99–108).

The main decisions in questionnaire design relate to the type of questions to be used and the overall format of the questionnaire (Easterby-Smith *et al* 1996, p119). It is important to distinguish between questions of 'fact' and questions of 'opinion'. Biographical data such as age, length of service or job title are factual and capable of a 'correct' answer, although there are sometimes problems with the last of these as people may define the job in a different way. Other questions may ask for opinions such as 'do you think you have enough say in decisions made at your work?' The answers to these sorts of question can vary significantly across a sample.

There is also a distinction between 'closed' (or forced-choice) and 'open' questions. The former – as in the question above – can be answered with a yes/no response. However, if the question is phrased as 'what do you see as the main functions of management development?' then the answer could be several lines long. Once all the data has been collected, it needs to be coded by assigning numbers to each answer category so that common answers can be aggregated (Bryman and Bell 2003, pp156–158). One of the problems with open questions (and unstructured interviews) is that when coding, the researcher has no idea whether omissions are deliberate or simply forgotten. For example, using the above question, where respondents omit to mention implementation of corporate strategy, it is not clear whether it is not regarded as one of the main functions, or whether the respondent forgot to include this in their answer.

With closed questions, yes/no responses may be rather crude and a Likert scale is commonly used providing some idea of the strength of opinion. A statement – such as 'do you think you have enough say in decisions made at your work?' – is provided and respondents are asked to indicate their views by choosing from the options available. Typically, a five-point Likert scale, or a six- or seven-point variant, would be used:

Strongly agree $\rightarrow$ Agree $\rightarrow$ Undecided $\rightarrow$ Disagree $\rightarrow$ Strongly disagree

There are certain general principles to follow when drafting a questionnaire (Easterby-Smith *et al* 1996, p120; Brewerton and Millward 2001, pp104–108; Bryman and Bell 2003, pp146–150), and it is essential to ensure that:

1   Questions are clear and unambiguous.

2   Questions are short.

3   Questions avoid jargon or specialist language.

4   'Double-barrelled' questions, in which the respondent is asked about two things in one question, are avoided.

5   'Leading' questions and 'presuming' questions that suggest indirectly what the right answer might be are avoided.

6   Personal questions are avoided unless essential to the research.

It is normal for questionnaires to begin with relatively simple, non-threatening and closed questions, before moving on to questions that are more involved, complex or 'open' towards the end of the document (Thietart *et al* 2001, p174). This is done to ensure that respondents are not discouraged from continuing with the questionnaire. There are also a number of issues relating to layout that are important in terms of achieving comprehensibility. Amongst the key issues identified by Brewerton and Millward (2001, pp107–108) are the following:

■   The instructions and covering letter need to be clear, outlining the background and aims of research, explaining why the respondent's involvement is important, as well as stressing confidentiality and anonymity.

■   The questionnaire should normally be able to be completed in no more than 45 minutes, and not be more than 10 pages in length.

■   The font type and size needs to be readable. Having tiny fonts to keep the number of pages down is not a good approach!

■ Correct spelling and grammar are critical to reassure the respondent that the researcher is competent and professional.

It is essential to 'pilot' the draft questionnaire to check that respondents are able to understand all the questions and that they make sense. It is also vitally important to ensure that respondents are able to answer questions in the way that was intended and that their replies are meaningful. If a large number of questionnaires are to be distributed, it is necessary to use statistical packages such as SPSS to help with the analysis. In this case, issues of scaling are also critically important. These need to be sorted out during the drafting of the questionnaire so as to avoid problems at a later stage in the analysis. It is impossible in this book to provide details of all the issues relating to questionnaire design and analysis, so researchers are referred to the standard texts indicated in the useful reading section.

> Consider the last time that you filled in a questionnaire, and try to recall how you felt about this. Does this experience help you to design questionnaires?

TRIANGULATION

Denzin's commitment to multiple triangulation is clear: 'if each method leads to different features of empirical reality, then no single method can ever completely capture all the relevant features of that reality'; hence, there is a need to 'learn to employ multiple methods in the analysis of the same empirical events' (1970, p13). Denzin articulates four basic types of triangulation: data, investigator, theory and methodology. By *data triangulation* he means that information should be collected from different people, at different times, and in different places, in order to create a fuller picture of a single event. At the same time, data needs to be drawn from a range of levels as well. *Investigator triangulation* is fairly straightforward, meaning that more than one researcher should be employed, wherever possible, on the data collection parts of a project so as to remove the potential bias that comes from a single person, and ensures greater reliability in observations. *Theoretical triangulation* requires researchers to approach the study with multiple perspectives and hypotheses in mind. In addition, it permits the widest possible use of theoretical findings. Finally, there is *methodological triangulation*, which can be within an individual method – for example by using separate scales in a questionnaire for measuring the same construct (say personality) – or between methods. Denzin regards the latter as essential because 'the flaws of one method are often the strengths of another and by combining methods, observers can achieve the best of each, while overcoming their unique deficiencies' (1970, p308). In sum, *multiple triangulation* combines all the features (data, investigator, theory, methods) simultaneously in analysing the same set of events.

Qualitative data is not always easy to analyse. Often large amounts of qualitative data are collected, but the researcher needs to make sense of it. Facts don't always speak for themselves, they have to be interpreted. Too often researchers/students simply reproduce unregurgitated the volume of material they have collected eg large extractions of quotes are provided or the student simply reports a frequency (eg 80 per cent of senior staff are male) without any comment. All too often projects contain a large amount of such *description* and too little *analysis*, yet it is the analysis that is the most important element, and should carry greater weight. Much relevant information can be presented in appendices, devoting more space to discussion and analysis in the main body of the report. Data needs to be linked with theory and the research questions. The first objective needs to be to reduce information and have a sense of control over what one has collected (Anderson 2004, p169). Analysis is a

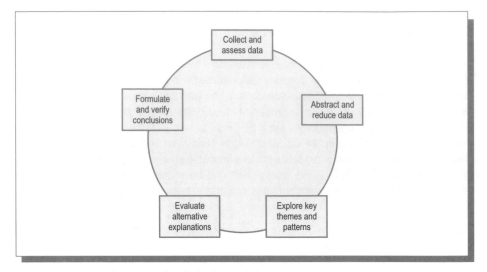

Figure 17 *Overview of the process of qualitative data analysis*
Source: Anderson V. *Research Methods in Human Resource Management*. London, CIPD. 2004. p170

process of thought that enables you to understand the nature of what is being investigated, the relationship between different variables in the literature, and the likely outcomes of particular actions or interventions. Analysis therefore involves finding answers to your research questions using the data you have gathered by asking questions such as 'what', 'why' and 'how' (Anderson 2004, p169).

Figure 17 gives an overview of the process of qualitative data analysis.

In short, one needs to transform the nature of the data one has collected in order to allow one to:

1   comprehend and manage them

2   merge related data drawn from different transcripts and notes

3   identify key themes or patterns from them for further exploration

4   develop and/or test hypotheses based on these apparent patterns or relationships

5   draw and verify conclusions (Saunders *et al* 2002, p382).

To reduce the volume of data one must attempt to categorise or code it. These categories/codes may come from the research questions, the literature or the researcher's own experience while gathering the data and could be about subject matter, attitudes, methods of work, characteristics of people and so on (Anderson 2004, p177). For example if explaining attitudes to and the implementation of performance-related pay, issues could be categorised as (a) the principles of performance-related pay and (b) its practice in operation. These may result in further categories such as management attitudes, training issues and so on. By reducing data to categories the processes of interpreting the data and determining emerging themes is simplified. This process may lead to re-examination of some categories and may result in their being integrated or combined. The process is complex and iterative, with some themes being apparent from early on, others emerging later. This analysis will then lead on to drawing up of conclusions, and it is important to look for alternative explanations at this stage. For example, are employees positive about performance-related pay as a principle, or because it resulted in £2000 extra for most workers. Do employees welcome teambriefing as an opportunity to engage in discussions or because it results in half an hour off normal work?

There are two basic ways of analysing such data: content analyses, with an emphasis on numbers and frequency, and grounded theory (see earlier) where the emphasis is on feel and intuition aiming to produce common or contradicting patterns as the basis for interpretation (Easterby-Smith *et al* 1996, p105).

According to Cresswell (2003, pp191–194) there are six steps to data analysis:

1   Organise and prepare the data for analysis. This involves transcribing interviews, material, typing up field notes and arranging the data into different types depending on the sources of information.

2   Read through all the data, obtain a general sense of the information and reflect on its overall meaning. What general ideas are being expressed? What is the general impression of the overall depth, credibility and use of the information?

3   Begin detailed analysis with a coding process. Coding is the process of organising the material into 'chunks' before bringing meaning to these. It involves taking text data, segmenting paragraphs into categories and labelling those categories. Researchers should analyse their data for material that can yield codes that address topics that readers would expect to find, codes that are surprising, and codes that address a larger theoretical perspective in the research. Obviously, there is an enormous range of codes that could be used depending on the research; they could include processes, activities, people's perceptions etc. The coding process can be enhanced by the used of computer qualitative software programs.

4   The coding process generates a description of the setting or people as well as categories or themes for analysis. Description involves a detailed rendering of information about people, places or events in a setting. Researchers can generate codes for this description. The coding can then be used to generate a small number of themes or categories.

5   Explain how the description and themes will be represented in the narrative. A story is needed to convey the findings of analysis, including a chronology of events, discussion of several themes and a discussion with interconnecting themes.

6   A final step in data analysis involves making an interpretation of the data including the lessons learned (Lincoln and Guba 1985).

PRESENTING FINDINGS: THE STRUCTURE OF THE REPORT

The precise form of the report obviously depends upon the subject matter, the individual writer and the terms of reference. The introduction would typically include something on terms of reference or hypotheses, and maybe a discussion of research methods, and a rough balance should be achieved between subsequent sections. It needs to be remembered that the report – especially if commissioned – can be seen as an exercise in persuasion and the researcher needs to do everything possible to ensure its presentation maximises impact.

A typical format would be:

■   *Executive summary* – A short report to management or the sponsoring organisation summarising the key points and recommendations. This is particularly pertinent where the report is to be presented to several audiences, some of which might not read the report in its entirety. For example, it would be hoped that senior management of the organisation in which the research took place and academics assessing the work would read it very carefully. On the other hand, managers at other organisations may wish only to consult the executive summary. Since the executive summary is likely to reach the widest possible audience, it is very important that it is well presented, clear and unambiguous.

- *Introduction* – A clear statement of the terms of reference for the project, and its principal objectives. This should indicate the way in which the topic has been formulated, the issues connected with the project, and how these have been interpreted and clarified. A summary of the structure of the report is helpful to the reader. It may be necessary at an early stage in the project to acquaint the reader with some background information that is relevant to a full understanding of the project argument. This may include some complex issues. If such information is detrimental to a fluent reading of the text, it could be presented as an appendix.

- *Literature review* – A concise and critical review of the relevant literature, appreciation of the range of theoretical bases upon which the study has drawn and an awareness of current practice in the matter being investigated. The review is not a separate part of the report; it should inform the research approach and needs to be re-examined in the conclusions so as to locate the findings within the wider body of knowledge about the subject.

- *Methodology* – An account of, and justification for, the methods (for example, qualitative and/or quantitative) selected. The writer should be able to demonstrate an understanding of the different methods and an appreciation of which methods are appropriate in particularly sets of circumstances. The influence of different methods on the results emerging from their investigations should be explained. For example, different results may be obtained by asking personnel managers and employees about the success of performance-related pay. The former may have designed and implemented the scheme whereas employees have it applied to them.

- *Data description and background* – An account of the investigation stating what has actually been done. It is crucial that data is presented in a concise and logical manner, and makes appropriate use of tables, statistics, quotations and observations, so as to guide the reader through the mass of information in the report. It is important not to mix together evidence and analysis in the same place but to deal with these things separately. Other people's work can provide evidence, but it must be clear which is the project work, and which is the work and findings of others. It is better to present project findings first, and then bring in other evidence in a separate analysis of these findings, and discussion of them.

- *Analysis and discussion* – This is the most important part of the report. It is about the significance of findings in terms of the overall project argument. It involves evaluating the project findings as well as the theoretical literature and other published work. Discussion is wide and speculative, as the wider meaning of the findings are analysed and interpreted to achieve different ways of understanding. It is important to be original and show initiative and imagination in the work, and not to hide 'ifs' and 'buts'. Also, when discussing findings from the fieldwork, it should be clear what the researcher is concluding and what others have claimed. In other words, if a company says it has implemented TQM, equal opportunities or empowerment, make it clear that this is what *they* claim, not necessarily what the researcher believes. Beware of using confidential, sensitive or personal material obtained from respondents, especially via the interview process.

■ *The conclusion* – This draws together the evidence from the investigation, and explains it with reference to the introduction and the literature survey and relates findings to the hypotheses or terms of reference for the project. There should be an explicit statement indicating the value of the investigation, and the way in which it supplements, refines or disputes existing wisdom. Researchers should also show their awareness of the limitations of the study, and indicate what they have personally learned from their investigation. This process of reflection is vital for researchers and it can help with CPD (Continuing Professional Development) because it may prevent similar mistakes being made.

■ *Recommendations* – Recommendations are usually presented as simple statements of follow-up actions. It is important to be specific, especially if asked to provide these. Vague statements about 'a need to review x and y', 'more thought needs to be given to z' or 'we should involve people more' are not really very helpful. If recommending greater involvement of staff then suggestions as to how to operationalise this are important. Also bear in mind that recommendations exist in a context: issues of practicality and affordability always need to be considered. If there are recommendations then these should not be confused with conclusions.

■ *Appendices* – These can be used for information which is necessary to provide a fuller understanding of the research, but would be a distraction to the key arguments if it were put in the main body of the text. Typically such material would be organisational documents, forms or internal publications central to the research, but which are not the researchers' own work. The status of such material should be clearly stated. However, information put into an appendix should not be there just for padding.

■ *References* – These need to be appropriate, accurate and easy to follow. They should provide details of the sources used, and they can help to provide the reader with a good understanding of the approach that has been taken as well as an indication of other sources that have been useful to the project.

The style of the report is also very important. The use of very brief *introductions* and *summaries* in each chapter, to link each stage of the argument in terms of its purpose and structure, will greatly help the reader. It may be useful to think of the report as a story: each section should follow from the previous one and be signposted. Good presentation will not redeem an unsatisfactory dissertation, but it help to make its processes and findings more accessible. Avoid the use of too many bullet points. These can be helpful – providing brief snapshots of some of the key issues but they may carry different weights. Think of the character of Hannibal Lecter in the film *Silence of the Lambs* and whether to invite him to dinner. He is educated, erudite, cultured and charming, and has exceptional knowledge of fine wine and food (all pluses). There may be just one downside – he might decide to eat you.

Having read this section, look again at the last report that you wrote, and critically review the process in terms of what you did, how you organised the report, and how it was presented. How can this reflective learning be used to improve your skills?

IMPLEMENTING RECOMMENDATIONS FOR CHANGE

Once project recommendations have been accepted, the HR manager is likely to be asked to implement these, and this involves management of change.

Unintended consequences

As an HR practitioner it is important to continually be aware that actions taken as a result of recommendations will have unintended consequences. Any action invariably impacts on other areas, and finding solutions to one problem in turn creates further unforeseen problems. For example, systems set up to ensure things run smoothly may gradually become more bureaucratic and become ends in themselves – and in some cases may be a sledgehammer to crack a nut. The application of a specific technique to improve a process becomes viewed as a universal panacea for all problems with the result that the user(s) become blinkered to the use of other more appropriate tools and techniques. A good example may be where senior management aim to get middle managers to take quality seriously. They may do this by setting up an elaborate appraisal system that middle managers do not have the time to implement. Similarly, payment systems introduced to motivate staff – such as payment by results (PBR) – may lead to increased output, but at the expense of quality.

Overcoming resistance to change

There is overwhelming evidence that the best way to reduce resistance to change is to involve those whom it is going to affect in the decision-making process. Individuals who have been involved in the diagnosis, planning, devising and implementation of change are far more likely to feel positively about it. In general, they will feel more committed and it should lead to speedier and improved implementation.

The ideal situation is where all the necessary information is freely available, and decisions are taken by consensus. There will, however, be occasions when it is not possible to be totally open (for example if some of the information is commercially sensitive). As Makin *et al* (1989) emphasise, the general rule should be that good communication and feedback channels should be established between the change agents and those who are to be affected. Even where there are short-term costs, such as need for retraining, it is necessary to show that there will be long-term benefits, such as improved pay, improved job security, better working conditions, or the award of more customer contracts. Obviously, it will be easier to effect change if there is a general climate of trust in the organisation, where people feel that their fears will be listened to, and their problems recognised and dealt with in a sympathetic manner.

HR managers as effective change agents

According to Buchanan and Boddy (1992, pp88–116), there are five competence clusters required for people to be effective change agents. The definition of competence adopted by the authors concerns actions and behaviours identified by change agents as contributing to their perceived effectiveness as change implementers. The framework below draws heavily on Buchanan and Boddy (pp92–93).

Goals

- *Sensitivity to changes* in key personnel, top management perceptions and market conditions, and to the way in which these impact on the goals of the project in hand are vital. The project does not take place in a vacuum and events will shape the direction of the project which itself may have unintended consequences.

■ *Clarity in specifying goals*, in defining the achievable, is important for internal communication and motivation (and external relationships). Goals need to be realistic and be seen as realistic.

■ *Flexibility* in responding to changes outside the control of the project manager is also important. This may require major shifts in project goals and management style, and risk taking in response to unforeseen events.

Roles

■ *Teambuilding abilities*, including bringing together key stake-holders and establishing effective working groups, to define and delegate respective responsibilities. The project should not be based on the effort of a single person.

■ *Networking skills* in establishing and maintaining appropriate contacts within and outside the organisation are usually crucial.

■ *Tolerance of ambiguity*, to be able to function comfortably, patiently and effectively in an uncertain environment is vital so the project manager can live with delay and disappointment.

Communication

■ *Effective communication* enables the project manager to transmit effectively to colleagues and subordinates the need for changes in project goals and in individual tasks and responsibilities.

■ *Interpersonal skills* – including selection, listening, collecting appropriate information, identifying the concerns of others and managing meetings – are also vital.

■ *Personal energy and enthusiasm*, in expressing plans and ideas.

■ Stimulating the motivation and commitment of others involved in the process.

Negotiation

■ *Vision* – Part of the project manager role is to sell plans and ideas to others.

■ *Negotiating* with key players for resources, or for changes in procedures, and to resolve conflict in a context of limited resources and varied agendas.

Managing-up

■ Project managers have to demonstrate *political awareness*, in identifying potential coalitions, and in balancing conflicting goals and perceptions.

■ *Influencing skills*, to gain commitment to project plans and ideas from potential sceptics and resisters are important, given the project manager may not be in a position to force through change.

■ A *helicopter perspective*, to stand back from the project and take a broader view of priorities, is required.

Based on their research, Buchanan and Boddy (1992, p108) argue that change management now places a much greater emphasis on these five competence clusters rather than traditional project management and content agenda skills.

Box 58 (page 404) lists Dawson's (2003) 10 points you might find helpful when managing change.

BOX 58   LESSONS IN MANAGING CHANGE

1 There are no simple universal prescriptions for how best to manage change.

2 Change strategies must be sensitive to people and context.

3 Major change takes time.

4 Different people experience change in different ways.

5 We can learn from all change experiences, not just the successful ones.

6 Employees need to be trained in new methods and procedures, often overlooked.

7 Communication must be ongoing and consistent.

8 Change strategies must be tailored to fit the substance and context.

9 Change is a political process.

10 Change involves the complex interaction of often contradictory processes.

Source: Dawson P. *Understanding Organisational Change*. London, Sage. 2003. pp173–175

CONCLUSIONS

This chapter has examined the topics of research and change management. HR managers today no longer simply act as administrative agents or 'clerks' of the work but play a role in the running of the organisation. Research has a vital role to play in this, and it is usually linked to a wider change management role.

In carrying out projects, the parameters are often clearly defined by those outside the function. However, allowing 'customers' to define the role of the HR function contains some dangers (Wilkinson and Marchington 1994). While most people would agree with Giles and Williams (1991, p29) that it is important to remind personnel departments 'to accept that their role is to serve their customers and not their egos', this begs the question of how customer needs are defined. If a narrow conformist role is adopted, where needs are defined by line managers, advice from HR function can often be rejected. In such circumstances, the function can do no more than reflect the competencies and values of line managers who expect it to adopt a passive role. A paradigm in which 'hard data' or meeting contractual obligations is required to justify personnel activity means that HR can lose its distinctive role. Thus we would argue that much depends on HR adopting a creative role in organisations. Simply responding to the requests of line managers may provide short-term credibility but in the longer run makes little contribution to organisational goals. The HR function is regarded by some managers as free from the typical conflicts that take place between production, marketing and design, and thus more likely to be 'objective' in its approach to managing change. This could offer real opportunities to help define the agenda.

USEFUL READING

Anderson V. *Research Methods in Human Resource Management*. London, CIPD. 2004.

Brewerton P. *and* Millward L. *Organisational Research Methods: A guide for students and researchers*. London, Sage. 2001.

Bryman A. *and* Bell E. *Business Research Methods*. Oxford, Oxford University Press. 2003.

Buchanan D. *and* Boddy D. *The Expertise of a Change Agent*. Hemel Hempstead, Prentice Hall. 1992.

Burnes B. *Managing Change*. London, Pitman Publishing. 2000.

Darwin J., Johnson P. *and* McAulay J. *Developing Strategies for Change*. London, Financial Times/Prentice-Hall. 2002.

Easterby Smith M., Thorpe R. *and* Lowe A. *Management Research: An introduction*. London, Sage. 1996.

Gill J. *and* Johnson P. *Research Methods for Managers*. London, Paul Chapman Publishing. 1997.

Saunders M., Lewis P. *and* Thornhill A. *Research Methods for Business Students*, 3rd edition. London, Financial Times/Prentice Hall. 2002.

Bibliography

Accounting for People: Report of the Task Force on Human Capital Management. Available at: www.accountingforpeople.gov.uk. 2003.

Ackers P. 'Pluralism', in T. Redman *and* A. Wilkinson (eds), *The Informed Student Guide to Human Resource Management.* London, Thomson Learning. 2002a.

Ackers P. 'Unitarism', in T. Redman *and* A. Wilkinson (eds), *The Informed Student Guide to Human Resource Management.* London, Thomson Learning. 2002b.

Ackers P. 'Employment ethics', in T. Redman *and* A. Wilkinson (eds), *Contemporary Human Resource Management.* London, Financial Times/Prentice Hall. 2001.

Ackers P., Marchington M., Wilkinson A. *and* Dundon T. 'Partnership and voice, with or without trade unions: changing UK management approaches to organisational participation', in M. Stuart *and* M. Martinez-Lucio (eds), *Partnership and Modernisation in Employment Relations.* London, Routledge. 2005.

Ackers P., Marchington M., Wilkinson A. *and* Goodman J. 'The use of cycles: explaining employee involvement in the 1990s', *Industrial Relations Journal*, Vol. 23, No. 4, 1992. pp268–283.

Ackers P. *and* Payne J. 'British trade unions and social partnership: rhetoric, reality and strategy', *International Journal of Human Resource Management*, Vol. 9, No. 3, 1998. pp529–549.

Ackers P. *and* Preston D. 'Born again: the ethics and efficacy of the conversion experience in contemporary management development', *Journal of Management Studies*, Vol. 34, No. 5, 1997. pp677–701.

Ackers P. *and* Wilkinson A. (eds), *Understanding Work and Employment: Industrial relations in transition.* Oxford, Oxford University Press. 2003.

Ackers P. *and* Wilkinson A. 'From employee involvement to social partnership: changing British management approaches to employment participation', *Croners Employee Relations Review*, Vol. 14, September 2000. pp3–10.

Ackroyd S. *and* Hughes J. *Data Collection in Context.* London, Longman. 1992.

Ackroyd S. *and* Procter S. 'British manufacturing organisation and workplace industrial relations: some attributes of the new flexible firm', *British Journal of Industrial Relations*, Vol. 36, No. 2, 1998. pp164–183.

Adams K. 'Externalisation versus specialisation: what is happening to personnel?', *Human Resource Management Journal*, Vol. 1, No. 4, 1991. pp40–54.

Adler N. *and* Ghadar F. 'Strategic human resource management: a global perspective', in R. Pierper (ed), *Human Resource Management: An international comparison.* Berlin, De Gruyter. 1990.

Advisory, Conciliation and Arbitration Service. *Advisory Handbook.* Available at: www.acas.org.uk. 2004.

Advisory, Conciliation and Arbitration Service. *Annual Report 2003–2004.* London, Acas. 2004.

Advisory, Conciliation and Arbitration Service. *Pay Systems.* London, Acas. 2003a.

Advisory, Conciliation and Arbitration Service. *Job Evaluation: An introduction.* London, Acas. 2003b.

ADVISORY, CONCILIATION AND ARBITRATION SERVICE. *Acas Code of Practice Disciplinary Practice and Grievance Procedures*. London, HMSO. 2003c.

ADVISORY, CONCILIATION AND ARBITRATION SERVICE. *Appraisal Related Pay*. London, Acas. 2002.

AHLSTRAND B. *The Quest for Productivity: A case study of Fawley after Flanders*. Cambridge, Cambridge University Press. 1990.

AIKIN O. 'Strictly invitation only', *People Management*, 6 July 2000. p20.

ALBERGA T., TYSON S. *and* PARSONS D. 'An evaluation of the Investors in People standard', *Human Resource Management Journal*, Vol. 7, No. 2, 1997. pp47–60.

ALMOND S. *and* HEALEY A. 'Mental health and absence from work: new evidence from the UK Quarterly Labour Force Survey', *Work, Employment and Society*, Vol. 17, No. 4, 2003. pp731–742.

ANDERMAN S. 'Overview: the law and the employment relationship', in B. TOWERS (ed), *The Handbook of Employment Relations, Law and Practice*. London, Kogan Page. 2003. pp83–105.

ANDERSON N. *and* OSTROFF C. 'Selection as socialization', in N. ANDERSON *and* P. HERRIOT (eds), *International Handbook of Selection and Assessment*. Chichester, John Wiley and Sons Ltd. 1997.

ANDERSON T. *and* METCALF H. *Diversity: Stacking up the evidence*. London, CIPD. 2003.

ANDERSEN V. *Research Methods in Human Resource Management*. London, CIPD. 2004.

APPELBAUM E., BAILEY T., BERG P. *and* KALLEBERG A. *Manufacturing Competitive Advantage: The effects of high performance work systems on plant performance and company outcomes*. New York, Cornell University Press. 2000.

ARAGON-SANCHEZ A., BARBA-ARAGON I. *and* SANZ-VALLE R., 'Effects of training on business results', *International Journal of Human Resource Management*, Vol. 14, No. 6, 2003. pp956–980.

ARMSTRONG M. *Employee Reward*, 3rd edition. London, CIPD. 2002.

ARMSTRONG M. *Employee Reward*, 2nd edition. London, CIPD. 1999.

ARMSTRONG M. *Personnel and the Bottom Line*. London, Institute of Personnel Management. 1989.

ARMSTRONG M. *and* BARON A. *Performance Management: Action and impact*. London, CIPD. 2004.

ARMSTRONG M. *and* BROWN D. *New Dimensions in Pay Management*. London, Kogan Page. 2001.

ARMSTRONG M. *and* MURLIS H. *Reward Management*, 4th edition. London, Kogan Page. 1998.

ARTHUR J. 'Effects of human resource systems on manufacturing performance and turnover', *Academy of Management Journal*, Vol. 37, No. 3, 1994. pp670–687.

ARTHUR J. *and* AIMAN-SMITH L. 'Gainsharing and organizational learning: an analysis of employee suggestions over time', *Academy of Management Journal*, Vol. 44, No. 4, 2001. pp737–754.

ARTHUR W., Woehr D. *and* GRAZIONO W. 'Personality testing in employment settings: problems and issues in the application of typical selection practices', *Personnel Review*, Vol. 30, No. 6, 2001. pp657–676.

ARTHURS A. *Recognising Emotional Labour: Is it a route to equal pay?* Paper presented at the ESRC Seminar Day on the Regulation of Service to Work, Loughborough University. 2003.

ARTHURS A. 'Job evaluation', in M. WARNER (ed), *International Encyclopaedia of Business and Management*, 2nd edition. London, Thomson Learning. 2002a.

ARTHURS A. 'Job evaluation', in T. REDMAN *and* A. WILKINSON (eds), *The Informed Student Guide to Human Resource Management*. London, Thomson Learning. 2002b.

ARTHURS A. 'Towards single status', *Journal of General Management*, Vol. 11, No.1, 1985. pp17–28.

ASHTON D., DAVIES B., FELSTEAD A. *and* GREEN F. *Work Skills in Britain*. Universities of Oxford and Warwick, SKOPE. 2002.

ASHTON D. *and* SUNG J. *Supporting Workplace Learning for High Performance Working*. Geneva, International Labour Office. 2002.

ATKINSON J. 'Flexibility of fragmentation? The United Kingdom labour market in the eighties', *Labour and Society*, Vol. 12, No. 1, 1987. pp87–105.

ATKINSON J. 'Manpower strategies for the flexible organisation', *Personnel Management*, August 1984. pp28–31.

ATKINSON J. *and* MEAGER N. 'Is flexibility a flash in the pan?', *Personnel Management*, September 1986. pp26–29.

BACH S. 'From performance appraisal to performance management', in S. BACH *and* K. SISSON (eds), *Personnel Management: A comprehensive guide to theory and practice*. Oxford, Blackwell. 2000.

BACH S. *and* SISSON K. (eds), *Personnel Management: A comprehensive guide to theory and practice*. Oxford, Blackwell. 2000.

BACON N. 'Human resource management and industrial relations', in P. ACKERS *and* A. WILKINSON (eds), *Understanding Work and Employment in Industrial Relations in Transition*. Oxford, Oxford University Press. 2003.

BACON N. 'Employee relations', in T. REDMAN *and* A. WILKINSON (eds), *Contemporary Human Resource Management*. London, Financial Times/Prentice Hall. 2001.

BACON N. 'Union derecognition and the new human relations: a steel industry case study', *Work, Employment and Society*, Vol. 13, No. 1, 1999. pp1–17.

BACON N. *and* BLYTON P. 'The Impact of teamwork on skills: employee porooptions of who gains and who loses', *Human Resource Management Journal*, Vol. 13, No. 2, 2003. pp13–29.

BAIRD L. *and* MESHOULAM I. 'Managing two fits of strategic human resource management', *Academy of Management Review*, Vol. 13, No. 1, 1988. pp116–128.

BAKER B. *and* COOPER J. 'Occupational testing and psychometric instruments: an ethical perspective', in D. WINSTANLEY *and* J. WOODALL (eds), *Ethical Issues in Contemporary HRM*. London, Macmillan, 2000. pp59–84.

BAKER D., GLYN A., HOWELL D. *and* SCHMITT J. 'Labour market institutions and unemployment: a critical assessment of the cross-country evidence', in D. HOWELL (ed), *Fighting Unemployment: the limits of free market orthodoxy*. Oxford, Oxford University Press. 2004.

BALDAMUS W. *Efficiency and Effort*. London, Tavistock. 1961.

BALDWIN T. *and* HALPIN T. 'Graduate glut devalues price of a degree', *The Times*, 29 March 2004. p1.

BANDURA A. *Social Learning Theory*. Englewood Cliffs, Prentice Hall. 1977.

BARCLAY J. 'Improving selection interviews with structure: organisations' use of "behavioural" interviews', *Personnel Review*, Vol. 30, No. 1, 2001. pp81–101.

BARKER J. 'Tightening the iron cage: Concertive control in self-managing teams', *Administrative Science Quarterly*, Vol. 38, 1993. pp408–437.

BARLOW G. 'Deficiencies and the perpetuation of power: latent functions in management appraisal', *Journal of Management Studies*, Vol. 26, No. 5, 1989. pp499–517.

BARNARD C., DEAKIN S. *and* HOBBS R. 'Opting out of the 48 hour week: employer necessity or individual choice?', *Industrial Law Journal,* Vol. 32, No. 4, 2003. pp223–252.

BARNEY J. 'Is the resource-based "view" a useful perspective for strategic management research? Yes', *Academy of Management Review*, Vol. 26, No. 1, 2001. pp41–56.

BARNEY J. 'Firm resources and sustained competitive advantage', *Journal of Management*, Vol. 17, No. 1, 1991. pp99–120.

BARRICK M., MOUNT M. *and* JUDGE A. 'Personality and performance at the beginning of the new millennium: what do we know and where do we go next?', *International Journal of Selection and Assessment*, Vol. 9, No. 1–2, 2001. pp9–30.

BARTELL A. 'Human resource management and organizational performance: evidence from retail banking', *Industrial and Labor Relations Review*, Vol. 5, No. 2, 2004. pp181–203.

BARTLETT C. *and* GHOSHAL S. *Managing Across Borders: The transnational solution*. Boston, Harvard Business School Press. 1989.

BATT R. 'Who benefits from teams? Comparing workers, supervisors and managers', *Industrial Relations*, Vol. 43, No. 1, 2004. pp183–212.

BATT R., COLVIN A. *and* KEEFE J. 'Employee voice, human resource practices, and quit rates: evidence from the telecommunications industry', *Industrial and Labor Relations Review*, Vol. 55, No. 4, 2002. pp573–594.

BATT R. *and* DOELLGAST V. 'Organizational performance in services', in D. HOLMAN, T. WALL, C. CLEGG, P. SPARROW *and* A. HOWARD (eds), *The New Workplace: A guide to the human impact of modern working practices*. London, Wiley. 2003.

BAXTER B. 'Consultancy expertise: a post-modern perspective', in H. SCARBROUGH (ed), *The Management of Expertise*. London, Macmillan. 1996.

BEARDWELL J. *and* WRIGHT, M. 'Recruitment and selection', in I. BEARDWELL, L. HOLDEN *and* T. CLAYDON (eds), *Human Resource Management: A contemporary approach*, 4th edition. London, Financial Times/Prentice Hall. 2004.

BEAUMONT G. *Review of 100 NVQs/SVQs*. London, DfEE. 1996.

BEAUMONT P. *The Decline of Trade Union Organisation*. London, Croom Helm. 1987.

BEAUMONT P. *and* BEE R. *Learning Needs Analysis and Evaluation*. London, CIPD. 2003.

BEER M., SPECTOR B., LAWRENCE P., QUINN MILLS D. *and* WALTON R. *Human Resource Management: A general manager's perspective*. Glencoe, Free Press. 1985.

BELAL A. 'Stakeholder accountability or stakeholder management: a review of U.K. firms' social and ethical accounting, auditing and reporting (SEAAR) practices', *Corporate Social Responsibility and Environmental Management*, Vol. 9, 2002. pp8–25.

Bell E., Taylor S. *and* Thorpe R. 'A step in the right direction? Investors in People and the learning organisation', *British Journal of Management*, Vol. 13, No. 2, 2002. pp161–171.

Bennett R. *Research Guides for Higher Degree Students*. Oxford, Thomson Publications. 1983.

Benson G. *and* Lawler E. 'Employee involvement: utilization, impacts, and future prospects', in D. Holman, T. Wall, C. Clegg, P. Sparrow *and* A. Howard (eds), *The New Workplace: A guide to the human impact of modern working practices*. London, Wiley. 2003.

Bercusson B. (ed), *European Labour Law and the EU Charter of Fundamental Rights*. Brussels, European Trade Union Institute. 2002.

Berg P. 'The effects of high performance work practices on job satisfaction in the United States steel industry', *Relations Industrial/Industrial Relations*, Vol. 54, 1999. pp111–135.

Bélanger J., Giles A. *and* Grenier J. 'Patterns of corporate influence in the host country: a study of ABB in Canada', *International Journal of Human Resource Management*, Vol. 14, No. 3, 2003. pp469–485.

Bird A. *and* Beechler S. 'Links between business strategy and HRM strategy in US-based Japanese subsidiaries: an empirical investigation', *Journal of International Business Studies*, First quarter 1995. pp23–46.

Blyton P. *and* Turnbull P. *The Dynamics of Employee Relations*, 3rd edition. London, Macmillan. 2004.

Bone A. 'Working time', in T. Redman *and* A. Wilkinson (eds), *The Informed Student Guide to Human Resource Management*. London, Thomson Learning. 2002.

Boselie P., Paauwe J. *and* Jansen P. 'Human resource management and performance: lessons from the Netherlands', *International Journal of Human Resource Management*, Vol. 12, No. 7, 2001. pp1107–1125.

Boselie P., Paauwe J. *and* Richardson R. 'Human resource management, institutional and organisational performance: a comparison of hospitals, hotels and local government', *International Journal of Human Resource Management*, Vol. 14, No. 8, 2003. pp1407–1429.

Bott D. 'Employment relations procedures', in B. Towers (ed), *The Handbook of Employment Relations, Law and Practice*, 4th edition. London, Kogan Page. 2003.

Bowey A. 'Gainsharing', in R. Thorpe *and* G. Homan (eds), *Strategic Reward Systems*. London, Financial Times/Prentice Hall. 2000.

Bowey A. *A Guide to Manpower Planning*. London, Macmillan. 1975.

Bowey A. *and* Thorpe R. 'Motivation and reward', in R. Thorpe *and* G. Homan (eds), *Strategic Reward Systems*. London, Financial Times/Prentice Hall. 2000.

Bowey A., Thorpe R., Mitchell F., Nicholls G., Gosnold D., Savery L. *and* Hellier P. *Effects of Incentive Payment Systems: UK 1977–1980*. Department of Employment Research Paper No. 36. London, HMSO. 1982.

Boxall P. 'Achieving competitive advantage through human resource strategy: towards a theory of industry dynamics', *Human Resource Management Review*, Vol. 8, No. 3, 1998. pp265–288.

Boxall P. 'The strategic HRM debate and the resource-based view of the firm', *Human Resource Management Journal*, Vol. 6, No. 3, 1996. pp59–75.

411

BOXALL P. *and* PURCELL J. *Strategy and Human Resource Management*. London, Palgrave Macmillan. 2003.

BOXALL P. *and* PURCELL J. 'Strategic human resource management: where have we come from and where are we going?', *International Journal of Management Reviews*, Vol. 2, No. 2, 2000. pp183–203.

BOXALL P. *and* STEENEVELD M. 'Human resource strategy and competitive advantage: a longitudinal study of engineering consultancies', *Journal of Management Studies*, Vol. 36, No. 4, 1999. pp443–463.

BOYATSIS R. *The Competent Manager: A model for effective performance*. New York, Wiley. 1982.

BRAMHAM J. *Human Resource Planning*. London, Institute of Personnel and Development. 1994.

BRAMHAM J. *Practical Manpower Planning*. London, Institute of Personnel Management. 1975.

BRAMLEY P. *Evaluating Training*. London, CIPD. 2003.

BRATTON J. *and* GOLD J. *Human Resource Management: Theory and practice*, 3rd edition. Basingstoke, Palgrave Macmillan. 2003.

BRAVERMAN J. *Labour and Monopoly Capital*. New York, Monthly Review Press. 1974.

BREAUGH J. *and* STARKE M. 'Research on employee recruitment: so many studies', *Journal of Management*, Vol. 26, No. 3, 2000. pp405–434.

BREWERTON P. *and* MILLWARD L. *Organisational Research Methods: A guide for students and researchers*. London, Sage. 2001.

BREWSTER C., GILL C. *and* RICHBELL S. 'Industrial relations policy: a framework for analysis', in K. THURLEY *and* S. WOOD (eds), *Industrial Relations and Management Strategy*. Cambridge, Cambridge University Press. 1983.

BROAD M. 'Nailing the serial skivers', *The Sunday Times*, 20 January 2002. p13.

BROWN D. *Reward Strategies: From intent to impact*. London, CIPD. 2001.

BROWN D. *and* ARMSTRONG M. *Paying for Contributions*. London, Kogan Page. 1999.

BROWN P. 'The opportunity trap: education and employment in a global economy', *European Educational Research Journal*, Vol. 2, No. 1, 2003. pp141–179.

BROWN P., GREEN A. *and* LAUDER H. *High Skills: Globalisation, competitiveness and skill formation*. Oxford, Oxford University Press. 2001.

BROWN P. *and* HESKETH A. *The Mismanagement of Talent: Employability, competition and careers in the knowledge-driven economy*. Oxford, Oxford University Press. 2004.

BROWN W. 'Putting partnership into practice in Britain', *British Journal of Industrial Relations*, Vol. 38, No. 2, 2000. pp299–316.

BROWN W. *Piecework Bargaining*. London: Heinemann, 1973.

BROWN W., DEAKIN S., HUDSON M., PRATTAN C. *and* RYAN P. 'The individualisation of employment contracts in Britain', *DTI Employment Relations Research Series*, No. 4. London, DTI. 1998.

BROWN W., MARGINSON P. *and* WALSH J. 'Management of pay', in P. EDWARDS (ed), *Industrial Relations*, 2nd edition. Oxford, Blackwell. 2003.

BROWN W. *and* WALSH J. 'Managing pay in Britain', in K. SISSON (ed), *Personnel Management*, 2nd edition. Oxford, Blackwell. 1994.

Bryman A. *and* Bell E. *Business Research Methods.* Oxford, Oxford University Press. 2003.

Bryson A. 'Managerial responsiveness to union and nonunion worker voice in Britain', *Industrial Relations,* Vol. 43, No. 1, 2004. pp213–241.

Buchanan D. *and* Boddy D. *The Expertise of a Change Agent.* Hemel Hempstead, Prentice Hall. 1992.

Buchanan D., Boddy D. *and* McCallum J. 'Getting in, getting on, getting out and getting back', in A. Bryman (ed), *Doing Research in Organisations.* London, Routledge. 1988.

Buchanan D. *and* Huczynski A. *Organizational Behaviour: An introductory text,* 5th edition. London, Financial Times/Prentice Hall. 2004.

Bullock A. *Report of the Committee Inquiry on Industrial Democracy.* London, HMSO. 1977.

Burawoy M. *Manufacturing Consent: Changes in the labour process under monopoly capitalism.* Chicago, University of Chicago Press. 1979.

Burchell B., Day D., Hudson M., Ladipo D., Mankelow R., Nolan J., Reed H., Wichert I. *and* Wilkinson F. *Job Insecurity and Work Intensification: Flexibility and the changing boundaries of work.* York, Joseph Rowntree Foundation. 1999.

Burgoyne J. 'Management development for the individual and organisation', *Personnel Management,* June 1988. pp40–44.

Burnes B. 'Managing change and changing managers from ABC to XYZ', *Journal of Management Development,* Vol. 22, No. 7, 2003. pp627–642.

Burnes B. *Managing Change.* London, Pitman Publishing. 2000.

Burton, M. 'The principles and factors guiding the CAC', *Employee Relations,* Vol. 24, No. 6, 2002. pp606–618.

Buyens D. *and* De Vos A. 'Perceptions of the value of the HR function', *Human Resource Management Journal,* Vol. 11, No. 3, 2001. pp53–89.

Caldwell R. 'The changing roles of personnel managers: old ambiguities, new uncertainties', *Journal of Management Studies,* Vol. 40, No. 4, 2003. pp983–1004.

Caldwell R. 'Champions, adapters, consultants and synergists: the new change agents in HRM', *Human Resource Management Journal,* Vol. 11, No. 3, 2001. pp39–52.

Callaghan G. *and* Thompson P. '"We recruit attitude": The selection and shaping of routine call centre labour', *Journal of Management Studies,* Vol. 39, No. 2, 2002. pp233–255.

Cannell M. 'Class struggle', *People Management,* 7 March 2002. p46.

Capizzi E. *Learning That Works: Accrediting the TUC programme.* Available at: www.tuc.org.uk. 2002.

Cappelli P. *and* Neumark D. 'Do "high-performance" work practices improve establishment-level outcomes?', *Industrial and Labor Relations Review,* Vol. 54, No. 4, 2001. pp737–776.

Carrington L. 'Just desserts', *People Management,* 29 January 2004. pp38–40.

Carroll M., Marchington M., Earnshaw J. *and* Taylor S. 'Recruitment in small firms: processes, methods and problems', *Employee Relations,* Vol. 21, No. 3, 1999. pp236–250.

Cassell C. 'Managing diversity', in T. Redman *and* A. Wilkinson (eds), *Contemporary Human Resource Management.* London, Financial Times/Prentice Hall. 2001.

Cassidy S. 'Teachers' pay bonus schemes wasteful', *The Independent,* 14 July 2001.

C<small>AULKIN</small> S. 'The time is now', *People Management*, 30 August 2001. pp32–34.

CEML. *Managers and Leaders: Raising our game.* London, Council for Excellence in Management and Leadership. Online version also available at: www.managementandleadershipcouncil.org/. 2002.

C<small>ENTRAL</small> A<small>RBITRATION</small> C<small>OMMITTEE</small>. *Annual Report.* London, CAC. 2004.

C<small>ERIN</small> P. 'Communication in corporate environmental reports', *Corporate Social Responsibility and Environmental Management*, Vol. 9, 2002. pp46–66.

C<small>ERTIFICATION</small> O<small>FFICER</small>. *Annual Report of the Certification Officer, 2003–4.* London, Certification Office for Trade Unions and Employers' Associations. 2004.

C<small>HANDLER</small> A. *Strategy and Structure: Chapters in the history of the American industrial enterprise.* Cambridge, MIT Press. 1962.

C<small>HARLWOOD</small> A. 'Willingness to unionise among non-union workers', in H. G<small>OSPEL</small> *and* S. W<small>OOD</small> (eds), *Representing workers: Union recognition and membership in Britain.* London, Routledge. 2003.

C<small>HARTERED</small> I<small>NSTITUTE</small> <small>OF</small> P<small>ERSONNEL</small> <small>AND</small> D<small>EVELOPMENT</small>. Professional Development Scheme Standards.

C<small>HARTERED</small> I<small>NSTITUTE</small> <small>OF</small> P<small>ERSONNEL</small> <small>AND</small> D<small>EVELOPMENT</small>. *Calling Time on Working Time?* London, CIPD. 2004a.

C<small>HARTERED</small> I<small>NSTITUTE</small> <small>OF</small> P<small>ERSONNEL</small> <small>AND</small> D<small>EVELOPMENT</small>. *Recruitment, Retention, and Turnover: A survey of the UK and Ireland.* London, CIPD. 2004b.

C<small>HARTERED</small> I<small>NSTITUTE</small> <small>OF</small> P<small>ERSONNEL</small> <small>AND</small> D<small>EVELOPMENT</small>. *Employee Absence 2004: A survey of management policy and practice.* London, CIPD. 2004c.

C<small>HARTERED</small> I<small>NSTITUTE</small> <small>OF</small> P<small>ERSONNEL</small> <small>AND</small> D<small>EVELOPMENT</small>. *Training and Development Survey Report.* London, CIPD. 2004d.

C<small>HARTERED</small> I<small>NSTITUTE</small> <small>OF</small> P<small>ERSONNEL</small> <small>AND</small> D<small>EVELOPMENT</small>. *Guide to the Employment Act 2002.* London, CIPD. 2004e.

C<small>HARTERED</small> I<small>NSTITUTE</small> <small>OF</small> P<small>ERSONNEL</small> <small>AND</small> D<small>EVELOPMENT</small>. *'Reward Management': A survey of policy and practice.* London, CIPD. 2004f.

C<small>HARTERED</small> I<small>NSTITUTE</small> <small>OF</small> P<small>ERSONNEL</small> <small>AND</small> D<small>EVELOPMENT</small>. *Employee Share Ownership Fact Sheet.* London, CIPD. 2004g.

C<small>HARTERED</small> I<small>NSTITUTE</small> <small>OF</small> P<small>ERSONNEL</small> <small>AND</small> D<small>EVELOPMENT</small>. *Corporate Social Responsibility and HR's Role.* London, CIPD. 2003a.

C<small>HARTERED</small> I<small>NSTITUTE</small> <small>OF</small> P<small>ERSONNEL</small> <small>AND</small> D<small>EVELOPMENT</small>. *Living to Work.* London, CIPD. 2003b.

C<small>HARTERED</small> I<small>NSTITUTE</small> <small>OF</small> P<small>ERSONNEL</small> <small>AND</small> D<small>EVELOPMENT</small>, *'Occupational Pensions': Strategic issues.* London, CIPD. 2003c.

C<small>HARTERED</small> I<small>NSTITUTE</small> <small>OF</small> P<small>ERSONNEL</small> <small>AND</small> D<small>EVELOPMENT</small>. *Who Learns at Work?* CIPD Survey Report. London, CIPD. 2002a.

C<small>HARTERED</small> I<small>NSTITUTE</small> <small>OF</small> P<small>ERSONNEL</small> <small>AND</small> D<small>EVELOPMENT</small>. *Quick Facts: Flexible benefits.* London, CIPD. 2002b.

C<small>HARTERED</small> I<small>NSTITUTE</small> <small>OF</small> P<small>ERSONNEL</small> <small>AND</small> D<small>EVELOPMENT</small>. *Developing Managers for Business Performance.* London, CIPD. 2002c.

C<small>HARTERED</small> I<small>NSTITUTE</small> <small>OF</small> P<small>ERSONNEL</small> <small>AND</small> D<small>EVELOPMENT</small>. *Work Life Balance Survey.* London, CIPD. 2002d.

CHARTERED INSTITUTE OF PERSONNEL AND DEVELOPMENT. *Recruitment Report*. London, CIPD. 2001a.

CHARTERED INSTITUTE OF PERSONNEL AND DEVELOPMENT. *Performance Through People: The new people management*. London, CIPD. 2001b.

CHARTERED INSTITUTE OF PERSONNEL AND DEVELOPMENT. *The Case for Good People Management: A summary of the research*. London, CIPD. 2001c.

CHARTERED INSTITUTE OF PERSONNEL AND DEVELOPMENT. *Survey of National Training and Development Practices*. London, CIPD. 2001d.

CHARTERED INSTITUTE OF PERSONNEL AND DEVELOPMENT. *Managing Diversity: Evidence from case studies*. London, CIPD. 1999.

CLAYDON T. 'Problematising partnership: the prospects for a co-operative bargaining agenda', in SPARROW P. *and* MARCHINGTON M. (eds), *Human Resource Management: The new agenda*. Financial Times Pitman, 1998. pp180–191.

CLAYDON T. *and* DOYLE M. 'Trusting me, trusting you? The ethics of employee empowerment', *Personnel Review*, Vol. 25, No. 6, 1996. pp13–25.

COFF R. 'Human assets and management dilemmas: coping with hazards on the road to resource-based theory', *Academy of Management Review*, Vol. 22, No. 2, 1997. pp374–402.

COLLIN A. 'Learning and development', in I. BEARDWELL, L. HOLDEN *and* T. CLAYDON (eds), *Human Resource Management: A contemporary approach*. Harlow, Pearson Education Limited. 2004.

COLLING T. 'Managing without unions', in P. EDWARDS (ed), *Industrial Relations*, 2nd edition. Oxford, Blackwell. 2003.

COLLING T. 'Tendering and outsourcing: working in the contract state?', in S. CORBY *and* G. WHITE (eds), *Employee Relations in the Public Services*. London, Routledge. 1999.

COMMISSION OF THE EUROPEAN COMMUNITIES. *Promoting a European Framework for Corporate Social Responsibility*. Green Paper. 2001.

COOK M. *Personnel Selection: Adding value through people*, 3rd edition. Chichester, Wiley. 1998.

COOKE F. L., EARNSHAW J., MARCHINGTON M. *and* RUBERY J. 'For better and for worse: transfer of undertaking and the reshaping of employment relations', *International Journal of Human Resource Management*, Vol. 15, No. 2, 2004a. pp276–294.

COOKE F. L., SHEN J., MCBRIDE A. *and* ZAFAR R. *Outsourcing HR: Implications for the role of the HR function and the workforce in the NHS*. A review conducted under the Policy Research Programme, Department of Health. 2004b.

CO-OPERATIVE BANK. *Sustainable Development: Partnership report 2002*. Manchester, Co-operative Bank. 2002.

COOPER C. 'Is education really to blame for the great British skills famine?', *People Management*, 9 August 2000. pp10–11.

COOPER D. *and* ROBERTSON I. *The Psychology of Personnel Selection*. London, Thomson. 2002.

COOPER D., ROBERTSON I. *and* TINLINE G. *Recruitment and Selection: A framework for success*. London, Thomson. 2003.

CORDERY J. 'Teamwork', in D. HOLMAN, T. WALL, C. CLEGG, P. SPARROW and A. HOWARD (eds), *The New Workplace: A guide to the human impact of modern working practices*. London, Wiley. 2003.

COUPAR W. and STEVENS S. 'Towards a new model of industrial partnership: beyond the HRM versus industrial relations argument', in P. SPARROW and M. MARCHINGTON (eds), *Human Resource Management: The new agenda*. London, Financial Times/Pitman. 1998.

COX A. 'The importance of employee participation in determining pay effectiveness', *International Journal of Management Reviews*, Vol. 2, No. 4, 2000. pp357–372.

CRAWSHAW M., DAVIS E. and KAY J. '"Being stuck in the middle" or "good food costs less at Sainsbury's"', *British Journal of Management*, Vol. 5, No. 1, 1994. pp19–32.

CRESSEY P. 'The influence of the European Union' in B. TOWERS (ed), *The Handbook of Employment Relations, Law and Practice*. London, Kogan Page. 2003.

CRESSEY P. 'European works councils in practice', *Human Resource Management Journal*, Vol. 8, No. 1, 1998. pp67–79.

CRESSWELL J. *Research Design: Qualitative, quantitative, and mixed methods approaches*, 2nd edition. London, Sage. 2003.

CRICHTON A. *Personnel Management in Context*. London, Batsford. 1968.

CROFTS P. 'Support key to success'. *People Management*, 3 June 2000. p55.

CROSBY P. *Quality is Free*. New York, Mentor. 1980.

CROUCH C., FINEGOLD D. and SAKO M. *Are Skills the Answer? The political economy of skill creation in advanced industrial nations*. Oxford, Oxford University Press. 2001.

CULLY M., WOODLAND S., O'REILLY A. and DIX G. *Britain at Work: As depicted by the 1998 Workplace Employee Relations Survey*. London, Routledge. 1999.

CULLY M., WOODLAND S., O'REILLY A., DIX G., MILLWARD N., BRYSON A. and FORTH, J. *The 1998 Workplace Employee Relations Survey: First findings*. London, Department of Trade and Industry. 1998.

CUNNINGHAM I. 'Back to reality', *People Management*, 8 April 2004. pp37–38.

CUNNINGHAM I. and HYMAN J. 'Devolving human resource responsibilities to the line: beginning of the end or a new beginning for personnel?', *Personnel Review*, Vol. 28, No. 1/2, 1999. pp9–27.

CUNNINGHAM I. and HYMAN J. 'Transforming the HRM vision into reality: the role of line managers and supervisors in implementing change', *Employee Relations*, Vol. 17, No. 8, 1995. pp5–20.

CURTIS S. and LUCAS R. 'A coincidence of needs? Employers and full-time students', *Employee Relations*, Vol. 23, No. 1, 2001. pp38–54.

CZERNY A. 'Tesco defends its sick-pay pilot', *People Management*, June 2004. p9.

DANFORD A., RICHARDSON M., STEWART P., TAILBY S. and UPCHURCH M. *Partnership, Mutuality and the One-way Street: A case study of aircraft workers*. Labour Process Conference, Bristol. 2003.

DARWIN J., JOHNSON P. and MCAULAY J. *Developing Strategies for Change*. London, Financial Times/Prentice Hall. 2002.

DAVIES J. 'Labour disputes in 2000', *Labour Market Trends*, Vol. 109, No. 6, June 2004. p302.

DAWSON P. *Understanding Organisational Change*. London, Sage. 2003.

DEAKIN S., HOBBS R., KONZELLMAN S. and WILKINSON F. 'Working corporations: corporate governance and innovation in labour-management partnerships in Britain', in M. STUART and M. MARTINEZ-LUCIO (eds), *Partnership and Modernisation in Employment Relations*. London, Routledge. 2004.

DEARING R. *Higher Education in the Learning Society*. National Committee of Inquiry into Higher Education. 1997.

DECI E. and FLASTE R. *Why We Do What We Do: The dynamics of personal autonomy*. New York, Penguin. 1996. p26.

DEEPHOUSE D. 'To be different, or to be the same? It's a question (and theory) of strategic balance', *Strategic Management Journal*, Vol. 20, 1999. pp147–166.

DELANEY J. and HUSELID M. 'The impact of human resource management practices on perceptions of organisational performance', *Academy of Management Journal*, Vol. 39, 1996. pp349–369.

DELBRIDGE R. *Life on the Line in Contemporary Manufacturing: The workplace experience of lean production and the 'Japanese' model*. Oxford, Oxford University Press. 1998.

DELERY J. and DOTY H. 'Modes of theorising in strategic human resource management: tests of universalistic, contingency and configurational performance predictions', *Academy of Management Journal*, Vol. 39, No. 4, 1996. pp802–835.

DENHAM N., ACKERS P. and TRAVERS C. 'Doing yourself out of a job? How middle managers cope with empowerment', *Employee Relations*, Vol. 19, No. 2, 1997. pp147–159.

DENNY C. 'Gazing in awe at executive salaries, US style', *The Guardian*, 23 August 2000.

DENZIN N. *Sociological Methods: A sourcebook*. New York, McGraw-Hill. 1978.

DENZIN N. *The Research Act*. Aldine: Chicago, 1970.

DEPARTMENT FOR EDUCATION AND EMPLOYMENT. *21st Century Skills: Realising our potential: individuals, employers, nation*. Available at: www.dfes.gov.uk. July 2003.

DEPARTMENT FOR EDUCATION AND EMPLOYMENT. *Learning and Training at Work 2000*. Available at: www.dfes.gov.uk. April 2001a.

DEPARTMENT FOR EDUCATION AND EMPLOYMENT. *Schools: Building on success*. Available at: www.dfes.gov.uk. 2001b.

DEPARTMENT FOR EDUCATION AND EMPLOYMENT. *Skills for All: Research for the National Skills Taskforce*. London, DfEE. 2000.

DEPARTMENT FOR EDUCATION AND SKILLS. *Disability Discrimination*. Available at: http://www.teachernet.gov.uk/management/atoz/d/disabilitydiscrimination/. 2004a.

DEPARTMENT FOR EDUCATION AND SKILLS. *Fitness to Teach*. Available at: http://www.teachernet.gov.uk/management/atoz/f/fitnesstoteach/. 2004b.

DEPARTMENT OF TRADE AND INDUSTRY. *Competing in the Global Economy: The Innovation Challenge*. Available at: www.dti.gov.uk/innovationreport/. December 2003.

DEPARTMENT OF TRADE AND INDUSTRY. *Business and Society: Corporate Social Responsibility Report 2002*. London, DTI. 2002a.

DEPARTMENT OF TRADE AND INDUSTRY. *High Performance Workplaces: A discussion paper*. London, DTI. 2002b.

DEPARTMENT FOR WORK AND PENSIONS. *Review of Employers' Liability Compulsory Insurance, Second Stage Report*. Available at: www.dwp.gov.uk. December 2003.

Devanna M., Fombrun C. and Tichy N. 'A framework for strategic human resource management', in C. Fombrun, N. Tichy and A. Devanna (eds), *Strategic Human Resource Management*. New York, Wiley. 1984.

Dex S. *Families and Work in the Twenty-first Century*. York, Joseph Rowntree Foundation. 2003.

Dickens L. 'Beyond the business case: a three-pronged approach to equality action', *Human Resource Management Journal*, Vol. 9, No. 1, 1999. pp9–19.

Dickens L. 'Individual statutory employment rights since 1997: constrained expansion'. *Employee Relations*, Vol. 24, No. 6, 2002, pp619–637.

Dickens L. and Hall M. 'Labour law and industrial relations: a new settlement', in P. Edwards (ed), *Industrial Relations*, 2nd edition. Oxford, Blackwell. 2003.

Dietz, G. 'Partnership and the development of trust in British workplaces', *Human Resource Management Journal*, Vol. 14, No. 1, 2004. pp5–24.

DiMaggio P. and Powell W. 'The iron cage revisited: institutional isomorphism and collective rationality in organisational fields', *American Sociological Review*, Vol. 48, 1983. pp147–160.

Dolton P. *Press release*. London, Institute of Education. 11 April 2003.

Donovan. *Royal Commission on Trade Unions and Employers Associations 1965–68*. Report Cmnd 3623. London, HMSO. 1968.

Doogan K. 'Insecurity and long-term unemployment', *Work, Employment and Society*, Vol. 15, No. 3. 2001. pp419–441.

Down S. and Smith D. 'It pays to be nice to people: Investors in People – the search for measurable benefits', *Personnel Review*, Vol. 27, No. 2, 1998. pp143–155.

Druker J. 'Wages systems', in G. White and J. Druker (eds), *Reward Management: A critical text*. London, Routledge. 2000.

Druker J. and Stanworth C. 'Partnerships and the private recruitment industry', *Human Resource Management Journal*, Vol. 11, No. 2, 2001. pp73–89.

Duncan C. 'Pay, payment systems and job evaluation', in B. Towers (ed), *A Handbook of Industrial Relations Practice*, 3rd edition. London, Kogan Page. 1992.

Dundon T. 'Recognition', in T. Redman and A. Wilkinson (eds), *The Informed Student Guide to Human Resource Management*. London, Thomson Learning. 2002a.

Dundon T. 'Employer opposition and union avoidance in the UK', *Industrial Relations Journal*, Vol. 33, No. 3, 2002b. pp234–245.

Dundon T. 'Policies and procedures', in T. Redman and A. Wilkinson (eds), *The Informed Student Guide to Human Resource Management*. London, Thomson Learning. 2002c.

Dundon T., Grugulis I. and Wilkinson, A. 'New management techniques in small and medium-sized enterprises', in T. Redman and A. Wilkinson (eds), *Contemporary Human Resource Management*. London, Financial Times/Prentice Hall. 2001.

Dundon T., Grugulis I. and Wilkinson A. 'Looking out of the black-hole: non-union relations in an SME', *Employee Relations*, Vol. 21, No. 3, 1999. pp251–266.

Dundon T. and Wilkinson A, 'Employment relations in SMEs', in B. Towers (ed), *Handbook of Industrial Relations*. London, Kogan Page. 2003.

DUNDON T., WILKINSON A., MARCHINGTON M. *and* ACKERS P. 'The meaning and purpose of employee voice', *International Journal of Human Resource Management*, Vol. 15, No. 6, 2004. pp1149–1170.

DUNN C. *and* WILKINSON A. 'Wish you were here: managing absence', *Personnel Review*, Vol. 31, No. 2, 2002. pp228–246.

EARNSHAW J. 'Unfair dismissal', in T. REDMAN *and* A. WILKINSON (eds), *The Informed Student Guide to Human Resource Management*. London, Thomson Learning. 2002.

EARNSHAW J. *and* COOPER C. *Stress and Employer Liability*. London, IPD. 1996.

EARNSHAW J., GOODMAN J., HARRISON R. *and* MARCHINGTON, M. 'Industrial tribunal workplace disciplinary procedures and employment practice', in *Employment Relations Research*, Series No. 2. London, DTI. 1998.

EARNSHAW J., MARCHINGTON L., RITCHIE E. *and* TORRINGTON D. 'Neither fish nor foul? An assessment of teacher capability procedures', *Industrial Relations Journal*, Vol. 35, No. 2, 2004. pp139–152.

EARNSHAW J., MARCHINGTON L., RITCHIE E. *and* TORRINGTON D. 'Are teacher capability procedures capable of improving performance', *Education Law Journal*, Vol. 3, No. 4, 2002a. pp225–235.

EARNSHAW J., MARCHINGTON M. *and* GOODMAN J. 'Unfair to whom? Discipline and dismissal in small establishments', *Industrial Relations Journal*, Vol. 31, No. 1, 2000. pp62–73.

EARNSHAW J., RITCHIE E., MARCHINGTON L., TORRINGTON D. *and* HARDY S. *Best Practice in Undertaking Teacher Capability Procedures*. London, DfES. 2002b.

EARNSHAW J., RUBERY J. *and* COOKE F. L. *Who is the Employer?* London, Institute of Employment Rights. 2002c.

EASTERBY SMITH M., THORPE R. *and* LOWE A. *Management Research: An introduction*. London, Sage. 1996.

EDWARDS C. 'Great returns', *People Management*, 6 May 2004. pp35–36.

EDWARDS P. 'The employment relationship in the field of industrial relations', in P. EDWARDS (ed), *Industrial Relations: Theory and practice in Britain*. Oxford, Blackwell. 2003a.

EDWARDS P. (ed), *Industrial Relations: Theory and practice in Britain*. Oxford, Blackwell. 2003b.

EDWARDS P. 'Discipline: towards trust and self-discipline', in S. BACH *and* K. SISSON (eds), *Personnel Management*, 3rd edition. Oxford, Blackwell. 2000.

EDWARDS P. *and* WRIGHT M. 'Human resource management and commitment: a case study of teamworking', in P. SPARROW *and* M. MARCHINGTON (eds), *Human Resource Management: The new agenda*. London, Pitman. 1998.

EDWARDS R. *Contested Terrain*. London, Heinemann. 1979.

ENGINEERING EMPLOYERS' FEDERATION *and* CHARTERED INSTITUTE OF PERSONNEL AND DEVELOPMENT. *Maximising Employee Potential and Business Performance: The role of high performance working*. London, EEF. Online version also available at: www.eef.org.uk. 2003.

EQUAL OPPORTUNITIES COMMISSION. *Code of Practice on Equal Pay*. London, EOC. 2003.

EQUAL OPPORTUNITIES COMMISSION. *Just Pay*. EOC. 2001.

EQUAL OPPORTUNITIES COMMISSION. *Good Practice Guide: Job evaluation schemes free of sex bias*. Manchester, EOC. 2000.

EUROPEAN COMMISSION. *Promoting a European Framework for Corporate Social Responsibility*. Green Paper. Commission of the European Communities. 2001.

EUROPEAN FOUNDATION FOR THE IMPROVEMENT OF LIVING AND WORKING CONDITIONS. *Part-time Work in Europe*. Available at: www.eurofound.eu.int/working/reports/ES0403TR01/ES0403TR01_1.htm. 2004.

EWING K. 'Labour law and industrial relations', in P. ACKERS *and* A. WILKINSON (eds), *Understanding Work and Employment: Industrial relations in transition*. Oxford, Oxford University Press. 2003.

FAIRCLOUGH M. *and* BIRKENSHAW C. 'Employee rights and management wrongs, mastering people management', *Financial Times*, 26 November 2001. pp4–5.

FARNHAM D. 'Employee relations', in T. REDMAN *and* A. WILKINSON (eds), *The Informed Student Guide to Human Resource Management*. London, Thomson Learning. 2002.

FARNHAM D. *Employee Relations in Context*, 4th edition. London, CIPD. 2000.

FARNHAM D. *Personnel in Context*. London, Institute of Personnel Management. 1990.

FELDMAN D. *and* KLAAS B. 'Internet job hunting: a field study of applicant experiences with on-line recruiting', *Human Resource Management*, Vol. 41, No. 2, 2002. pp175–192.

FELSTEAD A., GALLIE D. *and* GREEN F. *Work Skills in Britain 2001*. London, Department for Education and Skills. 2002.

FELSTEAD A., GREEN F. *and* MAYHEW K. *Getting the Measure of Training: A report on training statistics in Britain*. Leeds, Centre for Industrial Policy and Performance. 1997.

FELSTEAD A., JEWSON N., PHIZACKALEA A. *and* WALTERS S. 'Working at home: statistical evidence for seven key hypotheses', *Work, Employment and Society*, Vol. 15, No. 2, 2001. pp215–231.

FELSTEAD A., JEWSON N. *and* WALTERS S. 'Managerial control of employees working at home'. *British Journal of Industrial Relations*, Vol. 41, No. 2, 2003. pp241–264.

FENTON O'CREEVY M. 'Employee involvement and the middle manager: saboteur or scapegoat?', *Human Resource Management Journal*, Vol. 11, No. 1, 2001. pp24–40.

FERNER A. *and* HYMAN R. (eds), *Industrial Relations in the New Europe*. Oxford, Blackwell. 1998.

FERNER A. *and* QUINTANILLA J. 'Multinational, national business systems and HRM: the enduring influence of national identity or a process of Anglo-Saxonisation', *International Journal of Human Resource Management*, Vol. 9, No. 4, 1998. pp711–731.

FERNIE S., METCALF D. *and* WOODLAND S. *Does HRM Boost Employee–management Relations?* London, London School of Economics, Centre for Economic Performance and Industrial Relations Department. 1994.

FERRIN D. *and* DIRKS K. 'The use of rewards to increase and decrease trust: mediating processes and differential effects', *Organizational Science*, Vol. 14, No. 1, 2003. pp18–31.

FINCH J. and TREANOR J. 'Profits down, shares sinking, but boss on £7m says it's not enough', *The Guardian*, 18 November 2002.

FINCHAM R. *and* EVANS M. 'The consultants' offensive: reengineering – from fad to technique',

New Technology, Work and Employment, Vol. 14, No. 1, 1999. pp32–44.

FINEGOLD D. 'Creating self-sustaining high-skill ecosystems', *Oxford Review of Economic Policy*, Vol. 15, No. 1, 1999. pp60–79.

FINEGOLD D. *and* SOSKICE D. 'The failure of training in Britain: analysis and prescription', *Oxford Review of Economic Policy*, Vol. 15, No. 1, 1988. pp60–80.

FINEMAN S. *and* MANGHAM I. 'Data meanings and creativity', *Journal of Management Studies*, Vol. 20, No. 3, 1983. pp295–300.

FLETCHER C. *Appraisal and Feedback: Making performance review work*. London, CIPD. 2004.

FOMBRUN C., TICHY N. *and* DEVANNA M. (eds), *Strategic Human Resource Management*. New York, Wiley. 1984.

FORD R. *Motivation Through Work Itself*. New York, American Management Association. 1969.

FORDE C. 'Temporary arrangements: the activities of employment agencies in the UK', *Work, Employment and Society*, Vol. 15, No. 3, 2001. pp631–644.

FORDE C. *and* MACKENZIE R. 'Cementing skills: training and labour use in UK construction', *Human Resource Management Journal*, Vol. 14, No. 3, 2004. pp74–88.

FOWLER A. 'New directions in performance related pay', *Personnel Management*, Vol. 20, No. 11, 1988. pp30–34.

FOX A. *Beyond Contract*. London, Faber & Faber. 1974.

FOX A. *Industrial Sociology and Industrial Relations*. Royal Commission Research Paper No. 3. London, HMSO. 1966.

FRANKS O. *and* THOMPSON D. 'Mix 'n' match', *People Management*, 17 February 2000. pp40–43.

FRASER M. *Employment Interviewing*. London, McDonald & Evans. 1966.

FREEMAN R. 'Upping the stakes', *People Management*, 8 February 2001. pp24–29.

FREIDSON E. (ed), *The Professions and their Prospects*. London, Sage. 1973.

FRIEDMAN M. 'The social responsibility of business is to increase its profits', *The New York Times Magazine*, 13 September 1970. Reprinted in G. CHRYSSIDES *and* J. KALER (eds), *An Introduction to Business Ethics*. London, Chapman & Hall. 1993.

FROBEL P. *and* MARCHINGTON M. 'Teamworking structures and worker perceptions: a cross national study in pharmaceuticals', *International Journal of Human Resource Management*, Vol. 16, No. 2, 2005. pp90–110.

FRY B. *and* OSTERLOH M. *Successful Management by Motivation*. Berlin, Springer-Verlag. 2002.

FULLER A., MUNROE A. *and* RAINBIRD H. 'Introduction and overview', in H. RAINBIRD, A. FULLER, *and* A. MUNROE, *Workplace Learning in Context*. London, Routledge. 2004.

FULLER A. *and* UNWIN L. 'Creating a "Modern Apprenticeship": a critique of the UK's multi-sector, social inclusion approach', *Journal of Education and Work*, Vol. 16, No. 1, 2003. pp5–25.

FULLER A. *and* UNWIN L. 'Reconceptualising apprenticeship: exploring the relationship between work and learning', *Journal of Vocational Education and Training*, Vol. 50, No. 2, 1998. pp153–173.

GAGNE R. *The Conditions of Learning*. New York, Holt Saunders. 1977.

GALL G. 'Trade union recognition in Britain 1995–2002: turning a corner?', *Industrial Relations Journal,* Vol. 35, No. 3. 2004. pp249–270.

GALL G. 'Back to terms', *People Management*, 13 September 2001. pp40–42.

GALL G. *and* McKAY S. 'Developments in union recognition and derecognition in Britain 1994–1998', *British Journal of Industrial Relations*, Vol. 37, No. 4, 1999. pp601–614.

GALLIE D., WHITE M., CHENG Y. *and* TOMLINSON M. *Restructuring the Employment Relationship*. Oxford, Oxford University Press. 1998.

GAMBLE J., CULPEPPER R. *and* BLUBAUGH M. 'Esops and employee attitudes: the importance of empowerment and financial value', *Personnel Review*, Vol. 31, No. 1, 2002. pp9–26.

GANNON M. *Understanding Global Cultures*. London, Sage. 2000.

GAYMER, J. 'Making a molehill out of a mountain', *People Management*, 26 February 2004, p17.

GEARY J. 'New forms of work organisation', in P. EDWARDS (ed), *Industrial Relations*, 2nd edition. Oxford, Blackwell. 2003. pp338–367.

GEARY J. *and* DOBBINS A. 'Teamworking: a new dynamic in the pursuit of management control', *Human Resource Management Journal*, Vol. 11, No. 1, 2001. pp3–23.

GENNARD J. 'Employee relations public policy developments 1997–2001: a break with the past?', *Employee Relations*, Vol. 24, No. 6, 2002. pp.581–594.

GENNARD J. 'Europe is about far more than beef bans', *Employee Relations*, Vol. 22, No. 2, 2000. pp117–120.

GENNARD J. *and* JUDGE G. *Employee Relations*, 4th edition. London, CIPD. 2005.

GENNARD J. *and* JUDGE G. *Employee Relations*, 3rd edition. London, CIPD. 2002.

GENNARD J. *and* KELLY J. 'The unimportance of labels: the diffusion of the personnel/HRM function', *Industrial Relations Journal*, Vol. 28, No. 1, 1997. pp27–42.

GIBB S. 'The state of human resource management: evidence from employees' views of HRM systems and staff', *Employee Relations*, Vol. 23, No. 4, 2001. pp318–336.

GIGA S., COOPER C. *and* FARAGHER E. 'The development of a framework for a comprehensive approach to stress management interventions at work', *International Journal of Stress Management*. Vol. 10, No. 4, 2003. pp280–296.

GILES E. and WILLIAMS R. 'Can the personnel department survive quality management?', *Personnel Management*, Vol. 23, No. 4, 1991. pp28–33.

GILL J. *and* JOHNSON P. *Research Methods for Managers*. London, Paul Chapman Publishing. 1997.

GLASER B. *and* STRAUSS A. *The Discovery of Grounded Theory: Strategies for qualitative research*. New York, Adline De Gruyter. 1967.

GLEBBEEK A. *and* BAX E. 'Is high employee turnover really harmful? An empirical test using company records', *Academy of Management Journal,* Vol. 47, No. 2, 2004. pp277–286.

GLOVER C. 'The taking stock market', *People Management*, 6 December 2001. pp44–45.

GODARD J. 'A critical assessment of the high performance paradigm', *British Journal of Industrial Relations*, Vol. 42, No. 2, 2004. pp349–378.

GODFREY G., WILKINSON A., MARCHINGTON M. *and* DALE B. *Competitive Advantage Through*

People? Human resource policies in TQM firms. UMIST Working Paper. Manchester, UMIST. 1998.

GOLDTHORPE J., LOCKWOOD D., BECHOFER F. *and* PLATT J. *The Affluent Worker: Industrial attitudes and behaviour.* Cambridge, Cambridge University Press. 1968.

GOLLAN P. 'So what's the news? Management strategies towards non union employee representation at News International', *Industrial Relations Journal*, Vol. 33, No. 4, 2002. pp316–331.

GOLLAN P. *and* PERKINS S. 'A raised voice', *People Management*, 21 March 2002. pp46–49.

GOLZEN G. 'Award scheme comeback', *The Times*, 13 April 2000. p19.

GOODCHILD P. 'Savings grace', *People Management*, 9 October 2003. p18.

GOODMAN J. 'Building bridges and settling differences: collective conciliation and arbitration under Acas', in B. TOWERS *and* W. BROWN (eds), *Employment Relations in Britain: 25 years of the Advisory, Conciliation and Arbitration Service.* Oxford, Blackwell. 2000.

GOSPEL H. *and* PALMER G. *British Industrial Relations*, 2nd edition. London, Routledge. 1993.

GOSPEL H. *and* WOOD S. 'Representing workers in modern Britain', in H. GOSPEL *and* S. WOOD (eds), *Representing Workers: Union recognition and membership in Britain.* London, Routledge. 2003a.

GOSPEL H. *and* WOOD S. (eds), *Representing Workers: Union recognition and membership in Britain.* London, Routledge. 2003b.

GOSS D. *Principles of Human Resource Management.* London, Routledge. 1994.

GOSS D. *Small Business and Society.* London, Routledge. 1991.

GRANOVETTER M. 'Economic action and social structure: the problem of embeddedness', *American Journal of Sociology*, Vol. 91, No. 3, 1985. pp481–510.

GRANT R. *Contemporary Strategy Analysis.* Oxford, Blackwell. 1998.

GRATTON L. 'More than money', *People Management,* 29 January 2004. p23.

GRATTON L., HOPE-HAILEY V., STILES P. *and* TRUSS C. *Strategic Human Resource Management.* Oxford, Oxford University Press. 1999.

GRAY C. 'Growth orientation and the small firm', in K. CALEY, E. CHELL, F. CHITTENDEN *and* C. MASON (eds.), *Small Enterprise Development and Policy and Practice in Action.* London, Paul Chapman Publishing. 1992.

GRAY D. *and* MORGAN M. 'Modern Apprenticeships: filling the skills gap?', *Journal of Vocational Education and Training*, Vol. 50, No. 1, 1998. pp123–134.

GREEN F. 'It's been a hard day's night: the concentration and intensification of work in late twentieth-century Britain', *British Journal of Industrial Relations*, Vol. 39, No. 1, 2001. pp53–80.

GREEN F., MAYHEW K. *and* MOLLOY E. *Employer Perspectives Survey.* London, DfES. 2003.

GREER C., YOUNGBLOOD S. *and* GRAY D. 'Human resource management outsourcing: the make or buy decision', *The Academy of Management Executive*, Vol. 13, No. 3, 1999. pp85–96.

GRIMSHAW D. *and* CARROLL M. *Qualitative Research on Firms' Adjustments to the Minimum Wage.* Final report prepared for the Low Pay Commission. September 2002.

GRIMSHAW D., EARNSHAW J. *and* HEBSON G. 'Private sector provision of supply teachers: a case of legal swings and professional roundabouts', *Journal of Education Policy*, Vol. 18, No. 3, 2003. pp267–288.

GRINT K. 'What's wrong with performance appraisals? A critique and a suggestion', *Human Resource Management Journal*, Vol. 3, No. 3, 1993. pp61–77.

GRUGULIS I. 'The contribution of National Vocational Qualifications to the growth of skills in the UK', *British Journal of Industrial Relations*, Vol. 41, No. 3, 2003. pp457–475.

GRUGULIS I. 'The management NVQ: a critique of the myth of relevance', *Journal of Vocational Education and Training*, Vol. 52, No. 1. 2000. pp79–99.

GRUGULIS I. *and* BEVITT S. 'The impact of Investors in People: a case study of a hospital trust', *Human Resource Management Journal*, Vol. 12, No. 3, 2002. pp44–60.

THE GUARDIAN. 'Profits down, top pay up', *The Guardian*, 16 July 2001. p20.

GUEST D. 'Human resource management: when research confronts theory', *International Journal of Human Resource Management*, Vol. 12, No. 7, 2001a. pp1092–1106.

GUEST D. 'Industrial relations and human resource management,' in J. STOREY (ed), *HRM: A critical text*. London, Thomson Learning. 2001b.

GUEST D. 'Human resource management and performance: a review and research agenda', *International Journal of Human Resource Management*, Vol. 8, No. 3, 1997. pp263–276.

GUEST D. 'Personnel management: the end of orthodoxy?', *British Journal of Industrial Relations*, Vol. 29, No. 2, 1991. pp149–175.

GUEST D. 'Human resource management and industrial relations', *Journal of Management Studies*, Vol. 24, No. 5, 1987. pp503–521.

GUEST D. *and* CONWAY N. *Pressure at Work and the Psychological Contract: Research report*. London, CIPD. 2002.

GUEST D. *and* CONWAY N. 'Peering into the black hole: the downside of the new employment relations in the UK', *British Journal of Industrial Relations*, Vol. 37, No. 3, 1999. pp367–389.

GUEST D. *and* CONWAY N. *Fairness at Work and the Psychological Contract: Issues in people management*. London, Institute of Personnel and Development. 1998.

GUEST D. *and* HOQUE K. 'Yes, personnel does make a difference', *Personnel Management*, November, 1994a. pp40–44.

GUEST D. *and* HOQUE K. 'The good, the bad and the ugly: employment relations in new non-union workplace', *Human Resource Management Journal*, Vol. 5, No. 1, 1994b. pp1–14.

GUEST D. *and* KING Z. 'Power, innovation and problem-solving: the personnel managers' three steps to heaven?', *Journal of Management Studies*, Vol. 41, No. 3, 2004. pp401–423.

GUEST D. *and* KING Z. *Voices from the Boardroom: Senior executives' views on the relationship between HRM and performance*. London, CIPD. 2002.

GUEST D., MICHIE J., CONWAY, N. *and* SHEEHAN M. 'Human resource management and performance', *British Journal of Industrial Relations*, Vol. 41, No. 2, 2003, pp291–314.

GUEST D., MICHIE J., SHEEHAN M. *and* CONWAY N. *Employment Relations, HRM and Business Performance: An analysis of the 1998 workplace employee relations survey*. London, CIPD. 2000a.

GUEST D., MICHIE J., SHEEHAN M., CONWAY N. *and* METOCHI M. *Effective People Management: Initial findings of the Future of Work study*. London, CIPD. 2000b.

GUEST D. *and* PECCEI R. 'Partnership at work: mutuality and the balance of advantage', *British Journal of Industrial Relations*, Vol. 39, No. 2, 2001. pp207–236.

GUEST D. *and* PECCEI R. 'The nature and causes of effective human resource management', *British Journal of Industrial Relations*, Vol. 32, No. 2, 1994. pp219–242.

GUNNIGLE P., COLLINGS D. *and* MORLEY M. *Hosting the Multinational: Exploring the dynamics of industrial relations in US multinational subsidiaries in Ireland.* Employment Relations Research Unit Working Paper, University of Limerick. 2004.

HACKMAN J. *and* OLDHAM G. 'Motivation through the design of work: test of a theory', *Organisation Behaviour and Human Performance*, Vol. 16, 1976. pp250–279.

HALES, C. *and* GOUGH, O. 'Employee evaluations of company occupational pensions: HR implications', *Personnel Review*, Vol. 32, No. 3, 2003. pp319–340.

HALL L. *and* TORRINGTON D. 'Letting go or holding on – the devolution of operational personnel activities', *Human Resource Management Journal*, Vol. 8, No. 1, 1998. pp41–55.

HALL M., HOFFMAN A., MARGINSON P. *and* MULLER T. 'National influences on European Works Councils in UK and US based companies', *Human Resource Management Journal*, Vol. 13, No. 4, 2003. pp75–92.

HALPIN T. 'Vocational A levels fail Ofsted test', *The Times,* 29 March 2004. p4.

HAMBLIN A. *Evaluation and Control of Training.* Maidenhead, McGraw-Hill. 1974.

HAMEL G. *and* PRAHALAD C. K. *Competing for the Future.* Boston, Harvard Business School Press. 1994.

HANDY C. *Inside Organisations: 21 ideas for managers.* London, BBC Books. 1991.

HARRIS H., BREWSTER C. *and* SPARROW P. *International Human Resource Management.* London, CIPD. 2003.

HARRIS L. 'Rewarding employee performance: line managers' values, beliefs and perspectives', *International Journal of Human Resource Management*, Vol. 12, No. 7, 2001. pp1182–1192.

HARRISON R. *Learning and Development.* London, CIPD. 2002.

HASTINGS S. 'Grading systems and estimating value', in G. WHITE *and* J. DRUCKER (eds), *Reward Management: A critical text.* London, Routledge. 2000.

HATCHETT A. 'A test of determination', *People Management*, 8 February 2001. pp36–40.

HAWKINS K. *A Handbook of Industrial Relations Practice.* London, Kogan Page. 1979.

HAYNES P. *and* ALLEN M. 'Partnership as a union strategy: a preliminary evaluation', *Employee Relations*, Vol. 23, No. 2, 2001. pp164–187.

HEALTH AND SAFETY EXECUTIVE. *Beacons of Excellence in Stress Prevention.* HSE research report 133. Available at: www.hse.gov.uk/stress. 2004.

HEBSON G., GRIMSHAW D. *and* MARCHINGTON M. 'PPPs and the changing public sector ethos: case study evidence from the health and local authority sectors', *Work, Employment and Society*, Vol. 17, No. 3, 2003. pp483–503.

HEERY E. 'Partnership versus organising: alternative futures for British trade unionism', *Industrial Relations Journal*, Vol. 33, No. 1, 2002. pp20–35.

HEERY E. 'Trade unions and the management of reward', in G. WHITE *and* J. DRUCKER (eds), *Reward Management: A critical text.* London, Routledge. 2000.

HEERY E. 'The re-launch of the Trades Union Congress', *British Journal of Industrial Relations*, Vol. 36, No. 4, 1998. pp339–360.

HEERY E. and SALMON J. 'The insecurity thesis', in E. HEERY and J. SALMON (eds), *The Insecure Workforce*. London, Routledge. 2000.

HEERY E., SIMMS M., DELBRIDGE R., SALMON J. and SIMPSON D. 'The TUC's organising academy: an assessment', *Industrial Relations Journal*, Vol. 31, No. 5, 2000. pp400–415.

HELLER F., PUSIC E., STRAUSS G. and WILPERT B. *Organisational Participation: Myth and reality*. Oxford, Oxford University Press. 1998.

HENDRY C. *Human Resource Management: A strategic approach to employment*. London, Butterworth. 1994.

HENDRY C., WOODWARD S., BRADLEY P. and PERKINS S. 'Performance and rewards: cleaning out the stables', *Human Resource Management Journal*, Vol. 10, No. 3, 2000. pp46–62.

HERRIOT P. 'The role of the HRM function in building a new proposition for staff', in P. SPARROW and M. MARCHINGTON (eds), *Human Resource Management: The new agenda*. London, Financial Times/Pitman. 1998.

HERRIOT P. and PEMBERTON C. 'Facilitating new deals', *Human Resource Management Journal*, Vol. 7, No. 1, 1997. pp45–56.

HERZBERG F. 'Workers' needs: the same around world', *Industry Week*, 21 September 1987. pp29–32.

HERZBERG F. 'One more time: how do you motivate employees?', *Harvard Business Review*, Jan/Feb 1968. pp53–62.

HERZBERG F. *Work and the Nature of Man*. Cleveland, World Publishing. 1966.

HICKS-CLARKE D. and ILES, P. 'Climate for diversity and its effects on career and organisational attitudes and perceptions', *Personnel Review*, Vol. 29, No. 3. 2000. pp324–345.

HIGGINBOTTOM K. 'BP learns outsourcing lesson', *People Management*, 8 November 2001. p8.

HIGHAM J., HAYNES G., WRAGG C. and YEOMANS D. '14–19 Pathfinders: An evaluation of the first year'. Available at: www.dfes.gov.uk/14-19pathfinders. 2004.

HILL R. and STEWART J. 'Investors in People in small organisations: learning to stay the course?', *Journal of European Industrial Training,* Vol. 23, No. 6, 1999. pp286–299.

HILLAGE J., REGAN J. and MCLOUGHLIN K. *2002 Employers' Skill Survey*. DfES Research Brief RR372. 2002.

HILTON P. 'Using incentives to reward and motivate employees', *Personnel Management*, Vol. 24, No. 9, 1992. pp49–51.

HOFSTEDE G. *Cultures and Organizations*, 2nd edition. Thousand Oaks, Sage. 2001.

HOFSTEDE G. *Cultures and Organizations: Software of the mind*. London, McGraw-Hill. 1991.

HOFSTEDE G. *Culture's Consequences: International differences in work-related values*. London, Sage. 1980.

HOGARTH T. and HASLUCK C. *Net Costs of Modern Apprenticeship Training to Employers*. DfES Research Brief 418. 2003.

HOGARTH T., HASLUCK C., PIERRE G., WINTERBOTHAM M. and VIVIAN D. 'Work–life Balance 2000: Results from the baseline study', *IRS Labour Market Trends*, July 2001. pp371–373.

HOGARTH T. and WILSON R. *Skills Shortages, Vacancies, and Local Unemployment.* Available at: www.dfes.gov.uk. 2003.

HOLMAN D., WALL T., CLEGG C., SPARROW P. and HOWARD A. *The New Workplace: A guide to the human impact of modern working practices.* London, Wiley. 2003.

HOLME R. and WATTS P. *Corporate Social Responsibility: Making good business sense.* Geneva, World Business Council for Sustainable Development. 2000.

HOPE-HAILEY V., GRATTON L., McGOVERN P., STILES P. and TRUSS C. 'A chameleon function? HRM in the 90s', *Human Resource Management Journal*, Vol. 7, No. 3, 1997. pp5–18.

HOQUE K. 'All in all, it's just another plaque on the wall', *Journal of Management Studies*, Vol. 40, No. 2, 2003. pp543–571.

HOQUE K. *Human Resource Management in the Hotel Industry.* London, Routledge. 2000.

HOQUE K. 'Human resource management and performance in the UK hotel industry', *British Journal of Industrial Relations*, Vol. 37, No. 3, 1999. pp419–443.

HOSKISSON R., HITT M., WAN W. and YIU, D. 'Theory and research in strategic management', *Journal of Management*, Vol. 25, No. 3, 1999. pp417–456.

HOUSTON D. and MARKS G. 'The role of planning and workplace support in returning to work after maternity leave', *British Journal of Industrial Relations*, Vol. 41, No. 2, 2003. pp197–214.

HOWARD K., SHARP J. and PETERS J. *The Management of a Student Research Project*, 3rd edition. London, Gower/Open University. 2002.

HOWELL D. (ed), *Fighting Unemployment: The limits of free market orthodoxy.* Oxford, Oxford University Press. 2004.

HUDSON M. 'Disappearing pathways and the struggle for a fair day's pay', in B BURCHELL, D. LAPIDO and F. WILKINSON (eds), *Job Insecurity and Work Intensification.* London, Routledge. 2002a.

HUDSON M. 'Flexibility and the reorganisation of work', in B. BURCHELL, D. LAPIDO and F. WILKINSON (eds), *Job Insecurity and Work Intensification.* London, Routledge. 2002b.

HUNT J. and BARUCH Y. 'Developing top managers: the impact of interpersonal skills training', *Journal of Management Development*, Vol. 22, No. 8, 2003. pp729–752.

HUNT S. 'The resource-advantage theory of competition', *Journal of Management Inquiry*, Vol. 4, No. 4, 1995. pp317–332.

HUNTER L., McGREGOR A., MacINNES J. and SPROULL A. 'The flexible firm, strategy and segmentation', *British Journal of Industrial Relations*, Vol. 31, No. 3, 1993. pp383–407.

HUSELID M. 'The impact of human resource management practices on turnover, productivity and corporate financial performance', *Academy of Management Journal*, Vol. 38, No. 3, 1995. pp635–672.

HUSELID M. and BECKER B. 'Methodological issues in cross-sectional and panel estimates of the HR-firm performance link', *Industrial Relations*, Vol. 35, 1996. pp400–422.

HUSSEY D. *Strategic Management: From theory to implementation.* Oxford, Butterworth Heinemann. 1998.

HUTCHINSON S. and PURCELL J. *Bringing Policies to Life: The vital role of front line managers in people management.* London, CIPD. 2003.

HUTCHINSON S. *and* WOOD S. 'The UK experience', in *Institute of Personnel and Development, Personnel and the Line: Developing the new relationship*. London, IPD. 1995. pp3–42.

HUTTON W. *The Stakeholding Society*. Cambridge, Polity Press. 1998.

HYMAN J. 'Financial participation schemes', in G. WHITE *and* J. DRUCKER (eds), *Reward Management: A critical text*. London, Routledge. 2000.

HYMAN R. 'The future of employee representation', *British Journal of Industrial Relations*, Vol. 35, No. 3, 1997. pp309–336.

HYMAN J., BALDRY C., SCHOLARIOS D. *and* BUNZEL D. 'Work–life imbalance in call centres and software development', *British Journal of Industrial Relations*, Vol. 41, No. 2, 2003. pp215–239.

ICHNIOWSKI C., SHAW K. *and* PRENNUSHI G. 'The effects of human resource management practices on productivity: a study of steel finishing lines', *American Economic Review*, Vol. 87, 1997. pp291–313.

ILES P. 'Employee resourcing', in J. STOREY (ed), *Human Resource Management: A critical text*. London, Routledge. 2001.

ILES P. *and* ROBERTSON I. 'The impact of personnel selection procedures on candidates', in N. ANDERSON *and* P. HERRIOT (eds), *International Handbook of Selection and Assessment*. Chichester, John Wiley and Sons Ltd. 1997.

INCOMES DATA SERVICES. *HR Service Centres*. IDS Study 750. London, IDS. 2003.

INCOMES DATA SERVICES. *Bonus Schemes*. IDS Study 655. London, IDS. 1999.

INCOMES DATA SERVICES. *Flexible Benefits*. July 1998.

INVESTORS IN PEOPLE UK. *What is Investors in People?* Available at: www.investorsinpeople.co.uk. 2001.

INVOLVEMENT AND PARTICIPATION ASSOCIATION. *Towards Industrial Partnership: A new approach to relationships at work*. London, IPA. 1993.

IRS EMPLOYMENT REVIEW 807. *Learning and Development in the Workplace*. 3 September 2004. pp10–17.

IRS EMPLOYMENT REVIEW 804. *Recruiting with a Little Help from My Friends*. 23 July 2004. pp44–49.

IRS EMPLOYMENT REVIEW 802. *Human Capital Reporting: Proving the value of people*. 18 June 2004. pp9–15.

IRS EMPLOYMENT REVIEW 800. *Attendance and Absence*. 21 May 2004. p17.

IRS EMPLOYMENT REVIEW 799a. *Answering the Recruitment Call Online*. 7 May 2004. pp46–48.

IRS EMPLOYMENT REVIEW 799b. *HR Shapes Up Its Focus on Managing Absence*. 7 May 2004. pp18–20.

IRS EMPLOYMENT REVIEW 799c. *Pay the Strategic Way*. 7 May 2004. pp10–13.

IRS EMPLOYMENT REVIEW 797a. *The Working Time Regulations 1998*. 2 April 2004. pp51–59.

IRS EMPLOYMENT REVIEW 796a. *Aligning Business Strategy and HR for Competitive Advantage*. 19 March 2004. pp9–15.

IRS EMPLOYMENT REVIEW 796b. *Managing to Make the Best Hiring Choice*. 19 March 2004. pp43–48.

IRS EMPLOYMENT REVIEW 796c. *Managing Long-term Absence and Rehabilitation: Part 2*. 19 March 2004. pp18–24.

IRS EMPLOYMENT REVIEW 796d. *Data Briefing: Trade union membership*. 19 March 2004. p5.

IRS EMPLOYMENT REVIEW 795a. *HR Roles and Responsibilities: Climbing the admin mountain*. 5 March 2004. pp9–15.

IRS EMPLOYMENT REVIEW 795b. *Skills Triumph Over Experience*. 5 March 2004. pp4–5.

IRS EMPLOYMENT REVIEW 793a. *Welcome the New Multitasking All-purpose Management Expert*. 6 February 2004. pp8–13.

IRS EMPLOYMENT REVIEW 793b. *Measuring and Managing Labour Turnover: Part 1*. 6 February 2004. pp38–48.

IRS EMPLOYMENT REVIEW 793c. *Management Skills on Tap*. 6 February 2004. p14.

IRS EMPLOYMENT REVIEW 792a. *Recruiters March in Step with Online Recruitment*. 23 January 2004. pp44–48.

IRS EMPLOYMENT REVIEW 792b. *Civil Service Absence Cost £370 m in 2002*. 23 January 2004. pp20–21.

IRS EMPLOYMENT REVIEW 792c. *Attendance and Absence*. 23 January 2004. p17.

IRS EMPLOYMENT REVIEW 792d. *GPs are Sick of Sick Notes*. 23 January 2004. p18.

IRS EMPLOYMENT REVIEW 792e. *Putting Job Evaluation to Work: Tips from the front line*. 23 January 2004. pp8–15.

IRS EMPLOYMENT REVIEW 792f. *Thank You Goes a Long Way*. 23 January 2004. pp32–36.

IRS EMPLOYMENT REVIEW 791. *Picking the Best from the Rest*. 23 January 2004. pp42–48.

IRS EMPLOYMENT REVIEW 788a. *Graduate Recruitment 2003/4: Cutbacks and change*. 21 November 2003. pp40–49.

IRS EMPLOYMENT REVIEW 788b. *Rehabilitation is the Key to Employers' Liability Insurance*. 21 November 2003. pp20–21.

IRS EMPLOYMENT REVIEW 787A. *Outsourcing HR at Novo Nordisk*. 7 November 2003. pp19–21.

IRS EMPLOYMENT REVIEW 787b. *Where's the Evidence?* 7 November 2003. pp22–24.

IRS EMPLOYMENT REVIEW 786. *Adopting a Risk Management Approach to Manage Absence*. 17 October 2003. pp21–24.

IRS EMPLOYMENT REVIEW 785. *Employers Beg to Differ*. 3 October 2003. pp42–48.

IRS EMPLOYMENT REVIEW 784a. *Councils Count the Cost of Fairer Terms and Conditions*. 19 September 2003. pp8–16.

IRS EMPLOYMENT REVIEW 784b. *Work Related Absences are Growing Longer*. 19 September 2003. p19.

IRS EMPLOYMENT REVIEW 782. *Sharpening Up Recruitment and Selection with Competencies*. 15 August 2003. pp42–48.

IRS EMPLOYMENT REVIEW 778. *Discipline Procedures: Dawn of a new era?* June 2003. pp10–15.

IRS EMPLOYMENT REVIEW 774a. *Chasing Progress on Equal Pay*. 18 April 2003. pp19–22.

IRS EMPLOYMENT REVIEW 774b. *The Glimmer of a National Rehabilitation Service*. 18 April 2003. pp42–43.

IRS EMPLOYMENT REVIEW 772. *Induction to Perfection: The start of a beautiful friendship*. 21 March 2003. pp34–40.

IRS EMPLOYMENT REVIEW 769a. *Time to Talk: How and why employers conduct appraisals*. 7 February 2003. pp8–14.

IRS EMPLOYMENT REVIEW 769b. *Health, Safety, and Wellbeing*. 7 February 2003. p39.

IRS EMPLOYMENT REVIEW 769c. *Stress Risk Assessments and EAPs*. 7 February 2003. p40.

IRS EMPLOYMENT REVIEW 768. *Tackling Long-term Absence: Doncaster Council*. 24 January 2003. pp42–44.

IRS EMPLOYMENT REVIEW 762. *Managing Disability*. 21 October 2002. p9.

IRS EMPLOYMENT REVIEW 761. *Training: The vital statistics*. 7 October 2002. pp7–13.

IRS EMPLOYMENT REVIEW 759. *Mixed Practice for Pensions*. 9 September 2002. pp23–27.

IRS EMPLOYMENT REVIEW 756. *Corporate Accountability*. 2002. pp6–12.

IRS EMPLOYMENT REVIEW 754. *Measure for Measure*. 24 June 2002. pp8–13.

IRS EMPLOYMENT REVIEW 748. *Stormy Waters Ahead for Employers' Associations?* 25 March 2002. pp7–13.

IRS EMPLOYMENT REVIEW 742. *Benchmarking the HR Function: The IRS guide*. 17 December 2001. pp6–14.

IRS EMPLOYMENT REVIEW 740. *Developing HR Policies: A case of reinventing the wheel?* 19 November 2001. pp7–15.

IRS EMPLOYMENT REVIEW 735. 'Part-time working options and arrangements', *IRS Employment Trends 735*, September 2001. pp4–16.

IRS EMPLOYMENT REVIEW 732a. 'Think local: using jobcentres for recruitment', *IRS Employment Development Bulletin 139*, July 2001. pp12–16.

IRS EMPLOYMENT REVIEW 732b. 'Whatever happened to team reward?', *Pay and Benefits Bulletin 524*, July 2001. pp2–7.

IRS EMPLOYMENT REVIEW 727. 'Managing discipline at work', *IRS Employment Trends 727*, May 2001. pp5–11.

IRS EMPLOYMENT REVIEW 726. 'Airing a grievance: how to handle employee complaints', *IRS Employment Trends 726,* April 2001. pp6–16.

IRS EMPLOYMENT REVIEW 710. 'Single status: the story so far', *IRS Employment Trends 710*, August 2000. pp2–16.

IRS EMPLOYMENT REVIEW 703. 'In-store personnel managers balance Tesco's scorecard', *IRS Employment Trends 703*, May 2000. pp13–16.

IRS EMPLOYMENT REVIEW 698. 'Human resources consulting: friend or foe?', *IRS Employment Trends 698*, February 2000. pp7–12.

IRS EMPLOYMENT REVIEW 499. 'Civil service pay – from individual to team rewards', *IRS Pay and Benefits Bulletin 499*, July 2000. pp5–9.

IT TRAINING NEWS. 'New ITQ set to lift IT apprenticeships', *IT Training*, February 2004. p5.

JAMES P., CUNNINGHAM I. *and* DIBBEN P. 'Absence management and the issues of job retention and return to work', *Human Resource Management Journal*, Vol. 12, No. 2, 2002. pp82–94.

JOHNS T. *Report Writing as an Exercise in Persuasion*. London, CIPD. 1996.

JOHNSON A. 'Match making'. *People Management*, 9 October 2003. p24.

JOHNSON G. *and* SCHOLES K. *Exploring Corporate Strategy*. London, Prentice Hall. 2002.

JOHNSTONE S., WILKINSON A. *and* ACKERS P. 'Partnership paradoxes: a case study of an energy company', *Employee Relations*, Vol. 26, No. 4, 2004. pp353–376.

JONES A. *The Labour of Hours: Is managing time the route to smarter working?* London, The Work Foundation. 2004.

KAHN-FREUND O. 'Industrial relations and the law: retrospect and prospect', *British Journal of Industrial Relations*, Vol. 7, 1965. pp301–316.

KAHN-FREUND O. 'Labour law', in M. GINSBERG (ed), *Law and Opinion in England in the 20th Century*. London, Stevens. 1959.

KAMOCHE K. 'Strategic human resource management within a resource-capability view of the firm', *Journal of Management Studies*, Vol. 33, No. 2, 1996. pp213–233.

KANDOLA R. *and* FULLERTON J. *Diversity in Action: Managing the mosaic*. London, CIPD. 1998.

KAPLAN R. *and* NORTON D. *The Strategy-focused Organization: How balanced scorecard companies thrive in the new business environment*. Boston, HBS Press. 2001.

KAPLAN R. *and* NORTON D. 'Using the balanced scorecard as a strategic management system', *Harvard Business Review*, Jan–Feb, 1996. pp75–85.

KAUFMAN B. 'High-level employee involvement in Delta Airlines', *Human Resource Management*, Vol. 42, No. 2, 2003. pp175–190.

KEENOY T. 'Human resource management: rhetoric, reality and contradiction', *International Journal of Human Resource Management*, Vol. 1, No. 3, 1990. pp363–384.

KEEP E. 'The trouble with training', *People Management*, 3 April 2003a. p27.

KEEP E. *The State and Power: An elephant and a snake in the telephone box of English VET policy*. Paper presented to the ESRC Seminar Series on the history and philosophy of VET, University of Greenwich, London. 27 November 2003b.

KEEP E. 'The English vocational education and training debate – "fragile technologies" or opening the "black box": two competing visions of where we go next', *Journal of Education and Work*, Vol. 15, No. 4, 2002. pp457–479.

KEEP E. *If It Moves, It's a Skill: The changing meaning of skill in the UK context*. Paper presented at ESRC seminar The Changing Nature of Skills and Knowledge, UMIST, Manchester, 3–4 September 2001.

KEEP E. 'Learning organisations, lifelong learning and the mystery of the vanishing employers', *Economic Outlook*, Vol. 24, No. 4, 2000. pp18–26.

KEEP E. *and* RAINBIRD H. 'Towards the learning organisation', in S. BACH *and* K. SISSON (eds), *Personnel Management*. Oxford, Blackwell. 2000.

KELLIHER C. *and* PERRETT G. 'Business strategy and approaches to HRM: a case study of new developments in the UK restaurant industry', *Personnel Review*, Vol. 30, No. 4, 2001. pp421–437.

KELLY J. 'Social partnership arrangements in Britain', *Industrial Relations,* Vol. 43, No. 1, 2004. pp267–292.

KELLY J. *and* GENNARD J. 'Getting to the top: career paths of personnel directors', *Human Resource Management Journal*, Vol. 10, No. 3, 2000. pp22–37.

KESSLER I. 'Pay and performance', in B. TOWERS (ed), *The Handbook of Employment Relations Law and Practice*. London, Kogan Page. 2003.

KESSLER I. 'Reward system choices', in J. STOREY (ed), *Human Resource Management*. London, Routledge. 2001.

KESSLER I. 'Remuneration systems', in S. BACH *and* K. SISSON (eds), *Personnel Management*, 3rd edition. Oxford, Blackwell. 2000.

KESSLER I. 'Reward systems', in J. STOREY (ed), *Human Resource Management: A critical text*. London, Routledge. 1994.

KESSLER I. *and* PURCELL J. 'Individualism and collectivism', in P. EDWARDS (ed), *Industrial Relations*, 2nd edition. Oxford, Blackwell. 2003.

KINGSMILL D. *Accounting for People: Report of the Task Force on Human Capital Management*, presented to the Secretary of State for Trade and Industry. October 2003a.

KINGSMILL D. *The Kingsmill Review of Women's Pay and Employment*. Available at: www.kingsmillreview.gov.uk. 2003b.

KINNIE N., HUTCHINSON S. *and* PURCELL J. 'Fun and surveillance: the paradox of high commitment management in telephone call centres', *International Journal of Human Resource Management*, Vol. 11, No. 5, 2000. pp63–78.

KINNIE N., SWART J., RAYTON B., HUTCHINSON S. *and* PURCELL J. *HR policy and Performance: An occupational analysis*. Paper presented to the International Industrial Relations Association, HRM Study Group. Lisbon. September 2004.

KIRKBRIDE P. 'Management development: in search of a new role?', *Journal of Management Development*, Vol. 22, No. 2. 2003. pp171–180.

KIRKPATRICK D. 'Evaluation of training', in R. CRAIG *and* L. BITTELL (eds), *Training and Evaluation Handbook*. New York, McGraw Hill. 1967.

KLAAS B., MCCLENDON J. *and* GAINEY T. 'Outsourcing HR: the impact of organizational characteristics', *Human Resource Management*, Vol. 40, No. 2, 2001. pp125–138.

KLEIN J. 'Why supervisors resist employee involvement', *Harvard Business Review*, September/October, 1984. pp87–95.

KOCH M. *and* MCGRATH R. 'Improving labour productivity: human resource management policies do matter', *Strategic Management Journal*, Vol. 17, No. 5, 1996. pp335–353.

KOCHAN T. *and* BAROCCI T. *Human Resource Management and Industrial Relations*. Boston, Little Brown. 1985.

KOCHAN T., KATZ H. *and* CAPPELLI R. *The Transformation of American Industrial Relations*. New York, Basic Books. 1986.

KOCHAN T. *and* OSTERMAN P. *The Mutual Gains Enterprise*. London, Harvard Business School Press. 1994.

KOHN A. 'Why incentive plans cannot work', *Harvard Business Review*, September/October, 1993. pp54–63.

KOLB D., OSLAND J. *and* RUBIN I. *Organisational Behaviour: An experiential approach*, 6th edition. New Jersey, Prentice Hall. 1995.

LABOUR MARKET TRENDS. Central Statistical Office. London, Her Majesty's Stationery Office. (Monthly)

LABOUR MARKET TRENDS. 'Labour market update', Vol. 112, No. 7, July 2004. pp259–261.

LABOUR MARKET TRENDS. 'Self employment in the UK labour market', Vol. 111, No. 9, September 2003. pp441–451.

LANE C. *Management and Labour in Europe.* Aldershot, Edward Elgar. 1989.

LAWLER E. *Rewarding Excellence: Pay strategies for the new economy.* New York, Jossey Bass. 2000a.

LAWLER E. 'Pay strategy: new thinking for the new millennium', *Compensation and Benefits Review*, Vol. 32, No. 1, 2000b. p7.

LAWRENCE F. 'Sweatshop campaigners demand Gap boycott'. *The Guardian*, 22 November 2002. p10.

LAYARD R. *Happiness: Has social science a clue?* Lionel Robbins Memorial Lecture. London, London School of Economics. 3–5 March 2003.

LAZEAR E. *Personnel Economics.* Cambridge, MA, MIT Press. 1998.

LEARNING AND SKILLS COUNCIL. *The LSC Strategic Framework to 2004: Corporate plan.* Available at: www.lsc.gov.uk. 2004.

LEARNING AND SKILLS COUNCIL. *National Employer Skills Survey 2003: Key findings.* Available at: www.lsc.gov.uk. 2003a.

LEARNING AND SKILLS COUNCIL. *Skills in England 2002.* Available at: www.lsc.gov.uk. 2003b.

LEGGE K. 'The ethical context of HRM: the ethical organisation in the boundaryless world', in D. WINSTANLEY *and* J. WOODALL (eds), *Ethical Issues in Contemporary Human Resource Management.* London, Macmillan Business. 2000.

LEGGE K. *Human Resource Management: Rhetorics and realities.* London, Macmillan. 1995.

LEGGE K. *Power, Innovation and Problem Solving in Personnel Management.* London, McGraw Hill. 1978.

LEIGHTON P. *and* PROCTOR G. *Legal Essentials: Recruiting within the law.* London, CIPD. 2001.

LENGNICK HALL C. *and* LENGNICK HALL M. 'Strategic human resource management: a review of the literature and a proposed typology', *Academy of Management Review*, Vol. 13, No. 3, 1988. pp454–470.

LEONARD D. *Wellsprings of Knowledge: Building and sustaining the sources of innovation.* Boston, Harvard Business School Press. 1998.

LEOPOLD J. *Human Resources in Organisations.* London, Prentice Hall. 2002.

LEUNG A. 'Different ties for different needs: recruitment practices of entrepreneurial firms at different developmental phases', *Human Resource Management*, Vol. 42, No. 4, 2003. pp303–320.

LEWIS D. *and* SARGEANT M. *Essentials of Employment Law*, 8th edition. London, CIPD. 2004.

LEWIS P. 'Reward management', in T. REDMAN *and* A. WILKINSON (eds), *Contemporary Human Resource Management.* London, Financial Times/Pearson. 2001.

LEWIS P. 'Managing performance related pay based on evidence from the financial service sector', *Human Resource Management Journal*, Vol. 8, No. 2, 1998. pp66–77.

LIFF S. 'Manpower or human resource planning: what's in a name?', in S. BACH and K. SISSON (eds), *Personnel Management: A comprehensive guide to theory and practice*. Oxford, Blackwell. 2000.

LINCOLN Y. and GUBA E. *Naturalistic Inquiry*. California, Sage. 1985.

LLOYD C. 'Training and development deficiencies in "high skill" sectors', *Human Resource Management Journal,* Vol. 12, No. 2, 2002. pp64–81.

LOVAS B. and GHOSHAL S. 'Strategy as guided evolution', *Strategic Management Journal*, Vol. 21, No. 9, 2000. pp875–896.

LOW PAY COMMISSION. *The National Minimum Wage: Fourth annual report*. London, The Stationery Report. 2003.

LOWE J. 'Teambuilding via outdoor training: experiences from a UK automotive plant', *Human Resource Management Journal*, Vol. 2, No. 1, 1992. pp42–59.

LOWRY D. 'Performance management', in J. LEOPOLD (ed), *Human Resources in Organisations*. London, Prentice Hall. 2002.

LUNDY O. and COWLING A. *Strategic Human Resource Management*. London, Routledge. 1996.

LUPTON B. 'Pouring the coffee at interview? Personnel's role in the selection of doctors', *Personnel Review*, Vol. 29, No. 1, 2000. pp48–68.

LUPTON B. and SHAW S. 'Are public sector personnel managers the profession's poor relations?', *Human Resource Management Journal*, Vol. 11, No. 3, 2001. pp23–38.

LUTHANS F. and PETERSON S. '360-degree feedback with systematic coaching: empirical analysis suggests a winning combination', *Human Resource Management*, Vol. 42, No. 3, 2003. pp243–256.

LYNCH P. 'Time based pay', in R. THORPE and G. HOMAN (eds), *Strategic Reward Systems*. London, Financial Times/Prentice Hall. 2000.

MABEY C. 'Mapping management development practice', *Journal of Management Studies*, Vol. 39, No. 8, 2002. pp1139–1160.

MABEY C. 'Closing the circle: participant views of a 360 degree feedback programme', *Human Resource Management Journal*, Vol. 11, No. 1. 2001. pp41–53.

MACDUFFIE J. 'Human resource bundles and manufacturing performance: Organisational logic and flexible production systems in the world auto industry', *Industrial and Labor Relations Review*, Vol. 48, 1995. pp197–221.

MACHIN S. 'Trade union decline, new workplaces and new workers', in H. GOSPEL and S. WOOD (eds), *Representing Workers: Union recognition and membership in Britain*. London, Routledge. 2003.

MACLEOD D. 'E is for error', *Education Guardian*, 8 June 2004. pp18–19.

MAHONEY C. 'Firms fail to see how IIP boosts profits', *People Management*, 3 August 2000. pp8–9.

MAKIN P., COOPER C. and COX C. *Managing People at Work*. London, Routledge, 1989.

MAKINSON J. (Chair), *Incentives for Change: Rewarding performance in National Government Networks*. London, Public Services Productivity Panel, H.M. Treasury. 2000.

MALTZ A., SHENHAR A. and REILLY R. 'Beyond the balanced scorecard: refining the search for organisational success measures', *Long Range Planning*, Vol. 36, No. 2, 2003. pp187–204.

MANOCHA R. 'Well adjusted', *People Management*, 8 April 2004. pp26–30.

MANOCHA R. 'Catch 22', *People Management*, 9 October 2003. pp40–44.

MARCHINGTON L., EARNSHAW J., TORRINGTON D., *and* RITCHIE E. 'The local education authority's role in operating teacher capability procedures', *Educational Management Administration and Leadership*, Vol. 32, No. 1, 2004a. pp25–44.

MARCHINGTON M. 'Employee involvement: patterns and explanations', in B. HARLEY, J. HYMAN and P. THOMPSON (eds), *Participation and Democracy at Work: Essays in honour of Harvie Ramsay*. London, Palgrave. 2005.

MARCHINGTON M. 'Employee involvement at work', in J. STOREY (ed), *Human Resource Management: A critical text*, 2nd edition. London, Thomson. 2001.

MARCHINGTON M. 'Teamworking and employee involvement: terminology, evaluation and context', in S. PROCTER *and* F. MUELLER (eds), *Teamworking: Issues, concepts, and problems*. London, Blackwell. 1999.

MARCHINGTON M. 'Managing labour relations in a competitive environment', in A. STURDY, D. KNIGHTS *and* H. WILLMOTT (eds), *Skill and Consent: Contemporary studies on the labour process*. London, Routledge. 1992.

MARCHINGTON M., CARROLL M. *and* BOXALL P. 'Labour scarcity and the survival of small firms: a resource-based view of the road haulage industry', *Human Resource Management Journal*, Vol. 13, No. 4, 2003a. pp5–22.

MARCHINGTON M., COOKE F. *and* HEBSON G. 'Performing for the "customer": managing housing benefit operations across organisational boundaries', *Local Government Studies*, Vol. 29, No. 1, 2003b. pp51–74.

MARCHINGTON M., GOODMAN J., *and* BERRIDGE J. 'Employment relations in Britain', in G. BAMBER, R. LANSBURY *and* N. WAILES (eds), *International and Comparative Employment Relations*, 4th edition. Crows Nest, NSW, Allen & Unwin. 2004b.

MARCHINGTON M., GRIMSHAW D., RUBERY J. *and* WILLMOTT H. (eds), *Fragmenting Work: Blurring organisational boundaries and disordering hierarchies*. Oxford, Oxford University Press. 2004c.

MARCHINGTON M. *and* GRUGULIS I. '"Best practice" human resource management: perfect opportunity or dangerous illusion?', *International Journal of Human Resource Management*, Vol. 11, No. 4, 2000. pp905–925.

MARCHINGTON M. *and* Parker P. *Changing Patterns of Employee Relations*. Hemel Hempstead, Harvester Wheatsheaf. 1990.

MARCHINGTON M. *and* VINCENT S. 'Analysing the influence of institutional, organisational and interpersonal forces in shaping inter-organisational relations', *Journal of Management Studies*, Vol. 41, No. 6, 2004. pp1029–1056.

MARCHINGTON M. *and* WILKINSON A. 'Direct participation', in S. BACH *and* K. SISSON (eds), *Personnel Management: A comprehensive guide to theory and practice*. Oxford, Blackwell. 2005.

MARCHINGTON M., WILKINSON A., ACKERS P. *and* DUNDON A. *Management Choice and Employee Voice*. London, CIPD. 2001.

MARCHINGTON M., WILKINSON A., ACKERS P. *and* GOODMAN J. 'The influence of managerial relations on waves of employee involvement', *British Journal of Industrial Relations*, Vol. 31, No. 4, 1993a. pp543–576.

MARCHINGTON M., WILKINSON A. *and* DALE B. 'The case study report', in A. BARON (ed), *Quality: People management matters*. London, Institute of Personnel Management. 1993b.

MARGOLIS A. 'Licensed to skill', *People Management*, 26 June 2003. pp46–48.

MARLOW S. 'Regulating labour management in small firms', *Human Resource Management Journal*, Vol. 12, No. 3, 2002. pp1–25.

MARSDEN D. *Teachers Before the 'Threshold'*. Working Paper. London, Centre for Economic Performance. 2000.

MARSDEN D. *and* FRENCH A. *What a Performance: PRP in the public sector*. Working Paper. London, Centre for Economic Performance. 1998.

MARSDEN D., FRENCH S. *and* KUBO K. *Why Does Performance Pay De-motivate? Financial incentives versus performance appraisal*. Discussion Paper. London, LSE Centre for Economic Performance. 2000.

MARSH A. *and* McCARTHY W. *Disputes Procedures in Britain Royal Commission*. Research Paper No. 2, Part 2. London, HMSO. 1968.

MARTIN G. *and* BEAUMONT P. 'Diffusing "best practice" in multinational firms: prospects, practice and contestation', *International Journal of Human Resource Management*, Vol. 9, No. 4, 1998. pp671–695.

MARTINEZ-LUCIO M. *and* STUART. M. 'Assessing partnership: the prospects for, and challenges of, modernisation', *Employee Relations*, Vol. 24, No. 3, 2002. pp252–261.

MASLOW A. 'A theory of human motivation', *Psychological Review*, Vol. 50, 1943. pp370–396.

MAYO A. 'Called to account', *People Management*, 8 April 1999. p33.

MAYO A. 'Economic indicators of human resource management', in S. TYSON (ed), *Strategic Prospects for Human Resource Management*. London, Institute of Personnel and Development. 1995.

McBRIDE J. *and* STIRLING J. 'Partnership and process in the maritime construction industry', *Employee Relations*, Vol. 24, No. 3, 2002. pp290–304.

McEWEN N. 'Transforming HR: the practitioner's perspective', *Strategic HR Review*, Vol. 2. No. 1, 2002. pp18–23.

McGOVERN P. *and* HILL S. *The End of the Status Divide?* BUIRA Conference Paper, Leeds. 2003.

McGOVERN P., HOPE-HAILEY V., STILES P. *and* TRUSS C. 'Human resource management on the line?', *Human Resource Management Journal*, Vol. 7, No. 4, 1997. pp12–29.

McGREGOR D. *The Human Side of Enterprise*. New York, McGraw-Hill. 1960.

McKENNA E. *Business Psychology and Organisational Behaviour*, 3rd edition. Hove, Psychology Press. 2000.

McLEOD J. *Counselling in the Workplace: The facts*. Rugby, BACP. 2001.

McSWEENEY B. 'Hofstede's model of national cultural differences and their consequences: a triumph of faith – a failure of analysis', *Human Relations*, Vol. 55, No. 1, 2002. pp89–118.

MEGGINSON D. 'Style counsel revisited', *People Management*, 6 December 2001. p57.

MEGGINSON D. *and* WHITAKER V. *Continuing Professional Development*. London, CIPD. 2003.

MELLOR-CLARK N. 'The move to a new HR function'. Unpublished MSc dissertation, UMIST. 2004.

MERRICK N. 'Modern romance', *People Management*, 25 March 2004. pp16–17.

MERRICK N. 'Happy returns?', *People Management*, 6 March 2003. p16.

MILES M. 'Qualitative data as an attractive nuisance: the problem of analysis', *Administrative Science Quarterly*, Vol. 12, No. 4, 1979. pp590–601.

MILES A. and HUBERMAN A. *Analysing Qualitative Data: A source book for new methods.* London, Sage. 1984.

MILES R. and SNOW C. *Organisational Strategy, Structure and Process.* New York, McGraw Hill. 1978.

MILLWARD N., BRYSON A. and FORTH J. *All Change at Work: British employment relations 1980–1998, as portrayed by the Workplace Industrial Relations Survey series.* London, Routledge. 2000.

MILLWARD N., STEVENS M., SMART D. and HAWES W. *Workplace Industrial Relations in Transition.* Aldershot, Dartmouth Publishing. 1992.

MINTZBERG H. 'Crafting strategy', *Harvard Business Review*, July–August 1987. pp66–75.

MINTZBERG H. 'An emergent strategy of direct research', *Administrative Science Quarterly*, Vol. 24, No. 4, 1979. pp582–589.

MINTZBERG H. 'Patterns in strategy formation', *Management Science*, Vol. 24, No. 9, 1978. pp934–948.

MINTZBERG H., AHLSTRAND B. and LAMPEL J. *Strategy Safari: A guided tour through the wilds of strategic management.* London, Prentice Hall. 1998.

MITCHELL J. 'Case and situation analysis', *Sociological Review*, Vol. 31, No. 2, 1983. pp187–211.

MONGER J. 'Labour disputes in 2003', *Labour Market Trends*, Vol. 112, No. 6, June 2004. p236.

MONKS J. 'Trade unions, enterprise and the future', in P. SPARROW and M. MARCHINGTON (eds), *Human Resource Management: The new agenda.* London, Financial Times/Pitman. 1998.

MONKS, K. 'Models of personnel management: a means of understanding the diversity of personnel practices?', *Human Resource Management Journal*, Vol. 3, No. 2, 1993. pp29–41.

MORGAN G. *Images of Organisation.* Newbury Park, Sage. 1986.

MORLEY M. 'Gainsharing', in T. REDMAN and A. WILKINSON (eds), *The Informed Student Guide to Human Resource Management.* London, Thomson Learning. 2002a.

MORLEY M. 'Pensions', in T. REDMAN and A. WILKINSON (eds), *The Informed Student Guide to Human Resource Management.* London, Thomson Learning. 2002b.

MORRELL K., LOAN-CLARKE J. and WILKINSON A. 'Unweaving leaving: the use of models in the management of employee turnover', *International Journal of Management Reviews*, Vol. 3, No. 3, 2001. pp219–244.

MORRIS J., WILKINSON B. and MUNDAY M. 'Farewell to HRM? Personnel practices in Japanese manufacturing plants in the UK', *International Journal of Human Resource Management*, Vol. 11, No. 3, 2000. pp1047–1060.

MORTON B. and WILSON A. 'Double vision', *People Management*, 9 October 2003. pp37–38.

MORTON C. *Becoming World Class.* London, Macmillan. 1994.

MUELLER F. 'Human resources as strategic assets: an evolutionary resource-based theory', *Journal of Management Studies*, Vol. 33, No. 6, 1996. pp757–785.

MUELLER F. 'Societal effect, organisation effect and globalisation', *Organisation Studies*, Vol. 15, 1994. pp407–428.

MULLINS L. *Management and Organisational Behaviour*, 7th edition. London, Financial Times/Pitman. 2004.

MULLINS L. *Management and Organisational Behaviour*, 6th edition. London, Financial Times/Pitman. 2001.

MUMFORD A. 'Enhancing your learning skills – a note of guidance for managers', in S. WOOD (ed), *Continuous Development*. London, Institute of Personnel Management. 1988.

MUMFORD A. *and* GOLD J. *Management Development: Strategies for action*. London, CIPD. 2004.

NADLER D. *and* LAWLER E. 'Motivation: a diagnostic approach', in M. STEERS *and* L. PORTER (eds), *Motivation and Work Behaviour*, 2nd edition. New York, McGraw Hill. 1979.

NEWELL S. *and* SHACKLETON V. 'Selection and assessment as an interactive decision-action process', in T. REDMAN *and* A. WILKINSON (eds), *Contemporary Human Resource Management*. London, Financial Times/Prentice Hall. 2001.

NEWELL S. *and* SHACKLETON V. 'Recruitment and selection', in S. BACH *and* K. SISSON (eds), *Personnel Management: A comprehensive guide to theory and practice*. Oxford, Blackwell. 2000.

NEWELL S. *and* TANSLEY C. 'International uses of selection methods', *International Review of Industrial and Organisational Psychology*, Vol. 16, 2001. pp195–213.

NIJHOF A., FISSCHER O. *and* LOOISE J. 'Inclusive innovation: a research project on the inclusion of social responsibility', *Corporate Social Responsibility and Environmental Management*, Vol. 9, 2002. pp83–90.

NIVEN M. *Personnel Management, 1913–1963*. London, Institute of Personnel Management. 1967.

NOLAN P. *and* WOOD S. 'Mapping the future of work', *British Journal of Industrial Relations*, Vol. 41, No. 2, 2003. pp165–174.

NOON M. *and* BLYTON P. *The Realities of Work*. London, Macmillan Business. 2002.

NYHAN B., CRESSEY P., TOMASSINI M., KELLEHER M. *and* POELL R. 'European perspectives on the learning organisation', *Journal of European Industrial Training*, Vol. 28, No. 1, 2004. pp67–92.

OLIVER C. 'Sustainable competitive advantage: combining institutional and resource-based views', *Strategic Management Journal*, Vol. 18, No. 9, 1997. pp697–713.

OLIVER N. *and* WILKINSON B. *The Japanisation of British Industry*, 2nd edition. Oxford, Blackwell. 1992.

OXENBRIDGE S. *and* BROWN W. 'Developing partnership relationships: a case of leveraging power', in M. STUART *and* M. MARTINEZ-LUCIO (eds), *Partnership and Modernisation in Employment Relations*. London, Routledge. 2004.

PAAUWE J. *HRM and Performance: Achieving long term viability*. Oxford, Oxford University Press. 2004.

PAAUWE J. *and* BOSELIE P. 'Challenging "strategic HRM" and the relevance of the institutional setting', *Human Resource Management Journal*, Vol. 13, No. 3, 2003. pp56–70.

PATTERSON M., WEST M., LAWTHOM R. *and* NICKELL S. *Impact of People Management Practices on Business Performance*. London, Institute of Personnel and Development. 1997.

PEARN M. *and* KANDOLA R. *Job Analysis*. London, Institute of Personnel Management. 1993.

PECCEI R. *Human Resource Management and the Search for the Happy Workplace*. Rotterdam, Erasmus Research Institute of Management. 2003.

PEDLER M., BURGOYNE J. *and* BOYDELL T. *The Learning Company: A strategy for sustainable development*. London, McGraw-Hill. 1991.

PENDLETON A. 'Profit sharing and employee share ownership', in R. THORPE *and* G. HOMAN (eds), *Strategic Reward Systems*. Harlow, Financial Times/Prentice Hall. 2000.

PENDLETON A. *and* BREWSTER C. 'Portfolio workforce', *People Management*, 12 July 2001. pp38–40.

PENROSE E. *The Theory of the Growth of the Firm*. Oxford, Blackwell. 1959.

PERLMUTTER H. 'The tortuous evolution of the multinational corporation', *Columbia Journal of World Business*, Vol. 4, 1969. pp9–18.

PETTIGREW, A. 'Contextualist research and the study of organisational change processes', in E. LAWLER (ed), *Doing research that is useful in theory and practice*. New York, Jossey Bass. 1985.

PETTIGREW A. *The Politics of Organisational Decision Making*. London, Tavistock. 1973.

PFEFFER J. *The Human Equation: Building profits by putting people first*. Boston, Harvard Business School Press. 1998.

PFEFFER J. 'Pitfalls on the road to measurement: the dangerous liaison of human resources with the idea of accounting and finance', *Human Resource Management*, Vol. 36, No. 3, 1997. pp357–365.

PFEFFER J. *Competitive Advantage Through People*. Boston, Harvard Business School Press. 1994.

PICKARD, J. 'Should I stay or should I go?', *People Management*, 25 March 2004. pp31–36.

PICKARD J. 'Quietly confident', *People Management*, 9 October 2003a. pp16–17.

PICKARD J. 'A clearer provision', *People Management,* 12 June 2003b. pp28–32.

PITT G. *Employment Law*, 5th edition. London, Sweet & Maxwell. 2004.

PITT G. *Employment Law*, 4th edition. London, Sweet & Maxwell. 2000.

PLUMBLEY P. *Recruitment and Selection*. London, Institute of Personnel Management. 1991.

PORTER M. *Competitive Advantage: Creating and sustaining superior performance*. New York, Free Press. 1985.

POSTHUMA R., MORGESON F. *and* CAMPION M. 'Beyond employment interview validity: a comprehensive narrative review of recent research and trends over time', *Personnel Psychology*, Vol. 55, No. 1, 2002. pp1–81.

PRICE R. *and* PRICE L. 'Change and continuity in the status divide', in K. SISSON (ed), *Personnel Management in Britain*. Oxford, Blackwell. 1994.

PRICEWATERHOUSECOOPERS. *Global Human Capital Survey 2002, Executive Briefing*. 2002.

PRIEM R. *and* BUTLER J. 'Is the resource-based "view" a useful perspective for strategic management research?', *Academy of Management Review*, Vol. 26, No. 1, 2001. pp22–40.

PRIME MINISTER'S STRATEGY UNIT. *Prime Minister Welcomes Workforce Development Report.* Available at: www.number10.gov.uk/output/page3885.asp. 27 November 2001.

PRITCHARD H. 'Discrimination in employment', in B. TOWERS (ed), *The Handbook of Employment Relations, Law and Practice*, 4th edition. London, Kogan Page. 2003. pp47–67.

PRITCHARD R. *and* PAYNE S. 'Performance management practices and motivation', in D. HOLMAN, T. WALL, C. CLEGG, P. SPARROW *and* A. HOWARD (eds), *The New Workplace: A guide to the human impact of modern working practices*. London, Wiley. 2003.

PROCTER S. *and* CURRIE G. 'The role of the personnel function: roles, perceptions and processes in an NHS trust', *International Journal of Human Resource Management*, Vol. 10, No. 6, 1999. pp1077–1091.

PROCTER S. *and* MUELLER F. (eds), *Teamworking*. London, Macmillan. 2000.

PURCELL J. 'After collective bargaining? Acas in the age of human resource management', in B. TOWERS *and* W. BROWN (eds), *Employment Relations in Britain: 25 years of the Advisory, Conciliation and Arbitration Service*. Oxford, Blackwell. 2000.

PURCELL J. 'The search for best practice and best fit in human resource management: chimera or cul-de-sac?', *Human Resource Management Journal*, Vol. 9, No. 3, 1999. pp26–41.

PURCELL J. 'The impact of corporate strategy on human resource management', in J. STOREY (ed), *New Perspectives on Human Resource Management*. London, Routledge. 1989.

PURCELL J. *Good Industrial Relations: Theory and practice*. London, Macmillan. 1980.

PURCELL J. *and* AHLSTRAND B. *Human Resource Management in the Multi-divisional Company*. Oxford, Oxford University Press. 1994.

PURCELL J., KINNIE N., HUTCHINSON S., RAYTON B. *and* SWART J. *Understanding the People and Performance Link: Uunlocking the black box*. London, CIPD. 2003.

QUINN B., COOKE R. *and* KRIS A. *Shared Services: Mining for corporate gold*. London, Pearson Education. 2000.

QUINN J. 'Strategies for change', in J. QUINN, H. MINTZBERG *and* R. JAMES (eds), *The Strategy Process: Concepts, contexts, and cases*. Englewood Cliffs, NJ, Prentice Hall. 1988.

QUINN J. *Strategies for Change: Logical incrementalism*. Homewood, IL, Irwin. 1980.

QUINTANILLA J. *and* FERNER A. 'Multinationals and human resource management: between global convergence and national identity', *International Journal of Human Resource Management*, Vol. 14, No. 3, 2003. pp363–368.

RAINBIRD H. 'A further education', *People Management*, 11 September 2003. p48.

RAINBIRD H., FULLER A. *and* MUNRO A. *Workplace Learning in Context*. London, Routledge. 2004a.

RAINBIRD H. *and* MUNRO A. 'Workplace learning and the employment relationship in the public sector', *Human Resource Management Journal*, Vol. 13, No. 2, 2003a. pp30–44.

RAINBIRD H. *and* MUNRO A. 'Professional standards: how do people learn?', *People Management*, 20 November 2003b. p52.

RAINBIRD H., MUNRO A. *and* HOLLY L. 'Exploring the concept of employer demand for skills and qualifications: case studies from the public sector', in C. WARHURST, E. KEEP and I. GRUGULIS (eds), *The Skills That Matter*. Basingstoke, Palgrave. 2004b.

RAM M. 'Investors in People in small firms', *Personnel Review*, Vol. 29, No. 1, 2000. pp69–89.

RAM M. *Managing to Survive: Working lives in small firms*. Oxford, Blackwell. 1994.

RAMSAY H. and SCHOLARIOS D. 'Selective decisions: challenging orthodox analyses of the hiring process', *International Journal of Management Reviews*, Vol. 1, No. 4. 1999. pp63–89.

RAMSAY H., SCHOLARIOS D. and HARLEY B. 'Employees and high-performance work systems: testing inside the black box', *British Journal of Industrial Relations*, Vol. 38, No. 4, 2000. pp501–531.

RANA E. 'Council appraisals discriminate', *People Management*, 23 January 2003. p11.

RANA E. 'A head start', *People Management*, 7 March 2002. pp32–36.

RAUSCH E., SHERMAN H. and WASHBUSH J. B. 'Defining and assessing competencies for competency-based, outcome-focused management', *Journal of Management Development*, Vol. 21, No. 3/4, 2002. pp184–201.

REDMAN T. 'European Works Councils', in T. REDMAN and A. WILKINSON (eds), *The Informed Student Guide to Human Resource Management*. London, Thomson Learning. 2002.

REDMAN T. 'Performance appraisal', in T. REDMAN and A. WILKINSON (eds), *Contemporary Human Resource Management*. London, Financial Times/Prentice Hall. 2001.

REDMAN T. and WILKINSON A. (eds), *The Informed Student Guide to Human Resource Management*. London, Thomson Learning. 2002.

REDMAN T. and WILKINSON A. (eds), *Contemporary Human Resource Management*. London, Financial Times/Prentice Hall. 2001.

REID M., BARRINGTON H. and BROWN M. *Human Resource Development: Beyond training interventions*. London, CIPD. 2004.

REID P. 'EU social policy', *CIPD Quick Facts*, London, CIPD. 2000.

REILLY P. *HR Shared Service and the Realignment of HR*. Report 368. London, Institute of Employment Studies. 2000.

REMERY C., VAN DOORNE-HUISKES A. and SCHIPPERS J. 'Family-friendly policies in the Netherlands: the tripartite involvement', *Personnel Review*, Vol. 32, No. 4, 2003. pp456–473.

RENWICK D. 'Line manager involvement in HRM: an inside view', *Employee Relations*, Vol. 25, No. 3, 2003. pp262–280.

RENWICK D. and GENNARD J. 'Grievance and discipline', in T. REDMAN and A. WILKINSON (eds), *Contemporary Human Resource Management*. London, Financial Times/Prentice Hall. 2001.

REVANS R. *The Origins and Growth of Action Learning*. Bromley and Lund, Chartwell-Bratt. 1982.

REYNOLDS J. 'Method and madness', *People Management*, 4 April 2002. pp2–3.

REYNOLDS J., CALEY L. and MASON, R. *How Do People Learn?* Cambridge Programme for Industry research report. London, CIPD. 2002.

RITSON N. 'Corporate strategy and the role of HRM: critical cases in oil and chemicals', *Employee Relations*, Vol. 21, No. 2, 1999. pp159–175.

ROBERTS G. *Recruitment and Selection: A competency approach*. London, Institute of Personnel and Development. 1997.

ROBERTS Z. 'Referred pain', *People Management*, 20 May 2004. pp10–11.

ROBERTS Z. 'Get well sooner', *People Management*, 3 April 2003a. pp10–11.

ROBERTS Z. 'UK top managers pay league', *People Management on line,* 20 August 2003b.

ROBERTSON I. *and* SMITH M. 'Personnel selection', *Journal of Occupational and Organizational Psychology*, Vol. 74, No. 4, 2001. pp441–472.

ROBERTSON I., SMITH M. *and* COOPER D. *Motivation*. London, CIPD. 1992.

ROBINSON P. 'Explaining the relationship between flexible employment and labour market regulation', in A. FELSTEAD *and* N. JEWSON (eds), *Global Trends in Flexible Labour*. London, Macmillan. 1999.

ROCHE W. 'In search of commitment-oriented human resource management practices and the conditions that sustain them', *Journal of Management Studies*, Vol. 36, No. 5, 1999. pp653–678.

ROCHE W. *and* GEARY J. 'Advocates, critics and union involvement in workplace participation', *British Journal of Industrial Relations*, Vol. 40, No. 3, 2002. pp659–688.

RODGER A. *The Seven Point Plan*. London, National Institute for Industrial Psychology. 1952.

RODRIGUEZ J. *and* VENTURA J. 'Human resource management systems and organisational performance: an analysis of the Spanish manufacturing industry', *International Journal of Human Resource Management*, Vol. 14, No. 7, 2003. pp1206–1226.

ROGERS C. *Freedom to Learn*. Ohio, Charles and Merrill Publishing Company. 1969.

ROLLINSON D. 'Grievance', in T. REDMAN *and* A. WILKINSON (eds), *The Informed Student Guide to Human Resource Management*. London, Thomson Learning. 2002.

ROLLINSON D., BROADFIELD A. *and* EDWARDS D. *Organisational Behaviour and Analysis*. London, Addison-Wesley. 1998.

ROLPH J. 'Standard issue', *People Management*, 11 March 2004. pp34–38.

ROSE M. 'Good deal, bad deal? Job satisfaction in occupations', *Work, Employment and Society*, Vol. 17, No. 3, 2003. pp503–530.

ROSE M. *How Far Can I Trust It? Job satisfaction data in the WERS98 Employee Survey*. ESRC Future of Work Paper No. 6. Swindon, ESRC. 2000.

ROSE M. *Explaining and Forecasting Job Satisfaction: The contribution of occupational filing*. ESRC Future of Work Paper No. 3. Bath, ESRC. 1999.

ROSE M. *Industrial Behaviour*. Harmondsworth, Penguin, 1978.

ROUSSEAU C. *Psychological Contracts in Organisations: Understanding written and unwritten agreements*. Thousand Oaks, CA, Sage. 1995.

ROY D. 'Fear stuff, sweet stuff and evil stuff', in T. NICHOLS (ed), *Capital and Labour*. London, Fontana. 1980.

ROYLE T. 'Recruiting the acquiescent workforce: a comparative analysis of McDonald's in Germany and the UK', *Employee Relations*, Vol. 21, No. 6, 1999. pp540–555.

RUBERY J. 'Performance-related pay and the prospects for gender equity', *Journal of Management Studies*, Vol. 35, No. 5, 1995. pp637–654.

RUBERY J., CARROLL M., COOKE F. L., GRUGULIS I. and EARNSHAW J. 'Human resource management and the permeable organisation: the case of the multi-client call centre', *Journal of Management Studies*, Vol. 41, No. 7, 2004. pp1199–1222.

RUBERY J., COOKE F. L., EARNSHAW J. and MARCHINGTON M. 'Inter-organisational relations and employment in a multi-employer environment', *British Journal of Industrial Relations*, Vol. 41, No. 2, 2003. pp265–289.

RUBERY J., EARNSHAW J., MARCHINGTON M., COOKE F. and VINCENT S. 'Changing organisational forms and the employment relationship', *Journal of Management Studies*, Vol. 39, No. 5, 2002. pp645–672.

RUBERY J. and GRIMSHAW D. *The Organisation of Employment: An international perspective*. London, Palgrave. 2003.

RUGMAN A. and VERBEKE A. 'Edith Penrose's contribution to the resource-based view of strategic management', *Strategic Management Journal*, Vol. 23, No. 8, 2002. pp769–780.

RUTHERFORD M., BULLER P. and McMULLEN P. 'Human resource management over the life cycle of small to medium sized firms', *Human Resource Management*, Vol. 42, No. 4, 2003. pp321–335.

SADHEV K., VINNICOMBE S. and TYSON S. 'Downsizing and the changing role of HR', *International Journal of Human Resource Management*, Vol. 10, No. 5. 1999. pp906–923.

SADLER-SMITH E. and BADGER B. 'The HR practitioner's perspective on continuing professional development', *Human Resource Management Journal*, Vol. 8, No. 4, 1998. pp66–75.

SALAMAN G. 'Competences of managers, competences of leaders', in J. STOREY (ed), *Leadership in Organizations: Current issues and key trends*. London, Routledge. 2004.

SALAMON M. *Industrial Relations: Theory and practice*, 4th edition. Harlow, Financial Times/Prentice Hall. 2000.

SALGADO J. 'The big five personality dimensions and counterproductive behaviours', *International Journal of Selection and Assessment*, Vol. 10, No. 1/2, 2002. pp117–125.

SALONIEMI A., VIRTANEN P. and VAHTERA J. 'The work environment in fixed-term jobs: are poor psychosocial conditions inevitable?', *Work, Employment and Society*, Vol. 18, No. 1, 2004. pp193–208.

SANDBERG J. 'Understanding human competence at work: an interpretative approach', *The Academy of Management Journal*, Vol. 43, No. 1, 2000. pp9–26.

SANZ-VALLE R., SABATER-SANCHEZ R. and ARAGON-SANCHEZ A. 'Human resource management and business strategy links: an empirical study', *International Journal of Human Resource Management*, Vol. 10, No. 4, 1999. pp655–671.

SARGEANT M. 'Employee consultation', *Employee Relations*, Vol. 27, No. 5, 2001. pp483–497.

SAUNDERS M., LEWIS P. and THORNHILL A. *Research Methods for Business Students*, 3rd edition. London, Financial Times/Prentice Hall. 2002.

SCARBROUGH H. and KINNIE N. 'Barriers to the development of teamworking in UK firms', *Industrial Relations Journal*, Vol. 34, No. 2, 2003. pp135–149.

SCARBROUGH H. and SWAN J. *Case Studies in Knowledge Management*. London, CIPD. 1999.

SCASE R. 'Employment relations in small firms', in P. EDWARDS (ed), *Industrial Relations*, 2nd edition. Oxford, Blackwell. 2003.

SCASE R. and GOFFEE R. *Reluctant Managers: Their work and lifestyles*. London, Unwin Hyman. 1989.

SCHEIN E. *Career Dynamics: Matching individual and organisational needs*. Reading, MA, Addison Wesley. 1978.

SCHNEIDER S. and BARSOUX J. *Managing Across Cultures*. London, Financial Times/Prentice Hall. 1997.

SCHMIDT F. and HUNTER J. 'The validity and utility of selection methods in personnel psychology: practical and theoretical implications of 85 years of research findings', *Psychological Bulletin*, Vol. 124, No. 2, 1988. pp262–274.

SCHMITT J. and WADSWORTH J. 'Is the OECD jobs strategy behind US and British employment and unemployment success in the 1990s?', in D. R. HOWELL (ed), *Fighting Unemployment: The limits of free market orthodoxy*. Oxford, Oxford University Press. 2004.

SCHMITT N. and CHAN D. 'The status of research on applicant reactions to selection tests and its implications for managers', *International Journal of Management Reviews*, Vol. 1, No. 1. 1999. pp45–62.

SCHULER R. 'Strategic human resource management and industrial relations', *Human Relations*, Vol. 42, No. 2, 1989. pp157–184.

SCHULER R. and JACKSON S. 'Linking competitive strategies with human resource management', *Academy of Management Executive*, Vol. 1, No. 3, 1987. pp207–219.

SCHULER R., JACKSON S. and STOREY J. 'HRM and its link with strategic management', in J. STOREY (ed), *Human Resource Management: A critical text*, 2nd edition. London, Thomson Learning. 2001.

SCHUSTER J. and ZINGHEIM P. *The New Pay: Linking employee and organisational performance*. New York, Lexington. 1992.

SCOTT M., ROBERTS I., HOLROYD G. and SAWBRIDGE D. *Management and Industrial Relations in Small Firms*. Department of Employment Research Paper No. 70. London, HMSO. 1989.

SEARLE R. *Selection and Recruitment: A critical text*. Milton Keynes, Open University Press. 2003.

SEMLER R. *Maverick!* London, Arrow Business Books. 1993.

SENGE P. *The Fifth Discipline: The art and practice of the learning organisation*. London, Century. 1990.

SHAW S. and CLARK M. 'Women, pay and equal opportunities', in R. THORPE and G. HOMAN (eds), *Strategic Reward Systems*. Harlow, Financial Times/Prentice Hall. 2000.

SILVERMAN A. *Interpreting Qualitative Data*. London, Sage. 1993.

SIMONS P., GERMANS J. and RUIJTERS M. 'Forum for organisational learning: combining learning at work, organisational learning and training in new ways', *Journal of European Industrial Training*, Vol. 27, No. 1, 2003. pp41–49.

SISSON K. 'Human resource management and the personnel function', in J. STOREY (ed), *Human Resource Management: A critical text*, 2nd edition. London, Thomson. 2001.

SISSON K. 'In search of human resource management', *British Journal of Industrial Relations*, Vol. 31, No. 2, 1993. pp201–210.

Sisson K. *and* Marginson P. 'Management: systems structure and strategy', in P. Edwards (ed), *Industrial Relations*, 2nd edition. Oxford, Blackwell. 2003.

Sisson K. *and* Storey J. *The Realities of Human Resource Management*. Milton Keynes, Open University Press. 2000.

Sisson K. *and* Timperley S. 'From manpower planning to strategic human resource management?', in K. Sisson (ed), *Personnel Management: A comprehensive guide to theory and practice in Britain*. Oxford, Blackwell. 1994.

Skills Sector Development Agency. *Working Futures: Sectoral report 2003–04*. Available at: www.ssda.org.uk. 2004.

Sloman M. *Training in the Age of the Learner*. London, CIPD. 2003.

Sloman M. 'Plug but no play', *People Management*, 13 September 2001. p57.

Sloman M. *and* Rolph J. *E-learning: The change agenda*. London, CIPD. 2003.

Smethurst S. 'Ageism rife in UK workplaces'. *People Management*. 15 January 2004. p10.

Smethurst S. 'Empowerment: blood and simple', *People Management*, 20 March 2003. pp42–44.

Smith C., Daskalaki M., Elger T. *and* Brown D. 'Labour turnover and management retention strategies in new manufacturing plants', *International Journal of Human Resource Management*, Vol. 15, No. 2, 2004. pp371–396.

Smith I. 'Benefits', in G. White *and* J. Druker (eds), *Reward Management: A critical text*. London, Routledge. 2000a.

Smith I. 'Flexible plans for pay and benefits', in R. Thorpe *and* G. Homan (eds), *Strategic Reward Systems*. Harlow, Financial Times/Prentice Hall. 2000b.

Smith M. *and* Robertson I. *The Theory and Practice of Systematic Personnel Selection*. Basingstoke, Macmillan. 1993.

Smith P. 'Job evaluation', in R. Thorpe *and* G. Homan (eds), *Strategic Reward Systems*. London, Financial Times/Prentice Hall. 2000c.

Smith P. *and* Morton G. 'New labour's reform of Britain's employment law: the devil is not only in the detail but in the values and policy too', *British Journal Industrial Relations*, Vol. 39, No. 1, 2001. pp119–138.

Smithers R. 'Tests and training will be used to boost skills', *The Guardian,* 18 March 2004. p21.

Snape E., Redman T. *and* Bamber G. *Managing Managers: Strategies and techniques for human resource management*. Oxford, Blackwell. 1994.

Sparrow P., Brewster C. *and* Harris H. *Globalizing Human Resource Management*. London, Routledge. 2004.

Spilsbury M., Moralee J., Frost D. *and* Hillage J. *Evaluation of Investors in People in England and Wales*. Research Report No. 263. Brighton, Institute of Employment Studies. 1995.

Stairs M., Kandola B. *and* Sandford-Smith R. 'Slim picking', *People Management*, 28 December 2000. pp28–30.

Stammers R. *and* Patrick J. *The Psychology of Training*. London, Methuen. 1975.

Stansfield L. 'Continuing professional development', in T. Redman *and* A. Wilkinson (eds),

The Informed Student Guide to Human Resource Management. London, Thomson Learning. 2002.

STEERS R., MOWDAY R. and SHAPIRO D. 'The future of work motivation theory', *Academy of Management Review*, Vol. 29, No. 3, 2004. pp379–387.

STERN E. and SOMMERLAD E. *Workplace Learning, Culture and Performance*. London, CIPD. 1999.

STEWART J. 'Individual learning', in J. LEOPOLD (ed), *Human Resources in Organisations*. Harlow, Financial Times/Prentice Hall. 2002.

STILES P. 'The impact of the Board on strategy: an empirical investigation', *Journal of Management Studies*, Vol. 38, No. 5, 2001. pp627–650.

STIRLING J. and FITZGERALD I. 'European Works Councils: representing workers on the periphery', *Employee Relations*, Vol. 23, No. 1, 2001. pp13–25.

STOREY D. 'Exploring the link, among small firms, between management training and firm performance: a comparison between the UK and other OECD countries', *International Journal of Human Resource Management*, Vol. 15, No. 1. 2004. pp112–130.

STOREY J. (ed), *Human Resource Management: A critical text*, 2nd edition. London, Thomson. 2001.

STOREY J. *Developments in the Management of Human Resources*. Oxford, Blackwell. 1992.

STOREY J. (ed), *New Perspectives on Human Resource Management*. London, Routledge. 1989.

STOREY J. and SISSON K. *Managing Human Resources and Industrial Relations*. Buckingham, Open University Press. 1993.

STREDWICK J. 'Employee share schemes', in T. REDMAN and A. WILKINSON (eds), *The Informed Student Guide to Human Resource Management*. London, Thomson Learning. 2002.

STREECK W. 'The uncertainties of management and the management of uncertainty: employers, labour relations and industrial adjustment in the 1980s', *Work, Employment and Society*, Vol. 1, No. 3, 1987. pp281–308.

STURDY A., GRUGULIS I. and WILLMOTT H. (eds), *Customer Service: Empowerment and entrapment*. London, Palgrave. 2001.

SUFF R. and WILLIAMS S. 'The myth of mutuality? Employee perceptions of partnership at Borg Warner', *Employee Relations*, Vol. 26, No. 1, 2003. pp31–43.

SUTHERLAND J. and RAINBIRD H. 'Unions and workplace learning: conflict or cooperation with the employer?', in H. RAINBIRD (ed), *Training in the Workplace: Critical perspectives on learning at work*. Basingstoke, Macmillan Press Ltd. 2000.

SWART J. and KINNIE N. 'Knowledge-intensive firms: the influence of the client on HR systems', *Human Resource Management Journal*, Vol. 13, No. 3, 2003. pp37–55.

SWART J., KINNIE N. and PURCELL, J. *People and Performance in Knowledge Intensive Firms*. CIPD Research Report. London, CIPD. 2003.

TAILBY S. and WINCHESTER D. 'Management and trade unions: towards social partnership', in S. BACK and K. SISSON (eds), *Personnel Management*, 3rd edition. Oxford, Blackwell. 2000.

TANG T., KIM J. and TANG D. 'Does attitude toward money moderate the relationship between intrinsic job satisfaction and voluntary turnover?', *Human Relations*, Vol. 53, 2000. pp213–245.

TAPLIN I., WINTERTON J. *and* WINTERTON R. 'Understanding labour turnover in a labour-intensive industry: evidence from the British clothing industry', *Journal of Management Studies*, Vol. 40, No. 4, 2003. pp1021–1046.

TAYLOR P. *and* BAIN P. '"An assembly line in the head": work and employee relations in the call centre', *Industrial Relations Journal*, Vol. 30, No. 2, 1999. pp101–117.

TAYLOR P., HYMAN J., MULVEY G. *and* BAIN P. 'Work organisation, control and the experience of work in call centres', *Work Employment and Society*, Vol. 16, No. 1, 2002. pp133–150.

TAYLOR R. *The Future of Work–life Balance*. Swindon, ESRC. 2002a.

TAYLOR R. *The Future of Employment Relations*. Swindon, ESRC. 2002b.

TAYLOR S. *People Resourcing*. London, CIPD. 2002c.

TAYLOR S. 'Debates in reward management', in R. THORPE *and* G. HOLMAN (eds), *Strategic Reward Systems*. London, Financial Times/Prentice Hall. 2000a.

TAYLOR S. 'Occupational pensions', in R. THORPE *and* G. HOLMAN (eds), *Strategic Reward Systems*. London, Financial Times/Prentice Hall. 2000b.

TERRY M. 'Can "partnership" reverse the decline of British trade unions?', *Work Employment and Society*, Vol. 17, No. 3, 2003. pp459–472.

TERRY N. *and* WHITE P. 'Occupational pension schemes and their interaction with HRM', *Human Resource Management Journal*, Vol. 8, No. 4, 1998. pp20–36.

THIETART R. *et al. Doing Management Research*. London, Sage. 2001.

THOMASON G. *A Textbook of Industrial Relations Management*. London, Institute of Personnel Management. 1984.

THOMPSON M. 'Salary progression schemes', in G. WHITE *and* J. DRUKER (eds), *Reward Management: A critical text*. London, Routledge. 2000.

THOMPSON P. *Total Reward*. London, CIPD. 2002.

THOMPSON P. *and* McHUGH D. *Work Organisations: A critical introduction*, 3rd edition. London, Palgrave. 2002.

THOMPSON P. *and* MILSOME S. *Reward Determination in the UK: Research report*. London, CIPD. 2001.

THOMSON A., MABEY C., STOREY J., GRAY C. *and* ILES P. *Changing Patterns of Management Development*. Oxford, Blackwell. 2001.

THOMSON A. *and* MURRAY V. *Grievance Procedures*. Farnborough, Saxon House. 1976.

THORPE R., BOWEY A. *and* GOODRIDGE M. 'Auditing a remuneration system', in R. THORPE *and* G. HOMAN (eds), *Strategic Reward Systems*. London, Financial Times/Prentice Hall. 2000.

THORPE R. *and* HOMAN G. (eds), *Strategic Reward Systems*. London, Financial Times/Prentice Hall. 2000.

THURLEY K. *and* WOOD S. (eds), *Industrial Relations and Management Strategy*. Cambridge, Cambridge University Press. 1983.

TOPLIS J., DULEWICZ V. *and* FLETCHER C. *Psychological Testing: A manager's guide*. London, Institute of Personnel Management. 1994.

TORRINGTON D. 'Discipline', in M. POOLE *and* M. WARNER (eds), *IEBM Handbook of Human Resource Management*. London, International Thomson Press. 1998.

TORRINGTON D., EARNSHAW J., MARCHINGTON L. *and* RITCHIE E. *Tackling Under-performance in Teachers*. London, RoutledgeFalmer. 2003.

TORRINGTON D., HALL L. *and* TAYLOR S. *Human Resource Management*. London, Prentice Hall. 2002.

TOULSON, P. *and* DEWE P. 'HR accounting as a measurement tool', *Human Resource Management Journal*, Vol. 14, No. 2, 2004. pp75–90.

TOWERS B. 'Overview: the changing employment relationship', in B. TOWERS (ed), *The Handbook of Employment Relations, Law and Practice*. London, Kogan Page. 2003. pp7–23.

TOWERS B. *The Representation Gap: Change and reform in the British and American workplace*. Oxford, Oxford University Press. 1997.

TRADES UNION CONGRESS. *Learning Attracts New Women Union Reps*. Available at: www.tuc.org.uk/learning/tuc-7310-f0.cfm. November 2003.

TRADES UNION CONGRESS. *Partnership Works*. London, TUC. 2002.

TRADES UNION CONGRESS. *Partners for Progress*. London, TUC. 1999.

TRAPP R. 'A flying start', *People Management*, 6 February 2003. pp36–38.

TRAPP R. 'Main attraction', *People Management*, 25 October 2001. pp44–46.

TREANOR J., FINCH J. *and* MOORE C. 'Executive pay survey: £26 million puts Tesco at top of the table', *The Guardian*, 27 August 2004. p26.

TRUSS C., GRATTON L., HOPE-HAILEY V., McGOVERN P. *and* STYLES P. 'Soft and hard models of human resource management: a reappraisal', *Journal of Management Studies*, Vol. 34, No. 1, 1997. pp53–73.

TUCKMAN A. 'All together better? Single status and union recognition in the chemical industry', *Employee Relations*, Vol. 20, No. 2, 1998. pp132–149.

TULIP S. 'Flexible trend', *People Management*, 20 November 2003a. pp42–44.

TULIP S. 'Just rewards', *People Management*, 10 July 2003b. pp42–46.

TURBAN D. *and* CABLE D. 'Firm reputation and applicant pool characteristics', *Journal of Organizational Behavior*, Vol. 24, No. 6, 2003. pp733–751.

TURNER H. *Trade Union Growth, Structure and Policy: A comparative study of the cotton unions*. London, Allen & Unwin. 1962.

TYRELL, M. 'From backwater to mainstream: trends in SRI and sustainability reporting', in *Directions3: Trends in CSR reporting*. London, Salterbaxter & Context. 2003.

TYSON S. *and* FELL A. *Evaluating the Personnel Function*. London, Hutchinson. 1986.

ULRICH D. 'A new mandate for human resources', *Harvard Business Review*, Jan–Feb 1998. pp125–134.

ULRICH D. *Human Resource Champions: The next agenda for adding value and delivering results*. Boston, Harvard Business School Press. 1997.

UPTON R. 'Spread the word', *People Management*, 25 March 2004. pp42–43.

VAN MAANEN J. 'The fact of fiction in organisational ethnography', *Administrative Science Quarterly*, Vol. 24, No. 4, 1979. pp539–550.

VROOM V. *Work and Motivation*. Chichester, John Wiley. 1964.

WADDINGTON J. 'Trade union organisation', in P. EDWARDS (ed), *Industrial Relations: Theory and practice*. Oxford, Blackwell. 2003.

WADDINGTON J. *and* HOFFMAN R. (eds), *Trade Unions in Europe: Facing challenges and searching for solutions*. Brussels, European Trade Union Institute. 2000.

WADDINGTON J. *and* WHITSON C. 'Why do people join unions in a period of membership decline?', *British Journal of Industrial Relations*, Vol. 35, No. 4, 1997. pp515–546.

WALKER J. *Human Resource Strategy*. New York, McGraw Hill. 1992.

WALL T., MICHIE J., PATTERSON M., WOOD S., SHEEHAN M., CLEGG C. *and* WEST M. 'On the validity of subjective measures of company performance', *Personnel Psychology*, Vol. 57, 2004. pp95–118.

WALSH J. 'A happy reunion', *People Management*, 8 November 2001. pp33–36.

WALTON R. 'From control to commitment in the workplace', *Harvard Business Review*, Vol. 63, March–April 1985. pp76–84.

WARD K., GRIMSHAW D., RUBERY J. *and* BEYNON H. 'Dilemmas in the management of temporary work agency staff', *Human Resource Management Journal*, Vol. 11, No. 4, 2001. pp3–21.

WARHURST C., KEEP E. *and* GRUGULIS I. (eds), *The Skills That Matter*. Basingstoke, Palgrave. 2004.

WARHURST C. *and* NICKSON D. *Looking Good, Sounding Right: Style counselling in the new economy*. London, The Industrial Society. 2001.

WARHURST C. *and* THOMPSON P. 'Hands, hearts and minds: changing work and workers at the end of the century', in P. THOMPSON *and* C. WARHURST (eds), *Workplaces of the Future*. London, Macmillan Press. 1998.

WATKINS J. 'Retailers to revamp training', *People Management*, 1 May 2003. p7.

WATSON T. 'Recruitment and selection', in K. SISSON (ed), *Personnel Management: A comprehensive guide to theory and practice in Britain*. Oxford, Blackwell. 1994.

WATSON T. *Management, Organisation and Employment Strategy*. London, Routledge & Kegan Paul. 1986.

WATSON T. *The Personnel Managers: A study in the sociology of work and employment*. London, Routledge & Kegan Paul. 1977.

WERNERFELT B. 'A resource-based view of the firm', *Strategic Management Journal*, Vol. 5, No. 2, 1984. pp171–180.

WEST M., BORRILL C., DAWSON J., SCULLY J., CARTER M., ANELAY S., PATTERSON M. *and* WARING J. 'The link between the management of employees and patient mortality in acute hospitals', *International Journal of Human Resource Management*, Vol. 13, No. 8, 2002. pp1299–1310.

WHIDDETT S. 'Rules of engagement', *People Management*, 4 December 2003. pp29–30.

WHIDDETT S. *and* HOLLYFORDE S. *A Practical Guide to Competencies*. London, CIPD. 2003.

WHIDDETT S. *and* HOLLYFORDE S. *The Competencies Handbook*. London, Institute of Personnel and Development. 1999.

WHITE G. *and* DRUKER J. (eds), *Reward Management: A critical text*. London, Routledge. 2000.

WHITE M., HILL S., MILLS C. *and* SMEATON D. *Managing to Change? British workplaces and the future of work*. Basingstoke, Palgrave. 2004.

WHITFIELD K. *and* MCNABB R. 'Job evaluation and high performance work practices: compatible or conflictual?', *Journal of Management Studies*, Vol. 38, No. 2, 2001. pp293–312.

WHITTAKER J. 'Remaking the grade', *People Management*, 27 September 2001. pp44–46.

WHITTAKER S. *and* MARCHINGTON M. 'Devolving HR responsibility to the line: threat, opportunity or partnership?', *Employee Relations*, Vol. 25, No. 3, 2003, pp245–261.

WHITTINGTON R. *What is Strategy and Does It Matter?* London, Routledge. 1993.

WHITTINGTON R. *and* MAYER M. *Organising for Success in the Twenty-first Century.* London, CIPD. 2002.

WICKENS P. *The Road to Nissan: Flexibility, quality, teamwork.* London, Macmillan. 1987.

WILK S. *and* CAPPELLI P. 'Understanding the determinants of employer use of selection methods', *Personnel Psychology*, Vol. 56, No. 1, 2003. pp103–124.

WILKINSON A. 'Empowerment', in M. WARNER (ed), *International Encyclopaedia of Business and Management*, 2nd edition. London, Thomson. 2002. pp1720–1730.

WILKINSON A. 'Empowerment', in T. REDMAN *and* A. WILKINSON (eds), *Contemporary Human Resource Management*. London, Financial Times/Pitman, 2001. pp336–352.

WILKINSON A., DUNDON T., MARCHINGTON M. *and* ACKERS P. 'Changing patterns of employee voice', *Journal of Industrial Relations*, Vol. 46, No. 3, 2004. pp297–321.

WILKINSON A., GODFREY G. *and* MARCHINGTON M. 'Bouquets, brickbats and blinkers: total quality management and employee involvement in practice', *Organisational Studies*, Vol. 18, No. 5, 1997. pp799–819.

WILKINSON A. *and* MARCHINGTON M. 'Total quality management: instant pudding for the personnel function?', *Human Resource Management Journal*, Vol. 5, No. 1, 1994. pp33–49.

WILKINSON A., MARCHINGTON M. *and* ACKERS P. 'Strategies for human resource management: issues in larger and international firms', in R. HARRISON (ed), *Human Resource Management*. London, Addison-Wesley. 1993.

WILLIAMSON O. *Markets and Hierarchies: Analysis and antitrust implications*. New York, Free Press. 1975.

WILSON F. *Organisational Behaviour: An introduction*. Oxford, Oxford University Press. 1999.

WINTOUR P. 'Battle lines drawn for equality body', *The Guardian*, 23 July 2004, p11.

WITCHER B. *and* WILKINSON A. *What a Research Thesis Should Look Like*. Department of Management Working Paper. Norwich, University of East Anglia. 2002.

WOMACK J., JONES D. *and* ROOS D. *The Machine That Changed the World*. New York, Rawson Associates. 1990.

WOOD S. 'Organisational performance and manufacturing practices', in D. HOLMAN, T. WALL, C. CLEGG, P. SPARROW *and* A. HOWARD (eds), *The New Workplace: A guide to the human impact of modern working practices*. London, Wiley. 2003.

WOOD S. 'Learning through ACAS: the case of union recognition', in B. TOWERS *and* W. BROWN (eds), *Employment Relations in Britain: 25 years of the Advisory, Conciliation and Arbitration Service*. Oxford, Blackwell. 2000.

WOOD S. 'Human resource management and performance', *International Journal of Management Reviews*, Vol. 1, No. 4, 1999a. pp367–413.

Wood S. 'Getting the measure of the transformed high-performance organisation', *British Journal of Industrial Relations*, Vol. 37, No. 3, 1999b. pp391–418.

Wood S. 'The four pillars of human resource management: are they connected?', *Human Resource Management Journal*, Vol. 5, No. 5, 1995. pp49–59.

Wood S. *Continuous Development*. London, Institute of Personnel Management. 1988.

Wood S. and Albanese M. 'Can we speak of a high commitment management on the shop floor?', *Journal of Management Studies*, Vol. 32, No. 2, 1995. pp1–33.

Wood S. and de Menezes L. 'High commitment management in the UK: evidence from the Workplace Industrial Relations Survey and Employers' Manpower and Skills Survey', *Human Relations*, Vol. 51, No. 4, 1998. pp485–515.

Wood S. and Fenton O'Creevy M. 'Channel hopping', *People Management*, 25 November 1999. pp42–45.

Wood S., Moore S. and Ewing K. 'The impact of the trade union recognition procedure under the Employment Relations Act 2000–2', in H. Gospel and S. Wood (eds), *Representing Workers: Union recognition and membership in Britain*. London, Routledge. 2003.

Wragg E., Haynes G., Wragg C. and Chamberlain R. *Performance Pay for Teachers*. London, Routledge. 2004.

Wright A. *Reward Management in Context*. London, CIPD. 2004.

Wright P. and Gardner T. 'The human resource–firm performance relationship: methodological and theoretical challenges', in D. Holman, T. Wall, C. Clegg, P. Sparrow and A. Howard (eds), *The New Workplace: A guide to the human impact of modern working practices*. London, Wiley. 2003.

Wright P., McMahon G., and McWilliams A. 'Human resources and sustained competitive advantage: a resource-based perspective', *International Journal of Human Resource Management*, Vol. 5, No. 2, 1994. pp301–326.

Xu Z. 'It's a call centre, but it's a strange call centre: HRM and employment practices in HR service centres'. Unpublished MSc dissertation, UMIST. 2003.

Yin R. *Case Study Research: Design and methods*. London, Sage. 1984.

Yin R. 'The case study crisis: some answers', *Administrative Science Quarterly*, Vol. 26, No. 1, 1981. pp58–65.

Yong J. and Wilkinson A. 'The state of total quality management: a review', *International Journal of Human Resource Management*, Vol. 10, No. 1, 1999. pp137–161.

Youndt M., Snell S., Dean J. and Lepak D. 'Human resource management, manufacturing strategy, and firm performance', *Academy of Management Journal*, Vol. 39, 1996. pp836–866.

Zingheim P. and Schuster J. 'Pay it forward', *People Management*, 2002. pp32–34.

INDEX

Membership has its rewards

Join us online today as an Affiliate member and get immediate access to our member services. As a member you'll also be entitled to special discounts on our range of courses, conferences, books and training resources.

To find out more, visit www.cipd.co.uk/affiliate or call us on 020 8612 6208.